FIREARMS AND VIOLENCE

FIREARMS AND VIOLENCE
Issues of Public Policy

Edited by
DON B. KATES, JR.

Foreword by
JOHN KAPLAN

Pacific Studies in Public Policy

PACIFIC INSTITUTE FOR PUBLIC POLICY RESEARCH
San Francisco, California

International Standard Book Number: 0-88410-928-3 (CL)
0-88410-929-1 (PB)

Library of Congress Catalog Card Number: 83-25850

Printed in the United States of America

Library of Congress Cataloging in Publication Data

Main entry under title:

Firearms and violence.

  (Pacific studies in public policy)
  Includes bibliographies and index.
    1. Gun control—United States—Addresses, essays, lectures.
  2. Firearms ownership—United States—Addresses, essays, lectures.
  3. Gun control—United States—Public opinion—Addresses, essays,
  lectures.   4. Public opinion—United States—Addresses, essays, lectures.
  5. Firearms—Law and legislation—United States—Addresses, essays,
  lectures.   6. Violent crimes—United States—Addresses, essays, lectures.
  I. Kates, Don B., 1941-   II. Series.
  HV7436.F47 1984   363.3'3   83-25850
  ISBN 0-88410-922-4 (Ballinger)
  ISBN 0-88410-923-2 (Ballinger : pbk.)

To Essie, in memoriam; to Siva, in perpetuity.

PACIFIC INSTITUTE

FOR PUBLIC POLICY RESEARCH

The Pacific Institute for Public Policy Research is an independent, tax-exempt research and educational organization. The Institute's program is designed to broaden public understanding of the nature and effects of market processes and government policy.

With the bureaucratization and politicization of modern society, scholars, business and civic leaders, the media, policymakers, and the general public have too often been isolated from meaningful solutions to critical public issues. To facilitate a more active and enlightened discussion of such issues, the Pacific Institute sponsors in-depth studies into the nature of and possible solutions to major social, economic, and environmental problems. Undertaken regardless of the sanctity of any particular government program, or the customs, prejudices, or temper of the times, the Institute's studies aim to ensure that alternative approaches to currently problematic policy areas are fully evaluated, the best remedies discovered, and these findings made widely available. The results of this work are published as books and monographs, and form the basis for numerous conference and media programs.

Through this program of research and commentary, the Institute seeks to evaluate the premises and consequences of government policy, and provide the foundations necessary for constructive policy reform.

PACIFIC STUDIES IN PUBLIC POLICY

Forestlands
Public and Private
Edited by Robert T. Deacon and M. Bruce Johnson
Foreword by B. Delworth Gardner

Urban Transit
The Private Challenge to Public Transportation
Edited by Charles A. Lave
Foreword by John Meyer

Politics, Prices, and Petroleum
The Political Economy of Energy
By David Glasner
Foreword by Paul W. MacAvoy

Rights and Regulation
Ethical, Political, and Economic Issues
Edited by Tibor M. Machan and M. Bruce Johnson
Foreword by Aaron Wildavsky

Fugitive Industry
The Economics and Politics of Deindustrialization
By Richard B. McKenzie
Foreword by Finis Welch

Money in Crisis
The Federal Reserve, the Economy, and Monetary Reform
Edited by Barry N. Siegel
Foreword by Leland B. Yeager

Natural Resources
Bureaucratic Myths and Environmental Management
By Richard Stroup and John Baden
Foreword by William Niskanen

Water Rights
Scarce Resource Allocation, Bureaucracy,
and the Environment
Edited with an Introduction by Terry L. Anderson
Foreword by Jack Hirshleifer

Locking Up the Range
Federal Land Controls and Grazing
By Gary D. Libecap
Foreword by Jonathan R. T. Hughes

The Public School Monopoly
A Critical Analysis of Education and the State
in American Society
Edited by Robert B. Everhart
Foreword by Clarence J. Karier

Resolving the Housing Crisis
Government Policy, Decontrol, and the Public Interest
Edited with an Introduction by M. Bruce Johnson

FORTHCOMING

The American Family and the State

Stagflation and the Political Business Cycle

Rationing Health Care
Medical Licensing in the United States

Oil and Gas Leasing on the Outer Continental Shelf

Taxation and Capital Markets

Myth and Reality in the Welfare State

Electric Utility Regulation and the Energy Crisis

Crime, Police, and the Courts

Drugs in Society

For further information on the Pacific Institute's program and a catalog of publications, please contact:

PACIFIC INSTITUTE FOR PUBLIC POLICY RESEARCH
177 Post Street
San Francisco, California 94108

CONTENTS

PART VIII   POLITICAL AND SOCIAL ASPECTS
             OF GUN OWNERSHIP

Chapter 16
The Political Functions of Gun Control
— Raymond G. Kessler

LIST OF FIGURES

LIST OF TABLES

FOREWORD

The ideological battle over the issue of gun control is in itself a most interesting field of study. The vast preponderance of the literature has been dominated by one point of view. Despite the far closer vote on the issue when it has been submitted to elections, one would still gain the impression that almost all right-thinking people are in favor of major restrictions on firearms and that those on the other side are right-wing kooks. The defeat, then, of gun control proposals at the polls or in the legislatures is explained by the lobbying activities of "gun nuts" or the National Rifle Association, by the great amounts of money spent by those against the gun control measure, or by some technical defect in the particular enactment under consideration, which did not affect the basic soundness of the idea. With the publication of this book, it will be hard to maintain such a simple view of the world.

The argument for gun control has proceeded from a number of factual, legal, and moral premises — virtually each one of which is attacked in the following pages, though, of course, not all with equal degrees of success. For instance, one of the bases of the gun control argument is the view that guns are a cause of crime in the sense that if guns somehow did not exist we would have less crime, or at least less of certain kinds of crime. Like many of the individual propositions in the pro-gun-control argument, this seems quite plausible.

After all, we can easily call to mind the many crimes that involve the use of a gun. It is much more difficult to determine how many of these would have taken place anyway, with a different weapon had no gun been available, and how much more or less socially damaging the results would have been in that case. In addition, we have no way of knowing how many crimes were prevented by the use, possession, or even possible possession of guns by potential victims.

Of course, even if we knew these facts and they clearly proved that we would endure less social damage if no guns were in the private possession of citizens, this would not solidify the case for gun prohibition. We must remember that we are not considering which theoretically alternative state of the world is preferable but rather what would be the consequences of a particular government policy designed to approach what is felt to be the most desirable state. In practice, such a policy, like all governmental efforts to alter the behavior of citizens, will have costs as well as benefits. It will not be completely effective; insofar as it is effective, it will produce undesirable as well as desirable results; and, the intractability of human beings being what it is, the behavior of the subjects of the law may be such as to change the proportion of desirable and undesirable effects of gun ownership.

To put the matter less abstractly, let us assume that we were confident that the social disadvantages of private possession of firearms outweighed the advantages and, hence, passed a law prohibiting such an activity. Not only would such a law impose major costs of enforcement, including investigating, prosecuting, and punishing offenders, but the enforcement would not be complete. It is by no means a fanciful speculation to predict that, insofar as the incomplete enforcement of such a law would leave some citizens but not others in possession of firearms, those in possession of firearms would more likely be involved in the socially costlier aspects of gun ownership than in those aspects which are more beneficial. Thus, we would expect those who disobeyed such a law to be comparatively more involved in crime than in self-defense, protection of property against animal pests in rural areas, or those activities which we can justify because they give psychic satisfaction to the individual, such as hunting, target shooting, gun collecting, and deriving the feeling of safety that, realistic or not, gun ownership may give.

This comparative magnification of the harmful uses of guns is complicated by another facet of the problem: today, the beneficial, or at least socially harmless, owners of guns are far more numerous than those who impose costs upon society (even if the total costs imposed by the latter outweigh the benefits produced by the former). Even though the prohibition would reduce the number of beneficial or harmless users more than it would the socially costly ones, the disparity in numbers might still be great enough to prevent any concentration of law enforcement resources on the socially costly users who disobey the gun prohibition, without sweeping far more otherwise noncriminal gun offenders into our net.

In addition to the utilitarian considerations imposed by cost-benefit reasoning, there are other aspects to the debate over gun control. Once one concedes that there will be some who lose as well as some who benefit from a gun prohibition, it becomes clear that there are moral aspects to the decision. It is true that every law worth talking about harms some individuals while benefiting others, but here we are weighing a right as basic as any we can conceive of—self-protection. It would seem that we should at least consider whether a society should deprive some of its citizens of such a right in order to benefit others. It can be argued that severe restrictions on the individual's ability to protect him or herself with firearms may be moral only after society has done a tolerable job—or at least can promise credibly to do so—in reducing illegal violence to tolerable limits.

Moreover, we should consider whether there are in any event legal obstacles as well as moral ones to major gun control efforts. For some years, the Second Amendment to the Constitution has been regarded by the great majority of constitutional scholars as irrelevant to the issue of gun control. First of all, the wording of the amendment, with its mention of the necessity of "a well regulated militia," was thought to imply a state, rather than an individual, right. Second, the advocates of an interpretation of the Bill of Rights to protect the "right to keep and bear arms" were caught in a dilemma as to what "arms" were contemplated. If the amendment were given a static interpretation, all that "arms" meant was the weaponry available in 1789—muzzle loaders and flintlocks. On the other hand, if "arms" were given a dynamic interpretation, could the freedom granted by the amendment not literally encompass machine guns, mortars, and even hydrogen bombs? Obviously, neither of these two interpretations was satisfactory to those opposing efforts to disarm the citizenry, a fact that cast doubt on the validity of the whole effort to rely on the Second Amendment.

The constitutional issue today does not seem nearly as clear, however. As the following pages reveal, recent scholarship has made a strong case for the proposition that those who framed and adopted the Second Amendment were concerned about protecting the individual's right to bear arms as well as the right of the state to maintain a militia. Second, this and other research have produced the concept of "militia weapons," the very handguns and rifles that are at issue today, thus building the foundation for a constitutional argument that avoids the pitfalls of either the static or the dynamic interpretations that had made the constitutional issue so difficult for those who claimed the protection of the Second Amendment.

That is not to say that the constitutional issue is now clear the other way. First of all, the historical evidence is by no means all in, nor is what we have in any way conclusive. In addition, all that the Second Amendment in itself could do would be to invalidate certain gun control measures that might be adopted by the federal government; in order for the Constitution to restrain state laws, the Second Amendment would have to be incorporated into the Fourteenth. The research that might justify such a step has hardly begun, and it is fair to say that both Supreme Court precedents and the attitudes of the present members of the Court (the liberals can be expected to be, almost by reflex, in favor of gun control, while the conservatives have staked out a position in favor of states' rights) make this a hard uphill climb.

Perhaps even more difficult is the problem of what kinds of regulation are consistent with any legal right to keep and bear arms, should one be held to exist. The concept of militia weapons makes coherent the view that the government might ban ownership or possession of heavy weapons, but even if no complete ban on militia weapons could pass constitutional scrutiny, there still would remain the issue of what regulations might be imposed on those weapons which could not be completely banned. Thus, even if the courts could be convinced to change their minds on the Second Amendment issue, the way might still be left open for regulations prohibiting certain kinds of light weapons ("Saturday Night Specials"), withdrawing legal protection from certain potential gun owners (felons, those with a history of mental illness, juveniles, etc.) and requiring certain procedures of gun owners (not carrying their weapons in public places, not carrying concealed weapons, compulsory safety instruction, licensing based on competence, and gun registration).

Indeed, as a practical matter, the real dispute today is not over wholesale gun prohibition but rather over some step well short of this. Though the great majority of loosely worded gun control proposals have a strong prohibitionist flavor, virtually all stop short of attempting to ban all guns from private civilian possession. Probably the most extreme measure in the popular debate is a ban on handguns. And even when it is argued that handguns should be banned, the proposals usually make exception for security guards or for police permit procedures. In fact, since virtually everyone recognizes that in some situations firearms provide some social benefits (even if by merely giving their owners pleasure) and also do some social harm, the objective is generally to come up with some restriction that will improve the balance we presently have. In theory, of course, our present restrictions might already be greater than optimal, but, except for the complaints of unreasonable, unproductive and socially costly restrictions on gun collectors, such arguments are rarely heard, at least compared with the far more common arguments in favor of greater restrictions.

To some extent the failure to attempt to ban all firearms is based on a decision by the proponents of lesser measures that the best balance between the costs and benefits of gun control (including the costs and benefits of enforcing such a policy) could be reached without banning long guns. This view can easily be defended on the grounds that, at present, handguns proportionally impose much greater costs per weapon, in terms of homicides and other crimes, than do long guns; that the benefits of long gun ownership are greater, or at least not much less, than the costs; and that the costs of attempting to enforce a gun prohibition against a recalcitrant population, many of whom are located in rural areas, would be far in excess of the costs. On the other hand, it is perhaps not unduly cynical for one to believe that a major reason for not including a complete ban on long guns in gun control proposals is the fact that public opinion, though in favor of "gun control" in the abstract, seems strongly against any such measures that are "too burdensome," and, by virtually any view, a prohibition on long guns would be seen as failing this test.

Ironically, with the exception of those measures already in place, the gun control measure that seems to enjoy the greatest popular support today is gun registration. I say "ironically" because registration seems to create a worse balance of costs and benefits than does any comparable gun control measure. Indeed, a registration system for handguns might be more costly, considering its efficacy, than a complete prohibition. It is unfortunate that none of the following chapters concentrates on the issue of gun registration, but rather than leave such a basic issue unexplored, I will devote a certain amount of space to it here—more, arguably, than is appropriate in a foreword, though less than is necessary to do the job thoroughly.

The first point to note in discussing gun registration is that this term encompasses many very different kinds of arrangements. A registration system can be as simple as automobile registration, where the owner merely has to file a declaration containing name and address, the kind of gun owned, and its serial number. Registration, however, can be more complex; it can involve the owner's birth certificate, photograph, and perhaps fingerprints. A gun registration system could be designed that would be analogous to the driver licensing system. Such a system could require safety instruction, proficiency exams, and even psychological testing.

All of the above licensing and registration requirements are of the permissive variety, since upon completion of certain formalities, they allow anyone except people in relatively small proscribed categories to possess registered weapons. A licensing or registration system, however, could also be of the restrictive variety. Either some particular objective reason, such as employment as a security guard or ownership of a small business likely to be the target of crime, or the approval of the police would be required before an individual could possess a handgun. Needless to say, each of these means of registration would have its own costs, and as the registration became more complex, it would become increasingly expensive for the government to administer and for the citizen to obey.

Even if we used the simplest system, one analogous to auto registration, we should not anticipate the same ease of administration for gun registration. Automobile registration is easily enforced by the issuance of license plates which are visible to all on the highway; possession of an unregistered gun is private and would require the enforcement of the registration law in the same way as a prohibition against gun ownership. And we must remember that no one fears that automobile registration will be a prelude to the confiscation of his or her car. With respect to guns, however, the perception of many owners is quite different.

If many handgun owners did not register their weapons because of lethargy, fear, principle, parsimony, or ignorance, a gun registration system might become very costly. Proportional to their numbers, the unregistered owners would impose upon society many of the same costs that would result from a complete prohibition of guns.

However, the real problem with a law simply requiring the registration of handguns is that it would provide few benefits to balance its costs. A registration system that is not burdensome will not lower gun possession to any significant extent; indeed, it would not even be intended to do so. Those who possessed guns legally could register them with no trouble. If owners wished to avoid registration, one would expect that they would simply keep their guns without registering them, and it is especially hard to believe that those who possessed handguns for criminal purposes would be influenced by a registration requirement. Moreover, as registration becomes more burdensome, it takes on more of the characteristics of a prohibition—though probably at higher administrative cost.

Many people seem to feel that a major advantage of a registration system is that it would make it easier under some circumstances for the police to identify a firearm and trace it to its owner. There are several problems with this view. The gun crime of the otherwise law-abiding citizen is most likely to be the shooting of a relative or acquaintance in the heat of passion. In these cases, the police usually find both the gun and its owner quite easily. With respect to the criminal gun owner the problem is far more difficult, but a registration system is not of much help. Automobiles are sufficiently large that they can be and are built with a number of serial numbers in secret locations. The same cannot be done with handguns, and it is not difficult to remove the serial numbers of weapons. Second, guns whose possessors are unknown and which can be connected to a crime seldom fall into police hands. If weapons could be more easily traced, they would presumably be hidden or destroyed and would be confiscated by police even less often. Finally, competent criminals would exert considerable effort to obtain firearms that could not be traced to their crimes.

Of course, it would be helpful in tracking down criminals to have a registry of the bullets fired by each gun, since police do find bullets they cannot trace—often in homicide and robbery victims. The problem is that any method of registering guns by the particular markings on the bullets they fire would be hopelessly impractical. The markings change with the age of the gun, and in any event, we have no method of indexing the markings the way we do fingerprints. Hence, we would have no means of finding the few relevant patterns among the vast number that would be registered.

If the registration compromise does not address the problem of guns in our society, neither does the most popularly advanced alternative to gun control, high mandatory criminal penalties for the misuse of firearms. In theory, this makes some sense. Long sentences should have the effect of deterring more gun criminals and isolating for a longer time those who were not deterred. In addition, we could do this without having to catch and process more criminals, simply by raising the penalties for those we have caught. Unfortunately, deterrence seems to be affected more by the likelihood of apprehension than by the penalty if apprehended, and it is probable that the present sentences would be sufficient if those committing crimes with guns thought their chances of being caught were substantial enough—to the extent that they thought at all about the matter.

Part of the problem is that the criminal justice system is overloaded at all its stages, not merely at the police apprehension stage. Though a mandatory sentence system does not appear to require additional police work in terms of arresting criminals, it does put a considerably greater strain on the trial system. Restrictions on plea bargaining and on judicial leniency prevent precisely those activities which permit the courts to cope with their overload. Most people forget that the major effect of mandatory sentences and restrictions on plea bargaining is to induce a higher percentage of defendants to take their chances with going to trial, thus further overburdening the courts.

This effect can rather easily overtax our resources. If the percentage of defendants pleading guilty drops from 90 to 80 percent, the trial calendars must double, and twice as many courtrooms, judges, jurors, court officials, prosecutors, and defense attorneys will be necessary. And if the percentage of guilty pleas drops to 70 percent— a figure most citizens would still consider unacceptably high—our trial resources would have to be tripled.

Few people who are not directly involved in the system can appreciate the degree to which our criminal courts are already overcrowded. A recent editorial in a local newspaper gives details on a typical situation—in this case in one of California's most affluent counties:

> One day recently, Judge Stone's calendar listed a record 269 cases. A courthouse holding cell designed to accommodate 20 defendants was jammed with

100. The judge says they were unguarded because the sheriff didn't have enough deputies to assign one to the holding cell. . . .

Judge Stone estimates it could cost up to $1 million a year to provide Santa Clara County with enough prosecutors, public defenders and adult probation officers to keep the courts operating efficiently, which is to say justly. He doesn't know where the money will come from and, at this point, neither does the board of supervisors, which is facing the prospect of a budget deficit. . . .

A million dollars isn't going to build a new jail, but $1 million would go a long way torward clearing the Superior Court's criminal trial calendar, thus reassuring the public that the criminal justice system isn't about to collapse.[1]

Longer sentences, mandatory or not, for those who misuse guns, tend to have another effect. Because of the relatively minor effect deterrence measures seem to have on those most likely to misuse guns, the number of such criminals confined will gradually increase. To combat this, we may have to release other criminals, perhaps even more deserving of imprisonment, from our overcrowded institutions. The sizable number of other claimants on our criminal justice resources—drug sellers, muggers, knife rapists, and the like—are equally good candidates for further imprisonment as are criminals who use guns. Alternatively, we will have to spend more money building and maintaining additional correctional facilities. The problem with the latter solution is that each new space in a medium security institution costs upward of $100,000 today, and the yearly cost per prisoner averages around $15,000. It is by no means unreasonable for most legislators, albeit reluctantly, to decide that they can do better with their tax revenues.

Does this and what follows mean that the problem of gun control is insoluble? Perhaps not, but it does mean that the problem is far more complex than most of us have been willing to admit. With the publication of this work, it becomes impossible for any serious, thoughtful person to deny this, and indeed, to fail to appreciate just how inadequate our dialogue formerly was. For this reason we should extend our thanks to those who have made this work possible.

John Kaplan
Stanford University

1. *San Jose Mercury News*, 20 January 1981, p. 6B.

ACKNOWLEDGMENTS

Creation of this volume depended on the superb work of many fine people. In terms of constructive criticism as well as financial and logistical support, I am indebted to the Pacific Institute for Public Policy Research. In particular, I wish to express my gratitude to the Institute's President, David J. Theroux, who first encouraged me to undertake this project, and who greatly assisted throughout in refining the massive work involved. Charles W. Baird, M. Bruce Johnson, and Patrick Cox were most helpful in their excellent suggestions at the various stages of completion. Colleen Gilbride was irreplaceable in handling editorial and publication responsibilities, and Jo McLain deserves thanks for editing assistance.

In addition, the volume benefited from the trenchant reviews and learned comments of Alan Lizotte, William Marina, Mark Moore, Gordon Tullock, S. T. Byrd, David I. Caplan, Stephen Halbrook, Gary Kleck, and Leonard Liggio.

Don B. Kates, Jr.

INTRODUCTION

Don B. Kates, Jr.

Credible social-scientific study of firearms ownership and its implications has largely been confined to the last ten years, the enormous volume of the previous literature notwithstanding. The decade 1965 to 1975 had seen the publication of at least six books, over forty law review articles, and five congressional hearings devoted solely to criminological aspects of firearms ownership. As B. Bruce-Briggs acerbically observed in 1976, "From the amount of energy spent on the gun issue one might conclude that gun control is the key to the crime problem. Yet it is startling to note that no policy research worthy of the name has been done on the issue of gun control. The few attempts at serious work are of marginal competence at best, and tainted by obvious bias."[1] Another analyst (who has subsequently contributed some of the most important work in the field), although somewhat less dubious about the value of gun regulation, was in substantial agreement: "While the consistent failure of gun control proposals to pass Congress has often been blamed on lobbying efforts of the NRA, part of the problem may be that the case for more stringent gun control regulation has not been made in any scientific fashion."[2]

---

1. B. Bruce-Briggs, "The Great American Gun War," *The Public Interest* (Fall 1976).
2. P. Cook, "A Policy Perspective on Handgun Control," (Duke University, 1976). (Mimeo.)

The authors of this volume seek both to summarize and to augment present knowledge on the major policy implications of American firearms ownership and regulation. To accomplish this, the Pacific Institute for Public Policy Research commissioned papers on a coordinated set of topics from seventeen scholars, a few of whom were new to the field, though most were selected because of outstanding contributions already made. Indicative of the breadth of the issues involved is the fact that the contributors to this volume include not only criminologists but sociologists, economists, historians, philosophers, and constitutional and criminal law theorists.

The seventeen papers presented herein are arranged around eight central topics chosen because of their importance to policy evaluation of the gun control controversy in the United States. These topics are (1) public opinion on gun ownership and its regulation; (2) the relationship of popular to academic attitudes on gun regulation; (3) gun ownership as a possible cause of homicide and other criminal violence; (4) the viability and utility of specific prohibitionary proposals, concentrating particularly on handguns and the subspecies thereof commonly termed "Saturday Night Specials"; (5) assessment of the effectiveness of present gun controls; (6) widespread gun ownership as a means of deterring or preventing crime; (7) gun ownership as a constitutional right; and (8) the implications of conferring a monopoly of gun ownership on the police, the military, and those civilians they approve.

To place these issues in context, two overviews are provided. The first is by law professor Leroy Clark, who discusses some of the constitutional and legal implications of the gun prohibitions he advocates, and generally surveys the pre-1975 work supporting his position. The second overview is by sociologist David Bordua and criminologist Gary Kleck. An earlier article by Kleck that appeared in the *American Journal of Sociology* was the first methodologically sophisticated study of the relationship between gun ownership and homicide.[3] It lent weight to the prohibitionist position, finding that increased gun ownership accelerates homicide, at least modestly, while decreasing capital punishment does not. The present Kleck and Bordua piece provides a critical overview of five crucial and generally unexamined assumptions that will be exhaustively reviewed in this volume.

3. Gary Kleck, "Capital Punishment, Gun Ownership and Homicide," *American Journal of Sociology* 84 (1979): 882–910.

After these introductions, we move to the issue of public opinion and the oft-heard claim that legislators are swayed by hyperactive gun owner lobbying to ignore the apathetic majority's desire to ban guns. The papers presented herein suggest a more complex analysis: the majority favors not prohibition but only control designed to disarm criminals without denying law-abiding citizens the right to possess handguns for self-defense.

Professor Bordua's chapter attributes the gun lobby's victories to the fact that its antiprohibitionary arguments appeal to and capitalize upon the attitudes of most voters. When anti-gun organizations, under the impression that they enjoy majority support, have transferred the issue from the legislatures to the voters via the initiative process, they have suffered overwhelming defeat (California, 1982; Massachusetts, 1976). Developing the "culture conflict" explanation, sociologist William Tonso suggests that unswerving allegiance to handgun prohibition is a majority sentiment only among intellectuals and academicians.[4]

Addressing the next central issue—whether gun ownership creates homicide—Gary Kleck modifies the conclusions of his *American Journal of Sociology* article in light of subsequent and more extensive data. He finds gun homicide to be a phenomenon of small and discrete groups of criminally and/or violently inclined people; gun ownership by the general populace does not per se cause homicide. Thus, Kleck and Bordua propose that "gun control" strategies be directed against firearms possession by the violent, rather than against possession by the general populace.

The next topic is the viability/utility of prohibitions directed at either "Saturday Night Specials" or all handguns. Addressing viabil-

4. Cf. B. Bruce-Briggs (*supra* n. 1):

But underlying the gun control struggle is a fundamental division in our nation. The intensity of passion on this issue suggests to me that we are experiencing a sort of low-grade war going on between two alternative views of what America is and ought to be. On the one side are those who take bourgeois Europe as a model of a civilized society: a society just, equitable, and democratic; but well ordered, with the lines of responsibility and authority clearly drawn, and with decisions made rationally and correctly by intelligent men for the entire nation. To such people, hunting is atavistic, personal violence is shameful, and uncontrolled gun ownership is a blot upon civilization.

On the other side is a group of people who do not tend to be especially articulate or literate, and whose world view is rarely expressed in print. Their model is that of the independent frontiersman who takes care of himself and his family with no interference from the state. They are "conservative" in the sense that they cling to America's unique pre-modern tradition—a non-feudal society with a sort of medieval liberty writ large for everyman. To these people, "sociological" is an epithet. Life is tough and competitive. Manhood means responsibility and caring for your own.

ity, Kates's chapter suggests that a ban of all handguns would meet as great or greater noncompliance than did alcohol Prohibition and would be significantly more difficult to enforce. Addressing utility, Gary Kleck's next chapter takes up the single most important unexamined assumption in "gun control" theory: that depriving potential killers of handguns will result only in substitution of less deadly knives without any substitution of more deadly rifles and shotguns. Since handguns are only marginally more deadly than knives (and long guns are much more deadly than either), even a relatively small substitution of long guns in assaults could actually increase homicide.[5]

Conversely, Paula McClain's chapter suggests that a purchase ban on "Saturday Night Specials" alone could reach its more limited objective precisely because of the continued availability of more expensive, generally higher caliber and larger handguns. Few people would be inclined to buy cheaply made handguns illegally at inflated black market prices when better weapons could legally be purchased at about the same cost.

Moving to assessment of gun law effectiveness, economists Joseph Magaddino and Marshall Medoff conclude that present federal and state gun laws have had little value in reducing violence. In this connection, criminologist-economists Steven Balkin and John McDonald produce a model by which the effectiveness of handgun regulations may be evaluated.

In the next section, James Wright, coauthor of the single most important and exhaustive general study of gun control issues,[6] reaches the controversial conclusion that the incidence of successful citizen self-defense with handguns roughly approximates that of accident and criminal misuse.[7] Economist Bruce Benson expands on this

---

5. It should be noted that both these chapters, along with those of Magaddino and Medoff, Wright, and Balkin and McDonald contained herein, are revised versions of papers presented at the November 1981 annual meeting of the American Society of Criminology. Likewise, the Bordua chapter is a revision of one he presented at the 1980 annual meeting of the American Sociological Association and the Kleck-Bordua chapter is a revision of a paper presented there by Kleck.

6. J. Wright, P. Rossi, et al., *Weapons, Crime, and Violence in America: A Literature Review and Research Agenda* (Washington, D.C.: GPO, 1981). Also see J. Wright, P. Rossi, and K. Daly, *Under the Gun: Weapons, Crime, and Violence in America* (Hawthorne, N.Y.: Aldine, 1983).

7. Further evidence on this topic recently became available through a survey of 1,850 inmates in ten major state prisons across the nation completed by the Social and Demographic Research Institute of Massachusetts University. A substantial majority of prison-

theme, placing gun ownership in context among many other devices and activities he groups logically together as examples of increasing privatization of law enforcement.

The next section is devoted to the right to keep and bear arms. Laywer-philosopher Stephen Halbrook examines the relationship of the Second Amendment to the classical republican political tradition of the armed populace. Historian Joyce Malcolm examines the Second Amendment's English common law antecedents in light of her exhaustive research in original sources. Historian William Marina places the amendment in the context of weapons technology, which throughout the ages has made possible the triumph of popular regimes over authoritarian ones.

In the concluding section, lawyer-sociologist Raymond Kessler discusses the political functions of gun prohibition in suppressing opposition to government and in increasing the populace's dependence upon the police. Historian-criminologist Frank Morn traces how American police, having started out unarmed, became armed. Unlike British police, American departments were forced to arm as criminal violence continued and increased in the nineteenth century United States while it decreased in the United Kingdom.

Having outlined the volume's contents, completeness requires discussion of two further matters, which, though often argued, are so unscholarly as to not merit attention in the chapters included here. The first of these—the claim that foreign countries' low violence is attributable to their gun laws—is of less significance for the issues than as evidence for Tonso's reflections on how partisanship has affected scholarly treatment of them. Imagine how the liberal academics who argue this point would react to the equally preposterous attribution of low rates of Japanese and English violence to those countries not having the exclusionary rule or the host of other rights Americans accused of crime enjoy. Obviously American gun availability cannot explain a rate of violent crime *without guns* that exceeds the per capita rate for violence with every kind of weapon in Japan, England, and elsewhere.

The fact is that while low rates of gun possession and violence coincide in some countries, in others (e.g., Switzerland, Canada, and

---

ers who admitted to the commission of violent felonies indicated that they had at one time been wounded, caught, or scared off by a gun-armed civilian or that they knew of crimes which had been abandoned or averted because of knowledge or belief that the victim might be armed.

Israel), equally low violence rates coincide with rates of gun ownership that equal or exceed that of the United States. In yet other
countries (South Africa and Taiwan), homicide rates exceeding the
American rate coincide with anti-gun laws more stringent than
English and Japanese laws. As Professor Morn's police chapter notes,
England's violence declined so steadily in the early nineteenth century that its police were never forced to arm. In contrast, the period
from 1820 to 1920 saw various American states pioneering gun-
carrying laws, Saturday-Night-Special laws, permit requirements for
handgun ownership or purchase, and even blanket prohibitions
(all without notable success in stemming violence). During the same
period in England, which started out equally or more violent, only
the police were prohibited ownership or the carrying of weapons.
Yet England had become so peaceful by 1920 that handgun prohibition (adopted for the purpose of suppressing anarchists, bolsheviks,
and other such groups) elicited wide compliance because few people
thought they needed a weapon for self-defense. The conclusion to be
drawn is obvious—that the basic determinants of homicide and
violent crime relate to sociocultural, economic, and institutional
factors, not to gun laws or gun possession.

From the other side, it is sometimes suggested that we need not
worry about guns because they are involved in only a tiny fraction
of American crime. In a crudely quantitative sense, this is true. By
definition, the nonconfrontation crimes (e.g., auto theft), which constitute the numerical majority of reported felonies, do not involve
firearms. But clearly firearms are involved in a great number of the
most serious crimes, including approximately 13,000 murders and
some hundreds of thousands of violent felonies yearly. Whatever
dubiety may be justified as to the ameliorative value of any particular proposed gun control, to belittle the seriousness of firearms misuse is ridiculous.

The purpose of bringing together the chapters presented in the
volume is to explore the extent and causes of that misuse.

PART I

OVERVIEW– ASSESSING THE PROBLEM

Chapter 1

REDUCING FIREARMS AVAILABILITY
Constitutional Impediments to Effective Legislation and an Agenda for Research

Leroy D. Clark

INTRODUCTION: THE PAST RESEARCH

Banning firearms, a hotly debated issue, has figured in the considerations of two or three national commissions investigating violence and disorder in America. But the research in this area to aid the development of public policy has been limited to the most preliminary questions. Two kinds of data have been collected to date — opinion polls assaying the public attitudes toward various kinds of gun control proposals and studies both supporting and refuting the proposition that the availability of guns is a critical element in the level or escalation of violence in society.

Those who favor firearms prohibitions have developed some credible proof that there is some relationship between the extent of firearm ownership and the incidence of homicides, accidental deaths, and aggravated assaults.[1] The studies making this conclusion, however, are not without serious weaknesses. A prime problem with such research is that the raw data generally used — *FBI Uniform Crime Statistics* — were probably not collected with a view toward specifically

The author wishes to make it clear that the enclosed article is an attempt to explore legal problems which may confront a gun prohibition program, but that his overall assessment is that, for a host of other reasons not explored herein, gun prohibitions are desirable and necessary.

1. Editor's note: See Kleck, *infra*, for evidence on this point.

measuring the role of the gun in criminal activity; thus refined conclusions are difficult to make.

The major charge made against this research, however, is the failure of the authors to control variables that may be more causally linked to the illegal use of firearms than the mere extent of their availability. It is claimed, for example, that in a jurisdiction that severely restricts gun ownership, persons may use guns less, not because they are less available, but because such citizens are, by character, very different from persons in states that have not passed gun control legislation. It is also argued that the incidence of the misuse of guns is miniscule in relation to the total availability of guns. There are approximately 150 million firearms in the country, but only .002 percent of them figure in accidents or criminal attacks in any given year.[2] If one even assumed gun ownership was as high as three guns per person, this would still mean that 99.98 percent of gun owners posed no threat to themselves or others. It is possible that those persons who use firearms illegally or even accidentally may be a fairly discrete and peculiar portion of the population.[3]

While some claims may be legitimate that the research supporting the "availability" theory is incomplete, further research on the question in this form may not be warranted. Such criticisms could be leveled at any attempt to indicate general tendencies when complex human behavior is being studied on the basis of mass data. There are always some variables that have not been or cannot be controlled, and alternative speculations can always be offered to explain the same phenomena.

The research that suggests some possibility of a reduction of firearm deaths and injuries is strong enough to warrant some experimentation in gun confiscation. This is particularly true when one compares the potential gains and losses through a confiscation program. Even a small reduction of deaths and injuries has other consequences: the lives of talented contributors to society may be saved, less time is lost at work, less drain occurs on medical and legal resources. Further, confiscation, especially of handguns, would create little inconvenience with respect to recreation or hunting, and the self-defense needs of the average citizen are not enhanced in any significant way by the possession of a gun.[4]

2. Editor's note: Wright *infra*, provides detailed discussion of the numbers involved.

3. Editor's note: Kleck, *infra*, provides data confirming this speculation.

4. It is estimated that the homeowner was able to foil a burglary in only 2 out of every 1,000 burglaries. (*Firearms and Violence*, A Staff Report to the National Commission on the Causes and Prevention of Violence.)

THE PROBLEM OF ENFORCEMENT

While further research may not be needed on the "availability" theory, the fairly unsuccessful attempts to prohibit possession of two other substances that create public health problems (alcohol and drugs) indicate that the most serious question for future research is the nature of the problems of enforceability of a gun confiscation effort, even assuming one could secure passage of a "model" statute.

The suggestion that an analogy in research be drawn between prohibition of the 1920s and gun confiscation is apt because alcohol is very much a part of the "technology" of homicide and aggravated assault. In a study of data over a four-year period, it was found that 54 percent of the persons committing homicide had been drinking. Unlike the gun, alcohol may have played a potent role in the victim's precipitating the homicidal event, because in 52 percent of the cases the victim had been drinking. Since homicide frequently occurs between spouses and friends in heated arguments, one can speculate that the normal bonds of affection and relationship might have prevented the homicide were it not for the disinhibiting effect of the alcohol. Thus, if one were able to achieve widespread abstinence in the general population, one would expect an impact on the homicide and aggravated assault rate, even if guns were present.

Although there is a high degree of association between alcohol and crimes of violence, it is highly unlikely that anyone today would seriously propose a resumption of prohibition. Not only was enforcement impossible, because of the manifold and easily adopted means of evasion, but there were associated consequences that made the "Great Experiment" too costly. Organized crime reaped substantial revenues from entry into the illegal traffic, lower level police were corrupted through graft, and discriminatory enforcement developed.[5]

A similar fate has visited our stringent legislation on narcotic use. As federal and some state penalties were increased between 1968 and 1972 for persons involved in the trafficking of drugs, the

---

Editor's note: Kleck, *infra*, and Wright, *infra*, reach substantially different conclusions based on data that are both newer and much more extensive than that available to Newton and Zimring.)

5. Andrew Sinclair, *Prohibition: The Era of Excess* (Boston: Atlantic Monthly Press, 1962); U.S. National Commission on Law Observance and Enforcement, *Report on the Enforcement of Prohibition Law of the United States* (Washington, D.C.: GPO, 1931).

addict population rose from 65,000 to approximately 300,000 to 400,000.[6] This was also a period of heightened public attention and increased law enforcement efforts.

While there was some general sympathy for the victims of drug addiction, the primary public concern was the urban criminality generated by the addict to secure the financial resources for drugs. One recent study, however, shows that where "strict" enforcement has managed to temporarily diminish the supply of drugs, the immediate consequence was an *increase* in addict criminality in order to meet the higher prices being charged for scarcer drugs.[7] If there had been a more complete picture of the high cost and minimal impact of our policy of "tough" criminal legislation, our anti-drug policies might have been fashioned along very different lines.

While there may be some similarities between the enforcement problems that may be encountered in suppression of the traffic in guns and alcohol or drugs (willing seller and buyer, ability to conduct transactions under secret circumstances, etc.), they are not identical. For example, the imperativeness of need is probably substantially higher for the average addict than the average gun owners, thus making the enforcement problem substantially different. The suggestion here is that analogous information should be the starting point, and the differences should be actively explored to throw light on the potential effectiveness of a confiscation effort.

For example, prosecutors sometimes found it difficult to secure convictions during prohibition, even where they had substantial evidence of guilt, because juries or judges who were unsympathetic to the law simply refused to convict. This is probably not a problem in prosecuting "pushers" of addictive drugs. How would gun prohibitions fare with respect to this factor? It may be difficult to develop a research design to answer some of the questions, but one would want to know the areas in which juries might nullify the laws through a high level of acquittals,[8] and whether there are strategies of education that might reduce this impediment to enforcement.[9]

---

6. American Bar Association's Special Committee on Crime Prevention and Control, *New Perspectives on Urban Crime* 29 (1972).

7. Study done under the auspices of the Drug Abuse Council on the impact of drug enforcement in Detroit, Michigan.

8. If a statute carried a light penalty for trafficking illegally in guns, it would run the risk of having little deterrent impact if there was a great profit incentive to get into the trade. Higher sentences (above six months imprisonment) would give the defendant a right

RESEARCH ON FOREIGN COUNTRIES

Research that concludes by advocating ownership restrictions and that has been restricted to the United States has been faced with one major problem. An assumption has been made that legislation in a given jurisdiction, which on its face is restrictive of gun ownership, resulted in fewer guns in the hands of the local populace. This assumption may be unwarranted due to the fact that there are always nearby jurisdictions that allow firearms acquisition, and an interstate traffic may have developed in circumvention of the restrictive legislation in any area.

The problem is well illustrated by comparing two articles written by Zimring, one before the passage of the 1968 Federal Gun Control Act and another written after a seven-year experience with that Act. In the earlier piece, Zimring points to the fact that guns were used in only 23.4 percent of the robberies in New York City, whereas nationally guns were involved in 38.9 percent of reported robberies. This was in support of the theory that a lower supply of weapons would result in less armed criminal activity, and this lower supply was ostensibly due to the fact that New York City had a "rigid" Sullivan law prohibition.[10]

Zimring's later research, however, embarrasses his earlier assertion. First, one would expect that the availability of guns in New York City would be *lower* after 1968 because the federal legislation prohibited many forms of interstate sales that had previously been lawful. Thus, theoretically, evasion of the New York City law should have been made more difficult. However, Zimring's data show that the rate of handgun violence increased more rapidly after passage of the federal legislation in New York City and Boston, ostensibly "control jurisdictions," than in fifty-seven other citities, most of which had no prohibitory legislation. The present high levels of gun ownership, an active resale market, and the ease by which guns may

---

to trial by jury. *Baldwin v. New York*, 399 U.S. 66 (1970). The defendants would elect this route where they thought the local populace was opposed to gun control laws.

9. Editor's note: These issues are all addressed in Kates, *infra*, which explicitly follows Clark's suggestion of a comparison between alcohol prohibition and the banning of handguns.

10. F. Zimring, "Games with Guns and Statistics," *Wisconsin Law Review* (1968): 1113, 1118.

be carried across state lines all make it difficult to denominate a particular jurisdiction as one that has achieved a restricted supply of guns. This suggests that research limited to the United States may not be the best way to answer some of the law enforcement questions.

It seems more fruitful to have more extensive, comparative research, examining the European countries that have gun control legislation and comparing them to the American scene. Most comparisons of the United States and other countries are not very developed.[11] Even the little data of comparison are always qualified by statements that the conclusions proffered are compromised by the absence of a control on cultural differences. Research, therefore, is needed to isolate and identify the pertinent cultural factors so that meaningful comparisons can be made.[12]

The foreign experience may divulge information we do not have in the American context—namely, whether a black market develops, aimed at smuggling guns in from other countries. This might supply information about the cost of guns in such a market and whether there are law enforcement techniques to effectively suppress such traffic.

LEGAL BARRIERS TO EFFECTIVE LEGISLATION

The Second Amendment

Are there legal impediments to federal legislation that would seek to bar the average citizen from ownership or possession of a gun? Some advocates have proposed state or municipal prohibitions, but only

11. In Zimring's report to the Violence Commission, *supra* p.e, he relied on the text of foreign laws, which he stated he knew was "an insufficient basis for evaluating the quality of any country's firearms control system," at p. 119. Other data in his study were based on "unpublished" reports of the English Home Office at p. 124. The National Advisory Commission of Criminal Justice Standards and Goals: *A National Strategy to Reduce Crime* (1973) relied on statements from the Tokyo Police Department on handgun homicides in 1971.

12. Editor's note: The two most important studies available in English are Colin Greenwood's *Firearm Control: A Study of Armed Crime and Firearms Control in England and Wales* (London: Routledge and Kegan Paul, 1972) and Richard Harding's *Firearms and Violence in Australian Life* (Nedlands: U. of W. Aus. Press (1981). Other comparative materials appear in Don Kates' *Restricting Handguns: The Liberal Skeptics Speak Out* (Croton-on-Hudson, N.Y.: North River Press, 1979), Ch. 2, and Tonso, *infra*.

national controls could be effective.[13] The potential for undermining the enforcement efforts of a local jurisdiction, because of open traffic in other jurisdictions, is too great. Further, local options are the status quo now, and the rate of gun violence, even in jurisdictions that nominally prohibit widespread ownership of firearms, is alarming.

The Second Amendment to the U.S. Constitution has been put forward as a bar to federal gun control legislation. However, the most convincing scholarly comments[14] and the few Supreme Court decisions on the matter do not support that view. The amendment seems to have been a compromise extracted by those who were suspicious of a strong central government and wanted the states empowered to resist militarily any excessive attempts at seizure of power. The local state militias had been the backbone of resistance to the British, and the colonists also wanted to prevent the occurrence of the European experience of a strong king, with a standing army, who oppressed the citizenry. The Second Amendment was, therefore, adopted to prevent the federal government from passing legislation that would incapacitate the states from having organized militias. It is thus argued that the amendment is not directed toward protecting *private* ownership of guns, but only at preserving the *state's* capacity to mount an army.

The major argument against this view of the Second Amendment is that the legislative history did not focus sharply on the issue.[15] This was probably because at the time of the adoption of the amendment, the personal possession of firearms was very widespread. There were no thoughts of disarming the citizenry, irrespective of the fear of an unchecked central government, because the need for hunting, conquering, and defending against Indians was so palpable.[16] However, the Second Amendment is probably one that has become antiquated in its thrust due to the vast changes in the technology of the

13. Editor's note: Kates, *infra*, discusses this point but comes to the directly opposite conclusion that well-policed states and cities like New York are better able to enforce prohibitory legislation than would be the federal authorities who are presently unable to prevent the smuggling of large quantities of drugs and illegal aliens over the country's vast border areas.

14. A typical piece is R. Weatherup, "Standing Armies and Armed Citizens: An Historical Analysis of the Second Amendment," *Hastings Law Quarterly* 2 (1975): 961.

15. A most cogent development of the counterarguments appears in D. Hardy and J. Stompoly, "Of Arms and The Law," *Chicago-Kent Law Review* 51 (1974–75): 62–114.

16. Editor's note: These issues are detailed in Halbrook and Kates, *infra*. See also Malcolm, *infra*.

phenomena that it sought to control.[17] The state militias armed with 38s, 45s, or rifles would hardly be a match against a central government with tanks, fighter planes, and atomic weaponry. It is likely, therefore, that the Supreme Court will not find this amendment an impediment to federal arms control legislation that has some potential for increasing public safety.

Authority Under the Interstate Commerce Clause

While the Second Amendment may present no barrier to federal legislation, crime control under our federal system is primarily a function of the states. Thus, for the federal government to legislate in this area, there must be some affirmative constitutional authority to do so.

The basis usually offered for federal gun control laws is Congress' right to control interstate commerce. The Gun Control Act of 1968, which focuses on interstate transactions, has been held to be a constitutional exercise of authority. More difficult questions would arise, however, if the federal government tried to reach the sales and purchases that were solely intrastate, or tried to ban mere intrastate possession without any showing of a prior passage in interstate commerce. The Supreme Court in *U.S. v. Bass* avoided reaching the question, by interpreting the federal statute as requiring proof that the weapon had been involved in interstate commerce.[18] A subsequent case, however, has held that the present amendments to the federal legislation do not require that an interstate commerce nexus be demonstrated.[19] It is unclear whether this case thoroughly and seriously considered that nexus, as there was little discussion of it. This raises the question of whether the present court, with its different personnel, upon a fuller exploration of the question, might find otherwise.

The probable argument in support of the federal legislation is that no effective control is exercised over interstate transactions unless intrastate transactions are likewise brought under the federal statute. Congress technically has the legal authority to control intrastate

17. Position adopted in P. Feller and K. Gotting, "The Second Amendment, A Second Look," *Northwestern University Law Review* 61 (1966): 61.
18. *United States v. Bass*, 404 U.S. 336 (1971).
19. *Huddleston v. United States*, 415 U.S. 814 (1974).

transactions when they have this kind of impact on interstate commerce. The problem, however, is that there is very little in the legislative history of the 1968 Gun Control Act that lays a factual basis for this conclusion, and some courts have questioned whether federal legislation founded on the commerce clause is constitutional unless there is some such factual support. If it could be documented that, even with the 1968 Gun Control Act, there was a flow of weapons from jurisdictions where possession was lawful to jurisdictions where it was not, this might supply the factual basis that the courts have indicated is necessary, should federal legislation go further to ban intrastate possession.[20]

The Fifth Amendment

If federal legislation took the form of requiring the registration of weapons, the Fifth Amendment to the U.S. Constitution would play a role. Where ownership or possession of the gun was in violation of other federal or state laws, registration would require the person to give incriminating evidence against himself. Were this compelled disclosure used to prove a violation of the law against possession, the declarant would have a claim that his Fifth Amendment privilege against self-incrimination had been violated. This is, however, not an impediment to a registration statute, for the federal law could simply exempt those persons from registration who possess the firearms in violation of some other provision.

One might ask what the utility of a registration statute would be under such circumstances, for those who possess guns lawfully would register, and the criminal element would not. Further, it is unlikely that persons who intended to use their weapons in criminal activity

20. Editor's note: The matter was more thoroughly discussed in *Scarborough v. United States*, 431 U.S. 563 (1977), which strongly suggests that the interstate commerce power extends to prohibiting possession of any firearm that has at any time traveled in interstate commerce, i.e. has either been imported or been shipped across state lines. Since a substantial minority of American firearms are imported, and the rest are manufactured by a few firms, which are generally localized in the New England states, it would appear that most, if not all, firearms have the "minimal nexus" to interstate commerce of having at some time crossed a state or federal border. Moreover, it is at least arguable from existing precedents that the interstate commerce power would extend to confiscating even those firearms that have never crossed a state or federal border on the grounds that the metals and other materials out of which they are fabricated have moved in interstate commerce. See, for example, *Katzenbach v. McClung*, 379 U.S. 294 (1964).

would register them, even if the possession itself were not unlawful, and even if they were protected by the Fifth Amendment should they register. It has been argued, however, that persons who originally possess guns lawfully pass them on in sales or other transactions. If those persons register the gun and it is later recovered in a circumstance where it had been used unlawfully, one could use the original lawful owner of the gun to get a lead to its subsequent owners.

Should the unlikely occur and a person who intended to use the weapon in criminal activity actually register under the federal statute, this would not provide the person with an absolute shield against prosecution under any law that made possession illegal. While many federal statutes gave such total immunity in the past, the Supreme Court has recently said that it is not constitutionally mandated.[21] The government is only barred from using the compelled information, directly or indirectly, in a prosecution, but is permitted to prove the offense through any information that has been secured independently.

The Fourth Amendment

While the Fifth Amendment poses little in the way of an obstacle to gun control legislation, the Fourth Amendment, restricting searches and seizures, could be a serious barrier to enforcing a registration or confiscation program.

Should the bulk of persons who presently possess firearms resist registration or delivery of guns to appropriate officials in a confiscation program, collecting approximately 50 million handguns may be impossible in terms of police manpower. Even assuming substantial compliance (e.g. two thirds of the public), there would still be the problem of establishing the legal grounds for a search for the "holdouts." For the police to conduct a search of any premise for weapons they would have to satisfy the Fourth Amendment's "probable cause" standard—namely, they would have to get a warrant by presenting some credible information to a magistrate from which the court could infer that it was more likely than not that contraband was located on the premises to be searched. While the court has re-

21. *Kastigar v. United States*, 406 U.S. 441 (1972).

laxed the requirement of a warrant for the arrest of a *person* in a public place, the general rule with respect to the search of *premises* is still that, absent some exigent circumstances, the authorities must have a warrant issued by a magistrate prior to the entry.[22] The requirement of a warrant for the search of premises is insisted upon more where the premises is a private home, as opposed to a business establishment, and the available data suggest that a sizeable number of weapons is stored in homes.

How would the police secure the minimal information needed to obtain a valid search warrant? Since the premises in most instances would be a private home, only those persons who have lawful access to such premises or who are acquainted with the owner or tenant could normally supply this information. The Supreme Court has said that the State may insinuate an agent into a relationship with a citizen to secure the "probable cause" evidence, but again because of limitations on law enforcement resources, this effort will probably be limited to persons believed to be in the trafficking of the contraband, as opposed to large numbers of "consumers" of the product.[23] It is unlikely that others will come forth with information that could cause the arrest and conviction of friends and relatives.

There is a possibility of a warrantless seizure of a gun if it were being carried by a person in public, even if an officer did not have full "probable cause" for an arrest. However, the officer must subsequently describe some activity that created a "reasonable suspicion" that a violent crime was being contemplated in order to justify his or her "frisk" of the suspect and seizure of the gun.[24] Obviously this relaxed standard for a limited person-search would be of utility only against those in the preliminary stages of committing an offense and would not reach the average law-abiding citizen, even if he or she were carrying a weapon concealed on the person.

It was mentioned earlier that a study of foreign countries might provide information about the extent of gun smuggling from other countries. In a formal sense at least, the Fourth Amendment poses no problems, for the usual requirements of a search warrant and probable cause do not obtain in searching persons or property coming into the country from abroad. There are some limitations on very

22. *United States v. Watson*, 423 U.S. 411 (1975).
23. *United States v. White*, 401 U.S. 745 (1971).
24. *Terry v. Ohio*, 392 U.S. 1 (1968).

intrusive personal searches (body cavities), but this is more pertinent for contraband, like heroin, which may be carried in small packages and easily concealed. The major problems would entail the level of smuggling (modulated probably by its profitability) and the necessary expenditures in personnel and equipment to conduct surveillance. It is hoped that foreign research would supply some of the information here.

The legal impediments to recovery of weapons solely by law enforcement efforts, given their widespread possession by the public to date, suggest that it would be necessary to design, through research efforts, the kind of program that would encourage the gun-owning public to relinquish the weapons voluntarily. It would be helpful to know what the cost of a purchase-back program might be, and what other kind of educational influences might be brought to bear to achieve voluntary cooperation. In this light, obviously more research is needed into the psychology of gun ownership if confiscation, under our particular constitutional framework, would be difficult.

An aspect of the psychology of gun ownership to be explored involves its racial dimension. While there is some gross data that show that the accelerated increase in gun ownership among whites during the mid-1960s was in response to riots in urban areas, we also know that there was very little actual use of guns by rioters.[25] This was true even though guns have played a heavy role among blacks in intracommunity violence. Research is therefore suggested by these paradoxes. What is the precise nature of the fears of the white community that have prompted the inordinate purchase of guns, and how might they operate to resist any confiscation program? What is the incidence of gun ownership in the black community, and what different functions does gun ownership play in a ghettoized, low income area?

It may be extremely difficult to secure any adequate information on black ownership of guns, but even the difficulty of carrying forth such research would be informing with respect to the likely success of law enforcement efforts. Such research is particularly pertinent, since one of the most consistent advocates of the availability hypothesis suggested that "subcultural groups [may be] disproportionately associated with violence" and thus prompted a reformula-

25. Report of the National Advisory Commission on Civil Disorders, at 180.

tion of that hypothesis.[26] This conclusion was stated frankly to be a speculation and therefore unsupported by any hard research.

NONLEGAL ENFORCEMENT PROBLEMS

Another enforcement problem involves the "substitution" argument—namely, if only handguns were banned, would persons simply resort to other weapons to achieve the same results? The matter is in dispute now, and further research would be very helpful in gauging the actual impact of handgun prohibition. In part, it entails describing the mindset of the attacker—is it homicidal as Wolfgang believes, or is it ambivalent as Zimring hypothesizes?[27] In part, it depends on the availability of alternative weapons (knives, long guns, zip guns, etc.).

Those advocating gun control have rarely tried to include long guns in their confiscation proposals. This may be because of the legitimate functions of long guns (hunting), but it may also reflect political reality presented by a strong rifle lobby. Whatever the explanation, leaving long guns out of any confiscation program would seem to create further problems for any goal of substantially reducing gun violence. The long gun is primarily kept in the home; most gun attacks between spouses or relatives occur in the home; so one must hypothesize that a handgun has such unique features that it is unlikely that a person would substitute a long gun in a family altercation when the handgun is no longer available. If the long gun remains, there will be only minimal impact on the accident rate because long guns are the major source of these shootings.

All of the foregoing presents, in the opinion of the author, serious questions about the gun being the focus of serious anti-violence research. Given the durability of guns, their widespread ownership, and the leaps in purchases when consideration of gun control legislation threatens to shut off supply, the seemingly straightforward approach of confiscation may be beyond realization in the foreseeable future.

26. F. Zimring, "Firearms and Federal Law: The Gun Control Act of 1968," *Journal of Legal Studies* 133 (1975).

27. M. Wolfgang, *Patterns in Criminal Homicide* (Montclair, N.J.: Patterson Smith, 1958); Zimring, "Is Gun Control Likely to Reduce Violent Killings," *University of Chicago Law Review* 721 (1968): 35.

One is also left with the uneasy feeling, after reading much of the literature of gun control, that an easy answer is being pursued to hard questions and that the more difficult but fruitful approach will entail probing complex human behavior. The gun lobby may be using the phrase "Guns don't kill people, people kill people" as a diversionary tactic, but the limits, legal and otherwise, to effecting mass change in behavior may mandate more focussed research on the kinds of persons and groups that are more violence prone. This view suggests that research might be better aimed at the relationship that generates more gun violence than any other—the family. It not only presents a serious public problem, especially for women and children who are the prime victims, but is collaterally a police problem since 22 percent of police fatalities come from investigating family disputes.[28] Persons active in the field have set out an agenda of basic research needs ("Violence in the Family: An Assessment of Knowledge and Research Needs" [1976], by Richard J. Gelles, Murry A. Straus, and Suzanne K. Steinmertz[29]). There are also proposals for practical intervention in the family to reduce violence.[30]

28. R. Parnas, *The Police Response to Domestic Disturbance* (Wisconsin: n.p., 1967), p. 914.

29. Paper presented at the 1976 meetings of the American Association for the Advancement of Science; can be secured from Professor Gelles at the Department of Sociology, University of Rhode Island, Kingston, Rhode Island 02881.

30. Ms. Marjory Fields at the Brooklyn Legal Services Corp. has a proposal to provide legal, social work, and counseling services for women and children who have been assaulted by male members of the family. Professor Morton Bard of the City University of New York claims to have achieved a reduction in homicides and aggravated assaults for police intervening in family disputes.

Chapter 2

THE ASSUMPTIONS OF GUN CONTROL

Gary Kleck and David J. Bordua

INTRODUCTION

The gun control issue is complex, involving dozens of interrelated subissues and disputes. Some of the disputes are value disputes or conflicts over fundamental beliefs — a clash of cultures.[1] As such, the issues cannot be resolved solely on the basis of research evidence. However, many of the arguments for gun control depend on certain specific assumptions, sometimes explicitly stated, often left implicit, which can be evaluated on logical grounds and compared against the available research evidence. We have identified five of the more important assumptions of this sort and have attempted to subject them to this kind of examination. We take a predominantly critical stance toward these assumptions, because the dominant stance in much of the academic research community has been one unusually uncritical of gun control policies, in sharp contrast to its ordinarily skeptical view of other governmental policies restricting human behavior in one way or another.

The term "gun control" is very broad, referring to anything from increased penalties for use of guns in a felony to a total ban on ownership of firearms. There are dozens of basic gun control policies

This chapter is based on a paper originally presented at the annual meetings of the Midwest Sociological Society, April 26, 1979, in Chicago, Illinois.

1. *Wall Street Journal*, 7 June 1972, p. 14; and B. Bruce-Briggs, "The Great American Gun War," *Public Interest* 45 (Fall 1976): 37-62.

and thousands of possible combinations of these policies. Some are directed at ownership, others at illegal use, some at handguns, others at all firearms. We will concentrate in general on policies aimed at restricting or banning *ownership* of firearms, especially (but not exclusively) policies directed at handguns.

ASSUMPTION NUMBER 1

Guns are five times deadlier than the weapons most likely to be substituted for them in assaults where guns are not available.

This assumption is crucial to gun control arguments because opponents of gun control measures have claimed that where guns are unavailable, other weapons will be substituted for them and homicides will be committed with the alternative weapons at the same rate as would have occurred had guns been available. Gun control advocates counter this argument by saying that the substituted weapons will be less deadly, less technically effective for inflicting fatal injury than firearms, resulting in a lower assault fatality rate and therefore fewer homicides. Two assumptions are involved in the substitution argument of gun control advocates. The first is that knives are the most deadly of the likely substitute weapons and therefore would produce the largest possible substitution effect, and the second is that guns are approximately five times deadlier than knives.

If guns become harder to obtain or riskier to own, those who feel the greatest need to own guns will be the ones most likely either to retain their guns or to obtain the best available substitute they can afford. If a control policy directed at all guns is under consideration, knives might well be the most common substitute, since they seem to be the next most effective available weapon among those which could be used in the same sort of circumstances as guns. However, many of the policies currently advocated are directed solely at specific *types* of guns, especially handguns, or even more narrowly, the cheap handguns known as "Saturday Night Specials."

If denied one defensive device, a rational, highly motivated person would presumably acquire the next best substitute device. If handguns become harder to get, the next most satisfactory weapon, either for self-defense or for committing crimes, would be a rifle or shotgun, not a knife. These weapons are certainly more expensive than knives, but they are also much more effective for the person who desires a weapon because he or she feels unable to physically resist the average robber or rapist, who is most likely to be a strong male. Therefore, restriction of handgun ownership could result in a shift to rifles and shotguns for defensive purposes among those highly motivated,[2] and also to the use of sawed-off versions of these weapons for criminal purposes. If these weapons are deadlier than handguns (especially at close range, where most assaults occur), such a shift in weapon type would amount to an upgrading of weaponry and would tend to result in a higher assault fatality rate.

In a similar way, effective restrictions on the availability of cheap, small caliber handguns could cause a shift to more expensive handguns of better construction and larger caliber. Since larger caliber guns are deadlier,[3] this policy could also result in a higher assault fatality rate. Whether handgun restrictions would result in a net increase in the assault fatality rate would depend on what proportion of prospective assaulters would substitute knives for handguns and what proportion would substitute long guns. Kates and Benenson estimate that even if only 30 percent switched to long guns and the remaining 70 percent switched to knives, there would still be a substantial net increase in homicides.[4]

While firearms may be deadlier in assaults than knives, it is debatable just how much of the greater deadliness is due to the technical characteristics of the weapons and how much is due to differences in the intentions and intensity of motivation of the people who use the weapons. It may be that people who are more serious about committing deadly violence for that reason choose more "serious" weapons. However, Zimring claimed that not only are firearms five times as deadly as knives, but that the difference between gun and knife fatality rates cannot be attributed to differences in motivation or intention of the weapon's user.[5] As evidence of the latter claim he purports to show that gun and knife assaulters, described in Chicago

2. See Don B. Kates, Jr., "Reflections on the Relevancy of Gun Control," *Law and Liberty* 3 (Summer 1976): 1–3; and Kleck, *infra*, on this point.

3. Franklin E. Zimring, "The Medium is the Message: Firearm Caliber as a Determinant of Death from Assault," *Journal of Legal Studies* 1 (January 1972): 97–123.

4. Don B. Kates, Jr., and Mark K. Benenson, "Handgun Prohibition and Homicide: A Plausible Theory Meets the Intractible Facts," in Don B. Kates, Jr., ed., *Restricting Handguns: The Liberal Skeptics Speak Out* (Croton-on-Hudson, N.Y.: North River Press, 1979), pp. 11, 227. See Kleck, *infra*, for an extended analysis of this matter.

5. Franklin E. Zimring, "Is Gun Control Likely to Reduce Violent Killings?," *University of Chicago Law Review* 35 (Summer 1968): 721–37.

police records for 1967, were similar in type of motive, race, sex, and bodily location of the wounds they inflicted. However, by recomputing row percentages of gun and knife assaulters by sex in Zimring's Table 5, the reader can see that 87.3 percent of gun assaulters were male, while only 65.2 percent of the knife assaulters were male. The relationship between gender and violence is well known, and it is not implausible that male assaulters as a group are more intent on inflicting deadly violence than female assaulters. Weapon preference may be affected by sex role structured prior experience with, and attitides toward, firearms, and sex in turn may be related to seriousness of intent.

Zimring's early work does not allow detailed analysis of large numbers of gun and nongun assaults that are comparable in presumed degree of intent to kill, since the studies concern rather heterogeneous samples of assaults. However, a later study examined only assaults in robberies, presumably a much more homogeneous sample.[6] It indicated that guns were only 1.31 times as deadly as knives in armed robbery assaults (based on police data). Further, a medical study that concerned only abdominal wounds found a 3.1 percent mortality rate for stab wounds and a 9.8 percent mortality rate for gunshot wounds, indicating a three-to-one ratio.[7] Thus, even using fatality rates in the Zimring manner to measure the relative deadliness of different weapons leads to weaker conclusions than Zimring reached. However, the technique is fallacious in any case, since it erroneously assumes comparability of motives and intentions between users of different types of weapons. These considerations suggest that if knives were substituted for guns as a result of an effective gun control program, the savings in lives would be considerably less than would appear if the five-to-one deadliness ratio is believed.

ASSUMPTION NUMBER 2

Firearms ownership increases the rate of assaults because the sight of a gun can elicit aggression due to the learned association between guns and violence.

6. Franklin E. Zimring, "Determinants of the Death Rate from Robbery: A Detroit Time Study," *Journal of Legal Studies* 6 (June 1977): 317–32.

7. Harwell Wilson and Roger Sherman, "Civilian Penetrating Wounds of the Abdomen," *Annals of Surgery* 153 (January 1961): 640.

This assumption implies that not only does firearms use in assaults increase the deadliness of those assaults, but that the rate of assaults will also be higher because some assaults that would not otherwise have occurred will be stimulated by the presence of a gun. In two articles in the semipopular *Psychology Today*, Leonard Berkowitz made the argument explicit and summarized it with a slogan repeated by others since: "Guns not only permit violence, they can stimulate it as well. The finger pulls the trigger, but the trigger may also be pulling the finger."[8] Elsewhere, Berkowitz has argued that stimuli commonly associated with aggression, such as guns, can elicit aggression from people ready to aggress (i.e., angry people) when the stimuli are associated with an available target. By a process of classical conditioning, the repeated pairing of guns and aggression, in real life and in fiction, creates an association between guns and aggression. As a result, angered persons may respond with aggression when presented with the stimulus, guns. In addition to causing assaults that might not otherwise have occurred, guns may also cause increased *intensity* of attack, Berkowitz argued. The theoretical rationale for this notion was never made clear and Berkowitz seems to have dropped the idea since the original Berkowitz and Le Page article on the subject.[9]

The "weapons effect" studies are nearly all experimental studies, usually conducted in laboratories. Typically, confederates of the experimenters in some way anger the subjects, who are then given an opportunity to aggress against the confederates using electrical shocks, supposedly in the context of a "learning experiment." The key experimental condition is the presence of a weapon (usually a gun), toy weapon, or picture of a weapon, which either is or is not associated with the confederate.

Berkowitz and Le Page produced marginal support for the gun effect hypothesis: the "weapons effect" was observed for strongly angered subjects but not for weakly angered subjects; significant differences between control and experimental groups were observed for mean *number* of shocks given but not for mean *duration* of the shocks. Further research has elaborated, and to some extent under-

8. Leonard Berkowitz, "Impulse, Aggression and the Gun," *Psychology Today* 2 (September 1968): 22. See also Leonard Berkowitz, "How Guns Control Us," *Psychology Today* 15 (June 1981): 11–12.

9. Leonard Berkowitz and Anthony Le Page, "Weapons as Aggression-eliciting Stimuli," *Journal of Personality and Social Psychology* 7 (October 1967): 202–07.

cut, Berkowitz's original theoretical framework in several important ways. Studies have differentiated between groups that showed the weapons effect and other groups that did not, noted the importance of the differing meanings that people attach to guns, and more fully recognized the possibility of guns *inhibiting* aggression as well as eliciting it.

Turner and his associates thought that many people may not perceive guns as aggressive stimuli, especially if they have frequently been observed in nonaggressive contexts such as hunting or target shooting.[10] They devised a naturalistic experiment in which a pickup truck driven by a confederate would deliberately fail to move at a traffic light when the light turned green, obstructing traffic behind him. Horn honking by the drivers of the cars immediately behind the truck was the measure of aggression. The truck sometimes had a rifle in a gun rack, which was clearly visible from behind the truck, and sometimes did not. The rifle was paired with a large bumper sticker on the truck with either an aggressive connotation (the word "vengeance"), or a nonaggressive connotation (the word "friend"). Significantly more honking occurred when the rifle was given the aggressive connotation than when it was not given such a connotation. Further, the rifle paired with the nonaggressive meaning did *not* produce significantly more aggression than the no-rifle control condition (a fact Berkowitz unaccountably fails to mention in his 1981 *Psychology Today* discussion of this study). The validity of horn honking as a measure of aggression or its comparability to physical violence is unknown, and unfortunately the effect of gun meaning on the weapons effect has not been empirically evaluated with any other measure of aggression.

Given that virtually all of the personal experience with guns that most gun owners have is in predominantly nonaggressive recreational activities, these findings suggest that the weapons effect is largely limited either to people who do not own guns or to gun owners whose experience with guns is limited to circumstances of real-life aggression and/or to fictional violence (especially on television or in films).

Four experimental studies have produced findings largely inconsistent with the weapons effect hypothesis: Ellis et al., Page and

10. Charles W. Turner et al., "Naturalistic Studies of Aggressive Behavior: Aggressive Stimuli, Victim Visibility, and Horn Honking," *Journal of Personality and Social Psychology* 31 (June 1975): 1098–107.

Scheidt, Buss et al., and Turner and Simons (although the authors of the last study chose not to emphasize the negative weapons effect findings in their Table 1).[11] In two other studies, Fischer et al. found only a small (and statistically insignificant) weapons effect, and that only for people of low emotionality, while Turner and his colleagues found weapons effects only in a minority of experimental conditions and obtained results indicating inhibition of aggression more often than stimulation of aggression.[12]

The findings of Frodi, Leyens and Parke, and Page and O'Neal largely support the hypothesis.[13] However, Leyens and Parke used pictures of guns rather than actual weapons as stimuli and used as a measure of aggression the number of shocks subjects said they *wanted* to give to the confederates who had insulted them. The artificiality of these conditions and the dubious validity of the aggression measure makes the findings of questionable generalizability. Further, the Leyens and Parke study was conducted in Belgium and that of Frodi in Sweden. Since Europe has little tradition of widespread participation in gun-related recreational activities such as hunting, most European subjects are likely to have had real-life experience with firearms only in the context of the military or warfare, if at all.[14] Otherwise, their experience will have been limited to the fictional and largely aggression-laden contexts of television and films. Therefore, these studies may be of limited relevance to an evaluation of

11. D.P. Ellis et al., "Does the Trigger Pull the Finger? An Experimental Test of Weapons as Aggression-eliciting Stimuli," *Sociometry* 34 (December 1971): 453–65; Monte M. Page and Rick J. Scheidt, "Demand Awareness, Evaluation Apprehension, and Slightly Sophisticated Subjects," *Journal of Personality and Social Psychology* 10 (December 1971): 304–15; Arnold H. Buss et al., "Firing a Weapon and Aggression," *Journal of Personality and Social Psychology* 22 (June 1972): 296–302; and Charles W. Turner and Lynn Stanley Simons, "Effects of Subject Sophistication and Evaluation Apprehension on Aggressive Responses to Weapons," *Journal of Personality and Social Psychology* 30 (September 1974): 341–48.

12. D. Fischer and J. Kelm, "Knives as Aggression-eliciting Stimuli," *Psychological Reports* 24 (June 1969): 755–60; Turner et al., "Naturalistic Studies of Aggressive Behavior," pp. 1098–107.

13. A. Frodi, "The Effects of Exposure to Aggression-eliciting and Aggression-inhibiting Stimuli on Subsequent Aggression," *Goteburg Psychological Reports* 3, no. 8 (1973); J.P. Leyens and R.D. Parke, "Aggressive Slides Can Induce a Weapons Effect," *European Journal of Social Psychology* 5 (1975): 220–36; and David Page and Edgar O'Neal, "Weapons Effect Without Demand Characteristics," *Psychological Reports* 11 (August 1977): 29–30.

14. On the contrast between European and U.S. traditions of gun use see Lee Kennett and James LaVerne Anderson, *The Gun in America: The Origins of a National Dilemma* (Westport, Conn.: Greenwood Press, 1975).

the plausibility of the weapons effect hypothesis in the United States.

The social psychologist critics and defenders of the weapons effect hypothesis have clashed with each other primarily over technical issues. These largely inconclusive discussions focus on whether findings were due to demand characteristics of the experiments, such as subject awareness of experimenter expectations and subjects' anxiety at being evaluated on their aggressiveness. However, a more fundamental criticism can be made of almost all of these studies. In nearly all experimental studies of the weapons effect, the weapon was either associated with the potential victim of the aggression (the confederate) or was not associated with anyone in the experimental situation. Weapons were almost never in the possession of or associated with the potential aggressor (the subject). Yet the principal issue of relevance to gun violence is whether possession of a gun makes the *aggressor's* physical aggression more likely, not whether it makes the potential victim's aggression more likely. Thus, the social psychological literature does not address itself directly to the issue of gun owner aggression at all, but rather to the subsidiary issue of aggression directed *against* gun owners! And in the one study in which guns were linked to the experimental subjects, no weapons effect was found (subjects in this study fired BB guns before being evaluated for aggression).[15]

In a real-life setting of potential violence, where one person has a gun and the other does not, it seems highly likely that any potential aggression of the other will be inhibited by the fear of the consequences of assaulting the person with the gun far more than it will be stimulated by the sight of the gun. Consistent with this point, Fischer et al., Fraczek and Macaulay, and Turner et al. obtained results indicating significant inhibiting effects of weapons (knives in the Fischer et al. study and guns in the other two studies).[16] Fischer et al. found inhibiting effects for women, while Turner and his associates found inhibiting effects for men and women in a number of experimental conditions. Fraczek and Macauley found significant inhibiting effects of guns on highly emotional subjects, possibly be-

15. Buss et al., "Firing a Weapon and Aggression," pp. 296–302.

16. Fischer et al., "Knives as Aggression-eliciting Stimuli," pp. 755–60; Adam Fraczek and Jacqueline R. Macaulay, "Some Personality Factors in Reaction to Aggressive Stimuli," *Journal of Personality* 39 (June 1971): 163–77; and Turner et al., "Naturalistic Studies of Aggressive Behavior," pp. 1098–107.

cause such people have learned to fear the possible consequences of their own aggression. These findings, combined with the mixed findings regarding the eliciting of aggression, suggest that, for the population as a whole, guns are as likely to *inhibit* assaults as to incite them, and that gun ownership therefore has no net effect at all on the frequency of assaults.

ASSUMPTION NUMBER 3

People are only superficially motivated to acquire and own guns. Therefore, if guns are made more expensive, more difficult to obtain, or legally risky to own, people will do without them (i.e. the demand for guns is highly elastic).

The demand for guns is most elastic among those gun owners least highly motivated to acquire and retain them. If we assume that those motivated by fear of crime are on the average more highly motivated than those motivated by desire for recreation, in hunting or target shooting, then demand for guns is least elastic among those who own guns for self-defense. Consequently, we would expect the resistance to policies restricting firearms to be strongest (or at least very strong) among the most highly motivated defensive gun owners.

A large proportion of gun owners own guns for the purpose of protection or self-defense. A 1975 national survey found that for 55 percent of *all* gun owners, self-defense was at least one of the reasons they owned a gun, although some owners gave other reasons in addition to this one.[17] In two national surveys conducted in 1978, 21 percent and 25 percent of *all* gun owners said self-defense was the most important reason they owned a gun. Among the *handgun* owners, 45 percent owned their guns for this reason.[18] A 1977 survey of Illinois residents indicated that among persons who owned only handguns, 57 percent owned them exclusively for the purpose of protection, while another 10 percent indicated protection was their *main* purpose.[19] In a Florida survey, 54.5 percent of handgun owners said

17. U.S. Congress, Senate, "Gun Control," *Congressional Record* 121 (December 19, 1975): 9.
18. Decision/Making/Information (DMI), *Attitudes of the American Electorate Toward Gun Control* (Santa Ana, Calif.: DMI, 1979), p. 40.
19. David J. Bordua et al., *Patterns of Firearms Ownership, Use and Regulation in Illinois* (Springfield, Ill.: Illinois Law Enforcement Commission, 1979), p. 231.

protection was their primary purpose for purchasing the gun. Similar results were obtained in a survey of California handgun owners.[20]

Given the frequency of defensive ownership of firearms, it would not be surprising if laws restricting gun ownership would be met with widespread resistance and a low rate of compliance. This expectation is confirmed by survey data regarding anticipated rates of compliance. The Illinois survey asked respondents if they would comply if a law were passed requiring people to turn in their firearms to the federal government; 73 percent of gun owners stated they would not comply.[21] Further, the general public does not believe compliance with such a law would be very great: fully 95 percent of a general national sample of adults questioned in 1978 believed that only half or fewer of gun owners would comply with a law requiring a turn-in of handguns to the federal government. The same survey found that 71 percent of the general public believed that even with a registration of guns, half or fewer of gun owners would comply.[22] These data suggest that gun ownership for self-defense, especially handgun ownership, is highly inelastic and that voluntary compliance with restrictions of ownership would be discouragingly low, even in the general, predominantly noncriminal gun-owning population. Presumably, voluntary compliance among criminal gun owners would be far worse.

It is a truism that restricting ownership of firearms can have an effect on the homicide rate only to the extent that ownership is reduced or limited among those who are violence-prone. This must be true, since everyone who commits a homicide is by definition violence-prone, regardless of whether killers could be identified as violence-prone in advance of their killings. Therefore, it is crucial to know to what degree gun control laws will limit gun ownership within this group.

It can be hypothesized that killers are more likely to be found among the highly motivated defensive gun owners. This is because, we would argue, killers often perceive themselves as potential victims.[23] Such a view should not be surprising, since the distinction

---

20. California Bureau of Criminal Statistics, *A Synopsis of a California Poll of Handgun Ownership and Use* (Sacramento: California Department of Justice, 1977). See also Kleck, *infra.*

21. Bordua et al., *Patterns of Firearms Ownership.*

22. DMI, *Attitudes of the American Electorate*, p. 66.

23. For a related view, see Hans Toch, *Violent Men* (Chicago: Aldine, 1969).

between the killer and the victim in a homicidal episode often is simply a matter of who strikes the last or hardest blow in a mutual exchange of blows, or of who happens to first introduce a deadly weapon into the exchange.[24] Many killers actually come close to being victims themselves in exchanges initiated by persons who ultimately became the homicide victims. Further, if killers and victims are often both members of a subculture of violence, as Wolfgang and others have argued, and if they both reside in high crime areas where risks of victimization are high, it is to be expected that many gun acquisitions by people who eventually become killers were initially made for defensive reasons. Few homicides are premeditated,[25] and thus few guns are purchased with the goal in mind of killing a particular individual. Rather, it is reasonable to believe that the weapons were originally acquired for defensive purposes and only later were used to kill. Indeed, in a sample of Florida prisoners convicted of gun murder, 58.5 percent had originally acquired their guns for protection.[26]

Therefore, it is among violence-prone people that demand for guns is most inelastic, and it is they who would be the most likely to either violate gun laws or seek effective substitutes for prohibited weapons, whether they be handguns in general or Saturday Night Specials in particular. This would not, for the most part, be because they intend to use the weapons for criminal purposes, although that may also be true for a small minority of gun owners. Rather, it would be the result of a felt need for protection in an environment accurately perceived to be dangerous. If this analysis is correct, laws aimed at restricting gun ownership will be least successful in doing so precisely where they most need to succeed in order to produce a reduction in homicide.

24. Marvin E. Wolfgang, *Patterns in Criminal Homicide* (Philadelphia: University of Pennsylvania, 1958); David F. Luckenbill, "Criminal Homicide as a Situated Transaction," *Social Problems* 25 (December 1978): 175–86.
    25. Marvin E. Wolfgang and Franco Ferracuti, *The Subculture of Violence: Toward an Integrated Theory in Criminology* (New York: Tavistock, 1967), p. 14.
    26. Florida, *Final Report, Handgun Regulation Project* (Tallahassee: Florida Bureau of Criminal Justice Planning and Assistance, 1977), pp. 4–10.

ASSUMPTION NUMBER 4

People who buy guns for self-defense are the victims of self-deception and a mistaken belief in the protective efficacy of gun ownership. In fact, guns are useless for self-defense or protection of a home or business.

This assumption is crucial to gun control policy because without it opponents can claim that loss of self-defense guns by law-abiding citizens is an opportunity cost of gun control policy that would go a long way toward counterbalancing possible benefits in crime reduction. Persons who own guns for defensive purposes, unless they are totally irrational, clearly must at least *believe* their guns are useful for self-defense, regardless of the actual protective efficacy of guns. Consistent with this point, 83 percent of a 1978 national sample agreed with the statement that "Most people who have guns feel safer because of it."[27] Gun owners derive at the very least the real, albeit intangible, psychological benefit of decreased anxiety regarding criminal victimization. This is a benefit exactly analogous to one that life insurance provides. You do not purchase a policy so you can die and leave your family the insured sum; rather, the principal benefit is peace of mind. Likewise, the chief benefit of defensive gun ownership is not the actual *use* of guns for defense against criminals, but rather the peace of mind that is produced by the knowledge that the gun is available and *could* be used for defensive purposes if needed.

Gun control advocates argue that however real these psychological benefits may be, they nevertheless are largely illusory, because gun ownership does not in fact prevent crime victimization. The argument that guns are ineffective for self-defense has been put forth in its most complete form in the work of Matthew Yeager and his colleagues.[28] They compiled diverse bits and pieces of evidence, some relevant but much of it bearing little or no relationship to their stated issue of the efficacy of handguns as crime defensive devices. Because their work is cited by others, it is important to evaluate their

27. DMI, *Attitudes of the American Electorate*, p. 43.
28. Matthew G. Yeager, Joseph D. Alviani, and Nancy Loving, *How Well Does the Handgun Protect You and Your Family?* (Washington, D.C.: U.S. Conference of Mayors, 1976).

arguments and evidence where it is at least marginally relevant to the protection issue.

In connection with burglary, the authors present evidence indicating that burglary victims seldom have an opportunity to use a gun against a burglar because there is rarely any confrontation between victim and offender, and they show that almost no burglars are killed by homeowners. Yet, as Bruce-Briggs has wryly noted, "the measure of the effectiveness of self-defense is not in the number of bodies piled up on doorsteps, but in the property that is protected."[29] A more pertinent question is whether the victim's gun ownership somehow deters burglars from committing burglaries. It is not usually a matter of common knowledge, either in the general population or among burglars, that a particular homeowner owns a gun; therefore, a gun in a given residence is not likely to deter burglars from victimizing *that specific residence.* Consequently, evidence cited by Yeager and others regarding individual victim ownership of guns and burglary victimization is irrelevant to the deterrence issue.[30] However, it may very well be a matter of common knowledge (or belief) that certain neighborhoods are, in the *aggregate*, heavily armed, and it certainly is common knowledge that some regions of the United States, especially the South, are more heavily armed than others.[31] It therefore is conceivable that a potential burglar might either refrain from burglary altogether or commit fewer burglaries because of anxieties regarding the risks of being shot by an armed householder.

There is evidence that the risk of legal punishment for burglary, although very low in absolute terms, nevertheless exerts a deterrent effect on burglars. Several researchers have found that burglary rates are lower, *ceterus paribus*, where the probabilities of legal punishment are higher.[32] If the nonlegal risk of being shot by a homeowner is taken more seriously by burglars than the risks of legal punishment,

---

29. Bruce-Briggs, "The Great American Gun War," pp. 37–62.

30. Yeager et al., *How Well Does the Handgun Protect You and Your Family?*, p. 5.

31. For example, regarding a black neighborhood in Washington, D.C., see Ulf Hannerz, *Soulside: Inquiries in Ghetto Culture and Community* (New York: Columbia University Press, 1969), p. 80.

32. For example, Charles R. Tittle, "Crime Rates and Legal Sanctions," *Social Problems* 16 (Spring 1969): 409–23; Llad Phillips and Harold L. Votey, Jr., "An Economic Analysis of the Deterrent Effect of Law Enforcement on Criminal Activity," *Journal of Criminal Law, Criminology, and Police Science* 63 (September 1972): 330–42; and Isaac Ehrlich, "Participation in Illegitimate Activities: A Theoretical and Empirical Investigation," *Journal of Political Economy* 81 (May-June 1973): 521–65.

which are themselves rather low, this would imply that the perceived risk of being shot by a householder would also exert a deterrent effect.

The clearance and conviction rates for burglaries in the United States in 1976 were 16.8 percent and 27.8 percent respectively, giving an approximate risk of arrest and conviction for any given burglary reported to the police of 4.7 percent (0.168 × 0.278 × 100%).[33] An estimated total of 3,252,100 burglaries were reported to the police in 1975, out of a total of 8,223,000 as indicated by victimization surveys, indicating that only about 40 percent of burglaries were reported to the police.[34] Thus the overall risk of a burglar being arrested and convicted was only about 1.8 percent (.40 × .047 × 100%). If half of those burglars convicted received a prison sentence, then the risk of imprisonment was 0.9 percent. In 1964 (the last year for which relevant national data are available), the median prison term served for burglary was 20.1 months, a value that is probably lower now.[35] Therefore the legal risk that an average burglar in the United States faces is a 0.9 percent chance of serving a median prison sentence of 20 months. In short, the legal risks of burglary are low in absolute terms, yet they nevertheless seem to exert a deterrent effect on burglars and potential burglars.

On the other hand, the principal nonlegal risk a burglar faces is that of being shot, possibly fatally, by a homeowner armed with a gun. The probability of such an event occurring is also undoubtedly low, but it is certainly greater than zero. A Toronto victimization survey found that in 21 percent of burglaries, the burglar was confronted by a victim, indicating that opportunities to use a firearm would not be uncommon among burglary victims if they owned firearms.[36] Given the *seriousness* of the possible outcome, even a very slight probability of the event occurring may be taken very seriously by a potential burglar. For example, some professional robbers interviewed by Conklin stated that they began their careers committing

33. U.S. Federal Bureau of Investigation, *Uniform Crime Reports* (Washington, D.C.: GPO, 1977), pp. 162, 217.

34. Ibid., p. 37; and U.S. National Criminal Justice Information and Statistics Service (NCJISS), *Criminal Victimization in the United States, 1975; 1977* (Washington, D.C.: GPO, 1977), p. 17.

35. U.S. Federal Bureau of Prisons, *State Prisoners: Admissions and Releases, 1964* (Washington, D.C.: GPO, 1967), p. 52.

36. Irvin Waller and Norman Okijiro, *Burglary: The Victim and the Public* (Toronto: University of Toronto Press, 1978), p. 31.

burglaries but later gave up this type of crime because of "the risk of being trapped in a house by the police or *an armed occupant*" (emphasis added).[37] Therefore, even though burglars may not be deterred from victimizing particular households because of gun ownership, the knowledge that gun ownership is common in general, or in a given area, may very well exert a deterrent effect.

However, there is also some direct evidence that criminals do take victim gun ownership into consideration in planning crimes and choosing victims. Convicted robbers and burglars interviewed in a California prison stated that they would take into consideration the presence of weapons in a house or business and that they knew of specific cases where robberies were not committed because the prospective victim was known to be armed.[38] If this is so, then a reduction in gun ownership among potential crime victims, due to gun control measures, could conceivably have the perverse effect of actually *increasing* burglary.

Our discussion of deterrence of burglary is necessarily somewhat conjectural, due to the paucity of hard evidence. However, Yeager and his colleagues provide some evidence regarding self-protection and other crimes, in particular robberies, assaults, and rapes. Contrary to their interpretation, the weight of their relatively hard evidence contradicts the claim that guns are ineffective for self-defense. Unpublished data derived from victimization surveys were studied to determine the outcome of crimes where victims used various forms of self-protection. The surveys did not cover victim use of a gun specifically, but they did cover weapon use in general. Regarding robbery, Tables 5, 6, and 7 in the Yeager report indicate the following: (1) robberies were less likely to be completed if the victim used a weapon for self-protection, compared both to those who did not use any self-protection methods and to those who used alternative protection methods, such as running away, hitting or kicking, yelling, or reasoning with the criminal; (2) robbery victims who resisted with a weapon were no more likely to be injured than those who did not resist at all, and were even *less* likely to be injured than those who resisted by yelling, hitting or kicking, or holding onto their property. Presumably those who used guns were even more successful in pre-

---

37. John E. Conklin, *Robbery and the Criminal Justice System* (Philadelphia: Lippincott, 1972), p. 85.

38. H.L. Richardson, "Myth #2: Criminals Won't Have Guns," *True Magazine* (July 1975): 32ff.

venting completion of the crime and in avoiding injury than those using less intimidating weapons.

Regarding assault, the data presented in Tables 11 and 13 indicate that (1) assaults are less likely to be completed against victims who used weapons, as compared to those using no self-protection method, and (2) assault victims who used weapons were *less* likely to be injured than those who used no self-protection method.

Regarding rape, the authors have little direct evidence on the success of efforts to resist attackers with a weapon, since there are too few victims included in the victimization surveys for meaningful analysis. The authors do point out that most rapists are unarmed, yet they fail to draw the obvious inference that this would presumably give an armed victim an even greater chance of successfully resisting the attack.[39]

There are instances of widely publicized firearms training programs apparently producing dramatic reductions in crime in various cities, including rape in Orlando, Florida, in 1966, armed robberies in Highland Park, Michigan, in 1967, and grocery store robberies in Detroit.[40] While none of these apparent effects have been rigorously analyzed, they are at least suggestive of the possible crime deterrent effect of widespread gun ownership.

One of the few potentially persuasive points made by Yeager et al. is the simple observation that crime victims rarely get the opportunity to use a gun, even if they own one, especially when the crimes are committed away from the victim's home. Because of laws prohibiting or restricting the carrying of handguns in public places, most potential victims are not likely to get a chance to defend themselves with a gun if victimized away from home, unless they are willing to violate the law by carrying a concealed weapon.

Nevertheless, gun owners *do* have opportunities to use their guns in self-defense, whether at home or away from home. A 1978 national survey indicated that in 15 percent of U.S. households, some member of the household had, in the past, used a gun (even if it was

---

39. Yeager et al., *How Well Does the Handgun Protect You and Your Family?*, p. 32. On the value of guns in defending against rape compare Carol Ruth Silver and Don B. Kates, Jr., "Self-defense, Handgun Ownership, and the Independence of Women in a Violent, Sexist Society," in *Restricting Handguns: The Liberal Skeptics Speak Out*, ed. Don B. Kates, Jr. (Croton-on-Hudson, N.Y.: North River Press, 1979), pp. 164–65.

40. Neal Knox, "Should You Have a Home Defense Gun?," in Jim Woods, ed., *Guns & Ammo Guide to Guns for Home Defense* (Los Angeles: Peterson Publishing, 1975), pp. 108–9.

not fired) for self-protection against a person, excluding military service or police work.[41] A California survey found that 8.6 percent of handgun owners responding had used a handgun for self-protection.[42] A Toronto victimization survey found that 21 percent of the burglary victims caught burglars in the act, although few of the homeowners had guns, presumably because of generally low Canadian gun ownership.[43]

Even in connection with robberies, there is some opportunity for victims to use weapons to defend themselves. In 3.5 percent of robberies reported to victimization surveyors in eight U.S. cities in 1971–72, victims admitted using weapons (not necessarily firearms) for self-protection.[44] Presumably this is a conservative estimate, since many victims may be doubtful about the legality of their weapon use, and therefore reluctant to acknowledge it to government interviewers.

It is of course, a matter of personal judgment whether these opportunities for protective use of firearms occur with sufficient frequency to justify gun ownership for self-defense. Nevertheless, many potential crime victims apparently want to have the option of defending themselves with firearms against criminals should the necessity arise, however rare such a situation may be. Regardless of how one may feel about the desirability of using guns for defensive purposes, it cannot be claimed, on the basis of available evidence, that the belief in the protection efficacy of firearms is just the product of self-delusion.

ASSUMPTION NUMBER 5

(The myth of the noncriminal killer.) Homicides are largely unpredictable "crimes of passion" committed by ordinary individuals not distinguishable from other people. Everyone is potentially a killer, and we cannot tell in advance who is likely to kill and who is not. Therefore, control must be directed at all gun owners rather than select subgroups.

41. DMI, *Attitudes of the American Electorate*, p. 68.
42. California, *California Poll of Handgun Ownership*.
43. Waller and Okijiro, *Burglary*.
44. Yeager et al., *How Well Does the Handgun Protect You and Your Family?*

The position on gun control of the U.S. Conference of Mayors includes the following statement: "those who possess handguns cannot be divided into criminals and qualified gun owners."[45] The assumption is also made in the gun control positions of the AFL–CIO, Common Cause, and the Union of American Hebrew Congregations, among others.[46] This assumption is crucial to gun control proposals directed at all gun owners, rather than at just those who misuse their guns. If it is false, then opponents of gun control may argue that such "blanket" measures unnecessarily and unjustly deprive and punish law-abiding people along with criminals.

It is, of course, perfectly true that we cannot identify in advance specific individuals who will kill (or assault), either with or without a gun. The predictive technology simply does not exist and is not likely to exist in the near future.[47] And it is true that everyone is potentially a killer, in the sense that there is at least an infinitesimally small probability that any given person will commit a homicide. However, this does not mean that killers are randomly distributed through the population, or that some aggregates cannot be divided, if we so choose, into two distinct, nonoverlapping groups: those who have been convicted of a felony (or, more specifically, a violent felony) and those who have not. This is, in fact, a distinction already made in existing gun control law.[48] For example, the 1968 Gun Control Act makes it a federal crime punishable by two years in prison for any convicted felon to possess a firearm.[49]

Opponents of gun control argue that gun control will needlessly deprive ordinary citizens of guns, while leaving criminal misusers of guns armed. Because criminals will disobey gun laws just as they disobey other laws, gun control will fail to affect the small minority of the population that uses guns to commit violent crimes. Gun control supporters then reply that even if criminals remain armed, gun control will still help reduce homicides by disarming ordinary citizens who otherwise would have used guns in domestic assaults and other

---

45. Ibid., p. xiii.
46. Joseph D. Alviani and William R. Drake, *Handgun Control: Issues and Alternatives* (Washington, D.C.: U.S. Conference of Mayors, 1975).
47. See Ernest Wenk et al., "Can Violence Be Predicted?," *Crime and Delinquency* 18 (October 1972): 393–402.
48. For a summary of handgun law see Barnes Company, *Handgun Laws of the United States* (Fairfield, Conn.: Barnes Company, 1974).
49. U.S. Internal Revenue Service, *Gun Control Act of 1968* (Washington, D.C.: GPO, 1968), p. 8.

fights between persons who know each other. This argument has been phrased in a nicely explicit form by gun control advocate Leonard Berkowitz: "Gun control may not be too effective in protecting ordinary citizens against criminals or Presidents against assassins, but it may, nevertheless, save some ordinary citizens from other ordinary citizens like themselves." [50]

Proponents of gun control also perceive domestic homicides as being isolated outbursts of otherwise ordinary, nonviolent, noncriminal persons. Because intrafamily homicides constitute 17 percent of all U.S. homicides, gun control advocates argue that it therefore is important to restrict firearms among seemingly law-abiding persons as well as among convicted felons. [51]

Because most violent acts are not reported to the police, and many do not result in any kind of officially recorded action, whether an arrest, a conviction, or imprisonment, official records of the previous violence of homicide offenders represent only a fraction of the true statistics. Records of previous arrests for violent acts seriously underestimate the number of instances of previous violent behavior; records of prior convictions do so even more; and records of prior imprisonment do so still more. Nevertheless, it is useful to look at the evidence regarding officially recorded prior violence of known homicide offenders, in order to establish a minimum, baseline estimate of the prevalence of prior violence among killers.

The most representative available samples of known or suspected homicide offenders would be samples of homicide arrestees, since samples drawn at later points in the criminal justice process (e.g., samples of persons convicted or persons imprisoned) would be subject to case loss and various selection biases, including bias associated with prior criminal record. [52] There is little evidence concerning prior convictions for such samples. More usually, the data either concern prior arrests (and the proportion of arrestees with prior arrests would necessarily be larger than the proportion with prior felony convictions) or refer to samples of incarcerated persons, who would presumably be more recidivist than general samples of arrestees.

Wolfgang reviewed earlier studies of the prior records of homicide offenders, most of them done in the 1930s and 1940s. [53] In one sam-

---

50. Berkowitz, "How Guns Control Us," p. 11.
51. U.S. FBI, *Uniform Crime Reports* (1980), p. 11.
52. On this general point see Wolfgang, *Patterns in Criminal Homicide*, pp. 11-13.
53. Ibid., pp. 170-72, 183.

ple of persons *imprisoned* for homicide offenses, 82 percent had previous criminal convictions, while the figures were 98 percent and 32 percent for two other similar samples. In a sample of persons *convicted* of homicide offenses, 43 percent had previous convictions. Regarding prior record of *arrests*, three studies indicated that 54 percent, 50 percent, and 55 percent, respectively, of samples of homicide prisoners had previous arrests, while in Wolfgang's own sample of homicide arrestees, 64.4 percent had a record of prior arrests.[54] More recently the Careers in Crime data of the Uniform Crime Reports indicate that 77.9 percent of persons arrested for murder or nonnegligent manslaughter in 1970 had previous arrests, and 50.1 percent had prior convictions.[55] Among those homicide offenders arrested in the United States between 1970 and 1975, 67.6 percent had previous arrest records.[56]

The FBI is rather vague as to the types of crimes for which offenders were previously arrested or convicted. However, in special computer runs for the 1968 Eisenhower Commission, it was determined that 74.7 percent of persons arrested between 1964 and 1967 for criminal homicide had a record of previous arrests for "a major violent crime or burglary."[57] The Careers in Crime data can be questioned regarding sample representativeness, so some independent confirmation of these figures would be helpful. Data for New York City indicate that among those arrested for homicide in 1970, 64.7 percent had a prior arrest record and 40 percent had prior arrests for violent offenses.[58]

Considered as a whole, research evidence shows that the majority of homicide arrestees have prior arrest records. As a rough estimate, perhaps half of them have previous convictions of some sort, although the convictions were not necessarily for felonies. A reasonably conservative estimate of the fraction of homicide offenders with prior felony convictions might be about 25 percent.

Further, it should be noted that felony killings account for an increasingly large fraction of U.S. homicides. In 1964, 17 percent of

54. Ibid., p. 175.

55. U.S. FBI, *Uniform Crime Reports* (1971), p. 38.

56. U.S. FBI, *Uniform Crime Reports* (1976), p. 43.

57. Donald J. Mulvihill et al., *Crimes of Violence*. Task Force on Individual Acts of Violence, National Commission on the Causes and Prevention of Violence (Washington, D.C.: GPO, 1969).

58. Reuel Shinnar and Shlomo Shinnar, "The Effects of the Criminal Justice System on the Control of Crime," *Law and Society Review* 9 (Summer 1975): 596.

murders and nonnegligent manslaughters were known, or suspected to be, the result of other felonious activities. By 1976, the figure was 28 percent. Among the known felony killings in 1976, 42 percent resulted from robberies.[59] If robbers are more likely to have criminal records than persons who commit nonfelony killings, this suggests that the proportion of homicides committed by persons with prior convictions, who fit the popular stereotypes of a "real" criminal, is increasing. Therefore, the potential effect of well-enforced gun control policies aimed specifically at this group has been increasing as well.

Even arrest records grossly underestimate the extent of prior violent behavior of assaultive offenders, since for every arrest for a homicide or assault, there were at least six such crimes committed.[60] There is, however, another official indicator of prior violence that produces somewhat less underestimation: police records of patrol car "disturbance calls." A study of Kansas City killings found that 90 percent of the homicides had been preceded by past disturbances at the same address—disturbances which were serious enough that the police had to be called in—with a median number of five previous disturbance calls per address.[61] Thus killings are rarely isolated outbursts of previously nonviolent people but rather are usually part of a pattern of violence, engaged in by people who are known to the police, and presumably others, as violence-prone.

Assumption 5 is therefore false to the extent that most violent crimes are committed by persons with records of previous violence and criminal behavior, and there is thus significant potential for reducing homicide through measures aimed strictly at criminals. On the other hand, it remains to be seen whether these measures could be effectively enforced, how much substitution of nonprohibited weapons there would be, and how well private transfers (legal and illegal) of firearms from legal gun owners to criminals could be prevented.

59. U.S. FBI, *Uniform Crime Reports* (1965, 1977), p. 10.

60. According to the National Crime Survey victimization study, there were an estimated 4,664,000 simple and aggravated assaults in 1977 (U.S. NCJISS 1979: 20), while there were an estimated 718,980 arrests the same year for homicides and simple and aggravated assaults (U.S. FBI 1978: 172), giving a ratio of 6.5 crimes to every 1 arrest.

61. Marie G. Wilt et al., *Domestic Violence and the Police: Studies in Detroit and Kansas City* (Washington, D.C.: Police Foundations, 1977).

CONCLUSION

The research evidence reviewed in this chapter renders suspect some of the most crucial factual assumptions underlying arguments in favor of policies aimed at restricting the ownership of firearms. These assumptions have gone largely uncriticized and unquestioned by advocates of gun control measures and by social scientists working in the area of crime and violence. In this light, it is suggested that more thorough and rational evaluation of the potential consequences of suggested gun control policies is called for, with greater attention being focussed on the issues we have discussed, both by researchers and others who would seek to influence crime control policy.

SELECTED BIBLIOGRAPHY
(PART I)

Barnes Company. *Handgun Laws of the United States.* Fairfield, Conn.: Barnes Company, 1974.

Berkowitz, Leonard. "Impulse, Aggression and the Gun." *Psychology Today* 2 (September 1968): 19-22.

_____ . "How Guns Control Us." *Psychology Today* 15 (June 1981): 11-12.

Berkowitz, Leonard, and Anthony Le Page. "Weapons as Aggression-eliciting Stimuli." *Journal of Personality and Social Psychology* 7 (October 1967): 202-7.

Bordua, D.J.; A.J. Lizotte; G. Kleck; with Van Cagle. *Patterns of Firearms Ownership, Use and Regulation in Illinois.* Springfield: Illinois Law Enforcement Commission, 1979.

Bruce-Briggs, B. "The Great American Gun War." *Public Interest* 45 (Fall 1976): 37-62.

Buss, Arnold H.; Ann Booker; and Edith Buss. "Firing a Weapon and Aggression." *Journal of Personality and Social Psychology* 22 (June 1972): 296-302.

California Bureau of Criminal Statistics. *A Synopsis of a California Poll of Handgun Ownership and Use.* Sacramento: California Department of Justice, 1977.

"A Clash of Cultures." *Wall Street Journal,* 7 June 1972, p. 14.

Conklin, John E. *Robbery and the Criminal Justice System.* Philadelphia: Lippincott, 1972.

Decision/Making/Information (DMI). *Attitudes of the American Electorate Toward Gun Contol, 1978.* Santa Ana, Calif.: DMI, 1979.

Ehrlich, Isaac. "Participation in Illegitimate Activities: A Theoretical and Empirical Investigation." *Journal of Political Economy* 81 (May-June 1973): 521-65.

Ellis, D.P.; P. Weiner; and L. Miller III. "Does the Trigger Pull the Finger? An Experimental Test of Weapons as Aggression-eliciting Stimuli." *Sociometry* 34 (December 1971): 453-65.

Fischer, D.; J. Kelm; and A. Rose. "Knives as Aggression-eliciting Stimuli." *Psychological Reports* 24 (June 1969): 755-60.

Florida. *Final Report.* Handgun Regulation Project. Tallahassee: Florida Bureau of Criminal Justice Planning and Assistance, 1977.

Fraczek, Adam, and Jacqueline R. Macaulay. "Some Personality Factors in Reaction to Aggressive Stimuli." *Journal of Personality* 39 (June 1971): 163-77.

Frodi, A. "The Effects of Exposure to Aggression-eliciting and Aggression-inhibiting Stimuli on Subsequent Aggression." *Goteburg Psychological Reports* 3, no. 8, 1973.

Hannerz, Ulf. *Soulside: Inquiries in Ghetto Culture and Community.* New York: Columbia University Press, 1969.

Hardy, David T., and John Stompoly. "Of Arms and the Law." *Chicago-Kent Law Review* 51 (September 1974): 62-114.

Kates, Don B., Jr. "Reflections on the Relevancy of Gun Control." *Law and Liberty* 3 (Summer 1976): 1-3.

Kates, Don B., Jr., and Mark K. Benenson. "Handgun Prohibition and Homicide: A Plausible Theory Meets the Intractible Facts." In Don B. Kates, Jr., ed., *Restricting Handguns: The Liberal Skeptics Speak Out*, pp. 91-138. Croton-on-Hudson, N.Y.: North River Press, 1979.

Kennett, Lee, and James L. Anderson. *The Gun in America: The Origins of a National Dilemma.* Westport, Conn.: Greenwood Press, 1975.

Knox, Neal. "Should You Have a Home Defense Gun?" In Jim Woods, ed., *Guns & Ammo Guide to Guns for Home Defense.* Los Angeles: Petersen Publishing, 1975.

Leyens, J.P., and R.D. Park. "Aggressive Slides Can Induce a Weapons Effect." *European Journal of Social Psychology* 5 (1975): 220-36.

Luckenbill, David F. "Criminal Homicide as a Situated Transaction." *Social Problems* 25 (December 1978): 175-86.

Newton, George D., and Franklin Zimring. *Firearms and Violence in American Life.* A Staff Report of the Task Force on Firearms, National Commission on the Causes and Prevention of Violence. Washington, D.C.: Government Printing Office, 1969.

Page, David, and Edgar O'Neal. "Weapons Effect Without Demand Characteristics." *Psychological Reports* 11 (August 1977): 29-30.

Page, Monte M., and Rick J. Scheidt. "Demand Awareness, Evaluation Apprehension, and Slightly Sophisticated Subjects." *Journal of Personality and Social Psychology* 10 (December 1971): 304-15.

Phillips, Llad, and Harold L. Votey, Jr. "An Economic Analysis of the Deterrent Effect of Law Enforcement on Criminal Activity." *Journal of Criminal Law, Criminology, and Police Science* 63 (September 1972): 330-42.

Richardson, H.L. "Myth #2: Criminals Won't Have Guns." *True Magazine* (July 1975): 32ff.

Shinnar, Reuel, and Shlomo Shinnar. "The Effects of the Criminal Justice System on the Control of Crime." *Law and Society Review* 9 (Summer 1975): 581-611.

Silver, Carol Ruth, and Don B. Kates, Jr. "Self-defense, Handgun Ownership, and the Independence of Women in a Violent, Sexist Society." In Don B. Kates, Jr., ed., *Restricting Handguns: The Liberal Skeptics Speak Out*, pp. 139-69. Croton-on-Hudson, N.Y.: North River Press, 1979.

Tittle, Charles R. "Crime Rates and Legal Sanctions." *Social Problems* 16 (Spring 1969): 409-23.

Toch, Hans. *Violent Men.* Chicago: Aldine, 1969.

Turner, Charles W.; John F. Layton; and Lynn Stanley Simons. "Naturalistic Studies of Aggressive Behavior: Aggressive Stimuli, Victim Visibility, and Horn Honking." *Journal of Personality and Social Psychology* 31 (June 1975): 1098-107.

Turner, Charles W., and Lynn Stanley Simons. "Effects of Subject Sophistication and Evaluation Apprehension on Aggressive Responses to Weapons." *Journal of Personality and Social Psychology* 30 (September 1974): 341-48.

U.S. Congress. Senate. "Gun Control." *Congressional Record* 121 (December 19, 1975): 1-10.

U.S. Department of Justice, Federal Bureau of Investigation (FBI). *Crime in the United States (Uniform Crime Reports).* Washington, D.C.: Government Printing Office, 1965, 1971, 1976, 1977, 1980.

U.S. Department of Justice, Bureau of Prisons. *State Prisoners: Admissions and Releases, 1964.* Washington, D.C.: Government Printing Office, 1967.

U.S. Internal Revenue Service. *Gun Control Act of 1968.* Washington, D.C.: Government Printing Office, 1968.

U.S. National Criminal Justice Information and Statistics Service (NCJISS). *Criminal Victimization in the United States, 1975; 1977.* Washington, D.C.: Government Printing Office, 1977, 1979.

Waller, Irvin, and Norman Okijiro. *Burglary: The Victim and the Public.* Toronto: University of Toronto Press, 1978.

Wenk, Ernest; James Robinson; and Gerald Smith. "Can Violence Be Predicted?" *Crime and Delinquency* 18 (October 1972): 393-402.

Wilson, Harwell, and Roger Sherman. "Civilian Penetrating Wounds of the Abdomen." *Annals of Surgery* 153 (January 1961): 639-49.

Wilt, G.M.; J. Bannon; R.K. Breedlove; J.W. Kennish; D.M. Sandker; and R.K. Sawtell. *Domestic Violence and the Police: Studies in Detroit and Kansas City.* Washington, D.C.: Police Foundations, 1977.

Wolfgang, Marvin E. *Patterns in Criminal Homicide.* Philadelphia: University of Pennsylvania, 1958.

Wolfgang, Marvin E., and Franco Ferracuti. *The Subculture of Violence: Toward an Integrated Theory in Criminology.* New York: Tavistock, 1967.

Zimring, Franklin E. "Is Gun Control Likely to Reduce Violent Killings?" *University of Chicago Law Review* 35 (Summer 1968): 721-37.

_____ . "The Medium is the Message: Firearm Caliber as a Determinant of Death from Assault." *Journal of Legal Studies* 1 (January 1972): 97-123.

_____ . "Determinants of the Death Rate from Robbery: A Detroit Time Study." *Journal of Legal Studies* 6 (June 1977): 317-32.

PART II
PUBLIC OPINION AND ACADEMIC–INTELLECTUAL ATTITUDES

Chapter 3

GUN CONTROL AND OPINION MEASUREMENT
Adversary Polling and the
Construction of Social Meaning

David J. Bordua

INTRODUCTION

This chapter examines gun control as a public issue, especially as it appears in public opinion polls. The focus is not on what the public really thinks but on the use of opinion polls as weapons in the struggle over firearms ownership. The development of adversary polling, the seeming superiority of the cultural understanding of the so-called gun lobby, and the errors in cultural understanding of the pollers and gun control forces are discussed. The failure of the handgun ban referendum in Massachusetts in 1976 is used as an illustration of the interpretation. Data are from national surveys done by standard polling organizations, national surveys commissioned by lobbying groups, postreferendum poll data from Massachusetts, and a telephone survey of Illinois done by the author in 1977.

While opinion polling on public issues is hardly unusual in modern American society, the case of gun control and the polls presents some interesting features. Among these are two that this chapter will explore: adversary polling and the struggle to construct through polling a social meaning of firearms ownership. The chapter will focus largely on the efforts of the so-called gun lobby, as personified by the National Rifle Association. Although little attention is paid to small fluctuations in responses to survey questions, the reader should be aware that the analysis here really ends with data gathered in 1977, though some slightly later opinion data are referred to in the conclusion. The chapter refers, therefore, to a period prior to the murder of John Lennon and the attempt on the life of President Reagan.

BRIEF HISTORY OF GUN CONTROL POLLING

While the techniques of opinion measurement may be politically neutral—an assertion that can, in fact, be doubted—the persons and groups involved in opinion assessment in areas of controversy are not. A brief history of opinion measurement in the firearms area is shown in Table 3-1. Phase One is the long period of domination by "neutral" pollsters, such as Gallup, Harris, and the National Opinion Research Center, that is, where advocacy groups other than the pollsters themselves are not clearly visible. This activity continues through the other phases. The benchmark published product of this period was the 1972 summary article by Hazel Erskine in *Public Opinion Quarterly*, which first stated in the polling context that the people *wanted* gun control but the "gun lobby" prevented the people's will from being realized.[1] This construction—partly of the meaning of guns, partly of the political process—was to dominate the gun control forces until the Massachusetts referendum of 1976.

Phase Two is marked by the appearance in 1975 of sophisticated polling by the National Rifle Association (NRA) in what they call the DMI Poll. Stung by the assertions of Erskine and others, the NRA commissioned a "conservative" polling organization, Decision/Making/Information (DMI), to do a study of attitudes and opinions centering around private ownership of firearms. This first DMI study of registered voters was entered in the *Congressional Record* in 1975 as an obvious counter to assertions about public opinion and gun control.[2]

1. The publications that mark historical phases in gun control polling are cited in detail in Table 3-1, note a.
2. U.S. Congress, Senate, "Gun Control," *Congressional Record* 121 (December 19, 1975): 1-10.

Phase Three centers around the 1976 Massachusetts referendum on whether to prohibit private ownership of handguns. The benchmark product is the publication in 1977 by Holmberg and Clancy of *People vs. Handguns,* a postmortem analysis of the proposition's failure. The report included an after-poll specifically on the referendum by Cambridge Survey Research, Inc. (CSR), a "liberal" firm headed by Patrick Caddell. The firm name was later to change to Cambridge Reports, Inc. (CRI).

Phase Four in Table 3-1 is marked by the appearance of two major efforts. The first was a national poll done by Caddell (CRI) for the Center for the Study and Prevention of Handgun Violence (CSPHV) specifically on the subject of private ownership of handguns. The second is a pair of polls again for NRA by DMI in 1977 and 1978.

Table 3-1. Historical Phases in Gun Control Polling.

Phase	Characterized by	Benchmark[a]
One	Pro-control "neutral" pollsters	Erskine article, *POQ,* 1972
Two	Sophisticated NRA counter polling, 1975 (DMI Poll)	"Gun Control." *Congressional Record* 121, no. 189, Part II (1975)
Three	Massachusetts Handgun Ban Referendum (1976)	Holmberg and Clancy (1977), *People vs. Handguns.* Caddell—CSR Poll (1977)
Four	CRI—Caddell counter-counter poll for Center for the Study and Prevention of Handgun Violence (CSPHV), Second Round DMI Polls 1977, 1978.	Decision/Making/Information, *Attitude of the American Electorate Toward Gun Control, 1978.* (1979). Cambridge Reports, Inc., *An Analysis of Public Attitudes Toward Handgun Control* (1978).

a. Complete citations of the Benchmark publications are as follows: Phase One, Hazel Erskine, "The Polls: Gun Control," *Public Opinion Quarterly* 36 (1972): 455-69; Phase Two, United States Congress, Senate, "Gun Control," *Congressional Record* 121, no. 189, Part II (1975); Phase Three, Cambridge Survey Research, Inc. (CSR), "An Analysis of Political Attitudes in the Commonwealth of Massachusetts," mimeo (Cambridge, Mass.: Cambridge Survey Research, Inc., 1977), prepared for the United States Conference of Mayors. Judith Vandell Holmberg and Michael Clancy, *People vs. Handguns: The Campaign to Ban Handguns in Massachusetts* (Washington, D.C.: United States Conference of Mayors, Handgun Control Staff, 1977); Phase Four, Cambridge Reports, Inc. (CRI), "An Analysis of Public Attitudes Toward Handgun Control," mimeo (Cambridge, Mass.: Cambridge Reports, Inc., 1978), prepared for the Center for the Study and Prevention of Handgun Violence; Decision/Making/Information (DMI), "Attitudes of the American Electorate Toward Gun Control, 1978," mimeo (Santa Ana, California: Decision/Making/Information, 1979), prepared for the National Rifle Association.

DATA SOURCES FOR THE CHAPTER

Three opinion surveys provide the bulk of the data used in the chapter: the 1975 DMI study, the 1977 Caddell-CSR poll in Massachusetts, and a 1977 Illinois survey directed by the author.[3] The latter survey was part of a larger study of firearms ownership in Illinois, results of which have been reported in several places.[4] The Illinois public opinion data reported here, however, have not appeared elsewhere.

The Illinois data will be used to replicate the DMI results and also to extend their implications. The 1975 DMI data cards were supplied to the author by DMI. Unless otherwise noted, results are from the author's analysis of these data. In all comparable cases they agreed with those reported by DMI.

THEMES IN THE COUNTER CONSTRUCT

An important part of the gun control lobby's political construction is the idea that the public "wants" gun control and is prevented from getting it by the "gun lobby." The importance or priority attached to an issue by an interviewee is ordinarily referred to as salience, sometimes as intensity.[5]

3. The 1975 DMI study is reported in United States Congress, Senate, "Gun Control," *Congressional Record*, vol. 121, no. 189, Part 2 (1975). The 1977 Caddell-CSR poll is in Judith Vandell Holmberg and Michael Clancy, *People vs. Handguns: The Campaign to Ban Handguns in Massachusetts* (Washington, D.C.: U.S. Conference of Mayors, Handgun Control Staff, 1977), ch. 7.

4. David J. Bordua and Alan J. Lizotte, "A Subcultural Model of Legal Firearms Ownership in Illinois," *Law and Policy Quarterly* 2 (1979): 149–75; David J. Bordua et al., "Patterns of Firearms Ownership Use and Regulation in Illinois," mimeographed (Chicago: Illinois Law Enforcement Commission, 1979), pp. xviii, 253; Alan J. Lizotte and David J. Bordua, "Firearms Ownership for Sport and Protection: Two Divergent Models," *American Sociological Review* 45 (1980): 229–44; Alan J. Lizotte, David J. Bordua, and Carolyn White, "Firearms Ownership for Sport and Protection: Two Not so Divergent Models," *American Sociological Review* 46 (1981): 499–503.

5. Howard Schuman and Stanley Presser, "Attitude Measurement and the Gun Control Paradox," *Public Opinion Quarterly* 41 (1977): 427–37.

Salience

In the 1975 DMI poll, salience was measured in two ways: by open-ended funnelling questions and by a semistructured question. DMI asked two open-ended questions about problems facing the country and the community, respectively. For both, zero persons answered with anything related to guns or gun control, despite the fact that 13.5 percent of the DMI respondents mention crime as an important problem facing the country and 18.0 percent as an important problem facing their community. In Illinois in 1977, 13.3 percent volunteered crime as an important problem facing their community and 2.1 percent as an important problem facing them personally.

The NRA drew from these 1975 DMI results four important gains. First, it could plausibly argue that guns and gun control were *not* important in the public mind, thus reassuring anti-control congressmen. Second, since the public did not really *"want"* gun control, the gun lobby could not be plausibly painted as the evil conspirators who were thwarting the so-called will of the people. Indeed, and third, the NRA could turn the tables and argue that the insistence on public passion and gun lobby blockage by the gun control people constituted underhanded tactics, since there was no passion to block. Finally, the low salience construction helped the NRA to at least partially discredit the "neutral" pollsters.

The discovery that the people really did not "want" gun control was part of a major revitalization of the NRA that surfaced in 1977. Crucial to the change was the lift in morale that came from the realization that the gun lobby *represented* rather than contravened public opinion.[6]

In 1975 DMI asked, "In recent years there has been a sharp increase in the nation's crime rate. What steps do you think should be taken to reduce crime?" Ten percent answered with something codeable as "gun control." Here again is evidence of low salience. In addition it is evidence that *gun control* and *crime control* do not (or at least, did not) seem connected in popular thought. This is an important clue that without such contextual support, approval of such measures as firearms registration may be soft.

6. NRA Staff, "Concerned NRA Members Redirect their Association," *American Rifleman* 125 (1977): 16.

Ineffectiveness in Crime Control

The latter measure of salience shades off into the next theme: ineffectiveness against crime. Both the 1975 DMI and the 1977 Illinois surveys asked closed or "fully aided" questions at this juncture, but the formats differed considerably. DMI asked respondents to rank five kinds of actions that might reduce crime. "Register all Firearms and License Owners" was ranked first by 14.8 percent of the respondents. It was fourth of the five alternatives in terms of the number of first place choices. The 1977 Illinois Survey gave ten items and asked respondents to rate each on a five point scale of importance — Very Important, Somewhat Important, Not Very Important, Not At All Important. In terms of the percentage of respondents saying Very Important, "Strengthen Gun Control Laws" was seventh with 50 percent. Close, with almost the same percentage, were "Increase Police Patrols" and "Increasing Use of the Death Penalty." The big winners were "Strengthening the Family Unit," 85.4 percent; "Handling Cases Quicker," 84.8 percent; and "Longer Sentences," 70.5 percent. The lowest ranking of the ten, with 18 percent "Very Important," was "Keeping a Gun for Protection."

The results on this effectiveness theme seem quite sensitive to question format. The open-ended DMI question gives a low public effectiveness rating — 10 percent. The closed DMI gives a lowish figure, with gun control ranked fourth of five alternatives. The 1977 Illinois survey, which asked only for ratings, got 50 percent saying "Very Important," but this ranked seventh of ten.

DMI asked their national sample, "Just suppose congress passed a law requiring all guns to be turned in. Do you think such laws would be effective in reducing crime or not?" Twenty-five percent said "yes." However one might wish to cavil with this question, the response indicates a low level of public belief that even a quite severe form of gun control would reduce crime. This low level of belief can be related to the public's views on the relative importance of people as against guns as targets of crime control efforts. The item in DMI was, "If we are serious about solving crime and violence, we must concentrate more on people than on weapons." Sixty-three percent "Agreed Strongly," while another 28 percent "Just Agreed." A total of 91 percent prepared to give some sort of positive response.

The question is poor because it is difficult to interpret, although there are clearly echoes of "guns don't kill people/people kill people." Nevertheless, the response also indicates that the gun lobby, far from being a barrier to the expression of the public mind, may in fact be a rather accurate reflection of same. In any event, the NRA interpreted the 1975 DMI results with considerable justification to mean that the public did not see gun control as a very effective measure against crime—an important matter in later campaigns as the 1976 Massachusetts referendum was to prove.

Compliance

The DMI question on the crime-reducing effectiveness of a law requiring guns to be turned in may have gotten low approval in part because the public expected compliance to be low. The next theme or element in the gun lobby's construction is compliance, that is, public beliefs about probable levels of compliance with gun control laws.

Both studies (DMI 1975 and Illinois 1977) asked questions. Both asked respondents to estimate how many firearms owners would comply with a law that would require people to *turn in* all their firearms. Again the Illinois study followed DMI. In both studies the response alternatives were None, A Few, About Half, Most, All. Reported here is the proportion of respondents who think that half or fewer of firearms owners would comply on the "turn-in" question.

In Illinois we asked the "turn-in" compliance question and an additional one which specifically asked what the respondent him- or herself would do. Ninety-one percent of the Illinois respondents believed that half or fewer firearms owners would turn in their guns—a proportion almost exactly the same as the 90 percent in the DMI national sample. Three percent said they did not know. Dropping these from the analysis, 95 percent of the owners and 93 percent of the nonowners felt that half or fewer of firearms owners would comply. This indicates very little difference indeed between owners and nonowners—evidence that at least one belief about the symbolic importance of guns to gun owners is widely shared among owners and nonowners alike.

At the next step the Illinois survey asked, "How about you? Do you think you would comply?" Sixty-three percent of the sample said "Yes." In the final step in this chain we can compare owners and nonowners. The response to the question "Do you think you would comply?" is a researcher's dream. Seventy-three percent of the nonowners said Yes, 73 percent of the owners said No! Not only is there widespread consensus about the symbolic significance of guns to gun owners, but the consensus seems to be correct.

More directly germane to the matter of the politics of gun control, the population believes, in both surveys, that compliance would be low. This, of course, added significantly to the NRA's confidence that a proper construction of public opinion would be favorable to them.

Protection

The themes of fear and personal protection or self-defense are prominent in the published literature of gun ownership. Indeed, Kennett and Anderson have gone so far as to argue that over time a major justification for private arms has shifted from the fear that the citizens will need protection *from* the government to the fear that there will be no protection by the government.[7] We expected DMI to ask on the subject, and they did. The 1975 question and the responses of 630 owners are shown in Table 3-2.

It is a good question because it taps the subtlety of purposes for firearms ownership. Personal contacts with hunting and sport-shooting firearms owners indicate that there are many who have a "secondary" or "mixed" self-defense or protection purpose. It is a bad question because it is closed; it lists self-defense first, and three of the five alternatives include self-defense. It is a response format likely to produce a high estimate of the importance of self-defense among the meanings owners attach to their firearms. In any event, 17 percent of owners responded with what we can call primary or pure self-defense, while another 38 percent answered with what we will call secondary self-defense—for a total of 55 percent of owners in the DMI national sample prepared to give at least some kind of self-defense or protection-oriented reason for gun ownership. Thus if approximately half of the households in the country have a gun and approximately half of the owners (one to a household) when inter-

---

7. Lee Kennett and James Laverne Anderson, *The Gun in America: The Origins of a National Dilemma* (Westport, Conn.: Greenwood Press, 1975), pp. 148, 253.

Table 3-2. Reasons for Gun Ownership in 1975 DMI National Poll
(*N* = 1538).

Which One of the Following Choices Best Describes Why You Own a Gun?	
I own it for self-defense	17%
I own it for hunting	22
I own it for sport or target shooting	9
I own it mainly for hunting but I'm glad it's there for self-defense	24
I own it mainly for sport or target shooting but I'm glad it's there for self-defense	14
Other	10
Refused	5
Total	101%
Cases	(630)

Source: U.S. Congress, "Gun Control" (*121* : Pt. II, 1975) Proceedings and Debates of the 94th Congress, First Session.

viewed give some sort of protection-oriented response, then approximately one fourth of the country's households may be said to more or less vibrate to the theme of protection as it relates to gun ownership; a potential constituency, again, of great significance for the gun lobby.

While the DMI question is constructed in such a way as to perhaps exaggerate protection or self-defense as a "reason" for owning firearms, in another sense DMI minimizes the significance of the theme by asking the question only of gun owners. Evidence of an even greater potential potency of this theme comes from another DMI question asked of all respondents — "Do you personally feel that the presence of a gun in your home would make you feel more secure, or not?" Forty-five percent answered "Yes, more secure." As opposed to one quarter of households being potentially responsive to the protection theme when measured by the reasons given for gun ownership by owners, the answer to this "security" question indicates that just under *half* the population nationally may be so attuned.

The 1977 Illinois survey asked a similar question of *all* respondents. Responses are in Table 3-3. The results agree in a general sense with those reported by DMI. Half of the respondents (49.7 percent to be exact) answered that having a firearm to protect themselves against intruders is a good or very good idea. There is, of course, a difference between gun owners and nonowners, but even among nonowners the proportion selecting "good idea" or "very

Table 3-3.   Approval of Protective Firearms Ownership Among Illinois Respondents, 1977.

What Do You Think of the Idea of People Having a Firearm to Protect Themselves Against Intruders? Is it...

		Nonowners	Owners	Total
A very good idea		10.1%	23.1%	13.0%
A good idea		33.5	48.1	36.7
A bad idea		37.1	20.6	33.4
A very bad idea		19.3	8.1	16.9
	Total %	100.0%	99.9%	100.0%
	Cases	564	160	724

good idea" is 44 percent. Proportions of this size are all the more noteworthy since they are based on responses from both sexes. Both the DMI and Illinois studies then indicate considerable public approval of the general theme of privately owned guns as a source of security or protection, and this sentiment is by no means confined to firearms owners.

The Illinois survey attempted to discover the purposes for firearms ownership in a way that would be less open to criticism than is the DMI closed question. It simply asked, "For what purpose do you own the firearm(s)?" and left the responses completely open. If only one purpose was given, there was a probe—"Any other purpose?" If more than one purpose was given, with or without the probe, the respondent was asked, "What is your main purpose for owning the firearm(s)?" Twenty-nine percent of the owners volunteered "protection" or something codable as protection, either alone or with other "purposes." Seventy-two percent mentioned "Hunting or Other Recreation," with "Collecting" mentioned by 14 percent and "Other" by 16 percent. Thus hunting or other recreational use is far and away the most common purpose mentioned, with protection a rather distant second.

The 29 percent mention of protection in the 1977 Illinois survey is best compared with the total self-defense response in the DMI sample. Clearly 29 percent and 55 percent are far enough apart not to ignore. Some of the difference is undoubtedly due to question wording, some to the difference between Illinois and the national sample. Parenthetically, the finding in Illinois that protection ownership is predicted in part by county violent crime rate and personal

Table 3-4. Protection as Purpose for Firearms Ownership Among
Illinois Respondents[a] by Race and Sex, 1977.

Percent Who	Whites		Blacks	
	Male	Female	Male	Female
Own gun	43.2	8.0	20.0	11.8
Protection only	2.4	2.7	4.0	9.8
Mixed reason	6.2	.8	8.0	2.0
Cases	292	377	25	51

a. Age 18 and over.

fear of crime and not by racism or pro-violence attitudes cannot but
help the pro-gun ownership forces in their attempt to reinforce the
legitimacy of personal protection ownership.[8]

Indeed, simple tabular analysis of the protection-oriented owners
in Illinois gives the results shown in Table 3-4. The group with
the highest percentage owning a gun for protection only is black
women—not precisely the stereotyped paranoid male redneck gun-
nut. Black women constitute 6.7 percent of the Illinois sample and
21.7 percent of the protection-only owners. This kind of information will help make it possible for the gun lobby to portray "gun
control" as an attempt by the rich and safe to disarm the poor and/
or endangered.[9]

Civil Liberty: To Keep and Bear Arms

It is a fixed tenet of gun control activists that the right to keep and
bear arms as stated in the Second Amendment to the Constitution is
not personal but collective and applies only in the context of the
need for a "well-regulated militia." In this the gun control forces
believe themselves to be supported by standard authorities on the
Constitution. The discussion by Kennett and Anderson of the political significance of the varying interpretations is especially cogent.[10]

8. Lizotte and Bordua, "Firearms Ownership for Sport and Protection," and Lizotte,
and White, "Two Not So Divergent Models," pp. 499-503.
9. Don B. Kates, Jr., *Restricting Handguns: The Liberal Skeptics Speak Out* (Croton-
on-Hudson, N.Y.: North River Press, 1979), pp. 148-50, 153.
10. Kennett and Anderson, *The Gun in America*, ch. 3.

However backward it may seem to the anti-gun lobby, the "personal right" interpretation has been a cornerstone of the philosophy of firearms ownership in the United States. It is no surprise, then, that DMI, in a survey commissioned by the National Rifle Association, would ask questions on the subject. In brief, 81 percent of the respondents answered "Yes" to the question, "Do you believe that you as a citizen have a right to own a gun, or not?" Seventy-seven percent answered "Yes" to the question, "Do you believe that the Constitution gives you the right to keep and bear arms, or not?" The third question was, "Do you think that the 'right to keep and bear arms' applies to each individual citizen or only to the National Guard?" "Individual citizen" was selected by 75 percent, with "both" being offered by another 3 percent. Seventy-eight percent, then, accept the "personal right" interpretation.

Clearly when it comes to guns, the people and the gun control movement live under different constitutions. Just as clearly, the gun control movement must accept the fact that popular beliefs about the "right to keep and bear arms" may be a powerful force—if activated—working against extreme forms of gun control. It is perhaps a sign of the rather elitist views of gun control groups and the rather populist views of the gun lobby that the latter can conceive of a "popular" constitution. Pro-personal-right interpretations are beginning to appear in law review articles—another gun lobby assault on the certainties of the gun control movement.[11] In any event, results of the 1975 DMI poll enable the NRA to present the gun control movement as an attack on civil liberties.

Softness on Specific Gun Control Measures

The 1975 DMI study included a large number of questions on the subject of specific gun control measures. Of these, two were asked in the 1977 Illinois survey. Two have also been asked in other national surveys. Respondents were asked whether they favored or opposed (1) registration of each gun; (2) the necessity to get a police permit before buying a firearm; (3) giving the police the power to decide who may or may not own a firearm. This last item is rather ambigu-

---

11. David P. Caplan, "Restoring the Balance: The Second Amendment Revisited," *Fordham Urban Law Journal* 5 (1976): 31–53; and David T. Hardy and John Stompoly, "Of Arms and the Law," *Chicago-Kent Law Review* 51 (1974): 64–114.

ous. It was used in Illinois because DMI had used it. For brevity, we can refer to these as REGISTER, POLICE PERMIT, and POLICE DECIDE. On REGISTER, 76 percent of the Illinois sample was in favor. DMI did not ask this question. On POLICE PERMIT, 67 percent favored in Illinois and 78 percent in the DMI national sample. This question has been asked in other national surveys, and both the Illinois and DMI results are close to the results of the other surveys (which lends at least some rudimentary scientific credence to the procedure). Finally, on the POLICE DECIDE item, the percentage favoring in Illinois was 35 percent, while in the DMI survey it was 27 percent. The percentages were similar, which is gratifying, but more importantly the drop in proportion in favor is similar: large in both studies. The difference between POLICE PERMIT and POLICE DECIDE is 32 percent in Illinois and 51 percent in DMI's national sample. In both cases this represents a considerable drop, but it is much larger for the national sample.

The POLICE DECIDE item is ambiguous as I have mentioned, but it clearly is a "tougher" item than REGISTER or POLICE PERMIT. Of the three it much more clearly implies that some sizeable number of persons might not be able to own guns. It indicated to the NRA that gun control sentiment may fade when things get restrictive. It is potentially double barreled, however, in that a due process oriented respondent might object, regardless of feelings about guns. In any event, the drop in both studies between POLICE PERMIT and POLICE DECIDE leads to a justifiable suspicion that the interpretation by gun control activists that REGISTRATION and POLICE PERMIT mean "gun control" and that the public favors it may be quite misleading.

The Gun Lobby's Construct

By the end of 1975, then, the NRA had created, using modern polling techniques, a construction of the social meaning of firearms ownership and gun control that it could use in the cultural and political struggle. The fact that the DMI's 1975 results were immediately published in the *Congressional Record* indicates the intent. The construction goes as follows:

The public really does not care about gun control (*Low Salience*), thinks it would not help much against crime (*Ineffectiveness*), and also thinks protection ownership is a good idea (*Protection*). The public thinks that *Compliance* with strict gun control would be low, and public approval of stiff controls is *Soft*. Finally, and philosophically most importantly, the public believes in a personal right to "keep and bear arms." Gun control for the public is a *Civil Liberties* issue.

THE MASSACHUSETTS REFERENDUM

In what they originally billed as a major step in eventual national banning of private ownership of handguns, a group of strong gun control advocates were successful in having a ban proposition placed before the people of Massachusetts at the time of the national election in November 1976. Gun control forces were highly optimistic that the proposition would be approved. Massachusetts was the "most liberal" state in the union. Gun ownership rates were relatively low. The major newspaper in Boston, the *Boston Globe*, favored the ban, as did the Boston-based *Christian Science Monitor*, the *Washington Post*, and the *New York Times.*

The pro-ban movement was led by a group called People vs. Handguns, which had been established in early 1974 under the primary leadership of John J. Buckley, Sheriff of Middlesex County. The movement came to have major support from the Massachusetts League of Women Voters, the Massachusetts Council of Churches, and the Massachusetts Federation of Women's Clubs. The discussion of the Massachusetts referendum here is based mainly on the analysis published by supporters of the ban.[12] It is a very valuable source on the Massachusetts referendum but also on polling and the social movements on both sides of the gun control issue. A coauthor, Judith Vandell Holmberg, was Executive Director of People vs. Handguns.

Commissioner Robert Di Grazia of the Boston police and, of course, Sheriff Buckley both favored and spoke for the ban. Indeed, Sheriff Buckley was, as much as anyone, the prime mover in the attempt. A poll published two weeks before the November 2 election day by the Becker Research Corporation of Boston indicated that

---

12. Judith Vandell Holmberg and Michael Clancy, *People vs. Handguns: The Campaign to Ban Handguns in Massachusetts* (Washington, D.C.: United States Conference of Mayors Handgun Control Staff, 1977).

the vote could be close. Proponents of the ban proposition had a slight lead: 51 percent yes, 41 percent no, 8 percent undecided, but support had been fading. Gun control advocates in Massachusetts saw this as a golden opportunity to bypass the gun lobby and go directly to the people – the people whose will had so long been thwarted by the National Rifle Association. The closeness of the predicted result indicated that every effort should be made to "get out the vote." As cited in Holmberg and Clancy "Speaking for People vs. Handguns, Buckley said, 'For many years the legislature has listened to the small but loud voice of the gun lobby' and he urged the legislature to 'listen to the voice of the people.' "[13]

The outcome was defeat of the proposition by a vote of 1,669,945 to 743,014, a ratio of 2.25 to 1. Put another way, the proposition to ban private ownership of handguns was opposed by 69.2 percent of the 2,412,959 votes cast on the proposition. Eighty-six percent of the eligible electorate went to the polls. A full 77 percent of the eligible Massachusetts voters voted on the handgun proposition. The voice of the people, indeed!

All was not lost, however. Just as a poll had failed to predict the outcome, so another poll could help explain away defeat. A post-election survey of voters was partially interpreted, largely incorrectly as we will see later, as revealing that the major reason for opposing the proposition was the projected cost of paying for confiscated handguns. The estimates ranged from $40,000,000 (by proponents), to $400,000,000 (by opponents).

The NRA Decides to Fight

Another reason given for the defeat is that the gun lobby outcampaigned and outspent the gun control forces. Campaign they did, and they outspent by a minimum of $100,000 to $10,000.[14] But why take on the enemy where he seemed strongest? A loss in Massachusetts could have been attributed to the special circumstances there. On the other hand, a victory on the enemy's home ground would have been a real coup—as it turned out to be. The conservative strategy would have been to not contest, at least openly, and attribute a

13. Ibid.
14. *Boston Globe*, 3 November 1976.

loss to "liberal" Massachusetts. The maximum risk would be to contest openly and lose. The NRA chose to fight. Why?

Part of the answer lies in the fact that the basic strategic position of NRA is the obverse of the position of the gun control forces. They (the gun control forces) avow an incremental or salami slicing strategy—today Massachusetts, tomorrow . . . ? Today permits, tomorrow . . . ? The NRA therefore feels it must defend everywhere.

But another important part of the decision was that the NRA expected to win. Their interpretation of the 1975 DMI poll made them believe that *they* would win a direct appeal to the voters.

The Caddell Survey:
Postmortem on the Massachusetts Referendum

Discussion thus far has been based on a national poll commissioned by the gun lobby and conducted by a supposedly conservative polling organization (DMI); a survey in Illinois directed by a sociologist more attuned perhaps than most to populist values, but surely not in the pay of the gun lobby; and brief allusions to results of "standard" national polls. Where comparisons are possible, they are in substantial agreement. The analysis will now turn to results from a statewide poll commissioned by a group that is avowedly in favor of very strict handgun control—the Handgun Control Staff of the United States Conference of Mayors—and carried out in Massachusetts by Cambridge Survey Research Inc.

By the standards applied to NRA sponsorship and to DMI as an organization, this study is pro-gun control in sponsorship. The firm is owned by Patrick Caddell. If polling for Gerald Ford makes DMI a "conservative" survey research firm, then polling for Jimmy Carter makes Cambridge Research Associates, Inc., a "liberal" research firm. The NRA asked DMI to do a study to show them how to win; People vs. Handguns and the Conference of Mayors' Handgun Control Staff asked CSR to do a study to show them why they lost. Properly interpreted, the CSR study could help the extreme handgun control people to win in the future.

CSR interviewed 500 Massachusetts residents of voting age in a postmortem of the defeat of the handgun ban proposition. Interpretation of the results as well as presentation of considerable data are provided by Holmberg and Clancy.[15] This analysis relies on the presentation there.

In Chapter 8 of their book, Holmberg and Clancy do not follow very closely the obvious leads provided by the Caddell data of Chapter 7. When it came time to sum up the reasons for defeat of the proposition, they focussed on the issue of cost: "However, by the fall of 1976, the cost of the proposed handgun-buy-back program became the primary issue, overshadowing the handgun violence problem itself. Opponents exploited the cost factor in massive advertising campaigns." [16]

Their own data in Chapter 7 indicate otherwise: "The major reasons given by voters for opposing the handgun ban referendum was (sic) that it would be ineffective in reducing crime and would leave the law-abiding citizen unprotected. The constitutional argument (that the proposed law violated right-to-bear arms provisions of the Second Amendment) was also mentioned frequently." [17] The "reasons" referred to are those volunteered by respondents when asked why they voted against the handgun ban proposition. They therefore correspond roughly with the "unaided" or "open" questions asked by DMI.

A slight and conservative regrouping of the reasons to correspond roughly and where possible with the themes of the gun lobby construct yields the results in Table 3–5. These results are certainly not out of line with what is known from the 1975 DMI and 1977 Illinois results. If it is assumed that half of those who gave as their reason for opposition that guns were needed by people generally meant they were needed for protection, there would be roughly equal emphasis on Ineffectiveness Against Crime, Protection, and Civil Liberty. Holmberg and Clancy persist in attributing the defeat to public concern about money, despite the fact that only 5 percent volunteered that as a reason for a negative vote.

CONCLUSIONS

An earlier quotation from Sheriff John Buckley was basically wrong. When severe gun control is made salient and the public is approached

---

15. The study is Cambridge Survey Research, Inc., "An Analysis of Political Attitudes in the Commonwealth of Massachusetts," mimeographed (Cambridge, Mass.: Cambridge Survey Research, Inc., 1977), prepared for the United States Conference of Mayors. The interpretation is in Holmberg and Clancy, *People vs. Handguns*, ch. 7.

16. Holmberg and Clancy, *People vs. Handguns*, p. 88.

17. Ibid., p. 82.

Table 3-5.   Reasons Volunteered by Voters Opposing the Handgun Ban in the Massachusetts Referendum of November 1976.

Reasons	Percent
Ineffectiveness against crime	26
Right to own a gun	22
Protection	16
Guns are needed	19
By people generally	9
By police	5
By hunters	5
Too expensive	5
Other and don't know	13
Total reasons	101
Cases	(310)

Source: Cambridge Survey Research, Inc., *An Analysis of Political Attitudes in the Commonwealth of Massachusetts* (prepared for the United States Conference of Mayors, January, 1977). Quoted in Holmberg and Clancy (1977), p. 82. Sixteen categories of reasons in the original combined into eight. The telephone survey had an *N* of 500. The survey was done in December of 1976. The 310 respondents who recall voting against the ban are the base for this table.

directly, the gun lobby turns out to be more in tune with public opinion than do the civic disarmers. This same conclusion is reached based on a national NRA-sponsored poll by a "conservative" firm, DMI, in 1975; a somewhat populist professor's survey conducted in Illinois in 1977; and, with less analysis, a gun control movement sponsored poll conducted in Massachusetts in 1977 by a "liberal" firm, Cambridge Research Associates, Inc. To the implicit question about the adequacy of our science, the answer is that technically our science is quite good; similar operations produce similar results.

The political utility thus far of the gun lobby's construction of the meaning of private arms in the United States does not come from superior survey technology but from superior cultural and historical knowledge.

As previously mentioned, another approach to some of the problems raised here is a technical analysis of what survey researchers call intensity. Thus, in attempting to explain what they see as the "gun control paradox," Schuman and Presser argue that strict gun control has not been forthcoming despite public approval because of the greater intensity with which the beliefs of the anti-control populace are held.[18] The approach in this chapter has been more in terms of substantive cultural content and symbolic context, since it illustrates much more fundamentally the nature of the opposing constructions of social meaning. The implication of DMI's low salience finding, coupled with the rest of the analysis presented here, is that making the public as a whole more intense would probably benefit the gun lobby, depending heavily on specific times, places, and issues.

Making the gun control activists more intense would imply a shift in the politically relevant construct. The model of two intense competing elites with a relatively uninterested public is quite different from the Sheriff Buckley formulation. It then becomes in the interest of the control lobby to keep the public at large out of the process and for the gun lobby, with its larger number of activists plus contextual support in public opinion, to want the public included. Low salience among the public should benefit the gun control lobby if it emphasizes low visibility decisions in the public bureaucracy or local governing bodies, again depending heavily on specific times, places, and issues. The problem is more one of elite curtailment of a popular liberty about which the public is largely apathetic than of elite interference with a reform backed by passionate public desire.

This chapter set the modest goal of examining the constructs of social meaning fashioned by adversaries in the gun control struggle. Opinion poll data have loomed large in these fashionings. The chapter has specifically avoided any attempt to definitely answer the question, "What does the public really want?" To do so implies that the social scientist has an ability to construct reality separate from and superior to that of the social participants. To do so would also require at least another chapter. A beginning answer can be found, however, in recent work by James Wright.[19]

Wright has analyzed the surveys that are listed in Phase Four in Table 3-1, the 1977 and 1978 DMI and 1978 CRI polls. Wright does not address the issue of salience, and the reader would be well advised to read personally the results of the large number of questions. In attempting his own construction or interpretation of the "public mind," Wright analogizes guns to automobiles. Two quotations, differing a bit in tone will convey the thrust: "Measures more extreme

18. Schuman and Presser, "Attitude Measurement," pp. 427–37.
19. James D. Wright, "Public Opinion and Gun Control: A Comparison of Results from Two Recent National Surveys," *Annals of the American Academy of Political and Social Science* 455 (1981): 24–39.

than those currently used to regulate automobile ownership and use, in general, do not enjoy much public support."[20] "The underlying concept here seems to be that weapons, as automobiles, are intrinsically dangerous objects that governments ought to keep track of for that reason alone. Whether doing so would reduce the level of crime or violence in the society seems to be taken as a separate issue entirely."[21]

One final quotation will perhaps help explain what to some is inexplicable—the persistence and vitality of something like the gun lobby's construction of the social meaning of firearms in the United States:

> A strong body makes the mind strong. As to the species of exercise, I advise the gun. While this gives a moderate exercise to the body, it gives boldness, enterprise and independence to the mind. Games played with the ball and others of that nature, are too violent for the body and stamp no character on the mind. Let your gun, therefore, be the constant companion of your walks. Never think of taking a book with you.[22]

20. Ibid., p. 32.
21. Ibid., p. 39.
22. Thomas Jefferson, Letter to his nephew Peter Carr, 18 August 1775, *The Papers of Thomas Jefferson*, ed. Julian P. Boyd, vol. 8 (Princeton, N.J.: Princeton University Press, 1953), p. 407.

Chapter 4

SOCIAL PROBLEMS AND SAGECRAFT
Gun Control as a Case in Point

William R. Tonso

This chapter is not about the gun control issue per se. It is about the way the issue has typically been dealt with by those social scientists who, in one social scientific capacity or another, have had occasion to be concerned with it. Or, more accurately, this chapter focuses on the more publicized social scientific treatments of the gun control issue – those passed on to college students through social problems texts, anthologies, and monographs, and to the general public through magazine articles and the published findings of various social science assisted federal commissions on crime, violence, and civil disturbances. The chapter's objective is to point out some of the shortcomings of what will be referred to as the conventional social scientific approach to controversial social issues and social problems.

While the controversial issue examined here is gun control, other examples could conceivably have been used to make the same points: issues such as school busing, pornography, or the legalization of marijuana, or social problems such as discrimination, pollution, poverty, unemployment, or crime. There is a missionary aspect to the conventional approach to such issues and problems in that it often goes beyond analysis to lend, subtly or otherwise, supposedly scientifically based support to one means or other of coping with these phenomena. This support is disseminated through textbooks, commission findings, and so forth, and being "scientifically" based can be ignored only at the risk of one's being considered unenlightened. It will be argued, therefore, that the conventional social scientific treatments of controversial social phenomena often have much more in common with the work of those to whom Florian Znaniecki referred as "sages" than they have with social science, and consequently that such treatments obscure more than they reveal about the issues or problems with which they are dealing. The first part of the chapter describes the conventional social scientific treatment of the gun issue, places this treatment into social-cultural context, and finally links it to Znaniecki's comments on the social role of the sage. The second part points out, through a critique of the conventional treatment of the gun issue, how the concerns of the sage affect the social scientific enterprise, here defined broadly enough to include social history.[1]

SOCIAL SCIENCE OR SAGECRAFT?

It seems to be generally accepted that the civilian possession of firearms in the United States is widespread, but whether or not this state of affairs is desirable has been the subject of much controversy since the early part of the twentieth century.[2] The side of this controversy that has received the most publicity through the media, however, maintains that this widespread possession constitutes, if not a social problem unto itself, a major contributing factor to other social problems such as crime, violence, and civil disorder. It is hardly surprising, then, that efforts to bring the civilian possession of firearms under strict control and to reduce the number of firearms in civilian hands have also received a great deal of publicity through the media.

A perusal of the *Reader's Guide to Periodical Literature's* "Firearms — Laws and Regulations" section can give one some indication of the magnitude of this media support for gun controls. Since the latest major push for controls began in the early 1960s, articles on

1. While the tone of this chapter might seem polemical in places, its aim is not to argue against gun control. Though the author does personally oppose such controls, whether or not they are necessary or desirable is a political issue to him, rather than a social scientific issue. The chapter's polemics are not aimed at gun control, therefore, but at one-sided social science, which in this case is pro-gun-control.

2. Lee Kennett and James LaVerne Anderson, *The Gun in America: The Origins of a National Dilemma* (Westport, Conn.: Greenwood Press, 1975), ch. 7.

the subject in such news and general interest magazines as *Life, Time, Newsweek, The Saturday Evening Post, Reader's Digest, Harper's, Saturday Review, The Nation,* and *The New Republic* have been almost unanimous in their strong support of gun controls, with only the outdoor, gun, and libertarian magazines consistently taking an anticontrol stand. The national television networks have also been almost unanimous in their support of controls through various documentaries on the subject as well as through such television favorites as "Laugh-In," "All in the Family," and "Hawaii Five-O." The leading urban newspapers have all editorialized in favor of controls, the *Washington Post* once doing so for seventy-seven straight days,[3] as have many medium- and small-town newspapers and the syndicated columnists and political cartoonists appearing in them—Ann Landers, Art Buchwald, Jack Anderson, and Herblock, among others. Newspapers and magazines have also helped publicize the works of such procontrol authors as Carl Bakal and Robert Sherrill.[4] And even comic strips, such as "Goosemyer," "Tank McNamara," and "Doonesbury," have supported gun controls by ridiculing the anticontrol position.

While those responsible for the various newspaper editorials, columns, magazine articles, and TV documentaries that have over the years argued for controls have often looked to the "experts" on man and society—psychiatrists, psychologists, and sociologists—for assistance, by the middle 1960s the social sciences were starting to get more directly involved in the controversy. In response to the political assassinations and civil disturbances of the period, a number of federal commissions aimed at discovering and eradicating the causes of crime, violence, and civil disturbances were established, and these commissions were invariably assisted by social scientists. The commissions also invariably ended up recommending that strict gun controls be enacted as one means of reducing the amount of crime, violence, and civil disorder.[5]

Beginning with the federal commissions, the social scientific involvement with the gun control issue has extended increasingly to

3. Ibid., pp. 239, 312.
4. Carl Bakal, *The Right to Bear Arms* (New York: McGraw-Hill, 1966); Robert Sherrill, *The Saturday Night Special* (New York: Charter House, 1973).
5. See George D. Newton and Franklin E. Zimring, *Firearms and Violence in American Life*, a staff report to the National Commission on the Causes and Prevention of Violence (Washington, D.C.: GPO, 1969). This work is a prime example of such commission reports, and it includes a summary of several others, pp. 151–62.

monographs, textbooks, and anthologies which deal with various social problems and are aimed at the college market. Based on commission reports and the treatment that the gun issue has received in the various texts, and so forth, that have dealt with it, the sentiments concerning civilian firearms possession and gun control that have been transmitted through these various social science sources can be summarized as follows:

1. When the United States was being transformed from a raw wilderness to a modern, urban, industrial nation, passing through a rural, agricultural stage along the way, private citizens often had use for firearms if they were to provide themselves with food and/or protection.[6]

2. The United States no longer has a frontier, and in fact, it is now primarily urban and industrial rather than rural and agricultural. Consequently, the large number of firearms that have gotten and continue to get into civilian hands no longer serve any useful purpose and are more trouble than what they are worth. They no longer contribute to the establishment of law and order but actually undermine efforts to establish order, as the high rate of firearms-related crime shows.[7]

3. The United States is the only modern, urban, industrial nation that does not strictly regulate the civilian possession of firearms. The effectiveness of such controls is demonstrated by the fact that other modern, urban, industrial nations, all of which have them, have violent crime rates far lower than those of the United States.[8]

6. See Richard Hofstadter, "America as a Gun Culture," *American Heritage* (October 1970): 7, 10; Richard Hofstadter and Michael Wallace, eds., *American Violence: A Documentary History* (New York: Vintage Books, 1970), p. 24; Eugene W. Hollon, *Frontier Violence: Another Look* (New York: Oxford University Press, 1974), pp. 121–22; Charles H. McCaghy, *Deviant Behavior: Crime, Conflict, and Interest Groups* (New York: Macmillan, 1976), p. 125; Joseph Boskin, "The Essential American Soul: Violent," in Joseph Boskin, ed., *Issues in American Society* (Encino, Calif.: Glencoe, 1978), p. 43; Daniel Glazer, *Crime in Our Changing Society* (New York: Holt, Rinehart and Winston, 1978), p. 201; Charles E. Silberman, *Criminal Violence, Criminal Justice* (New York: Vintage Books, 1978), pp. 48–49; and Newton and Zimring, *Firearms and Violence in American Life*.

7. See Kenneth Westhues, *First Sociology* (New York: McGraw-Hill, 1982), pp. 457, 460–62; Newton and Zimring, *Firearms and Violence in American Life*; Hofstadter, "America as a Gun Culture"; Hofstadter and Wallace, *American Violence*, pp. 25–26; Hollen, *Frontier Violence*, pp. 121–22; McCaghy, *Deviant Behavior*, p. 125; Boskin, "The Essential American Soul," p. 48; Glazer, *Crime in Our Changing Society*, p. 260; and Silberman, *Criminal Violence*, pp. 80–81.

8. See Amitai Etzioni, "Violence," in Robert K. Merton and Robert Nisbet, eds., *Contemporary Social Problems* (New York: Harcourt Brace Jovanovich, 1971), p. 740;

4. It is obvious, therefore, that the United States is badly in need of strict gun controls that at a minimum would require the registration of all privately owned firearms, and licenses and identification cards for all firearms owners, plus a drastic reduction of the number of privately owned handguns.[9]

5. The pollsters have shown that considerably more than half of the populace supports all of these measures and that as many as three fourths support some of them.[10]

6. The only reason that such regulations have not been enacted into law is that the domestic firearms industry and the National Rifle Association have, through well-organized lobbying efforts, been able to take advantage of the weaknesses of the federal system of government to block such legislation.[11]

Lamar Empey, "American Society and Criminal Justice Reform," in Abraham S. Blumberg, ed., *Current Perspectives on Criminal Behavior: Original Essays in Criminology* (New York: Oxford University Press, 1974), pp. 295–96; Arthur S. Shostak, ed., *Modern Social Reforms: Solving Today's Social Problems* (New York: Macmillan, 1974): p. 291; Rodney Stark, *Social Problems* (New York: Random House, 1975), p. 226; Martin R. Haskell and Lewis Yablonsky, *Crime and Delinquency* (Chicago: Rand McNally, 1978), pp. 340–41; Michael S. Bassis, Richard J. Gelles, and Ann Levine, *Social Problems* (New York: Harcourt Brace Jovanovich, 1982), p. 477; Donald Light, Jr., and Suzanne Keller, *Sociology*, 3rd ed. (New York: Alfred A. Knopf, 1982), p. 254; Newton and Zimring, *Firearms and Violence in American Life*, pp. 119–28; Hofstadter, "America as a Gun Culture," p. 82; Hofstadter and Wallace, *American Violence*, p. 26; and Hollon, *Frontier Violence*, p. 122.

9. See Joseph Julian, *Social Problems* (New York: Appleton-Century-Croft, 1973), pp. 481–82; Marvin E. Wolfgang, "Violent Behavior," in Abraham S. Blumberg, ed., *Current Perspectives on Criminal Behavior: Original Essays on Criminology* (New York: Oxford University Press, 1974), p. 246; Frank Scarpitti, *Social Problems* (New York: Holt, Rinehart and Winston, 1974), p. 431; President's Commission on Law Enforcement and the Administration of Justice, "Control of Firearms," in Rose Giallombardo, ed., *Contemporary Social Issues: A Reader* (Santa Barbara, Calif.: Hamilton, 1975), pp. 176–77; Hugh Barlow, *Introduction to Criminology* (Boston: Little, Brown and Company, 1978), p. 116; Jeffrey H. Reiman, *The Rich Get Richer and the Poor Get Prison: Ideology, Class, and Criminal Justice* (New York: John Wiley and Sons, 1979), pp. 192–93; Newton and Zimring, *Firearms and Violence in American Life*, pp. 139–48; Hofstadter, "America as a Gun Culture"; Hofstadter and Wallace, *American Violence*, pp. 25–26; Etzioni, "Violence," p. 740; Empey, "Criminal Justice Reform," p. 296; Stark, *Social Problems*, pp. 226–27; McCaghy, *Deviant Behavior*, p. 126; Boskin, "The Essential American Soul," p. 48; Glazer, *Crime in Our Changing Society*, pp. 260–64; Haskell and Yablonsky, *Crime and Delinquency*, p. 752; and Bassis, Gelles, and Levine, *Social Problems*, p. 477.

10. See Michael J. Harrington, "The Politics of Gun Control," in Phillip Whitten, ed., *Readings in Sociology: Contemporary Perspectives* (New York: Harper and Row, 1979), p. 257; Newton and Zimring, *Firearms and Violence in American Society*, p. 152; Shostak, *Modern Social Reforms*, p. 292; President's Commission, "Control of Firearms," p. 174; Stark, *Social Problems*, p. 227; McCaghy, *Deviant Behavior*, p. 126; and Glazer, *Crime in Our Changing Society*, p. 262.

11. See Hofstadter, "America as a Gun Culture," p. 85; Etzioni, "Violence," pp. 739–40; Julian, *Social Problems*, p. 481; Scarpitti, *Social Problems*, p. 431; President's Commis-

7. This opposition to obviously needed firearms regulations, though thus far effective, is self-serving, irresponsible, irrational, unenlightened, reactionary, uninformed, etc.[12]

The impression given by the foregoing is that through historical research, cross-cultural comparisons of crime rates, and the scientific analysis of public opinion, social scientists have been able to establish definitely that the United States would benefit significantly from gun controls, that the majority of Americans want such controls, and consequently, that opposition to such controls is self-serving or unreasonable. But there are things about the conventional social scientific analysis of the gun control issue that make one wonder about the impartiality of those engaged in it. First, it should be noted that the conventional social science position on gun control summarized earlier is identical to the position that procontrollers have taken for years without social scientific assistance. In fact, it is not uncommon for nonsocial scientific, nonscholarly, procontrol, antigun polemics such as *The Right to Bear Arms*, by irate citizen Carl Bakal, and *Saturday Night Special*, by "investigative reporter" Robert Sherrill, to be cited in social science textbook analyses of the gun issue.[13] And when such sources are cited, no mention is made of the acknowledged procontrol, antigun sentiments of their authors.

A second interesting aspect of the conventional social scientific treatment of the gun issue is that qualification of the material presented on the subject is rare to nonexistent. Poll findings are accepted at face value, although there is good social scientific cause to do otherwise.[14] Similarly, cross-cultural comparisons of firearms-related

sion, "Control of Firearms," pp. 174–75; Stark, *Social Problems*, p. 227; McCaghy, *Deviant Behavior*, pp. 127–29; Barlow, *Introduction to Criminology*, p. 115; Glazer; *Crime in Our Changing Society*, p. 262; Haskell and Yablonsky, *Crime and Delinquency*, p. 341; and Harrington, "The Politics of Gun Control."

12. See Newton and Zimring, *Firearms and Violence in American Life*, pp. 195–99; Hofstadter, "America as a Gun Culture"; Hofstadter and Wallace, *American Violence*, p. 25; Etzioni, "Violence," pp. 739–40; Julian, *Social Problems*, p. 481; Shostak, *Modern Social Reforms*, pp. 278–92; President's Commission, "Control of Firearms," pp. 174–75; Stark, *Social Problems*, p. 227; McCaghy, *Deviant Behavior*, pp. 127–29; Barlow, *Introduction to Criminology*, p. 115; Haskell and Yablonsky, *Crime and Delinquency*, p. 341; and Harrington, "The Politics of Gun Control."

13. See Hofstadter and Wallace, *American Violence*, p. 26; Barlow, *Introduction to Criminology*, p. 143; Glazer, *Crime in Our Changing Society*, pp. 213, 261, 262, 263; Haskell and Yalbonsky, *Crime and Delinquency*, p. 340; and Joseph F. Sheley, *Understanding Crime: Concepts, Issues, Decisions* (Belmont, Calif.: Wadsworth, 1979), p. 229.

14. See President's Commission, "Control of Firearms," p. 174; Glazer, *Crime in Our Changing Society*, pp. 261–62; Shostak, *Modern Social Reforms*, p. 292; McCaghy, *Deviant Behavior*, p. 126; and Harrington, "The Politics of Gun Control," p. 257.

crime rates are made with no consideration given to factors having little or nothing to do with gun controls that might help account for cross-cultural differences between such rates.[15]

Finally, it is worthy of consideration that the conventional social scientific treatment of the gun issue makes no attempt to put the control controversy into social, cultural, and historical perspective in order to foster nonjudgmental understanding of the sentiments and vested interests of both those who support controls and those who oppose them. Occasional attempts are made to present the anti-control position along with the procontrol position,[16] but no effort is made to uncover the vested interests of the people who subscribe to these conflicting views of control, and one is seldom left in doubt concerning which position is the most sophisticated, informed, and logical. Similarly, the gun's place in American history is sometimes examined by conventional social scientists,[17] but its survival is obviously viewed as unfortunate and is explained in terms of cultural lag.

In other words, the conventional social scientific treatment of gun control leaves much to be desired if its goal is the scientific illumination of this controversial issue. Why? To answer this question it is helpful to put both the issue and those studying it into social, cultural, and historical context, as the conventional have been so reluctant to do; a very unconventional work by social historians Lee Kennett and James LaVerne Anderson provides a starting point for such an effort. In *The Gun in America: The Origins of a National Dilemma*, Kennett and Anderson make no policy recommendations or insinuations. They simply fit the gun into American history, demonstrating along the way how the pro and anticontrol factions evolved and came into conflict with each other as the United States became ever more urban and industrial, and less rural and agricultural. They conclude that the trends are against the gun, but they do

15. See Newton and Zimring, *Firearms and Violence in American Life*, pp. 119–28; Hofstadter, "America as a Gun Culture," p. 82; Hofstadter and Wallace, *American Violence*, p. 26; Etzioni, "Violence," p. 740; Empey, "American Society," pp. 295–96; Hollon, *Frontier Violence*, p. 122; Stark, *Social Problems*, p. 226; Haskell and Yablonsky, *Crime and Delinquency*, pp. 340–41.

16. See Shostak, *Modern Social Reforms*, pp. 287–92; and McCaghy, *Deviant Behavior*, pp. 124–29. McCaghy handles the gun control issue in a more evenhanded manner in a recent textbook, *Crime in American Society* (New York: Macmillan, 1980), pp. 112–15. Though he still accepts much that is questionable about public opinion polls, handgun usage, and so forth, in this book McCaghy does question the practicality and effectiveness of gun controls.

17. See Hofstadter, "America as a Gun Culture"; and Hollon, *Frontier Violence*, pp. 106–23.

not hint that American society will be either better or worse off if this is the case.

While Kennett and Anderson make no attempt to delineate the role that the social sciences have played in the gun control controversy, their treatment of the phenomenon in terms of culture conflict is quite suggestive along these lines. Taking their lead from a *Wall Street Journal* article dealing with gun control, they argue that the controversy is best seen "as a skirmish in the larger battle over the nation's cultural values, a battle in which 'cosmopolitan America' is pitted against 'bedrock America.' "[18] Expanding on the differences between the world views of these two Americas and commenting on the appropriateness of the labels applied to them, Kennett and Anderson continue:

> The terms are apt; they could be used to describe the protagonists when the Sullivan Law was debated fifty years ago. Pro-gun spokesmen have long been addicted to those assaults on the liberal establishment in which Spiro Agnew excelled, and those in the other camp have not always concealed their contempt for the 'shirtsleeve crowd.' Cosmopolitan America foresees a new age when guns and the need for them will disappear; bedrock America conceives of it as 1984. Cosmopolitan America has always been concerned about its international image; bedrock America has always been nativist. Shortly after Robert Kennedy's assassination, Gunnar Myrdal reportedly said that if the Constitution allowed such indiscriminate ownership of guns, 'then to hell with the Constitution.' Cosmopolitan America would have found this food for sober reflection; bedrock America, without reflection, would have said: "To hell with Gunnar Myrdal."[19]

If, as Kennett and Anderson argue, the gun controversy is "a skirmish in the larger battle over the nation's cultural values," a battle pitting cosmopolitan America's life styles, world views, and ways of interpreting reality against those of bedrock America, it is hardly surprising that the conventional social scientific treatment of the control issue amounts to an unquestioning scientific stamp of approval of the media-supported procontrol stand. Kennett and Anderson make no claim that the "cultural battle lines" between the two Americas are rigidly fixed. In fact, they claim that "sophisticated America and shirtsleeve America war in all of us."[20]

18. Kennett and Anderson, *The Gun in America*, p. 254.
19. Ibid., pp. 254–55.
20. Ibid., p. 255.

While the two Americas may war in many of us—all is surely an exaggeration—one gets the impression that the purest cosmopolitanism is likely to be found in the urban, highly educated (degreed might be more appropriate), philosophically and politically liberal, upper-middle class; the purest bedrockism is likely to be found in the rural and small town, less degreed, philosophically and politically conservative, lower-middle and working classes.[21] If this is the case, at the very cosmopolitan-sophisticated core of cosmopolitan-sophisticated America, along with those who control the nation's media — or at least the national television networks, large circulation metropolitan newspapers, general interest periodicals, and major publishing houses—are the American intellectual elite. And of course, the American intellectual elite includes not only the nation's "top" writers, journalists, and other such literary folk, but its "top" educators, scholars, and scientists, social and otherwise, as well. Cosmopolitan America, therefore, is not only generally more adept at articulating its views than is bedrock America; it also possesses the means to place its views before bedrock as well as cosmopolitan America; *Reader's Digest* and TV for the former; *New Republic* and college social science courses for the latter. Through its scholarly and scientific connections, cosmopolitan America can also coat these views with a thick veneer of what passes for impartial scientific authority: consider the gun control issue and the conventional social scientific treatment of it as a case in point.

That the media, the scholarly-intellectual community, and even the social scientific subcommunity of the latter are, for the most part, part of what the *Wall Street Journal* and Kennett and Anderson have referred to as cosmopolitan America, rather than impartial observers and interpreters of and reporters on the passing scene, has been noted by a number of maverick social scientists. Sociologist, Roman Catholic priest, and columnist Andrew Greeley, himself a strong supporter of strict gun controls, has claimed that the intellectual community—social scientists not excluded—has all the characteristics of an ethnic group, including divisive factions and an ethnocentrism that encourages it to look down upon rather than attempt to understand the nonintellectual "masses."[22] Michael Lerner, while

21. Ibid., p. 254; and *American Rifleman* Staff; "Pro-gun Poll Comes as Revelation," *The American Rifleman* (February 1976): 16-17.
22. Andrew M. Greeley, *Why Can't They Be Like Us?* (New York: Dutton, 1970) ch. 10.

a graduate student in political science and psychology at Yale, claimed in an even more scathing polemic that the "upper classes" are extremely prejudiced against the lower-middle class and that "one of the strongest supports for this upper-class, 'respectable' bigotry lies in the academic field of psychology."[23] Clearly including social scientists, sociologist Stanislav Andrzejewski has noted that liberal intellectuals are not as tolerant as they think they are when it comes to dealing with those who do not subscribe to their Liberal-Humanitarian religion or participate in their "supranational culture."[24] And sociologist Peter Berger has written about the rising "New Class" of knowledge producers, symbol- rather than thing-manipulators, who have class vested interests of their own. According to Berger, "institutionally, prestige universities and other centers of knowledge production (such as think tanks) are centers of New Class power, while publishing houses, periodicals, and foundations serve as distributing agencies."[25] He goes on to point out that the New Class has a vested interest in government intervention because the greater part of its livelihood is derived "from public-sector employment. . . . Because government interventions have to be legitimated in terms of social ills, the New Class has a vested interest in portraying American society as a whole, and specific aspects of that society, in negative terms."[26]

In other words, to these critics and analysts of the knowledge-producing and disseminating class to which they themselves belong, knowledge producers and disseminators in general tend to be so bound up with the world views, life styles, values, and vested interests of their own urban, upper-middle class, degreed, liberal, sophisticated, cosmopolitan lives that their analyses of various controversial social issues and problems might be expected to be somewhat one-sided and aimed at promoting their own cosmopolitan interests. If this is the case, such knowledge producers and disseminators are involved in what might be called "sagecraft" in behalf of the cosmopolitan America of which they are not only an integral but a central part. "The original status of the sage lies within his party," according to Florian Znaniecki, "and his original function consists in rationalizing and justifying intellectually the collective tendencies of his party.

23. Michael Lerner, "Respectable Bigotry," *The American Scholar* (Autumn 1969): 608.

24. Stanislav Andrzejewski, *Military Organization and Society* (London: Routledge and Kegan Paul, 1954), pp. 13–14.

25. Peter L. Berger, "Ethics and the Present Class Struggle," *World View* (April 1978): 7.

26. Ibid., p. 10.

It is his duty to 'prove' by 'scientific' arguments that his party is right and its opponents are wrong."[27]

In order to perform his duty, the sage must demonstrate that his party's position is right because it is based on truth, and that the opposition's stand is wrong because it is based on error. "There is no doubt but that he can perform this task to the satisfaction of himself and his adherents," says Znaniecki, "for in the vast multiplicity of diverse cultural data it is always possible to find facts which, 'properly' interpreted, prove that the generalizations he accepts as true are true and that those he rejects as false are false."[28] Of course, the sage is likely to be opposed by the sages of the other side. Unless opposition sages can be silenced, the sage must call their reasoning and/or facts into question.

If the knowledge producers and disseminators form the core of cosmopolitan America, as suggested in the aforementioned, it is hardly surprising that the social scientific treatment of the gun issue that has been publicized through federal commissions and college social problems books is identical to the procontrol stand almost unanimously supported by the media. Neither is it surprising that such treatments do not critically examine poll findings, cross-cultural comparisons of crime rates, and so forth, that can be used to support controls; nor that they invariably fail to put the control controversy into social, cultural, and historical context examining the vested interests of the pro as well as the anticontrol factions. That sagecraft, purposeful or the inadvertent product of cosmopolitan ethnocentrism, helps account for such oversights is suggested by statements made by two prominent sociologists associated with a federal commission headed by Milton Eisenhower. In spite of the fact that his own research ten years earlier had found no correlation between the availability of guns and the incidence of gun crime, one of these, Marvin E. Wolfgang, stated in a letter to the editor of *Time* magazine: "My personal choice for legislation is to remove all guns from private possession. I would favor statutory provisions that require all guns to be turned in to public authorities."[29] The other, Morris Janowitz, is in complete agreement: "I see no reason . . . why anyone in a democracy should own a weapon."[30]

27. Florian Znaniecki, *The Social Role of the Man of Knowledge* (New York: Harper & Row, 1968), pp. 72–73.
28. Ibid., p. 74.
29. Marvin E. Wolfgang, "Letters to the Editor," *Time* (July 5, 1968): 6.
30. See "The Gun Under Fire," *Time* (June 21, 1968): 17.

Inadvertent or otherwise, a sage orientation results in social scientific analysis that is social scientific in name only. The social scientist who is primarily concerned with "rationalizing and justifying intellectually the collective tendencies of his party," rather than with shedding as much light as possible on a complex social phenomenon is quite limited. He or she is not likely to consider personal position as part of the phenomenon being studied, or to recognize how one's ideological position restricts one's vision.

SAGECRAFT AND THE SOCIAL SCIENTIFIC ENTERPRISE

While it is being suggested that those social scientists responsible for the conventional social scientific treatment of the gun control issue are acting as sages in behalf of a cosmopolitan America that is generally antigun, no claim is made that they are, in most cases at least, consciously doing so. It would not be surprising to find that most of those social scientists assisting federal commissions or passing information concerning the phenomenon to students through textbooks actually feel that they are letting the facts—crime rates, poll results, and so forth—speak for themselves. The point being made is that such social scientists have been inclined to take too much for granted about the gun issue, possibly due to their own cosmopolitan world views, life styles, values, and vested interests, and in doing so they have provided "scientific" support—sage fashion—for the cosmopolitan tendencies that they not only share but help to create. A few examples should suffice to demonstrate how such cosmopolitan ethnocentrism and the sage orientation it encourages can affect the social scientific enterprise.

Consider the late Richard Hofstadter's attempt to explain the widespread civilian possession of firearms in the United States. Along the way, as he attempted to discredit the "frontier past" explanation for a state of affairs that he clearly considered to be deplorable, Hofstadter noted that the American frontier experience could not account for the persistence of what he referred to as the American gun culture, since the frontier faded away several generations ago. "Why," Hofstadter asked, "did the United States alone among industrial societies cling to the idea that a substantially unregulated supply of guns among its city populations is a safe and acceptable thing."[31]

31. Hofstadter, "America as a Gun Culture," p. 82.

Canada and Australia have had frontiers, and Japan has had a violent past, he reminds us, yet the gun homicide, suicide, and accident rates for these nations are far lower than those for the United States. Hofstadter credits the "rigorous gun laws" that Japan (the land of hara-kiri) has adopted as it has modernized with producing that country's extremely low gun homicide and suicide rates. "In sum," he states, "other societies, in the course of industrial and urban development have succeeded in modifying their old gun habits, and we have not."[32]

The preceding is typical of the conventional social scientific use of cross-cultural comparisons to support gun controls. The facts have apparently been allowed to speak for themselves. But interestingly enough, the conventional never tell us anything about the "old gun habits" of other nations that gun controls have supposedly modified. In fact, the conventional not only do not tell us anything about these "old gun habits," but they show no sign that they are familiar with them or that they have made any attempt to become so. Hofstadter, for example, simply assumed that Japan's "old gun habits" were similar to ours because of that nation's tradition of feudal and military violence, and that Australia's and Canada's were similar to ours because both nations have had frontiers. Such assumptions certainly amount to convenient lapses of scholarly curiosity, since the works of various scholars who have not involved themselves with the gun control controversy—firearms historians, students of Japanese history and those who have compared frontiers—give us no reason to believe that the "old gun habits" of these nations were anything like ours.

With respect to Japan, if we are to accept what other scholars have written on the subject, firearms were used extensively in the feudal wars after having been brought to Japan by the Portuguese toward the middle of the sixteenth century, but the populace as a whole never seemed to have become familiar with them.[33] The sword remained the most respected weapon through the 250 years of relatively peaceful Tokugawa rule down to rather recent times. During this period, partly due to traditional concerns and partly due to official policy, little or no effort was made to improve firearms, and

32. Ibid.

33. See Noel Perrin, *Giving Up the Gun: Japan's Reversion to the Sword, 1543-1879* (Boston: Godine, 1979). See also George Sansom, *Japan: A Short Cultural History* (New York: D. Appleton-Century, 1936), pp. 412–13; and *A History of Japan 1334-1615*, vol. 2 (Stanford, Calif.: Stanford University Press, 1961), pp. 263–64.

when Perry "reopened" Japan to the rest of the world in the middle of the nineteenth century, the Japanese were still using matchlock guns of the same basic variety as those to which they had been introduced by the Portuguese 300 years earlier. What "old gun habits" did the Japanese have to modify as they became urban and industrial? Why should "rigorous gun laws" that came with "modernization" be credited with producing a low gun-related homicide rate when, prior to "modernization," Japan had relegated the gun to the status of plaything of the wealthy and had shown little or no concern for developing it as a weapon? Similarly, how can such laws be credited with producing a low gun-related suicide rate in a tradition-bound land where the honored way to commit harakiri was with a knife?

With regard to Canada and Australia, scholars who have compared them have found many differences between the Canadian and Australian frontiers and our own—differences that may account for dissimilar patterns of firearms usage between those of our frontier and the others. Except for the trouble that the French experienced with the Iroquois Confederacy in eastern Canada during the eighteenth century, for instance, neither Canadian nor Australian frontiersmen encountered the formidable aboriginal opposition that Americans encountered on the fringes of settlement for some 250 years of "recurring pioneering experience."[34] In fact, neither the Canadian nor the Australian frontier experience could even be described as recurring. Part of the Canadian east was simply transported west after the railroads penetrated the Laurentian Shield in the late nineteenth century; in Australia, pioneer expansion was stopped short in the mid-nineteenth century by the uninhabitable interior deserts.[35] Centralized police forces, for another example, were reasonably effective in Canada[36] and Australia, though hardly popular in the latter,[37] while

34. Ray Allen Billington, "Frontiers," in C. Vann Woodward, ed., *The Comparative Approach to American History* (New York: Basic Books, 1968), p. 79. See also Richard A. Preston and Sydney F. Wise, *Men in Arms: A History of Warfare and Its Interrelationships with Western Society* (New York: Praeger Publishers, 1970), pp. 165–66.

35. Billington, "Frontiers," p. 79.

36. See Seymour Martin Lipset, "The 'Newness' of the New Nations," in C. Vann Woodward, ed., *The Comparative Approach to American History* (New York: Basic Books, 1968), p. 70; and Paul F. Sharp, *Whoop-Up Country: The Canadian American West, 1865–1885* (Minneapolis: University of Minnesota Press, 1955), p. 110.

37. See H.C. Allen, *Bush and Backwoods: A Comparison of the Frontier in Australia and the United States* (Sydney: Angus and Robertson, 1959), p. 103; and Russel Ward, *The Australian Legend* (New York: Oxford University Press, 1958), p. 144.

"law and order" was often brought to American frontier communities through vigilante action,[38] a phenomenon hardly known on the other two frontiers. In short, it would seem that American frontiersmen over a period of 250 or so years were required to rely more heavily on their firearms for their own protection than were their Canadian and Australian counterparts.

But Hofstadter not only was not aware of, or conveniently overlooked, differences between frontiers that might have produced dissimilar "old gun habits" in these various ex-frontier nations; he also overlooked differences that developed behind the frontiers in these nations — differences that also might have had some bearing on the forms these "habits" took and on their preservation. To compare modern firearms-related crime rates of formerly frontier nations without considering the differences in the magnitude of the transformations that these nations have experienced is to "stack the deck" sage-fashion in favor of one's own cause rather than to attempt to foster understanding. When one considers that the United States, 3,615,122 square miles in area to Canada's 3,851,809 and Australia's 2,967,909, has almost five times the population and over eight times the Gross National Product of Canada and Australia combined, it is obvious that much more has occurred behind the frontier here than in either of the other nations. And it seems generally agreed that this American transformation generated much more social disruption and civil strife than has resulted from the lesser transformations in Canada and Australia. What were the Canadian or Australian equivalents of our Revolutionary and Civil Wars, for example — conflicts that set neighbor against neighbor and lasted at that level long after the battlefields had grown silent? When did either Canada or Australia have racial, ethnic, or labor wars to approach those that Americans have waged against each other behind the frontier?

In other words, the passing of the frontier in the United States did not appreciably reduce the risk to life and limb that Americans have created for each other, so, given the political nature of law enforcement that conflict theorists take such delight in exploring, why is it surprising that many Americans continue to look to the gun for protection as well as for recreation? How can Canadian and Australian gun laws be credited with producing lower gun-related crime rates than ours by modifying "old gun habits" assumed to have been simi-

38. See Richard Maxwell Brown, *Strains of Violence: Historical Studies of American Violence and Vigilantism* (New York: Oxford University Press, 1975).

lar to ours, when there seems to be good reason to believe that neither their frontiers nor what came afterward actually produced "old gun habits" like ours?

Hofstadter's comments on the modified "old gun habits" of other nations appeared in an *American Heritage* article entitled "America as a Gun Culture." This article developed a theme first mentioned in Hofstadter's introduction to an anthology he and Michael Wallace edited, entitled *American Violence: A Documentary History.*[39] If his assumptions concerning the "old gun habits" of other nations have been challenged in the scholarly literature on the gun issue published to date, such challenges have received little publicity.

Another example of the selective perception that scholarly supporters of gun controls carry into their cross-cultural comparisons of crime rates is provided by a social science assisted staff report submitted to the National Commission on the Causes and Prevention of Violence, headed by Milton Eisenhower. This report, directed by George D. Newton and Franklin E. Zimring, pointed out that of the four homicides per 100,000 persons recorded in England and Wales in 1967, only one out of each four involved the use of a firearm.[40] In the United States during the same period, sixty-one crimes of this sort were recorded per 100,000 persons, with thirty-eight of each sixty-one involving the use of firearms. Similarly, in England and Wales, ninety-seven robberies per 100,000 persons were recorded, with only six of each ninety-seven involving firearms, while in the United States 1020 robberies per 100,000 persons were recorded, with 372 out of each 1020 involving the use of firearms.

To the extent that one is inclined to take statistics at face value, these figures are interesting. Suppose that no American citizen had possessed a firearm in 1967, and let us assume that none of the crimes in which firearms were used that year would have been committed if a firearm had not been available—a questionable assumption, to say the least. Subtracting the firearms-related crimes from the others, we find that the United States still would have led England and Wales in homicides twenty-three to four per 100,000 (5.8 to 1) and in robberies 648 to ninety-seven per 100,000 (6.7 to 1). A scholar interested in shedding light on a complex issue might wonder, then, if it is English gun laws or the differences between English and

39. Hofstadter and Wallace, *American Violence*, pp. 5, 25–27.
40. Newton and Zimring, *Firearms and Violence in American Life*, p. 124.

American societies that are responsible for the lower rate of firearms-related crime in England and Wales. Newton and Zimring acknowledge this possibility but do not dwell on it, since they are building the case for controls. A scholar might also point out that the passing of the frontier has not, according to these figures, removed the sorts of threats that humans create for one another from the United States (and these threatening conditions have continued not simply because of the absence of strong firearms regulations). A procontrol sage, of course, would hardly be expected to consider seriously either of these issues, but Newton and Zimring and the social scientists who assisted them were supposedly searching for "truths" upon which to base policy recommendations.[41] It should be mentioned that Marvin Wolfgang, whose strong procontrol sentiments have been mentioned, was one of the social scientists associated with the report.

As the conventional have been inclined to take too much for granted about firearms use, past and present, in other parts of the world, they have also been inclined to accept uncritically and pass on Gallup and Harris poll results that invariably show that there is a great deal of public support for various gun control measures. Sociologist Rodney Stark, for example, wrote the following in his college-level social problems text: "The failure of national, state, and local governments to enact strict gun-control legislation offers considerable insight into the American political process. For decades a dedicated minority has had its will over an apathetic majority. What does the majority believe?"[42] Looking to the public opinion polls for the answer to his question, Stark noted that 84 percent of those polled on gun control by Gallup in 1938 believed that " 'all owners of pistols and revolvers should be required to register with the Government' "; that 75 percent of those polled in 1959 "(and 65 percent of gun owners) believed no one should be permitted to buy a gun without a police permit"; and that "no poll conducted in the United States has ever found that more than a third of those polled opposed tough gun controls."[43] This same message, as has been noted, can be found in other social problems texts and anthology reading, always presented in a matter-of-fact manner as if the poll findings are indisputable. But poll findings are not indisputable, as anyone familiar

41. Ibid., p. iii.
42. Stark, *Social Problems*, p. 227.
43. Ibid.

with the measurement and interpretation problems encountered by survey researchers is likely to be aware.

To claim that the "apathetic majority" believes that we should have "tough gun controls" of some type or other implies that we know that the people concerned have seriously considered the issue, taken a stand in favor of controls, but been unwilling to put forth the effort required to get them enacted. But might we not just as easily conclude that the majority is inactive because most of those who are a part of it have seldom given any consideration at all to the issue and are really not particularly committed to controls? The apparent overwhelming pro-control support reported by the polls does not preclude this interpretation. The appearance of support might be the product of one or both of the following:

1. Even if an individual has given little or no consideration to the gun control issue, and consequently is not committed to either a pro or anticontrol stand, once he has decided to cooperate with the pollsters, he or she must make some effort to answer their questions. And, given the situation, it would hardly be surprising for the responses to support tough gun laws. Though not committed, the individual may quite understandably feel that this is the response expected. Survey researchers are familiar with the measurement problems posed by "social desirability" responses,[44] and with the overwhelming media support for controls, the possibility that such responses may have inflated the procontrol column of the polls can scarcely be dismissed. The way the questions are posed, the demeanor of the interviewer, and recent news events may also tend to make the pro-control response seem to be the expected response. Who but the most dedicated opponent of controls could tell an urbane interviewer that he or she was against tough gun controls after a presidential assassination involving the use of a firearm?

2. Apart from the social desirability response issue, the way that single questions or a series of questions are posed can, inadvertently or otherwise, elicit the responses desired by those commissioning the polls. Thus the Harris and Gallup polls, commissioned by the pro-control media, ask whether the respondent is for tough gun controls and invariably find that most Americans want the controls that the media support. On the other hand, the less-publicized survey con-

---

44. See Derek L. Phillips, *Abandoning Method: Sociological Studies in Methodology* (San Francisco: Jossey-Bass, 1973), pp. 38–59.

ducted for the anti-control National Rifle Association by Decision/ Making/Information (DMI), a California-based opinion measuring firm, asked simply "What should be done to reduce crime?" When only 11 percent suggested that gun laws were needed, DMI reported that "the lack of gun control laws is not spontaneously mentioned as either a national problem or a local problem by a significant number of citizens. Their attention had to be called to the issue before they expressed an opinion."[45] Once their attention was called to the issue, 73 percent answered that they did not believe that even firearms confiscation would reduce crime, and 68 percent answered that they felt that most gun owners would not turn in their guns if the federal government demanded that they do so. Not surprisingly, the bias built into the DMI poll satisfied the NRA. When NBC made the mistake of asking similar questions, they found that 59 percent of those polled answered that a handgun ban would not reduce crime and 11 percent answered that it would increase crime.[46] Certainly this was a tactical error in the war between the sages.

Even if we assume that the interviewer's questions have tapped the "true feelings" of the American public on a given issue, however, we are still faced with the problem of interpretation. It may be that the majority of Americans, after carefully thinking over the issue, support tougher gun controls. It may also be, given what appears to be an American, or at least a bedrock, tendency to view crime in terms of "us good guys" against "those bad guys,"[47] that many such supporters, particularly those who are firearms owners, do not consider the possibility that they themselves may be adversely affected by such laws. After all, the police would never deny them permission to acquire or possess the firearm of their choice—only the "bad guys" would be affected. This assumption may shed light on the apparent paradox noted by Kennett and Anderson: according to the polls, most Americans support gun controls at the same time that most would use their guns against urban rioters.[48] What response would Gallup and Harris receive if they asked those being interviewed if they would support firearms regulations even though there was a good chance that those regulations would restrict their own possession and usage of firearms?

45. *American Rifleman* Staff, "Pro-gun Poll," p. 16.
46. NBC Special, "Violence in America," 1977.
47. Kennett and Anderson, *The Gun in America*, p. 252.
48. Ibid., p. 255.

Many social scientists are aware of the problems associated with polls and survey research in general, and in fact, the preceding commentary is largely based on Armand L. Mauss and Milton Rokeach's critique of a 1976 Gallup poll. The purpose these two sociologists give for their critique is as follows: "We would like to suggest a number of considerations that should be kept in mind by the intelligent and sophisticated reader in assessing the significance of survey results like these, and then offer a few opinions of our own about their meanings."[49] This objective could certainly be considered praiseworthy, an example of the scientific, inquiring mind at its best, taking for granted no more than necessary, and helping others to examine that which they might have overlooked. The poll findings being critiqued, however, had nothing to do with gun control. Significantly, the poll chosen for critical examination dealt with religious beliefs and had found, among other things, "that 94 percent of Americans still believe in God," and that "69 percent believe in immortality." Bedrock America, of course, might be expected to revel in these findings, but ultra-cosmopolitan America would probably find them disconcerting. And also significantly, the critique appeared in *The Humanist*, the journal of the ultra-cosmopolitan secular humanists. When poll findings indicating that the majority of Americans favor strong gun controls are cited in texts and commission reports, they are not accompanied by "considerations that should be kept in mind by the intelligent and sophisticated reader in assessing the significance of survey results."

As the conventional have been inclined to take too much for granted about the use of firearms past and present in other parts of the world, and to accept uncritically and pass on Gallup and Harris poll findings, so have they been reluctant to treat the gun issue as some of their number have treated other controversial social issues. Edwin M. Schur, for example, has claimed that categories of victimless crimes have been created through the outlawing of abortion, homosexuality, and the use of certain drugs. He has argued that such laws are unenforceable, and that they may have unwelcome side effects—the establishment of "the economic basis for black-market operations," or the production of "situations in which police effi-

---

49. Armand Mauss and Milton Rokeach, "Pollsters as Prophets," *The Humanist* (May-June 1977): 48–51.

ciency is impaired and police corruption encouraged."[50] While bedrock America might find such an argument hard to accept, cosmopolitan America would probably tend to agree with it.

If the argument holds for laws against the use of certain drugs, and so forth, does it not also hold for attempts to regulate firearms possession? Those who do not register their guns when registration is required, or who do not turn in their handguns when handgun possession is banned become classifiable as criminal even though they have not misused firearms or committed other acts classifiable as serious crimes. How would gun control affect police efficiency? The more difficult it becomes to acquire firearms legally, the more valuable supposedly confidential firearms registration and owner registration lists become to professional burglars who wish to locate firearms for illegal sale; hence, more temptation is placed in the way of those officials charged with guarding such records. If an attempt is made to disarm the populace, the guns that the police are able to confiscate become valuable items. How many will be filtered back into private hands via the black market? How could gun controls not foster official and police corruption? When laws are difficult to enforce, as attorney Don B. Kates, Jr., has noted, "enforcement becomes progressively more haphazard until at last the laws are used only against those who are unpopular with the police."[51] How could gun control not lead to selective enforcement and discrimination against minorities and the poor? It would seem that Schur, of all people, would be in a position to recognize that if this argument concerning the creation of victimless crime categories and their side effects holds for any attempts to regulate behavior, it holds as well for gun control. But not surprisingly, the recognition seems to have escaped him, as it has other social scientists, and he has even indicated that he believes gun controls could play a significant part in reducing violence and civil disorder.[52] Need more be said concerning the restricted vision that cosmopolitan ethnocentrism and sagecraft can impose on the social scientific enterprise?

50. Edwin M. Schur, *Crimes Without Victims: Deviant Behavior and Public Policy—Abortion, Homosexuality, Drug Addiction* (Englewood Cliffs, N.J.: Prentice-Hall, 1965), p. 6.

51. Don B. Kates, Jr., "Handgun Control: Prohibition Revisited," *Inquiry* (December 5, 1977): 21.

52. Edwin M. Schur, *Our Criminal Society: The Sociological and Legal Sources of Crime in America* (Englewood Cliffs, N.J.: Prentice-Hall, 1969), pp. 143, 237.

SUMMARY

Using the gun control issue as a case in point, this chapter has argued that the conventional social scientific treatment of controversial social phenomena often has much more in common with sagecraft than it does with social science. The social scientific treatment of the gun issue passed on to the general public through magazine articles, textbooks, and the published findings of various social science assisted federal commissions is identical to the pro-gun control argument generally accepted by that segment of American society with which the more prominent social scientists are more likely to identify — urban, degreed, philosophically and politically liberal, upper-middle class, or cosmopolitan America. While the cosmopolitan ethnocentrism of the social scientists involved may help to account for their treatment of the control issue, in lending "scientific" support to the pro-gun control position of cosmopolitan America, these social scientists are still serving the vested interests of their party.

Firearms historians, students of frontiers, and other scholars not dealing directly with the gun control issue have shown in various ways that patterns of firearms use and the social factors accounting for them have differed significantly from one part of the world to another. Textbook and federal commission treatments of the gun issue, apparently completely oblivious to such considerations, continue to credit gun controls with "modifying the old gun habits" of other modern nations and thereby reducing their gun crime rates. Many social scientists are aware of the problems associated with public opinion polls and survey research in general, but textbook and commission citations of poll results supportive of gun controls are never accompanied by hints to the "intelligent and sophisticated reader" interested "in assessing the significance of survey results." Some social scientists have concerned themselves with making students and the public aware of the social repercussions arising from the creation of victimless crime categories, but these same individuals do not seem to believe that attempts to regulate firearms possession would create such a category. It would certainly appear that cosmopolitan ethnocentrism and the sage orientation that it fosters do little to encourage the intellectual curiosity and skepticism so vital to the social scientific enterprise.

SELECTED BIBLIOGRAPHY (PART II)

Allen, H.C. *Bush and Backwoods: A Comparison of the Frontiers in Australia and the United States.* Sydney: Angus and Robertson, 1959.

Andrzejewski, Stanislav. *Military Organization and Society.* London: Routledge and Kegan Paul, 1954.

Berger, Peter L. "Ethics and the Present Class Struggle." *World View* (April 1978): 6-11.

Billington, Ray Allen. "Frontiers." In C. Vann Woodward, ed., *The Comparative Approach to American History*, pp. 75-90. New York: Basic Books, 1968.

Bordua, David J., and Alan J. Lizotte. "A Subcultural Model of Legal Firearms Ownership in Illinois." *Law and Public Policy Quarterly* 2 (April 1979): 147-75.

Bordua, D.J.; A.J. Lizotte; G. Kleck; with Van Cagle. *Patterns of Firearms Ownership, Use and Regulation in Illinois.* Springfield: Illinois Law Enforcement Commission, 1979.

Boyd, Julian P., ed. *The Papers of Thomas Jefferson*, vol. 8. Princeton, N.J.: Princeton University Press, 1953, p. 407.

Brown, Richard Maxwell. *Strain of Violence: Historical Studies of American Violence and Vigilantism.* New York: Oxford University Press, 1975.

Bruce-Briggs, B. "The Great American Gun War." *Public Interest* 45 (Fall 1976): 37-62.

_____., ed. *The New Class.* New Brunswick, N.J.: Transaction Books, 1979.

Cambridge Reports, Inc. *An Analysis of Public Attitudes Toward Handgun Control.* Cambridge, Mass.: Cambridge Reports, Inc., 1978. (Prepared for the Center for the Study and Prevention of Handgun Violence.)

Cambridge Survey Research, Inc. *An Analysis of Political Attitudes in the Commonwealth of Massachusetts.* Cambridge, Mass.: Cambridge Survey Research, Inc., 1977. (Prepared for the United States Conference of Mayors.)

Caplan, David P. "Restoring the Balance: The Second Amendment Revisited." *Fordham Urban Law Journal* 5 (1976): 31-53.

Decision/Making/Information (DMI). *Attitudes of the American Electorate Toward Gun Control, 1978.* Santa Ana, Calif.: DMI, 1979.

Erskine, Hazel. "The Polls: Gun Control." *Public Opinion Quarterly* 36 (Summer 1972): 455-69.

Greeley, Andrew M. *Why Can't They Be Like Us: America's White Ethnic Groups.* New York: Dutton, 1970.

Greenwood, Colin. *Firearms Control: A Study of Armed Crime and Firearms Control in England and Wales.* London: Routledge and Kegan Paul, 1972.

Hardy, David T., and John Stompoly. "Of Arms and the Law." *Chicago-Kent Law Review* 51 (September 1974): 62-114.

Harrington, Michael J. "The Politics of Gun Control." In Phillip Whitten, ed., *Readings in Sociology: Contemporary Perspectives*, pp. 255-59. New York: Harper and Row, 1979.

Hofstadter, Richard. "America as a Gun Culture." *American Heritage* (October 1970): 4-11ff.

Hollon, W. Eugene. *Frontier Violence: Another Look.* New York: Oxford University Press, 1974.

Holmberg, Judith Vandell, and Michael Clancy. *People vs. Handguns: The Campaign to Ban Handguns in Massachusetts.* Washington, D.C.: United States Conference of Mayors, Handgun Control Staff, 1977.

Kates, Don B., Jr. "Handgun Control: Prohibition Revisited." *Inquiry* (December 5, 1977): 20-23.

_____., ed. *Restricting Handguns: The Liberal Skeptics Speak Out.* Croton-on-Hudson, N.Y.: North River Press, 1979.

Kennett, Lee, and James L. Anderson. *The Gun in America: The Origins of a National Dilemma.* Westport, Conn.: Greenwood Press, 1975.

Kessler, Raymond G. "Enforcement Problems of Gun Control: A Victimless Crime Analysis." *Criminal Law Bulletin* 16 (March-April 1980): 131-49.

Kukla, Robert B. *Gun Control.* Harrisburg, Penn.: Stackpole Books, 1973.

Lerner, Michael. "Respectable Bigotry." *American Scholar* (Autumn 1969): 606-17.

Lipset, Seymour Martin. "The 'Newness' of the New Nation." In C. Vann Woodward, ed., *The Comparative Approach to American History*, pp. 62-74. New York: Basic Books, 1968.

Lizotte, Alan J., and David J. Bordua. "Firearms Ownership for Sport and Protection: Two Divergent Models." *American Sociological Review* 45 (April 1980): 229-44.

Lizotte, Alan J.; David J. Bordua; and Carolyn S. White. "Firearms Ownership for Sport and Protection: Two Not So Divergent Models." *American Sociological Review* 46 (August 1981): 499-503.

Mauss, Armand, and Milton Rokeach. "Pollsters as Prophets." *The Humanist* (May-June 1977): 48-51.

Newton, George D., and Franklin Zimring. *Firearms and Violence in American Life.* A Staff Report of the Task Force on Firearms, National Commission on the Causes and Prevention of Violence. Washington, D.C.: Government Printing Office, 1969.

NRA Staff. "Concerned NRA Members Redirect Their Association." *American Rifleman* 125 (1977): 16-17.

O'Connor, James F., and Alan J. Lizotte. "The Southern Subculture of Violence Thesis and Patterns of Gun Ownership." *Social Problems* 25 (1978): 420-29.

Perrin, Noel. *Giving Up the Gun: Japan's Reversion to the Sword, 1543-1879.* Boston: Godine, 1979.

Phillips, Derek L. *Abandoning Method: Sociological Studies in Methodology.* San Francisco: Jossey-Bass, 1973.

Preston, Richard A., and Sydney F. Wise. *Men in Arms: A History of Warfare and Its Interrelationships with Western Society.* New York: Praeger, 1970.

Schuman, Howard, and Stanley Presser. "Attitude Measurement and the Gun Control Paradox." *Public Opinion Quarterly* 41 (1977): 427-37.

Schur, Edwin M. *Crimes Without Victims: Deviant Behavior and Public Policy— Abortion, Homosexuality, Drug Addiction.* Englewood Cliffs, N.J.: Prentice-Hall, 1965.

Sharp, Paul F. *Whoop-Up Country: The Canadian-American West, 1865-1885.* Minneapolis: University of Minnesota Press, 1955.

Tonso, William R. *Gun and Society: The Social and Existential Roots of the American Attachment to Firearms.* Washington, D.C.: University Press of America, 1982.

_____. "Media Culture and Guns." *The Quill* (March 1983): 17-20.

U.S. Congress. Senate. "Gun Control." *Congressional Record* 121 (December 19, 1975): 1-10.

Ward, Russel. *The Australian Legend.* New York: Oxford University Press, 1958.

Wright, James D. "Public Opinion and Gun Control: A Comparison of Results from Two Recent National Surveys." *Annals of the American Academy of Political and Social Science* 455 (May 1981): 24-39.

Wright, James D., and Linda L. Marston. "The Ownership of the Means of Destruction: Weapons in the United States." *Social Problems* 23 (October 1975): 93-107.

Wright, James D.; Peter H. Rossi; and Kathleen Daly. *Under the Gun: Weapons, Crime, and Violence in America.* Hawthorne, N.Y.: Aldine, 1983.

Znaniecki, Florian. *The Social Role of the Man of Knowledge.* New York: Harper and Row, 1968.

PART III

GUN OWNERSHIP AS A CAUSE OF VIOLENT CRIME

Chapter 5

THE RELATIONSHIP BETWEEN GUN OWNERSHIP LEVELS AND RATES OF VIOLENCE IN THE UNITED STATES

Gary Kleck

How are levels of gun ownership and rates of violence related? If we are to believe the conclusions of the Task Force on Firearms of the 1968 Eisenhower Commission, the answer is a simple one: "More Firearms—More Firearms Violence."[1] However, it is worth noting that even in their enthusiastically pro-gun-control report nowhere is it explicitly stated that increases in gun ownership *caused*, even partially, the increases in violent crime of the 1960s, although it is certainly implied throughout. The slogan just quoted is carefully phrased in such a way as to clearly suggest such an interpretation to the casual reader, without actually committing its authors to a claim they could not (or at least did not) support. Virtually all of the evidence marshalled to establish the association between gun ownership and violence could just as easily be interpreted as showing that more gun violence leads to more people acquiring guns for defensive purposes rather than the reverse (see especially their chapter 7). Yet the authors never acknowledged this alternative interpretation, despite devoting an entire chapter to the subject of firearms and self-defense, where they noted that home defense is a major reason why many people acquire and own guns!

---

1. George D. Newton and Franklin Zimring, *Firearms and Violence in American Life.* A Staff Report of the Task Force on Firearms, National Commission on the Causes and Prevention of Violence (Washington, D.C.: GPO, 1969), p. xiii.

There is no logically necessary relationship between levels of gun ownership and interpersonal violence, or even between levels of gun ownership and gun violence. Clearly, most people who own guns do not use them for inflicting harm on others, and many people commit acts of violence without using guns. It is possible for gun violence to decrease while at the same time gun ownership is increasing, as indeed happened in the United States during the 1950s.[2] Gun ownership can increase among people who are very unlikely to be violent, with or without weapons, while remaining constant among those social groups where interpersonal violence is relatively common, producing no change in the homicide rate. Guns, like other objects, do not have any meaning in themselves but only the meaning that is attached to them by people, a meaning that varies between social groups and between social situations. Some people, in some situations, may identify a gun as an instrument of interpersonal violence, a way of establishing dominance, or a method of settling a dispute; other people, in other situations, may not attach any such meaning. The mere possession of a gun alone does not necessarily make deadly violence more likely, and thus the connection between levels of gun ownership and violence is one that must be evaluated empirically.

This chapter is in part an update and elaboration of an earlier investigation of the relationship between trends in gun ownership and homicide rates in the United States.[3] Two questions are addressed:

1. To what extent, if any, do levels of gun ownership in the general population affect U.S. homicide rates?
2. To what extent, if any, do crime rates affect levels of gun ownership?

The earlier paper covered the 1947–1973 period, while this chapter covers five additional years, spanning the period from 1947 to 1978. This change has not been a trivial one, as it has resulted in the need to modify some of the earlier paper's findings regarding the effect of gun ownership on homicide rates. In addition, I will examine the

---

2. Gun ownership increased from an estimated 38,127 guns per 100,000 resident population in 1950 to an estimated 43,061 in 1960, while homicide deaths from firearms declined from 2.75 per 100,000 resident population in 1950 to 2.57 in 1960, and total homicides per 100,000 resident population declined from 5.23 to 4.70 during the same period.

3. Gary Kleck, "Capital Punishment, Gun Ownership, and Homicide," *American Journal of Sociology* 84 (January 1979): 882–910.

effect of gun ownership on robbery rates and test Franklin Zimring's "new guns" hypothesis, to be discussed later.[4]

PREVIOUS RESEARCH

There are two ways in which gun ownership could lead to greater violence and death. First, the availability of guns could conceivably increase the frequency of assaults by facilitating or stimulating attacks that would not otherwise have occurred. Berkowitz has argued that the sight of a gun can elicit aggression from angered people because people have been conditioned to associate guns and aggression.[5] This has been labelled the "weapons effect." The evidence regarding the hypothesis has been critiqued elsewhere, and it was concluded that the available evidence does not support the hypothesis and that for the population as a whole, guns are as likely to inhibit assaults as to incite them.[6]

Second, the availability of guns could increase the fraction of assaults that result in death (the assault fatality rate) because guns are deadlier than knives and other weapons commonly used in assaults. This hypothesis has considerably more support than the weapons effect hypothesis, but it is not known, even approximately, how much deadlier guns are than knives or other weapons. Simple comparisons of fatality rates of assaults involving the different weapons cannot be used to estimate the difference, contrary to the efforts of some to do so.[7] This kind of comparison has produced widely differing results, some indicating that guns may be as little as 1.31 times as deadly as knives, when comparable assaulters in comparable situations are compared.[8] Since handgun assaults (the predominant

---

4. Franklin E. Zimring, "Firearms and Federal Law: The Gun Control Act of 1968," *Journal of Legal Studies* 4 (January 1975): 133-98; Franklin E. Zimring, "Street Crime and New Guns: Some Implications for Firearms Control," *Journal of Criminal Justice* 4 (Summer 1976): 95-107.

5. Leonard Berkowitz, "Impulse, Aggression and the Gun," *Psychology Today* 2 (September 1968): 19-22; idem., "How Guns Control Us," *Psychology Today* 15 (June 1981): 11-12.

6. Kleck and Bordua, *infra*.

7. Kleck, *infra*; Franklin E. Zimring, "Is Gun Control Likely to Reduce Violent Killings?," *University of Chicago Law Review* 35 (Summer 1968): 721-37.

8. Franklin E. Zimring, "Determinants of the Death Rate from Robbery: A Detroit Time Study," *Journal of Legal Studies* 6 (June 1977): 317-32.

type of gun assault) are fatal only about 3 percent of the time and usually involve small caliber, and therefore less deadly, types of guns, it is not implausible that the difference is actually quite slight.[9] Thus, it is not obvious that we should expect any significant relationship between levels of gun ownership and assaultive violence in the United States.

The previous studies of the aggregate relationship between crime rates and gun ownership levels have been less than satisfactory. Newton and Zimring claimed to have found that more guns means more gun violence.[10] Their analysis was methodologically crude, relying on simple zero-order correlations between gun ownership and gun use in violence, thus ignoring other factors that could influence gun use, and the possibility that more violence produces more gun ownership, rather than the reverse.

Murray's cross-sectional analysis indicated no relationship between gun ownership and state homicide rates, but Phillips and Votey's time-series analysis indicated a positive relationship.[11] However, neither study developed any explicit model of homicide causation. Both treated gun ownership as if it were an exogenous variable, even though it is reasonable to suspect a simultaneous reciprocal relationship between gun ownership and crime, in which case gun ownership would have to be specified as endogenous. Further, Murray used survey measures of gun ownership that he acknowledged to be of doubtful accuracy.

Neither Seitz nor Fisher had any direct measure of gun ownership, and both in fact included homicide or assault rates as component items in their gun ownership factors, producing an artifactual association between the rate of violence and their "gun ownership" scores.[12] Further, both authors ignored the possibility of a reciprocal relationship between homicide and gun ownership. Therefore, neither study's findings of a positive relationship between violence and gun ownership can be clearly interpreted.

9. Kleck, *infra.*

10. Newton and Zimring, *Firearms and Violence in American Life.*

11. Douglas R. Murray, "Handguns, Gun Control Laws, and Firearms Violence," *Social Problems* 23 (October 1975): 81–93; Llad Phillips and Harold L. Votey, Jr., "Handguns and Homicide: Minimizing Losses and the Costs of Control," *Journal of Legal Studies* 5 (June 1976): 463–78.

12. Steven T. Seitz, "Firearms, Homicides, and Gun Control Effectiveness," *Law and Society Review* 6 (May 1972): 595–614; Joseph C. Fisher, "Homicide in Detroit: The Role of Firearms," *Criminology* 14 (November 1976): 387–400.

The best cross-sectional study of the effect of gun ownership on levels of violence is that of Cook, yet it suffers from two of the same problems as the previous studies.[13] His regression analysis of fifty U.S. cities in 1974–1975 found that a gun density variable was positively and significantly related to both gun robbery rates and robbery murder rates (but not the overall robbery rate), controlling for a variety of other variables. Like Seitz and Fisher, he had no direct measure of gun density, since there is none available for cities. Instead, he used an index consisting of two components, both indicators of relative frequency of gun *use* (or citizen preference for using guns), rather than ownership itself.

A far more serious problem, however, has to do with his specification of the relationship between crime rates and gun density. Cook implicitly assumes that robbery rates have no influence on a citizen's acquisition of guns and therefore no effect on gun density, allowing him to interpret a positive relationship between the two variables as indicating the effect of gun density on robbery rates. The assumption is clearly unwarranted, and if untrue, would bias the coefficients computed, due to identification problems. Cook's finding that gun density relates to gun robbery rates but not nongun robbery rates accords perfectly with a fear-of-crime interpretation: citizens acquire guns in response to reports of gun robberies, because they are frightening and/or more likely to be reported in the newspapers and on television, while not being affected by the frequency of nongun robberies, because they are viewed as less serious or frightening and/or are less widely reported through the news media. Therefore Cook's conclusion that gun density affects gun robbery rates is premature, and the meaning of his regression results is unclear.

My own previous investigation attempted to deal with these difficulties by developing a model of homicide rate and gun ownership trends that specified a reciprocal relationship between the two variables, with each positively affecting the other.[14] The model was estimated using U.S. data for each of the years from 1947 to 1973, and each variable showed a significant positive effect on the other, suggesting that increases in gun ownership levels cause increases in the homicide rate, while increases in crime in turn cause more people to

---

13. Philip J. Cook, "The Effect of Gun Availability on Robbery and Robbery Murder: A Cross-Section Study of Fifty Cities," in Robert H. Haveman and B. Bruce Zellner, eds., *Policy Studies Review Annual*, vol. 3, pp. 743–81 (Beverly Hills, Calif.: Sage, 1979).
14. Kleck, "Capital Punishment."

acquire guns, presumably because they fear crime and/or believe they need guns for home defense or self-defense.

Do higher levels of crime and violence cause higher levels of gun ownership? A considerable variety of evidence can be brought to bear on this question. Many survey studies of gun ownership include questions asking gun owners why they own guns, and one of the answer categories is always "defense," "protection," or something similar. Some studies ask only for the respondent's main reason for owning, while the better studies distinguish between defense as the main or primary reason for owning and as a secondary or tertiary reason, and include separate breakdowns of the results for handguns. Unfortunately, only the study conducted by Bordua et al. reported results for respondents who personally own guns; the rest of the studies asked the reasons-for-ownership question of anyone who reports *household* ownership.[15] Consequently, they ask the question of many wives whose husbands own guns and who therefore can only provide an indirect report on why the guns are owned. Using the household as the unit of analysis thereby produces additional error in measuring reasons for ownership.

The percentage of gun-owning households who own for defensive reasons is reported in Table 5–1. When the reason-for-ownership question is asked regarding guns in general, anywhere from 27 to 34 percent of the households report owning guns *primarily* for defense (ignoring the clearly deviant Ennis results), while between 28 and 65 percent report owning either primarily or secondarily for defense, in those surveys which permitted respondents to give both primary and secondary reasons. When the question is asked specifically about handguns, between 43 and 67 percent respond as owning primarily for defensive reasons, and in the single study that asked for secondary reasons for handgun ownership, over 73 percent indicate owning either primarily or secondarily for defense. Therefore it is clear that defense or protection is a very common reason for owning guns in general, and that it is the *dominant* reason, although clearly not the only one, for owning handguns in the United States. These results certainly suggest that increases in crime and violence should cause increases in gun ownership among that fraction of the population which believes gun ownership is an acceptable response to crime.

15. David J. Bordua et al., *Patterns of Firearms Ownership, Use and Regulation in Illinois* (Springfield, Ill.: Illinois Law Enforcement Commission, 1979).

Table 5-1. Fraction of Gun-owning Households that Own for Defensive Reasons.

Study	Date of Survey	Coverage	Percent Reporting Defense or Protection (primary reason/secondary, tertiary reason) Among Those Owning:	
			Any Guns	Handguns
Ennis (1967)	June, 1966	U.S. adults	78[a,b]	—
DMI (U.S. Congress 1976: 9)	Oct., 1975	U.S. registered voters	17/38	—
Center for Political Studies, University of Michigan (1976)	1976	U.S. adults	46[c]	—
Florida (1977, Sect. II)	Spring, 1977	Fla. adults	—	54.5
California (1977)	Spring, 1976	Calif. adults	—	55.5
Bordua et al. (1979: 224, 231)	May, 1977	Illinois adults	19.8/8.4	66.7/6.7[d]
Cambridge Reports (1978: 18)	April–May, 1978	U.S. adults	—	43 (and 8% for law enf.)
DMI (1979), survey 1	May–June, 1978	U.S. registered voters	25/40	—
survey 2	Dec., 1978	U.S. registered voters	21	45
L.A. Times Poll	Jan., 1981	U.S. adults	34	—

a. Where there is no slash between percentages, this indicates respondents were allowed to give only one reason, presumably the most important one.

b. 37% of *all* households reported they owned a gun for protection of the household, even if it had other purposes as well. Since 47.4% of U.S. households in a 1966 Gallup survey (no. 733) admitted gun ownership (not 59% as erroneously reported in Newton and Zimring 1969: 6), about 0.37/0.474 or 78% of all gun-owning households own guns for protection. Unfortunately, since a disproportionate number of persons in this sample were crime victims (Newton and Zimring 1969: 176), it is likely that protection ownership is exaggerated.

c. The 1976 NORC survey showed 48% of all households owned guns. The CPS survey found that 22% of all households owned a gun for protection. Therefore, 22/48 = 46% of gun-owning households have a gun for which one of the purposes, not necessarily the primary one, is protection.

d. Among persons who own only handguns and no other type of gun. The figures from this study refer to respondents who said they personally owned a gun, rather than to those who merely report a gun in their household or home.

They do not necessarily mean that it is *fear* of crime which causes all defensive gun acquisition, since a person can get a gun simply as a matter of prudence, "just in case," without feeling particularly strongly about it or experiencing any anxiety about potential victimization.

Some survey studies have directly investigated the issue of whether gun ownership is affected or produced by fear of crime, prior victimization, or the actual or perceived level of crime. Three of these studies (Wright and Marston, Williams and McGrath, De Fronzo) can be discussed together, since they are all based on the same source of data, the General Social Surveys in the mid-1970s of the National Opinion Research Center. While these surveys were not specifically designed to investigate gun ownership, they did include a question asking if anyone in the respondent's household owned a gun and another question asking what type of gun it was.

All of these studies found that fear of crime was not positively related to gun ownership, although Wright and Marston nonetheless concluded that gun ownership is related to "anticipation and expectation of crime."[16] Wright and Marston found that gun ownership was related to prior victimization for only two of four types of victimization, while Williams and McGrath and De Fronzo found no significant relationship between victimization and general gun ownership.[17]

All of the studies suffer from common deficiencies, which render their findings suspect. First, fear of crime is very crudely measured by a single item—whether the respondent was afraid to walk in his/her neighborhood at night. This hardly includes all or even most of the important dimensions of fear of crime. Second, a problem is introduced by the household ownership of guns: researchers could not know if the respondent personally owned a gun. Yet the fear and victimization items referred only to the respondent, making it difficult to link up both these variables and gun ownership. Any lack of relationship could be attributed to the fact that the variables refer to different persons, since when a female respondent reports household gun ownership, the guns are usually owned by her husband.

16. James D. Wright and Linda L. Marston, "The Ownership of the Means of Destruction: Weapons in the United States," *Social Problems* 23 (October 1975): 101.

17. Ibid., p. 102; J. Sherwood Williams and John H. McGrath III, "Why People Own Guns," *Journal of Communication* 26 (Autumn 1976): 27; James DeFronzo, "Fear of Crime and Handgun Ownership," *Criminology* 17 (November 1979): 337.

In order to avoid this problem, the researchers created another one: they omitted females from the sample. Thus they could usually correctly infer the respondent's personal ownership from reported household ownership. Unfortunately, this procedure amounted to selectively removing fully half of the sample, the half most likely to report fear of crime and, more importantly, the half that is proportionately most likely to own guns specifically for defensive reasons, that is, those related to fear of crime. Data from Bordua et al. indicate that 53 percent of female gun owners own guns primarily or secondarily for protection, while the figure is only 21 percent for men.[18] This selective removal of cases in a manner systematically related to both gun ownership and fear of crime hopelessly biases the sample against the fear-gun ownership hypothesis.

Of these three studies, only Williams and McGrath separately analyzed the relationship between fear or victimization and ownership of *pistols*. Since handguns are the gun type most likely to be owned for protection reasons (see Table 5–1), ownership of pistols is presumably the most likely type of ownership to be related to fear and victimization. That such a distinction is important is confirmed by the authors' findings, which show that although general gun ownership is unrelated to fear and victimization, pistol ownership is positively and significantly related to both.[19]

Finally, and most seriously, the interpretation of the results of these studies is obscured by the failure to control for income when examining the relationship between fear or victimization and gun ownership.[20] The fear hypothesis, like most hypotheses in criminology, is a multivariate one, contingent upon a *ceterus paribus* assumption: those more fearful of crime or those previously victimized are more likely to own guns, *other things being equal.* Those with more income are obviously more able to buy guns, independent of their motivation to do so.[21] Income is also systematically related to fear of crime and victimization: those with more income are better able to locate their residences in more desirable, less crime-ridden areas. Thus the effect of income on both gun ownership and fear and victimization is a suppression effect, which can create a false impression

---

18. Bordua et al., *Patterns of Firearms Ownership*, p. 225.

19. Williams and McGrath, "Why People Own Guns," p. 29.

20. However, Williams and McGrath (1976: 28) controlled for "class," breaking it down into only two categories, low and high. They did not explain how class was measured.

21. Wright and Marston, "The Ownership of the Means of Destruction," pp. 97, 99.

of nonrelationship. If fear and victimization have a positive effect on gun ownership when income is controlled, this effect would be hidden in an examination of the zero-order relationship between fear or victimization and gun ownership, because increases in income cause both increased gun ownership and decreased fear and victimization risks. Thus, while it is true that crime victims and those who fear crime are not more likely to own guns, this does not mean that fear and victimization do not have positive effects on gun ownership, contrary to the conclusions drawn by the authors of these studies.

Two less elaborate studies deserve mention, for the sake of completeness. Caetano found a positive but nonsignificant relationship between prior victimization and gun ownership, but the study concerned a sample of 467 night students enrolled at a California college, a sample not representative of any larger population.[22]

Northwood et al. studied 400 persons who applied for permits to carry concealed weapons in Seattle in 1972, and hence their study is of some marginal relevance to our subject.[23] Applicants were asked to indicate on their application forms why they needed to carry a concealed weapon. Most applicants gave only one or two reasons, and the two most common reasons were protection related: 50.3 percent gave personal protection as a reason, and 26.5 percent gave protection at place of employment as a reason. Although applicants apparently were not directly asked whether they had been crime victims in the past, fully 18.5 percent spontaneously volunteered the information that they had indeed been victimized. Yet, astoundingly, the authors chose to phrase their conclusion from these findings as follows: "the fact that *only* (my emphasis) 18.5 percent of the applicants claim prior victimization as a reason for carrying a concealed weapon suggests that this factor alone is not sufficient to explain gun application behavior in general." The authors do not explain by what criterion they judge 18.5 percent to be a small figure, nor do they cite anyone foolish enough to think that prior victimization is the only factor explaining either gun application behavior or gun carrying. The evidence presented by the authors, as distinguished from their interpretation of it, clearly supports the hypothesis that fear or

22. Donald F. Caetano, "The Domestic Arms Race," *Journal of Communication* 29 (Spring 1979): 39–46.

23. Lawrence K. Northwood et al., "Law-abiding One-man Armies," *Society* 16 (November–December 1978): 69–74.

anticipation of victimization, as well as actual prior victimization, can at least partially account for gun carrying.

Clearly the best survey study of gun ownership, that of Lizotte and Bordua, avoided all of the problems discussed in relation to the others.[24] Lizotte and Bordua measured gun ownership at the individual as well as household level, controlled for income, used a five-item measure of victimization and a three-item measure of fear of crime, and measured attitudes toward violence, home defense, and blacks. In addition, they explicated the relationships among actual levels of crime, perceived levels of crime, fear of crime, victimization, and gun ownership for protection. They found that county crime rates positively affect respondent's perceived level of crime, which positively affects fear of crime, which in turn has a significant positive effect on gun ownership for protection. In addition, victimization was found to have a significant positive effect on fear, which then affected gun ownership. Wright and Marston artificially contrasted two factors potentially affecting gun ownership, stating that anticipation and expectation of crime is a more important determinant than actual experiences with crime.[25] The Lizotte and Bordua findings indicate that it would be more accurate to say that actual experience with crime (i.e., prior victimization) is itself a determinant of the anticipation or fear of crime, which is in turn an important determinant of weapons ownership.

Lizotte and Bordua found that while the proximity of blacks to the respondent's area was positively related to the perceived level of crime, racist attitudes were not, indicating that blacks served as a symbol or indicator of crime levels and thus indirectly affected gun ownership, but that racist attitudes were neither direct nor indirect causes of gun ownership. Northwood et al. had interpreted the relationship between the percentage of blacks and concealed weapons permit application rates in areas of Seattle as evidence of a response to "perceived racial threat," but the Lizotte and Bordua results make

---

24. Alan J. Lizotte and David J. Bordua, "Firearms Ownership for Sport and Protection: Two Divergent Models," *American Sociological Review* 45 (April 1980): 229–43. See also Alan J. Lizotte et al., "Firearms Ownership for Sport and Protection: Two Not So Divergent Models," *American Sociological Review* 46 (August 1981): 499–503. The results in Lizotte and Bordua (1980) were erroneous, based on a faulty computer program. Their corrected results were presented in Lizotte et al. (1981), and it is the corrected results that are discussed here.

25. Wright and Marston, "The Ownership of the Means of Destruction," p. 101.

it clear that it would be considerably less misleading if this were called a "perceived crime threat."

Other researchers have attempted to measure the effect of crime on gun ownership using data on aggregate levels of these two variables, determining the statistical relationship between crime rates and gun ownership in either a cross-sectional or time-series analysis. Clotfelter pooled time-series and cross-sectional data on five states over differing time periods in the 1960s and 1970s regarding crime rates and a handgun acquisition variable that apparently measured handgun sales, applications for permits to purchase handguns or the granting of permits to purchase handguns.[26] (Clotfelter is not clear on which of these was measured, or even whether the same thing was measured for all of the states). He found no significant relationship between the murder rate or the rate of other violent crimes and handgun acquisitions when a time trend variable was included, although the rate of violent crimes other than murder was significantly and positively related to handgun acquisitions when the trend variable was not included. Handgun acquisitions were found to be related to frequency of riots in the United States, although not to riots within the states themselves.

Regardless of what Clotfelter's gun acquisition variable was, it is clear that it measured only recorded, legal transfers. It has been found that even in noncriminal general population samples within states with fairly strong gun control laws, a large percentage of the guns owned were acquired illegally.[27] Bordua and his colleagues found that illegal ownership in Illinois was most common among persons owning handguns (those most likely to be defensive owners) and least common among those who owned rifles and shotguns only.[28] This strongly suggests that applications for permits to legally own or buy handguns may be a poor indicator of the demand for defensive guns, and that Clotfelter's mixed findings may indicate little about the general relationship between crime and the acquisition of handguns in general.

Bordua and Lizotte studied the relationship between rates of legal ownership of firearms and crime rates in Illinois counties in 1976.[29]

26. Charles T. Clotfelter, "Crime, Disorders and the Demand for Handguns: An Empirical Analysis," *Law and Policy Quarterly* 3 (1981): 425–46.

27. Bordua et al., *Patterns of Firearms Ownership*, p. 160.

28. Ibid., p. 175.

29. David J. Bordua and Alan J. Lizotte, "A Subcultural Model of Legal Firearms Ownership in Illinois," *Law and Policy Quarterly* 2 (April 1979): 147–75.

They found that crime rates had no effect on rates of legal ownership among men but did have significant positive effects on legal ownership among women, consistent with our earlier observation that women are more likely to own guns for defensive reasons than men. Because the data did not permit them to do so, the authors could not isolate handgun ownership and determine the effect of crime rates on such ownership. Since rifles and shotguns are far more numerous than handguns, and male owners more numerous than female owners, it is not surprising that crime rates showed no effect on the ownership measure, especially when it is noted that the authors emphasize that they measured only legal ownership and not total ownership levels.

Northwood et al. compared rates of crime reported to the police for census tracts with rates of concealed weapons permit applications.[30] Without reporting any data, they rather vaguely stated that "the results suggest a low and statistically insignificant relationship (of crime rates) to gun application rates." However, this finding is of little significance, since it may simply be a consequence of measurement instability. Since only about 2,400 people applied for a permit in the period studied, with these scattered over 121 census tracts, there were an average of about 20 permit applications per tract. Measurement of such an extremely rare event is necessarily erratic and unstable, and is therefore unlikely to show a relationship to any variable, regardless of what may cause people to apply for permits to carry concealed weapons.

In a sophisticated time-series analysis of the issuance of handgun licenses to purchase handguns in Detroit, McDowall and Loftin found that Detroit residents "purchase more handguns when violent crime and civil disorders reduced confidence in collective security, and fewer when these conditions abated."[31] Futhermore, they responded to variations in police strength, buying fewer handguns when it rose and more when it fell.

My own time-series analysis of trends in gun ownership, discussed earlier, found a significant positive effect of both the homicide rate and the robbery rate on levels of handgun ownership, and a significant positive effect of the homicide rate on levels of general gun ownership.[32] Using my data, extended to 1977, and a somewhat dif-

30. Northwood et al., "Law-abiding One-man Armies."
31. David McDowall and Colin Loftin, "Collective Security and the Demand for Legal Handguns," Institute for Social Research, University of Michigan, 1982. (Unpublished.)
32. Kleck, "Capital Punishment."

ferent estimation technique, Magaddino and Medoff *(infra)* obtained a similar result with respect to the effect of the homicide rate on the level of handgun ownership. These studies are superior to the other aggregate studies because they use actual estimates of the stock of firearms or handguns available, based on cumulations of production and importation figures, rather than indirect measures based on the

Table 5-2. Cumulated Stock of Firearms in the United States, 1947-1978.[a]

			All Firearms	Handguns
	Total Stock of All Firearms	*Total Stock of Handguns*	*1000 Resident Population*	*1000 Resident Population*
1947	50,543,473	13,098,619	350.8	91.3
1948	53,203,031	13,542,653	362.6	92.7
1949	55,406,460	13,805,157	371.1	92.9
1950	57,902,081	14,083,195	381.3	93.5
1951	59,988,664	14,431,568	389.6	94.1
1952	61,946,315	14,885,797	396.1	95.6
1953	63,945,235	15,301,654	402.3	96.7
1954	65,945,235	15,678,109	405.0	97.3
1955	67,387,135	16,107,346	408.2	98.0
1956	69,435,933	16,642,310	413.1	99.5
1957	71,416,509	17,180,342	417.2	100.8
1958	73,163,450	17,699,704	420.1	102.1
1959	75,338,188	18,348,376	425.3	103.9
1960	77,501,065	18,951,219	430.6	105.4
1961	79,536,616	19,512,961	434.6	106.6
1962	81,602,984	20,111,610	439.3	108.3
1963	83,834,808	20,787,672	444.8	110.3
1964	86,357,701	21,531,945	451.8	112.6
1965	89,478,922	22,545,245	462.4	116.5
1966	93,000,989	22,758,062	475.5	121.5
1967	97,087,751	25,431,479	491.7	128.8
1968	102,302,251	27,846,203	513.1	139.7
1969	107,111,820	29,571,586	532.0	146.8
1970	111,917,733	31,244,813	549.4	153.3
1971	116,928,781	33,022,675	567.3	160.1
1972	122,304,980	35,129,558	587.7	168.7
1973	128,016,673	36,910,819	610.3	175.9
1974	134,587,281	39,086,637	637.0	184.9
1975	139,915,125	41,081,714	657.1	192.8
1976	145,650,789	43,108,403	678.5	200.8
1977	150,748,000	45,022,453	696.7	208.1
1978	156,164,518	46,994,951	715.6	215.3

a. As of the end of each calendar year, assuming unmeasured losses from stock equal unmeasured increments.

use of guns, and because they take account of the possibly reciprocal relationship between gun ownership and crime rates.

Finally, one of the simplest pieces of information suggesting that crime rates have an effect on ownership is the fact that from 1968 to 1978, over 21 million handguns were manufactured or imported into the United States (see Table 5–2), amounting to about an 85 percent increase in the available stock, while the *Uniform Crime Reports* crime index rate increased by 52 percent.[33]

In sum, the weight of the available evidence considered as a whole indicates that when either individual-level survey studies or aggregate-level studies are done properly, they indicate that many gun owners, and most handgun owners, own guns for defensive or protective reasons, that fear of crime and prior victimization are significantly and positively related to gun ownership, and that crime rates have a positive effect on levels of gun ownership, especially handgun ownership.

ANALYSIS OF U.S. HOMICIDE AND GUN OWNERSHIP TRENDS, 1947–1978

In my earlier study of trends in homicide and gun ownership, I developed a four-equation simultaneous model, with the homicide rate, gun ownership rate, homicide arrest clearance rate, and homicide conviction rate as endogenous variables, and estimated the model using the two-stage least-squares method on annual data for the United States from 1947 to 1973.[34] The present study updates the data set to include five additional years, 1974 to 1978. The only other major change has been the deletion of the conviction rate equation. The FBI stopped gathering data on convictions after 1977, but this was not the major reason I deleted it. In the earlier article I had noted the erratic properties of the measure.[35] By the mid-1970s

33. U.S. Federal Bureau of Investigation (FBI), *Uniform Crime Reports, 1960–1980* (Washington, D.C.: GPO, 1979). Wright et al. have argued that noncrime factors account for most of the handgun increases during this period, but my replication of their work (available from the author) indicates that such factors account for only 18 percent of the handgun rise. See James D. Wright et al., *Under the Gun* (New York: Aldine, 1983), pp. 45–101.

34. For further details see Kleck, "Capital Punishment." For an explanation of simultaneous equations methods, see John Johnston, *Econometric Methods* (New York: McGraw-Hill, 1972), pp. 341–420.

35. Kleck, "Capital Punishment," pp. 904, 906.

the measure showed improbably variable trends: 41 percent in 1974, 48 percent the next year, 44 percent the next, and back up to 52 percent the next.[36] Although the variable was still negatively related to the homicide rate when the model was estimated on the 1947–1978 data set, its coefficient was statistically insignificant and showed large standard errors. As it seemed to contribute mostly measurement error to the model, it was deleted.

The variables included in the model are listed and described in Table 5-3, and their place in the model can be seen by consulting Table 5-4. The rationale for the inclusion of the variables other than the gun measures is contained in Kleck (1979) and will not be repeated here. The relationship between the homicide rate and gun ownership rates is specified as a simultaneous reciprocal one, with guns pushing up the homicide rate and the rate of homicide (and other crimes) pushing up gun ownership. One other variable specified as affecting the homicide rate is the robbery rate. In 1978, 10 to 13 percent of homicides occurred in connection with robberies, so an increased robbery rate could directly contribute to the homicide rate.[37] One important effect of the inclusion of this variable is that it "absorbs" some of the effect of gun ownership levels on the homicide rate. If gun ownership rates positively affect robbery rates, which in turn affect homicide rates, then the inclusion of the robbery rate in the homicide equation accounts for some of the effect of gun ownership on homicide and should result in a smaller coefficient of the gun variable than would be the case without the robbery rate. This hypothesis will be tested later.

Besides the homicide rate, several other variables were specified as affecting the gun variables: the gun variable lagged one year, the median family income in the total guns and long gun equations, the income of families in the 20th percentile of the income distribution in the handgun equation, hunting license holders per 100,000 population in the total guns equation and the long gun equation, and the robbery rate in the handgun equation. Neither of the latter two variables proved to be significant in their respective equations, although they were for the 1947–1973 data set, and thus were deleted. The median family income variable reflects the ability of the average family to purchase a gun and thus should positively affect the total and

---

36. U.S. FBI, *Uniform Crime Reports, 1975–1978.*
37. U.S. FBI, *Uniform Crime Reports, 1979.*

Table 5-3. Variables Used in Analysis.

Symbol	Variable	Mean (ln)	SD (ln)	Mean (Natural Values)
H	(Homicides — [executions and police homicides])/100,000 resident population	1.791	0.302	6.286
G1	Estimated total firearms/100,000 resident population	10.771	0.208	48,711
G2	Estimated handguns/100,000 resident population	9.426	0.285	12,942
G3	Estimated long guns/100,000 resident population	10.468	0.180	35,768
G4	New handguns added to existing stock in year t	—	—	1,067,518
C	UCR percent of murders and nonnegligent manslaughters known to the police cleared by arrest (for total cities)	4.480	0.066	88.388
Y	Persons aged 15–24/100,000 resident population	9.644	0.138	15,573
I	State and federal sentenced prisoners present at the end of the year/100,000 resident population	4.700	0.092	110,424
R	Robberies/100,000 resident population	4.445	0.569	101,028
P	Percent of families with incomes less than $3,000 in constant 1974 dollars	2.233	0.452	10.303
F	Median family income in constant 1974 dollars	9.192	0.242	10,103
D	Income of families in the 20th percentile of the income distribution in 1974 dollars	8.444	0.453	4,984
S	Holders of hunting licenses/100,000 resident population	8.974	0.062	7,913
A	Total motor vehicle registrations/100,000 resident population	10.699	0.260	45,819

Note: Variables refer to the United States, each year 1947–1978.

Table 5-4. Unstandardized Structural Equation Coefficients for Complete Model (Ratio of Coefficients to their SEs in Parentheses).

Equation Number	Dependent Variable	Intercept	$\ln \hat{G1}$	$\ln \hat{C}$	$\ln Y$	$\ln I$	$\ln R$	$\ln P$	D-W / df	SEE / Σe_i^2
1	$\ln H$	3.378	0.986 (0.53)	-1.846 (-6.40)	0.621 (5.40)	-0.472 (-5.53)	0.302 (5.90)	0.228 (5.48)	2.31 / 25	0.0198 / 0.0098
2	$\ln G1$	0.513	$\ln \hat{H}$ 0.56 (6.64)	$\ln G1_{t-1}$ .912 (46.10)		$\ln F$ 0.039 (3.14)			1.55 / 28	0.0064 / 0.0011
3	$\ln C$	2.194	$\ln \hat{H}$ -0.047 (-1.84)	$\ln C_{t-1}$ .652 (5.03)		$\ln A$ -0.052 (-2.69)			1.96 / 28	0.0154 / 0.0066

Equation Number	Dependent Variable	Intercept	$\ln \hat{G2}$	$\ln \hat{C}$	$\ln Y$	$\ln I$	$\ln R$	$\ln P$	D-W / df	SEE / Σe_i^2
4	$\ln H$	1.727	0.122 (0.56)	-1.572 (-4.21)	0.644 (6.04)	-0.446 (-4.89)	0.301 (4.26)	0.227 (5.37)	2.40 / 25	0.0213 / 0.0113
5	$\ln G2$	-0.073	$\ln \hat{H}$ 0.060 (3.02)	$\ln G2_{t-1}$ 0.898 (32.41)	$\ln D$ 0.111 (6.21)				1.80 / 28	0.0114 / 0.0036
6	$\ln C$	2.228	$\ln \hat{H}$ -0.049 (-1.91)	$\ln C_{t-1}$ 0.644 (4.99)	$\ln A$ -0.051 (-2.69)				1.93 / 28	0.0154 / 0.0066

long gun rates. The income of the 20th percentile reflects the income level of the poor. Since a larger percentage of guns bought by the poor are handguns than is the case for wealthier persons, we would expect the income of the poor to be more closely related to handgun levels than to levels of other gun types.

The measurement of gun ownership in the United States consisted of cumulating the annual totals of firearms manufactured by domestic manufacturers for private sale in the United States and those imported for private sale in order to estimate the total stock of guns available, and then dividing this figure by the resident population for each year in order to obtain a per capita figure. This procedure was carried out for total firearms, for handguns alone, and for long guns alone. The measurement method does not take account of losses of firearms due to destruction, misplacement, or deterioration, but the numbers of such guns over the short period of time studied (1947-1978) would in any case be very small compared with the total gun stock. Perhaps the most serious shortcoming of the data used for this measure was that for 1947-1968 there was no count of imports of firearm "actions" (trigger and bolt or lever) and other parts that could be assembled into workable guns.[38] It might also be pointed out that data used by the Firearms Task Force to estimate the total of guns manufactured and imported before 1918 were rather incomplete, and therefore the cumulated total subsequent to that period is likely to be an underestimate. However this is not important for our purposes, since we are only interested in trends in the stock of guns since 1947, rather than the absolute level of the stock.

RESULTS

The statistical results of the estimation of two of the models are presented in Table 5-4. The upper half of the table, with equations (1) through (3), contains the results for the version of the model in which the included gun variable is the total gun ownership rate and

---

38. For other limitations of the data covering 1947–1968, see Newton and Zimring, *Firearms and Violence in American Life*, pp. 171–72. Data on gun production and importation after 1972 were gathered by the U.S. Bureau of Alcohol, Tobacco and Firearms, and *do* cover "actions." Sources of data for other variables in this analysis may be obtained by writing to the author.

all of the variables are expressed in natural logs.[39] The lower half, with equations (4) through (6), contains the results for the model in which the gun variable is the handgun ownership rate, and again the model is in the natural log format. In the last two columns of Table 5-4, four descriptive statistics are given: D-W, the Durbin-Watson statistic,[40] is a measurement of autocorrelation of the disturbances in an ·equation;[41] SEE is the standard error of estimate, that is, the standard deviation of the error term of the equation; df is the degrees of freedom of the equation; and Σe_i^2 is the sum of the squared residuals, a measure of the fit of the equation to the data.[42]

Each model contains three equations, one for each of the endogenous variables: H, the homicide rate; G, gun ownership; and C, the homicide arrest clearance rate. As an aid to interpreting the tables, equation (1) is written out in full:

$$\ln H = 3.378 + 0.986 \ln \hat{G1} - 1.846 \ln \hat{C} + 0.621 \ln Y$$
$$\quad\quad\quad\quad (0.53) \quad\quad\quad (-6.40) \quad\quad (5.40)$$

$$-0.472 \ln I + 0.302 \ln R + 0.228 \ln P + e_H$$
$$(-5.53) \quad\quad (5.90) \quad\quad\quad (5.48)$$

39. The rationale for converting the variables into natural logs can be found in Kleck, "Capital Punishment," pp. 896-97, 904-905. It is sufficient to say here that the natural log form of the equations produces a better fit to the data, as measured by the sum of the squared residuals, compared to the equations with variables expressed in their ordinary natural values. Total guns is the sum of long guns (rifles and shotguns) and handguns. Both long guns and handguns per capita cannot be included in the same equation because of their high collinearity (their zero-order correlation is 0.97).

40. The Durbin-Watson statistic is itself biased in the presence of autocorrelated residuals when there are lagged endogenous variables included in the equations, as is the case here. While there is no basis in statistical theory for applying the D-W test, simulation studies by Taylor and Wilson (1964) have shown that it nonetheless is quite powerful in detecting autocorrelation in such situations when the upper value of d was used to define the critical region for the test. This is what was done in the recent study. The 1 percent upper limit for the statistic (n = 32) is 1.69. Nearly all of the D-W values exceed this, and thus the null hypothesis of no autocorrelation rarely had to be rejected, although there is a possibility of autocorrelation in some of the gun equations.

41. For a discussion of autocorrelation and the D-W statistic, see Johnston, *Econometric Methods*, pp. 243-66.

42. The reader will notice that the adjusted R^2 statistic reported in connection with ordinary least-squares estimation is not reported here. This is because the R^2 statistic for structural equations estimated with two-stage least-squares is not directly relevant or meaningful for such equations in the same way it is for ordinary least-squares. In fact, the structural equation R^2 can approach infinity or even take on negative values (Bassman 1962). The adjusted R^2 (corrected for degrees of freedom) for the *first*-stage homicide equations was invariably at least 0.99.

where ln denotes the natural logarithm of each variable, e_H is the residual for the homicide equation, the coefficients are unstandardized coefficients, and the variables are as defined in Table 5-3. The number in parentheses below each regression coefficient is the ratio of the coefficient to its standard error.[43]

The coefficients presented in Table 5-4 are generally consistent in direction with the predictions of our theoretical model. The arrest clearance rate shows a significant negative effect, supporting a general deterrence hypothesis. Further, the measure of incapacitation, I, shows a significant negative effect on the homicide rate independent of the clearance rate, supporting the hypothesis of an incapacitative effect of imprisonment on the homicide rate. The age structure, robbery rate, and poverty variables all had positive, significant coefficients, again as expected.

The gun results indicate that, contrary to what was found for the 1947-1973 data set, the coefficient indicating the effect of gun ownership on the homicide rate is not statistically significant, when either the total guns measure or the handgun measure is used. On the other hand, the 1947-1978 results confirm those of the 1947-1973 data set regarding the effect of the homicide rate on the gun ownership rate. The homicide coefficients in the total gun, long guns, and handgun ownership equations are positive and significant.

Clearly the difference between this and the earlier study in time points in the data set produced different results regarding the apparent effect of gun ownership on the homicide rate. The shift in results is magnified even further when the model is estimated only on later time points, from 1952 to 1978. The homicide equation for this data set is contained in Table 5-5, equation (2). (Equation (1) is simply a repetition of equation (1) in Table 5-4, included here for ease of comparison.) The gun variable's coefficient is even more contradictory to the conventionally expected result, even turning negative, although still insignificant. While the model cannot be estimated only on time points in the 1960s and 1970s, because there would be too few degrees of freedom for stable estimation, the results indicate that when data points from this period predominate in the sample,

---

43. With ordinary least-squares estimation, this ratio would be a t-ratio, but since the small sample properties of the TSLS estimator are not defined, the ratio is assumed to have a normal distribution and is therefore called a z-ratio. A z-ratio of 1.645 or higher is significant at the 5 percent level (one-tailed test), while a value of 1.282 is significant at the 10 percent level.

Table 5-5. Unstandardized Structural Equation Coefficients for Homicide Equations (Ratio of Coefficients to their SEs in Parentheses).

Equation Number	Gun Variable Used[a]	Intercept	$\hat{G}$	$\hat{C}$	Y	I	R	P	D-W df	SEE Σe_i^2
1	ln G1	3.378	0.099 (0.53)	-1.846 (-6.40)	0.621 (5.40)	-0.472 (-5.53)	0.302 (5.90)	0.228 (5.48)	2.33 / 25	0.0198 / 0.0098
2	ln G1 (1952-78)	12.751	-0.750 (-0.98)	-2.518 (-2.75)	0.728 (3.21)	-0.219 (-1.08)	0.455 (3.58)	0.179 (2.06)	1.73 / 20	0.0227 / 0.0103
3	G1	18.129	-3.0×10^{-5} (-1.11)	-0.151 (-4.88)	0.0001 (2.46)	-0.018 (-3.48)	0.024 (7.98)	0.060 (3.06)	1.75 / 25	0.1365 / 0.4658
4	ln G2	1.727	0.122 (0.56)	-1.572 (-4.21)	0.644 (6.04)	-0.446 (-4.89)	0.301 (4.26)	0.227 (5.37)	2.40 / 25	0.0213 / 0.0113
5	G2	19.047	-0.0001 (-1.39)	-0.166 (-4.43)	0.0001 (3.12)	-0.017 (-3.20)	0.025 (7.28)	0.063 (4.10)	1.79 / 25	0.1330 / 0.4422
6	ln G3	3.042	0.121 (0.63)	-1.841 (-6.30)	0.634 (5.00)	-0.478 (-5.16)	0.302 (5.98)	0.233 (5.11)	2.32 / 25	0.0213 / 0.0113
7	G3	13.326	-1.3×10^{-5} (-0.31)	-0.113 (-3.53)	1.7×10^{-4} (2.72)	-0.019 (-3.15)	0.023 (6.96)	0.070 (2.82)	1.67 / 25	0.1618 / 0.6545
8	ln G1 (with t)	0.413	0.205 (0.70)	-1.531 (-3.13)	0.666 (5.34)	-0.417 (-2.83)	0.304 (5.47)	0.184 (1.25)	2.41 / 24	0.0211 / 0.0107
9	none	3.672		-1.747 (-3.86)	0.613 (4.31)	-0.410 (-4.25)	0.335 (6.82)	0.208 (6.00)	1.88 / 26	0.0292 / 0.0171
10	ln G2 (exogenous)	1.094	0.172 (0.84)	-1.519 (-3.82)	0.649 (5.70)	-0.462 (-5.10)	0.286 (4.20)	0.235 (5.61)	1.96 / 25	0.0226 / 0.0102
11	ln G1 (R omitted)	-0.776	0.735 (4.91)	-2.356 (-6.03)	0.884 (7.62)	-0.847 (-11.25)		0.292 (6.18)	1.78 / 26	0.0250 / 0.0162
12	G4	13.558	-2.6×10^{-7} (-1.09)	-0.112 (-4.85)	0.0002 (3.58)	-0.025 (-5.92)	0.022 (11.86)	0.053 (2.11)	1.82 / 25	0.1334 / 0.4449

a. See Table 5-4 for description of variables. Where gun variable is in natural values, all other variables are also in natural values.

the results are more inconsistent with the hypothesis that higher general gun ownership levels lead to higher homicide rates. When data points from before the mid-1960s predominated, the results showed gun levels positively affecting homicide levels, but when they became a minority, in the 1947–1978 set, the results did *not* show any significant effect. This strongly suggests that something changed in the 1960s or 1970s regarding the patterns of ownership and criminal use of guns. This matter will be explored later.

Equation (3) is the same as equation (1), except that all the variables are expressed in their ordinary natural values. They again show no significant effect of gun ownership on homicide rates, while results for the rest of the model remained substantially unchanged. The results therefore are not dependent on the functional form of the equations. Equation (4) is the same as equation 4 in Table 5–4, again repeated for ease of comparison. When the handgun rate is included in the model in its natural value form (equation 5), it again shows no significant effect. In equations (6) and (7), the long gun variable is in natural log and natural value forms, respectively, and shows no effect in either case. Given the relative infrequency of the use of long guns in homicide, this result should, in any case, not be surprising.

In equation (8) the model was estimated including a time trend variable, as a way of controlling for omitted variables which show a consistent trend over time and could account for the apparent effects of variables included in the model. The trend variable was found to have an insignificant coefficient (not shown, but equal to -0.003, z-ratio $= -0.35$), and the coefficients of the other variables in the model remained in the same direction and statistically significant (except for the P coefficient, $p = 0.11$). The gun variable still shows no significant effect on the homicide rate.

Because the gun variables were unrelated to the homicide rate, the model was estimated without the gun variable. The results are in equation (9). As was done in the earlier paper, the adequacy of the basic model is tested by using it to forecast the homicide rate for 1979, one year in advance of the data set on which the model was estimated. When the 1979 values for the predictor variables are substituted into equation (9), the value of the natural log homicide rate forecast by the model is 2.3158. In fact, the natural log of the homicide rate for 1979 was 2.2750. The error of prediction was therefore 0.0408, a 1.79 percent error. Since the error is only 1.44 times the size of the SEE of the equation, we conclude that the causal structure we have modeled could have generated the observed 1979 homicide rate and that our model is satisfactory.[44]

If the homicide rate was assumed to not influence the gun ownership rate, then we would treat the gun variable as exogenous. Equation (10) shows the results of estimation of the model with the handgun ownership rate treated as exogenous. As with the other equations, its coefficient is insignificant, indicating no effect of general levels of handgun ownership on the homicide rate.

We hypothesized that some of the influence of gun ownership rates on homicide rates is indirect, through their effect on robbery rates. In equation (11), this is confirmed. When the robbery rate is omitted from the model, and therefore not controlled for, the gun ownership variable does show a significant effect on the homicide rate. To test whether gun levels did indeed affect robbery rates, we estimated a robbery equation with the gun variable included as a predictor variable, and obtained the following robbery equation:

$$\ln R = 10.939 + 0.500 \ln R_{t-1} + 1.091 \ln G1 + 0.499 \ln Y - 0.719 \ln I + e_i$$
$$\quad (4.13) \qquad\quad (4.51) \qquad (1.81) \qquad (-4.44)$$

Thus, gun ownership levels appear to affect robbery rates, which in turn affect homicide rates, although the general level of gun ownership does not *directly* affect the homicide rate.

Results Regarding the New Guns Hypothesis

Some critics have argued that it would do no good to ban the further manufacture or importation of guns, since the available stock is so huge that it would easily meet the needs of future criminal users of guns. Apparently in response to this argument, gun control advocate Franklin Zimring has suggested that decreasing the annual inflow of guns, in particular handguns, would reduce gun-related crime and would even have an effect disproportionate to the magnitude of the gun reduction.[45] He bases this belief on the results of gun-tracing efforts which indicate that a disproportionately large fraction of "crime" handguns confiscated by police (mostly in connection with

44. For a discussion of a similar forecasting procedure applied to crime rates, see Kenneth C. Land and Marcus Felson, "A General Framework for Building Dynamic Macro Social Indicator Models: Including an Analysis of Changes in Crime Rates and Police Expenditures," *American Journal of Sociology* 82 (November 1976): 565–604.

45. Zimring, "Street Crime and New Guns," p. 103.

illegal carrying arrests) are new guns, originally sold to their first owner within a few years of the time they were confiscated. The belief that rates of introduction of new handguns have a disproportionately large impact on gun-related crime rates is called by Zimring the "new guns" hypothesis. The term implies that it is either the newness of the guns themselves, or something related to the newness, which puts them at high risk of criminal use.

Zimring is never explicit about why he thinks new handguns are disproportionately represented among crime guns. One plausible explanation would be simply that newer guns are held by different, more crime-prone sorts of persons than older guns. Since Zimring, as a gun control advocate, has emphasized guns themselves as important in contributing to crime, rather than the sorts of people who use them, his reluctance to state his hypothesis explicitly in this form is understandable. Were he to do so, he would be placing himself uncomfortably close to those whose slogan is "guns don't kill, people kill." In any case, he says nothing about possible differences between the kinds of people who own older and newer guns.

It is probably the case that new guns are owned in disproportionate numbers by younger people, regardless of either their reasons for ownership or their inclinations toward criminal behavior. Obviously they have reached the age of acquiring their first gun relatively recently, while older people reached that age a longer time ago and therefore are more likely to have possessed guns a long time. Given that 45 percent of persons arrested for homicide and 73 percent of those arrested for robbery in 1980 were under age twenty-five, this alone could account for the disproportionately large fraction of new guns involved in crime. If this is the explanation, then the rate of introduction of new handguns should show no relationship to the rate of gun-related crimes.

The results of the test of the "new guns" hypothesis are presented in equation (12) of Table 5 – 5. The gun variable included in this equation is simply the number of new handguns introduced in the United States in year t. The results are contrary to Zimring's hypothesis. The number of new handguns introduced in year t is not related to the homicide rate in year t. Since the number of new guns added in years t – 1 or t – 2 would be even less "new," they would logically be even less likely to show a relationship to the homicide rate.

The robbery equation was also estimated with the number of new handguns added in year t as the gun variable. It was found that this variable had no significant effect on the robbery rate. Thus the "new guns" hypothesis is rejected in regard to both homicide and robbery, the two most serious gun-related crimes.

Results Regarding the Effect of Crime on Gun Ownership

The gun equations that correspond to the homicide equations presented in Table 5-5 are contained in Table 5-6. They generally show that, as expected, the homicide rate has a positive and significant effect on gun ownership levels, suggesting that at least some significant fraction of gun ownership is a response to crime. The equations are numbered to correspond to those in Table 5-5. Equation (1) is a repetition of equation (2) in Table 5-4. Equation (2) is the same as equation (1), but estimated over the period 1952 to 1978. It shows that for a period dominated more by years in the 1960s and 1970s, the homicide variable shows an even stronger effect on the gun ownership. Equations (4) and (5) are the gun equations when the model was estimated with handgun ownership as the gun variable, and equations (6) and (7) are the gun equations when long gun ownership is used. They all show a significant positive effect of homicide on gun ownership, even though long guns are usually not described by their owners as primarily owned for defensive reasons. However, since there is some long gun ownership among owners who say protection is a secondary reason for owning, the result is not entirely surprising.[46] Further, it may be that gun owners state reasons for ownership that reflect popular or stereotypical reasons for owning guns. In short, they give the conventional reason they think the interviewer expects to hear, even when they own their guns for purposes that other types are conventionally thought to serve better. If so, protection-oriented ownership of long guns may be more common than is indicated by ownership surveys.

Equation (10) was estimated using ordinary least squares, with homicide omitted. The lagged robbery rate was included as an exogenous variable, and it shows a significant effect on handgun ownership levels. In equation (12), homicide has a barely significant effect on yearly additions of new handguns. Equation (13) merely serves to demonstrate why S, the measure of hunting demand for guns, was

---

46. Bordua et al., *Patterns of Firearms Ownership*, p. 231.

Table 5-6. Unstandardized Structural Equation Coefficients for Gun Equations (Ratio of Coefficients to their SEs in Parentheses).

Equation Number	Gun Variable Used[a]	Intercept	G_{t-1}	$\hat{H}$	F	D	Other Variables	D-W df	SEE Σe_i^2
1	ln G1	0.513	0.912 (46.10)	0.056 (6.64)	0.039 (3.14)			1.55 28	0.0064 0.0011
2	ln G1 (1952–78)	2.737	0.756 (13.35)	0.180 (5.40)	−0.044 (−0.98)			1.37 23	0.0168 0.0065
3	G1	474.395	0.940 (45.51)	393.378 (4.95)	0.198 (3.03)			1.61 28	349.8 3.4×10^6
4	ln G1	−0.073	0.898 (32.41)	0.060 (3.02)		0.111 (6.21)		1.80 28	0.0114 0.0036
5	G2	−909.305	0.951 (30.42)	91.520 (1.67)		0.262 (4.64)		1.98 28	191.6 1.0×10^6
6	ln G3	0.907	0.935 (48.79)	0.051 (8.12)	-7.6×10^{-4} (−0.05)		−0.032 (−1.19)	1.61 27	0.0051 0.0007
7	G3	1431.183	0.951 (52.17)	279.211 (7.03)	0.022 (0.42)		−0.117 (−0.95)	1.60 27	192.0 2.3×10^5
10	ln G2 (exogenous)	0.203	0.952 (18.08)			0.010 (1.18)	0.043 (1.65)	0.95 28	0.0169 0.0080
12	G4	-1.2×10^6	−5.531 (0.08)	1.8×10^5 (1.33)		234.935 (2.41)		1.79 28	5.0×10^5 6.2×10^{12}
13	ln G1	0.676	0.917 (41.96)	0.055 (6.18)	0.033 (2.01)		−0.018 (−0.54)	1.49 27	0.0063 0.0011
14	ln G2	0.176	0.880 (27.81)	0.017 (0.41)		0.092 (3.81)	0.039 (1.22)	1.88 27	0.0112 0.0034

a. See Table 5-4 for description of variables. See text for identification of "other variables." The G_{t-1} in each case is the lagged version of whatever gun variable was used in that equation. Where the gun variable is indicated as being in natural logs, all the other variables on that equation are as well. Gun equation 12 is virtually identical to equation 1 and so has been omitted. There is no gun equation 9, since homicide equation 9 had no gun variable.

not included in the gun equations. Contrary to the 1947–1978 results, hunting did not show any significant effect on gun ownership. This could indicate the increasing predominance of defensive, non-recreational reasons for gun ownership in the later years of the period. In equation (14), both homicide and robbery are included in a handgun equation, and it is found that neither shows a significant coefficient. However, either of the variables included singly in the handgun equation did show a significant effect on ownership levels. It seems reasonably clear that this is due to multicollinearity: the homicide and robbery rates are so highly correlated that both "account" for the same share of the variability in gun ownership. Therefore either of the two can be included in the gun equation, but not both. It is thus statistically impossible to estimate the relative effects of the two crime variables on handgun ownership levels within the current research model.[47]

THE CHANGING CHARACTER OF U. S. GUN OWNERSHIP

Why is it that in a data set dominated by years prior to 1964, gun ownership in the general population appeared to have a significant positive effect on the homicide rate, while in the 1947–1978 set, dominated by cases from the 1960s and 1970s, there was no such effect apparent? I propose that the apparent discrepancy is due to

47. There could be an identifiability problem with our model. If underidentified, coefficients can be biased, possibly enough to produce estimated coefficients that appear significant when they are not, or even to reverse their sign (Johnston 1972). In order to avoid this problem, we must include in the model variables that can reasonably be expected to directly affect H, the homicide rate, but not G, the level of gun ownership, and variables that directly affect G but not H (such variables are called "instruments"). While we have the former (e.g., C, I), it is debatable whether we have the latter. Virtually no variable for which national data are available affects G without also having some possibility of directly affecting H as well. In our earlier study (Kleck 1979), S, the hunting license holder rate, served as a good instrument since it should directly affect G but not H. However, for the 1947–1978 data set it proved unrelated to G. It is unclear whether F, median family income, is an adequate instrument, although it clearly should affect G. Since it measures the population's capacity to buy goods, including firearms, it could conceivably affect H as well. Although not itself a measure of poverty, it is certainly related to homicide. Without alternative instruments to test and with no a priori theoretical certainty about what variables do or do not affect H and G, we cannot definitely say whether the model is underidentified, and thus this Chapter's conclusions regarding the relationship between two variables are necessarily tentative in direct proportion to our uncertainty on this point.

a change in the pattern of ownership of firearms that occurred in the 1960s.

The vast majority of gun owners never commit a serious crime of violence with their guns. Although at least half of America's 80 million households own a gun, and there may be more than 160 million guns in circulation by now, it is doubtful if even 200,000 different guns or gun owners are involved in serious violent gun crimes in any given year.[48] Since our measure of gun ownership describes the general population rather than any crime-prone segment of it, it is largely a measure of gun ownership among the law-abiding and non-violent. Levels of *legal* gun ownership have been found to be unrelated to rates of violent crime in a cross-sectional analysis.[49] Therefore the only reason why such a measure would show an effect of gun ownership on homicide would be if it served as an indicator of ownership within the violence-prone segment of the population. The difference in results found between data sets could be due to the possibility that trends in general gun ownership and ownership among the violence-prone roughly paralleled each other up until the 1960s, but that they no longer did so in more recent years. In particular, it seems likely that ownership among low income and nonwhite people began to increase even faster than in the rest of the population around the mid-1960s. Thus, as time went on, the general level of gun ownership became an increasingly poor indicator of gun ownership among the violence-prone and consequently showed less of a relationship with the homicide rate for time periods dominated by later years.

The best evidence of changing firearms ownership patterns would be national survey evidence which compared reported gun ownership among persons with arrest or conviction records for crimes of violence with ownership among those without such records. Unfortunately, I know of no published national survey that has made such a comparison, and there certainly are not enough of such surveys to show whether trends among the two groups differ. A second-best strategy would involve examination of reported gun ownership among the poor and among blacks. Between 1952 and 1978, from 49 to 66 percent of homicide arrestees were black, although blacks con-

---

48. Hazel Erskine, "The Polls: Gun Control," *Public Opinion Quarterly* 36 (Summer 1972): 455–69.

49. Bordua and Lizotte, "A Subcultural Model."

stituted only 11 to 12 percent of the U.S. population.[50] For seventeen cities studied in 1967, 87 percent of homicide arrestees were blue-collar workers, service, farm or domestic workers, housewives (presumably most of these were wives of men with occupations similar to the male arrestees), or were unemployed.[51] Serious violence, including gun violence, is heavily concentrated among low income and nonwhite people, and thus gun ownership trends among these groups are especially crucial.

Before 1966 there were almost no national surveys that included a gun ownership question which would allow us to establish some benchmark levels of ownership, and after 1966, although I know of at least twenty such surveys, there have been almost no analyses that published breakdowns by income groups.[52] A few breakdowns by race have been published, but these show extremely erratic trends; this is not surprising, since typical national surveys, with a total sample size of 1,200, often contain only about 30 to 70 gun-owning black households. Reported handgun ownership in U.S. white households increased from 16 percent in 1972 to 25 percent in 1978, while it increased even more sharply in black households over the same period, from 11 percent in 1972 to 23 percent in 1978, supporting the hypothesis that gun ownership trends in groups with high rates of violence were diverging from those for the rest of the population.[53]

A more indirect, but perhaps more reliable kind of evidence of changing ownership patterns is found in data on the criminal use of firearms. Trends in the relative frequency with which homicides are committed with a firearm can serve as a rough indicator of trends in the relative availability of firearms among the violence-prone, although it is also a product of weapon preference. Table 5–7 shows that the relative frequency of gun use in homicide remained almost constant until 1964, then increased sharply, from 57.5 percent in 1964 to a peak of 68.7 percent in 1974. Further, the percentage of

50. U.S. FBI, *Uniform Crime Reports, 1953-1979.*

51. D.J. Mulvihill and M.M. Tumin, with L.A. Curtis, *Crimes of Violence.* Task Force on Individual Acts of Violence, National Commission on the Causes and Prevention of Violence (Washington, D.C.: GPO, 1969), p. 27.

52. The study by Wright and Marston, "The Ownership of the Means of Destruction," is a prominent exception.

53. Gallup poll no. 852 in George H. Gallup, *The Gallup Poll: Public Opinion, 1972-1977* (Wilmington, Del.: Scholarly Resources, 1978); Cambridge Reports, Inc., *An Analysis of Public Attitudes Toward Handgun Control* (Philadelphia, Penn.: Center for the Study and Prevention of Handgun Violence, 1978).

Table 5-7. Firearms Use in Homicides, by Race of Victim, 1960-1978.

Year	*Percent of Homicides by Firearms*			*Percent Black Homicides by Guns*
	Total	*Black*	*White*	*Percent White Homicides by Guns*
1960	56.7	54.0	60.1	0.90
1961	57.3	54.7	60.2	0.91
1962	56.4	55.3	59.0	0.94
1963	57.2	56.3	59.2	0.95
1964	57.5	56.8	59.2	0.96
1965	59.0	58.8	59.9	0.98
1966	60.6	62.0	59.7	1.04
1967	63.9	65.3	62.7	1.04
1968	65.7	67.6	64.3	1.05
1969	67.3	70.4	64.3	1.09
1970	67.9	71.0	64.9	1.09
1971	67.6	70.8	64.5	1.10
1972	69.2	73.8	64.7	1.14
1973	68.5	72.6	64.8	1.12
1974	68.7	71.4	66.5	1.07
1975	67.1	70.7	64.2	1.10
1976	65.3	68.8	62.7	1.10
1977	(62.5)[a]	—	—	—
1978	(63.6)[a]	—	—	—

a. Figures drawn from UCRs (U.S. FBI 1978; 1979).

Note: Killings by policemen in the line of duty and executions were excluded from homicide figures. Black homicide figures for 1947-1949 actually refer to *nonwhite* homicide victims; the differences are negligible.

Sources: U.S. National Center for Health Statistics, *Vital Statistics of the United States*, annual issues for 1947-1977; U.S. NCHS, *Monthly Vital Statistics Report, Advance Report Final Mortality Statistics, 1974; 1975*; U.S. Bureau of the Census, *Current Population Reports*, Series P-25, nos. 311, 519, 614.

gun use increased far more among blacks than among whites. Because over 90 percent of homicides are intraracial, the victim's race can be used to indicate the offender's race with little error.[54] Therefore vital statistics data on weapon use in homicide deaths can accurately indicate trends in the relative use of guns in homicides among whites and blacks. The percent of homicides committed with guns among blacks increased by 17 percentage points, from 56.8 to 73.8 percent between 1964 and 1972, while the increase was only 5.5 percentage points among whites over the same period.

Criminals' proportional use of guns increased in connection with aggravated assaults as well during this period, according to FBI data. While only 15 percent of aggravated assaults reported to the police

54. U.S. FBI, *Uniform Crime Reports, 1979*, p. 10.

Table 5-8.   Weapon Carrying, 1960–1978.

Percent of total arrests that were for illegal weapons carrying, possession, etc.

Year		Year	
1960	0.96	1970	1.48
1961	0.95	1971	1.56
1962	0.97	1972	1.65
1963	0.98	1973	1.72
1964	1.03	1974	1.88 = peak
1965	1.08	1975	1.79
1966	1.16	1976	1.53
1967	1.32	1977	1.50
1968	1.51	1978	1.54
1969	1.54		

Source: U.S. FBI, *Uniform Crime Reports*, 1961–1979.

in 1964 were committed with a gun, this figure reached a peak of 25.7 percent in 1973.[55] Parallel figures on the percentages of robberies that were armed robberies indicate an increase after 1967, peaking in 1972. Thus the use of guns by criminals in general was increasing from 1964 to the early and mid-1970s.

There is also some indirect evidence that the frequency of the carrying of firearms and other weapons increased in a manner that almost exactly paralleled the trends in relative gun use in crimes. Arrests on illegal weapons charges rarely occur other than as a result of an arrest or search regarding some other crime, that is, "incident" to some other matter.[56] Therefore, weapons arrests as a percentage of total arrests can serve as a rough indicator of the relative frequency with which police found persons searched to be illegally carrying weapons. Data for this indicator, presented in Table 5-8, show a sharp increase beginning in 1964 and a peak in 1974. If these trends regarding weapons in general apply to guns as well, it suggests that illegal carrying of firearms, as well as ownership of guns, increased during this period among those people most inclined to commit acts of violence. Thus the hypothesis that gun ownership was increasing faster among the violence-prone during the 1960s and 1970s than within the general population is consistently, albeit indirectly, supported.

55. U.S. FBI, *Uniform Crime Reports, 1965; 1974.*
56. Bordua et al., *Patterns of Firearms Ownership*, sec. 3.

CONCLUSIONS

The general level of gun ownership in our society has no direct effect on the homicide rate (although it has an indirect effect on homicide through its significant positive effect on robbery rates, which in turn positively affect homicide rates). How can such a statement be true when over 60 percent of the homicides committed in the United States in the last thirty years were committed with firearms? These seem to be mutually incompatible observations, especially to people who believe the latter fact to be prima facie evidence of the need for highly restrictive versions of gun control. A few simple statements can summarize and tie together the available evidence in a way which makes it clear that there are no contradictions between these observations.

The following statements seem to be supported by, or at least consistent with, the best available evidence regarding the effects of gun ownership on homicide rates:

1. Most gun ownership is for legal purposes. Most of the guns owned are long guns, which are primarily owned for recreational reasons unrelated to crime. Only a small percentage of guns or gun owners are involved in crimes; this is true even for handguns.
2. Gun ownership among the law-abiding has no effect on the homicide rate. Killers almost invariably have records of prior violence, and it is a myth that guns are commonly used in family arguments and assaults between previously law-abiding people (see Kleck and Bordua *infra*).
3. From (1) and (2) we should expect that *general* levels of gun ownership should show no effect on the homicide rate, and this is indeed what our analysis has found.
4. Ownership of guns among the violence-prone *is* related to homicide rates, because when an assault occurs (for reasons largely unrelated to gun ownership) it is somewhat more likely to produce a fatality if it involves a gun. However, we have no direct measure of such ownership levels; the only measure we *do* have is of general, largely noncriminal ownership.

These conclusions imply that gun ownership among the law-abiding poses no direct risk of crime or violence in the community. Thus the only justification for disarming the majority of the population is for the sake of denying violence-prone persons easy access (presumably mostly through theft) to firearms owned by the law-abiding. In effect, the justification runs this way: we must deny guns to the 99 percent of the population who will never commit a serious act of violence in their lives in order to produce some marginal reduction in the ease of access to guns among the 1 percent who will commit such an act. Understandably, the argument is rarely phrased quite so baldly by advocates of gun or handgun prohibition, or of near approximations such as restrictive licensing.

On the other hand, these conclusions are perfectly compatible with more moderate gun control strategies, such as permissive licensing or laws restricting the open or concealed carrying of firearms. Such laws have the potential of being both just and at least modestly effective precisely because they are focussed and concentrated in their intended impact in a way that corresponds with the way in which the problem of violence, both gun and nongun, is focussed and concentrated. Violence is not uniformly or randomly distributed through the population, nor should its remedies be so distributed.

Regarding the effect of homicide and other crimes on levels of gun ownership, our conclusions are straightforward. General levels of ownership either of all gun types, handguns only, or long guns only are all positively affected by crime rates. Either the homicide rate or the robbery rate shows a significant positive effect on gun ownership levels (although both cannot be included in the same equation and still show positive effects, due to the problem of multicollinearity). These aggregate-level findings accord well with the best of the individual-level studies, in particular that of Lizotte and Bordua.[57]

It seems clear that, although most gun ownership is motivated by recreational and sport concerns, a significant part of it is oriented toward protection of the self, family, and home, and is a response to reported rates of crime, sometimes to prior victimization, and to the fear of victimization that these engender. The conclusions probably apply to both the law-abiding and the non-law-abiding, although no study of this subject has distinguished between the two groups. However, logically we would expect that if there is any difference between the two groups, it is the non-law-abiding whose gun ownership is most strongly motivated by victimization and fear of future victimization, simply because they are the most likely to live in dangerous neighborhoods, among other people as dangerous as themselves.

57. Lizotte and Bordua, "Firearms Ownership for Sport and Protection"; Lizotte et al., "Firearms Ownership for Sport and Protection."

SELECTED BIBLIOGRAPHY (PART III)

Bassman, R.L. "Letter to the Editor." *Econometrica* 30 (October 1962): 824-26.

Berkowitz, Leonard. "Impulse, Aggression and the Gun." *Psychology Today* 2 (September 1968): 19-22.

____ . "How Guns Control Us." *Psychology Today* 15 (June 1981): 11-12.

Bordua, David J., and Alan J. Lizotte. "A Subcultural Model of Legal Firearms Ownership in Illinois." *Law and Public Policy Quarterly* 2 (April 1979): 147-75.

Bordua, D.J.; A.J. Lizotte; G. Kleck; with Van Cagle. *Patterns of Firearms Ownership, Use and Regulation in Illinois.* Springfield: Illinois Law Enforcement Commission, 1979.

Caetano, Donald F. "The Domestic Arms Race." *Journal of Communication* 29 (Spring 1979): 39-46.

California Bureau of Criminal Justice Statistics. *A Synopsis of a California Poll of Handgun Ownership and Use.* Sacramento: California Department of Justice, 1977.

Cambridge Reports, Inc. *An Analysis of Public Attitudes Toward Handgun Control.* Cambridge, Mass.: Cambridge Reports, Inc., 1978. (Prepared for the Center for the Study and Prevention of Handgun Violence).

Center for Political Studies. *1976 American Election Survey.* Ann Arbor: University of Michigan Press, 1976.

Clotfelter, Charles T. "Crime, Disorders and the Demand for Handguns: An Empirical Analysis." *Law and Policy Quarterly* 3 (1981): 425-46.

Cook, Philip J. "The Effect of Gun Availability on Robbery and Robbery Murder: A Cross-Section Study of Fifty Cities." In Robert H. Haveman and

B. Bruce Zellner, eds., *Policy Studies Review Annual*, vol. 3, pp. 743-81. Beverly Hills, Calif.: Sage, 1979.

DeFronzo, James. "Fear of Crime and Handgun Ownership." *Criminology* 17 (November 1979): 331-40.

Decision/Making/Information (DMI). *Attitudes of the American Electorate Toward Gun Control 1978.* Santa Ana, Calif.: DMI, 1979.

Ennis, Philip. *Criminal Victimization in the U.S.* A report to the President's Commission on Law Enforcement and the Administration of Justice. Washington, D.C.: Government Printing Office, 1967.

Erskine, Hazel. "The Polls: Gun Control." *Public Opinion Quarterly* 36 (Summer 1972): 455-69.

Feagin, J.R. "Home Defense and the Police: Black and White Perspectives." *American Behavioral Scientist* 13 (May 1970): 797-814.

Fisher, Joseph C. "Homicide in Detroit: The Role of Firearms." *Criminology* 14 (November 1976): 387-400.

Florida. *Final Report, Handgun Regulation Project.* Tallahasse: Florida Bureau of Criminal Justice Planning and Assistance, 1977.

Gallup, George H. *The Gallup Poll: Public Opinion, 1972-1977.* Wilmington, Del.: Scholarly Resources, 1978.

Johnston, John. *Econometric Methods.* New York: McGraw-Hill, 1972.

Kleck, Gary. "Capital Punishment, Gun Ownership, and Homicide." *American Journal of Sociology* 84 (January 1979): 882-910.

Land, Kenneth C., and Marcus Felson. "A General Framework for Building Dynamic Macro Social Indicator Models: Including an Analysis of Changes in Crime Rates and Police Expenditures." *American Journal of Sociology* 82 (November 1976): 565-604.

Lizotte, Alan J., and David J. Bordua. "Firearms Ownership for Sport and Protection: Two Divergent Models." *American Sociological Review* 45 (April 1980): 229-43.

Lizotte, Alan J.; David J. Bordua; and Carolyn S. White. "Firearms Ownership for Sport and Protection: Two Not So Divergent Models." *American Sociological Review* 46 (August 1981): 499-503.

McDowall, David, and Colin Loftin. "Collective Security and the Demand for Legal Handguns." Institute for Social Research, University of Michigan, 1982. (Unpublished.)

Mulvihill, Donald J.; Melvin M. Tumin; with Lynn A. Curtis. *Crimes of Violence.* Task Force on Individual Acts of Violence, National Commission on the Causes and Prevention of Violence. Washington, D.C.: Government Printing Office, 1969.

Murray, Douglas R. "Handguns, Gun Control Laws, and Firearms Violence." *Social Problems* 23 (October 1975): 81-93.

National Opinion Research Center (NORC). *National Data Program for the Social Sciences, Codebook for the Spring General Social Survey.* Chicago: National Opinion Research Center, 1973-1977.

Newton, George D., and Franklin Zimring. *Firearms and Violence in American Life.* A Staff Report of the Task Force on Firearms, National Commission on the Causes and Prevention of Violence. Washington, D.C.: Government Printing Office, 1969.

Northwood, Lawrence K.; Richard Westgard; and Charles E. Barb, Jr. "Law-abiding One-man Armies." *Society* 16 (November–December 1978): 69-74.

Phillips, Llad, and Harold L. Votey, Jr. "Handguns and Homicide: Minimizing Losses and the Costs of Control." *Journal of Legal Studies* 5 (June 1976): 463-78.

Seitz, Steven T. "Firearms, Homicides, and Gun Control Effectiveness." *Law and Society Review* 6 (May 1972): 595-614.

Taylor, L.D., and T.A. Wilson. "Three-pass Least Squares: A Method for Estimating Models with Lagged Dependent Variables." *Review of Economics and Statistics* 46 (1964): 329-46.

"The Times Poll: Fear of Crime Triggers Rise in Gun Sales." *Los Angeles Times*, 22 February 1981, p. 1.

U.S. Bureau of Alcohol, Tobacco and Firearms. "Quarterly Firearms Manufacturing and Exportation Report." Consolidated Fiscal Year Report, 1977-81. (Unpublished.)

U.S. Comproller General. *Handgun Control: Effectiveness and Costs.* A Report to the Congress. Washington, D.C.: Government Printing Office, 1978.

U.S. Department of Commerce, Bureau of the Census. *Statistical Abstract of the United States.* Washington, D.C.: Government Printing Office, 1970, 1971, 1981.

U.S. Department of Commerce. *1972 Census of Manufacturers.* vol. 2, pt. 2. Washington, D.C.: Government Printing Office, 1977, pp. 34E-15.

U.S. Department of Justice, Federal Bureau of Investigation (FBI). *Crime in the United States (Uniform Crime Reports).* Washington, D.C.: Government Printing Office, 1961-1981.

Williams, J. Sherwood, and John H. McGrath III. "Why People Own Guns." *Journal of Communication* 26 (Autumn 1976): 22-30.

Wright, James D., and Linda L. Marston. "The Ownership of the Means of Destruction: Weapons in the United States." *Social Problems* 23 (October 1975): 93-107.

Zimring, Franklin E. "Is Gun Control Likely to Reduce Violent Killings?" *University of Chicago Law Review* 35 (Summer 1968): 721-37.

_____ . "Firearms and Federal Law: The Gun Control Act of 1968." *Journal of Legal Studies* 4 (January 1975): 133-98.

_____ . "Street Crime and New Guns: Some Implications for Firearms Control." *Journal of Criminal Justice* 4 (Summer 1976): 95-107.

_____ . "Determinants of the Death Rate from Robbery: A Detroit Time Study." *Journal of Legal Studies* 6 (June 1977): 317-32.

PART IV

HANDGUN-ONLY CONTROL

Chapter 6

HANDGUN BANNING IN LIGHT OF THE PROHIBITION EXPERIENCE

Don B. Kates, Jr.

How small of all that human hearts endure
That part which laws or kings can cause or cure.
— Samuel Johnson

Many prominent persons and organizations have suggested that substantial reduction in violence would follow from the prohibition of civilian handgun ownership.[1] Though the argument is generally encountered in the abstract, the specific prohibitory mechanism most often envisioned is a federal permit requirement for handgun ownership. Administration would be modeled on that traditional in New York City so that it would be futile for the ordinary citizen to apply for a permit.

Administrative modeling of a permit system will vary according to the public policy it is intended to implement. Newton and Zimring use the term "permissive" licensing for systems like those of Illinois, Massachusetts and Connecticut under which the administrative agency cannot refuse a permit to any citizen who meets the statutorily defined criteria.[2] The purpose of such an administrative model

---

1. J.D. Alviani and W.R. Drake, *Handgun Control . . . Issues and Alternatives* (Cleveland: U.S. Conference of Mayors, 1975), pp. 38–54; George D. Newton and Franklin E. Zimring, *Firearms and Violence in American Life* (Washington, D.C.: GPO, 1970); Carl Bakal, *The Right to Bear Arms* (New York: McGraw-Hill, 1966); R.J. Riley, "Shooting to Kill the Handgun: Time to Martyr Another American 'Hero,'" *Journal of Urban Law* 51 (1974): 491–524.

2. Newton and Zimring, *Firearms and Violence in American Life.*

is simply to exclude small fixed categories (generally minors, the insane, and prior felons) without reducing handgun availability to the vast majority of citizens.

But if the purpose is to eliminate or drastically reduce handgun availability to the general population, resort must be made to what Newton and Zimring call "restrictive" licensing. New York State's Sullivan law has long served as the primary example of restrictive licensing, particularly as administered in New York City. Under that administrative model (1) Every presumption is against issuance of a permit; (2) The burden rests on the applicant to show that he or she not only meets the general criteria prescribed by statute but meets additional general criteria prescribed by the police department and criteria that individual licensing officers impose at their own discretion; (3) Even if these qualifications are established, the applicant must also satisfy the licensing official that he or she has an important enough reason to want a handgun. (At one time, for instance, the New York City Department took the position that target shooting was not an important enough reason.) Finally, irrespective of the applicant's personal qualifications or need, the police may deny permits on the basis that a sufficient number have already been issued to others.[3]

Thus federal authorities would face the task of confiscating the 99 percent of the present handgun stock (estimated at upwards of 54 million) for which permits would not be issued.[4] Excepting alco-

---

3. See generally Carol Ruth Silver and Don B. Kates, Jr., "Self-Defense, Handgun Ownership and the Independence of Women in a Violent, Sexist Society," in Don B. Kates, Jr., ed., *Restricting Handguns: The Liberal Skeptics Speak Out* (Croton-On-Hudson: North River Press, 1979); David T. Hardy and Kenneth Chotiner, "The Potentiality for Civil Liberties Violations in the Enforcement of Handgun Prohibition," in Don B. Kates, Jr., ed., *Restricting Handguns: The Liberal Skeptics Speak Out* (Croton-On-Hudson: North River Press, 1979).

As can readily be perceived, such an administrative model allows for drastic reduction of (legal) handgun ownership. At the same time the police retain maximum flexibility to confer permits on those whom they think appropriate without having to resort to the subterfuge common in some countries of enrolling such citizens as reserve or "special" officers. The concept of handgun prohibition, as used in this chapter, refers to this restrictive model, or any other system of restriction whose purpose is to reduce the civilian handgun stock by 50 percent or more.

4. This estimate has been reached by combining the 1968 Eisenhower Commission finding that domestic production since 1899, plus imports since 1918, approximated 28 million handguns with the average of 2 million handguns per year that have been imported and/or domestically produced in the period since 1968. See discussion J. Wright et al., *Weapons, Crime, and Violence: A Literature Review and Research Agenda* (Washington, D.C.: GPO, 1981), ch. 2. Wright et al. point out that we do not know how many guns have

hol Prohibition, it is difficult to recall a federal attempt to eradicate so popular a commodity. Certainly neither marijuana, cocaine, nor heroin had even remotely the same popularity when Congress prohibited each of them as does the handgun now.

It is surprising that no commentator seems to have anticipated, or responded to, Leroy Clark's suggestion (see Chapter 1) that a comparison to alcohol Prohibition might prove enlightening. For reasons that are not entirely clear, the scholarly literature in this emotionally tinged area has tended to eschew discussion of the question of enforceability. Newton and Zimring (1970), the fountainhead prohibitionist argument, barely acknowledge the issue.[5] R.J. Riley's 10,000 word jeremiad against the handgun is similar.[6] Indeed, Riley's devotion of an entire paragraph to the issue (he recommends "strict" enforcement) is unusually prolix. Much of the exhortatory scholarship in the area espouses prohibition without any attention at all to the question of enforceability. Robert Sherrill, though himself strongly sympathetic to the prohibitionist viewpoint, refers derisively to an eminent cosympathizer's impassioned plea that Congress outlaw handguns, "and then figure out how to seize them in the days ahead."[7]

---

become unserviceable, been confiscated, or been thrown away since 1899. But these "downside" lacunae must be balanced against the facts: we also do not know how many guns have been brought back by returning servicemen, by tourists and immigrants, or, before 1918, by importers, subsequent import figures are very shaky; and in most states, police resell to the public guns they have confiscated.

Thus, shaky as they are, the Eisenhower Commission and Statistical Abstract figures on domestic production and commercial importation (less commercial exportation) of handguns are the only partially reliable supply-side figures. For the reasons stated they may be either substantially above or substantially below the total national handgun stock. In this state of the data it seems not wholly unreasonable to simply assume that the unknown factors offset each other.

5. Newton and Zimring (1970) was one of the staff reports of the Eisenhower Commission. In fairness to Professor Zimring, he recently emphasized to me in a personal communication that he had opposed the inclusion in that report of the Eisenhower Commission's recommendation of handgun prohibition. The report as he wrote it was simply an exploration of the harms attendant upon firearms ownership. As he was not necessarily proposing any particular legislative response to those harms, he did not feel it incumbent upon him to discuss the enforceability of a program he does not endorse. He has stressed the need for substantial change in public consciousness as a prerequisite to substantial reduction in the handgun stock. See Franklin E. Zimring, "Handguns in the 21st Century: Alternative Policy Futures," *Annals of the American Academy of Political and Social Science* 455 (1981): 1-10.

6. Riley, "Shooting to Kill."

7. Robert Sherrill, *The Saturday Night Special* (New York: Charter House, 1973).

Believing that exploration of enforceability should precede, rather than follow, the enactment of a ban, the present chapter responds to Leroy Clark's suggestion. The following subtopics will be covered: (1) the theoretical arguments that alcohol Prohibition and handgun prohibition (respectively) would reduce violent crime and mortality; (2) comparison of the potential risk of detection for violators of both bans as bearing upon the likelihood of voluntary compliance with each; (3) public perception of the legitimacy of each ban as bearing upon the likelihood of voluntary compliance with each; and (4) comparison of physical and market factors relating to enforceability of each ban against the noncompliant.

ARGUMENTS FOR REDUCING VIOLENT CRIME AND MORTALITY BY BANNING (RESPECTIVELY) ALCOHOL AND HANDGUNS

Prohibition is so thoroughly discredited that few remember the arguments of its proponents, or even their identities. But from the 1830s on, the Temperance Movement enjoyed the support of most of the progressive social and political figures of each successive generation. Proponents included Susan B. Anthony (whose political life began as a temperance lecturer), William Lloyd Garrison, Frederick Douglass, Horace Mann, Henry Ward Beecher, Lyman Beecher, Abraham Lincoln, Elizabeth Cady Stanton, Horace Greeley, Jane Addams, Nelson Miles, William Jennings Bryan, Gifford Pinchot, and Eleanor Roosevelt. In contrast to this array of luminaries, the anti-Prohibition forces centered around the liquor industry (often described as the "Liquor Lobby"), which could be dismissed as self-interested, and sometimes as reactionary, underhanded, and corrupt.[8]

The argument for Prohibition admixed religious and abstract moral consideration with an acute perception of the role alcohol plays in mortality and violent crime. Temperance advocates believed that liquor accounted for much of the incidence of sex crime, robbery, mob violence, and all varieties of homicide.[9] Liquor was par-

8. For instance, believing that women would inevitably vote for Prohibition, liquor interests lobbied intensively against women's suffrage, sometimes going to the extreme of subverting voting officials where women's suffrage issues appeared on the ballot. R. Tremain, *The Fight for Women's Rights* (New York: Ballantine, 1973), pp. 97–98.

9. A. Sinclair, *Prohibition: Era of Excess* (Boston: Little, Brown, 1962), pp. 17, 220; Paul E. Isaac, *Prohibition and Politics in Tennessee* (Nashville: University of Tennessee, 1965), pp. 147–50.

ticularly blamed for domestic and acquaintance homicide. Typifying the reformers' views was a cartoon depicting a husband being arrested in front of his children while his wife lies on the floor, a broken bottle beside her head. Entitled "The Bottle," its caption reads, "The husband, in a state of furious drunkenness, kills his wife with the instrument of all their misery."[10]

Prohibition advocates even went so far as to compile extensive statistics purporting to show sharp decreases in crime as a result of the Volstead Act.[11] Evaluation of these ancient statistics would be as pointless as it would be difficult, for modern evidence amply demonstrates the link between alcohol and various forms of mortality and violent crime. Since the link between handguns and crime is frequently argued as justifying handgun prohibition, it may be instructive to compare the respective degrees of linkage. Over the past five years, handguns have been involved in up to 50 percent of all murders[12]; in comparison, "most studies show that up to 86 percent of offenders have been drinking when the murder was committed."[13] (Comparing ten earlier studies showing between 19 percent and 83 percent of homicide offenders to have been drinking, Donald Goodwin calculated the median in alcohol involvement as 54 percent.[14]) Almost 41 percent of robberies are committed with firearms, primarily handguns[15]; in comparison "one study estimates alcohol involvement as high as 72 percent in robbery offenders."[16] Firearms, primarily handguns, are used by 5 to 12 percent of rape perpetrators[17];

10. Lithograph by D.W. Moody from Harry T. Peters Lithography Collection "America on Stone" in Smithsonian Institution. Reprinted under the topic "Prohibition" in the *United States Encyclopedia of History* (Philadelphia: Curtis, 1968).

Analysis and quotation of nineteenth century criminological thought on liquor as a cause of crime can be found in Arthur Fink's historiographical work, *Causes of Crime* (New York: Barnes, 1938), pp. 76–94.

11. D.L. Colvin, *Prohibition in the United States* (New York: Doran, 1926), pp. 477–78; Jane Addams, *The Second Twenty Years At Hull House* (New York: Macmillan, 1930), p. 221.

12. Federal Bureau of Investigation, *Uniform Crime Reports* (Washington, D.C.: GPO, 1974–1979).

13. U.S. Department of Health, Education and Welfare (HEW), *Alcohol and Health: Third Special Report to the U.S. Congress* (Washington, D.C.: U.S. Public Health Service, 1978), p. 64.

14. Donald W. Goodwin, "Alcohol in Suicide and Homicide," *Quarterly Journal of Studies on Alcohol* 35 (1973): 151.

15. See, for example, *Uniform Crime Report, 1978*, p. 19.

16. *Alcohol and Health: Third Special Report to the U.S. Congress, 1978*, p. 64.

17. United States Department of Justice, *Criminal Victimization in the United States* (Washington, D.C.: GPO, 1979), p. 23; United States Department of Justice, *Rape Victimization in 26 American Cities* (Washington, D.C.: GPO, 1980), pp. 56–57.

in comparison, about 50 percent of rape perpetrators had been drinking before the crime.[18]

Roughly similar theories are advanced regarding a "causative" connection between liquor and handguns (respectively) and violent crime, particularly homicide. It is argued that each alters the psyche: a drinker's inhibitions are lowered by liquor; one who carries a weapon is conditioned to expect violence and/or to react to situations violently. Regarding the psychological effects of weapons possession there is, as yet, no empirical evidence.[19] As to psychological effects of alcohol, experimental evidence does suggest heightening of aggression in some subjects,[20] and a study of former heroin addicts showed significant increase in violence among those who had turned to liquor as a substitute.[21]

A special caveat is necessary in evaluating such arguments because of the distortionary effect caused by their exclusive focus on criminal behavior. When the focus is thus narrowed, involvement of either liquor or handguns may seem significant enough to be "causative." But if the focus is broadened to include all alcohol users and handgun possessors (respectively), the relationship to crime becomes insignificant. Comparing the number of homicides involving handguns to the total handgun stock, it is apparent that less than 1 in 5,400 (0.018%) handguns are used to murder.[22] Although liquor-related homicides are somewhat more frequent, and the number of heavy drinkers is much smaller than the number of people who have ready access to handguns, the proportion (0.081%) of heavy drinkers who murder is still very small.[23] Thus, if there is a "causative" relation-

---

18. Richard T. Rada, "Alcohol and Rape," *Medical Aspects of Human Sexuality* 9 (1975): 48-65.

19. Gary Kleck, "Capital Punishment, Gun Ownership and Homicide," *American Journal of Sociology* 84 (1979): 882-910.

20. HEW, *Alcohol and Health: Third Special Report to the U.S. Congress*; F.P. Taylor et al., "The Effects of Alcohol and Delta-9-Tetrahydrocannabinol on Human Physical Aggression," *Aggressive Behavior* 2 (1976): 153-61.

21. L.Z. Freedman, "Methadone and Alcohol," *Alcoholism Digest* 4 (1975): 256.

22. This ratio is obtained by dividing the estimated number of handguns (54 million) by 10,000 which, plus or minus, is the figure at which handgun homicide has stood annually over the past five years. A ratio of 5,400 to 1 somewhat exaggerates the proportion of all handguns that are involved in homicides. It is not the case that 10,000 handguns are used in each year's 10,000 handgun homicides. Sometimes multiple homicides were committed by one person with the same handgun.

23. From survey and other data it is estimated that approximately 13.3 million Americans aged fourteen or over can be classified as heavy drinkers, including alcoholics. If 10,800 homicides per year (54% of the approximately 20,000 homicides annually) are committed

ship at all, it appears to exist only among a very small proportion of handgun owners or heavy drinkers. These seem to be highly atypical of the rest.

This point deserves discussion at length because it contradicts what is probably the most commonly heard argument for handgun prohibition: Conceding that assassins, terrorists and common criminals will not obey a ban, nevertheless most homicides are committed by ordinary citizens in the heat of a momentary anger and only because of the availability of a handgun they keep loaded around the home for protection.

If this characterization of murderers were accurate, banning handguns would seem an appealingly simple means of reducing domestic and acquaintance homicide. Most killings are not, however, perpetrated by the average noncriminal citizen, whose law-obedient mentality (it is believed) would induce him to give up handguns in response to a ban.[24]

The involvement of liquor and handguns (respectively) in types of mortality other than intentional homicide is well known. Handguns are used in about one half of all suicides yearly[25]; liquor is involved

---

under the influence of alcohol, this would average out to a little less than 1 homicide per every 1,231 heavy drinkers.

That figure overrepresents the ratio of heavy drinkers to homicides, since some of the homicides that are liquor-related may have been committed by people who would be classified in the HEW statistics as light or moderate drinkers. The impossibility of establishing precise mathematical comparisons is evident, and those offered in the preceding paragraph should be taken as suggestive only. The point is that, while the involvement of alcohol in homicide is great, the proportion of heavy drinkers and/or alcoholics who commit homicide is insignificant.

24. "The great majority of [family] killings are among poor, restless, alcoholic, troubled people, usually with long criminal records. Applying the domestic homicide rate of these people to the presumably upstanding citizens whom they prey upon is seriously misleading." A. Swersey and E. Enloe, *Homicide in Harlem* (New York: Rand Institute, 1975), p. 17: "We estimate that the great majority of both perpetrators and victims of assaults and homicides had previous arrests, probably over 80% or more." Kleck *supra* n. 19 and sources there cited.

Moreover, a murderer's prior arrest record is likely to substantially underrepresent his or her real prior violence history. Unlike robbers, who generally strike at strangers, murderers' prior violence may have been directed against relatives or acquaintances, that is, the same kinds of people they end up killing. Such prior violent incidents may have never led to arrest or conviction, either because the victim did not press charges or because the police refused to interfere in "a family affair." A study of domestic homicide in Kansas City revealed that in 85 percent of cases the police had been summoned at least once before the killing occurred; and in 50 percent of the cases, the police were called five or more times before the actual murder. G. Wilt et al., *Domestic Violence and the Police* (Washington, D.C.: Police Foundation, 1977).

25. Newton and Zimring, *Firearms and Violence in American Life*, p. 33.

in about one third of them.[26] Handgun accidents take between 200 to 250 lives per year[27]; liquor is involved in approximately 53,000 accidental deaths per year, including 25,000 automobile fatalities, 9,800 fatal falls, 7,200 industrial accidents, 5,500 burn deaths, and 3,500 drownings.[28] Overall, handguns are involved in approximately 25,000 violent deaths yearly (homicide, suicide, and accident), while liquor is involved in approximagely 75,000. Adding in fatalities resulting from liquor-related physical ailments, liquor is estimated to be involved in about 11 percent of all deaths each year, while handguns are involved in a little over 1 percent.[29]

Thus the "life-saving" argument for banning handguns is roughly comparable to that for banning alcohol. Equally important, however, is the often unspoken assumption that something in the commodity

26. James L. Luke, "Cause of Death in Alcoholics," *Addictions* 5 (1976): 22-23; L. Riddick and James L. Luke, "Alcohol-associated Deaths in the District of Columbia," *Journal of Forensic Sciences* 23 (1978): 493-502.

27. National Safety Council, Safety Education Data Sheet no. 3 (revised): *FIREARMS* (1974), p. 5. Based on 1971-1973 data, this paper placed fatal firearms accidents at 2,500 annually, with handguns accounting for 10 percent of the fatalities (i.e., 250). Subsequently there has been a progressive decline in accidental firearms fatalities to 1,800 per year. National Safety Council, *ACCIDENT FACTS* (1980), p. 7. Although no separate figure is given for handgun accident fatalities, they presumably continue to represent approximately 10 percent of the total, that is, approximately 200 deaths per year.

Advocates of handgun prohibition often ascribe all accidental firearms fatalities to the handgun, thereby exaggerating the handgun accident fatality total by a factor of ten. See, for example, Sam Fields, "Handgun Prohibition and Social Necessity," *St. Louis University Law Journal* 23 (1979): 34-61. They then compound this error by arguing that, in addition to its presumed crime-reductive effect, a handgun ban would reduce firearms fatalities because it "would significantly alter the firearms habits of law-abiding citizens" in that they would keep loaded shotguns and rifles in their homes and offices instead of handguns (Fields, ibid.).

In fact, one of the potential costs of a handgun prohibition is that it would substantially increase accidental fatalities if it caused substantial substitution of long guns for handguns as self-defense weapons. Long guns are not only far more deadly than handguns, but they are also more difficult to secure from inquisitive children and much easier for a child to accidentally discharge. Shotgun accidents take five times as many lives as do handgun accidents, although the number of handguns is roughly the same and the handgun has replaced the shotgun as the weapon kept loaded in the home for defense. In the 1930s, when handgun ownership was relatively rare and long guns were the primary self-defense weapon kept in the home, the per capita rate of accidental firearm fatalities was well above the present rate. Indeed, the per capita rate of accidental firearm fatalities has progressively declined over the past twenty-five years as the handgun has replaced the long gun as the weapon kept loaded for home defense. Mark Benenson, "A Controlled Look at Gun Controls," *New York Law Forum* 14 (1968): 720; John Kaplan, "The Wisdom of Gun Prohibition," *Annals Of The American Academy of Political and Social Sciences* 455 (1981): 17.

28. Compare HEW, *Alcohol and Health* to *ACCIDENT FACTS*, 1980 edition, at n. 27, *supra.*

29. HEW, *Alcohol and Health*, p. xi.

to be prohibited is so inherently correlative to the mortality and other evils involved that prohibition will not just result in some likely substitute commodity producing the same evils. Thus it is assumed that, if handguns were prohibited, murderers could not readily turn to the use of shotguns, knives, and other weapons; if liquor were prohibited, the same evils would not occur under the influence of marijuana, heroin, barbituates, etc. While the assumption that substitution would not result in the same evils is quite controversial with respect to handgun prohibition,[30] common knowledge and experimental evidence at least partially validate it in regard to alcohol.[31] Prohibition was termed the Great Experiment because, inter alia, it was designed to test this no-substitution assumption. But this part of the experiment proved abortive because noncompliance was so widespread that drinkers seem to have had little occasion to resort to substitutes for liquor.

LIKELIHOOD OF VOLUNTARY COMPLIANCE IN RELATION TO COMPARATIVE RISKS OF NONCOMPLIANCE

David Bordua and Alan Lizotte divide gun owners into three subgroups, according to their reasons for owning: sport-collection, protection, and criminal. Drinkers may also be divided into three subgroups: moderate or social, heavy, and alcoholics. The comparison that most readily suggests itself is of the moderate or social drinker to the sport-collection handgun owner. Without putting too much emphasis on the point, it is evident that the members of both subgroups are attracted to their respective commodities primarily by pleasure.[32]

---

30. Compare Don B. Kates, Jr., "Reflections of the Relevancy of 'Gun Control,' " *Criminal Law Bulletin* 13 (1977): 122–23; Don B. Kates, Jr., "Some Remarks on the Prohibition of Handguns," *St. Louis University Law Journal* 23 (1979): 20–23; and David T. Hardy and Don B. Kates, Jr., "Handgun Availability and the Social Harms of Robbery: Recent Data and Some Projections," in Don B. Kates, Jr., ed., *Restricting Handguns*, p. 127 (arguing that long guns could readily be substituted for handguns in most homicide situations) to Sam Fields, "Handgun Prohibition," pp. 42–43 (arguing the opposite). See Kleck (Chapter 7 in this volume) calculating that homicide would increase if a handgun ban resulted in the totel elimination of handgun woundings, but long guns were substituted in 19 percent of the woundings previously involving handgun bullets.

31. Taylor et al., "The Effects of Alcohol."

32. David J. Bordua and Alan Lizotte, "A Sub-Cultural Model of Legal Firearms Ownership in Illinois," *Law and Policy Quarterly* 1 (1979): 147–75; Alan Lizotte and David

But comparing such an incentive to the respective risks makes it evident that violation of Prohibition by social drinkers was far likelier than would be violation of a handgun ban by the sport or collection handgun owners. Of course the social drinker ran risks by obtaining liquor and drinking with friends. But this did not involve the same magnitude of "visibility" that would be run by anyone so foolish as to continue target shooting or hunting with handguns after a ban, or even by a well-known collector who failed to turn in his weapons. Thus the inherent enforceability of a handgun ban appears substantially to exceed that of alcohol prohibition, at least with the sport- or collection-minded handgun owner.

Among the other subgroups of handgun owners and drinkers, the incentive for violation is not pleasure but necessity or perceived necessity. The most extreme case is that of the alcoholic, to whom, by definition, alcohol is a physical necessity. The heavy drinker's dependency is psychological rather than physical, but it may also manifest itself in acute cravings. In the case of handguns, the value that a criminal is likely to place upon them, prohibitory legislation notwithstanding, is obvious. For protection owners, the handgun provides an important sense of security, which is reified into a belief that it vitally protects the physical safety of the owners and their loved ones. (For present purposes it is unnecessary to inquire into the objective validity of this belief. Protection owners have the same incentive to violate a ban whether or not their subjective belief that the handgun offers protection is well founded.[33])

Bordua, "Firearms Ownership for Sport and Protection: Two Divergent Models," *American Sociological Review* 45 (1980): 229–44; 46 (1980): 499–503.

33. The exhortatory literature on handgun prohibition tends to dismiss people who want firearms for self-protection as ignorant, neurotic, or hysterical, at best. See, for example, Emanuel Tanay, "Neurotic Attachment to Guns," *The Five Minute Hour* (n.p., 1976), p. 3; Robert E. Burns, "Sex Education Belongs in the Gun Store," *U.S. Catholic Magazine* 44 (August 1979): 2; Robert F. Drinan, "Gun Control: The Good Outweighs the Evil," *Civil Liberties Review* 3 (1976): 51; Tom Wicker, " 'Legitimate' Handguns Assure Supply for Criminals," *Baltimore Evening Sun* (15 December 1980). But for the purpose of evaluating the likelihood that protection owners would comply with a handgun prohibition, an attempt to analyze their motivation may be more useful. Peter A. Lake's "Shooting to Kill," *Esquire* (February 1981), is an article by a self-described liberal journalist and A.C.L.U. member. He relates that he enrolled in a handgun self-defense course because of an experience in which he called the police emergency number to report a robbery in progress, only to be answered by a recording to the effect that all lines were busy and calls would be taken in the order received.

There is evidence that this experience is not atypical in Los Angeles ("LAPD Morale Down as Crime Rate Rises," *Los Angeles Times*, 16 January 1981); or elsewhere ("When

Thus the incentives for the protection (or criminal) owner to violate a ban, though perhaps less than those for an alcoholic to violate Prohibition, seem at least as great as those for the heavy drinker to do so. Weighing the incentives against the countervailing consideration of risk of detection, a handgun ban would seem significantly less likely to elicit voluntary compliance than Prohibition. For a heavy drinker to continue drinking under Prohibition necessitated obtaining an infinite succession of new suppliers, each involving some risk of detection. But a handgun is a single purchase item, which, with proper care, will endure throughout the life of its owner and far beyond the seventh generation of descendants.[34] (Of course, if the prospective violator happened to already own one of the 54 million

---

You Can't Count on a Cop," *San Francisco Examiner*, 12 June 1981), particularly as local tax revenues decline and federal and state financial support is withdrawn. See, for example, *Newsweek* (March 23, 1981), p. 50: "Many city [police] forces are in a terrible bind. In Los Angeles only 600 patrolmen cruise the streets. In Houston, the city is so large that cops take 25 minutes to answer the average emergency call. In New Jersey, state troopers were called in this month to patrol the streets of Trenton because local police can't keep up with the volume."

Understandably, readers might gain the impression that personal armament is the only real protection available for themselves and their families. Moreover, this may be reinforced by contact with police officers, whom many citizens would regard as authoritative advisers on the subject. Of over 5,000 officers who responded to a 1977 poll, 64 percent felt that an armed citizenry deters crime, and 86 percent stated that, if they were private citizens, they would keep a firearm for self-defense. (Crime Control Research Project, 1601 115th Street, S.E. Suite 155, Bellevue, Washington). These results may be subject to question, since the poll was done for an organization that opposes handgun prohibition. But in 1976, police chiefs and high ranking administrators were polled nationwide by the Research Division of the Boston Police Department, which was then headed by Robert diGrazia, an outspoken proponent of handgun prohibition. *Boston Police Department, Handgun Control: A Survey of the Leading Law Enforcement Officials in the Country* found that "A substantial majority of the respondents looked favorably upon the general possession of handguns by the citizenry (excludes those with criminal records and a history of mental instability). Strong approval was also elicited from the police administrators concerning possession of handguns in the home or place of business."

Indeed, by a bare majority, the respondents endorsed the idea that the citizenry be allowed to actually carry firearms with them at all times for self-protection. In answer to another question, the respondents opined that officers lower ranking than themselves would be even less favorably disposed toward "gun control."

Thus, to the extent that protection owners exchange opinions with the very people who are supposed to be enforcing the handgun prohibition, they are likely to be confirmed in their belief that it is an unjustifiable impediment to the security of themselves and their family.

34. Arguably, many turn-of-the-century firearms have been effectively destroyed, not through overuse but by the rust and corrosion resulting from disuse and lack of owner interest. In contrast, owners who would willfully defy a handgun prohibition are presum-

handguns now in circulation, he or she could simply keep it, thereby avoiding even the risk involved in a single purchase.)

Unlike the firearm itself, ammunition does eventually lose its potency. But those who keep handguns purely for crime or self-defense would need no great amount of ammunition (in contrast, once again, to the avid target shooter who may fire as many as 10,000 rounds per year). The risk of detection involved in purchasing a handful of ammunition for criminal or self-defense purposes once every generation cannot be compared to that involved in the regular purchases of liquor that millions made during Prohibition.

Fully as important as the abstract risk of detection is the likelihood that detection will actually result in condign punishment. One factor promoting Prohibition violations in certain areas was the knowledge that, even if violators were caught, juries would not convict them or judges would not severely punish them.[35] Otherwise law-abiding people who might contemplate violating a handgun ban could reasonably believe that even if caught they would not be severely punished. Court records establish that judges and juries in a number of major cities will not severely punish such people for violation even of present, less onerous (and less controversial) laws against actually carrying a handgun.[36] The intractable human factors involved in such prosecutions are poignantly described by a judge of a court handling only gun law violations.[37] He notes that most defendants coming before him have no criminal record; they are secretaries, shopkeepers, the elderly—often people who have previously been victimized by violent crime—who carry guns because they are vulnerable, terrified, and have no other way of protecting themselves. Unable to bring himself to send such people to prison, Judge Shields imposes only a modest fine. A popular article uses a quote from another judge of the same court as its subtitle: " 'I can't send this man to jail,' the judge said, 'People are afraid so they carry guns.' "[38]

---

ably sufficiently motivated to provide the minimum maintenance necessary so that the gun would last indefinitely. Newton and Zimring, *Firearms and Violence*, p. 5; Benenson, "Controlled Look at Gun Controls," p. 719.

35. See Chapter 1.

36. Note: "Some Observations on the Disposition of CCW Cases in Detroit," *Michigan Law Review* 74 (1976): 614–43; James Beha, "And *Nobody* Can Get You Out," mimeograph (Cambridge, Mass.: Harvard Law School, 1976), pp. xvii, 200. A somewhat revised version appears in *Boston University Law Review* (1977): pp. 96, 289.

37. David J. Shields, "Two Judges Look at Gun Control," *Chicago Bar Record, January–February 1976* (1976): 180–85.

Such judicial attitudes should not be confused with approval of handguns. These judges actively support the idea of a national handgun ban, perhaps on the theory that the responsibility for enforcement will fall upon the federal courts rather than their own. Concluding a study of judicial enforcement, Paul Bendis and Steven Balkin comment: "Based on the Chicago data, it is difficult to argue [either that present] gun laws do not work or that stronger gun laws are needed. . . . It is very possible that, if gun laws do potentially reduce gun-related crime, the present laws are all that is needed if they are enforced. What good would stronger gun laws do when the courts have demonstrated that they will not enforce them?"[39]

---

38. Jack Star, "Why the Gun Law Doesn't Work," *Chicago Magazine* (February 1978): 128–31, 241. In response to the problem of actual or perceived judicial lenience, it has been proposed that defiance of a handgun prohibition can be deterred by a mandatory penalty scheme. A year in a federal prison would be a mandatory sentence which the judge must impose on any defendant convicted of having a handgun without a permit. The viability of such a penalty scheme is discussed in the text.

39. Paul Bendis and Steven Balkin, "A Look at Gun Control Enforcement," *Journal of Police Science and Administration* 7 (1979): 439–48. The complex factors (including public pressure) leading to judicial nullification when firearms prohibitions impact upon a non-criminal who is protecting him or herself with an illegal gun are illustrated in an article that appeared in the *New York Daily News*, 17 June 1977. Titled "Where Survival is a Crime," it refers to an incident involving a crippled, middle-aged black cab driver. While he was preparing dinner, his Harlem tenement home was broken into by a junkie. Demanding money, the junkie beat him about the head with a lead pipe until the cabbie managed to reach his "Saturday Night Special" and kill the attacker. The *Daily News* goes on to criticize the cabbie's arrest for illegal handgun ownership in rather unmeasured terms:

Willie, holding his hurt head, went into a paddy wagon full of murderers and muggers and pimps and went downtown to sit with them in a detention pen. Willie must have thought he was in Russia. . . . Willie, of course, had no gun permit. To get one in New York City, you need to know somebody. Willie doesn't know anybody. All he knows is that he had to defend himself. Our politicians don't give a damn about Willie, any more than they give a damn about you. They ride in limos and carry guns. Judges are politicians. In New York, as the street axiom says, the only thing harder to find than a judge without a piece is a mugger with a conscience.

Contrary to what might be implied from this outpouring, the *Daily News* does not oppose handgun prohibition. Indeed, it repeatedly editorialized in equally unmeasured terms for Mayor Koch's proposal that owners of unlicensed handguns be mandatorily punished by a year in prison—a proposal that the *New York Times* opposed as too harsh in that most of the people punished would be like the cabbie. The juxtaposition between the article on the cabbie and the mandatory imprisonment editorials highlights the insoluble conundrum of "gun control" enforcement. The *Daily News* supports enactment of the harshest possible anti-gun measures and then denounces them when they are actually enforced.

PERCEIVED LEGITIMACY OR ILLEGITIMACY OF THE PROHIBITION AS BEARING UPON THE LIKELIHOOD OF VOLUNTARY COMPLIANCE

Though important, the considerations discussed thus far would be dispositive only as to noncompliance with a handgun ban by those who define themselves as criminals. People who define themselves as law-abiding generally obey the laws they regard as legitimate — even if they have strong incentives toward disobedience and even though they think it unlikely that they would be caught disobeying. It appears that Prohibition was, in fact, obeyed by millions, particularly in its earliest stage. Disobedience to Prohibition became endemic only as those inclined toward noncompliance came increasingly to accept rationalizations suggesting that Prohibition was an illegitimate law. These rationalizations were twofold: (1) that Prohibition was minority legislation foisted on the public by a well-organized clique of do-gooders while the Doughboys were overseas, unable to vote for their rights; and (2) that Prohibition was a gross imposition upon personal liberty that no real American would abide.

The first rationalization would obviously not come into play in relation to the legitimacy of a handgun ban. But the second would seem as applicable to a handgun ban as to Prohibition for those who find such arguments appealing.[40] Indeed, there is a related rationale for violating a handgun ban which might have even more popular

---

40. B. Bruce-Briggs, "The Great American Gun War," *Public Interest* 45 (Fall 1976): 37–62. Bruce-Briggs suggests that "underlying the gun control struggle is a fundamental division in our nation."

[A] sort of low grade [war] is going on between two alternative views of what America is and ought to be. On the one side are those who take bourgeois Europe as a model of a civilized society: A society just, equitable, and democratic; but well ordered, with the lines of responsibility and authority clearly drawn, and with decisions made rationally and correctly by intelligent men for the entire nation. To such people, hunting is atavistic, personal violence is shameful, and uncontrolled gun ownership is a blot on civilization.

On the other side is a group of people who do not tend to be especially articulate or literate, and whose world view is rarely expressed in print. Their model is that of the independent frontiersman who takes care of himself and his family with no interference from the state. They are "conservative" in the sense that they cling to America's unique pre-modern tradition — a non-feudal society with a sort of medieval liberty writ large for everyman.

Holders of this second world view would seem particularly susceptible to virtually all of the rationalizations for violation of a handgun ban discussed in the text.

appeal than did the similar argument against Prohibition. This rationalization is that a government that cannot protect its citizens has no right to prevent them from trying to protect themselves and their families.

Yet another related rationale, of perhaps even more importance, is the likely popular perception of the constitutional illegitimacy of a handgun ban under the Second Amendment. In both the national polls that have asked the question, the overwhelming majority response (predictably including most, if not all, protection owners) has been that citizens have an inalienable right to keep and bear arms.[41] Of course, this "popular" interpretation of the Constitution might be corroded by a contrary interpretation of the Second Amendment by the United States Supreme Court. Unfortunately, for at least some protection owners, such a contrary interpretation would impugn not their view of the Constitution, but their belief in the Supreme Court and perhaps in government as a whole.[42] The "popular" view of the Second Amendment has considerably more historical support than do many unpopular (though often socially desirable) Supreme Court interpretations of other provisions of the Constitution.[43] Nor are many protection owners likely to accept Chief Justice Hughes' dictum, "we are under a constitution, but the constitution is what the judges say it is . . . ," as a nomothetic prescription rather than a mere statement of fact. In any event, the con-

41. Decision/Making/Information (DMI), *Attitudes of the American Electorate Toward Gun Control* (Santa Ana, Calif.: DMI, 1978).

42. In note 40, *supra*, Bruce-Briggs is quoted contrasting the cosmopolitan, European world view of those who wish to ban firearms to the world view that predominates among handgun owners. Bruce-Briggs continues with the following in reference to the ideological "hardcore" of gun owners:

> They ask, because they do not understand the other side, "why do these people want to disarm us?" They consider themselves no threat to anyone; they are not criminals, not revolutionaries. But slowly, as they become politicized, they find an analysis that fits the phenomenon they experience: Someone fears their having guns, someone is afraid of their defending their families, property and liberty. Nasty things may happen if these people begin to feel that they are cornered.

43. Compare Halbrook (Chapter 13), Malcolm (Chapter 14) and Hardy, "The Second Amendment as a Restraint on State and Federal Firearms," in Kates, ed., *Restricting Handguns*, pp. 171–85 (all relative to the Second Amendment) to C. Amtieau, A. Downey, and E. Roberts, *Freedom From Federal Establishment* (Milkwaukee, Wisc.: Bruce, 1964) (regarding the original meaning of the Establishment Cause of the First Amendment); L. Levy, *Legacy of Suppression* (Cambridge: Harvard University Press, 1960) (regarding the original meaning of free expression guarantees of the First Amendment); and Fairman, "Does the Fourteenth Amendment Incorporate the Bill of Rights: The Original Understanding," *Stanford Law Review* 2 (1949): 3.

stitutional argument against the legitimacy of a handgun ban is considerably stronger than was that against Prohibition, whose constitutionality had been assured by its enactment as a constitutional amendment.

Also of great significance, at least within "popular" conceptions of the Constitution, would be issues of equality and fairness versus elitism. Even under New York City's extremely stringent administration, some citizens are able to obtain permits not only to own but even to carry handguns for protection. Several years ago the local affiliate of the National Rifle Association obtained from a sympathizer in the police what purported to be a list of those holding such "carry permits." According to official policy, a "carry permit" should have been granted only upon the applicant's showing a "unique need" for self-defense. Yet the list was predominantly made up of individuals noted less for the perilousness of their life styles, than for wealth, social prominence, and political influence. Highly, and ironically, visible on the list were a number of well-known "gun control" advocates.[44]

Contrary to the implication drawn by the NRA affiliate, this revelation did not demonstrate the inherent iniquity of handgun permit laws. It only illustrates the inevitability that important people, influential people, will obtain special privileges in any governmental program, including many programs that nevertheless clearly serve the interest of the general public. Deplorable as it is, tax loopholes from

44. Although under New York law handgun permits are supposed to be matters of public record, the New York City Police Department refused to allow reporters access to them or to confirm or deny issuance of permits to any of the persons whose names had been leaked. Several of the named individuals admitted that they did have permits, including Arthur Ochs Sulzberger, publisher of the *New York Times*, which has frequently editorialized for handgun prohibition via a federal permit law. Other proponents of such legislation who allegedly had permits included Nelson, David, Winthrop and John Jay Rockefeller, John Lindsay, and the husband of Dr. Joyce Brothers – she having often argued that firearms ownership is indicative of male sexual inadequacy or dysfunction. Silver and Kates, *Restricting Handguns*, p. 153.

New York City police opened their files four years later, only after an order was obtained from New York's highest court by a reporter for the *Wall Street Journal*. Reporters assigned to cull the newly opened files described permit holders as "entertainers, publishers, media stars, politicians of all stripes." "Permit 29,000 to Pack Guns," *New York Daily News*, 22 June 1981. Among those listed at this time were Arthur Godfrey, William Buckley, Laurance Rockefeller, Lyman Bloomingdale, and, of course, the *New York Times'* A.O. Sulzberger. Surprisingly the *New York Times* did not cover the issue either at the time of the original leak in 1977 or in 1981 after the *Wall Street Journal* obtained its precedential decision in the New York courts.

which the rich get most advantage, farm subsidies from which giant agri-corporations are in the position to gain most advantage, "pork barrel" projects for the districts of influential legislators, favoritism in the granting of licenses, special considerations to prominent people (and/or their children) caught in petty crime and the like are inevitably going to occur in any government. If laws or programs serving legitimate public ends are to be condemned because they incidentally create opportunities for special privilege (opportunities that will multiply far beyond the ability of reforms to keep pace), there will be neither laws nor programs.

The true significance of such revelations is their adverse effect on voluntary compliance with a handgun ban by the ordinary citizen. Not even the most virulent opponent of Prohibition could have claimed that Jane Addams and William Jennings Bryan were only inveighing against the evil of liquor in order to establish a system whereby they could secretly tipple while ordinary citizens went dry. Allied to the issue of elitism/equality is the effect of such revelations on the belief that handguns are indeed useful for self-defense. It is only natural (however empirically irrelevant) for that belief to seem validated when opinion leaders who have preached for years against protection ownership turn out to have been opposing it only for people who do not have the influence they use to get a protection gun for themselves.

Thus such revelations simultaneously reinforce the perceived need for having a protection gun and undermine the perceived legitimacy of ownership restrictions. When people whose lives are spent in mansions, high security buildings, and chauffeured limousines are accorded gun permits which ordinary citizens condemned to live and/or work in high crime areas are denied, those citizens are likely to assume that government places a higher value on the lives of the wealthy or influential than on theirs. Needless to say, ordinary citizens are unlikely either to concur in that valuation or to feel many qualms about violating a law which they deem expressive of it.

PHYSICAL AND MARKET FACTORS AFFECTING ENFORCEABILITY

The longevity of the handgun makes the difficulty of enforcing a ban incomparably greater than the difficulty of enforcing alcohol Prohibition. No matter how opposed to Prohibition some might have been, after their stock of liquor was consumed, continued violation entailed the considerable effort, and/or attendant risk of detection, involved in home manufacture or outside purchasing of liquor. In contrast, each of the approximately 54 million present civilian handguns will continue in private circulation unless and until the authorities succeed in confiscating it or its possessors voluntarily surrender it.

The previous discussion suggests that there may be substantial failure of voluntary compliance with a ban. It is obviously impossible to predict (either in terms of guns surrendered or percentage of gun owners surrendering them) the extent of voluntary compliance a handgun ban would receive. Perhaps the best estimate derives from a 1975 poll in which registered voters were asked what degree of compliance a federal ban would elicit. Nine percent of the respondents thought that no gun owners would comply; 59 percent thought a "few/some" would comply; and 24 percent thought that half would. Thus 92 percent of the respondents thought that half or less of the present gun owners would comply with a ban.[45] It is tempting, but dubious, to correlate this with the same poll's finding that about 50 percent of all handgun-owning respondents gave self-defense as their reason for having the weapon. But it is not necessary to resort to statistical legerdemain to predict that the percentage of noncompliance will be approximately coterminous with the percentage of protection ownership.

Since those whom the handgun ban principally targets are the least likely to voluntarily comply with it, the question becomes, How successful is an involuntary confiscation effort likely to be? On the basis of New York City's experience, the answer must be "not very." After nearly seven decades of strictly enforced handgun prohibition, the generally accepted police estimate of illegal handguns in New York City is 2 million.[46] Beyond the sheer magnitude of the figure is its comparative significance. The ratio of handguns to population is 1 to 3.5 in New York City, whereas in the rest of the country (where handgun ownership is generally legal) it is only 1 to 5.[47]

This comparison is further accentuated by reference to the dichotomy between protection and sporting handgun owners. In the coun-

45. DMI, *Attitudes of American Electorate*, 1975.

46. Hardy and Kates, "Handgun Availability," in Kates, ed., *Restricting Handguns*, p. 132.

47. Wright et al., *Weapons, Crime, and Violence*.

try as a whole it appears that only about 50 percent of all handgun owners have their weapons for protection, with the rest being sport users.[48] But it would be naive to think that many of New York City's 2 million illegal handguns are kept for hunting squirrels in Central Park. It may be theorized that, but for the ban, protection ownership would be even greater in the city. But it remains the case, not only that the ratio of handgun owners to population is significantly greater in New York City than in the rest of the country, but that the proportion of handguns owned for protection (rather than sport) is enormously greater. The existence of this situation after seventy years of highly restrictive permit policy is strong evidence both of the unlikelihood of voluntary compliance by the protection minded and of the difficulties of enforcing involuntary confiscation against them.

It is often suggested that New York City's situation reflects no more than the inherent impossibility of controlling firearms ownership on a state rather than a national level. Whether federal regulation might be more viable for preventing the transportation of *additional* handguns from areas in which they are not legal into New York State is addressed in the following discussion. But it is difficult to see how a federal ban would be any more successful in decreasing or eliminating the number of illegal handguns presently in New York City than the New York State ban which has been in effect since 1911. The federal ban would be even more unenforceable in the rest of the country, which is far less well policed than is New York City.[49]

By the same token, it is not clear that expanding the area of prohibition from New York State to the nation as a whole would even prevent additional handgun acquisition, at least among Americans who want them for crime or protection purposes. Geographical expansion would require enforcement in areas less well policed than New York City and along a 12,000 mile border. If handguns were illegally imported at the same volume as marijuana is estimated to be, approximately 20 million of the size used to slay John Lennon

48. Ibid., ch. 3.

49. As of 1979, it was computed that New York City had almost 4 officers per 1,000 population. The average number of law enforcement employees per 1,000 population for all cities in the nation was 2.5; for cities over 250,000 it was 3.4; and for the nation in general it was 2.1. FBI, *Uniform Crime Report, 1979*, pp. 232, 249.

would enter the country each year.[50] Of course, the number of people seeking to buy handguns for crime or protection would not support a market of 20 million per year. Even now, when handguns may legally be purchased in all but six states, less than 2.5 million new ones are sold annually,[51] and a large proportion of those are sold to the sporting-collection owners who would presumably comply with a ban.[52] But whatever the demand for illegally imported handguns, it seems unlikely that the federal government could prevent its satisfaction when it cannot prevent either in excess of 1 million illegal immigrants or 10,000 metric tons of marijuana from crossing its borders every year.

Illegally imported handguns would probably be inordinately expensive. But millions of people are willing to pay far more for the privilege of smoking marijuana year after year. It seems likely that people who consider handguns necessary to preserving their lives would willingly undertake one exorbitant transaction to obtain a handgun that they can keep indefinitely. Moreover, perversely enough, a handgun ban might make illegal weapons available at prices below the present cost of legal sale—just as cheap moonshine sold during Prohibition for less than good liquor had cost before it.

Any competent machinist can produce a serviceable pot metal copy of a modern handgun at a fraction of the cost of manufacturing it out of high grade materials in a factory subject to government

---

50. Federal law enforcement officials estimate that 10,000 metric tons (22,036,000 pounds) of marijuana are imported annually. "The Pot Trade," *Wall Street Journal*, 16 July 1980.

Because marijuana is much more compressible than handguns, it is not possible to precisely project from this figure a comparability as to the number of handguns that could be illegally imported with an equivalent amount of effort. If weight alone be considered, approximately 22,000,000 handguns comparable to the .38 special Charter Arms "Undercover" used in the Lennon slaying could be imported each year. In estimating importation at 20,000,000, I am deducting 2,000,000 as a crude proxy for the noncompressibility of handguns in comparison to marijuana. Likewise, I have used the Lennon gun as an example because its combination of comparatively small size and large caliber would seem to epitomize the optimum handgun likely to be imported illegally for protection or crime in a nation where handguns were illegal. Of course, types and models of handguns differ markedly from each other in size and weight. It may be expected that smuggled guns would represent rather a mixed bag. Thus it may be relevant to note that, using weight as an index alone, the estimated 22,036,000 pounds of marijuana imported yearly would equate to 8.81 million very large handguns (equivalent to the .45 automatic now used by the United States Army) or 39.4 million very small handguns (equivalent to the small, cheap imported .25 caliber F.I.E.).

51. See note 4, *supra.*

52. Wright et al., *Weapons, Crime, and Violence.*

taxation, regulation, and record-keeping requirements. Vietnamese and Pakistani peasants regularly produce firearms in "cottage manufacture" environments with far less sophisticated tooling and energy sources than are available in millions of American home workshops.[53] Such weapons are markedly inferior to commercial firearms in that they are inaccurate and have a "life expectancy" of no more than a few hundred rounds.

At present, when the cheapest foreign import handgun provides reasonable reliability, target accuracy, and a life expectancy of 25,000 to 50,000 shots for $80.00 to $100.00, there is no market for pot metal handguns. But with handguns banned, it is reasonable to anticipate that, out of the millions who possess sufficient resources to do so, thousands of entrepreneurs will take advantage of the opportunity to produce pot metal weapons, at a few dollars cost to themselves, which can be sold on the black market for $60 to $75 to those who want them for protection or crime. However unsatisfactory such weapons might be for target shooters, they would suffice for self-defense or crime, activities which are normally carried on at point blank range and require only a few shots, if any.

It is sometimes suggested that a more viable prohibitory alternative would concentrate on the sale or possession of ammunition. B. Bruce-Briggs provides the following evaluation:

> Whereas firearms are easily manufactured and last indefinitely, modern ammunition requires sophisticated manufacturing facilities and has a shorter shelf life [20 to 30 years] . . . But a strategy directed against ammunition is also flawed. Hundreds of thousands of Americans "handload" ammunition at home from commercially purchased shells, powder, and bullets in order to

---

53. The 1981 catalog for Paladin Press (publishers of "The Action Library") offers the following titles and descriptions under the subject of "weapons": Bill Holmes' *Home Workshop Guns for Defense and Resistance*, vol. 2, *The Handgun* ("The complete home workshop guide to making your own handgun. Offered are two complete firearms designs, one for a semi- or full automatic. . . . In addition to explaining how each part and section of the gun is made, the subjects of heat treatment and blueing are discussed thoroughly. Holmes emphasizes the use of improvised materials and suggests many alternative workshop gun smithing tips." $8.00); *Automatic and Concealable Firearms Design Book*, vol. 1 ("Ten weapons are presented, seven of which are totally improvised." $12.00); *Automatic and Concealable Firearms Design Book*, vol. 2 ("Offers ten new firearms for the home gun smith or machinist." $12.00).

Cottage-manufactured firearms – ranging from the most primitive single shot "zip gun" to very sophisticated revolvers or semiautomatic handguns – have occasioned a substantial literature. See discussion in Hardy and Kates, "Handgun Availability," in Kates, ed., *Restricting Handguns*, pp. 130–31.

obtain the sort of load they desire. Shell cartridges last forever and there are untold billions in circulation. Lead and steel bullets can be made by anyone with a stove or a file. So it would be necessary to close off powder sales as well. Smokeless powder would be extremely difficult to make at home, but the old style black powder that fired weapons for 500 years can be manufactured by any kid with a chemistry set. Besides, any ammunition cut off would be preceded by long debate and bitter fight—during which time everyone would stock up. Also, thefts from the military, National Guard and police would continue to be a major source of ammunition.[54]

It should be noted that the proposal Bruce-Briggs is evaluating is one calling for the prohibition of *all* firearms and therefore *all* ammunition. If only handgun ammunition were banned, handloaders could continue getting smokeless powder by draining it out of rifle and shotgun cartridges. Moreover a demand for ammunition would simply produce a black market based on unlawful manufacture of it. John Kaplan notes that smokeless powder "is simpler to make than any of the illegal drugs being manufactured in the laboratories all over the United States. The difficulty of manufacturing ammunition lies somewhat closer to distilling liquor than to making PCP or amphetamines."[55]

BEYOND THE PROHIBITION ANALOGY

The analogy between a handgun ban and alcohol Prohibition is inherently limited. In some ways firearms are subject to different methods of detection than liquor, and the technology of detection has improved since the era of Prohibition.[56] Thus it has been proposed that police could be equipped with metal detectors such as

54. Bruce-Briggs, "Great American Gun War," p. 52.
55. John Kaplan, "Controlling Firearms," *Cleveland State University Law Review* 28 (1979): 1–28.
56. Additionally, opponents of handgun ownership may have available an argument about self-defense more persuasive than any of the arguments that temperance advocates used with drinkers. Sam Fields, spokesman for the National Coalition to Ban Handguns, emphasizes the self-defense superiority of the shotgun over handguns because it is more likely not only to stop, but actually to kill, an assailant. Derisively referring to incidents publicized by the National Rifle Association in which householders armed with handguns routed or captured robbers, he notes that, "A 12-gauge shotgun, on the other hand, would offer more defense while permanently ending the intruder's crime career." Fields, "Handgun Prohibition," p. 41. See also Sherrill, *Saturday Night Special*, p. 275. In contrast, no temperance advocate seems to have thought of arguing the superiority of substitutes like opium, morphine, or cocaine to alcohol.

are now encountered in airports.[57] Flying squads could suddenly descend upon strategically chosen neighborhoods, assemble the airport-like metal detector "door frames" while any pedestrians seen are rounded up and herded through the machines.

However appealing such a scheme may appear at first blush, there are substantial difficulties. Stepping through the door frame itself is not too time consuming. But if it registers metal, a protracted manual search must ensue. Based on the airport experience, in more than 95 percent of the cases the positive registered by the machine proves false; upon manual search the metal detected is found to consist of keys, coins, pens, pocket knives, and so forth, rather than a gun.[58] The cost of employing (or diverting from other duties) enough police officers to round up and hold citizens in lineups, direct them through machines, and detain and manually search those registered would be prohibitive.

Also, the constitutionality of this scheme is, at best, dubious. Courts have (not without difficulty) upheld the use of such machines at airports on the rationale that no one is forced to enter them; to do so is simply a condition that those who elect to travel by air voluntarily accept. Although courts have sometimes gone to considerable lengths to justify the constitutionality of searches for guns, they are unlikely to adopt a doctrine that anyone who steps out of his or her house is volunteering to be dragnetted into a line and forced through a metal detector. Finally, as a political matter it is unlikely that the American people would stand for being held in long lineups, and then subjected to manual searches, every time they leave home to go to work, to the market, or on some other errand. (Of course it is predictable that the flying squads' attentions would primarily concentrate upon neighborhoods whose racial, ethnic, and eco-

---

57. This and the other proposals discussed previously for detecting illegal handgun ownership are set out in Hardy and Chotiner, "Potentiality for Civil Liberties Violation," pp. 196–99, 206–09. Except as otherwise noted, all descriptive material has been derived from their treatment.

58. An additional value (or disadvantage, depending upon one's attitude towards expansion of police power vis-à-vis the citizenry) is that every false positive "provides the police a convenient excuse to search and question, which could uncover not only firearm offenses but a whole host of commodity type violations and other criminal activity as well." Hardy and Chotiner, "Potentiality for Civil Liberties Violations," p. 208. They cite the fact that 80 to 90 percent of arrests made in connection with airport metal detectors and manual searches were for possession of drugs, as well as arrests of illegal aliens and AWOL soldiers discovered through ID checks.

nomic characteristics minimized the capacity for effective political resistance.)

Moreover, the metal detector approach would only operate against the transportation of handguns by pedestrians. It would not remove guns from homes and other buildings where most homicides occur, nor would it prevent their transportation by automobile. One proposal to supplement the metal detector system is the payment of bounties for people to turn in their neighbors and relatives. David Hardy and Kenneth Chotiner note that, "a report to the Governor of Massachusetts strongly advocated a proposal to confiscate all handguns in the state, offering bounties as the lynch pin of the enforcement effort. The report went so far as to lay out guidelines: Informers might remain anonymous, giving code names or numbers. When a tip resulted in confiscation, an appropriate notice would be given, and the person giving the code would be paid."[59]

One is reminded of Pavel Morozov, a fourteen-year-old boy posthumously lionized by Stalin because he was murdered for having turned in his father as a violator of Soviet farm collectivization policies.[60] Beyond the philosophical objection is the practical one that such methods have already proven unavailing in other contexts. The strongly prohibitionist author of a Police Foundation study has suggested that gun laws be enforced by the methods used in marijuana cases.[61] But the amount of success such methods have had in the inherently far easier task of preventing access to marijuana speaks for itself.[62]

The Honorable Malcolm Wilkey, a federal appellate judge, has suggested that anti-gun laws would be enforceable but only if police were not burdened by the normal restraints on illegal search and seizure. Taken literally, this would allow police to break into and search any house, stop and search any person or vehicle randomly or at whim, without warrant or reasonable suspicion.[63] Judge Wilkey

59. Hardy and Chotiner, "Potentiality for Civil Liberties Violations," p. 207.

60. H. Smith, *The Russians* (New York: New York Times Book Co., 1976), p. 162.

61. Steven Brill, *Firearm Abuse: A Research and Policy Report* (Washington, D.C.: Police Foundation, 1977).

62. The continued buying and possession of marijuana, as of alcohol during Prohibition, by millions of consumers is easier to detect and/or interdict since it requires an infinite succession of purchases, unlike a handgun, which is a single purchase item. See discussion in text.

63. *Wall Street Journal*, 7 October 1977, p. 14. The subsequent killing of John Lennon brought forth a torrent of "ban the gun" editorials, which included some unusually specific

makes no attempt to defend the constitutionality of his proposal, frankly calling upon the Supreme Court to simply suspend the Fourth Amendment insofar as enforcing gun laws is concerned. But the Supreme Court is unlikely to follow this advice, however desirable its members might feel a handgun ban to be. Nor would whatever benefits a ban might confer outweigh the cost of abrogating constitutional restraints upon illegal police behavior.

Yet another proposal is to terrify the resisters into compliance by congressionally mandating a minimum of one year in prison (without probation or parole) for illegal handgun possession.[64] However theoretically fearsome, such a penalty scheme would be undercut by its patent impracticability. As gun ban opponents would quickly announce, if only 0.2 percent of the likely violators were to be convicted, they would fill up one sixth of the prison cells in the combined federal and all-state prison system.[65] This system is already so overcrowded that courts are enjoining the addition of new inmates as cruel and unusual punishment violative of the Eighth Amendment. Are one-sixth of the convicted felons in the United States going to be released in order to incarcerate 50,000 otherwise

---

suggestions as to how this should be enforced. See, for example, *Columbia* (Mo.) *Daily Tribune*, 22 December 1980, p. 6 ("unlimited search and seizure . . . the police will have to be given the right to frisk anyone for hidden guns at any time and any place."), Michael Killian, "Gun Control Requires That We All Face the Realities," *Chicago Tribune*, 14 December 1980.

64. Legislation mandating a year term for ownership of a handgun without a Sullivan Law permit was recently introduced at the behest of the Mayor and Police Commissioner of New York City; it failed after New York's Correction Services Commissioner testified that New York's prisons would not be able to house convicted violators.

65. For the purpose of making these calculations I am assuming the number of handguns to be 54,000,000 and the rate of likely violation of a ban to be 50 percent. Compare the 1975 DMI poll, in which 92 percent of the respondents (gun owners and non-gun owners alike) estimated that less than half of gun owners would comply with a ban. Bordua (Chapter 3) reports that 73 percent of the Illinois gun owners he surveyed in 1977 stated that they would not comply with a prohibition. Hardy and Chotiner ("Potentiality for Civil Liberties Violations," p. 201) suggest that noncompliance with firearms registration laws (which gun owners often view as a prelude to confiscation) provides a useful index to the proportion of handgun owners who would defy a national prohibition. They cite police estimates that two-thirds of the gun owners in Chicago have refused to comply with the 1968 Illinois registration requirements; statewide the estimate is 75 percent noncompliance. Cleveland authorities estimate noncompliance with a 1976 municipal registration ordinance at 88 percent. (But noncompliance, particularly with the local Cleveland ordinance, may reflect ignorance of the law's existence rather than defiance.)

law-abiding citizens who have been convicted of violating a handgun ban?[66]

Of course, to convict them, they must first be tried. Faced with a mandatory year sentence, the defendants will have every reason to demand a jury trial and to take advantage of all conceivable delays and appeals. A demand for jury trial by 0.2 percent (or even 0.02%) of the handgun ban violators would completely incapacitate the federal court system. Even if processing of all other criminal and civil cases were suspended, and the resources of every United States District Court devoted only to trying gun law cases, many such defendants would probably end up winning motions to dismiss for failure to meet the constitutional requirement of speedy trial.

The result is easily forseeable, particularly when the defendants will generally be highly sympathetic—secretaries, shopkeepers, the elderly—ordinary decent people who keep handguns because they are terrified and live or work in areas where the police cannot control violence.[67] Congress can require that judges send such people to prison—if they are convicted. But Congress cannot require juries to convict them. Neither can it prevent judges from inventing technicalities to dismiss the prosecutions. Nor can it prevent prosecutors from refusing to prosecute out of sympathy for the defendants, or because a conviction in a particular case is less likely to deter violation of the law than a highly publicized acquittal or judicial dismissal is to encourage violators.[68]

CONCLUSION

The foregoing analysis should not be misunderstood as suggesting that a ban would have no effect upon handgun ownership. If the purpose of the ban were simply to reduce total civilian handgun ownership, it would likely meet with substantial success. The up to 50 percent of owners who do not want a handgun for either crime or self-

---

66. An article in the *Los Angeles Times* (5 February 1982, p. 19) cites California Governor Edmund Brown to the effect that "courts in 39 other states have ordered a reduction in inmate populations or the improvement of overcrowded prisons." These remarks were made in urging approval of a $495 million bond issue for new prisons, Brown stating that 29,000 California convicts are "jammed" into cells built for 24,000 and that the Department of Corrections anticipates 45,000 prisoners by 1986.

67. Shields, "Two Judges Look at Gun Control," pp. 180–85.

68. Kaplan, "Controlling Firearms," p. 12.

defense might surrender theirs, particularly if, as is someti. gested, market value were to be paid for each gun surrendere would most people interested in handguns only for sport-colle. purposes subsequently evade the ban by acquiring handguns on t. black market.

But a ban that reduces handgun ownership serves no purpose unless it thereby reduces violence. To do this it would have to reach beyond the sport-collection user to disarm the person who keeps a gun loaded for for self-protection or crime. We may assume that some protection owners will voluntarily comply with the law, though they feel it deprives them of a tool necessary to their family's safety. But the critical question for the homicide-reductive value of a ban is not its effect upon the most law-abiding of the protection owners. Nor is the question even the lack of effect upon those protection owners who would disobey and rationalize that the ban was unconstitutional or otherwise illegitimate. The critical question is whether, and how, a handgun ban would impact on the 1 in 5,400 handgun owners who commit murder. This 0.018 percent must be assumed to be the least responsive of all handgun owners to law—particularly since independent evidence suggests that they are likely to have long prior histories of impulsive violence against those around them.[69]

To present a convincing case for homicide reduction, proponents must demonstrate that handgun prohibition would be enforceable as a practical matter against this 0.018 percent whose handgun ownership "causes" them to murder. Unfortunately, prohibition advocates have failed to address this issue. Indeed, even among those who hold that handgun availability "causes" murder, belief in the homicide-reductive effect of a ban seems to vary inversely to the amount of attention that each author gives to the issue of enforceability. Compare the optimism of Robert Drinan and J. R. Riley to the pessimistic discussions of Arych Neier, Donald Lunde, and Robert Sherrill.[70]

---

69. See note 24, *supra.*
70. Drinan, "Gun Control"; R.J. Riley, "Shooting to Kill"; Arych Neier, *Crime and Punishment: A Radical Solution* (New York: Stein and Day, 1975); Donald T. Lunde, *Murder and Madness* (San Francisco: San Francisco Book Company, 1976); Sherrill, *Saturday Night Special*, pp. 271-74.

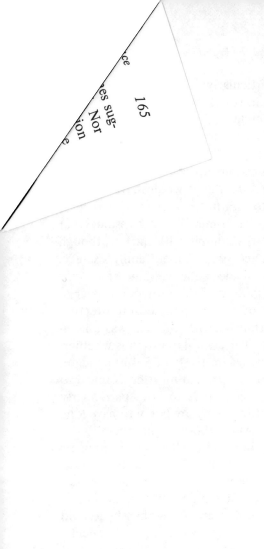

165

ce

es sug-

Nor

ion

Chapter 7

HANDGUN-ONLY GUN CONTROL
A Policy Disaster in the Making

Gary Kleck

Until the late 1960s debates over gun control generally concerned firearms of all kinds, without distinguishing between handguns and other guns.[1] However, around 1968, debate and policy suggestions for dealing with gun crime began to focus more and more exclusively on handguns.[2] In fact, recent gun control advocates often take great pains to make clear that they are not interested in restricting long guns (shotguns and rifles) and that hunters and sport shooters who use long guns therefore have nothing to fear from them.[3] Dozens of influential national organizations have come out in favor of banning, with limited exceptions, the private ownership of handguns only. These include the U.S. Conference of Mayors, Common Cause, the NAACP, the Committee for Economic Development, National Alliance for Safer Cities, National Council of Jewish Women, Unitarian Universalist Association, as well as organizations devoted exclusively

1. U.S. Congress, *Hearings Before the Subcommittee to Investigate Juvenile Delinquency of the Committee on the Judiciary, U.S. Senate, 89th Congress, Pursuant to S. Res. 53,* testimony June 8, July 1 (Washington, D.C.: GPO, 1965).

2. For a sampling of proposed federal legislation focusing exclusively on handguns, including at least three bills that would prohibit nearly all private ownership of handguns (HR 40, HR 2313, and S 2153), see Joseph D. Alviani and William R. Drake, *Handgun Control . . . Issues and Alternatives* (Washington, D.C.: U.S. Conference of Mayors, 1975), pp. 55–57.

3. Sam Fields, "Handgun Prohibition and Social Necessity," *St. Louis University Law Journal* 23 (1979): 35–36.

to handgun control, such as the National Coalition to Ban Handguns, National Council to Control Handgun, and dozens of others.[4]

Somewhat less extreme proposals severely limit legal ownership of handguns while applying only minimal restrictions to long gun ownership. For example, in perhaps the most influential official report ever done on gun control, the Task Force on Firearms of the 1968 National Commission on the Causes and Prevention of Violence recommended a restrictive licensing system for handguns combined with a permissive one for rifles and shotguns. Under this arrangement, nearly everyone would be denied handgun licenses except for the small minority who could show some special need for a handgun (household protection would not constitute such a need), while virtually everyone would be allowed licenses for long guns, except for those in prohibited classes, such as persons convicted of, or under indictment for, a violent crime, fugitives, addicts, mental incompetents, and minors.[5] Since only about one half of persons who commit homicides have prior convictions of any kind, this means that about half of all potential killers (at least among nonaddicted mentally competent adults) would qualify for legal long gun ownership but not for legal handgun ownership under the Task Force proposal.[6]

This shift to an emphasis on handguns appears to have occurred for several reasons. First, there was a growing recognition of the much greater frequency with which handguns were used in crimes relative to long guns, a predominance that increased through the 1960s and 1970s.[7] Second, there were several political assassinations and attempted assassinations committed with handguns during this period, including the killing of Senator Robert F. Kennedy and the attacks on President Gerald Ford and on Presidential candidate George Wallace. Third, there was a less dramatic but equally significant recognition of the political and tactical advantages of generally ignoring long guns and thereby blunting criticism that gun control

4. For policy statements of these organizations, see U.S. Congress, *Hearings on Firearms Legislation Before the Subcommittee on Crime of the Committee on the Judiciary, House of Representatives, 94th Congress* (Washington, D.C.: GPO, 1975), pp. 714–18; Alviani and Drake, *Handgun Control*, pp. 48–54.

5. George D. Newton and Franklin Zimring, *Firearms and Violence in American Life* (Washington, D.C.: GPO, 1969), pp. 143–45.

6. Kleck and Bordua, *infra.*

7. For example, in 1964, about 39 percent of homicides were committed with handguns and 55 percent were committed with guns of any type. By 1974, these figures had risen to 54 percent and 68 percent, respectively.

efforts were aimed at law-abiding hunters and sport shooters as much as criminal users of firearms. When gun control was directed at all types of firearms, opposition to the proposed control measures did not just come from organizations that were philosophically opposed to all interference with private ownership of firearms, like the National Rifle Association (NRA). The transcripts of congressional hearings are filled with testimony from hunting, conservation, and sport shooting associations opposed to one or another provision of laws directed at long guns as well as handguns (U.S. Congress 1965, 1967). By focusing only on handguns, gun control supporters could plausibly contend that their proposals did not involve any significant interference in the legitimate sporting use of firearms, thereby undercutting the basis for at least some of the political opposition to gun control.

Critics of the control measures directed at all types of firearms used to argue that if guns were restricted, the same people who would have killed with guns would use some other weapon to achieve the same end, and thus no lives would be saved. Supporters of gun control would then counterargue that the weapons likely to be substituted, such as knives or clubs, were less deadly, and therefore a smaller fraction of those assaulted would die. Thus lives would be saved, even if the same number of assaults occurred, since most assaulters, it was argued, did not have a single-minded intention to kill regardless of how difficult it might be to do so.[8]

However, the shift in emphasis to handgun-only control measures has led to a new substitution issue. Senator Thomas Dodd, Don Kates, and others have suggested that when and where handguns become more difficult to obtain, long guns will be substituted.[9] This substitution issue is radically different from the earlier one because the weapons that would be substituted are *more* deadly than the prohibited weapons, not less, and it is therefore conceivable than handgun restrictions could *increase* the number of homicide deaths.[10]

8. Franklin E. Zimring, "Is Gun Control Likely to Reduce Violent Killings?" *University of Chicago Law Review* 35 (Summer 1968): 721–37.

9. U.S. Congress, *Juvenile Delinquency*, 1965, p. 454; idem., *Hearings Before the Subcommittee to Investigate Juvenile Delinquency of the Committee on the Judiciary, U.S. Senate, 91st Congress, Pursuant to S. Res. 48*, testimony July 29 (Washington, D.C.: GPO, 1969), pp. 161–65; Don B. Kates, Jr., "Reflections on the Relevancy of Gun Control," *Law and Liberty* 3 (Summer 1976): 1–3.

10. See David T. Hardy and John Stompoly, "Of Arms and the Law," *Chicago-Kent Review 51* (Summer 1974): 62–114; Don B. Kates, Jr. and Mark K. Benenson, "Handgun

This simple but crucial point of more deadly alternative weapons has apparently not been recognized by some advocates of handgun control: "handguns are more dangerous weapons—they are more likely to result in death or serious injury than any other weapon."[11]

Whether substitution of long guns for handguns would produce an increase or decrease in the homicide rate would be dependent on two factors: how much deadlier long guns are compared to handguns and how large a fraction of assaulters who otherwise would have used handguns, had they been available, would substitute long guns. Handgun control advocates have tended to agree that long guns are deadlier, but they also argue that there would be little substitution.[12] However, to the best of my knowledge, none of them has suggested that there would be *no* substitution whatsoever. Thus in defending handgun-only control policies, their implicit line of reasoning seems to be that although some substitution would occur, it would be small enough so that a net decrease in homicide could still occur despite the greater fatality rate of those assaults involving substituted long guns.

In the influential Task Force report on firearms to the National Violence Commission, Newton and Zimring asserted that a national system of restrictive handgun licensing "would not appear to risk a massive shift to the use of long guns in crime."[13] The authors did not provide any evidence for this claim, nor did they define "massive." However, the day after the task force report was released, Zimring was vigorously interrogated regarding the substitution issue by Senator Thomas Dodd in Senate hearings on firearms legislation. Zimring responded, "My guess would be that no more than a third of handgun violent assaults in the city would be supplanted with long gun crime."[14] He apparently considered one third to be a small substitution fraction, and he clearly believed that handgun restrictions would be successful even with that much substitution. However, in a brief analysis, Kates and Benenson asserted that even if only 30 percent substituted long guns for handguns, and the rest substituted

---

Prohibition and Homicide: A Plausible Theory Meets the Intractible Facts," in Don B. Kates, Jr., ed., *Restricting Handguns: The Liberal Skeptics Speak Out* (Croton-on-Hudson, N.Y.: North River Press, 1979), pp. 109–17.

11. Testimony of G. Marie Wilt in U.S. Congress, *Hearings on Firearms Legislation*, p. 1020.

12. Fields, "Handgun Prohibition and Social Necessity."

13. Newton and Zimring, *Firearms and Violence in American Life.*

14. U.S. Congress, *Juvenile Delinquency*, 1969, p. 163.

knives, there would still be a substantial increase in homicides, assuming that long guns are four times as deadly as handguns.[15]

This chapter will follow up on their line of analysis, attempting to specify more precisely the trade-off relationship between the relative deadliness of handguns and long guns on the one hand, and the fraction substituting long guns (the "substitution fraction") on the other. It will also attempt to systematically determine, purely on the basis of technical characteristics of the weapons and ammunition involved, the relative deadliness of the two weapon types, and to examine how extensive substitution is likely to be, on the basis of the circumstances of homicidal assaults and the motives of handgun owners. The analysis will assume that handgun-only control policies can somehow remove and keep handguns from violence-prone people, that is, those who will commit a serious assault sometime in the future. Of course, if handguns *cannot* be denied to the violence-prone segment of the population, then the policy is clearly worthless for reducing homicide. We will be evaluating handgun control policies under the extreme assumption that they will be *completely* effective in denying handguns to the violence-prone, however this might be achieved. The discussion will be applicable to any public policy aimed at restricting only handguns, from a licensing system to total prohibition.

THE RELATIONSHIP BETWEEN FATALITY RATES AND THE SUBSTITUTION FRACTION

The first step in determining the relationship between the substitution fraction and the relative deadliness of long guns and handguns will be to compute fatality rates of different weapon types. However, as will be made clear in a later section, fatality rates cannot be used to establish the relative deadliness of weapons independent of the characteristics of the persons who use them. Therefore our alternative strategy will be to compute an approximate handgun fatality rate, then assume the long gun fatality rate to be various multiples (the "deadliness ratio") of the handgun rate. In short, we will allow the deadliness ratio to take on various assumed values and then deter-

15. Kates and Benenson, "Handgun Prohibition and Homicide," pp. 110–11.

mine what substitution fraction would have to be attained in order to achieve a saving in lives.

Table 7-1 contains the data used to estimate assault fatality rates (AFR), that is, the fraction of assaults with weapons of a given type that result in death. Two data sources were used. The F.B.I's *Uniform Crime Reports* (UCRs) provide data on fatal assaults (homicides) by weapon type, making the distinction between handguns and long guns. Although the UCRs contain data on aggravated assaults, they do not count the number of simple (nonaggravated) assaults and count only those aggravated assaults reported to the police. Therefore, a second source of data is used which counts both aggravated and simple assaults, both those reported to the police and those not reported: the National Crime Surveys (NCS) of victimization. All data refer to the United States for 1977, the latest year for which data were available from both sources. Unfortunately neither data source distinguishes long gun assaults from handgun assaults, and it is therefore impossible to directly compute fatality rates by gun type. In order to compute an approximate handgun fatality rate, we need to know the number of nonfatal handgun assaults and thus must somehow determine what fraction of the nonfatal gun assaults counted in victimization data were handgun assaults.

Table 7-1 indicates that the AFR for all gun attacks is 0.02557. The technical analysis later in the chapter will make it clear that long guns are at least several times deadlier than handguns, and thus the handgun AFR must be smaller than the long gun AFR. Since all gun attacks are either handgun attacks or long gun attacks, this means that the handgun AFR and long gun AFR must be such that in combination they produce a total gun AFR of 0.02557. Therefore we must allocate the estimated 455,356 nonfatal gun assaults so that the resulting long gun AFR is several times larger than the handgun AFR and the handgun AFR is smaller than 0.02557.

Of *fatal* gun assaults (gun homicides), we know that 76 percent were committed with handguns

$$\left(\frac{0.48}{0.48 + 0.15} = 0.76 \right).$$

If handguns are less deadly than long guns, they would predominate among *non*fatal gun assaults to an even greater extent. Therefore, let us assume that 90 percent of the nonfatal gun assaults were handgun

Table 7-1. Data for Computation of Assault Fatality Rates (AFRs) by Weapon Type (U.S., 1977).

	Total	With Weapon	Gun	Handgun	Long Gun	Nongun
Homicides	19,120	94.5%/18,068	62.5%/11,950	48%/9,105	15%/2,845	37.5%/6,118
Aggravated Assaults	1,738,000	93.4%/1,623,292	26.2%/455,356	n.a.	n.a.	1,282,644
Simple Assaults[a]	2,926,000	—	—	—	—	2,926,000
Total Assaults (1 + 2 + 3)	4,683,120	1,293,389	467,306	n.a.	n.a.	4,214,762
AFR = (1)/(4)	0.00408	0.01101	0.02557	n.a.	n.a.	0.00145

a. Under the victimization survey classification scheme, no simple assaults involve a weapon, since these assaults are all classified as aggravated. Simple assaults also include attempted assaults without a weapon, while aggravated assaults include attempted assaults with a weapon, whether or not any injury was actually inflicted.

Sources: Homicide data: U.S. Federal Bureau of Investigation, *Crime in the United States 1977* (Washington, D.C.: U.S. Government Printing Office, 1978): 8, 10.

Assault data: U.S. National Criminal Justice Information and Statistics Service, *Criminal Victimization in the United States* (Washington, D.C.: U.S. Government Printing Office, 1979): 20, 52, 53.

assaults, giving us 409,820 handgun and 45,536 long gun nonfatal assaults. Using these figures and the homicide figures by gun type in Table 7-1, we compute AFRs of 0.05880 for long guns and 0.02173 for handguns, satisfying the criteria we have mentioned. Because the assumption regarding the distribution of nonfatal gun assaults by gun type is debatable, it should be emphasized here that the assumption is not crucial regarding the estimated relative deadliness of the two gun types. It was only made in order to obtain an approximate hand-gun AFR. We will later allow the relative deadliness ratio to take on a wide range of plausible values, allowing the long gun AFR to be from 1.5 to 10 times as high as the handgun AFR.

There were 9,105 fatal handgun assaults in 1977, and we have estimated that there were 409,820 nonfatal handgun assaults, for a total of 418,925 handgun assaults. Let us make the optimistic assumption that a handgun-only control policy could be devised which would be completely effective in removing handguns from the hands of persons who otherwise would have used them in assaults. Since handgun control supporters acknowledge that control measures would not reduce the motivation or desire to kill or assault, we will first assume that the number of assaults would be unaffected.[16] This assumption will later be relaxed somewhat. However, lives could be saved by the control policy if less deadly weapons were used, so that the average AFR was reduced for those assaults which still occurred. The same assaults that would have occurred without the policy would still occur with it, but with different weapons involved. Some would involve hands or feet, or knives, or other weapons presumably less deadly than handguns, while others would involve shotguns or rifles, weapons more deadly than handguns. Thus some fraction of the assaults (X) would be subject to the long gun AFR, while the rest (1 – X) would be subject to the nongun AFR, computed to be 0.00145 in Table 7-1.

In order for the hypothetical handgun control policy to be a success, the resulting number of homicides would have to be lower than the number that actually resulted from handgun assaults in 1977 (the year from which our data are drawn), 9,105. To express the relationship between the substitution fraction X and the long gun-to-handgun deadliness ratio Y, we can write an equation that would obtain if the

---

16. For example, Lynn Curtis, *Criminal Violence: National Patterns and Behavior* (Lexington, Mass.: Lexington Books, 1974), p. 169. See also Kleck and Bordua, *infra*, on "weapons effect."

handgun control policy produced neither more homicides nor fewer, but rather the same number that occurred without the policy. If the estimated handgun AFR is 0.02173, then the long gun AFR would be (0.02173 times Y), and it would apply to (418,925 times X) assaults where a long gun was substituted. The nongun AFR of 0.00145 would apply to the rest of the assaults where knives, fists, and so forth, would be substituted for handguns, that is (418,925 times (1 — X)) assaults:

$$0.02173 \text{ Y } (418,925 \text{ X}) + 0.00145 (418,925 (1 - \text{X})) = 9,105$$

This reduces to:

$$X = \frac{8,497.56}{9,103.24 \text{ Y} - 607.44} \tag{1}$$

Now we can make various assumptions about how deadly long guns are compared to handguns (the ratio Y) and compute how large the long gun substitution fraction could be without producing a gain in homicides. For example, if we assume long guns are four times deadlier than handguns, we substitute four for Y, and compute X to be 0.2373. Thus, if the assumed deadliness ratio is accurate, the handgun-only control policy would save lives only if fewer than 23.73 percent of those violence-prone persons who otherwise would have used handguns substitute long guns in the assaults.

However, not everyone would agree that long guns are four times deadlier than handguns. Therefore Table 7–2 shows the resulting

Table 7–2. The Relationship Between the Substitution Fraction X and the Relative Deadliness Ratio Y.

Assumed Value of Y	Computed X	Computed X'
1.5	0.6513	0.8839
2.0	0.4828	0.6553
3.0	0.3182	0.4319
4.0	0.2373	0.3221
5.0	0.1892	0.2568
6.0	0.1573	0.2135
8.0	0.1177	0.1597
10.0	0.0940	0.1275

Note: X' is the same as X, but assuming that handgun controls could produce a 25 percent reduction among assaults that otherwise would have been handgun assaults.

values for X computed using various other assumed values of Y. The results indicate that if Zimring is right in expecting as much as one third substitution in assaults (X = 0.333), then even if long guns were only three times as deadly as handguns (Y = 3.0), handgun-only restrictions would result in an *increase* in homicides! However, we do not know what the deadliness ratio is, nor can we know for sure how much substitution of long guns is likely to occur, since Zimring was only guessing. Table 7-2 indicates that if the deadliness ratio or the substitution fraction is low enough, handgun-only restrictions could still save lives (e.g. if Y is only 2.0 and X remained below 0.4828). Therefore, it is necessary to determine plausible values of X and Y.

Let us now relax the assumption that handgun-only controls would only affect choice of weapon, but not the overall rate of assaults. Suppose that among assaults which, under noncontrol circumstances, would have involved handguns, 25 percent would not occur under control conditions. This could conceivably occur because some potential offenders would not be bold enough or strong enough to assault another person without a gun of some kind, yet would also be unable to substitute a long gun. For example, in many assaults which occur impulsively in public places, in order to use a gun the offender would have had to have brought it into the situation as a matter of daily routine, a difficult and unlikely practice with a long gun, even a sawed-off one. If a 25 percent reduction occurred, equation (1) would be modified by substituting 314,194 (75 percent of the original number of handgun assaults) for 418,925, and the equation would reduce to:

$$X' = \frac{8,649.19}{6,827.43 \, Y - 455.581} \tag{2}$$

where X' is the substitution fraction assuming a 25 percent reduction in assaults. The computed values of X' are shown in Table 7-2. The reader can see that the substitution fraction figures increase somewhat over X. For example, under this optimistic assumption of assault reductions, and assuming long guns are only three times as deadly as handguns, a handgun-only control policy would still reduce homicides only if the substitution fraction could be kept under 0.4319.

THE RELATIVE DEADLINESS OF HANDGUNS AND LONG GUNS

One way to compare the deadliness of different weapons is to compare the fractions of assaults of each kind that result in death, that is, to compare AFRs. Indeed this was essentially the procedure used by other researchers in the past in comparing guns and knives.[17] It is a misleading technique. Fatality rates not only reflect the deadliness of the weapons but also the intentions and intensity of motivation of the users of the weapons. It seems obvious that people who are more serious about inflicting serious, even fatal injury are likelier to use more deadly weapons. This is confirmed by analysis of Zimring's own data.[18]

This evidence makes it amply clear that it would be pointless to compare actual observed assault fatality rates of handguns and long guns in order to determine relative deadliness, even if adequate data were available for such an effort, since the fatality rates are not just the result of the deadliness of the weapons themselves. What is needed instead is a systematic evaluation of the characteristics of the firearms themselves and their ammunition in order to determine relative deadliness on a technical basis, independent of the intentions and strength of motivation of the users of weapons.

A concept closely related to deadliness has been developed for military and law enforcement purposes to determine the relative merits of different types of handguns. This is the concept of "stopping power," a measure of the likelihood of a single shot from a given weapon immediately incapacitating a human attacker with a solid torso hit. While not identical to the likelihood of killing a person, stopping power of a weapon should clearly be positively correlated with deadliness, possibly highly correlated, and should be adequate for our comparative purposes.

Measures of stopping power have been developed using formulae that take into account factors such as muzzle velocity, cross-sectional area, mass, and shape of the bullet used in a given weapon. The formulae have not been used to compare handguns with long guns but rather to compare different handgun cartridges with each other. However, with some modification, the same procedures can be applied to long guns.

17. For example, Zimring, "Is Gun Control Likely to Reduce Violent Killings?"
18. See Kleck and Bordua, *infra.*

At least four different measures of stopping power have been developed. We will be applying the results of Hatcher's work.[19] The other studies' results cannot be used for comparing handgun ammunition with long gun ammunition since they did not produce a mathematical formula that summarizes deadliness or stopping power based on characteristics of the ammunition. Rather, they only made empirical measures of the loss of kinetic energy or the size of simulated wound cavities produced when specific handgun cartridges were fired into blocks of ballistic gelatin.[20]

Hatcher's relative stopping power (RSP) was measured by a formula which reduces to:

$$RSP = \frac{mVAs}{450}$$

where   m   = bullet weight (in grains)

            V   = muzzle velocity (feet per second)

            A   = cross-sectional area of bullet (square inches)

            s   = coefficient of shape and material of bullet [21]

                                                                             (3)

The coefficient s ranges from 0.9 to 1.25, and reflects the differing degrees of damage inflicted by different shapes of bullets and the different materials of which they are made. (A bullet is the projectile part of a cartridge, the part actually fired from a gun barrel, not the whole cartridge.) For example, a flat bullet inflicts more damage than a rounded one, and a pointed bullet generally produces less damage than either of the other two.

For any given gun type, there are many different calibers (generally, the inside diameter of the barrel, and therefore approximately the diameter of the cartridge and its bullet), and for each caliber (or gauge, for shotguns), there are many different kinds of ammunition,

19. Julian S. Hatcher, *Textbook of Pistols and Revolvers* (Marines, Onslow County, N.C.: Small Arms Technical Publishing, 1935).

20. The other three are Vincent J.M. Di Maio et al., "A Comparison of the Wounding Effects of Commercially Available Handgun Ammunition Suitable for Police Use," *FBI Law Enforcement Bulletin* 43 (December 1974): 3–8; and idem., "The Effectiveness of Snub-Nose Revolvers and Small Automatic Pistols," *FBI Law Enforcement Bulletin 44* (June 1975): 10–13; R.C. Dobbyn et al., *An Evaluation of Police Handgun Ammunition: Summary Report* (Washington, D.C.: GPO, 1975); and Caroll E. Peters, *Defensive Handgun Effectiveness* (Manchester, Tenn.: Author, 1977).

21. Peters, *Defensive Handgun Effectiveness*, p. 25.

differing somewhat in weight, amount of powder, and shape of bullet or other projectile. In the following analysis, the practice has been to use data on typical, very common cartridges or shotshells for each weapon type and caliber. Furthermore, in order to obtain a conservative estimate of the long gun-to-handgun deadliness ratio, whenever there was more than one type of ammunition for a given caliber and gun type, the most powerful one was chosen for handguns and the least powerful one for long guns.

Table 7-3 displays the data used to compute RSP values for handguns. These values range from 3.9 for the .22 caliber cartridge, to 142.3 for the .44 magnum. Since we want to know the average stopping power of the handguns that are used in assaults, we computed an average for all calibers by weighting each cartridge's RSP by the fraction of handgun assaults that involve that caliber, based on Zimring's data on assaults reported to the Chicago police in 1970.[22] The sum of these weighted RSPs is the weighted average RSP for handguns, 19.474. Table 7-1 helps explain why the fatality rate of handgun assaults is as low as it is. Small caliber weapons, .32 caliber and below, accounted for 67 percent of the handgun assaults. Only 3 percent of the assaults were committed with large caliber (.357 and up) handguns. Legislation designed to limit availability of cheap, small caliber "Saturday Night Specials" could change this situation, causing a substitution of larger caliber handguns where these are left relatively unregulated and thereby producing an "upgrading" of weaponry parallel to the substitution of long guns for handguns where handguns in general are restricted.

There are dozens of different calibers of rifles and rifle cartridges, and for each caliber there are many different varieties of cartridge, with different shapes and weights of bullets and different muzzle velocities. This would make the computation of RSPs extremely arduous if we attempted to cover all of them. However, it is impossible to know in what fraction of assaults each gun-cartridge type would be used as a substitute for handguns. Therefore, since we cannot compute a weighted average RSP as we did with handguns, we computed RSPs for selected cartridges, including a very weak one, an extremely powerful one, and some common intermediate ones.

---

22. See Table 6 in Franklin E. Zimring, "The Medium is the Message: Firearm Caliber as a Determinant of Death from Assault," *Journal of Legal Studies* 1 (January 1972): 97–123.

Table 7-3.   Relative Stopping Power (RSP) of Handguns.

Caliber	Type[a]	m Bullet Weight (grains)	V Muzzle Velocity (ft./sec.)	A Bore Area (sq. in.)	s Coefficient of Shape, Material	RSP	Proportion Used in Gun Assaults	RSP Times Proportion
.22	Long rifle	40	1125	.039	1.00	3.9	.38	1.482
.25	ACP	50	810	.049	0.90	3.9	.13	0.507
.32	.32–20	100	1030	.076	1.10	19.0	.16	3.040
.38	S & W sp.	158	1090	.102	1.00	38.8	.30	11.640
.357	Magnum	158	1410	.102	1.10	55.2 }		
.44	Keith semi-wadcutter	240	1250	.146	1.25	142.3 }	.03	2.805[b]
.45	ACP	230	850	.159	0.90	82.9 }		
							Sum =	19.474

a. See Cooper (1979: 51) for details.

b. Because Zimring's data do not distinguish between different large caliber handguns, we have averaged the RSPs for .357, .44, and .45 cartridges and multiplied this average (93.5) times the combined proportion .03.

Sources: Ammunition data: Jeff Cooper, *Jeff Cooper on Handguns* (Los Angeles: Peterson, 1979): 51.
Gun use in assaults: Franklin E. Zimring, "The Medium is the Message: Firearm Caliber as a Determinant of Death from Assault," *Journal of Legal Studies* (January 1972): 103.

The smallest of all common rifle cartridges is the .22 caliber. The example in Table 7-4 has an RSP of 10.2, even smaller than the weighted average for handgun cartridges, while the .223 caliber has an RSP of 12.4. On the other hand, the largest cartridge in Table 7-4, the .458 big game cartridge, has an RSP of 312.4, more than sixteen times as high as the handgun average. The other cartridges, very common middle caliber examples, have RSPs of 27.5, 35.4, 46.9, and 62.3; they are thus about one and a half to three times as powerful as handgun cartridges. In computing rifle RSP values, the coefficient of shape and material of the bullet (s) was assumed to be 0.8 in all cases. Rifle bullets are generally more pointed than handgun bullets, decreasing their stopping power. Since this is a smaller s value than for any handgun, the assumption is again a conservative one, in that it tends to minimize the estimated deadliness of long guns relative to handguns. The relative deadliness of rifles is also underestimated for another reason. If a bullet tumbles end over end as it enters a human body, a longer bullet will produce a larger wound cavity and be more likely to cause death. Since rifle bullets are longer than handgun bullets, this means we have not taken into account a source of greater rifle deadliness and thereby contributed to underestimating the deadliness ratio.

These particular cartridge calibers were chosen for the analysis because they are the most common calibers, as indicated by the number of varieties that appear in the *Shooter's Bible* catalog.[23] We cannot know which of these are most likely to be substituted for handguns when such substitution occurs, but if gun acquisition is at all rational, it would be reasonable to expect that both those gun owners who want guns for self-defense and those who intend to use them for criminal purposes would choose the larger caliber guns, since these are obviously more powerful and appropriate. This is especially true when one considers the types of weapons recommended for home defense by experts writing on the subject in the popular gun magazines; the deadlier types of long guns are those that are recommended. For example, in perhaps the most widely read guide to home defense guns, all but one of four experts recommended 12 gauge shotguns for home defense, and two of these three specifically recommended loading them with buckshot, the deadliest type of shotshell load.[24]

23. Robert F. Scott, *Shooter's Bible* (South Hackensack, N.J.: Stoeger, 1980).

24. Garry James, *Guns and Ammo Guide to Guns for Home Defense* (Los Angeles; Peterson, 1975), pp. 43–53.

Table 7-4. Relative Stopping Power (RSP) of Rifles.

Caliber	Type	m	V	A	s	RSP
22	Hornet Super-X soft point	45	2690	.038	.8	10.2
223	Remington Super-X pointed soft point	55	3240	.039	.8	12.4
243	Win. Super-X	80	3420	.046	.8	22.6
270	Win. Super-X pointed soft point	100	3480	.057	.8	35.4
7 mm	Remington Mag. Super-X power-point soft point	125	3310	.059	.8	43.9
30	30 Carbine hollow soft point	110	1990	.071	.8	27.5
300	Win. Mag. Super-X pointed soft point	150	3290	.071	.8	62.3
30–30	Win. Super-X open point expanding	150	2390	.071	.8	45.1
30–06	Springfield Super-X pointed soft point	110	3380	.071	.8	46.9
303	Savage Super-X silvertip expanding	190	1940	.072	.8	47.3
308	Win. Super-X pointed soft point	110	3280	.075	.8	47.8
338	Win. Mag. Super-X power-point soft point	200	2960	.090	.8	94.7
458	Win. Mag. Super-X	500	2120	.165	.8	310.9

All cartridges are Winchester-Western center fire rifle cartridges.

Source: Robert F. Scott, *Shooter's Bible*, 1980 ed. (South Hackensack, N.J.: Stoeger, 1979) 504–506.

The method for computing RSPs for shotguns is somewhat different from that for handguns and rifles. In contrast to the latter weapons, the shotgun usually fires a shotshell, which typically contains anywhere from fifteen to several hundred small pellets. Our modified procedure assumes that the total RSP of a shotshell would simply be the RSP for a single pellet, multiplied by the number of pellets in the shotshell.[25] Shotguns can also fire rifled slugs, which are heavy single projectiles that offer greater accuracy than shotshells. The data for computation of RSPs of shotshells and rifled slugs are contained in Table 7–5.

The smallest common gauge (an indicator of shotgun barrel diameter) shotgun is the .410 gauge, and the smallest common shot size is number 9 birdshot. The computed RSP for the .410 gauge shotshell with number 9 shot is 3.8, smaller than that of the .32 caliber handgun. On the other hand, a big 12 gauge shotgun shell with the largest size pellets, 00 ("double ought") buckshot, has an RSP of 185.8, more than nine times as high as the handgun average. Likewise, a 12 gauge shotgun loaded with number 1 pellets has an RSP more than six times the handgun average. A middle size gauge (12), loaded with a typical load (number 5 shot) for shooting common game like ducks, squirrels, and rabbits, has an RSP of 20.8, about the same as the handgun average. The rifled slugs, even for the smallest shotguns, have very large RSPs, anywhere from two and a half to twenty-nine times as high as the handgun average. Once again, how much deadlier we expect substituted long guns to be, compared to handguns, depends on which long guns we consider. The most common shotshells used for hunting yield RSPs about the same as the handgun RSP. However, the most common hunting load is not likely to be the most common load used for defensive or criminal purposes, and it is for the latter two reasons that handgun assaulters have handguns. As with rifles, it is highly probable that the more powerful shotgun loads are more likely to be substituted for handguns by potential assaulters, when substitution occurs.

There is little published information on specific types of long guns used in assaults. The only detailed published data I know of were

---

25. In computing RSP values for shotgun pellets and rifled slugs, an s value of 1.0 has been assumed in all cases, since these are generally rounded projectiles and 1 is the value Hatcher assigned to round-nose handgun bullets. See Peters, *Defensive Handgun Effecitveness*, p. 25.

Table 7-5. Relative Stopping Power (RSP) of Shotguns.

				Shotshells						RSP	
Gauge	Shot Size	Weight of Shot (oz.)	Number of Pellets	m Weight per Pellet (grains)	Pellet Diameter (inches)	V Muzzle Velocity (ft./sec.)	s	A		Each Pellet	Total, Shotshell
.410	9	11/16	402	0.7482	.08	1135	1	.0050		0.0094	3.8
20	6	3/4	169	1.9416	.11	1210	1	.0095		0.0496	8.4
16	4	1 1/8	152	3.2381	.13	1185	1	.0133		0.1132	17.2
12	5	1 1/2	255	2.5735	.12	1260[a]	1	.0113		0.0815	20.8
12	1 Buck	1.46	16	40.0000	.30	1260[a]	1	.0707		7.9168	126.7
12	00 Buck	1.85	15	53.8462	.33	1210[a]	1	.0855		12.3836	185.8

Rifled Slugs

Gauge	Weight (oz.)	Diameter	m Weight (grains)	V	A	RSP
20	5/8	.615	273.4375	1600	.2971	288.8
16	4/5	.662	350.0000	1600	.3442	428.3
12	7/8	.729	382.8125	1600	.4174	568.1

All shotgun ammunition is Winchester Western.

a. Estimates based on figures for 12 gauge shotshells with smaller pellets but similar total shot weight, from Wallack (1977: 158).

Sources: Robert F. Scott, *Shooter's Bible*, 1980 ed. (South Hackensack, N.J.: Stoeger, 1979): 477, 481, 482. L. R. Wallack, *American Shotgun Design and Performance* (New York: Winchester, 1977): 109, 157, 158.

drawn from 970 Chicago homicide cases in 1974.[26] Among killings committed with long guns of known caliber or gauge, 56 percent involved 12 gauge shotguns, 8 percent lesser gauge shotguns, 24 percent .22 caliber rifles, and 12 percent middle caliber rifles (30, 30-30, or 303 caliber). Thus, the deadliest variety of long gun predominates, although this was partially counterbalanced by the substantial minority of cases which involved small caliber rifles. Let us assume that the persons substituting long guns where handguns are legally restricted would use the same long gun types, in roughly the same proportions, as the Chicago homicide sample. Then, based on these data and the corresponding RSP values in Tables 7-4 and 7-5, it would be reasonable to expect the long gun-to-handgun deadliness ratio to be about three or four.

None of this technical analysis of the deadliness of different types of firearms takes into account the relative accuracy of handguns and long guns. All firearms authorities agree long guns are more accurate than handguns, although the difference has not been precisely quantified. This suggests that a smaller percentage of shots fired by persons armed with handguns will strike their target than shots fired by long gun assaulters. The difference in accuracy will undoubtedly be less significant at the short ranges at which gun assaults usually occur than at typical hunting or target-shooting distances. But even at short ranges there is considerable room for increases in accuracy, since handgun shooting can be very inaccurate. Even among presumably trained police officers, stories of repeated misses with handguns at short range in stressful situations are not rare.[27] This is not ordinarily due to deficiencies of the gun in hitting what it is pointed at (intrinsic accuracy) but rather to deficiencies in the ability of the shooter to accurately point a short-barrelled gun (practical accuracy), especially in stressful situations.[28] Thus, once again our estimation of the relative deadliness of long guns and handguns is a conservative one in that it does not take account of the higher percentage of long gun shots that will hit their targets, especially in vital areas, compared to handgun shots.

26. U.S. Congress, *Hearings on Firearms Legislation*, p. 826.
27. John Van Maanen, "Beyond Account: The Personal Impact of Police Shootings," *The Annals* 452 (1980): 149-50.
28. Jeff Cooper, *Jeff Cooper on Handguns* (Los Angeles: Peterson, 1979); Hardy and Stompoly, "Of Arms and the Law," pp. 111-12.

PROBABLE VALUES OF THE
SUBSTITUTION FRACTION

In the following discussion it should be kept in mind that substitution of long guns for handguns as defense or crime weapons can occur in two different ways. First, persons who either already own a handgun or who are considering acquiring one could acquire a long gun as a substitute and thus would have a long gun instead of a handgun available should a violent incident occur. Second, among persons who already owned both handguns and long guns before handgun controls were imposed, some would be deprived of the handguns, leaving only long guns to be used in future assaults which might otherwise have involved only handguns.

What fraction of violence-prone persons who otherwise would have used handguns in assaults would substitute long guns if handguns were effectively denied to them? We must necessarily speculate here, but we can obtain at least an approximation of the range of probable values for the substitution fraction by examining the motives of handgun owners for acquiring the guns and the circumstances in which some of them use the weapons to assault other people.

Among noncriminal owners of handguns, the most common single reason for owning pistols is protection or self-defense. In various surveys of the general population, between 45 and 67 percent of handgun owners reported defense or protection was the main reason for their ownership of a handgun.[29] This clearly suggests that, even among noncriminal handgun owners, a large fraction of owners have an emotionally potent reason for having the weapon, and thus an equally potent reason for seeking an equally effective substitute. However, the general population is not of greatest concern for our purposes, because the effects of gun control measures on rates of violent crime will only occur to the extent that access to guns is limited among the assault-prone segment of the population.

If those who use guns in assaults live in high crime areas, then handgun ownership for protection should be even higher among this group than among the general population of handgun owners. Available evidence confirms this. A study of low income blacks arrested for illegal weapon carrying found that 70 percent of those arrested

29. See Kleck, *infra.*

were carrying weapons because they were anticipating attack.[30] And in a sample of Florida convicted felons, 58.5 percent of the gun murderers and 56.7 percent of the gun assaulters had originally purchased their handguns for protection, not specifically to commit some particular crime. Even among the burglars interviewed, 58.3 percent originally acquired their handguns for protection.[31] It therefore is clear that among the segment of handgun owners who must be affected in order to influence gun homicides, handguns are mainly owned because the owners fear for the safety of themselves and those around them. Thus, potential gun abusers have a very powerful motive for obtaining effective substitutes if handguns become unavailable to them.

It might be argued that expense would be a factor limiting substitution. Indeed, it is probable that many defensive gun owners have handguns because they believe they are cheaper than shotguns or rifles. Perhaps the greater size of long guns suggests greater expense. It is questionable how true this is, since cheap shotguns can be obtained for $50 or less, while the average retail price of handguns used in crimes in 1975 was $100.[32] (By now, due to inflation, the handgun figure has undoubtedly increased.)

Further, if handguns were legally restricted, the price of handguns in the resulting black market would skyrocket. A conservative estimate of the average price of an illegal handgun might be double that of a legal one, or about $200.[33] In contrast, even the moderately expensive semiautomatic shotgun can be purchased for about $200, a pump shotgun for $110, and a semiautomatic clip-fed rifle for $150. (These price figures come from a handgun control advocate arguing *against* the substitution thesis.[34]) While these weapons are often more expensive than typical crime handguns *now*, they would not necessarily be so after significant handgun controls were imposed. Ironically, the controls would erase much of the slight existing price differential and thereby make the deadlier weapons more attractive to potential gun abusers.

30. Leroy G. Schultz, "Why the Negro Carries Weapons," *Journal of Criminal Law, Criminology, and Police Science* 53 (December 1962): 477.

31. Florida, *Final Report, Handgun Regulation Project* (Tallahassee: Florida Bureau of Criminal Justice Planning and Assistance, 1977), App. 4-10.

32. Steven Brill, *Firearm Abuse: A Research and Policy Report* (Washington, D.C.: Police Foundation, 1977), p. 60.

33. Ibid., p. 58.

34. Fields, "Handgun Prohibition and Social Necessity," p. 45.

Even for very low income persons currently armed with very cheap handguns (or persons who would in the future want to obtain such guns), it seems doubtful that a price differential of even forty or fifty dollars (if such a differential could somehow be maintained) would deter the acquisition of long guns, especially among persons who believe their lives depend on being effectively armed. Further, if a handgun control measure involved compensation for guns confiscated, handgun owners affected could simply put the compensation money toward the purchase of a long gun.

Long guns differ from handguns not only in being deadlier but also in being larger and therefore less concealable. It is clear that it would be harder for defensive gun owners to casually and routinely carry long guns on their persons, even if the guns were cut down, as they can with handguns. Therefore, assaults that occur in circumstances where a gun would have to be carried on the offender's person in order for it to be available would be at least somewhat less likely to involve a gun if handguns were restricted and only long guns were easily available. It is these homicides which might be prevented by handgun restrictions, even if handgun owners and would-be owners acquired long guns, simply because of the greater inconvenience of routinely carrying a long gun. In short, substitution of long guns in *assaults* could thereby be less than substitution in *ownership*. The question is, how common are homicides like these we have described?

Homicides that occur in the home of the offender are clearly assaults in which long guns could be used just about as easily as handguns. A long gun can be kept in a closet, under a bed, or next to the door just as easily as a handgun can be kept in a bureau drawer. A large number of homicide studies have examined the location of the killings and whether they occurred in a home or residence; although most of them do not distinguish the offender's home from the victim's or some other person's home, three studies make this distinction. Harlan found that 59 percent of the homicides occurred in a home and 33 percent of the total were committed in the offender's home (or the home of both the offender and the victim, where they lived in the same residence).[35] Wolfgang found that 50.9 percent of the killings occurred in a home, and 29 percent occurred in the home

---

35. Howard Harlan, "Five Hundred Homicides," *Journal of Criminal Law and Criminology* 40 (March–April 1959): 741.

of the offender.[36] The District of Columbia Crime Commission stated that 4 percent of the killings occurred in the offender's home, while another 51 percent occurred in the victim's home, but the 51 percent apparently includes killings that occurred in the home of both the offender *and* victim.[37] In the Wolfgang study, of all killings in the home of the victim, 60.3 percent were committed in the home of both offender and victim, while in the Harlan study, this figure was 56.5 percent. Therefore we can estimate that, of the 51 percent of the D.C. homicides committed in the victim's home, about 58 percent were in the home of both offender and victim—about 30 percent of all the killings. Adding in the 4 percent that occurred in the home of the offender only results in an estimated 34 percent occurring in either the offender's or both the offender's and the victim's home. Thus the three studies indicate that 33 percent, 29 percent, and 34 percent of these samples of homicides occurred in the home of the offender, or on the average, 32 percent.

Even among homicides that occur in homes other than the offender's, long guns could be substituted. Since it is often the victim of a homicidal exchange of violence who is the first to introduce a weapon into the encounter, this would indicate that where homicide victims had previously substituted long guns for handguns for protection, a long gun could be made available to the offender by the victim.[38] A survey of Florida prisoners found that 6 percent of the gun murderers interviewed and 10 percent of the gun assaulters had used the victim's gun in the offenses for which they had been convicted.[39] This same consideration would apply to homicides that occur in the home of a third party, if the location of the host's weapon is either apparent or otherwise known to either the offender or victim.

There is a small but important segment of handgun owners not covered in the general population owner surveys: persons who use handguns to facilitate the commission of robberies, burglaries, rapes, and other felonies. For lack of a better term, we will refer to these handgun users as "assault-plus" gun users. Their use of handguns is primarily instrumental, used to help in obtaining property (or in the

36. Marvin E. Wolfgang, *Patterns in Criminal Homicide* (Philadelphia: University of Pennsylvania, 1958), p. 123.

37. District of Columbia Crime Commission, *Report of the President's Commission on Crime in the District of Columbia* (Washington, D.C.: GPO, 1966), p. 42.

38. Wolfgang, *Patterns in Criminal Homicide*, pp. 252–65.

39. Florida, *Final Report*, App. 4–3.

case of rapes, participation in sexual acts). Nevertheless, the felons' original motives for acquiring the guns may overlap those of the assaultive users and noncriminal users of guns, in that they may have originally obtained the gun primarily for protection in a dangerous neighborhood and only secondarily to facilitate crimes. This group may end up using handguns in assaults either in the context of a typical fight- or quarrel-instigated shooting, or in the context of a robbery or other felony, in order to intimidate a victim, eliminate witnesses, or to attack victims who resist. Would there be extensive substitution of long guns among these "assault-plus" gun users, especially among those who would use the guns in robberies?

In homicides that occur in connection with robberies and felonies other than assaultive crimes, the offender does not have to routinely carry a long gun on a daily basis in order for it to be introduced into as assault. Rather, he can make deliberate advance arrangements to have the weapon available for the purpose of furthering a nonassaultive crime such as a robbery, and then use it to assault his victim if necessary. Considerations of convenience in these premeditated, short-term situations are of slight importance.

Fields has argued that long guns would not generally be substituted in robberies and other felony situations because the guns have one or more deficiencies as crime weapons compared to handguns.[40] Before considering these claims, it should be noted that Fields has apparently misunderstood the logic of the substitution thesis. Kates and Benenson and others argue that *if* handguns are not available to felons, they will substitute long guns.[41] Therefore it is irrelevant how applicable long guns are to robberies and other felonies *compared to handguns*, since the thesis assumes handguns will be effectively kept from felons. Or course, if handgun control advocates assert that handguns will *not* be kept from robbers and other criminals, then the principal rationale for handgun control collapses, and they essentially are in agreement with their opponents who assert that control efforts will be ineffective in keeping handguns out of criminal hands. The appropriate comparison for Fields to have made would have been between long guns and various nongun weapons such as knives, clubs, fists, and so forth. Such a comparison would obviously indicate long guns to be the superior crime weapon in all respects except concealability and cost.

40. Fields, "Handgun Prohibition and Social Necessity."
41. Kates and Benenson, "Handgun Prohibition and Homicide."

Fields asserts that various types of long guns are less applicable to criminal purposes because they lack one or more of the desirable attributes that handguns have: concealability, multiple rapid fire, portability, and easy reload. Several of these attributes, however, are largely irrelevant to criminal applicability. Multiple fire and ease of reloading are unnecessary attributes of robbery weapons, since guns are not fired even once during the vast majority of robberies and are rarely fired more than once. For example, Cook's study of street robberies found that the victims of gun robberies were attacked in only 18.9 percent of the cases (and some of these might have been attacks with nongun weapons where the offender had both gun and nongun weapons) and the victim was actually shot in only 1.9 percent of the cases.[42] In those cases where a shot was fired, it seems likely that only one shot was fired in the majority of instances, given the low frequency of shooting overall.

Concealability is a significant characteristic affecting applicability of weapons to criminal uses, and it is certainly true that handguns are more concealable than long guns. Undoubtedly this, and the belief in the greater expense of long guns, largely explains why long guns are infrequently used in robberies. Where handguns are available, why use a long gun? However, we are examining the hypothetical situation where handguns have somehow been effectively denied to at least some robbers and other criminal users of handguns. Therefore, the crucial issue is whether long guns are *sufficiently* concealable to be substituted for handguns in robberies, not whether they are *more* concealable than handguns.

Although arguing against the substitution thesis, Fields's own data indicate that there are shotguns that can be sawed off to a length of 9 inches (double barrel), or 20 inches (pump or semiautomatic), while various types of rifles can be sawed off to lengths of 20, 14, 10, and even 7 inches![43] However, shortening the barrel reduces muzzle velocity, thereby reducing RSP. For example, the muzzle velocity of a shotgun drops 7.5 feet per second for every inch the barrel is reduced below 30 inches.[44] Thus if a shotgun were cut down to 20 inches total length, with a barrel of 14 inches, its muzzle veloc-

42. Philip J. Cook, *Does the Weapon Matter? An Evaluation of a Weapons-emphasis Policy in the Prosecution of Violent Offenders* (Washington, D.C.: Institute for Law and Social Research, 1979), p. 35.

43. Sam Fields, "Handgun Prohibition and Social Necessity," *St. Louis University Law Journal* 23 (1979): 35–61.

44. Jack O'Connor, *The Shotgun Book* (New York: Alfred A. Knopf, 1978), p. 226.

ity would drop 120 feet per second, reducing its RSP by about 10 percent. However, this still leaves more stopping power than any criminal would need in order to carry out a crime.

Even if robbers believed that they needed multiple rapid fire as well as concealability, Field's data indicate that there are several long gun types that offer this combination of traits, as well as being far deadlier than handguns. For example, the semiautomatic clip-fed rifle offers up to twenty rounds, without any action needed between shots, can be cut down to 7 inches, and can be bought for $150. The pump shotgun allows five to seven rounds, can be cut down to 20 inches, and costs only $110, although multiple fire requires a quick pump action between shots. The semiautomatic shotgun offers five to six shots *without* the action between shots, can also be cut down to 20 inches, and is priced at a level comparable to that of a black market handgun, $200.[45]

A criminal intending to commit a robbery, burglary, or rape can easily devise a method of hooking a sawed-off shotgun or rifle inside an overcoat or sport jacket. A weapon measuring anywhere from 7 to 20 inches in length would be invisible to a passing citizen, potential victim, or patrolman passing in a cruiser. Given a choice between acquiring a shotgun and cutting it down, and either robbing without a gun or giving up robbery altogether, it seems highly doubtful that many robbers would choose the latter. Thus, long guns seem eminently applicable to felonies under conditions where handguns become hard to obtain but long guns are left unrestricted.

In 1979, 22.2 percent of the criminal homicides reported to the police were committed in connection with a felony or suspected felony, most of them robberies.[46] Since few of these felonies would be committed in the offender's home, this group of homicides is essentially nonoverlapping with the 32 percent of homicides that occur in the killer's residence. By adding these percentages, we can say that in 54 percent of the homicide circumstances, a long gun is substitutable, and that in an unknown additional fraction of the killings, a long gun belonging to the victim or to a third party, and kept in the home, could have been used as easily as a handgun.

In addition, many of the remaining homicides occur *near* the residence of one of the participants, in or near a vehicle belonging to one

45. Fields, "Handgun Prohibition and Social Necessity," p. 45.
46. U.S. Federal Bureau of Investigation (FBI), *Crime in the United States, 1979* (Washington, D.C.: GPO, 1980), p. 12.

of them, or in some other location where a long gun could easily be available.[47] For example, Curtis's unusually detailed breakdown of homicide locations shows that, in addition to the 34.5 percent that occur in someone's home, 4.2 percent occur in the immediate area around a residence (some presumably near the offender's residence), 2.3 percent occur in a private transport vehicle, and another 29.8 occur in various other outside locations, which could be near the home or vehicle of either the offender or victim.

Only in the 26.5 percent of the homicides that occurred in non-residential inside locations can we be reasonably confident that most of the killings were committed in circumstances where use of a long gun would be difficult. And because Curtis's data on location covers all types of homicides, some felony killings are included in this 26.5 percent and thus are situations where a long gun could have deliberately been introduced according to previous plan. Therefore we can make a rough estimate that anywhere from 54 percent to about 80 percent of homicides occur in circumstances that would easily permit the use of a long gun.

This conclusion is confirmed by the only study I know of that examined in detail the manner in which weapons are introduced into homicidal situations. Luckenbill found that only sixteen out of seventy, or about 23 percent of the homicide offenders studied, had carried a weapon into the homicidal situation as a matter of daily routine.[48] In the remaining cases, the offenders had either carried a weapon into the situation on the assumption they might confront the eventual victim (nine cases), or temporarily had left the situation to get a weapon, or had transformed an existing prop (e.g., a telephone) into a lethal weapon (forty-five cases). It could be argued that some of the nine cases where the offender anticipated confrontation with the victim were cases where long gun substitution would have been difficult. Therefore, between forty-five and fifty-four of the seventy cases or 64–77 percent, involved circumstances permitting long gun substitution either through planned confrontation with the victim, through use of an available long gun (especially in homes of the victim or offender), or by leaving the situation temporarily to secure a long gun. In any of these situations, the lesser conceala-

---

47. In the South and in rural areas, the sight of a gun rack in a pickup truck, often with a shotgun or rifle in place, is commonplace, although virtually unknown to city dwellers.

48. David F. Luckenbill, "Criminal Homicide as a Situated Transaction," *Social Problems* (December 1978): 184.

bility of long guns would not pose any significant obstacle to their use.

It seems clear that persons who currently own (or in the future would want to own) handguns would find long guns an adequate, albeit not ideal, substitute in the event access to handguns was restricted while long guns were left relatively unrestricted. It is also clear that the majority of homicides occur in circumstances that would easily permit the introduction of long guns if the participants had acquired them. However, it is impossible to say for certain the extent to which such substitution *would* occur. We can certainly say that there is little to *prevent* substitution from occurring in the majority of assaults and can note that persons who believe handguns are useful for defensive or criminal purposes are likely to believe the same regarding long guns.

The likely extent of substitution of one gun type for another can be judged by considering the experience of states like New York and Massachusetts that have significantly restricted the purchase of guns by their citizens. Where such in-state sales have been restricted, millions of residents have, in effect, substituted out-of-state guns for in-state guns, a fact widely acknowledged by gun control advocates. Studies of guns confiscated by police show that an estimated 87 percent of the guns used in crimes in Massachusetts came from other states, while 65 percent of a sample of domestic handguns confiscated by New York City police came from outside the state, a state where the residents of New York City alone were estimated in 1973 to own at least one million guns, the great majority of them illegal.[49] Many people are thus willing to go to the added trouble, expense, and even legal risk of buying guns out-of-state (a violation of the federal Gun Control Act of 1968) or buying guns in-state from black market dealers. In contrast, handgun-only laws would ordinarily place *no* significant barriers to long gun acquisition, and long gun substitution would therefore involve even less added trouble or expense, and certainly less legal risk, than substitution of out-of-state guns for in-state guns. In short, it seems reasonable to expect that long gun substitution would be at least as massive as that experienced in states which have restricted purchases of guns.

49. Franklin E. Zimring, "Firearms and Federal Law: The Gun Control Act of 1968," *Journal of Legal Studies* 4 (January 1975): 175; Vera Institute of Justice, *Felony Arrests* (New York: Longman, 1981), p. 115.

CONCLUSIONS AND POLICY IMPLICATIONS

Our conclusions can be summarized as follows:

1. Based only on the characteristics of the weapons themselves, the long guns likeliest to be substituted for handguns for either defensive or criminal purposes are about three or four times as deadly as the handguns currently used in assaults, as well as being more accurate.

2. While we cannot know with precision what fraction of violence-prone handgun owners or would-be owners would substitute long guns if handguns were denied to them, the circumstances in which homicides occur would easily *permit* long guns to be substituted in anywhere from 54 percent to about 80 percent of the cases. Further, since many long guns would be no more expensive than black market handguns under handgun control conditions, cost would not be much of a deterrent to substitution. Even now, cheap shotguns can be had for $50. Various types of sawed-off shotguns and rifles offer sufficient concealability and more than sufficient deadliness to commit robberies and other gun felonies, as well as offering multiple rapid fire for the minority of robbers who might believe this to be necessary. Therefore, long guns are eminently substitutable for handguns in virtually all felony killing situations.

3. The principal motives for handgun ownership among those who misuse handguns are self-defense and facilitation of nonassaultive crimes like robbery. That is, such persons own handguns either because they fear for their lives or safety, or because they want to use them to commit other crimes. Therefore, if handguns are restricted and long guns left relatively unrestricted, there would seem no reason why the vast majority of these violence-prone handgun owners and would-be owners would not substitute long guns. Among the defensive owners, fear would be ample motivation to substitute, while among criminal users, the desire to continue their criminal careers and the advantages of having a firearm in robberies and other crimes would indicate substitution to be the rational course of action.

4. The relationship between the long gun-to-handgun deadliness ratio, Y, and the substitution fraction, X, is expressed in the following equation:

$$X = \frac{8,497.56}{9,103.24 \; Y \; 607.44}$$

Based on the values of X that result if we assume Y to be even the smallest value it seems likely to take on, 3.0, the handgun-only control policy would save lives only if fewer than 31.8 percent of the violence-prone handgun owners and would-be owners substituted long guns (see Table 7-2). Given the results of our analysis of motives for handgun ownership among this group, and the circumstances in which homicides occur, this is highly unlikely. However, if we assume that this group will substitute the deadlier varieties of long guns and long gun ammunition, and Y is set at 5.0, then a handgun-only control policy would save lives only if fewer than 18.9 percent substituted long guns. This seems even more improbable.

The hope that handgun-only controls can reduce homicide is thus dependent on highly improbable combinations of expectations, for example, that long guns are only twice as deadly as handguns *and* that fewer than 48.3 percent will substitute. While the latter expectation *might* be true, under a "best case" hypothesis, it is very doubtful if the former would be true as well. Advocates of handgun-only controls must hope that the population of handgun owners and would-be owners are a nonrational group of persons, who either will seek no effective substitute if handguns are denied to them or will obtain a substitute (i.e., a long gun) but, counterrationally, will choose a less effective variety of long gun.

This imagery of unmotivated, irrational gun ownership makes sense only to people who believe that no sensible person would own a gun in the first place, and that certainly no sensible person would believe that a gun has any defensive value. However, regardless of the objective value of guns for defensive purposes (see Chapter 2), defensive handgun owners obviously *do* believe the weapons are of value for protection. This in turn indicates that effective substitutes for handguns will be sought, if neither considerations of expense nor legal obstacles interfere. And since people believe that long guns are more effective defensive devices than knives, clubs, or other nongun weapons, this suggests that long gun substitution *will* occur where handgun-only controls are imposed.

The probability of handgun-only policies reducing violence thus seems low. However, it may sometimes make sense to try policies with slim hopes of success, if the potential benefits of a successful policy are great enough. This would certainly be the case if, as some advocates have asserted, handgun control could save thousands of lives. Unfortunately, the consequences of failure of this policy are not merely the loss of time, money, and effort, as with some public policies. An unsuccessful handgun control policy would not just be unproductive — it would be counterproductive, costing more human lives than it saves. People would needlessly die in long gun assaults who would have lived had only a handgun been involved, the victims of well-intended reformers who chose not to look too closely at the perverse consequences of the policies they favored.

Given the political opposition to gun control policies aimed at all firearms, and the probable disastrous consequences of handguns-only controls, it might seem that little can be done to reduce the criminal use of firearms. Nevertheless, there is a way out of this dilemma. Gun controls can be simultaneously broadened and narrowed in focus. On the one hand, they should be broadened to include all types of firearms, not just handguns, in order to avoid the problems we have outlined. On the other hand, they must be narrowed to focus only on the ownership, carrying, and use of firearms by persons known to be at high risk of misusing firearms. By leaving the legitimate gun owner alone, this provides the political support needed to achieve modest controls and avoids needlessly criminalizing millions of otherwise law-abiding citizens who would defy laws that they believe unjustly penalize them as much as criminal users of guns.

This combination of emphases suggests a well-enforced permissive licensing system which would grant firearms-owning licenses to all adults who wanted them, except to those who had been convicted of a violent crime within the past seven years (or some other appropriate period). These persons would be denied firearms of *any* kind. This is an old suggestion, which has already been put into law in a number of states, among them Illinois. However, the Illinois statutes have received virtually no enforcement. Arrests for possession of a firearm without a license occur very infrequently, and then apparently only are made incident to arrest for some other offense.[50]

We do not know how well an *adequately enforced* permissive licensing system would work, since it has never been tried. Enforcement of illegal gun possession laws appears to be predominantly reactive and the by-product of enforcement of other laws: police wait until an offense becomes apparent to them and then decide whether to make a weapons arrest in addition to the arrest for the

50. David J. Bordua et al., *Patterns of Firearms Ownership, Use and Regulation in Illinois* (Springfield: Illinois Law Enforcement Commission, 1979), sec. 3.

crime that originally drew their attention. Even this sort of arrest, made when someone arrested for another offense is found to be in illegal possession of a gun, occurs rarely. Over a five year period, an average of only 269 arrests were made per year for illegal possession (distinct from carrying) of a firearm in Illinois, a state where there were an estimated 5 million guns owned in 1977 and where 28 percent of the gun owners interviewed in a statewide survey admitted they owned guns but did not have the required license.[51]

The most effective enforcement of such a system would be targeted at high risk groups, especially persons on parole or probation after convictions for violent offenses. Proactive efforts could be made by police, probation, and parole officers to check for illegal gun possession in these groups. This would be deliberately discriminatory, in the sense that it would be intended to discriminate between those likely to misuse firearms and those not, in order to deter the possession and carrying of firearms in the high risk group. Mandatory penalties might be established for violations of such a law.

This suggestion has been made in connection with broader laws, but it is pointless if prosecutors and judges are motivated to evade them. Such evasion would occur when a law is directed at legitimate gun users as much as criminal users or where the penalties are perceived as excessively severe.[52] When judges are sentencing murderers to five year prison sentences and they know the offenders will be released after serving two years, it strikes them as somewhat bizarre to impose even a one year sentence on otherwise law-abiding first offenders whose only crime was illegal possession of a firearm for self-defense. However if the law were directed only at such violence-prone persons as those convicted of violent crimes, prosecutorial and judicial nullification of mandatory penalty provisions should be reduced, while still providing penalties possibly significant enough to deter gun possession.

Such licensing systems can be established at the state level, with each state deciding whether it needs them or not. The needs of New York City for firearms control are not those of North Dakota. Thus a uniform federal licensing system is unnecessary. What is needed at the federal level is a more stringent revision of the 1968 Gun Control

---

51. Ibid., pp. 79, 101, 160.
52. David J. Shields, "Two Judges Look at Gun Control," *Chicago Bar Record* 57 (January–February 1976): 180–85.

Act that would effectively restrict transfers of firearms between residents of different states who are not licensed dealers. This would make it possible for state licensing systems to effectively restrict access of firearms to high risk residents within their own borders, in those states where such controls are needed.[53]

This system of gun control would not eliminate all, or even most, gun homicides. Most criminals would still obtain guns, and some previously law-abiding citizens would commit gun homicides (although this is far less common than is widely believed—see Chapter 2). However, if well-funded enforcement efforts were made, there would certainly be more hope of making significant reductions in gun violence than would result from attempts to deny handguns to law-abiding citizens.

It should be emphasized that the arguments presented in this chapter apply to *any* kind of legal controls intended to restrict access to handguns without restricting access to long guns. These might include licensing of handgun owners, regulation of trafficking in handguns, and prohibition of handguns. The conclusion to be drawn from the data presented is that it would be a mistake to apply any such controls unless equally effective restrictions are applied to access to long guns. Either restrict access to all firearms or to none of them— along the middle course lies disaster.

---

53. This is essentially the stance taken by Hardy and Stompoly, "Of Arms and the Law," pp. 52–53.

Chapter 8

PROHIBITING THE "SATURDAY NIGHT SPECIAL" A Feasible Policy Option?

Paula D. McClain

Among the numerous policy questions addressed in the last decade, few have generated as much controversy and debate as the issue of gun regulation. Research indicates that at least one half of all American households are armed, and the number of guns privately owned was recently estimated at more than 140 million. Additionally, American gun manufacturers are estimated to produce approximately 4 million long guns (rifles and shotguns) and 2 million handguns annually.[1]

The increase in violent crimes over the past several decades, particularly firearm crimes, has resulted in considerable research focusing on the relationship between firearms ownership, firearms regulation, and violence. Two contradictory perspectives are reflected in these studies. One view suggests that legislation drastically reducing firearms ownership would be among the most effective means of reducing criminal violence in American society.[2] The contrasting

I wish to acknowledge my research assistant, Michael J. Gilbert, for his assistance in gathering background information for this chapter, and to thank Albert K. Karnig for his helpful comments.

1. J.D. Wright, P.H. Rossi, and E. Weber-Burdin. *Weapons, Crime and Violence in America* (Washington, D.C.: National Institute of Justice, 1981).

2. See, for example, Franklin Zimring, "Is Gun Control Likely to Reduce Violent Crime?" *University of Chicago Law Review* 35 (Summer 1968): 721–731; Steven T. Seitz, "Firearms, Homicide and Gun Control Effectiveness," *Law and Society Review* 6 (May 1972): 593–613; Llad Phillips, Harold L. Votey, Jr., and John Howell, "Handguns and

view contends that even moderate gun control would have limited value and views the costs of more drastic prohibitionary or confiscatory measur ∴s as outweighing the likely benefits.[3]

The controversy becomes even more complex in light of the various proposals for regulation itself. Should the object be to deny or reduce access to firearms to the entire populace or only to felons, juveniles, and other high risk groups? What should be regulated? All firearms?[4] Just handguns? Or only "Saturday Night Specials"? The arguments for and against each option are numerous. This chapter will focus on one option: prohibition of firearms identified as "Saturday Night Specials," and will examine arguments for and against the feasibility of implementing this policy option.

DEFINING THE "SATURDAY NIGHT SPECIAL"

The term "Saturday Night Specials" (SNS), although commonly used, has no universal definition. It usually refers to two groups of characteristics of the weapon: (1) short barrel, low caliber, and small size, which maximizes concealability; and (2) cheap construction from low tensile strength materials, which minimizes the price. The Bureau of Alcohol, Tobacco and Firearms (BATF), in its 1974 report entitled "Project Identification," attempted to reduce these perceived characteristics to specifics by defining SNS as handguns that met three basic criteria: (1) retailed for less than $50.00; (2) were .32 caliber or lower; and (3) had a barrel length of 3 inches or less.[5] It has been argued that the SNS, defined in this manner, has no legitimate use. Its low tensile strength prevents prolonged use in target shooting, and its short barrel precludes handgun hunting. Moreover,

---

Homicide: Minimizing Losses and the Costs of Control," *Journal of Legal Studies* 5 (June 1976): 463–478; and Joseph C. Fisher, "Homicide in Detroit: The Role of Firearms," *Criminology* 14 (November 1976): 387–400.

3. See Kleck and Bordua, Chapter 2 in this volume, as well as D. Murray, "Handguns, Gun Control Laws and Firearm Violence," *Social Problems* 23 (October 1975): 81–95; B. Bruce-Briggs, "The Great American Gun War," *Public Interest* 45 (Fall 1976): 38–62; Bruce Danto, "Firearms and Violence," *International Journal of Offender Therapy and Comparative Criminology* 2 (1979): 135–145; and John Kaplan, "Controlling Firearms," *Cleveland State Law Review* 28 (1979): 1–28.

4. The term "firearm" denotes the category of weapons that includes both handguns and long guns.

5. Bureau of Alcohol, Tobacco and Firearms, *Project Identification: A Study of Handguns Used in Crime* (Washington, D.C.: Department of Treasury, 1974), pp. 6–7.

its short barrel does not provide the velocity, nor does its low caliber provide the bullet size necessary to develop adequate "stopping power" for the weapon to be used for self-defense purposes.

Dade County, Florida, which prohibits the sale of "Saturday Night Specials," defines them along lines similar to BATF's. An SNS is any firearm that is .32 caliber or smaller, has a barrel length less than three inches, *except* those whose frame is an investment-cast or forged high tensile alloy. On the other hand, Minnesota, which also prohibits the sale of SNS, has a much broader definition. An SNS means a pistol having a frame, barrel, cylinder, slide, or breech-lock (a) of any material having a melting point of less than 1,000 degrees Fahrenheit; or (b) of any material having an ultimate tensile strength of less than 55,000 pounds per square inch; or (c) of any powdered metal having a density of less than 7.5 grams per cubic centimeter. Still another definition is utilized by Hapeville, Georgia, in its law prohibiting the sale and possession of SNS. Any .22 caliber pistol, revolver, or derringer with a barrel length of 3 inches or less, which sells at retail for less than $39.00, is prohibited.[6]

The myriad of definitions has implications for a host of policy problems, particularly if the prohibition were to extend beyond manufacturing, importation, and retail sales to the confiscation of privately owned weapons. Manufacturers and importers would have the necessary knowledge of tensile strength, melting point, price, and other relevant characteristics of firearms to comply with legislative and administrative guidelines if these were the definitional criteria of SNS.[7] On the other hand, ordinary citizens most likely would lack this type of information on their handguns. The use of a worth or price criterion, instead of tensile strength or melting point standard, might cause difficulties for individuals who might not know the current equivalency value of a handgun purchased years prior and/or whose production has been discontinued. It appears that any measure which sought to confiscate privately owned SNS would require

---

6. Bureau of Alcohol, Tobacco and Firearms, *State Laws and Published Ordinances: Firearms* (Washington, D.C.: Department of Treasury, 1980), pp. 45, 58, 115.

7. The Federal Gun Control Act of 1968 seeks to prevent the importation of SNS and gives enforcement authority to the Bureau of Alcohol, Tobacco and Firearms. In this regard, BATF has developed a "Factoring-Criteria-for-Weapons" test, which uses a point system based on barrel length, overall length, frame construction, unloaded weapon weight, caliber, safety features, and miscellaneous equipment. Foreign handguns failing to meet the minimum point standard cannot be imported.

the compilation of an exhaustive list of the hundreds of models of handguns made by various manufacturers in the last half-century.

HANDGUNS, SATURDAY NIGHT SPECIALS, AND VIOLENCE

Handguns have been emphasized in gun control proposals and actual legislation because they are involved in a substantial portion of violent crimes and the majority of gun-related violence.[8] Many believe that handguns identified as "Saturday Night Specials" are disproportionately involved in such violence. The staff report of the National Commission on the Causes and Prevention of Violence found that firearms arc commonly involved in three of the four major categories of crime causing injury or death—homicide, aggravated assault, and armed robbery.[9] Empirical data on the proportion of violent crimes committed with handguns, particularly SNS, unfortunately is almost nonexistent. The FBI's *Uniform Crime Reports* display annual data on firearms used in homicide, aggravated assault, and robbery. Only for the latter category, however, is the firearm category broken down by type of firearm, handgun and long gun. Although some more intensive studies of homicide and other violent crime do provide a breakdown of *type* of weapon, few have information on the caliber of weapon, much less barrel length, price, tensile or melting point characteristics. Some limited information is available, however.

In 1974, the Bureau of Alcohol, Tobacco and Firearms undertook a study, "Project Identification," to trace and determine the types of guns used in crimes and recovered by the police in sixteen cities. The study also sought to identify the weapons' sources of origin.[10] In the sixteen cities, a total of 10,617 crime guns was submitted by the police for tracing. Of this total, 7,815 or 74 percent were traced successfully. Forty-five percent or 3,486 of the weapons successfully traced could be classified as "Saturday Night Specials." (BATF used the three criteria discussed earlier—barrel length of 3 inches or less,

8. See figures cited in Kates, Chapter 6 in this volume.

9. G. Newton and F. Zimring, *Firearms and Violence in America* (Washington, D.C.: National Commission on the Causes and Prevention of Violence, 1968), p. 44.

10. The sixteen cities were New York, NY; Atlanta, GA; Detroit, MI; New Orleans, LA; Dallas, TX; Denver, CO; Kansas City, KS; Philadelphia, PA; Oakland, CA; Miami/Dade County, FL; Minneapolis/St. Paul, MN; Seattle, WA; Boston, MA; Charlotte, NC; Louisville, KY; and Los Angeles, CA.

a caliber of .32 or less, and a retail price of less than $50.00.) Atlanta had the largest portion of SNS, 56.3 percent; while St. Paul, Minnesota, had the smallest, 18 percent.[11]

Brill regards these BATF data as an unreliable index of firearms use and actual violence for several reasons. First, approximately one fourth of the firearms were not crime guns but were either found by police or turned in by individuals. Second, the crime of illegal possession of a firearm is the dominant crime for which the firearms were confiscated. Third, some police departments submitted a small number of firearms owned by police officers.[12]

Brill's own study on crime handguns confiscated by police in seven cities attempted to ameliorate his criticisms of BATF's study by limiting the weapons to those involved in actual crimes. Handguns were categorized by whether they were more or less than .32 caliber.[13] Brill's findings are presented in Table 8-1. The data show that SNS were approximately one third of the crime handguns confiscated by the police, except in Boston where the figure was closer to one fourth. Brill concluded from his data that higher caliber handguns (greater than .32 caliber) are involved in crime with approximately the same frequency as lower caliber handguns. Unfortunately, the data available on the guns did not include any details of barrel length, but only their brand and caliber, from which rough inferences of price could be made.

Another problem with Brill's conclusions is the omission of .32 caliber handguns as SNS. If we define SNS as including .32 caliber weapons — as well as those lower than .32 caliber — then there is evidence of substantial involvement of SNS in crime. For example, the proportion of SNS use ranges from a high in Baltimore of 71.5 percent to a low in Boston of 41.6 percent. If we view the data in this manner, Brill's conclusions would be altered. In most cities, SNS were the predominant crime weapons, but in others there was more of a combination of small and large handguns.

In a study of black homicide in six cities, Rose and McClain obtained data on the caliber of weapons used in cases of black homicide victims in St. Louis, Missouri, for 1970, 1973, and 1975.[14] The data

11. BATF (1974), pp. 8, 12.

12. Steven Brill, *Firearm Abuse: A Research and Policy Report* (Washington, D.C.: Police Foundation, 1977), pp. 23–25. Also see Kates's discussion, Chapter 6 in this volume.

13. Brill, *Firearm Abuse.*

14. H.M. Rose and P.D. McClain, *Black Homicide and the Urban Environment* (Washington, D.C.: National Institute of Mental Health, 1981).

Table 8-1. Confiscated Handguns by Caliber for Atlanta, Baltimore, Boston, Chicago, Philadelphia, San Francisco, and Washington, D.C., 1974.

City	< .32	.32	> .32	Unknown	Total Number
Atlanta	40.1%	18.8%	41.1%	—	197
Baltimore	42.9	28.6	28.6	—	42
Boston	28.2	13.6	55.5	2.7%	110
Chicago	32.7	18.2	46.6	2.5	1,778
Philadelphia	31.3	30.3	38.4	—	294
San Francisco	36.5	11.7	48.7	3.0	230
Washington, D.C.	39.3	20.4	37.4	2.9	206

Source: Steven Brill, *Firearm Abuse: A Research and Policy Report* (Washington, D.C.: Police Foundation, 1977).

are broken down by relationship of victim to offender—family, acquaintance, stranger, and unknown. The findings are displayed in Table 8-2. In 1970, 39.6 percent of black family homicides were committed with handguns of .32 caliber or less. In homicides in which an acquaintance was the murderer, 37.7 percent were committed with .32 or less caliber handguns. Further, these firearms were used in 18.9 percent of stranger-perpetrated homicides and in 7.2 percent of the homicides in which the offender was unknown. In 1973, 20 percent of the family homicides were committed with .32 caliber or less handguns, as were 23.3 percent of the acquaintance murders. In 1975, 19.2 percent of black family homicides were committed with these weapons, as were 24.2 percent of acquaintance-perpetrated homicides.[15]

Some overall conclusions are possible. At least three fourths of black homicides in St. Louis for 1970, 1973, and 1975 were *firearm* homicides. Of that figure, at least 60 percent or more were *handgun* homicides in each of those years. Even with the missing data on handgun type in 1970, .32 caliber or less handguns were used in more than one third of the handgun homicides. In 1973 and 1977, they were used in less than one fifth of the handgun homicides. Based on these limited data, it appears that smaller caliber handguns are not used in homicides as often as larger caliber weapons, at least

15. Ibid.

Table 8-2. Caliber of Handguns Used in Black Homicides in St. Louis, 1970, 1973, and 1975.

| Caliber | *1970* | | | | |
	Family (N = 38)	*Acquaintance (N = 106)*	*Stranger (N = 64)*	*Unknown (N = 69)*	*Total (N = 277)*
.45	—	—	—	—	—
.38	15.9% (6)	18% (19)	36% (23)	10.1% (7)	19.9% (55)
.357	—	—	—	—	—
.9 mm	—	—	—	—	—
.32	13.2 (5)	13.2% (14)	7.9% (5)	2.9% (2)	9.4% (26)
.30	2.6% (1)	—	—	—	.4% (1)
.25	7.9% (3)	9.4% (10)	—	2.9% (2)	5.4% (15)
.22	15.8% (6)	15.1% (16)	11% (7)	1.4% (1)	10.8% (30)
Handgun type unknown	2.6% (1)	1% (1)	17.1% (11)	45% (4)	15.9% (44)
Long gun	18.4% (7)	13.2% (14)	7.9% (5)	5.8% (4)	10.8% (30)
Long gun type unknown	—	6.6% (7)	—	1.4% (1)	2.8% (8)
Total	29	81	51	48	209

Total firearms homicides	= 75.5%
Handgun homicides	= 82%
SNS (.32 caliber and less) homicides	= 34.4%

(Table 8-2. continued overleaf)

as reflected in the homicides of blacks in St. Louis during the 1970-1975 time period.

The conclusions of the three data sets—BATF, Brill, and Rose and McClain—appear to differ. The data sets are not comparable. Both in conjunction and alone, the three studies do not provide strong evidence that smaller caliber handguns are more often used in crime than are larger caliber weapons. Nevertheless, the data *do not* suggest trivial involvement in criminal activity.

Table 8-2. continued

Caliber	Family (N = 25)	Acquaintance (N = 90)	Stranger (N = 69)	Unknown (N = 46)	Total (N = 230)
		1973			
.45	—	—	1.4% (1)	—	—
.38	36% (9)	28.8% (26)	14.5% (10)	8.7% (4)	21.3% (49)
.357	—	1.1% (1)	—	—	.4% (1)
.9 mm	—	—	1.4% (1)	—	—
.32	16% (4)	8.9% (8)	7.2% (5)	8.7% (4)	9.1% (21)
.30	—	—	—	—	—
.25	—	3.3% (3)	5.8% (4)	—	2.2% (5)
.22	4% (1)	11.1% (10)	4.3% (3)	2.2% (1)	6.6% (15)
Handgun type unknown	—	4.4% (4)	30.4% (21)	56.5% (26)	22.2% (51)
Long gun	16% (4)	15.5% (14)	8.7% (6)	10.9% (5)	12.6% (29)
Long gun type unknown	4% (1)	3.3% (3)	1.4% (1)	—	2.2% (5)
Total	19	69	52	40	176

Total firearm homicides = 76.5%
Handgun homicides = 61.7%
SNS homicides = 17.8%

FEDERAL AND STATE FIREARMS LEGISLATION

It has been estimated that between the three levels of government—
federal, state, and municipal—there are 20,000 or more firearms laws
of one type or another.[16] In addition to banning importation of
SNS, federal law prohibits acquisition or possession of any type of
firearm by felons, juveniles, the mentally ill, and various other special

16. Wright et al., *Weapons, Crime and Violence in America.*

Table 8-2. continued

| | | 1975 | | | |
Caliber	Family (N = 26)	Acquaintance (N = 116)	Stranger (N = 51)	Unknown (N = 64)	Total (N = 257)
.45	3.8% (1)	5.2% (6)	2% (1)	3.1% (2)	3.5% (9)
.38	19.2% (5)	26.7% (31)	39.2% (20)	11% (7)	25% (63)
.357	—	—	—	—	—
.9 mm	—	.9% (1)	—	—	.4% (1)
.32	—	15.5% (18)	5.9% (3)	9.4% (6)	10.5% (27)
.30	—	.9% (1)	—	—	.4% (1)
.25	3.8% (1)	.9% (1)	—	—	.8% (2)
.22	15.4% (4)	5.2% (6)	5.9% (3)	1.6% (1)	5.4% (14)
Handgun type unknown	3.8% (1)	13.8% (16)	15.7% (8)	50% (32)	22.2% (57)
Long gun	7.7% (2)	13% (15)	5.9% (3)	1.6% (1)	8.2% (21)
Long gun type unknown	—	1.7% (2)	5.9% (3)	1.6% (1)	2.3% (6)
Total	14	97	41	49	201

Total firearm homicides = 78.2%

Handgun homicides = 67.7%

SNS homicides = 17.1%

Source: St. Louis Police Department records.

groups prohibited from firearms ownership.[17] Illinois, South Carolina, and Minnesota prohibit the sale of SNS, as they variously define them. Michigan, New York, and New Jersey require a permit to purchase or possess a handgun; Illinois and Massachusetts require firearm owners to obtain an identification card, which is not avail-

17. F. Zimring, "Firearms and Federal Law: The Gun Control Act of 1968," *Journal of Legal Studies* 6 (January 1075): 133–98.

able to certain prohibited categories; while Hawaii, North Carolina, and certain counties of Virginia require a permit to purchase.[18]

In the last several years, in particular, many municipalities have aggressively attacked the handgun issue by adopting handgun prohibitions. In 1981, the Village of Morton Grove, Illinois, prohibited handgun ownership altogether, an example that the cities of San Francisco and Berkeley, California, and Evanston, Illinois, shortly followed, while Chicago totally banned the purchasing of handguns by its residents.[19] In 1975, the District of Columbia passed legislation that prohibits the purchase, sale, transfer, and, with one exception, possession of handguns by District residents other than law enforcement officers or members of the military. The exception allows individuals to retain possession of handguns and long guns if they had registered them under the District's 1968 registration law.

The D.C. law, among other things, requires all firearm purchasers to file for a registration certificate with the Metropolitan Police Department. The procedure calls for a police screening to determine eligibility. Registrants are also required to provide photographs and fingerprints, pass a vision test, pass a written test pertaining to knowledge of firearms laws and safe use of weapons, and present evidence of the absence of any physical disabilities that would preclude safe use of a weapon. Moreover, in order for a firearm to be maintained in the home, it must be unloaded and disassembled or bound by a trigger-locking device.[20]

EVALUATING EFFECTIVENESS OF GUN CONTROL LAWS

Sabatier and Mazmanian, in an article on policy implementation, contend that a statute constitutes a fundamental policy decision, in that it indicates the problem(s) being addressed and stipulates the objective(s) to be pursued.[21] In further explanation, they state —

18. See discussion of permit systems and administrative models in Kates, Chapter 6 in this volume.

19. Cf. *Quilici v. Morton Grove*, F.2d (7 Cir. 1982) upholding ordinance against both state and federal constitutional challenge; *Doe v. City and County of San Francisco*, Cal. App. 3rd (1982) invalidating the handgun ordinance as violative of state law.

20. Edward D. Jones, III, "The District of Columbia's Firearms Control Regulations Act of 1975: The Toughest Handgun Control Law in the United States—Or Is It?" *Annals of the American Academy of Political and Social Science* 455 (May 1981): 138-49.

21. Paul Sabatier and Daniel Mazmanian, "The Implementation of Public Policy: A Framework of Analysis," *Policy Studies Journal* 8 (Special Issue 1980): 538-60.

Explicitly or implicitly, a statute implies an underlying causal theory. Given a stipulated objective and the assignment of certain rights and responsibilities to various implementing institutions, the target groups will behave in the prescribed fashion and the objective will be attained. Within this theory, however, there are two separate components: "technical validity" and "implementation effectiveness." The former refers to the relationship between target group behavior and the attainment of statutory objectives.... The latter concerns the ability of implementing institutions to produce the requisite behavioral changes in the target groups, preferably with a minimum of adverse side effects. Both components must be valid if statutory objectives are to be attained.[22]

The point to be emphasized is that if the underlying assumptions of a statute are not understood or not valid and the goals are not clearly identified, implementation and evaluation are difficult at best, impossible at worst.

A major problem in evaluating the effectiveness of gun legislation is that many evaluators fail to identify or differentiate between short- and long-term objectives. Wright et al. differentiate among three broad classes of anticipated effects—intermediate effects, end effects, and side effects.[23] *Intermediate effects* are those anticipated within the gun distribution system and in the patterns of gun distribution and usage. *End effects* are anticipated effects that are the desired outcomes of the legislation. *Side effects* are effects that are not necessarily intended but which are also a consequence of the legislation. These may be either positive or negative, or both positive and negative. Table 8–3, taken from Wright et al., shows the possible end effects, intermediate effects, and side effects that might be considered in the assessment of firearm legislation.

Much of the evaluation literature on the effectiveness of gun control laws tends to utilize a narrow definition of effectiveness. Geisel, Roll, and Wettick measured the extent of effectiveness of gun control legislation by the extent to which differences in death and crime rates among the states and cities could be explained by the differences in gun control legislation.[24] The authors established controls for the influence of other factors that could influence death and

---

22. Ibid.

23. Wright et al., *Weapons, Crime and Violence in America.*

24. M.S. Geisel, R. Roll, and R.S. Wettick, "The Effectiveness of State and Local Regulation of Handguns: A Statistical Analysis," *Duke Law Journal* (1969): 647–76.

Table 8-3. Desired End Effects, Intermediate Effects, and Side Effects of Gun Control Regulation.

I. Desired end effects:

  A. Reduction in use of weapons in crime
  B. Reduction in stock of weapons held by private households
  C. Reduction in weapons in accidental injuries
  D. Reduction in stock held by "criminals"
  E. Reduction in stock of certain types of weapons (e.g., handguns, Saturday Night Specials," and so forth)

II. Desired intermediate effects:

  A. Regulating the weapons production system
    1. Restrictions on the manufacture of weapons
    2. Restrictions on the import of weapons
  B. Regulating the distribution system
    1. Restrictions on the sale and transfer of weapons
  C. Regulating possession
    1. Restrictions on ownership
  D. Regulating usage
    1. Restrictions on carrying weapons
  E. Raising the costs of weapons ownership and use
  F. Raising the penalties for improper usage

III. Possible side effects:

  A. Substitution of other weapons for firearms in crime
  B. Creation of illegal manufacturing, distribution, and transfer systems
  C. Higher costs to the criminal justice system
  D. Higher costs to the administering agency
  E. Higher costs to weapons users

Source: James D. Wright, Peter H. Rossi, Kathleen Daly, and Eleanor Weber-Burdin, *Weapons, Crime and Violence in America* (Washington, D.C.: National Institute of Justice, 1981), p. 508.

crime rates, such as per capita income, education, and population density. They limited their study to state and local laws regulating handguns. They did not include laws that regulated use of firearms at particular times or places, laws that regulated the discharge of firearms, and laws that made the use of firearms in connection with other illegal conduct unlawful. Their results showed that handgun control legislation is most effective in reducing the number of suicides and accidents by firearm; less effective in reducing the number of homicides. It is generally ineffective in reducing the number of other crimes. They conclude that these results suggest that stringent gun control legislation does indeed reduce the number of persons possessing firearms.

Jones evaluated the effectiveness of the Washington, D.C., Firearm Control Regulation Act of 1975 by utilizing FBI crime statistics for Washington, D.C., and Baltimore, Maryland, for 1974 and 1978.[25] He found that the legislation had a beneficial impact on handgun homicide. Jones concluded that the Act, by constraining the availability of handguns and requiring handguns to be inoperative in the home, would reduce the relative frequency of "within family" and "outside family" handgun homicides. He did not find, however, that the Act would have much impact on felony murder. The evidence suggested that criminal offenders would easily acquire handguns through alternative sources, principally by private transfer, theft, or interstate purchase.

Several other studies, however, have found no link between gun regulation and reduced crime. Murray's study of census data from all fifty states examined the effects of gun control legislation on violent crime.[26] He reported that these laws have no apparent effect on either handgun ownership or on crime rates. He further suggested that in the absence of any significant relationship, gun control legislation is totally irrelevant to its stated purpose.[27] DeZee, criticizing Murray's methodology, reached similar conclusions using later data on the states' gun regulation laws and reduced violent crime rates.[28] In a study focusing on armed robbery in the nation's fifty largest cities, Cook found that state regulations requiring purchase permits had little if any direct effect on robbery rates.[29]

Another approach to evaluating the effectiveness of hypothetical gun regulation statutes involves the "substitution hypothesis," which contends that if handguns were banned, long guns probably would be substituted. Even a partial substitution of long guns would increase the homicide rate because long guns are more deadly than hand-

---

25. Jones, "The District of Columbia's Firearms Control Regulations Act of 1975."

26. Murray, "Handguns, Gun Control Laws and Firearm Violence."

27. Ibid.

28. M. DeZee, "Gun Control Legislation: Impact and Ideology," *Law and Policy Quarterly* (Spring 1983). [Editor's note: For another study reaching similar conclusions, see Magaddino and Medoff, Chapter 9 in this volume.]

29. Phillip J. Cook, "The Effect of Gun Availability on Robbery and Robbery Murder: A Cross-Section Study of Fifty Cities," in *Policy Studies Review Annual* (Beverly Hills, Calif.: Sage Publications, 1980), pp. 743–81.

guns.[30] Kleck and Bordua (Chapter 2) suggest that a criminal intent upon committing a robbery, assault, or rape will saw off the barrel of a shotgun to make it concealable. They further argue that legislation designed to outlaw "Saturday Night Specials" would cause a substitution of larger caliber handguns in robberies and assaults. Additionally, Kates (Chapter 6) suggests the danger of accidental deaths in the home would also increase if loaded long guns were kept in the home for self-protection rather than handguns.

The narrow definitions and diverse measures of effectiveness, and different research methodologies utilized in the numerous evaluation studies, lead to little consensus on the effectiveness of gun regulation laws in general, and handgun prohibition in particular. In view of the fractured evidence on effectiveness, how should one evaluate, in a theoretical rather than an empirical manner, the feasibility of prohibiting "Saturday Night Specials"? One approach would be to utilize a variant of the Wright et al. framework for evaluating gun regulation laws, concentrating specifically on "Saturday Night Specials."

AN ILLUSTRATIVE CASE OF GUN CONTROL

At this time, there appears to be little likelihood of enacting national legislation that would curtail the use of all or even most handguns. Such legislation is unlikely because of the lack of sufficiently intense political support and the organized efforts of special interest groups that oppose gun legislation. It is possible, however, that enough political support might be marshalled for national legislation prohibiting the manufacture, sale, and importation of "Saturday Night Specials," because SNS have little utility for sport shooters or other legitimate users. Would such gun prohibition constitute a useful policy option? Many factors would impinge on such an assessment. Let us use the ban on SNS as an illustration of the complexities involved in determining the impact (effectiveness) of any gun control policy short of total gun prohibition.

---

30. See D.B. Kates, Jr. and Mark K. Benenson, "Handgun Prohibition and Homicide: A Plausible Theory Meets The Intractible Facts," in Don B. Kates, ed., *Restricting Handguns: The Liberal Skeptics Speak Out* (Croton-on-Hudson, N.Y.: North River Press, 1979); David T. Hardy and John Stompoly, "Of Arms and the Law," *Chicago-Kent Law Review* 51 (1974): 52–114; and Kleck and Bordua, Chapter 2 in this volume.

A carefully tailored ban on SNS could well be enforceable, particularly if the prohibition were only on the manufacture, importation, and sale of SNS. (This assumes, of course, that a definition of SNS can be agreed upon.) There might be no penalty or only a minor fine for possession. What would be the desired intermediate and end effects, and what possible side effects would follow a prohibition of SNS structured in this fashion? Let us examine two competing scenarios, one in favor of and the other opposed to this prohibition.

Scenario #1: The Case for the Ban

Proponents of prohibition of SNS would see the key anticipated *intermediate* effect as the cessation of the manufacture, sale, and importation of SNS—and thus reduction in the number of SNS. The absence of a penalty for possession would make it unnecessary for police to search for SNS among the general population; they would need only to confiscate and destroy them whenever they discovered them in the normal course of performing their other duties. Ordinary citizens would simply have their weapons confiscated when found. Criminals caught with an SNS, on the other hand, would be subject to the current laws and penalties concerning possession, carrying, and use of a firearm in the commission of a crime.

The primary undesirable *side* effect would be the possible development of illegal manufacturing and sales markets. A prohibition on SNS would significantly increase the price of these guns available through illegal means. It is doubtful, therefore, that a law-abiding citizen would buy an illegal SNS when he/she could purchase a legal, larger caliber handgun for the same price. Therefore, the extent of these illegal markets would probably be minimal.[31]

The foremost desired *end* effect from a prohibition of SNS would be the reduction of gun-related violence. It is highly likely that the number of SNS in circulation would be reduced significantly with a prohibition on their manufacture, sale, and importation, particularly if SNS were destroyed when confiscated. The reduction in stock might then make it more difficult, by making it more expensive, for

---

31. Prohibition legislation that is carefully tailored to minimize the intrusion on ordinary citizens, and which leaves them the option of purchasing more expensive larger caliber handguns avoids most or all of the objections raised by Kates in Chapter 6 to a program of prohibition/confiscation of all handguns.

criminals to secure weapons. If substitution did occur, knives and other less lethal weapons would be the most common substitutes — thus reducing the growth of violence and diminishing violent crime.[32] If SNS were not replaced with larger caliber handguns or long guns, then a decrease in the number of guns in circulation would lead to a corresponding reduction in the number of gun-related accidental injuries and deaths. Additionally, some categories of expressive homicide, for example, family and acquaintance, might also be decreased. Moreover, from a consumer standpoint, SNS prohibition would ensure that individuals who want firearms for home protection would not purchase unsafe, cheap handguns. Thus, the prohibition would be in the best interest of the public.

Scenario #2: The Case Against the Ban

The opposing viewpoint might contend that the case for the ban is weak. Rather, opponents of control would argue that as long as larger caliber handguns and shotguns and rifles are not prohibited, individuals intent upon committing a crime will be likely to find substitutes for SNS. One could easily saw off the barrel of a larger caliber handgun or shotgun or rifle to make it more concealable. Zimring suggests that a .38 caliber handgun is several times more likely to kill than a .22 or a .25.[33] Kleck makes similar suggestions with regard to the probability of death with the substitution of shotguns for handguns.[34] Therefore, if prohibition of SNS did lead to the purchase of more formidable weapons, and if these were used in crime, then it is possible that a ban on SNS could actually increase the number of injuries or deaths from robberies and assaults. A similar increase may occur in family and acquaintance homicides if large caliber handguns or shotguns and rifles are kept in the home in place of SNS. Consequently, there is some reason to be pessimistic about a dramatic decrease in violent crime.

For sake of argument, let us assume that a reduction in the stock of SNS is achievable. Even if the ban on SNS were successful, oppo-

---

32. Seitz, "Firearms, Homicide and Gun Control Effectiveness"; and Zimring, "Is Gun Control Likely to Reduce Violent Crime?"

33. Franklin Zimring, "Firearms and Federal Law: The Gun Control Act of 1968," *Journal of Legal Studies* 6 (January 1975): 133–98.

34. See Kleck, Ch. 7 in this volume.

nents would argue that a reduction in stock would simply result in an increase in deaths from robbery and assault caused by the probable substitution of larger caliber handguns or shotguns and rifles. Hence, what may be perceived to be a positive intermediate result—the reduction in the number of SNS—could conceivably lead to a deleterious end result—an actual increase in the number of gun-related deaths from crimes and from accidents.

SUMMARY

Two competing and plausible arguments have been presented, suggesting some possible impacts of a national prohibition on SNS. What is painfully clear from these two arguments is that there is little agreement on the potential impact of national legislation banning the manufacture and distribution of SNS. The *key* issue is the substitution effect. Proponents of SNS prohibition either see little substitution occurring or envision substitution with less lethal weapons, such as knives. Opponents contend that significant substitution would occur, more lethal weapons would be the substitutes, and more death would ensue.

We lack true experimental conditions on which to base firm assessment of possible national impacts. Some state and local governments have prohibited SNS, but these jurisdictions are contiguous with others that have no controls. Thus, population shifts, as well as illegal trafficking in SNS, make it impossible to develop effective state and local statutes. Indeed, the very ineffectiveness of state and local prohibition is used by proponents to argue that only national legislation promises success; and the failures are used by opponents to argue that national legislation would also be ineffective. This lack of information on the effects of a national prohibition on "Saturday Night Specials" indicates the need for more empirical research, particularly on the extent of substitution that would possibly occur. If future research indicates that the substitution effect would be minimal, then prohibition of SNS may be in order. If, on the other hand, the substitution effect would be great, then prohibition of SNS may not be "good" public policy and other avenues should be explored. In light of the difficulties involved in constructing and measuring the substitution effect, empirical evidence on which to decide whether or not to prohibit SNS may be extremely difficult to obtain.

SELECTED BIBLIOGRAPHY
(PART IV)

Alviani, Joseph D., and William R. Drake. *Handgun Control: Issues and Alternatives.* Washington, D.C.: United States Conference of Mayors, 1975.

"Attitudes Toward Gun Control: Overview of a National Survey of the American Electorate, October 1975." *Congressional Record* 121, no. 189 (December 19, 1975), part II.

Bordua, David J., and Alan J. Lizotte. "A Subcultural Model of Legal Firearms Ownership in Illinois." *Law and Public Policy Quarterly* 2 (April 1979): 147-75.

Bordua, D.J.; A.J. Lizotte; G. Kleck; with Van Cagle. *Patterns of Firearms Ownership, Use and Regulation in Illinois.* Springfield: Illinois Law Enforcement Commission, 1979.

Brill, Steven. *Firearm Abuse: A Research and Policy Report.* Washington, D.C.: Police Foundation, 1977.

Bruce-Briggs, B. "The Great American Gun War." *Public Interest* 45 (Fall 1976): 37-62.

Bureau of Alcohol, Tobacco and Firearms. *Project Identification: A Study of Handguns Used in Crime.* Washington, D.C.: Department of Treasury, 1974.

_____. *State Laws and Published Ordinances: Firearms.* Washington, D.C.: Department of Treasury, 1980.

Cook, Philip J. *Does the Weapon Matter? An Evaluation of a Weapons-emphasis Policy in the Prosecution of Violent Offenders.* Washington, D.C.: Institute for Law and Social Research, 1979.

_____. "The Effect of Gun Availability on Robbery and Robbery Murder: A Cross-section Study of Fifty Cities." In Robert Haveman and B. Bruce Zellner, eds., *Policy Studies Review Annual*, vol. 3, pp. 743-81. Beverly Hills, Calif.: Sage Publications, 1979.

Cooper, Jeff. *Jeff Cooper on Handguns*. Los Angeles: Petersen, 1979.

Curtis, Lynn. *Criminal Violence: National Patterns and Behavior*. Lexington, Mass.: Lexington Books, 1974.

Danto, Bruce. "Firearms and Violence." *International Journal of Offender Therapy and Comparative Criminology* 2 (1979): 135-45.

DeZee, M. "Gun Control Legislation: Impact and Ideology." *Law and Policy Quarterly* 5 (Spring 1983).

Di Maio, Vincent J.M. "The Effectiveness of Snub-Nose Revolvers and Small Automatic Pistols." *FBI Law Enforcement Bulletin* 44 (June 1975): 10-13.

Di Maio, Vincent J.M. et al. "A Comparison of the Wounding Effects of Commercially Available Handgun Ammunition Suitable for Police Use." *FBI Law Enforcement Bulletin* 43 (December 1974): 3-8.

District of Columbia Crime Commission. *Report of the President's Commission on Crime in the District of Columbia*. Washington, D.C.: Government Printing Office, 1966.

Dobbyn, R.C.; W.J. Bruchey; and L.D. Shubin. *An Evaluation of Police Handgun Ammunition: Summary Report*. Washington, D.C.: Government Printing Office, 1975.

Fields, Sam. "Handgun Prohibition and Social Necessity." *St. Louis University Law Journal* 23 (1979): 35-61.

"Firearms: Their Contribution to Violent Deaths in California." Sacramento, Calif.: Bureau of Criminal Statistics, 1977. (Unpublished.)

Fisher, Joseph C. "Homicide in Detroit: The Role of Firearms." *Criminology* 14 (November 1976): 387-400.

Florida. *Final Report, Handgun Regulation Project*. Tallahassee: Florida Bureau of Criminal Justice Planning and Assistance, 1977.

Geisel, Martin S.; Richard Roll; and R.S. Wettick, Jr. "The Effectiveness of State and Local Regulation of Handguns: A Statistical Analysis." *Duke Law Journal* (August 1969): 647-76.

Greenwood, Colin. *Firearms Control: A Study of Armed Crime and Firearms Control in England and Wales*. London: Routledge and Kegan Paul, 1972.

Hardy, David T. "Firearms Ownership and Regulation: Tackling an Old Problem with Renewed Vigor." *William and Mary Law Review* 20 (Winter 1978): 235-90.

Hardy, David T., and John Stompoly. "Of Arms and the Law." *Chicago-Kent Law Review* 51 (September 1974): 62-114.

Harlan, Howard. "Five Hundred Homicides." *Journal of Criminal Law and Criminology* 40 (March-April 1950): 736-52.

Hatcher, Julian S. *Textbook of Pistols and Revolvers*. Marines, N.C.: Small Arms Technical Publishing, 1935.

James, Garry. *Guns and Ammo Guide to Guns for Home Defense.* Los Angeles: Petersen, 1975.

Jones, Edward D. III. "The District of Columbia's Firearms Control Regulations Act of 1975: The Toughest Handgun Control Law in the United States—Or Is It?" *Annals of the American Academy of Political and Social Science* 455 (May 1981): 138-49.

Kaplan, John. "Controlling Firearms." *Cleveland State University Law Review* 28 (1979): 1-28.

Kates, Don B., Jr. "Reflections on the Relevancy of Gun Control." *Law and Liberty* 3 (Summer 1976): 1-3.

Kates, Don B., Jr., and Mark K. Benenson. "Handgun Prohibition and Homicide: A Plausible Theory Meets the Intractible Facts." In Don B. Kates, Jr., ed., *Restricting Handguns: The Liberal Skeptics Speak Out*, pp. 91-138. Croton-on-Hudson, N.Y.: North River Press, 1979.

Kessler, Raymond G. "Enforcement Problems of Gun Control: A Victimless Crime Analysis." *Criminal Law Bulletin* 16 (March-April 1980): 131-49.

Lizotte, Alan J., and David J. Bordua. "Firearms Ownership for Sport and Protection: Two Divergent Models." *American Sociological Review* 45 (April 1980): 229-44.

Murray, Douglas R. "Handguns, Gun Control Laws, and Firearms Violence." *Social Problems* 23 (October 1975): 81-93.

Newton, George D., and Franklin Zimring. *Firearms and Violence in American Life.* A Staff Report of the Task Force on Firearms, National Commission on the Causes and Prevention of Violence. Washington, D.C.: Government Printing Office, 1969.

O'Connor, Jack. *The Shotgun Book.* New York: Alfred A. Knopf, 1978.

Peters, Caroll E. *Defensive Handgun Effectiveness.* Manchester, Tenn.: Author, 1977.

Phillips, Llad; Harold L. Votey; and John Howell. "Handguns and Homicide: Minimizing Losses and the Costs of Control." *Journal of Legal Studies* 5 (July 1976): 463-78.

Rose, Harold M., and Paula D. McClain. *Black Homicide and the Urban Environment.* Washington, D.C.: National Institute of Mental Health, 1981.

Sabatier, Paul, and Daniel Mazmanian. "The Implementation of Public Policy: A Framework of Analysis." *Policy Studies Journal* 8 (Special Issue 1980): 538-60.

Schultz, Leroy G. "Why the Negro Carries Weapons." *Journal of Criminal Law, Criminology, and Police Science* 53 (December 1962): 476-83.

Scott, Robert F. *Shooter's Bible.* South Hackensack, N.J.: Stoeger, 1980.

Seitz, Steven T. "Firearms, Homicides, and Gun Control Effectiveness." *Law and Society Review* 6 (May 1972): 593-614.

Shields, David J. "Two Judges Look at Gun Control." *Chicago Bar Record* 57 (January-February 1976): 180-85.

A *Synopsis of a California Poll of Handgun Ownership and Use*. Sacramento, Calif.: Bureau of Criminal Statistics, 1977.

U.S. Congress. *Hearings Before the Subcommittee to Investigate Juvenile Delinquency of the Committee on the Judiciary, U.S. Senate, 89th Congress, Pursuant to S. Res. 53.* Testimony June 8, July 1. Washington, D.C.: Government Printing Office, 1965.

_____. *Hearings Before the Subcommittee to Investigate Juvenile Delinquency of the Committee on the Judiciary, U.S. Senate, 90th Congress, Pursuant to S. Res. 35.* Washington, D.C.: Government Printing Office, 1967.

_____. Senate. *Congressional Record–Senate.* 90th Congress, second session, vol. 114. Washington, D.C.: Government Printing Office, 1968.

_____. *Hearings Before the Subcommittee to Investigate Juvenile Delinquency of the Committee on the Judiciary, U.S. Senate, 91st Congress, Pursuant to S. Res. 48.* Testimony July 19. Washington, D.C.: Government Printing Office, 1969.

_____. *Hearings on Firearms Legislation Before the Subcommittee on Crime of the Committee on the Judiciary, House of Representatives, 94th Congress.* Washington, D.C.: Government Printing Office, 1975.

U.S. Department of Justice, Federal Bureau of Investigation (FBI). *Crime in the United States (Uniform Crime Reports).* Washington, D.C.: Government Printing Office, yearly.

U.S. National Criminal Justice Information and Statistics Service (NCJISS). *Criminal Victimization in the United States, 1975; 1977.* Washington, D.C.: Government Printing Office, 1977, 1979.

Van Maanen, John. "Beyond Account: The Personal Impact of Police Shootings." *The Annals* 452 (1980): 145–56; and in Vera Institute of Justice. *Felony Arrests.* New York: Longman, 1981.

Wallack, L.R. *American Shotgun Design and Performance.* New York: Winchester Press, 1977.

Wolfgang, Marvin E. *Patterns in Criminal Homicide.* Philadelphia: University of Pennsylvania, 1958.

Wright, James D.; Peter H. Rossi; Eleanor Weber-Burdin; and Kathleen Daly. *Weapons, Crime, and Violence in America: A Literature Review and Research Agenda.* Washington, D.C.: National Institute of Justice, 1981.

Zimring, Franklin E. "Is Gun Control Likely to Reduce Violent Killings?" *University of Chicago Law Review* 35 (Summer 1968): 721–37.

_____. "The Medium is the Message: Firearm Caliber as a Determinant of Death from Assault." *Journal of Legal Studies* 1 (January 1972): 97–123.

_____. "Firearms and Federal Law: The Gun Control Act of 1968." *Journal of Legal Studies* 6 (January 1975): 133–98.

_____. "Determinants of the Death Rate from Robbery: A Detroit Time Study." *Journal of Legal Studies* 6 (June 1977): 317–32.

PART V

GUN LAWS AND REDUCTION OF VIOLENCE

Chapter 9

AN EMPIRICAL ANALYSIS OF FEDERAL AND STATE FIREARM CONTROL LAWS

Joseph P. Magaddino and Marshall H. Medoff

INTRODUCTION

The political assassinations, civil disorders, and increasing crime rates of the past two decades have created a new awareness concerning the degree of lawlessness and violence present in society. This awareness has led many to view the lack of comprehensive control over the private ownership of firearms as a major contributing factor to the breakdown of social order. The firearm, and particularly the handgun, is viewed as facilitating the commission and increasing the incidence of the most violent crimes. The widespread availability of firearms is thought to increase and intensify the level of violence, and has led many to demand additional governmental regulations and control of firearms. In 1968, the U.S. Congress enacted statutes governing the possession, transfer, and manufacture of various types of firearms and destructive devices. This body of legislation was the first substantial change in firearm control since the enactment of the Federal Firearms Act of 1934. Passage of this legislation represented the culmination of five years of public debate on firearm control laws. At the same time, substantial pressure was brought forth at the

This study is a combined version of two separate unpublished studies, "Firearm Control Laws and Violent Crimes: An Empirical Analysis" and "Handguns, Homicides, and the Gun Control Act of 1968."

state and municipal level of government to alter the law regulating the ownership and acquisition of firearms.[1]

Proponents argue that firearm control laws, by limiting the access and availability of firearms, reduce violent crimes. Additionally, certain firearm control laws, such as record keeping or registration, increase the effectiveness of law enforcement authorities in tracing a firearm used in the commission of a crime. Opponents, in addition to challenging Constitutional issues, view firearm control as a program that inherently exhibits a perverse effect on the desired goal of crime reduction. They argue an arms buildup by the citizenry will have a greater effect in deterring crime than an arms limitation, since an arms buildup represents an increase in the private supply of protection through potential victim retaliation.

Unfortunately, research on this major social issue has yielded inconsistent and contradictory results. Much of the early research examined the relationship between the level of firearm ownership and the rate of violent crimes. Newton and Zimring, in a widely cited study, conclude that more firearms leads to more gun-related crimes on the basis of a positive zero-order correlation they found between gun ownership and gun use in violence.[2] However, many have argued that there is inconclusive evidence for the conclusion claimed by Newton and Zimring, since their methodology ignored causation as well as any other social factors that could account for gun use. Zimring examined the impact of the Federal Crime Control Act of 1968 and found that after passage of the law handgun violence continued to grow but at a slightly slower rate than in the period prior to the law.[3] Phillips, Votey, and Howell, using an explicit model of homicide causation, found a significant positive relationship over time between the stock of handguns per capita and the rate of homicide offenses.[4] However, their model ignored all the social factors that are related to high crime rates.

Implicit in this method of research is the belief that firearm laws cause a reduction in gun availability and concomitantly reduce the

1. For a review of these issues, see B. Bruce-Briggs, "The Great American Gun War," *Public Interest* 45 (Fall 1976): 1–20.

2. George D. Newton and Franklin E. Zimring, *Firearms and Violence in American Life* (Washington, D.C.: GPO, 1970).

3. Franklin E. Zimring, "Firearms and Federal Law: The Gun Control Act of 1968," *Journal of Legal Studies* 4 (January 1975): 133–98.

4. L. Phillips, H. L. Votey, and J. Howell, "Handguns and Homicide: Minimizing Losses and the Costs of Control," *Journal of Legal Studies* 5 (June 1976): 463–78.

incidence of violent crimes. As Zimring has stated: "... any countermeasure that succeeded in reducing gun availability in robbery appears likely to reduce both the number of robberies and the death rate per thousand robberies."[5] However, because of data constraints researchers have been unable to directly estimate the relationship between firearm control laws and gun availability and have had to concentrate on the relationship between firearm control laws and the rate of violent crimes.

The President's Commission on Law Enforcement and Administration of Justice found that gun-related crime rates in cities thought to have strict firearm laws (Chicago and New York) were less than the violent crime rates in cities thought to have weaker firearm laws (Dallas and Phoenix).[6] On the basis of this sample of only four cities the Commission concluded that stringent firearm control laws resulted in lower homicide rates.

Using a more sophisticated methodology, Geisel, Roll, and Wettick used multiple regression analysis to statistically evaluate the effectiveness of state firearm control laws.[7] Their model assigned numerical values to various types of state firearm control laws in order to arrive at a firearm control index. Controlling for state socioeconomic characteristics (age, education, race, income), they found a significantly negative relationship between a state's homicide rate and their index of firearm control laws and concluded that gun control laws have a significant role in lessening acts of violence. In a subsequent study, Murray argued that the weights derived by Geisel, Roll, and Wettick were picking up the variation explained by other factors not included in their model.[8] Using a comparable methodology that controlled for more social factors, Murray found that gun control laws had no statistically significant impact on reducing the rates of violence associated with firearms.

Deutsch and Alt examined the impact the 1975 Massachusetts Gun Control Law had on the occurrences of homicide, armed rob-

5. Franklin E. Zimring, "Determinants of the Death Rate from Robbery: A Detroit Time Study," *Journal of Legal Studies* 6 (June 1977): 317–32.

6. U.S. President's Commission on Law Enforcement and Administration of Justice, *The Challenge of Crime in a Free Society* (Washington, D.C.: GPO, 1967).

7. M.S. Geisel, R. Roll, and S. Wettick, "The Effectiveness of State and Local Regulation of Handguns: A Statistical Analysis," *Duke Law Journal* (August 1969): 647–76.

8. Douglas R. Murray, "Handguns, Gun Control Laws and Firearm Violence," *Social Problems* 23 (October 1975): 81-92.

bery, and gun assaults.[9] Their results showed that the level of gun assaults and armed robbery significantly decreased six months after the enactment of the law, while there was no significant change in the homicide rate. However, Hay and McCleary argued that the Deutsch and Alt result was due to methodological artifacts, and further that not enough time had elapsed to accurately measure the impact of the law.[10] Reanalyzing the Deutsch and Alt data using a different statistical technique, Hay and McCleary found the evidence to be inconclusive.

Although many of the aforementioned studies emphasize the causal linkages between social factors and crime, what is conspicuous is the absence of any variables measuring differences in the effectiveness of law enforcement agencies, the judicial system, and other factors in the criminal justice system. Since the deterrent effect of the criminal justice system is omitted, it is unclear what elements produce the differences in the rates of violence, beyond those that can be attributed to social factors. Such differences may be due to firearm control laws or may reflect differences in the level of deterrence.

The first section of this chapter examines the efficacy of state firearm control laws. The methodology used in this study differs from previous studies on state firearm laws in that the analysis explicitly incorporates deterrence variables as well as social factors, using the economic framework of criminal choice developed by Becker.[11] The second section analyzes the impact of the Federal Gun Control Act of 1968. Specifically, we will (1) address whether, and to what extent, the Federal Gun Control Act of 1968 affected the rate of handgun acquisition, (2) analyze the impact of the Federal Gun Control Act of 1968 upon the homicide rate, and (3) examine the relationship between violent crime and the availability of handguns.

9. Stuart J. Deutsch and Francis B. Alt, "The Effect of Massachusetts' Gun Control Law on Gun-Related Crimes in the City of Boston," *Evaluation Quarterly* 1 (November 1977): 543–68.

10. Richard A. Hay and Richard McCleary, "Box-Tiao Time Series Model for Impact Assessment: A Comment on the Recent Work of Deutsch and Alt," *Evaluation Quarterly* 3 (May 1979): 277–314.

11. G.S. Becker, "Crime and Punishment: An Economic Analysis." *Journal of Political Economy* 82 (March/April 1968): 526–36.

STATE FIREARM CONTROL LAWS
AND VIOLENT CRIMES

Historically, state governments have enacted firearm control laws for two reasons: (1) to regulate the conditions of firearm use (i.e., discharging weapons within city limits, from vehicles, near roads, etc.); and (2) to keep firearms out of the hands of undesirable and irresponsible individuals. In order to achieve these goals, special restrictions are imposed upon the consumer with respect to the acquisition, ownership, and use of firearms. Since firearms provide consumers access to legitimate activities such as hunting, target shooting, and so forth, enforcement of these restrictions entails procedures to limit misuse of firearms or to segregate illegitimate users of firearms.

Before attempting to define the most important and widespread of these strategies, two caveats are in order. First, most of the restrictions discussed apply only to private citizens and not to law enforcement officers. Second, the variation between state laws cannot be too greatly emphasized. All states have some kind of "gun control" law, however minimal. Typically, states have adopted firearm control measures in the following broad categories: market restrictions, registration or record keeping, licensing, and prohibitions.

Market Restrictions. Many states require dealers of firearms to be licensed, which often involves a license fee or tax. Presumably the purpose of this is to be able to enumerate and identify dealers and to assure that they are not disreputable individuals. A consequence of such licensing is to limit the number of retailers, importers, and manufacturers of firearms. As in other areas of regulation, the net effect is to increase the money cost and time cost of the regulated good. Since such a law does not deny anyone access to a firearm, one could argue that states adopting dealer licensing programs are attempting to restrict the supply of firearms by pricing marginal firearm users out of the market.

Registration or Record Keeping. Registration or record keeping simply records information regarding firearm ownership and does not attempt to segregate out illegitimate users. These laws require the firearm dealer to record all transactions with a full description of the firearm, caliber, serial number, and other information, as well as the identity of the purchaser. Some states require these records to be kept by the dealer on the premises. Others require that the records be maintained by a law enforcement agency.

It is claimed that record keeping facilitates retrieval of information concerning lost or stolen firearms and increases the efficiency of the police in solving crimes that involve firearms. Registration may also reduce the number of criminal acts involving firearms and lessen the severity of the consequences, since it is argued that criminals will select a substitute weapon for a registered firearm and thus reduce the likelihood of serious injury.

Whether or not intended, one of the effects of registration or record keeping, as with dealer licensing, is to increase dealers' money cost and time cost of doing business. Though these laws do not deny anyone access to a firearm, it could be argued that their effect is to restrict the supply of firearms as dealers attempt to pass the additional cost on to consumers, thereby pricing marginal firearms users out of the market.

Firearm Licensing. Firearm licensing is an attempt to segregate potential firearm misusers from legitimate users. Firearm licensing laws may regulate the purchase, the right to carry a firearm, or both.

Most license to purchase or to own programs require the applicant simply to establish that he or she is not a member of a restricted class (i.e., minor, felon, mentally incompetent, etc.). Although not formally listed as licensing, the applications to purchase laws instituted by several states attempt to achieve the same goals and are administered in the same fashion as licensing laws.

The variation in both the design of the law and its implementation or administration is diverse among the states. Many states have designed and implemented a licensing system that the literature describes as "permissive" or mandatory licensure. Under this system, only those having a permit or "identification card" can purchase a firearm. But the necessary document *must* be issued to them upon application if they do not fall within one of the prohibited or restricted classes. They are then at liberty to purchase firearms upon presentation of this document (which must be periodically renewed) to a dealer or other seller.

Other states have adopted "restrictive" or discretionary licensure programs. Under these programs, an individual desiring to purchase a handgun must apply separately and successively for each handgun desired. Even though the person does not fall within whatever classes the state has prohibited from owning handguns, the police have discretion to deny the permit for whatever reasons they deem appropriate. These may include particular aspects of the applicant's life that they regard as undesirable (i.e., lack of "good moral character") or may relate to the legitimacy or importance of the given need for a handgun.

The license to carry or the license to carry concealed is the most common form of state licensing firearm regulation. In general, this restriction requires the applicant to demonstrate that the carrying of a firearm is essential to his or her well-being or the conduct of employment.

In attempting to reduce impulsive violence, some states have enacted a waiting period between the time a purchase is requested and the time the actual receipt of the firearm takes place. This "cooling off" period typically varies between forty-eight hours and two weeks. In some states, the waiting period is the obverse of the permissive licensure program. After a customer has indicated to a dealer the desire to purchase a handgun (or firearm), the dealer is required to transmit information regarding the prospective sale to the police, who in turn investigate the prospective purchaser's background. The sale can be consummated only if the prospective purchaser does not fall within one of the classes specifically restricted from owning handguns (or firearms).

Prohibition. Many states attempt to control firearm use by laws defining the place and manner in which firearms may be legally used. The most common examples of this law are the prohibitions against carrying a firearm on one's person or in a vehicle. Some states prohibit the carrying of a firearm concealed on the person, while others prohibit carrying either concealed or openly. Exemptions may be made where the weapon is carried on the owner's own property and to or from a shooting range, repair shop, etc. In some states the carrying prohibition is absolute. In others the public authorities have discretion to issue licenses to carry (or carry concealed) in cases they deem appropriate.

Rationale of Criminal Choice

The paradigm of economic analysis is that individuals make choices to secure their largest net advantage. In terms of activity choice, the individual estimates the present discounted value of the expected net returns associated with one activity and compares the difference with the net returns of other activities. The individual selects the activity that appears to have the highest net return.

In his seminal work, Gary Becker argued that this paradigm could be applied in analyzing the criminal choice.[12] Confronted by the mutually exclusive alternatives of illegal and legal activities, an individual either would select the legal activity; would be indifferent between the two; or would select the illegal activity provided the expected utility of the legal activity was greater than, equal to, or less than the expected utility of the illegal activity. The work of Becker suggests that the individual behavioral supply function of illegal offenses depends upon the probability of conviction and the monetary equivalent of punishment confronting an individual engaged in an illegal activity, pecuniary and nonpecuniary returns of illegal and legal activities, and the etiological characteristics of the individual.

Becker's theoretical framework yields the result that the higher the perceived probability of apprehension, or the greater the severity of penalty for the crime, the lower the crime rate. The lower the expected rewards of an illegal activity or the greater the expected rewards from the legal activity, the lower the offense rate. Furthermore, the motivation for all violent crimes is not the same. In crimes against property such as robbery, offenders are motivated by a desire for self-enrichment; while in crimes against persons such as homicide and aggravated assault, most offenders are primarily motivated by anger, passion, or hate. Ehrlich suggests that because of these motivation differences one should treat crimes against persons as nonmarket activities (as opposed to wealth-generating activities).[13] In making this distinction, the basic implications of the model remain unchanged.

The Model

If firearm control advocates are correct, firearm regulations should increase the monetary cost and the time cost of obtaining firearms

---

12. Ibid.
13. Isaac Ehrlich, "Participation in Illegitimate Activities: A Theoretical and Empirical Investigation," *Journal of Political Economy* 81 (May/June 1973): 521–65.

and thus discourage their use.[14] To test the hypothesis that firearm control laws reduce violent crime necessitates comparisons of offense rates between states, controlling for differences in firearm laws, deterrence, and etiological factors. The method selected was to estimate the aggregate supply of homicides, robbery, and aggravated assaults across U.S. states for 1960 and for 1970.[15] It was assumed that Becker's behavioral supply function of illegal offenses takes the following explicit form:

$$(Q/N)_i = AP_i^a \; TS_i^b \; INC_i^c \; POV_i^d \; ED_i^e \; LFP_i^f \; NW_i^g \; UN_i^h \; AGE_i^j$$

$$i = 1, \ldots, 50 \qquad (1)$$

The dependent variable (Q/N) is defined as each state's homicide rate (robbery rate, aggravated assault rate) per 100,000 population. The desired statistic (P) to quantify the probability an individual offender will be apprehended and convicted is the percentage of offenses cleared by conviction. However, no judicial agency reports the number of offenses cleared by conviction. In order to approximate this variable, one may select either the percentage of offenses cleared by commitment into state and federal prisons or the percentage of offenses cleared by arrest. In the 1960 cross-section, court commitments were used to measure the probability of conviction, and the percentage of offenses cleared by arrest was used for the 1970 cross section. The variable for 1970 was changed due to the fact that sixteen states failed to report court commitments for the offenses studied in 1970.[16] The severity of punishment (TS) is taken to be the median time served for each offense by state.

---

14. An additional hypothesis is that a reduction in the use of firearms (or handguns) in crime will reduce the incidence or severity of crime. For purposes of the present research, however, it is unnecessary to differentiate these hypotheses. If state gun control laws are found to reduce the incidence or severity of crime, both hypotheses would seem validated. If state laws do not have that effect, our research does not allow identification of why not.

15. The Federal Bureau of Investigation defines these crimes as follows: (i) homicides are all willful killings without due process; (ii) robbery is the stealing or taking anything of value from a person by use of force or threat of force; (iii) aggravated assault is the unlawful attack by one person upon another for the purpose of inflicting severe bodily injury. Other crimes such as hijacking, kidnapping, and so forth, involve firearm misuse, as do suicides and accidents. These activities were excluded from the analysis, since their frequency of occurrence is low and/or they have unique characteristics that require them to be treated separately.

16. The 1970 data on arrests, which is unpublished FBI data, was made available to one of the authors for an earlier study. Since the variables in the 1960 and 1970 cross sections

Following Ehrlich, state median income (INC) was used as a proxy for the marginal returns to illegal activities.[17] The higher a state's median income, the greater the payoff from criminal activities. The marginal returns from legal activities (POV) was measured by the percentage of families in each state below the federally defined level of poverty. The greater the percentage of families in poverty, the smaller the returns from legitimate activities and the greater the incentive to participate in criminal activities.

The etiological factors were education, unemployment, labor force participation, percentage nonwhite, and age distribution.[18] The median number of years of schooling (ED) was thought to be negatively related to the crime rates considered, since education provides one with a comparative advantage in producing private protection against these crimes. Labor force participation rates of urban males between ages 24-34 (LFP) was included to take into account the fact that the greater the time spent in legitimate activities, the less time available for illegitimate activities. Similarly, the unemployment rate (UN) among urban males between ages 35-39 was included as a measure of legitimate market opportunities. To standardize for those demographic groupings where violence is most likely to be found, the percentage of nonwhites (NW) in the population and the percentage of males in the age group 24-29 (AGE) were included in the regressions.[19]

Finally, a binary variable was used to represent each state's firearm control laws. The value one was given to a state that had a dealer licensing law (DL), license to carry (LC), dealer record keeping (DRK), government record keeping (GRK), prohibition against carrying or carrying a concealed weapon (PRBT), firearm licensing (FL), or waiting period to purchase (WAIT); a zero was given otherwise.[20]

---

are not identically measured, we are not able to pool the data and investigate the net differences over the period. The logic for including the two cross sections was to meet the possible objection that a study of one cross section may result in a statistical artifact. While expanding the study to include two cross sections does not prove that the results are not artifacts, the similarity in results over the two cross sections reduces this likelihood.

17. Ehrlich, "Participation in Illegitimate Activities."

18. A theoretical justification for the inclusion of these variables is given in Ehrlich, "Participation in Illegitimate Activities."

19. Marvin E. Wolfgang, *Patterns in Criminal Homicide* (Philadelphia: University of Pennsylvania, 1958).

20. For a complete listing of state firearm control laws, see J.P. Magaddino, "Economic Analysis of State Gun Control Laws" (Ph.D. dissertation, Virginia Polytechnic Institute, 1972).

Empirical Results

Since the probability of apprehension is determined simultaneously with the offense rate, equation (1) was transformed to natural logarithms and estimated by two-stage least squares. The exogenous variables assumed to be excluded from equation (1) were the percentage of each state's population living in an urban area, police protection expenditures per capita, and the number of males per 100 females. The empirical results for homicides, robbery, and aggravated assaults in 1960 and 1970 are reported in Table 9-1. For both 1960 and 1970, the deterrence variables are found to have a significantly negative impact on personal (homicide and aggravated assault) and property (robbery) crime. An increase in either the probability or severity of punishment reduces the incentive to participate in an illegal activity.

In both the homicide and aggravated assault equation, income, unemployment, and labor force participation (1970 only) are not significantly different from zero. This is consistent with the hypothesis that personal crimes are activities that are not motivated by wealth considerations. In both the 1960 and 1970 robbery equations, the proxy for illegal returns, income, has a significantly positive effect on the rate of robberies. The positive but insignificant coefficient on unemployment weakly suggests that as legal market opportunities diminish, individuals are more likely to turn to robbery. Similarly, labor force participation is found to be inversely related to robberies, but this variable is significant for 1960 only.

For the three types of crimes, education is found to have a significantly negative impact only for personal crimes in 1970. This suggests that individuals were aware of the high crime rates in the sixties and reacted accordingly by increasing their personal defenses against homicides and aggravated assaults.

The percentage of families in poverty was significantly different from zero for the robbery and aggravated assault equations in 1960 only. The negative sign indicates that in 1960 participants in violent crimes tended to come from the more affluent economic classes.

Finally, not one of the seven state firearm control law variables is found to be significantly different from zero in any of the three crime equations for either 1960 or 1970. In other words, states with firearm control laws are found not to have statistically significant

Table 9-1. Regression Results for Specific Crimes in 1970 and 1960.

| | Crime and Year | | | | | |
| | Homicide | | Robbery | | Assault | |
Variables	1970	1960	1970	1960	1970	1960
Constant	10.73 (0.346)	40.37 (0.998)	2.021 (0.04)	66.27 (1.69)*	18.75 (0.56)	105.6 (2.51)***
P	-0.4403 (1.73)*	-0.4586 (2.29)**	-0.5625 (2.07)**	-0.7088 (4.91)***	-0.3818 (1.70)*	-0.4196 (4.22)***
TS	-0.2456 (2.13)**	-0.5085 (1.84)*	-0.0508 (0.13)	-0.5101 (1.76)*	-0.2909 (1.80)*	-0.4196 (2.43)**
INC	1.492 (1.43)	0.7639 (1.19)	4.706 (3.42)***	0.7331 (2.21)**	1.769 (1.48)	-0.0880 (0.13)
POV	-0.1518 (.48)	-0.3648 (1.50)	-0.0717 (0.16)	-0.4698 (2.23)**	0.1588 (0.49)	-0.4606 (1.96)*
NW	0.5032 (5.86)***	0.4915 (5.56)***	0.5790 (4.35)***	0.4134 (5.24)***	0.3013 (2.97)***	0.4454 (4.62)***
ED	-4.588 (2.65)***	0.4876 (0.36)	-2.931 (1.22)	-1.983 (1.56)	-3.658 (1.85)*	1.171 (0.89)
UN	0.2712 (0.90)	0.2977 (1.21)	0.0679 (0.16)	0.3217 (1.43)	0.3563 (1.08)	0.1390 (0.57)
LFP	-1.771 (0.24)	-7.388 (0.79)	-6.260 (0.62)	-16.23 (1.83)*	-4.248 (0.53)	-22.78 (2.38)**
AGE	-0.9209 (1.47)	0.6129 (0.86)	-2.403 (2.52)**	0.1371 (0.18)	-0.6653 (0.96)	0.3699 (0.46)

DL	−0.1573 (0.85)	−0.3329 (1.31)	−0.1307 (0.51)	−0.3611 (1.40)	−0.1911 (0.96)	−0.3362 (1.34)
LC	−0.0053 (0.03)	−0.1174 (0.63)	0.0660 (0.29)	0.0115 (0.96)	−0.0412 (0.25)	−0.1435 (0.75)
DRK	0.0858 (0.39)	0.0205 (0.10)	0.0084 (0.02)	−0.0956 (0.51)	0.1612 (0.66)	0.1339 (0.68)
GRK	−0.3703 (1.37)	0.0129 (0.05)	−0.3514 (1.05)	0.0988 (0.49)	−0.3310 (1.41)	−0.1340 (0.55)
PRBT	−0.4024 (0.87)	0.1001 (0.67)	−0.2928 (0.46)	0.1542 (1.07)	−0.5578 (0.55)	0.0115 (0.07)
FL	0.0634 (0.26)	−0.1404 (0.51)	0.1688 (0.51)	0.1954 (0.80)	0.0711 (0.27)	0.2251 (0.79)
WAIT	0.0817 (0.45)	0.0725 (0.30)	−0.0020 (0.01)	0.0166 (0.07)	0.1195 (0.61)	0.1172 (0.46)
R^2	0.78	0.83	0.76	0.81	0.63	0.84

Note: Absolute value of *t*-statistics in parentheses: * indicates coefficient significant at 0.10 level; ** at 0.05 level; *** at 0.01 level.

lower rates of homicides, robberies, or aggravated assaults than states without such laws.

Alternative Specifications of Firearm Control Laws

It might be argued that the use of dummy variables to represent state firearm control laws is fallacious since laws are not self-enforcing. Even though state firearm control laws are virtually identical in content, enforcement of these laws may differ. States enforcing their laws more vigorously impose higher real costs on potential firearm users and consequently should have lower rates of violent crimes.

The National Rifle Association has designated six states as having restrictive firearm control laws.[21] Restrictive states allow only those individuals who are able to clearly demonstrate a legitimate need (security guards, law enforcement personnel, etc.) the right to purchase and use a firearm. Typically, these states are characterized by high permit rejection rates, and personal or home defense is not considered a legitimate reason for owning a firearm.

To test for the possibility of state differences in the level of enforcement, equation (1) was reestimated with the state firearm control dummy variables replaced by a dummy variable (RSTRCT) which is equal to one for the six states designated as having restrictive firearm control laws and zero otherwise. The regression results are given in Table 9–2.

None of the partial regression coefficients in Table 9–2, Column 1, are significantly different from zero. States with so-called restrictive firearm control laws are not found to have significantly lower crime rates relative to other states.

It is possible that using a binary variable to represent a state's firearm control law does not adequately control for the existence of a firearm control program in each state. This hypothesis suggests that an index would be more appropriate in representing a state's overall firearm control program. To test for this possibility, the weights and procedure utilized in the study by Geisel, Roll, and Wettick were used to construct a firearm control law index for each state in 1960 and 1970.[22] This index was substituted for the state firearm control

21. The six states are Hawaii, Michigan, Missouri, New Jersey, New York, and North Carolina.

22. The index was determined as follows: each firearm control law in their study was assigned a weight (e.g., dealer licensing was assigned a weight of 8) and the index for each

Table 9–2. **Partial Regression Coefficients for Restrictive States and for Firearm Index on Specific Offenses in 1970 and 1960.**

Offense and Year	RSTRCT	Firearm Index
Homicide		
1970	−0.1361 (0.67)	−0.2399 (2.36)**
1960	−0.1048 (0.43)	−0.1421 (2.03)**
Robbery		
1970	0.0109 (0.04)	−0.2157 (1.41)
1960	0.1201 (0.55)	0.0912 (1.31)
Assault		
1970	−0.0959 (0.44)	−0.1793 (1.29)
1960	0.2178 (0.95)	0.0041 (0.07)

Note: Absolute value of *t*-statistics in parentheses; **indicates significant at 0.05 level.

dummy variables in equation (1). The partial regression coefficients are presented in Column 2 of Table 9–2.

In both 1960 and 1970, the firearm index is not significantly different from zero for either robbery or aggravated assault. However, in both 1960 and 1970, the firearm index is statistically negative in the homicide equation. This would seem to confirm the conclusion in the study by Geisel, Roll, and Wettick that nationwide imposition of increased controls would substantially reduce the rate of homicides.

However, it has been argued by Hardy and Stompoly that the index developed by Geisel, Roll, and Wettick actually measures the effect of regional variations in cultural attitudes toward violence.[23] That is, the so-called "frontier ethic" present in the South and Southwest tends to promote higher homicide rates in those regions. Thus it is possible that states with a large firearm index tended to

state was equal to $\sum w_i x_i$, all i, where w_i is the weight assigned to firearm control law i and x_i equals one if that state had firearm control law and zero otherwise.

23. David T. Hardy and John Stompoly, "Of Arms and the Law," *Chicago-Kent Law Review* 51 (Summer 1974): 62–114.

Table 9-3. Partial Regression Coefficients of Firearm Index and
Region on Homicides in 1970 and 1960.

Year	Firearm Index	Region
1970	-0.1584	0.4391
	(1.41)	(2.47)**
1960	-0.0528	0.5698
	(0.75)	(2.97)**

Note: Absolute value of *t*-statistics in parentheses; **indicates significant at 0.05 level.

have lower homicide rates, not because of the presence of any controls, but rather because the index was measuring their lesser tendencies toward violence.

In order to test the validity of this hypothesis, equation (1) was reestimated for 1960 and 1970 with the firearm control index and a dummy variable (REGION) equal to one for states in the South and the Southwest and zero otherwise. If the firearm index is actually measuring regional variations in homicidal proclivities, controlling for region should reduce the impact of the firearm index. The partial regression coefficients for the firearm control index and REGION are reported in Table 9-3.

For both 1960 and 1970, the variable REGION was positive and significantly different from zero. Further, the introduction of REGION reduces the value of the coefficient on the firearm index by 34 percent in 1970 and 63 percent in 1960, and in both years the firearm index becomes statistically insignificant. This is consistent with the hypothesis that the firearm control index was actually measuring cultural differences in homicidal tendencies between states. Controlling for these differences found the firearm index to have no impact on the rate of homicides.

Summary of State Firearm Control Laws and Violent Crimes

In order to determine the effectiveness of state firearm control laws in reducing the level of violent crimes, the supply of homicides, robberies, and aggravated assaults was estimated across states for 1970 and 1960. The theoretical approach used in this study differs from previous studies on firearm laws in that the analysis explicitly incorporates the probability and severity of punishment as well as economic and demographic variables. The empirical results found that the null hypothesis that the existing firearm laws have no significant impact on the rate of violent crimes could not be rejected. Alternative specifications of state firearm control laws left this conclusion unchanged.

HANDGUNS, HOMICIDES, AND THE GUN CONTROL ACT OF 1968

The assassination of President John F. Kennedy and the urban violence of the 1960s dramatically called attention to the role and use of firearms in American society. These events, followed by the assassinations of Martin Luther King and Robert Kennedy, provided the major impetus for enactment of federal firearms control in 1968. The belief of the 90th Congress regarding the necessity for controlling weapons was reflected in the language describing the statute's objectives:

> (1) provide support to Federal, State and local law enforcement officials in their fight against crime and violence . . . (2) the ease with which any person can acquire firearms . . . is a significant factor in the prevalence of lawlessness . . . (3) there is a causal relationship between the easy availability of firearms . . . and . . . youthful criminal behavior and (4) the large volume of relatively inexpensive pistols and revolvers (including military surplus weapons) imported into the United States has contributed greatly to lawlessness and the Nation's law enforcement problem.[24]

To address these issues, the Gun Control Act of 1968 contained three major provisions:

Licensing. The Federal licensing of individuals to manufacture or deal in firearms was mandated, and a ban was placed on all interstate transportation of weapons to or from individuals who were not licensed by the U.S. Department of the Treasury as dealers, manufacturers, importers or collectors.[25] The ban on interstate transporta-

---

24. 18 U.S.C.A. 8, 929, p. 104.

25. This provision of the Act essentially grants all federal license holders a monopoly position in commerce. The value of this monopoly position is dependent upon how vigo-

tion was the focal point of this legislation in that it attempted to assist state and local law enforcement efforts. It has been a long and widely held belief that jurisdictions with strict laws governing the acquisition and ownership of firearms had their efforts undermined if neighboring jurisdictions had easy firearm access. To remedy this shortcoming of federalism, the Act required dealers to verify whether a customer was a state resident. Dealers were required to record all sales and deliveries with the name, age, and place of residence of the purchaser and a complete description of the weapon sold. These records were to be kept at the licensee's place of business and were to be made available to the U.S. Department of Treasury or to local and state police upon request of the Secretary of the Treasury. Many viewed the record-keeping provision of the Act as an attempt to enhance law enforcement information and ultimately increase the probability of apprehension of all criminals who use firearms in their crimes.[26]

Prohibitions. Licensees were prohibited from knowingly transferring particular firearms or ammunition to certain groups classified as irresponsible or potentially dangerous. Specifically denied access were all persons eighteen years or under from the purchase or possession of any firearm or ammunition; all persons under twenty-one years of age from the purchase or possession of a handgun; all persons who are under indictment, convicted felons, fugitives from justice, drug addicts and users (including marijuana), mentally defective or committed individuals, from the purchase or possession of any firearm or ammunition. The enforceability of this provision of the Act is *ex post* in nature. An individual seeking to purchase a firearm is required to sign a statement that he or she does not fall within any

---

rously the Treasury Department restricts new entry. As with other monopoly positions, such legislation will raise the relative price of handguns.

26. While no one contests what the law attempts to accomplish, there is disagreement as to whether or not the record-keeping provision significantly raises the productivity of the criminal justice system or is cost effective. Testing this hypothesis is beyond the scope of the present study since (1) this research is confined to homicides and it is possible that the record-keeping provision raises the probability of apprehension and conviction of other crimes and (2) the statistical method employed does not allow one to analyze the record-keeping provision in isolation from other provisions of the Act. Regardless of the view of the effectiveness of record keeping, the provision restricting residents to purchase handguns, if they so choose, only from firms located within their state further enhances the monopoly position of licensed local dealers. Prior to the passage of the Act, a significant source of competition to local dealers was national mail order dealers.

of the above-described classes. An ineligible individual could purchase a firearm by supplying false information. However, the record-keeping requirements made it possible for law enforcement officials to prosecute such an individual if apprehended with a firearm.

Import Restrictions. The importation of relatively inexpensive fire-arms was prohibited unless the Secretary of the Treasury certified the firearm was being imported for scientific, research, or training purposes, was a curio or museum piece, or was particularly suitable or readily adaptable to sporting purposes. The importation ban was expressly designed to reduce access to foreign-produced, low-priced handguns.[27] In limiting availability of the so-called "Saturday Night Special," Congress was attempting to control a weapon that it perceived as being cheap, plentiful, and a significant cause of escalating rates of violent crime.

Handgun Ownership and the Impact of the Gun Control Act of 1968

Since one of the express purposes of the Gun Control Act of 1968 was to reduce the availability of handguns, it is of interest to question what impact the law had on the rate of civilian handgun acquisition. Implicit in much of the discussion of gun control is the premise that no one would purchase a handgun other than to use it in the commission of a crime. This assumes that the purchase of a weapon is somehow different from the purchase of any other kind of con-

27. One might argue that the importation ban was simply an attempt to protect U.S. manufacturers against foreign competition. In "Firearms and Federal Law" Zimring argues against this interpretation, reasoning that if the limitation of imports was merely "protectionist" legislation, then the exemption of weapons suitable for "sporting purposes" makes no sense, since it allows for the importation of rifles and shotguns. In attempting to explain the rationale for passage of this legislation one need not adopt the narrow view of "protectionist" legislation or the view that legislators were motivated by a genuine concern for public safety, since the important theoretical work of A. Downs, *An Economic Theory of Democracy* (New York: Harper & Row, 1957); James M. Buchanan and Gordon Tullock, *The Calculus of Consent* (Ann Arbor: University of Michigan Press, 1962); Sam Peltzman, "Toward a More General Theory of Regulation," *Journal of Law and Economics* 29 (August 1976): 211–40; and the subsequent empirical research strongly suggest that the behavior of legislators and regulators can be better explained from the view point of building broad-based coalitions. Whatever the intent of the importation restrictions, the actual effect of this legislation was to greatly reduce the number of imported handguns and greatly increase the demand for domestic handguns.

sumer durable good. It has been suggested that the examination of handgun purchases should proceed identically to the methodology one follows in examining the purchases of any other consumer durable good. This line of reasoning implies the civilian purchases of handguns depend upon the level of income, recreational attitudes of the population, urbanization, age distribution, the level of violent crime, and the stock of previously purchased handguns. The estimated equation was assumed to take the following explicit form[28]:

$$
\begin{aligned}
\log H1_t = \ & a_0 + a_1 \log YP_t + a_2 \log HTL_t + a_3 \log A2549_t \\
& + a_4 \log NW_t + a_5 \log OVC_{t-1} + a_6 T_t \\
& + a_7 \log H2_{t-1} + a_8 \ ACT \qquad\qquad t = 1947\text{-}1977
\end{aligned}
$$

$$(2)$$

The dependent variable, $H1_t$, is defined as the number of handguns purchased per thousand resident civilian population in period t. YP_t is the real permanent income per capita, and, assuming handguns are a normal good, one would anticipate a positive relationship between permanent income and handgun purchases. To measure the sporting use of handguns, hunting licenses per thousand resident civilian population, HTL_t, is included. It might be argued that handguns are of little value in hunting. However, hunting licenses may be a proxy for outdoor recreation. If the trend in "outdoor recreation" is representative of other recreational activities, then this variable should be positively related to handgun purchases regardless of whether handguns *per se* are valuable hunting weapons. Alternatively, one might argue that handguns represent a hunting weapon or that individuals with hunting licenses are also likely to purchase handguns (Wright, 1982). In either case, one would anticipate a positive relationship between hunting licenses and handgun purchases.

To account for sociodemographic variation over time, the percentage of the population between the ages of twenty-five and forty-nine, A2549, and the proportion of nonwhites in the residential civilian population, NW_t, are included. The inclusion of NW_t deserves special comment. In attempting to explain variations in handgun purchases over time, one needs to control for possible variations in be-

---

28. The functional form of this equation is based on the theoretical and empirical work of Stone and Rowe in their classic study "The Durability of Consumer's Durable Goods," *Econometrica* 28 (April 1960): 407-16.

havior between rural and urban areas. Ideally, one should include the fraction of the population in urban areas as an independent variable. Because available data on urban population are not sufficient for estimation, we use the proportion of nonwhites as a crude proxy for urbanization.[29]

To test whether or not individuals purchase handguns as a reaction to violent crimes, the aggregate of the seven major violent crimes occurring in the previous period, OVC_{t-1}, is included in the regression.[30] If one of the primary motivations for handgun acquisition is self-protection, then one would anticipate a positive relationship between the rate of criminal activity in the previous period and the rate of handgun purchases in the current period. The variable T is included to measure the trend variation over time. The additional purchases of handguns are also dependent upon the stock of handguns held at the beginning of the current period. The variable $H2_{t-1}$, is the cumulative number of handguns per thousand resident civilian population held in period $t-1$. Other things being equal, the larger the existing stock, the lower the purchases of handguns will be. Finally, the variable ACT is included to measure the impact of the Gun Control Act of 1968, being equal to zero for the years 1947–1968 and equal to one thereafter. If the Gun Control Act of 1968 was successful in achieving its express goal of reducing the availability of handguns, then one would anticipate a negative relationship between the variable ACT and handgun acquisition.

Equation (2) is estimated using ordinary least squares, and the results are exhibited in Table 9–4.[31] Permanent income, hunting licenses, and urbanization are found to have a positive and significant effect on handgun purchases. While the fraction of the population between twenty-five and forty-nine is positive, it is not statistically

29. For similar usages of this variable, see, for example, Isaac Ehrlich, "The Deterrent Effect of Capital Punishment: A Question of Life and Death," *American Economic Review* 65 (June 1975) and S.A. Hoenack and W.C. Weiler, "A Structural Model of Murder Behavior and the Criminal Justice System," *American Economic Review* 70 (June 1980): 327–40.

30. The FBI's seven index crime rates are homicide, rape, assault, robbery, burglary, larceny, and auto theft.

31. Since price is an important variable in explaining the variations in the purchase of consumer durable goods, a price variable was added to equation (2). Unfortunately, no data exists on the average price of handguns, so a proxy variable was employed. The proxy variable used was the GNP price deflator for consumer durable goods. The empirical results were virtually identical to those exhibited in Table 9–4, except that the price variable was statistically insignificant.

Table 9-4. Regression Table for Handgun Purchases: 1947-1977.

Independent Variables	Coefficient
Constant	-65.059 (-5.01)***
log YP_t	7.312 (3.52)***
log HTL_t	2.557 (2.28)***
log $A2549_t$	4.816 (1.60)
log NW_t	14.398 (2.31)**
log OVC_t	1.267 (2.34)**
T	-0.185 (-2.61)***
log $H2_{t-1}$	-6.664 (-3.88)***
ACT	0.327 (2.09)***
R^2 (adj)	0.971

Note: The number in parentheses below the coefficient is the value of the t-statistic; ***significant at 0.01 level; **significant at 0.05 level.

different from zero. Handgun purchases are found to be significantly and inversely related to the stock of handguns at the beginning of the period. The time trend variable indicates that there has been, *ceteris paribus*, a statistically significant decline in handgun purchases per thousand resident civilian population.[32] Furthermore, it appears that handgun purchases are systematically related to rising violent crime rates.

Finally, if the primary attempt of the Gun Control Act of 1968 was to reduce the purchase of handguns, then the regression results

32. This should not be misunderstood as meaning that handgun purchasing has declined in absolute number. What the analysis indicates is that if all the other factors affecting handgun acquisition had remained unchanged over the period studied, there would have been a decline in handgun purchases over time. Many have made references to the steady increase in handgun purchases that have occurred over time. However, our empirical results indicate that the increase in handgun purchases is not due to the passage of time, but instead the increase is related to changes in other factors in the model.

indicate that the Act has not only failed to achieve this desired result, but there has been a significant increase in handgun purchases since its enactment. It is possible that the buying populace forms adaptive expectations about the potential for future restrictive legislation. If this is so, then anticipating more restrictive legislation encouraged the populace to purchase more handguns after the passage of the Act.

This result does not necessarily imply that the Gun Control Act has been a failure; it is possible that the firearm control legislation selectively reduced the rate of handgun ownership among the high risk users. If the rate of handgun ownership was reduced among the high risk users, even though an overall increase in "legitimate" user purchases occurred, then the proper test of impact of the Gun Control Act is to examine its effect on homicide and not on handgun acquisition alone.[33]

The Structural Model

Zimring, in a widely cited study, qualitatively analyzed the Gun Control Act of 1968 by focusing on the rate of growth of handgun homicides and firearm assaults over the 1966–1973 period.[34] His results indicated that the Act was marginally effective in reducing the percentage of homicides attributable to handguns and the number of assaults attributable to firearms.

There are several difficulties with the approach adopted by Zimring. To infer that a change in the rate of growth of the selected variables is a function of the Gun Control Act of 1968 implicitly argues that all other variables affecting the rates of crime remain relatively the same over the period of investigation. However, a study of the time trend of the variables one normally would associate with violent crime fails to substantiate Zimring's implicit assumption. Furthermore, Zimring's results are based on an investigation of fifty-seven cities with populations of 250,000 or more. Unfortunately, his sampling procedure excluded twenty-one states, and since the popula-

33. If there exists a subcultural group within society that is more prone toward violent activity, then lower than average rates of handgun ownership may not be sufficient to reduce violent activity. Assuming this hypothesis is correct, the major impact of the Gun Control Act of 1968 would be upon criminal activity and not necessarily handgun sales.

34. Zimring, "Firearms and Federal Law."

tion in the excluded states is less urbanized, Zimring's procedure is biased toward states with lower firearm ownership rates than states with higher firearm ownership rates. More importantly, Zimring's methodology totally ignores differences in the effectiveness of law enforcement agencies, the judicial system, and other factors in the criminal justice system. Consequently, his results must be regarded as tenuous.

To test the impact of the Gun Control Act of 1968 on the homicide rate one must account for the many variables besides gun availability which influence crimes in order to isolate the effects of the legislation. A structural model based on the economic framework of criminal choice developed by Becker (1968) was formulated and estimated for U.S. data over the period 1947-1977. The advantage of the structural model over the approach adopted by Zimring is that it explicitly treats the homicide rate as a complex problem by incorporating the deterrent effect of the criminal justice system. It focuses not only on the variables affecting criminal behavior but also upon society's reaction to that behavior in terms of the probability of being arrested and convicted, the punishment meted out, firearm acquisition, expenditures on law enforcement, etc. The basic structural model of equations, except for the handgun equation, is the model developed by Hoenack and Weiler.[35]

The Murder Supply Structural Equation

$$Q/N = a_{10} + a_{11} \log Pa + a_{12} \log Pc \mid a + a_{13} \log Pe \mid c$$
$$+ a_{14} \log A1419 + a_{15} \log L + a_{16} \log YP$$
$$+ a_{17} T + a_{18} \log ALC + a_{19} \log H + a_{1,10} ACT$$

(3)

The dependent variable, Q/N, was the number of observed murders per thousand resident civilian population. The variables Pa, $Pc \mid a$, and $Pe \mid c$ represent the deterrent effects of the criminal justice system

35. Hoenack and Weiler, "A Structural Model of Murder Behavior and the Criminal Justice System." Similar economic modelling of criminal activity, including homicides, has been done by R.A. Carr-Hill and N.H. Stern, "An Econometric Model of the Supply and Control of Recorded Offenses in England and Wales," *Journal of Public Economics* 2 (November 1973): 289–318; Ehrlich, "Participation in Illegitimate Activitities"; "The Deterrent Effect of Capital Punishment," *American Economic Review* 65 (June 1975): 397–417; and K.I. Wolpin, "An Economic Analysis of Crime and Punishment in England and Wales," 1894–1967," *Journal of Political Economy* 86 (October 1978): 815–40.

being equal to the perceived probability of arrest, the conditional probability of being convicted given arrest, and the conditional probability of being executed given conviction, respectively. Economic theory suggests that an increase in the probability or severity of various punishments for murder will decrease (relative to the expected utility from an alternative independent activity) the expected utility from murder or from activities that may result in murder.[36]

The percentage of the population between the ages of fourteen and nineteen, A1419, is included to test whether the differential treatment of juvenile offenders has any effect on the supply of violent crime. Permanent income, YP, is a measure of the marginal returns to illegal activities. The greater the permanent income of the society, the larger the payoff to illegal activities. Labor force participation, L, is included to take into account that higher rates of labor force participation implies, *ceteris paribus*, less time to engage in illegitimate activities. The variable T is included to measure the trend variation over time.

Many have argued that alcohol consumption reduces inhibitions, impairs the ability to reason, etc., and thereby increases the degree of violent behavior among some groups of individuals.[37] To account for this behavior, alcohol consumption in gallons per person aged fifteen and above, ALC, is included to test this hypothesis. Two separate measures of handgun availability, H, are employed. The yearly handgun purchases per thousand resident civilian population, H1, is introduced to test Zimring's hypothesis that the rate at which new handguns enter the market has a greater impact on homicide rates than the stock of older handguns.[38] The *cumulative number* of handguns per thousand resident civilian population, H2, is used to test whether the cumulative number of handguns available affects the homicide rate. With either measure H1 or H2, conventional thinking posits a positive relationship between these variables and the murder rate.

The variable ACT was added to equation (3) to test whether or not the Gun Control Act of 1968 selectively reduced the availability of handguns to high risk users. If the Gun Control Act achieved its expressed objective, then this legislation would have lowered the rate of homicides in the post–1968 period. As before, ACT is measured as a dummy variable being equal to one for the years 1969–1977 and

36. Ehrlich, "The Deterrent Effect of Capital Punishment."
37. See Kates, *infra*.
38. Zimring, "Firearms and Federal Law."

zero otherwise. Due to space limitations, only the murder supply structural equation, which is estimated in the full context of the model, is described in the text; the remaining equations of the model are contained in the Appendix.

Estimates of the Murder Supply Structural Equation. Due to the simultaneous nature of the system of equations of the model and the presence of autocorrelation in time-series data, equation (3) is estimated by using two-stage Cochrane-Orcutt.[39] The empirical estimates of the coefficients of equation (3) and the t-statistics are presented in column 1 of Table 9-5.

The estimates of the murder supply equation generally support the hypothesis that the deterrent effect of legal sanctions reduces the homicide rate. Greater certainty of apprehension, conviction, and execution are found to have a significant inverse effect on the murder rate.[40] The coefficient for permanent income is significantly positive, while the coefficients for labor force participation and time trend are significantly negative. The fraction of the population in the age range of fourteen to nineteen is not significantly related to the number of murders. Particularly noteworthy is the finding that alcohol consumption is directly related to the rate of homicides. This finding is consistent with those who have hypothesized that the consumption of alcohol is a significant causal factor of violent behavior. Yearly handgun purchases are found not to significantly contribute to more violence. This result contradicts Zimring's hypothesis that "new handguns" are more likely to contribute to acts of violence. Statistical significance aside, the negative coefficient of yearly handgun purchases as well as the fact that the estimated coefficient is one and a half times its standard error strongly suggests that handgun purchases serve as a deterrent to homicides and introduces the possibility that there exists a simultaneous relationship between yearly handgun purchases and the homicide rate.[41] Finally, the coefficient on ACT is not significantly different from zero, suggesting that the

39. A complete description of autocorrelation and the Cochrane-Orcutt estimation procedure is given in J. Johnston, *Econometric Methods* (New York: McGraw-Hill, 1972).

40. The empirical results indicate that capital punishment reduces homicides. However, since we exclude other forms of punishment, this research offers no comment as to whether or not capital punishment is cost effective.

41. Newton and Zimring make reference to this point in *Firearms and Violence in American Life*, p. 21, but ignore its theoretical and empirical implications.

Table 9-5. Two-stage Cochrane-Orcutt Regression Results for Homicides: 1947-1977.

Independent Variables	Dependent Variable	
	Q/N (1)	Q/N (2)
Constant	-0.8905 (-2.01)**	-0.4280 (-0.87)
log Pa	-0.0781 (-2.40)††	-0.0549 (-1.47)†
log Pc | a	-0.0069 (-1.35)†	-0.0099 (-1.79)††
log Pe | c	-0.0006 (-1.82)††	-0.0005 (-1.44)†
log A1419	-0.0176 (-0.85)	-0.0132 (-0.60)
log L	-0.1776 (-1.70)†	-0.1723 (-1.70)††
log YP	0.3484 (6.09)**	0.2673 (4.98)**
T	-0.0111 (-6.08)††	-0.0093 (-5.47)††
log ALC	0.0133 (1.91)††	0.0184 (2.60)††
log H_1	-0.0039 (-1.56)	——
log H_2	—	0.0348 (1.73)*
ACT	0.0029 (1.17)	-0.0009 (-0.31)
R^2 (adj)	0.989	0.986

Note: Value of t-statistics in parentheses below each coefficient; ** significant at 0.05 level (two-tail test); * significant at 0.10 level (two-tail test); †† significant at 0.05 level (one-tail test); † significant at 0.10 level (one-tail test).

Gun Control Act of 1968 did not selectively reduce the access of handguns to high risk users.

It has been argued, however, that the murder rate may be related to the cumulative number of handguns owned rather than the rate of handgun acquisition. This reasoning suggests that the very existence of a large stock of handguns creates an environment conducive to murders. Accordingly, equation (3) in the model is reestimated using two-stage Cochrane-Orcutt with the handgun stock, H2, replacing handgun purchases, H1. These results are given in column 2 of Table 9-5.

As can be seen, the coefficients and the levels of significance of all the other variables in equation (3), except H2 and ACT, remained virtually unchanged.[42] The stock of handgun ownership is found to have a significant and positive impact on the homicide rate. It is incorrect, however, to conclude from this information that the handgun stock is a *cause* of murder, for two reasons. First, it is not inconceivable that increases in the handgun stock occurred in those groups of individuals most prone toward violence. Zimring, in fact, suggests that it is possible that, rather than the general patterns of handgun ownership contributing to violence, the increase in handgun ownership among subcultural groups disproportionately associated with violence is the basis of the problem.[43] Second, the homicide rate may affect the level of handgun ownership in the same way as it can be argued that the level of handgun ownership affects the homicide rate. In other words, greater handgun ownership may have been motivated by fear of crime, violence, and civil disorders. Thus, lower levels of handgun ownership may not be, as alleged by some, a sufficient condition for lower homicide rates. Finally, the coefficient on ACT reaffirms the conclusion that the Gun Control Act of 1968 did not have a statistically or numerically significant impact on the level of homicides.[44]

As suggested previously, the simultaneous relationship between yearly handgun purchases and the homicide rate implies that the ordinary least squares estimates of equation (2) are biased and inconsistent. Accordingly, equation (2) is reestimated using two-stage Cochrane-Orcutt within the context of the structural model. The empirical results appear in column 1 of Table 9-6.

---

42. Use of gross handgun stock figures assumes that over time handguns neither deteriorate, become obsolete, or are misplaced. Wright, *infra*, has estimated the net handgun stock figures assuming that the average lifetime of a privately owned firearm is fifty years. Using net handgun stock as H2, equation (3) was reestimated and the empirical results remained virtually identical.

43. Zimring, "Firearms and Federal Law."

44. One might argue that the Gun Control Act of 1968 was strictly designed to reduce access and availability to handguns rather than to have any direct effect on the homicide rate. Equation (3) was reestimated without ACT, and the empirical results, within either H1 or H2 included, remained virtually identical.

Table 9-6. Two-Stage Cochrane-Orcutt and Ordinary Least Squares Regression Results for Handgun Purchases: 1947-1977.

Independent Variables	Coefficient (Cochrane-Orcutt)	Coefficient (Ordinary Least Squares)
Constant	-45.586 (-2.17)**	-65.059 (-5.01)***
log YP_t	4.042 (1.03)	7.312 (3.52)***
log HTL_t	0.895 (0.79)	2.557 (2.28)
log $A2549_t$	8.915 (2.67)**	4.816 (1.60)
log NW_t	1.468 (0.22)	14.398 (2.31)**
log $(Q/N)_t$	18.698 (1.88)*	—
log OVC_t	—	1.267 (2.34)**
T	0.146 (0.78)	-0.185 (-2.61)**
log $H2_{t-1}$	-7.678 (-4.29)***	-6.664 (-3.88)***
ACT	0.484 (3.52)***	0.327 (2.09)**
R^2 (adj)	0.977	0.971

Note: Value of t-statistics in parentheses below each coefficient; *** significant at 0.01 level; ** significant at 0.05 level; * significant at 0.10 level. The ordinary least squares coefficients in Column 2 are reproduced from Table 9-1.

In contrast to the earlier results (reprinted in column 2 of Table 9-6), hunting licenses, permanent income, time trend, and urbanization are now found to be statistically insignificant. The fraction of the population between the ages of twenty-five and forty-nine is now significant and positively related to the rate of handgun acquisition, and the handgun stock is still significantly and inversely related to the rate of handgun acquisition. The homicide rate is found to be significantly positive, suggesting that the murder rate affects handgun purchases. Further, the coefficient of ACT is still significantly positive, reinforcing the earlier conclusion that the Federal Gun Control Act of 1968 not only did not reduce the rate of handgun acquisition, it may have had an "announcement effect" which resulted in citizens, because of fears or expectations of more restrictive legislation, purchasing handguns at dramatically higher rates.

Summary of Analysis of the Gun Control Act of 1968

The objective of this section was to analyze the impact of the Gun Control Act of 1968 on the rate of handgun acquisition and the homicide rate. We examined yearly handgun purchases using the methodology normally followed in examining the purchases of any other consumer durable good. A single equation model was used that controlled for various socioeconomic factors, the cumulative stock of handguns, and an index of violent crimes; our results showed that there had been a significant increase in handgun purchases since the enactment of the Federal Gun Control Act of 1968. We suggest that this may have occurred because the populace anticipated more restrictive legislation. However, this result did not necessarily imply that the Gun Control Act of 1968 was a failure. It might have been that the Gun Control Act of 1968 reduced the rate of handgun acquisition to groups classified as potentially dangerous or prone toward violence. If the rate of handgun acquisition was reduced among these high risk users, even though there was an overall increase in purchases, then the impact of the Gun Control Act of 1968 would affect the rate or number of homicides rather than the handgun acquisition alone.

To isolate the effect of the Gun Control Act on the homicide rate requires that homicide be treated as part of an interrelated system taking into account the effectiveness of law enforcement, the judicial system, the punishment meted out, expenditures available to the criminal justice system, and handgun availability. A structural model was formulated and the homicide equation was estimated within the context of this model. Our results indicate that the Gun Control Act of 1968 did not reduce the homicide rate, and that yearly handgun purchases were not significantly related to homicide rates.

Since many have suggested that the homicide rate is related to the cumulative number of handguns owned rather than the rate of yearly purchases, the homicide equation was reestimated within the context of the structural system of equations, using the stock of handguns rather than yearly handgun purchases. The results showed that, again, the Gun Control Act of 1968 did not have a statistically or numerically significant impact on the homicide rate. We did find, as alleged by proponents of gun control legislation, that the cumulative number of handguns owned did have a significantly positive impact on the homicide rate. However, such a finding does not necessarily imply that the cumulative level of handgun ownership is a cause of homicides. It is entirely possible that the level of handgun ownership and the homicide rate mutually interact (i.e., greater handgun ownership being a reaction to higher violent crime rates). To account for this mutual dependency, the yearly handgun acquisition equation was reestimated within the context of the structural system of equations. Our results indicate that the homicide rate has a positive impact on yearly handgun purchases. Further, we still find that the Gun Control Act of 1968 did not reduce the rate of handgun purchases.

POLICY IMPLICATIONS

From the viewpoint of society, the key policy question is whether federal and state firearm control laws are an effective method of reducing violent crimes. On the basis of both a 1960 and 1970 cross-sectional study of state violent crime rates, the null hypothesis that the existing state firearm laws have no significant impact on the rate of violent crimes could not be rejected. The crucial theoretical and methodological issue in analyzing the effectiveness of state firearm control laws is the causal relationship between firearm availability and violent crimes. If researchers could affirmatively establish that increases in gun availability cause increases in violent crimes, then decision makers need only focus on methods of reducing access to firearms. Unfortunately, there is no logically necessary causal relationship between firearms and violent crimes. For example, it is entirely possible that firearm availability is independent of the violent crime rate, that is, it is possible for firearm availability to increase and the violent crime rates to fall. In fact, during the 1950s and early 1960s, this is precisely what happened.[45] Thus, the conclusion reached in this study may reflect the fact that current firearm laws, for whatever reasons, do not effectively limit access, or that homi-

45. Magaddino, "Economic Analysis of State Gun Control Laws."

cide rates are independent of the level of gun ownership. Researchers to date have either overlooked or been unable to unambiguously distinguish between these two competing hypotheses.

An analysis of the 1947–1977 time period found that the Federal Gun Control Act of 1968 neither reduced the rate of handguns purchases nor reduced the rate of homicide. This result and the previous conclusion on state firearm control laws does not imply that firearm control laws in general are necessarily ineffective in reducing violent crime rates. It may well be that more stringent firearm laws, increased or stricter enforcement of the laws, or a different set of firearm laws would have yielded the desired social results. Our study merely shows that existing firearm control laws do not accomplish the social goals explicit in their adoption.

The most important aspect of this study is the structural model that treats homicides and handgun ownership as a complex problem that encompasses the behavior of murderers, society, and the criminal justice system. Previous research on gun ownership and on gun control suffers from the methodological shortcoming of ignoring the interdependence of many of the key variables.[46] Such research does not contribute to greater understanding and is open to the criticism that it has been dictated more by ideology than by detached scholarship.

It must also be understood that theoretical modelling and empirical testing of such models is only the first step in determining appropriate public policy. Even after identifying the causal relationships involved in the criminal choice-criminal justice system, a second stage of the analysis will require specification of the cost associated with each proposal for preventing criminal behavior. As there are many such proposals competing for a limited amount of criminal justice resources, yet a third stage of analysis may require comparison of the costs and benefits between competing potential solutions. In short, it is suggested that effective public policy in this area requires extensive and mature deliberation. Legislators who instead react reflexively to increases in violent crime and wanton acts of violence are likely to effect no more than a cosmetic panacea to the violence in American life.

46. See, for example, the empirical studies of Geisel, Rolls, and Wettick, "The Effectiveness of State and Local Regulation of Firearm Violence"; U.S. President's Commission on Law Enforcement and Administration of Justice, *The Challenge of Crime in a Free Society*; and P.M. Sommers, "Deterrence and Gun Control: An Empirical Analysis," *Atlantic Economic Journal* 8 (December 1980): 89–94.

APPENDIX
STRUCTURAL MODEL

The complete structural model used to estimate the murder supply structural equation was as follows [for a complete theoretical justification of model see Hoenack and Weiler (1980)]:

The Murder Supply Function

$$Q/N = a_{10} + a_{11} \log Pa + a_{12} \log Pc \mid a + a_{13} \log Pe \mid c$$
$$+ a_{14} \log A1419 + a_{15} \log L + a_{16} \log YP$$
$$+ a_{17} T + a_{18} \log ALC + a_{19} \log H + a_{1,10} ACT \tag{1}$$

The Production Equations

$$\log Pa = a_{30} + a_{31} \log Q + a_{32} \log POL + a_{33} \log NW \tag{2}$$

$$\log Pc \mid a = a_{40} + a_{41} \log ARST + a_{42} \log R + a_{43} \log NW \tag{3}$$

$$\log Pe \mid c = a_{50} + a_{51} \log CONV + a_{52} \log R + a_{53} CL$$
$$+ a_{54} T \times \log CONV_{t-1} + a_{55} \log A1419 \tag{4}$$

The Expenditure Equations

$$\log R = a_{60} + a_{61} \log Q + a_{62} \log YP + a_{63} \log N$$
$$+ a_{64} \log A2549 + a_{65} \log NW + a_{66} \log A50PLUS$$
$$+ a_{67} \log Q_{t-1} + a_{68} \log Q_{t-2}$$
$$+ a_{69} \log OVC_{t-1} + a_{6,10} \log OVC_{t-2} \tag{5}$$

$$\log POL = a_{70} + a_{71} \log Q + a_{72} \log YP + a_{73} \log N$$
$$+ a_{74} \log A2549 + a_{75} \log NW + a_{76} \log A50PLUS$$
$$+ a_{77} \log Q_{t-1} + a_{78} \log Q_{t-2}$$
$$+ a_{79} \log OVC_{t-1} + a_{7,10} \log OVC_{t-2} \tag{6}$$

The Handgun Equation

$$H1 = a_{80} + a_{81} \log YP + a_{82} \log HTL + a_{83} \log A2549$$
$$+ a_{84} \log NW + a_{85} \log (Q/N) + a_{86} T$$
$$+ a_{87} \log H2 + a_{88} ACT \tag{7}$$

Variable Identification

Endogenous Variables

Q = number of observed murders

ARST = arrests for observed murders

CONV = convictions for observed murders

Pa = probability of apprehension

$Pc \mid a$ = the conditional probability of conviction given apprehension

$Pe \mid c$ = the conditional probability of execution given conviction

H1 = handgun purchases per thousand resident civilian population

R = total resources available to the criminal justice system

POL = resources available to police only

Exogenous Variables

YP = real permanent income per capita

L = proportion of the population in the labor force

T = chronological time

N = resident civilian population

ALC = alcohol consumption per person aged fifteen or above (in gallons)

NW = proportion of the population that is nonwhite

H2 = handgun stock per thousand resident civilian population

HTL = hunting licenses per thousand resident civilian population

CL = dummy variable representing class action appeals taking the value one for 1965–1969 and zero otherwise

A1419 = proportion of the population aged fourteen to nineteen

A2549 = proportion of the population aged twenty-five to forty-nine

A50PLUS = proportion of the population aged fifty years or more

OVC = index of other violent crimes

ACT = dummy variable representing the Gun Control Act of 1968, taking the value zero from 1947–1968 and one from 1969–1977

Chapter 10

A MARKET ANALYSIS FOR HANDGUNS AND GUN CONTROL ISSUES

Steven Balkin and John F. McDonald

INTRODUCTION

There have been numerous theoretical and empirical attempts to analyze (1) the impact of handgun control efforts on the quantity of handguns that people hold; (2) the impact of the quantity of handguns on the crime rate; and (3) the combination of (1) and (2): the impact of handgun control efforts on the crime rate. All three approaches allude to a market for handguns, but no one has yet formally stated a market model for handguns that is developed from standard economic theory and that can be used as a theoretical anchor for attempts to analyze gun control issues.

The objective of this chapter will be to familiarize persons engaged in gun control research and consumers interested in gun control issues with the development of a market model for handguns. We will *not* be using our theoretical models to determine the advisability of additional handgun control efforts, but we will use our models to show what assumptions must be made *a priori* to expect that additional handgun control effort will reduce the quantity of handguns. The interested parties may thus make those assumptions needed to advance their views and may thereby know what to look for empirically when testing theory related to handgun control.

The authors thank M. Bruce Johnson, Don B. Kates, Jr., William D. White, and Joseph D. Nicol for helpful comments on an earlier version of this chapter.

We do not claim that our models represent the only possible derivations of handgun market models. Others in this field can build their cwn using our framework as the basic approach, and they can change sectors, assumptions, equations, and time frames to suit their analytical needs. Forcing researchers to state explicitly the underlying theoretical mechanisms they are working with can elevate the debate on handgun control issues by clarifying what people disagree about so that the items of disagreement can then be scrutinized and empirically tested. While the underlying theoretical models in this chapter imply the direction of relationship between the variables of interest, they do not imply the magnitude of relationship. They can imply the signs of the elasticities and derivatives but not the absolute size. In trying to reach at least two different audiences, we hope that the mathematically oriented reader not find the analytics too pedantic and that the non-mathematical readers find the chapter not too obtuse. For this latter group, the mathematical analysis should be viewed as backdrop and they are encouraged to read on to the verbal explanations.

We begin by deriving the demand functions for handguns for the three relevant sectors: recreational use, criminal use, and citizen self-protection use. Next, we develop a simple analysis of the aggregate handgun market and then portray it in its disaggregative form among the three relevant sectors. We call it a "simple" analysis because it assumes away the durable goods nature of handguns to allow portrayal of the comparative statics analysis of the handgun market. This model is formulated in common supply and demand terms, and its operation is described with the usual introductory-level economics market graphs. The third section delves into the durable goods nature of handguns and describes the supply function for various time frames: market period, short run, and long run. That section examines the possible changing patterns of handgun ownership during the transition from one long-run equilibrium position to another.

Throughout our analysis we employ a variety of symbols to enable us to portray hypothesized relationships in mathematical form. A table of symbols is provided at the end of the chapter to assist the reader.

A MODEL OF THE DEMAND FOR HANDGUNS

In any formal model in the social sciences it is necessary to introduce simplifying assumptions so that the model is analytically manageable and empirically testable. In the analysis of handguns we must first make decisions concerning the nature of the commodity under study. Handguns are relatively complicated goods in that they vary appreciably in features such as caliber, accuracy, general quality of workmanship, etc. The development of a model to explain this variety would be of interest (as similar models for housing and autos are of interest), but our purpose is different.

Ultimately we are concerned with the *number* of handguns in the hands of private citizens. The quality *mix* of a given number of handguns is of secondary importance to us.[1] Therefore we shall assume that all working handguns are homogeneous in quality and that, as a consequence, there is a single market price for a working handgun. We shall leave for future research the demonstration that the relaxation of this assumption may make an important difference to the conclusions of the analysis.

We shall assume that there are three distinct segments of the demand for handguns: recreational users, criminals, and citizens who demand handguns for self-protection.[2] Each group shall be examined in turn. Throughout this analysis the commodity demanded is really a flow of handgun services per unit of time, and the price is the price of a unit of these services. If we assume, as we do in the next section, that handguns are nondurable, then a handgun is the same thing as a unit of handgun services for a time period. In a later section we relax the assumption of nondurability and assume that the services provided by a stock of handguns are proportional to that stock.

Recreational Demand

People who demand handguns for recreational purposes can be assumed to maximize a utility function that includes recreation as

---

1. The quality level does have important implications which relate to the useful life of a given stock of handguns. This issue concerns the durability nature of handguns which we discuss in a later section.

2. See Lizotte and Bordua (1980) for empirical evidence that recreational demand and self-protection demand can be considered to be separate segments of total demand.

one of the goods. Recreation is "produced" by combining handguns and other purchased goods with recreational time. Formally, the problem is to maximize utility subject to income and time constraints, or maximize

$$U = U(W, R, L) \tag{1}$$

subject to

$$Y = W + P_g G_r + W_r + F_g \tag{2}$$

$$R = R(T_r, G_r, W_r) \tag{3}$$

and $\qquad T = T_r + L \tag{4}$

where $\quad Y \quad=\quad$ income

$\quad\quad\quad W \quad=\quad$ all-purpose consumer good (with price = 1.0)

$\quad\quad\quad R \quad=\quad$ an index of the quantity of the good recreation

$\quad\quad\quad L \quad=\quad$ other leisure time (not recreation time)

$\quad\quad\quad P_g \quad=\quad$ price of handguns

$\quad\quad\quad G_r \quad=\quad$ quantity of recreational handguns

$\quad\quad\quad W_r \quad=\quad$ quantity of other recreational purchases (price = 1.0)

$\quad\quad\quad F_g \quad=\quad$ expected value of punishment for possession of a handgun (which could be zero)[3]

$\quad\quad\quad T \quad=\quad$ time budget

$\quad\quad\quad T_r \quad=\quad$ recreation time

This consumer choice problem implies that the demand for handguns for recreational use can be expressed as

$$G_r = G_r(Y, P_g, F_g, T) \tag{5}$$

---

3. The expected value of the punishment is the level of punishment (e.g., a fine) multiplied by the probability of being caught and found guilty of the offense. The mere possession of a handgun is, of course, currently not illegal in most locations in the United States. Throughout this chapter we will generally consider punishment or handgun control effort calibrated in expected value terms. This permits us to consider changes in certainty or severity of punishment as one variable. For convenience, a difference in behavioral response to certainty versus severity of punishment is assumed away by the assumption of risk neutrality.

To carry out our analysis we assume that the expected value of punishment can be changed. However, if harsher penalties are imposed but the police and courts reduce the probability of arrest and conviction by the same percent as the increase in penalties, the expected value of punishment will not change. For a discussion on the difficulties of changing levels of enforcement, see Bendis and Balkin (1979).

The prices of W and W_r are not included in equations (1) through (5) because they are assumed to be unity. This assumption implies that changes in P_g should be thought of as changes in the price of handguns relative to other prices. We presume that the effects of increases in Y and T on G_r are positive and the effects of increases in P_g and F_g on G_r are negative.[4]

In this analysis, handguns are demanded as inputs into the production of the final consumer good recreation. The elasticity of demand for recreational handguns, $(dG_r/dP_g)(P_g/G_r)$, is greater the greater is the elasticity of demand for recreation and the greater is the ease with which he other inputs into the production of recreation can be substituted for handguns.[5] Our conjecture is that other inputs, such as long guns and other recreational equipment, can easily be substituted for handguns in recreational uses. Thus it is likely that a policy that appreciably increases P_g (or makes handguns illegal—increases F_g) will cause a marked decline in the use of handguns for recreational purposes; recreational demand is expected to be relatively elastic.

Criminal Demand

The criminal segment of the demand for handguns consists of those persons who would obtain handguns for the purpose of committing crimes such as burglary, robbery, and premeditated murder.[6] Such individuals make all or part of their livelihood through crime. For simplicity, we assume that the criminal produces income by combining time spent in the planning and perpetration of crimes with pur-

---

4. The signing of the variables in the demand function depends on the matrix of income and substitution effect partial derivatives generated from the maximization problem. Ambiguity as to the sign of a relationship in the demand function is possible. We are signing the variables on the basis of what we consider reasonable assumptions to make for this matrix (e.g., handguns are not a Giffen good; offenders do not have a backward bending labor supply curve). Limitations of space do not permit us to fully explain this standard analysis. For a treatment of this see Henderson and Quandt (1971: 26–39).

5. The elasticity of demand for recreation is $(dR/dP_r)(P_r/R)$, where P_r is the "price" of recreation. The price of a unit of recreation depends upon the prices of the inputs into the production of recreation, handguns, recreational time, etc.

6. We define offenders as those who are at the margin of committing a crime, *ex ante*. Citizens or recreational users may ultimately become offenders through improper use of their handguns, but they were not intending to commit a (premeditated) crime.

chased inputs such as handguns and other tools of the trade. Net income for the offender is

$$Y_o = Y_s(T_o, G_o, W_o) - P_g G_o - P_w W_o - F_g \qquad (6)$$

Net income is gross income, Y_s, minus expenses. Y_s is a positive function of T_o, time devoted to criminal activity; G_o, handguns; and W_o, other purchased inputs.[7] Expenses are $P_g G_o$, expenditures for handgun acquisition; $P_w W_o$, expenditures for other purchased inputs; and F_g, the expected value of punishment for possessing handguns. If the offender is apprehended, income is $Y_o - F$, where F is the value of the penalty suffered for commission of a violent crime. In evaluating the worth of crime, the offender also considers J, the probability of apprehension and punishment for commission of a violent crime. We further assume that the offender is neutral to risk.

This assumption permits us to formulate that the offender maximizes a utility function (U) which includes the expected value of net income and leisure time (L) as arguments. In particular, the offender maximizes

$$U = U(E(Y), L) \qquad (7)$$

subject to $T = T_o + L$, where

$$E(Y) = (1 - J)Y_o + J(Y_o - F) \qquad (8)$$

This analysis implies that there is a demand for handguns by offenders which can be written

$$G_o = G_o(P_g, T, F_g, J, F) \qquad (9)$$

We presume that increases in P_g, F_g, J, and F reduce the demand for handguns, and an increase in T increases G_o. The price of W_o is assumed to be unity, and thus does not appear in equation (9).

The elasticity of demand for handguns for criminal purposes is greater the greater is the ease with which inputs into the production of Y_o can be substituted for handguns. Our conjecture is that, because handguns are easily concealed and are very effective weapons for obtaining victim compliance, other weapons such as long guns

7. Cook (1979) uses a similar approach to derive offender demand for handguns. The offender considers the present value of the prospective increase in net robbery earnings from owning a handgun. His conclusion for the offender concurs with our assumption that the acquisition of a handgun is likely to increase illicit income.

and knives are imperfect substitutes for handguns. The offender could spend more time in planning and perpetration as a substitute for a handgun; however, the extent to which such a substitution is possible may also be limited. While the elasticity of demand for handguns may vary with the type of illegal intent, the aforementioned conjectures lead to the expectation that the overall elasticity of demand for handguns for criminal purpose is relatively low. In any event, the effectiveness of handgun controls on the amount of crime committed with weapons depends crucially on these parameters of the crime-income "production function." More knowledge of this relationship is needed.

Self-Protection Demand

Probably the largest segment of the demand for handguns stems from the perception by many citizens that handguns are needed to protect life and property. More technically, handguns are an input into the production of self-protection. Self-protection can also be produced by other purchased inputs, such as locks and non-handgun weapons, and by the use of time to avoid risky situations or to invest in self-defense courses. It seems that the degree of substitutability for handguns in the production of self-protection is between that of recreation and crime production. The formal analysis is essentially the same as in the case of the demand for handguns for recreational purposes. The demand for handguns for self-protection can be expressed as

$$G_c = G_c(Y, P_g, T, C, F_g) \tag{10}$$

where Y is the income of citizens, T is the time budget, and C is a crime rate. The prices of other purchased goods are assumed to be unity, so these prices do not appear in this demand equation. We presume that increases in Y, T, and C will increase G_c, while increases in P_g and F_g reduce G_c. In the analysis that follows, the time budget T will be assumed to be constant for all demanders of handguns in a given segment of the market and will be dropped from the demand equations (5), (9), and (10).

Aggregate Demand

Each of the three segments of demand has its own submarket demand curve, which is simply the number of individuals in each segment multiplied by the demand curve of the representative individual. We interpret equations (5), (9), and (10) as being demand curves for these representative individuals.

For simplicity of exposition we have portrayed each individual potential user of handguns as falling into one of three mutually exclusive demand sectors. Of course it is likely that some individuals may have multipurpose uses for handguns. Particularly, offenders can be expected to purchase handguns for self-protection as well as for illegal income-earning purposes. They are likely to perceive, more than the other groups, dangers in the real world. A more precise definition of the three subsectors would place those who have any criminal purpose for owning handguns in the "offender" sector; those who have no criminal purpose for owning a handgun but whose primary purpose for owning a handgun is for sport or collecting would be placed in the "recreation" sector; those who have no criminal purpose for owning a handgun but whose primary purpose for owning a handgun is for protection would be placed in the "self-protection" sector.

While this slightly more complex definition of the sectors of demand for handguns is more realistic, our assumptions about the relative elasticity of the three groups still hold. The total market demand for handguns is now derived by adding together the market demands for the three segments, yielding a demand equation

$$G = G(P_g, Y, F_g, J, F, C) \tag{11}$$

The price elasticity of total demand for handguns, or (dG/dP_g) (P_g/G) is the weighted average of the price elasticities of the three segments, where the weights are the quantities demanded in each market segment as a percentage of total market demand. From the previous derivations of three sectors of handgun demand, we have conjectured that recreational demand has the relatively highest price elasticity, followed by self-protection demand, and offender demand has the relatively lowest elasticity. We use this in the next section in our analysis of the effects of handgun control in the disaggregated market.

A MARKET ANALYSIS OF HANDGUN CONTROL

In the previous section the behavior of handgun demanders was derived using standard utility theory. In this section, for convenience and simplicity, the durable goods nature of handguns will be assumed away and a simple market model will be used to examine handgun control issues. Using the working assumption that handguns are a nondurable good, consumable in the period that they are purchased, makes for a simple depiction of handgun control analysis and does not significantly alter the basic findings. In a durable handguns context one can view the changes in market position, derived in this section, as the change from one long-run equilibrium position to another. A model of durable handguns is contained in the next section.

While the term "handgun control" is used in its generic sense as any policy that affects the supply or demand for handguns, the clearest interpretation for market analysis is to consider it as an outright prohibition policy. Other kinds of handgun controls exist in a myriad of types, such as licensing and registration arrangements, penalties for carrying handguns, and penalties for using handguns in the commission of a crime. To the extent that these other types of handgun control mechanisms act like a total or partial prohibition or affect demand or supply relationships, the following analysis would also apply to them. It is left to future research to determine the differential impact among the types of handgun controls.

A Simple Market Model

Figure 10-1 depicts a simple market model of handguns where there is some price elasticity to both the market supply and demand functions. The market price (P_1) and quantity (G_1) of handguns occurs at the intersection of the supply and demand curves. The market will be in equilibrium at that point because the behaviors of both suppliers and demanders are consistent with each other. There is no shortage or surplus to cause either of the sectors to change the amount they are willing to buy or sell. As was discussed in the previous section, the underlying market model can be expressed as

$$G_d = G_d \; (\overset{-}{P_g}, \; \overset{+}{Y}, \; \overset{-}{F_g}, \; \overset{-}{J}, \; \overset{-}{F}, \; \overset{+}{C}) \tag{12}$$

$$G_s = G_s \; (\overset{+}{P_g}, \; \overset{-}{F_s}, \; B_s) \tag{13}$$

$$G_d = G_s \tag{14}$$

Figure 10-1. The Market for Handguns.

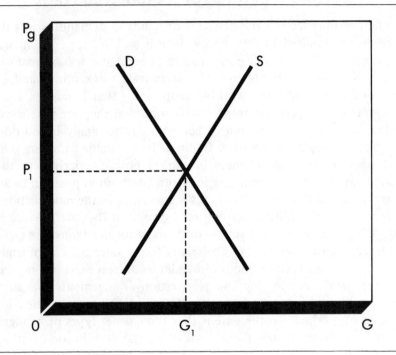

where

G_d = quantity of handguns demanded

P_g = price of handguns

Y = income of citizens

F_g = expected value of penalty for handgun possession

J = probability that criminals are apprehended and punished for violent offenses

F = penalty paid by criminals

C = crime rate

G_s = quantity of handguns supplied

F_s = expected value of punishment for producing and/or selling handguns

B_s = a vector of other influences that would affect the supply of handguns (e.g., prices of inputs, technology of producing guns)

The signs above the variables indicate the expected effect of an increase in the variable in question.

The supply side of the model, the handgun industry, as embodied in equation (13), is assumed to be a conventional perfectly competitive industry. Each producer and/or seller of handguns is assumed to take the market price as given and to maximize economic profits. The supply curve indicates how the quantity of handguns supplied varies with the price holding constant the input prices (labor, materials, etc.), the technology of producing handguns, and the expected value of the penalty attached to production or sale of handguns.

According to the conventional Becker-Ehrlich supply of crime model, potential offenders are expected to be responsive to punishment.[8] Increases in the certainty or severity of punishment (*ceteris paribus*) are expected to reduce offending behavior. Punishment acts like a demand or input price. The greater is the price that must be paid for participating in an illegal activity, the less participation in that activity. However, solutions for the underlying maximization problem can yield for some offenders an elasticity of response to punishment that is nonnegative.[9]

We will start off assuming that in the aggregate there is some elasticity of response to punishment for violating handgun control laws, which means that, in mathematical terms:

$$\frac{\partial G_d}{\partial F_g} < 0; \frac{\partial G_s}{\partial F_s} < 0$$

Thus if regulations were imposed against the purchase-possession and/or sales of handguns which implied a sanction if caught, supply and/or demand curves would shift to the left, respectively. If both functions possess some price elasticity, the market quantity would then decrease. The determination of the size of the decrease is an empirical matter. Economic theory can lead us to the expectation that the market quantity of handguns would decrease if sanctions were imposed for purchase and sales. The effect on the market price of handguns of these shifts is ambiguous. It would depend on the relative magnitude of these shifts to the left.

8. G. Becker, "Crime and Punishment," *Journal of Political Economy* 76 (1968): 169–217; I. Ehrlich, "Participation in Illegitimate Activities," *Journal of Political Economy* 81 (1973): 521–65.

9. M. Block and J. Heineke, "A Labor Theoretic Analysis of the Criminal Choice," *American Economic Review* 65 (1975): 314–25.

Figure 10-2.   Change in the Market for Handguns with the Imposition of Handgun Prohibition.

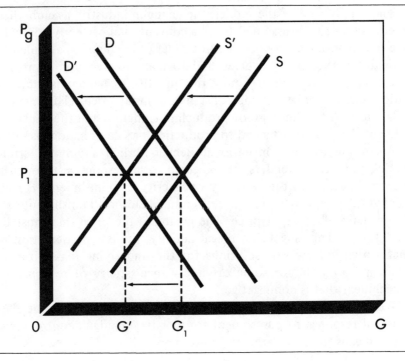

For a graphical example of this we will assume that Figure 10-1 represents the market for handguns when there are no regulations at all, and that we now impose handgun regulations such that it is illegal to purchase or sell handguns. This new situation is represented by Figure 10-2, where the new supply and demand curves S' and D' represent the behavior of suppliers and demanders of *illegal* handguns. The market quantity has decreased from G_1 to G'. When the commodity in a market is illegal, its transactions are referred to as a "black market." Imposing regulations against the purchase and sales of a commodity does not necessarily eliminate its use. However, it is expected that it will reduce the market quantity to below what it would be if it were legal to make market transactions.[10]

10. Besides the existing stock of handguns that is not given up, illegal supply is expected to be produced from three sources: formerly legal producers of handguns who now produce illegally, new domestic producers of illegal handguns, and foreign handguns imported illegally. Hardy and Kates (1979) have suggested an interesting possibility that soon after the initial shock of a handgun prohibition the (illegal) supply function will shift back to the

Figure 10-3. Elimination of the Market for Handguns.

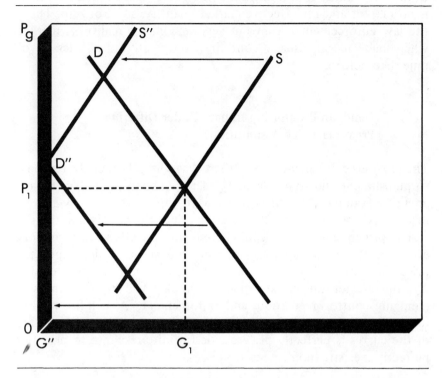

Two extreme outcomes are also possible. If the elasticity of response to punishments were zero for both producers and consumers, then no shift in the curves would occur and there would be no change in market quantity. This does not seem a likely outcome, considering past experiences for commodities that were made illegal.

Another possibility is that the elasticity response to punishment is very large, such that both curves shift considerably to the left and no longer intersect. If that occurs, then the market has been eliminated. While this is the intent of much effort of criminal legislation and law enforcement policy, this is also unlikely to occur. The graphical depiction of this possibility is presented in Figure 10-3. The supply curve shifted to the left from S to S″, and the demand curve shifted

right. This may occur if a cottage industry develops to produce illegal handguns and becomes efficient at producing low quality handguns such that more handguns are offered for sale at each price. While we expect the illegal handgun industry to become more efficient as time passes, it still may not become efficient enough to shift the supply curve back to or beyond the old legal supply curve. Analysis of this cottage industry argument would involve consideration of markets for two types of handguns, differing in quality.

to the left from D to D″. Since the new curves do not intersect, there is no market and the effective market quantity is G″, or zero. This is the law enforcement dream but very seldom the reality. A market, when made illegal, usually continues to operate but at a lesser volume than before.

Handgun Prohibition Impact Under Differing Price Elasticity Assumptions

The previous cases assumed that there was some elasticity of response to punishment and some elasticity of response to price. We are now going to examine the effects of leftward shifts of the supply and demand curves separately under differing price elasticity assumptions.

The principle to be explicated here is that the effects of regulatory effort on the market quantity of handguns are dependent upon the price elasticities of demand and supply. The greater the price elasticity, the greater the market quantity impact will be to changes in handgun control regulation and enforcement. A helpful way to understand these principles is to consider the polar cases where either of the curves is perfectly price elastic (infinite response to price) or perfectly inelastic (no response to price).

The Case of Perfectly Inelastic Demand. We first assume that the supply price elasticity is greater than zero but that the demand function has the characteristic of being perfectly price inelastic. This would be represented by the market graphically displayed in Figure 10-4. The market quantity is G_1 and the market price is P_1. In such a case, if a prohibition against sales were instituted, the supply curve would shift to the left. The demand curve would not shift since, in our example, there is no enforcement change against purchasers or users. This situation is displayed in Figure 10-5. The supply curve shifts from S to S′, and the total impact of this is only to cause the price to rise, from P_1 to P′. The market quantity remains the same as before.

Considering a possible sequencing for this situation can more clearly reveal why handgun control enforcement, in this case, has had no impact. For example, use as a case that the particular handgun control policy change is a confiscation in each time period of guns equal to amount $G_1 - G^*$. This is a pedagogically useful example to

Figure 10-4. The Market for Handguns with Perfectly Inelastic Demand.

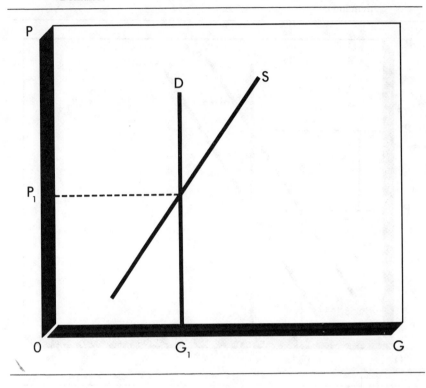

choose, but the implication occurs for any increase in regulatory effort on the supply side in a market where the demand curve is perfectly price inelastic. The immediate effect of the confiscation is to shift the supply curve to the left by the amount of the handguns confiscated. At the old price, P_1, there is a shortage of guns, but this shortage is only transitory. The shortage is of the amount $G_1 - G^*$. That is, at price P_1, only G^* amount of guns will be supplied at the same time (and price) that consumers want G_1 amount of guns. This shortage is only transitory because price will be bid up due to the shortage and because there is some elasticity of supply response to price.

Suppliers will increase the production of handguns to make up the amount of the shortage, motivated by increased prices they now receive for handgun sales. The market will again return to equilibrium but at a higher price, P', and the market quantity, after full adjust-

Figure 10-5. Change in the Market for Handguns due to Increased Handgun Control Effort on the Supply Side (with perfectly inelastic demand).

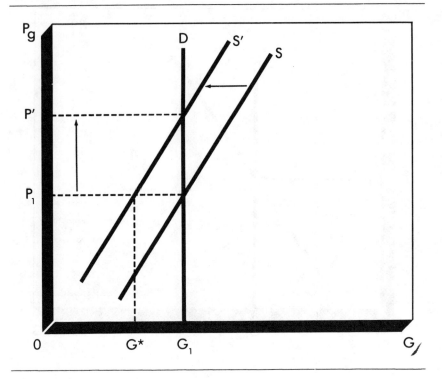

ment, returns to the old quantity, G_1. This is a situation where the market has replaced the amount lost due to the supply shock by the full amount of the shock. A 100 percent replacement effect occurs.

The driving force for this 100 percent replacement effect is our assumption of demand behavior which says that purchasers are intent about having G_1 amount of handguns regardless of what they have to pay for them. If such a situation occurs, handgun control regulations on the supply side will have no impact. Of course, there is a transitory impact of temporarily decreasing the amount of handguns, but this will last only as long as it takes suppliers to produce enough to replace them.

Such an assumption, using the assumption of perfectly price inelastic demand, is not too farfetched. For example, in self-protection demand, a citizen does not need to own many handguns to achieve the sense of sufficient protection. Usually one will do. The price of one handgun is a very small part of the citizen's budget. If people perceive a crime wave and they also perceive formal law enforcement to be weak, they may feel an intense need to own a handgun, as that may be their only and perhaps ultimate form of *expected* protection.

All of the above implies a highly price inelastic demand for handguns and also probably a highly punishment inelastic demand for handguns. If there is some price elasticity to the demand for handguns, though a very low one, a 100 percent replacement effect will not occur. A substantial replacement will, however, occur. That is, if demanders exhibit some price elasticity, only part of the initial shock (in our case it is the confiscation amount) will be replaced. The more price elastic the demand for handguns is, the smaller the replacement effect will be and thus the greater will be the permanent impact on the market quantity of handguns. If demand were perfectly price elastic (infinite responsiveness to price—a very unlikely assumption for the handgun market) the full amount of the shock on the supply side would be incurred on the market quantity of handguns.

Thus, we conclude that the more price elastic is the demand for handguns, the more effective will be a prohibition effect that initially impacts on the supply side of the gun market. Therefore, when considering proposals that impact initially on the supply side of the market, one should measure the price elasticity of demand for handguns to determine the expected effectiveness of such a policy.

The Case of Perfectly Elastic Supply. In the case of perfectly elastic supply, we assume that there is a finite, nonzero price elasticity for demanders but perfect price elasticity for sellers. This means that suppliers at a going price are willing to sell as many handguns as users want. This could occur as the result of technologies to produce handguns being widely known, generating constant returns to scale for the industry. Suppliers, to increase the quantity of handguns sold, can, if they need to, merely purchase extra plant and equipment to begin producing additional handguns at the established average cost—which is constant for everyone. New producers can easily enter the market and start production at the existing cost structures. This case is graphically displayed in Figure 10-6.

The market is in equilibrium at price P_1 and quantity G_1. A prohibition against handgun supply would have no effect in the market if

Figure 10-6. The Market for Handguns with Perfectly Elastic Supply.

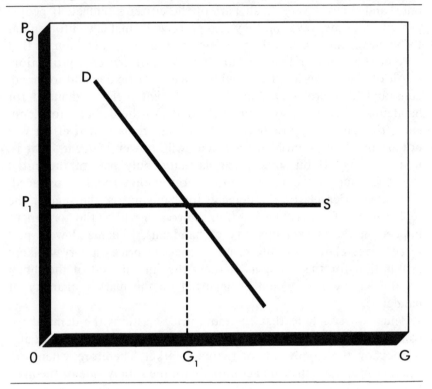

producers eliminated from the market by law enforcement were just replaced by new producers taking up the production slack. This comparative statics model has no time dimensions, so our assumption of a perfectly price elastic supply curve implies instantaneous replacement of suppliers. However, the situation is likely to be different because legal sanctions imposed by a prohibition affect business costs. The curve is now set at a higher price due to the increase in costs induced because suppliers face an increase in the expected value of punishment, an additional business cost. This circumstance is portrayed in Figure 10-7.

Increasing the costs of production, due to increased enforcement effort, shifts the horizontal supply curve upward. This results in the rise in market price from P_1 to P' and a decrease in market quantity of handguns from G_1 to G'. Notice again, though, that the size of the impact on market quantity depends on the elasticity of demand. A

Figure 10-7. Change in the Market for Handguns due to Increased Handgun Control Effort on the Supply Side (with perfectly elastic supply).

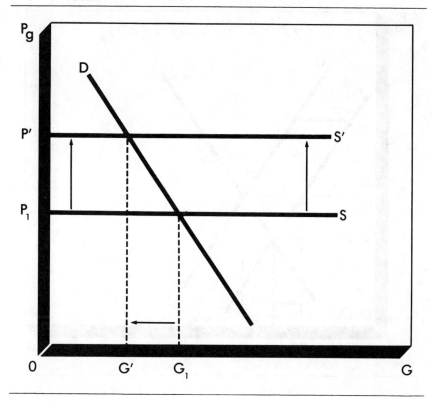

steeper demand curve (a more inelastic demand curve) would have generated a smaller decrease in market quantity induced by that supply shock.

The good news for handgun prohibition advocates is that when supply is perfectly price elastic, impacts of enforcement on the demand side will have maximal impact. That is, if increased enforcement against the demand side causes the amount of handguns demanded (at each price) to decline by a certain amount, the market quantity of handguns will decline by that same amount. Normally, when the supply curve has some price elasticity, a leftward shift (decrease) in demand causes a decline in the market quantity by an amount less than the demand shift. This is displayed in Figure 10-8.

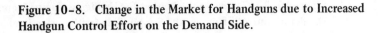

Figure 10-8.   Change in the Market for Handguns due to Increased Handgun Control Effort on the Demand Side.

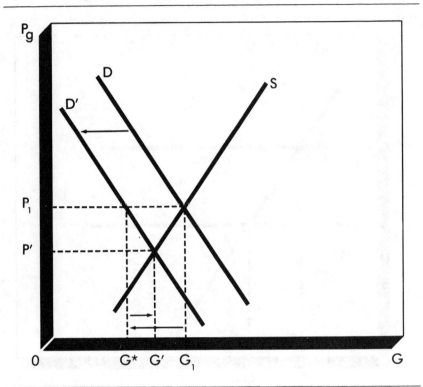

The initial impact of the demand curve shifting from D to D' (at P_1) is for a surplus of handguns to occur of amount $G_1 - G^*$. However, that surplus is only transitory. The surplus causes price to fall, and as it does, suppliers cut back on production but demanders increase their quantity demanded—this time in a response to price. Eventually the market will return to equilibrium at market price P' and market quantity G'. The market quantity of handguns has not decreased by the full impact of the initial shock on demanders of handguns because price has decreased simultaneously. This caused *some* of those demanders who dropped out of the markets on account of the increased handgun control effort directed at them to return or be replaced by some new demanders.

If the supply function has the characteristic of perfect price elasticity, a leftward shift in demand will have its full impact on the

Figure 10-9.   Change in the Market for Handguns due to Increased Handgun Control Effort on the Demand Side (with perfectly elastic supply).

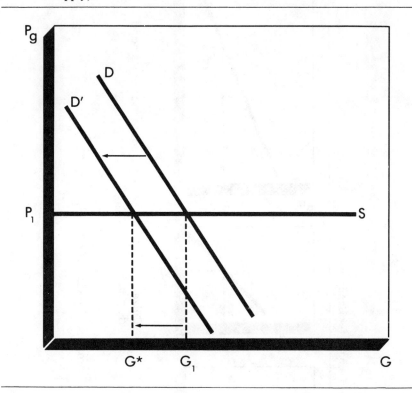

market quantity. This is shown in Figure 10-9. The more price elastic is the supply curve, the greater will be the impacts of increased handgun control effort on the market quantity.

The Impact of Handgun Prohibition on the Demand Sectors

The aggregate market demand for handguns is comprised of three types of users: recreational-sports users, offenders, and private citizens using guns for self-protection. The underlying theory used to derive the demand functions for the different users was presented in an earlier section. Figure 10-10 presents a graphical depiction of the

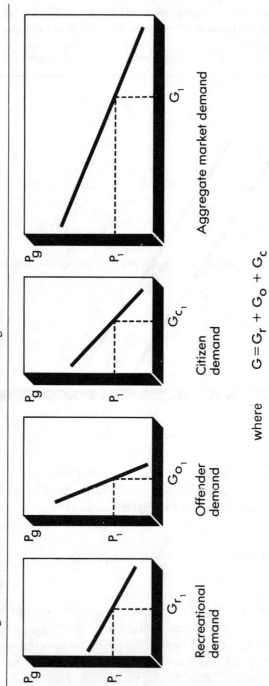

Figure 10–10. Sectors of the Market Demand for Handguns.

three sectors for the demand of handguns and shows how they determine the aggregate demand for handguns. At each price, the quantity of handguns demanded is obtained for the different sectors and then added. For example, at price P_1, in Figure 10-10, each sector demands a certain quantity of handguns, and the total aggregate market demand for handguns is merely the summation of the individual demand sectors:

$$G_1 = G_{r_1} + G_{o_1} + G_{c_1} \qquad (15)$$

Notice that we have drawn the slopes of the demand curves differently for the different sectors.[11] We have drawn the demand curves this way to reflect our basic assumptions of the relative price elasticity of demand for handguns among the different users. We assume that recreational users have the most price elastic demand for handguns because they can easily switch to other types of weapons or other types of activities for outdoor recreation. It is also primarily the long gun rather than the handgun that is used for most hunting or shooting recreation.

The demand curve for offender users is drawn to reflect our assumption that handguns are an important piece of equipment for committing crime. There is relatively less opportunity for offenders to choose weapons other than handguns, and there is restricted ability to switch to other legal or illegal occupations where a handgun would not be crucial. Therefore we have drawn the demand curve to be very steep—to reflect its high degree of price inelasticity.[12]

---

11. The concepts of demand curve slope (absolute marginal rate of change) and price elasticity (percentage marginal rate of change) are similar but not identical. Assumptions of the relative magnitudes of elasticity translate into the same assumptions of relative magnitudes of slope, if the subsector market quantities are approximately the same. We expect that the subsector market quantities for the offender sector are substantially smaller than for the other two sectors. The offender sector is assumed to have the smallest elasticity and is also assumed to have the smallest subsector size, but the two effects are offsetting, to imply that the offender sector may not have the smallest relative slope. Also, demand curves are conventionally drawn to have "price on the vertical axis and "quantity" on the horizontal axis. However, slope is still considered to be $\frac{dQ}{dP}$.

12. It has been suggested that persons could easily switch to using a sawed-off long gun as a substitute for a handgun. Doing this involves preplanning and incurring the risk of additional federal penalties for owning a sawed-off long gun. While a sawed-off long gun is a partial substitute for a handgun, it is not a perfect substitute. A sawed-off long gun is bulkier to carry and thus it is less concealable than a handgun. Long guns (sawed-off or intact) would seem to be more easily substituted in the home than in a public place. In the event of

The price elasticity of demand for self-protection by ordinary citizens is assumed to have an amount of price elasticity somewhere between the relatively high price elasticity of recreational users and the relatively low price elasticity of offenders. Ownership of a handgun for ordinary citizens is more important than for recreational users because it is related to self-protection rather than sport, and there are less substitutes available for citizens compared to recreational users. Handgun ownership is likewise more important for offenders than for citizens because offenders need handguns to earn income (and possibly for self-protection also) and because citizens have more substitutes available (alarms, private guards, exposure avoidance).

Effects of a Price Increase on Demand for Handguns

The impact of increased handgun control effort can be analyzed by characterizing that as the cause for an increase in the price of handguns. This would occur, for example, if there were a prohibition on the supply side of the handgun market forcing the price of handguns (now the black market price) to increase. This increase in price causes the quantity demanded to decrease. Using the same assumptions about price elasticity that were used for Figure 10-10, the graphical depiction of the quantity reductions in handguns in the aggregate and among the different demand sectors is portrayed in Figure 10-11.

The increase in the price of handguns from P_1 to P_2 causes the aggregate market demand for handguns to decline from G_1 to G_2. This decrease in the aggregate demand for handguns is comprised of the sum of the decreases in the different sectors. The different sectors do *not* decrease by the same amount. The largest contribution to the decrease in the quantity demanded for handguns in this example is from the recreational users because their demand has the flattest

---

a handgun prohibition, self-protection handgun users would likely switch to long guns to a greater extent than would offenders. Some offenders who are deterred from using a handgun or who are priced out of the handgun market may switch to a sawed-off long gun, but a 100 percent substitution effect is unlikely. While a handgun prohibition is expected to reduce the number of handguns owned for all segments of the market, it would seem useful to research the extent of weapon substitution, particularly substitution to the long gun, and its effective uses (Hardy and Kates 1979).

Figure 10-11. Sectors of the Market Demand for Handguns: Effects of a Price Increase (induced by an increase in gun control effort on the supply side).

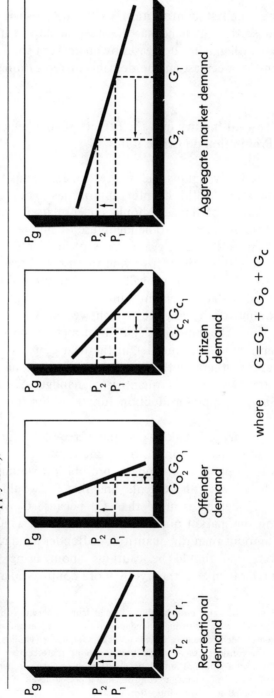

where $G = G_r + G_o + G_c$

slope. The smallest contribution to the decrease is from offender users because their demand has the steepest slope. Citizens' quantity demanded for handguns decreases by an amount somewhere between the amount of decrease in the demand of recreational and offender users.

Toward Inquiry into the Effects of Handgun Prohibition on Crime Rates

While theoretically linking the market for handguns to crime rates is beyond the scope of this chapter, approaches to doing so will be suggested. A model of linkage should concern itself with at least two types of incidents relative to handgun use. A simple model, for example, could include two relevant types of incidents: intentional premeditated low skill crimes involving the use of firearms, committed only by offenders, which we call C_1; and unpremeditated crimes of violence (and perhaps accidents) involving the use of firearms, which can be committed by anyone, which we call C_2. Examples of C_1 incidents would be gun robbery and murder for profit. Examples of C_2 incidents would be murder in the heat of passion and someone hurting self or others by the accidential firing of a handgun. One can presume that the market quantity of handguns is an explanatory variable in the supply-production functions for these two types of incidents.

A straightforward linking of the three-sector handgun market (from the previous section) to the crime supply functions for C_1 and C_2 tends to imply that a handgun prohibition would result in a decrease in both types of incidents, and that C_2 would decrease more than C_1. C_2 decreases more than C_1 because C_2 depends, ceteris paribus, on the market quantity of all handguns, which decreases by a greater amount than the quantity of offender handguns.[13]

However, one should be cautious about using such a simple straightforward linkage theory. A more complex analysis should be

---

13. Evaluation of harm brought about by handgun ownership is only one part of the analysis for consideration of stronger handgun control effort. One must consider the costs of enforcement needed to achieve various levels of compliance (Phillips, Votey, and Howell 1976). Through consideration of these two functions (enforcement costs and handgun harm) in setting up a minimization of social cost problem, one can determine the optimal amount of enforcement for handgun control. Only if present levels of handgun enforcement are below the optimal amount is more effort needed.

used which takes into account markets for other weapons, simultaneities between crime rates and the demand for handguns, interrelationships between the handgun holdings among the various sectors, and a larger set of crime rates. For example, a handgun prohibition is likely to increase the holdings of other weapons such as long guns and knives. Even though complete substitution is not expected, the distribution of crime rate changes among various types of incidents is expected to change, depending on the mix of alternative weapons. Crimes involving handguns are likely to decrease, but crimes involving the use of other weapons and crimes without weapons are likely to increase. The impact of a handgun prohibition on the overall crime rate may be ambiguous.[14]

A handgun prohibition, reducing handgun holdings, which directly reduces crime rates, is also expected to indirectly affect handgun demand because handgun demand includes crime rates as explanatory variables. Further, a change in handgun holdings of offenders may likely change the demand for handguns by citizens, and a change in handgun holdings by citizens may likely change the handgun holdings of offenders and their willingness to commit crime.

What is required is that such a general equilibrium model be constructed and the comparative statics properties examined to determine the ultimate qualitative effect of handgun control effort on a set of crime rates and the distribution of weapons holdings among the various sectors of demand. Since building such a model is likely to involve the use of a large set of underlying behavioral assumptions, the robustness of the model should be probed by relaxing different assumptions to determine which assumptions that may be questionable are also crucial to the results. A simulation approach, which includes magnitude estimates of parameters, would also seem useful to probe for the likely effects of handgun control on crime rates. Research along the lines described is already being undertaken by the authors.

THE MARKET FOR DURABLE HANDGUNS

The previous section examined the market for nondurable handguns. Since handguns last beyond the period in which they are purchased,

14. P. J. Cook, "The Effect of Gun Availability on Violent Crime Patterns," *Annals of the American Academy of Political and Social Sciences* 455 (1981): 63–79.

we can consider the demand for handguns as the demand for a desired stock. The demand for new handguns in the current market is derived from an increase in the demand for the desired stock and from purchases to replace handguns that have become lost or broken.[15] This framework is analogous to the analysis that can be used to examine the market for any durable good (e.g., autos, refrigerators, etc.). Alternatively, we can consider the demand-for-handgun functions previously derived as the demand for handgun services per time period. Since the rental market for handguns has heretofore been limited, one can only obtain handgun services by purchasing a handgun, a relatively small-budget purchase. This allows us to translate the demand for handgun services into a demand for the stock of handguns. The amount of handgun services per time period will be assumed to be proportional to the stock of working handguns.[16]

In order to understand the durable nature of the handgun market, it is useful to conceive of the supply side of the market in three "time frames": the market period, the short run, and the long run. We define these three time periods as follows:

1. The market period is the period in which the number of handguns is fixed and the amount of services provided by that stock is fixed. The price determined in the market period holds only momentarily, and provides the inducement for supply changes in the short run and the long run.
2. Short run is the period in which resources can be used to repair handguns that fall into disrepair, but new handguns cannot be produced.
3. Long run is the period in which new handguns can be added to the stock.

---

15. Part of the source of handguns, especially for offenders, is stolen handguns. This phenomenon does not reduce the total stock of handguns; it just redistributes it between different users. If handgun controls raise the price of handguns and this forces some offenders to steal rather than purchase handguns, it still raises the effective cost to those offenders, who now pay a greater acquisition cost for handguns in terms of search and risk costs.

16. A prohibition on handguns is expected to reduce the actual and desired stock of handguns. If a handgun rental market should develop on account of this, a lower stock of handguns could be providing more handgun services per stock unit than previously. Since renting an illegal handgun would require search and information costs, handguns probably will not be utilized as often as before the prohibition, when the greater stock provided more convenient use. But if an expanded handgun rental market should occur, one can expect offenses committed with a handgun to fall proportionately less than the decrease in the total stock available to offenders.

Figure 10-12. The Market for Durable Handguns.

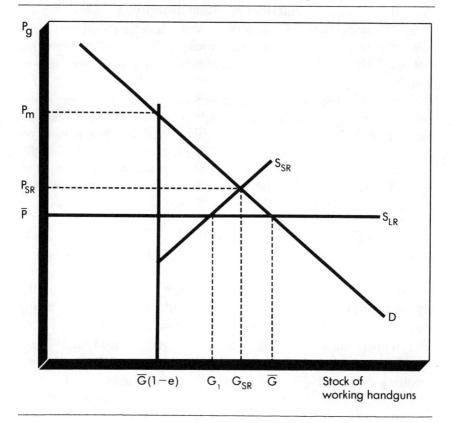

These time frames are simply a fictional analytical device. Actually, new handguns can probably be produced as readily as some broken handguns can be repaired. We shall assume that a fixed percentage, e, of all handguns falls into disrepair per time period.[17] The failure and severity of that failure are considered to be random events.

All of these notions can be illustrated on a simple diagram. In Figure 10-12 we have depicted a simple market for handguns in a given time period. The demand curve is labelled D, and the long-run

17. Zimring's (1976) analysis of the age distribution of confiscated handguns finds that a large proportion of handguns are of recent vintage. Policies that focus on controlling current new supply would then seem more efficacious because either the existing handgun stock can be expected to wear out rapidly (e is high) or growth in demand is inhibited.

supply is S_{LR}, which is assumed to reflect constant returns to scale at the industry level. Equilibrium price and quantity in the long run are $\overline{P}$ and $\overline{G}$, respectively. In each time period handguns fall into disrepair at rate e, implying that the supply of working handguns has fallen to $\overline{G}(1 - e)$. In the next market period the price of the $\overline{G}(1 - e)$ handguns is P_m.

However, in the short run, handguns can be repaired. Some handguns can be repaired at low cost, while others require major repairs. Indeed, as with any durable good, some handguns will require repairs that exceed the price of a new handgun. The short-run supply curve S_{SR} has been drawn to reflect these assumptions. The height of S_{SR} equals the cost of repair, and the handguns that have fallen into disrepair have been ranked from the least to the most expensive repair requirements.

In the short run, the price and quantity of working handguns will be established at P_{SR} and G_{SR} respectively. This time frame is conceived to reflect what would occur in the absence of new handgun production. In this context, part of the depreciated stock would be repaired $[G_{SR} - \overline{G}(1 - e)]$, and part would be removed from the stock in the short run $(\overline{G} - G_{SR})$. This price, P_{SR}, will, in the long run, induce the production of new handguns until $\overline{P}$ and $\overline{G}$ are reached once again. The new long-run equilibrium will be reached by repairing $G_1 - \overline{G}(1 - e)$ old handguns and producing $\overline{G} - G_1$ new handguns. In this long-run time frame, fewer handguns are repaired because handgun consumers find it more economical to buy new handguns when the price of repair exceeds the price of new handguns. With fewer repairs but with greater new purchases, handgun consumers are able to replace fully the depreciated stock to return to their original desired stock of handguns.

Now consider the handgun control measures examined in the previous section. We assume that both the supply of and demand for handguns are shifted by the increased expected value of punishment for handgun possession, ownership, production, and sale. In Figure 10-13 the demand for handguns is reduced from D to D′, and the long-run supply shifts from S_{LR} to S'_{LR}. The long-run equilibrium price and quantity will shift from $\overline{P}, \overline{G}$ to $\overline{P}', \overline{G}'$. However, the transition to the new long-run equilibrium will take a long time because of the durable nature of handguns.

In the market period immediately following the imposition of increased penalties, the price of handguns will fall to P_m. The stock

Figure 10-13. Change in the Market for Durable Handguns due to Increased Handgun Control Effort.

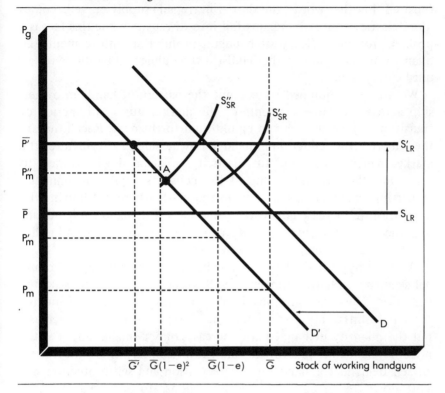

of $\overline{G}$ handguns will fall into disrepair at rate e, so $\overline{G}(1-e)$ becomes the stock of working handguns in the next market period, leading to a price of P'_m. In this time period there is no incentive to repair the broken handguns because the short-run supply has shifted to S'_{SR}. However, in the next time period the stock of working handguns is further reduced to $\overline{G}(1-e)^2$, giving a market period price of P''_m. This additional depreciation induces repair of some handguns along short-run supply curve S''_{SR} to reach a short-run equilibrium at point A.

This process of depreciation and repair of some of the broken handguns will continue until the new long-run equilibrium at $\overline{P}', \overline{G}'$ is finally reached. The rate at which this new equilibrium is reached depends upon the rate of depreciation, e, and the elasticity of the short-run (repair) supply curve. It should be noted that it may not be initially economical to repair some handguns that are broken, but as further depreciation of the stock takes place, these handguns may be repaired. In other words, the short-run (repair) supply curve becomes more elastic as more handguns fall into disrepair. While this fact is a problem for the efficacy of handgun prohibition enforcement, the quantity of handguns in the hands of the public will continue to fall until $\bar{G}'$ is reached.

We are now equipped to examine the pattern of handgun owner-ship across the three segments of the market during the period of transition from one long-run equilibrium to the next. Recall that, in the long run, the reduction in handgun ownership in a segment of the market will depend upon the elasticity of demand with respect to price and the expected value of the penalties applied to handgun ownership, possession, and use. In the market period following the imposition of increased expected penalties, the demand for handguns is reduced but the total quantity of handguns is fixed. This implies that the price of handguns in the market period decreases.

We have hypothesized that the demand for handguns by the crimi-nal segment is relatively inelastic with respect to price and expected penalties. These assumptions imply that the criminal demand for handguns shifts only a small amount as expected penalties increase, but the quantity demanded also increases only a small amount as the price of handguns falls in the market period. By the same token, citizen demand for handguns for recreation and self-protection will shift down by greater amounts in response to increased expected penalties and will be more responsive to reductions in the market price. It is thus not clear whether there will be any significant redis-tribution of handguns through the (illegal) used handgun market in the market period. Indeed, if the expected penalty for the use of a handgun in the commission of a crime is increased appreciably, crimi-nals may hold fewer handguns and citizens more handguns in the market period.[18]

However, as depreciation of the stock proceeds at rate e and the market price rises toward its eventual long-run equilibrium, the seg-ment of the market with the most price elastic demand curve will exhibit the greatest percentage decline in the quantity of handguns

18. The market period would appear to be the correct "time period" for the govern-ment to offer to purchase handguns in order to reduce the total stock. The price offered, must at least exceed the temporary market period price for the buy-back policy to have any impact.

owned. In other words, the subsequent declines in percentage terms will be largest in the recreational demand segment, next largest in the self-protection demand segment, and least in the criminal segment. The main point of this analysis of the transition to long-run equilibrium is that, assuming that increased handgun control measures reduce demand at a given price and increase the supply price in the long run, criminals may not increase their ownership of handguns at any time in this transition period. Whether criminals initially increase their ownership of handguns in the market period depends upon the elasticity of demand with respect to expected penalties versus the price elasticity.

SUMMARY AND CONCLUSIONS

This chapter has developed an analysis of handgun control policy around a traditional market economics framework. We have provided such an analysis so that the discussion of gun control issues can be more focused. We believe that progress in discussions of public policy issues depends upon the ability of the participants to state clearly their underlying assumptions and conceptual frameworks so their views can be subjected to tests for logical consistency and empirical relevance.

We have characterized handguns as a homogeneous commodity with a single market price. While the quality *level* of handguns is an important variable because it determines the rate at which handguns fall into disrepair, we assumed the quality mix was only of secondary importance.

Our demand model for handguns consists of three segments: recreational demand, criminal demand, and self-protection demand. It seemed plausible to assume that criminals' demand is relatively insensitive to variations in the price and expected value of penalties for handgun ownership. Recreational demand is probably the most sensitive of the three segments to these hypothetical variations, and the responsiveness of self-protection demand falls somewhere between the other two.

The basic analysis that follows from these assumptions has significant implications:

1. The ability of "supply side" controls (increased expected value of the penalty for handgun production and/or sale) to reduce the

total quantity of handguns held depends upon the responsiveness of price to this policy and the responsiveness of demand to the change in price. Supply side controls cannot and should not be analyzed independently of demand side responses.

2. The reduction of the number of handguns induced by supply side controls will be distributed across the three segments of demand according to the slopes of the three subsector demand curves. To the extent that increased handgun control effort reduces handguns held by the public, our model suggests that, in the long run, recreational use will decline the most and offender use will decline the least.

3. The efficacy of "demand side" controls (increased expected value of penalties for handgun ownership or possession) depends upon the responsiveness of demand to this policy measure. It is likely that relative responsiveness to demand side penalties will be similar to the relative demand responsiveness to price.

4. The efficacy of handgun control measures also depends upon the speed with which increased handgun control efforts induce a new long-run equilibrium (with fewer handguns). We have developed a model of durable handguns to identify the key parameters that determine this speed of adjustment. Clearly a key element is the rate at which handguns fall into disrepair or rust. In addition, the function describing repair costs is an important part of the analysis.

We hope that our analysis will prove helpful to three groups. For the researcher, we have identified several empirical questions that need to be answered to predict the impact of handgun control policy suggestions. For advocates of handgun prohibition, we have shown in the context of market economics what assumptions must be made to expect that their policies will reduce the number of handguns. For opponents of additional handgun controls, we have shown under what conditions additional handgun control effort will have no or minimal impact on the quantity of handguns.

TABLE OF SYMBOLS

B_s = a vector of other influences that would affect the supply of handguns (e.g., prices of inputs, technology)

C = crime rate

C_1 = crime rate for premeditated violent offenses involving firearms

C_2 = rate of unpremeditated violent acts and accidents involving firearms

e = percentage of handguns that fall into disrepair per time period

E = price elasticity of demand

$E(Y)$ = expected value of income

F = level of punishment for commission of a premeditated violent offense with the use of a firearm

F_g = expected value of punishment for possession of a handgun

F_s = expected value of punishment for producing and/or selling handguns

G = quantity of handguns

$\bar{G}$ = long-run quantity of handguns

G_c = quantity of handguns used by citizens for self-protection

G_d = quantity of handguns demanded

G_o = quantity of handguns used by offenders

G_r = quantity of recreational handguns

G_s = quantity of handguns supplied

G_{SR} = short-run quantity of handguns

J = probability of punishment for commission of a premeditated violent offense with the use of a firearm

L = other leisure time (not recreation time)

SELECTED BIBLIOGRAPHY
(PART V)

Becker, G.S. "Crime and Punishment: An Economic Approach." *Journal of Political Economy* 82 (March/April 1968): 526-36.

Bendis, P., and S. Balkin. "A Look at Gun Control Enforcement." *Journal of Police Science and Administration* 7 (1979): 439-48.

Block, M., and J. Heineke. "A Labor Theoretic Analysis of the Criminal Choice." *American Economic Review* 65 (1975): 314-25.

Bruce-Briggs, B. "The Great American Gun War." *Public Interest* 45 (Fall 1976): 1-20.

Buchanan, J.M., and G. Tullock. *The Calculus of Consent.* Ann Arbor: University of Michigan Press, 1962.

Carr-Hill, R.A., and N.H. Stern. "An Econometric Model of the Supply and Control of Recorded Offenses in England and Wales." *Journal of Public Economics* 2 (November 1973): 289-318.

Cochrane, D., and G.H. Orcutt. "Application of Least-Squares Regressions to Relationships Containing Auto-Correlated Error Terms." *Journal of the American Statistical Association* 44 (January 1949): 32-61.

Cook, Philip J. "A Strategic Choice Analysis of Robbery." In Wesley G. Skogan, ed., *Sample Surveys of the Victims of Crime*, pp. 173-87. Cambridge, Mass.: Ballinger, 1976.

_____ . "The Effect of Gun Availability on Robbery and Robbery Murder: A Cross-section Study of Fifty Cities." In Robert Haveman and B. Bruce Zellner, eds., *Policy Studies Review Annual*, vol. 3, pp. 743-81. Beverly Hills, Calif.: Sage Publications, 1979.

_____ . "The Effect of Gun Availability on Violent Crime Patterns." *Annals of the Academy of Political and Social Sciences* 455 (May 1981): 63-79.

Deutsch, Stuart J., and Francis B. Alt. "The Effect of Massachusetts' Gun Control Law on Gun-Related Crimes in the City of Boston." *Evaluation Quarterly* 1 (November 1977): 543-68.

Downs, A. *An Economic Theory of Democracy.* New York: Harper & Row, 1957.

Efron, V.; M. Kelly; and C. Gurioli. *Statistics on Consumption of Alcohol and on Alcoholism.* New Brunswick, N.J.: Rutgers Center for Alcohol Studies, 1974.

Ehrlich, Isaac. "Participation in Illegitimate Activities: A Theoretical and Empirical Investigation." *Journal of Political Economy* 81 (May-June 1973): 521-65.

_____ . "The Deterrent Effect of Capital Punishment: A Question of Life and Death." *American Economic Review* 65 (June 1975): 397-417.

Geisel, Martin S.; Richard Roll; and R.S. Wettick, Jr. "The Effectiveness of State and Local Regulation of Handguns: A Statistical Analysis." *Duke Law Journal* (August 1969): 647-76.

Hardy, David T., and Don B. Kates, Jr. "Handgun Availability and the Social Harms of Robbery: Recent Data and Some Projections." In Don B. Kates, Jr., *Restricting Handguns: The Liberal Skeptics Speak Out*, pp. 118-38. Croton-on-Hudson, N.Y.: North River Press, 1979.

Hardy, David T., and John Stompoly. "Of Arms and the Law." *Chicago-Kent Law Review* 51 (September 1974): 62-114.

Hay, Richard A., and Richard McCleary. "Box-Tiao Time Series Model for Impact Assessment: A Comment on the Recent Work of Deutsch and Alt." *Evaluation Quarterly* 3 (May 1979): 277-314.

Henderson, J., and R. Quandt. *Microeconomic Theory: A Mathematical Approach.* New York: McGraw-Hill, 1971.

Hoenack, S.A., and W.C. Weiler. "A Structural Model of Murder Behavior and the Criminal Justice System." *American Economic Review* 70 (June 1980): 327-40.

Johnston, John. *Econometric Methods.* New York: McGraw-Hill, 1972.

Lizotte, Alan J., and David J. Bordua. "Firearms Ownership for Sport and Protection: Two Divergent Models." *American Sociological Review* 45 (April 1980): 229-44.

Magaddino, J.P. "Economic Analysis of State Gun Control Laws." Ph.D. dissertation, Virginia Polytechnic Institute, 1972.

Murray, Douglas R. "Handguns, Gun Control Laws, and Firearm Violence." *Social Problems* 23 (October 1975): 81-92.

Newton, George D., and Franklin Zimring. *Firearms and Violence in American Life.* A Staff Report of the Task Force on Firearms, National Commission on the Causes and Prevention of Violence. Washington, D.C.: Government Printing Office, 1970.

Peltzman, S. "Toward a More General Theory of Regulation." *Journal of Law and Economics* 29 (August 1976): 211-40.

Phillips, Llad; Harold L. Votey; and John Howell. "Handguns and Homicide: Minimizing Losses and the Costs of Control." *Journal of Legal Studies* 5 (June 1976): 463-78.

Sommers, P.M. "Deterrence and Gun Control: An Empirical Analysis." *Atlantic Economic Journal* 8 (December 1980): 89-94.

Stone, R., and D.A. Rowe. "The Durability of Consumer's Durable Goods." *Econometrica* 28 (April 1960): 407-16.

U.S. Department of Commerce, Bureau of the Census. *Current Population Reports.* Various numbers. Washington, D.C.: Government Printing Office.

_____. *Governmental Finances.* Various numbers. Washington, D.C.: Government Printing Office.

_____. *Historical Statistics of the United States: Colonial Times to 1970.* Washington, D.C.: Government Printing Office.

_____. *Statistical Abstract of the United States.* Washington, D.C.: Government Printing Office, 1970, 1971, 1981.

U.S. Department of Commerce. *Survey of Current Business.* Various numbers. Washington, D.C.: Government Printing Office.

U.S. Department of Interior, U.S. Fish and Wildlife Service. *Federal Aid in Fish and Wildlife Restoration.* Various numbers. Washington, D.C.: Government Printing Office.

U.S. Department of Justice, Bureau of Prisons. *National Prisons Statistics Bulletin.* Various numbers. Published prior to 1950 by Bureau of Census. Washington, D.C.: Government Printing Office.

_____. *National Prisoner Statistics, State Prisoners: Admissions and Releases, 1970.* Washington, D.C.: Government Printing Office, 1972.

U.S. Department of Justice, Federal Bureau of Investigation (FBI). *Crime in the United States (Uniform Crime Reports).* Washington, D.C.: Government Printing Office, yearly.

U.S. Department of Labor. *Employment and Earnings and Monthly Report on the Labor Force.* Various numbers. Washington, D.C.: Government Printing Office.

U.S. Department of Labor, Bureau of Labor Statistics. *Handbook of Labor Statistics, 1978.* Washington, D.C.: Government Printing Office, 1978.

U.S. President's Commission on Law Enforcement and Administration of Justice. *The Challenge of Crime in a Free Society.* Washington, D.C.: Government Printing Office, 1967.

Wolfgang, Marvin E. *Patterns in Criminal Homicide.* Philadelphia: University of Pennsylvania, 1958.

Wolpin, K.I. "An Economic Analysis of Crime and Punishment in England and Wales, 1894-1967." *Journal of Political Economy* 86 (October 1978): 815-40.

Zimring, Franklin E. "Firearms and Federal Law: The Gun Control Act of 1968." *Journal of Legal Studies* 4 (January 1975): 133-98.

_____ . "Street Crime and New Guns: Some Implications for Firearms Control." *Journal of Criminal Justice* 4 (Summer 1976): 95-107.

_____ . "Determinants of the Death Rate from Robbery: A Detroit Time Study." *Journal of Legal Studies* 6 (June 1977): 317-32.

PART VI

GUN OWNERSHIP AND CRIME DETERRENCE

Chapter 11

THE OWNERSHIP OF FIREARMS FOR REASONS OF SELF-DEFENSE

James D. Wright

INTRODUCTION

It is often remarked that the United States has among the most heavily armed private populations in the Western world, and further, that the rates of crime and violence are also generally higher here than in any other advanced Western nation. The relationship between these two observations has been the object of much avid speculation and debate, and of some empirical research. Here, I focus on one aspect of this relationship, namely the utility of private firearms in deterring or resisting crime and, more generally, the ownership of firearms for reasons of self-defense.[1]

It is commonly supposed that many of the 120 million or so privately possessed firearms are owned primarily as a means of protecting self and family from crime, violence, disorder, and the related

The research reported in this chapter was supported by a grant from the National Institute of Justice, United States Department of Justice, Washington, D.C. Findings, analyses, interpretations, opinions, and conclusions expressed here are exclusively those of the author and do not necessarily reflect the view of the Institute or the United States Government.

1. In general, three hypotheses relating guns and crime have been entertained: (1) that guns are a cause of crime, (2) that guns are an effect of crime, and (3) that guns are a deterrent to crime. Only (3) is addressed here. Evidence bearing on the other two hypotheses is reviewed and assessed in Wright et al., *Weapons, Crime, and Violence in America* (Washington, D.C.: National Institute of Justice, 1981), ch. 7, from which the present chapter has also been adapted.

pathologies of modern, especially modern urban, life.[2] The fear of crime and violence is frequently posited as *the* explanation for the sharp increase in private weaponry over the past decade.[3] The reasons people give for owning firearms is one topic (among a relatively few) for which credible research evidence exists, and this evidence is reviewed in some detail in the following section of this chapter.

Does a gun actually afford its owner any protection from crime and violence? The answer to this question has, at least so far, been more a matter of faith than a topic of empirical research. Persons opposed to stricter controls over civilian firearms frequently argue that such controls would affect only the law-abiding, that criminals intent on arming themselves would continue to do so, and thus, that stricter controls would only heighten the advantage of criminals over victims. A key assumption in this argument is clearly that a gun is an efficacious defense against criminal violence. Persons favoring stricter controls grant as an obvious point that many people own guns for reasons of self-defense, but they argue that the actual benefit is more psychological than real: people "feel safer" if they have a gun, but in fact they are not. In most cases, the argument is taken one step further: although people may feel safer if they have a gun in the home, they are in fact considerably less safe; the firearm actually adds to the potential lethality of the environment because of the risk of a serious firearm accident or of a "heat of the moment" shooting.

The "evidence" produced on either side of this issue is thin and unpersuasive. The evidence that guns actually deter some crime con-

2. The figure of 120 million firearms presently in private hands in the United States is several tens of millions lower than the estimates commonly encountered elsewhere, which often run as high as 165 or even 180 million. (Estimates as high as a billion have actually appeared in print, but there is no *evidence* suggesting a number any higher than 180 million at the outside.) The figure used in the text results from a reanalysis and reconsideration of the various sources of evidence that go into all existing estimates and may thus be seen as a reasonable compromise value. Details of the estimate are published in Wright et al., *Weapons, Crime, and Violence in America*, ch. 2.

3. Sources arguing this theme include George D. Newton and Franklin E. Zimring, *Firearms and Violence in American Life* (Washington, D.C.: GPO, 1969); Lawrence Northwood et al., "Law-abiding One-man Armies," *Society* 16 (November–December 1978): 69–74; Jeffrey H. Spiegler and John J. Sweeney, *Gun Abuse in Ohio* (Cleveland, Ohio: Governmental Research Institute, 1975); Joseph D. Alviani and William R. Drake, *Handgun Control: Issues and Alternatives* (Washington, D.C.: U.S. Conference of Mayors, 1975); and many others. Despite the commonness of the claim, there is no solid evidence to support it; see James D. Wright, "The Recent Weapons Trend and the Putative 'Need' for Gun Control" (Paper read at the American Sociological Association meetings, August 1980); or Wright et al., *Weapons, Crime, and Violence in America*, chs. 3–5, for the appropriate analyses.

sists mainly of the recounting of instances and episodes where this was clearly the case, for example, cases of rapes or burglaries that were thwarted by "The Armed Citizen."[4] No credible (that is, statistically generalizable) evidence on the rate at which crimes are deterred by private firearms has ever been produced; that the number so deterred is "high" is, as has already been stated, an article of faith. However, the counterargument — that guns detract from, more than they add to, the safety of the home environment — is also not based on any credible evidence. Many of the arguments advanced on this point are either immaterial or, if they bear on the topic at all, are empirically vacuous. Reasons for these conclusions are stated in the third section of this chapter.

There are good theoretical and methodological reasons why the actual deterrence effects of private weaponry will never be perfectly known, these due mainly to the difficulties of detecting (that is, measuring) the rate at which crimes do not occur. This aside, the actual uses of firearms for self-protection, being behavioral matters, can be known in some detail. Indeed, the matter has been explored in depth in two recent national surveys, and the resulting evidence on the self-protective uses of weapons is reviewed and summarized in the final section of this chapter.

REASONS FOR OWNERSHIP

All credible evidence converges on the conclusion that the total number of firearms currently in private hands in the United States is in the range of 100 to 140 million, with 120 million total as a plausible compromise value.[5] Many of these weapons are owned for hunting and sport shooting, some are owned mainly as collectors items, some are possessed because of the requirements of one's job, and

---

4. This is the title of the column in *American Rifleman* (the official NRA publication) where these reports are collected and published.

5. See Wright et al., *Weapons, Crime, and Violence in America*, ch. 2. This is an estimate of the total number of weapons possessed, not an estimate of the number of persons or households possessing at least one weapon. There is very good evidence, derived from national surveys dating back to at least 1959, that roughly half the households in the United States possess at least one weapon. The best available estimate, based on 1978 data discussed more fully later in the text, is that the average such household possesses slightly more than three firearms in total.

some are owned primarily to provide protection or self-defense. How widespread are these various categories of ownership?

There is, of necessity, some inherent ambiguity in answering this question. First, unless one is content to infer ownership reasons from characteristics of the firearms themselves (i.e., to assume, as an example, that all handguns are owned for defensive or protective reasons), then any credible answer to the question will depend on what gun owners themselves say about their motives, and the answers they give may be disingenuous or dissimulating.[6] Second, firearms might well be owned for a variety of reasons—some sporting, others self-defensive—in which case the concern would have to be with the main or primary reason. A final ambiguity is simply that any firearm, whatever the main reason for owning it, could, should the situation arise, be used for self-defense. In the limiting (but obviously uninteresting) case, then, *all* firearms are defensive firearms in that they *could* be used to thwart the criminal designs of others.

Many surveys have asked gun owners why they own their weapons. The most recent nationally generalizable evidence on the topic is that contained in a 1978 poll conducted by Decision/Making/Information, Inc., under contract to the National Rifle Association.[7] Respondents to the survey were first asked whether they owned any guns, and if they did, a follow-up was asked: "I have a list of reasons why people own guns. Please listen while I read it and then tell me

6. It is easy to exaggerate in such matters. Most of the people who do serious survey work are far more impressed by what people are willing to reveal about themselves than by what they find it necessary to conceal. The number of people who flatly refuse to answer a gun ownership question in national surveys amounts, typically, to about 1 percent of the total sample; the percentage who refuse a question on family income is typically ten times higher. Certainly, the whole matter of owning guns (for whatever reason) is doubtlessly more "threatening" or "socially undesirable" among the people who do *not* own guns than among the people who do. Drawing briefly on personal experience (always hazardous, to be sure), I confess that I have never met a gun owner who was the least bit ashamed or embarrassed about it.

7. DMI, *Attitudes of the American Electorate Toward Gun Control* (Santa Ana, Calif.: DMI, 1978). For a more extensive secondary analysis of the DMI data, see James D. Wright, "Public Opinion and Gun Control," *Annals of the American Academy of Political and Social Science* 455 (May 1981): 24–39; or Wright et al., *Weapons, Crime, and Violence in America*, chs. 7 and 13. Although the amount of technical data supplied in the DMI report is rather meager, the study appears to have been done in accordance with recognized professional research standards. It is important to keep in mind that the DMI study is based on a sample of registered voters, not of all U.S. adults, and is therefore somewhat "biased" in favor of white, middle-class, middle-aged respondents (persons who are more likely to be registered to vote). All the sample demographics from the survey compare favorably (within a percentage point or two) with equivalent data from the Current Population Survey.

Table 11-1. Reasons for Gun Ownership.[a]

	All Guns	Handguns Only
Self-Defense at Home	20	40
Protection at Work	1	5
Law Enforcement or Security Job	3	8
Part of a Gun Collection	7	14
Target Shooting	10	17
Hunting	54	9
Just Like to Have One	3	6
Missing Data (DK, NA, etc.)	2	1
	100%	100%

a. The question reads: "I have a list of reasons why people own guns. Please listen while I read it and then tell me the most important reason *you* have a gun."

Source: DMI, 1979: 40; all results are from DMI's December 1978 poll.

the most important reason *you* have a gun." Results from the item are shown in Table 11-1, first for all gun owners, then for handgun owners only.

These results bear discussing in some detail. Focussing first on the "All Guns" column, we note that hunting is by far the most commonly given reason for owning a gun, mentioned by 54 percent of all owners. Other sport and recreational answers (collecting, target shooting) are given by an addition 17 percent. Total sport and recreational answers therefore amount to between two thirds and three quarters of all answers. "Self-defense at home" is explicitly mentioned as the "most important" ownership reason by just one in five; some sort of work-related reason is given by 4 percent; and the remaining 5 percent either "just like to have one" or gave no answer to the question. As a generalization, we can conclude that sport ownership exceeds ownership for reasons of self-protection among all gun owners by a factor of about 3 to 1. Similar percentages are reported in all other credible studies of the topic.[8]

In the DMI survey, just under half of all respondents reported owning a gun, and similar percentages have been reported in all other national surveys that have asked a gun ownership question.[9] If half

8. Most of the important literature on the topic is reviewed and summarized in Wright et al., *Weapons, Crime, and Violence in America*, chs. 5–7; no study suggests that more than a third of all guns are owned mainly for self-defense; all studies, without exception, report sport and recreation as the leading ownership reasons.

9. The first gun ownership question in a national survey appeared in a Gallup poll of 1959, and the question has been included in scores of national surveys since, including

of all households are armed, and 20 percent of those that are armed keep a weapon mainly for self-defense, then we are dealing roughly with a tenth of the nation's households who possess a firearm primarily for defense or protection reasons. Perhaps the most remarkable fact about the ownership of firearms for reasons of self-defense is thus that it is not a very widespread practice, in contrast to much of the alarmist imagery one encounters in the literature.[10]

The DMI question, of course, asks for the "most important" ownership reason, and many weapons owned primarily for sport or recreation could well be maintained for self-defense as a secondary reason. In other words, the DMI question gives a lower boundary for the ownership of defensive weaponry. An upper boundary is supplied by the 1976 American National Election Survey conducted by the Center for Political Studies at the University of Michigan. In a late section of the survey, respondents were asked about various "precautions" they had taken to "be safe from crime." One item asked whether respondents kept "a gun for purposes of protection." Of the respondents who answered the question ($N = 2,381$), 22 percent said "yes." Since this is a percentage of all respondents, and since only about half the respondents would be from households owning any gun for any reason, the proportion among gun-possessing households would thus be about 44 percent. We may thus conclude that the proportion of gun-owning households who keep a gun, either primarily or secondarily, for purposes of protection is somewhere between 20 and 40 percent, with the corresponding percentages for all U.S. households being 10 to 20 percent. Even at the outside, then, we are

---

several of the General Social Surveys (annual surveys by the National Opinion Research Center). The lowest ownership percentage ever recorded in a national survey is 42 percent, and the highest 58 percent. For details, see Wright et al., *Weapons, Crime, and Violence in America*, ch. 5, Table 5-1.

10. For example, "The unfortunate cycle continues: the rise in street crime causes nervous people to buy guns for protection, and those very guns eventually cause more accidents, more crime, and more national paranoia. This deadly cycle must be broken." (This passage is from a well-known pro-gun-control tract, *A Shooting Gallery Called America*.) Elsewhere, one will encounter the phrase, "the domestic arms race." In many of the more polemical tracts, the impression imparted is that virtually all the guns in the country are owned for protection against crime — certain proof that something must be done to control them. Because these are apparently widespread impressions, I emphasize in the text that the ownership of a gun primarily for protection or self-defense is relatively uncommon. Still, it is a fact that we are dealing, literally, with millions and millions of "protection" guns; in absolute numbers, in other words, the phenomenon is hardly rare.

dealing with a phenomenon that characterizes fewer than a quarter of all U.S. households.[11]

In the DMI and most other surveys, about half the gun owners (or about a quarter of the total sample) report that they own a handgun, and the reasons given for handgun ownership vary somewhat (although not remarkably so) from those given among "all owners." The most common reason given for owning a handgun is "self-defense at home," mentioned by 40 percent. Another 13 percent offer some job-related reason. Significantly, another 40 percent also give some sort of sport or recreational reason for owning their handgun: 17 percent mention target shooting, 14 percent mention gun collecting, and 9 percent mention hunting, which sums to 40 percent overall. It is thus a second remarkable fact that even handguns are as likely to be owned for sport and recreation as they are to be owned for protection or self-defense, this despite the very widespread assertion that handguns have *no* legitimate sport or recreational application.[12]

It is an easy, but perhaps misleading, assumption that "defense" or "protection" means defense or protection against other human beings, that is, protection against human crime and violence. It is well known, however, that firearms ownership is primarily a small town and rural phenomenon, and that ownership falls off sharply as city size increases.[13] It is therefore certain that at least some fraction of the defensive ownership of weapons is for defense against the various unfriendly fauna often encountered in the rural environment: snakes, rabid animals, rats, foxes, coyotes, etc.[14] The precise magni-

11. The rest of the SRC results are also of some interest. Of the total sample who answered the question sequence, 12 percent said they had "bought a dog for purposes of protection," 30 percent had "put new locks on windows or doors," 5 percent had put "an alarm system" in their car or home, and, as noted in the text, 22 percent "kept a gun for purposes of protection." By far the most common "defense" was to "stay away from certain areas" in the town or city, 54 percent mentioning this as a measure they had taken.

12. Given the utter certainty with which this point is advanced in the pro-gun-control literature, it is worth mention that no credible study of the sport and recreational uses of handguns has ever been undertaken. The DMI evidence on this point is at best fragmentary but suggests a very substantial sporting handgun use. A more extended discussion of the point is to be found in Wright et al., *Weapons, Crime, and Violence in America*, ch. 5.

13. Wright, *Weapons, Crime, and Violence in America*, ch. 6.

14. To persons reared in an urban environment, the idea that people own guns for protection against animals will seem anachronistic at best, bizarre at worst. Foxes and coyotes, however, remain a serious threat to farmers and their livestock more or less everywhere in the United States. Poisonous snakes, likewise, can be found virtually anywhere outside a metropolitan area, and in some areas of the South, alligators have reappeared as a serious

tude of this fraction is unknown, since, so far as I know, no national survey has asked the appropriate follow-up question. The DMI survey did ask respondents whether they had ever "had to use" their firearm for self-defense, and for those responding yes, a follow-up asked whether that was defense against animals or against other humans. How defensive firearms actually get used is, at best, an imperfect indicator of why they are owned, but it is perhaps of some importance that about *half* the people who reported a defensive weapons use also reported that it was in defense against an animal.

The most extensive and sophisticated inquiry into the characteristics of sporting versus defensive weapons owners is that of Lizotte and Bordua, an analysis based, unfortunately, on data only for the state of Illinois.[15] Ownership for sport displays all the characteristics normally associated with a "subculture." For example, the best predictor, by far, of the sporting ownership of a firearm is whether one's parent owned a gun, strongly suggesting some early childhood socialization into a "gun culture." A similar result has been reported in several other studies.[16] Ownership for protection also displays some signs of a subculture but responds primarily to so-called "structural variables," chiefly the rate of violent crime in the county of residence.[17]

---

problem. Every barn and silo in the world, and every landfill or dump area, will contain a population of rats. Skunks, raccoons, and porcupines are also occasionally a problem, even in urban areas; rooting around in urban trash cans is a favorite activity of all three species. Anyone who has ever awakened some fine summer Southern morning to a yard crawling with rattlesnakes would find the ownership of a gun for protection against them an eminently sensible strategy.

15. Alan J. Lizotte and David J. Bordua, "Firearms Ownership for Sport and Protection," *American Sociological Review* 45 (April 1980), 229–44.

16. For a review of the relevant studies on "socialization" as the primary factor in adult gun ownership, see Wright et al., *Weapons, Crime, and Violence in America*, ch. 6. All studies to have inquired into the matter (e.g., Lizotte and Bordua, "Firearms Ownership for Sport and Protection"; Alan Marks and Shannon C. Stokes, "Socialization, Firearms, and Suicide," *Social Problems* 23 [June 1976] : 622–29; Edward Deiner and Kenneth W. Kerber, "Personality Characteristics of American Gun Owners," *Journal of Social Psychology* 107 [1979] : 227–38) report that parent's gun ownership is the single best predictor of respondent's gun ownership, especially ownership for sport and recreation.

17. Interestingly, several studies (e.g., James D. Wright and Linda Marston, "The Ownership of the Means of Destruction," *Social Problems* 23 [October 1975] : 93–107; Sherwood J. Williams and John H. McGrath, "Why People Own Guns," *Journal of Communication* 26 [Autumn 1976] : 22–30; Lizotte and Bordua, "Firearms Ownership for Sport and Protection," pp. 229–44; Lizotte et al., "Firearms Ownership for Sport and Protection," *American Sociological Review* 46 [August 1981] : 499–503) report that there is no significant tendency for persons who have been victimized by crime to own guns at a greater rate than

THE EFFICACY OF FIREARMS AS A DEFENSE AGAINST CRIME

About half the households in the United States are armed, and of this half, somewhere between 20 and 40 percent are armed mainly for reasons of "protection," whether against animals or other people. Are the armed households actually safer against crime? Do the risks of such firearms ownership exceed the crime-reductive benefits?

For a variety of reasons, these are exceedingly difficult questions to answer. Some of the reasons are strictly logical. For example, it is self-evident that a deterred crime is a relatively undetected crime. This would be less true of crimes deterred "in process" (i.e., burglars frightened off by homeowners brandishing weapons) because, presumably, at least some such incidents would be reported to the police. But crimes that are never even attempted because of advance knowledge that the potential victim is armed (i.e., the burglary that does *not* occur because the homeowner is a well-known marksman) would never appear in any data source. And even if it could be shown that certain types of crimes were just as common in areas with a high density of private weaponry as in areas where this density is low, the argument might still be made that the rate of crime would nonetheless be *higher yet* in the heavily armed areas were the citizenry not quite so well armed. As is well known, the "deterrence" effect even of relatively direct criminal sanctions (e.g., sentencing) is notoriously difficult to estimate. Estimating the deterrence effects of private weponry is certain to be even more difficult.

The point being made is even more general. Relative to most other advanced Western nations, the citizenry of the United States is heavily armed, and it is also victimized by criminal violence more frequently than are the populations of most similar nations. Despite the high crime rates that now exist, it is certainly a logical possibility that these rates would be higher still were it not for the generally

---

those who have not; victimization, in other words, is itself uncorrelated with gun ownership. Still, the Lizotte-Bordua finding is that the protective ownership of guns is higher in counties with high crime rates than in other counties. From these two findings, it would apparently follow that much defensive weaponry is owned by people living in high crime areas but who have themselves not been victimized, which would suggest that it is the fear of crime more than the experience of crime that causes protective gun ownership. Data in Lizotte et al., "Firearms Ownership for Sport and Protection," pp. 499–503 are consistent with this interpretation.

widespread ownership of firearms by private citizens. In this sense, the most important single source of "crime deterrence" because of private weapons ownership would be in essence undetectable in any research design: namely, the deterrence of vast numbers of crimes that do not occur simply because the people who might otherwise commit them fear the possibility of being shot in the process.

The idea being advanced here is perhaps not so far-fetched as it might initially seem. We find it easy to believe, for example, that many people choose not to engage in crime because they fear being apprehended, convicted, and sentenced for the crime. As bad as "doing time" might be, it is certainly a lesser consequence than being seriously wounded or, for that matter, shot to death by one's intended victim. The "cost" of justice meted out by an armed potential victim is conceivably much greater than the "cost" of the punishments that would be enforced by the criminal justice system, so far as the offender would be concerned.

Granting in advance, then, that some of the potentially most important "crime reductive" effects of private weaponry are more or less intrinsically unmeasurable, what evidence is there that private weapons are or are not an effective defense against crime?[18] The argument that firearms are *not* an effective crime deterrent is typically made on the basis of two kinds of evidence: (1) that much crime occurs in situations or locations where the victim's ownership of a gun would be irrelevant to the prevention of the crime, and (2) that the number of criminals actually shot in the process by their intended victims is very low.

Concerning the first of these, little need be said. The burglary of an unoccupied residence, the most common situation of home burglary, is clearly not deterrable by any firearms kept in the home, since there is no one home to use them. Likewise, unless persons walk the streets armed (and some do, as will be discussed), then private weaponry is not going to deter much of any street crime. But neither of these obvious facts tells us anything about the effectiveness of firearms in deterring crimes that are potentially deterrable, which is the more important issue.

The matter of home burglary warrants a related comment. It is well known that about 90 percent of all home burglaries occur when

---

18. It is something of a misstatement to say that some of these effects are "unmeasurable." Many of them might be measured, or at least estimated roughly, by asking a sample of criminals about their fears and expectations.

no one is at home. One might wonder why this is the case, and in speculating along such lines, one would sooner or later arrive at the hypothesis that burglars may avoid occupied residences in part because they fear an encounter with an armed inhabitant. Episodic evidence from career burglars suggests that this is not a remote or implausible hypothesis.[19] In this framework, the fact that 90 percent of all burglaries occur in unoccupied residences might be taken as evidence for a substantial crime-reductive effect of private firearms.

It is also true that very few burglaries, robberies, or rapes are accompanied by the victim shooting the offender.[20] Newton and Zimring note, for example, that over the period 1964–1968, roughly 2 burglaries in 1000 were foiled by the intended victim shooting at the burglar; thus, some 99.8 percent of them were not.[21] For robbery, the figure is much higher, but still low in absolute terms: their data suggest that about 2 percent of all robberies "result in the firearms injury or death of the robber."[22] Yeager and associates report similar results.[23]

Since most (90%) home burglaries occur when no one is at home, the presented evidence for home burglary is somewhat misleading. If 2 in 1000 home burglaries are foiled by the victim's use of a firearm, and about 900 in 1000 occur with no one at home, then the actual rate for burglaries committed with a person in the home would perforce be similar to that for home robbery—on the order of 2 percent.

19. See, for example, John Crown's column in the *Atlanta Constitution* for Saturday, April 15, 1978. Crown recounts a letter received from a convict in Atlanta, apparently genuine, who opines in glorious detail that "there is no one in this world that would like to see gun control brought into force more so than the criminal." The author of the letter goes on to affirm that he does a considerable "casing" of each potential job (he claims more than 150 robberies in his career) "to ensure myself that there wasn't a gun on the premises except my own." Similar episodic evidence can be had from many sources; systematic and generalizable evidence, unfortunately, can be had from none, as of this writing.

20. For example, Newton and Zimring, *Firearms and Violence in American Life*, pp. 62–65; Matthew G. Yeager et al., *How Well Does the Handgun Protect You and Your Family?* (Washington, D.C.: U.S. Conference of Mayors, 1976).

21. The figure 2 per 1,000 is a comparison between the number of burglars shot or wounded in the course of the crime and the total number of burglaries reported to the police. Burglars who were shot at but got away and were never subsequently apprehended would presumably not appear in these data as deterred crimes, and so the calculated figure may be too low. Also, it is possible that many burglars are frightened off by the homeowner brandishing a weapon; these, presumably, should also count as deterred crimes but would not appear as such in these data. (All these points also apply to the calculated deterrence rate for robbery, as discussed in the text.)

22. Newton and Zimring, *Firearms and Violence in American Life*, p. 63.

23. Yeager et al., *How Well Does the Handgun Protect You and Your Family?*

We may thus conclude that the risk to a criminal victimizing an occupied residence of being shot at by the intended victim is roughly 0.02.

This seems a relatively low risk in absolute terms, and one might therefore question whether a risk of this magnitude ever prevents potential burglars or robbers from getting into the business. Interestingly enough, however, this magnitude of risk apparently *exceeds* the risk to a burglar of being apprehended, charged, prosecuted, convicted, and sentenced for the crime.[24] In 1976, "the overall risk of a burglar being arrested and convicted was only about 1.8 percent for any given burglary. If half . . . received a prison sentence, then the risk of imprisonment was 0.9 percent." Since there is reason, and some evidence to suppose that the possibility of imprisonment, however slight, deters at least some robbery and burglary (in the sense that it discourages people from ever robbing or burglarizing), and since the possibility of being shot at and wounded or killed appears to be on the same order of magnitude, then it is certainly plausible that at least some potential robberies and burglaries never occur because the people who would otherwise commit them fear the possibility of being shot by the intended victim.[25]

It must also be noted that the "deterrence" rates (more precisely, the probabilities of being shot at) given above are conservative estimates at best. Criminals who were simply frightened off by the intended victim brandishing or discharging a firearm would be counted in these data only if the incident were reported to the police; many such incidents, presumably, are not. Silver and Kates have remarked, not unreasonably, that "citizens keep [guns] not to kill with, but to defend themselves. Success is measured as much by the number of criminals wounded, captured, or driven off without a shot being fired, as by the number killed."[26] The *actual* number of violent crimes that are foiled by private arms is simply unknown, but is

24. Gary Kleck, "Guns, Homicide, and Gun Control" (Paper read at the annual meeting of the Midwest Sociological Society, Minneapolis, Minn., 1979), pp. 11–12.

25. For example, Charles R. Tittle, "Crime Rates and Legal Sanctions," *Social Problems* 16 (1969): 409–23; Isaac Ehrlich, "Participation in Illegitimate Activities," *Journal of Political Economy* 81 (1973): 521–65. See also Philip J. Cook, "The Effect of Gun Availability on Robbery and Robbery Murder," in Robert Haveman and B. Bruce Zellner, eds., *Policy Studies Review Annual*, vol. 3 (Beverly Hills, Calif.: Sage, 1979), pp. 743–81.

26. Carol Silver and Don B. Kates, Jr., "Self-Defense, Handgun Ownership, and the Independence of Women in a Violent, Sexist Society," in Don B. Kates, Jr., ed., *Restricting Handguns* (Croton-on-Hudson: North River Press, 1978), p. 157.

almost certainly higher than the numbers suggested in the previous paragraphs, and to emphasize, even those numbers approximate or exceed the numbers of burglars or robbers who are apprehended, convicted, and actually jailed for the crime.

Evidence from the criminal victimization surveys can also be used to examine the effectiveness of victim resistance to crime, whether by firearms or other means. Evidence reported by Yeager and others suggests that the use of a weapon against a robber is an effective deterrent in some cases. Robberies, that is, are less likely to be successful if the intended victim takes self-defensive measures (55%) than if not (85%).[27] Thus, "use of a weapon for self-protection may be the most effective means of resisting a robbery."[28] On the other hand, the opportunity to use a weapon to defend against a robbery is rare, since most robbery occurs on the street with the victim unarmed, and it is also true that the death or injury of the victim is more likely if he or she resists than if not.[29]

So far as can be determined, there is no systematic evidence available on the deterrence of crimes against businesses that results from weapons kept on the premises. One study, cited by Newton and Zimring, did show that roughly one small business in four has a gun on the premises for defense against crime.[30]

Studies examining the relationship between criminal victimization and gun ownership were mentioned in note 17. In general, no demonstrable relationship exists, that is, the criminally victimized are no more or less likely to own a gun that the nonvictimized, all else equal. If private weapons ownership were an effective crime deterrent, then we would expect less crime against armed than against unarmed households, which the data, in general, do not show. But in this sense, weapons ownership would only function as a deterrent if the criminal knew in advance that the intended victim was armed, not a very likely possibility.

27. Yeager et al., *How Well Does the Handgun Protect You and Your Family?*; see also Philip J. Cook, "Reducing Injury and Death Rates in Robbery," *Policy Analysis* 6 (Winter 1980): 21–45.

28. Yeager et al., *How Well Does the Handgun Protect You and Your Family?*, p. 1.

29. Cook, "Reducing Injury and Death Rates in Robbery"; idem., "The Effect of Gun Availability on Violent Crime Patterns," *Annals of the Academy of Political and Social Sciences* 455 (May 1981): 63–79; see also Wright et al., *Weapons, Crime, and Violence in America*, ch. 11.

30. Newton and Zimring, *Firearms and Violence in American Life*, p. 66.

On the other hand, Kleck has pointed out that while criminals may not know whether any specific household is armed, they might know that some areas of a state or city are more heavily armed than others and avoid them accordingly.[31] In this case, we would expect less crime against households located in neighborhoods where the rate of weapons ownership was known to be high. This, however, must remain a speculative possibility since no relevant data are known to exist.

Concerning the deterrence of aggravated assaults, the scanty evidence available suggests that assaults are *less* likely to be completed if the victim uses a weapon than if no protective measures are taken.[32]

Other types of potentially deterrable crime—for example, homicides, rapes, and so on—have not been extensively studied in this framework; there is, for example, no existing estimate of the rate at which rapes are foiled by an armed potential victim.[33] So on these matters, nothing empirical may be said.

It was noted earlier that two types of evidence were commonly cited as proof *against* the defensive efficacy of private weapons. To summarize briefly, the first line of evidence must be dismissed as irrelevant to the issue and the second as seriously misleading. That much crime occurs in situations where the victim's gun could not be used says nothing about the efficacy of the gun in situations where it could be used. In the relatively few cases where the opportunity to defend oneself with a gun is present, the evidence suggests that one is somewhat less likely to be successfully victimized if one is armed than if one is not. And likewise, the mere fact that relatively few criminals are actually shot in the process of crime is misleading as an indicator of the rate at which crime is deterred by private weapons ownership. Many crimes are effectively deterred by the victim's gun long before any shots are fired; and perhaps more importantly, there are at least as many crimes "thwarted" by the victim actually shooting at the offender as there are offenders who are apprehended and imprisoned for their offense. As a general conclusion, then, I suggest that such evidence as there is on crime deterrence by private weap-

31. Kleck, "Guns, Homicide, and Gun Control."
32. Ibid., p. 13; Yeager et al., *How Well Does the Handgun Protect You and Your Family?*
33. Silver and Kates, "Self-Defense, Handgun Ownership, and the Independence of Women."

onry does *not* support the argument that guns are useless in defense against crime.[34]

There is, of course, a series of counterarguments that must also be considered. One might grant, for example, that in at least some circumstances or situations, at least some types of crime can be successfully deterred (or defended against) by the use of a gun, but might at the same time argue that the benefits of so doing are greatly outweighed by the costs of keeping a gun for protection in the home. This raises the exceedingly complex issue of the relative costs and benefits of defensive weapons ownership, or in other words, the *expected utilities* and *disutilities* of keeping a firearm in the home.

A utility is defined by two independently variable parameters: the first is the *value* of some outcome, and the second is the *probability* that such an outcome would be realized. The expected utility, then, is the value times the probability. To use expected utilities as predictors of behavior, it perhaps goes without saying that both the values and the probabilities are those as *perceived* by the individual, whether they bear any realistic relationship to the true values and the true probabilities or not.

The counterargument can now be restated in slightly more technical terms: whatever the expected utility is of keeping a gun for protection in the home (and let us grant that it is non-zero), the expected disutility is much greater. And for this reason, a sensible person would *not* keep a gun for protection in the home, however effective it might otherwise be as a defense against crime.

One version of this counterargument appears in the pro-gun-control pamphlet of Yeager et al.[35] "The probability of being robbed, raped, or assaulted is low enough to seriously call into question the need for Americans to keep loaded guns on their persons or in their homes." Even if a gun is an effective deterrent against these crimes, in other words, the probability of being victimized by any of them is sufficiently low that the expected utility of keeping a gun is likewise very low.[36]

---

34. The victimization data show rather clearly that the probability of a successful victimization goes down, but that the probability of injury or death to the victim goes up, if any sort of defensive measure is taken. For crimes potentially deterrable by a private gun, then, the apparent tradeoff is between a slightly lower "completion" rate and a somewhat higher probability of suffering bodily harm.

35. Yeager et al., *How Well Does the Handgun Protect You and Your Family?*, p. 1.

36. The remark about "loaded guns" bears a passing comment. It is a very common presumption—but only that—that many (or most) people keep their firearms loaded and ready

There are several points to mention in this connection. First, the probability of criminal victimization is somewhat higher than Yeager's depiction suggests. The 1977 General Social Survey (conducted by the National Opinion Research Center), for example, found that about 9 percent of their national sample of households had been broken into, or had had something taken from them through use of force, *in the previous year.* Criminal victimization surveys routinely get similar results. For an American family picked at random, in other words, the probability of being victimized by crime in any given year is on the order of 10 percent and over five years would therefore be on the order of 50 percent, all else equal. To put these odds in a comparative framework, the probability to the same family of being victimized by a natural disaster (flood, tornado, hurricane, or earthquake) in the same year would be on the order of 1 to 2 percent, or some five to ten times less risk.[37] So far as I know, however, nobody has seriously argued that because the risk from natural hazards is so small, no protective measures need be taken against them.

One implication of Yeager's point is assuredly that the expected utility of a firearm kept for protection against crime is higher where the crime rate is higher and lower elsewhere. In areas where crime is high (for example, big cities, or black neighborhoods within big cities), the case against a defensive firearm is therefore correspondingly more difficult to maintain.

In the same vein, it is often argued that the risk of a serious firearms accident is a cost of keeping a gun in the home, and that this probability exceeds the probability that the gun would ever actually be used to foil a crime. Again, the expected disutility (a serious or fatal accident) is, it is argued, greater than the expected utility (actually preventing a crime). The National Health Survey gives a reasonable estimate of the number of firearms accidents that occur annually; the figure is about 183,000 (plus or minus several tens of thousands, to be sure).[38] Many (perhaps most) of these accidents result in trivial injuries, some in very serious injuries, and a small fraction of

---

for use. The proportion who actually do so is a matter about which not one shred of evidence exists. Certainly, some people keep them loaded and at hand; others keep them unloaded, disassembled, and in locked cabinets. It would be very useful to know the relative proportions.

37. Wright et al., *After the Clean-Up* (Beverly Hills, Calif.: Sage, 1979).

38. Wright et al., *Weapons, Crime, and Violence in America*, p. 294.

them result in death. (The number of accidental firearms *deaths* per annum is on the order of 2,000.) It would be a very great convenience to know the corresponding number of crimes deterred by private weapons in the average year, because if this number were known with equivalent precision, then the argument that there are many more accidents than deterred crimes could be assessed. However, this number is not known, as I have stressed in an earlier section of this chapter. That it is lower than the number of serious accidents is, therefore, an article of faith.

One often hears it claimed that a handgun kept in the home is six times more likely to be involved in the accidental death of a family member than to be involved in the death of a robber, burglar, or intruder. The study on which this estimate is based is that of Rushford et al., an analysis of shooting deaths in Cleveland.[39] In examining these data, Silver and Kates discovered, remarkably, that the data on "accidental deaths" apparently included firearms suicides along with fatal firearms accidents, which greatly inflates the numerator of the comparison.[40] In fact, according to these authors, the ratio of handgun suicides to accidental handgun deaths is on the order of 44 to 1, and if this is true, then the probability of actually shooting and killing a felon would be several times higher than the probability of an accidental death to a family member. (Just how much higher this probability would have to be to tip the cost-benefit equation in favor of owning the gun would, of course, depend on the value assigned to the life of a family member, an issue I shall not even attempt to address.)

Still, it is obvious that the probability of an accident involving the gun is a cost of owning it (whether it is owned for defense or for any other reason). This cost, however, can only be weighed against the probable benefits. It is well known that children are far more likely to be involved in a firearms accident than adults; among young males, firearms accidents are the third leading cause of accidental death. To a family with many small children, living in an area of little or no crime, reason would probably argue against owning a weapon for self-defense. If, on the other hand, one had no young children in the household and lived in a high-crime area, reason would probably

39. Norman Rushford et al., "Accidental Firearms Fatalities in a Metropolitan County (1958–1973)," *Am ·ican Journal of Epidemiology* 100 (1975): 499–505.

40. Silver and Kates, "Self-Defense, Handgun Ownership, and the Independence of Women," p. 152.

lead to an opposite conclusion. In any case, it is apparent that the "rationality" of a gun kept in the home for defense is going to vary quite substantially, depending on specific household circumstances. The extreme position, that no gun should be kept in any home for defensive purposes, is not adequately sensitive to the sharp contours present on the risk map. In a household with no small children, where the adults present are familiar with the operation of small arms, and where reasonable safety precautions are taken, the risk of a firearms accident is almost certainly negligible.[41]

Another "cost" sometimes advanced in arguing against the defensive ownership of weapons is the increased probability of a "heat of the moment" shooting. In this connection, it is often claimed (accurately, as it happens) that most homicides involve persons known to one another before the incident, most commonly relatives and family members. Just how many homicides result from the "heat of the moment" use of an available firearm, and how many result from a determined intention to kill, remains largely an open question, but it *is* clear that no one has yet demonstrated the former to be vastly more numerous than the latter, despite the very widespread assertions one encounters to this effect.[42] In the ordinary course of events, the only people one would have any reason to kill would be family, relatives, friends, and acquaintances, so the simple fact that most homicides involve family or friends is, in itself, not adequate evidence that the deaths were not also willful or intentional.

There are many people for whom the death of a spouse or their children would be the worst imaginable happening, something they

41. It is fair to assume that *most* people who own small arms are indeed familiar with their operation, use, safety features, and so on. As I noted earlier, much weapons ownership is a function of early childhood socialization, so many adult weapons owners will have had experiences with firearms from childhood. In one study of college students, 76 percent of the southern males and 55 percent of the northern males reported having fired a gun by the age of twelve (Marks and Stokes, "Socialization, Firearms, and Suicide"). It is also relevant that veterans are somewhat more likely to own a gun than nonveterans, and certainly, most veterans would be expected to be familiar with guns.

42. The relevant studies are reviewed in Wright et al., *Weapons, Crime, and Violence in America*, ch. 11. Most of the evidence commonly cited in behalf of the hypothesis that most homicide is "ambiguously motivated" (i.e., does not result from a willful determination to kill) turns out, on serious inspection, not to bear on the matter of intent, one way or the other. There is relatively good evidence to suggest, in contrast, that much family homicide, at least, is the culminating event in a long history of interpersonal violence and abuse among the parties, rather than an isolated ("heat of the moment") outburst occurring among normally placid and loving individuals. See Kleck "Guns, Homicide, and Gun Control" for some evidence on this point.

would try to avoid whatever the costs. People who feel this way and who fear a gun accident (or a "heat of the moment" shooting) above all else will often flatly refuse to keep a gun in their home for any reason, and under these circumstances, this counts as a supremely rational decision so far as they are concerned. In their minds, in other words, there is no conceivable benefit to owning a gun that would outweigh the costs of an injury to or the death of a loved one.

But there are many other people who love their spouses and children just as much but who are familiar with small arms and confident that with the appropriate safeguards they can keep a gun in the home safely, and who believe (rightly or wrongly) that the more pressing threat to the lives of their loved ones is a crazed intruder. These people will often flatly refuse not to keep a gun in the home: in their minds, the worst imaginable happening is to be defenseless in the face of a threat to the lives or well-being of their loved ones. Under these circumstances, this also must be counted as a supremely rational decision so far as these families are concerned. In their minds, there is no conceivable cost in owning a gun that would outweigh the cost of not being able to defend the family were such a situation to arise.

The point I wish to make in this connection is that both these situations derive ultimately from equal amounts of love and concern for one's family and differ only in what is perceived to be the greater threat. We might want to question the accuracy of these perceptions, but not, I think, the "purity" of the underlying motive.

It is often argued (with, incidentally, little supporting data) that the only discernible benefit of defensive gun ownership is psychological—that people who own guns for protection "feel safer," even if, in fact, they are not. This argument is misleading in at least three ways: (1) The idea that people are actually not safer from crime if they own a gun exaggerates the state of the evidence seriously. So far as the victimization evidence is concerned, people who keep a gun for protection probably are somewhat safer from crime than those who do not, simply because it appears that a firearm is an effective defense against at least some crimes in at least some circumstances. (2) Likewise, there is little evidence to support the common claim that the costs borne by defensive gun ownership (in terms of accidents, "heat of the moment" shootings, and so on) greatly exceed the benefits. In certain cases, the costs are close to zero, and in certain other cases, the potential benefits are very much greater than zero. Whether the "real" cost-benefit equation tips toward or away from owning a gun for self-defense is going to depend very directly on the particular circumstances and conditions of the household in question and therefore does not admit of a single solution that would be equally applicable to all households in all situations.

(3) Let us assume for the moment that neither (1) nor (2) held, and that the *only* benefit of a defensive firearm is the enhanced feeling of psychological safety. In modern society such is *not* a trivial benefit. Let us imagine a person who, for $25, has picked up a complete piece of junk: a .22 caliber imported revolver with a loose cylinder and a likely lifetime of fewer than another hundred rounds. In the event of a crime, a baseball bat or a box of rocks would be a superior weapon! This notwithstanding, if the person feels safer because he or she now "has a gun," and if, as a result of feeling safer, that person leads a happier or more satisfying or less fearful existence, then the gun has made a direct and unmistakable contribution to the overall quality of that person's life, at very little cost. It is, in other words, hard to see why the psychological benefit should be so heavily discounted, especially since, in the final analysis, all benefits are either psychological or no benefit at all.

THE USE OF FIREARMS IN SELF-DEFENSE

If the real or potential deterrent effects of privately possessed weaponry are necessarily difficult to determine, the actual *use* of private weapons in self-defense is not. Indeed, two recent national surveys have explored this issue in some detail, and it is appropriate to conclude the present chapter with a review of the more relevant findings.

The two surveys are the 1978 DMI survey and a survey conducted in the same year by Cambridge Reports, Inc. (Patrick Caddell's polling company), under commission to the Center for the Study and Prevention of Handgun Violence. Both surveys are focussed rather more directly on public opinion about gun control than on the uses of weapons in self-defense; a comparison of the public opinion results is contained in Wright.[43] But both also have at least some information on the uses to which private weapons are put. Most of Caddell's questions along these lines focus on handgun accidents and on respondents' experiences with handgun threats or attacks. DMI's questions, in contrast, focus heavily on the use of weapons by respondents for their own self-defense.

---

43. Wright, "Public Opinion and Gun Control," pp. 24–39.

Table 11-2 shows the relevant question sequence and marginal results from the Caddell survey. Consistent with other studies, 24 percent of Caddell's respondents say they possess a handgun, 17 percent (of the total, or 71 percent of the handgun owners only) say they own a handgun "for protection or self-defense," and 7 percent (of the total, or 29% of the handgun owners only) say that they carry their handgun with them for protection outside the home. Likewise, 3 percent of the total sample (or 13% of the handgun owners only) have "had to use" their weapon in self-defense; two thirds of those who have "had to use" their weapon in this manner actually fired it. It thus appears that 2 percent of the total adult population of the country has at some time in their lives actually fired a *handgun* in self-defense.[44]

The data on accidents, threats, and attacks suggest that about 4 percent of the respondents have been involved in a handgun accident, half of the incidents resulting in personal injury. Likewise, 10 percent report that a family member has been involved in such an accident, and 15 percent report a similar experience for a "close personal friend." Caddell's data suggest that 5 percent of the adults in the United States have had a family member *killed* in a handgun accident, and 7 percent have had a close friend *killed* in the same manner.[45] The evidence on handgun threats and attacks is similar: 11 percent of the respondents say they have personally experienced such an attack, 13 percent report such an attack for a member of the family other than themselves, and 19 percent report such an attack

44. At least some of this 2 percent would consist of persons using handguns in the course of their jobs; recall from Table 11-1 that somewhere between 8 percent and 13 percent of all privately owned handguns are owned primarily for employment-related reasons.

45. Caddell's figures for death from handgun accident and attack seem on the surface to be inordinately high. They are probably inflated to some extent by what is known in the survey literature as the "good respondent" syndrome, i.e., by the tendency of small fractions of the population to provide the answer that they think the investigator wishes to hear. It must also be kept in mind, however, that the frame of reference provided by the question is very broad: "Has *anyone* in your family *ever* been involved. . . ." In this case, "ever" could conceivably stretch back two or three generations (to, for example, grandparents and great-grandparents), and "anyone in your family" could include not just persons in the immediate family but also aunts, uncles, cousins, and various other extended family members. Keeping these frames of reference in mind, the numbers from the Caddell survey are more plausible. Rephrasing slightly, imagine a single individual killed in a handgun accident or attack. That person would have two parents, four grandparents, unknown numbers of aunts, uncles, and cousins, and possibly some children who could then accurately report that a family member had, indeed, been killed in a handgun mishap. Note further that if the person were married, all the equivalent in-laws could, again accurately, make the same report.

Table 11-2.   Data on Weapons Experience and Use from the Caddell Survey.

[IF "YES" TO THE HANDGUN OWNERSHIP QUESTION]
Do you ever carry that handgun or pistol outside of the house with you for protection or not?

YES	7%
NOT SURE	4
NO	15
DON'T OWN HANDGUN	77

Do you own a handgun for protection or self-defense purposes? [IF YES] Have you ever had to use it?

YES, TO THREATEN	1%
YES, AND I FIRED	2
YES, BUT NEVER USED IT	14
NO TO FIRST QUESTION	83

[IF "YES" TO ABOVE]
Where did you use it?

AT HOME	1%
AT BUSINESS	—
ON THE STREET	—
PUBLIC FACILITIES	1
OTHER PLACES	1
INAPPLICABLE	97

Have you ever been involved in a handgun accident? [IF YES] Were you injured or not?

YES, NOT INJURED	2%
YES, INJURED	2
NO, NEVER	96

Has anyone in your family ever been involved in a handgun accident? [IF YES] Were they injured or not?

YES, NOT INJURED	2%
YES, INJURED	3
YES, KILLED	5
NO, NEVER	89

Has a close friend ever been involved in a handgun accident? [IF YES] Were they injured or not?

YES, NOT INJURED	2%
YES, INJURED	6
YES, KILLED	7
NO, NEVER	85

(*Table 11-2. continued on next page*)

Table 11-2. continued

Have you ever been attacked or threatened with a handgun? [IF YES] Were you injured or not?

YES, NOT INJURED	9%
YES, INJURED	2
NO, NEVER	89

Has anyone in your family, beside yourself, ever been attacked or threatened with a handgun? [IF YES] Were they injured or not?

YES, NOT INJURED	7%
YES, INJURED	2
YES, KILLED	3
NO, NEVER	88

Has a close personal friend ever been attacked or threatened with a handgun? [IF YES] Were they injured or not?

YES, NOT INJURED	9%
YES, INJURED	6
YES, KILLED	4
NO, NEVER	82

on a close personal friend.[46] Roughly half of all these attacks are said to have resulted in personal injury or death.

Some of these data bear directly on an earlier theme. About 2 percent of the nation's adults have fired a handgun in self-defense, and an equivalent proportion have been involved in a handgun accident serious enough to result in personal injury (or worse). The comparison here is obviously imprecise, but the implication would apparently be that the true ratio of "serious accidents to deterrence" is more on the order of one to one than the "six to one" figure encountered frequently in the literature.

Table 11-3 presents the DMI data on weapons experience and uses. None of the DMI questions are precisely comparable to any of Caddell's, so direct comparisons between results are hazardous. Also, all of Caddell's questions ask about *handguns*, whereas the DMI items deal with all guns irrespective of type. A further important difference is that Caddell's questions on self-defensive weapons uses ask for

---

46. The NORC General Social Surveys have periodically asked, "Have you ever been threatened with a gun, or shot at?" The percentage responding "yes" varies between 16 and 20 percent, or somewhat higher than Caddell's 11 percent (for respondents only). Caddell's question, however, stipulates a *handgun* threat or attack, whereas the NORC item says nothing about the kind of gun, which would account for the difference in observed results.

Table 11-3.   Data on Weapons Experience and Use from the DMI Surveys.

Face-to-Face Survey

Have you yourself or a member of your household ever used a gun, even if it wasn't fired, for self-protection or for protection of property at home, at work, or elsewhere (except in military service or police work)?

YES	15%
NO	85

[IF YES TO THE ABOVE QUESTION]
Was the incident important enough to report to the police?

YES	31%
NO	66
DON'T KNOW	3

Was the gun fired in the incident?

YES	40%
NO	56
DON'T KNOW	5

Was anyone killed or injured?

YES	9%
NO	86
DON'T KNOW	6

[ALL RESPONDENTS]
Has anyone else you know personally ever used a gun, even if it wasn't fired, for self-protection . . . (AS ABOVE)

YES	27%
NO	73

[IF YES TO THE ABOVE]
Was the incident important enough to be reported to the police?

YES	52%
NO	47
DON'T KNOW	2

Was the gun fired in the incident?

YES	47%
NO	52
DON'T KNOW	1

Was anyone killed or injured?

YES	24%
NO	74
DON'T KNOW	1

Table 11-3. continued

Telephone Survey

Have you yourself or a member of your household ever used a gun, even if it wasn't fired, for self-protection . . . (AS ABOVE)? [IF YES] Was this to protect against an animal or a person?

YES, AN ANIMAL	5%
YES, A PERSON	5
YES, BOTH	2
NO	88

And, have you, yourself, ever been in a situation where you needed a gun to protect yourself or your family or property but there was no gun available? [IF YES] Was this to protect against an animal or a person?

YES, AN ANIMAL	1%
YES, A PERSON	8
YES, BOTH	1
NO	90

information only about the *respondent*, whereas the corresponding DMI questions ask about both the respondent and the respondent's family members.

According to the DMI data, 15 percent of all registered voters (or their family members) have "used a gun" for self-defense or other protective reasons at some point in their lives; in the DMI telephone poll, the corresponding percentage for an identical question was 12 percent. The telephone survey shows that roughly half of these defensive weapons uses are to protect against a person. Of the 15 percent reporting a defensive weapons use in the face-to-face survey, 31 percent say the incident was important enough to report to the police. The weapon was actually fired, it appears, in 40 percent of the incidents; 9 percent of the incidents apparently resulted in injury or death (presumably, to the offender). A parallel series of questions about personal friends produces similar, but uniformly higher, numbers on all items.

The DMI face-to-face survey thus suggests that 6 percent of all registered voters *or their families* $(0.40 \times 0.15 = 0.06)$ have, at some point in their lives, fired a weapon *of some sort* in self-defense; this finding is thus not inconsistent with Caddell's finding that 2 percent of all U.S. adults have *themselves* fired a *handgun* in self-defense. There is, in short, no serious disparity between the two findings.

DMI's telephone poll reveals another finding that figures promi- nently in their report; 10 percent of the DMI respondents say they can recall a situation where they "needed a gun but no gun was available." (Caddell has no comparable item with which this result might be compared.) Most of these incidents, it appears, involved a person rather than an animal.

Despite the differences between these surveys, both touch enough common ground to sustain at least a few conclusions. First, as shown in all other studies, some 20 to 25 percent of all U.S. households possess a handgun, and about twice that percentage possess a weapon of some sort. Second, many (although certainly not all) handguns are owned for purposes of protection or self-defense; approximately 40 percent of the handgun owners in both surveys cite self-defense or protection as the primary reason they possess the weapon, and some additional percentage cite this as a secondary reason. Third, at least some of the weapons that are owned for self-defense are actu- ally used for this purpose at some point: perhaps as many as 15 per- cent of all registered voters or their families have "used" a gun for self-defense; a rather lower percentage (7% in the Caddell survey) carry their weapons with them for defense outside the home; a lower percentage still say that they personally have "had to use" their handguns for self-defense (which is clearly a more restrictive phrasing than simply "used"); and the proportion of U.S. adults that have actually fired a weapon in self-defense is somewhere in the range of 2 to 6 percent. Fourth, the incidence of firearms accidents and hand- gun threats and attacks is at least as prevalent as, but not sharply more prevalent than, the incidence of weapons uses for self-defense.

SUMMARY

It is often said that "ownership of handguns by private citizens for self-protection against crime appears to provide more of a psy- chological belief in safety than actual deterrence to criminal behav- ior."[47] This conclusion is misleading in several related ways:

(1) The vast bulk of private weaponry is not owned for "self-pro- tection" but for other reasons.

---

47. Yeager et al., *How Well Does the Handgun Protect You and Your Family?*, p. 35.

(2) Of the weaponry possessed specifically and primarily for defense (perhaps 25% or so of the total armament), some is not for "self-protection against crime" but for protection against animals; evidence from DMI intimates that this factor might account for as much as half the total defensive ownership.

(3) In modern society a "psychological belief in safety" probably ought not be dismissed as a trivial benefit. If people feel safer because they own a gun and in turn lead happier lives because they feel safer and more secure, then their guns make a direct and nontrivial contribution to their overall quality of life.

(4) That private weapons are inefficacious crime deterrents has *not* been established directly in any source. In the case of crimes occurring in circumstances where they are potentially deterrable by a private gun, the evidence suggests, in contrast, at least some modest deterrent effects. (To be sure, most crimes do occur in what might be referred to as nondeterrable situations.)

(5) In owning a gun for protection (or for any other reason), a homeowner runs some risk that the weapon will be involved in an accident, or will be involved in a "heat of the moment" shooting, or will be stolen and used for criminal reasons by someone else. All of these are definitely costs incurred in owning a defensive firearm, costs that must be weighed against any potential benefits. By the same token, in choosing not to own a gun for protection, the homeowner runs some risk of being unable to deter crime (or defend against crimes) that he or she would otherwise be able to foil, and this is a cost of not owning the gun that has to be weighed against any potential benefits. In general, both costs and benefits are far too variable across households with varying characteristics to allow one to say in some general and all-embracing way whether families "should" or "should not" keep guns for protection in the home.

(6) At least some of the people who own guns for self-defense actually use them for that purpose; the precise percentage is, of course, very difficult to determine, as are the ensuing effects on crime and violence in the society as a whole. It is certainly possible that the high rates of crime and violence that predominate in the United States are due primarily to the widespread ownership of guns. But it is also possible that the widespread ownership of guns keeps the rates of crime and violence well below what they might otherwise be. At present, there is no good evidence anywhere that would allow one to choose decisively between these possibilities.

Chapter 12

GUNS FOR PROTECTION AND OTHER PRIVATE SECTOR RESPONSES TO THE FEAR OF RISING CRIME

Bruce L. Benson

INTRODUCTION

The relationship between firearms and violent crime rates is analogous to the relationship between jogging (or, more correctly, jogging shoes) and heart attacks. Every year many people in this country have heart attacks while jogging. Similarly, every year many people use firearms while committing violent crimes. Advocates of gun control contend that elimination of firearms will reduce violent crime. The same logic should lead to an argument for making jogging (or better yet, some tool of joggers like jogging shoes, since guns are tools of the criminals) illegal in order to reduce heart attacks.

Of course, we know that jogging (or jogging shoes) does not cause heart attacks. If a person who has a heart attack while jogging did not jog, he would have it the next time he shoveled the snow off his sidewalk, or changed a flat tire, or got overly nervous at work, and so forth. The person has a heart attack because he has heart disease, after all, not because he is jogging. Similarly, individuals who commit violent crimes with firearms generally would have committed a similar crime with a knife or a club or some other tool. The economic theory of crime teaches us that the typical criminal commits crimes because his or her socioeconomic position implies that the potential benefits of committing the crime (in terms of income or satisfaction) will exceed the potential costs (in terms of the probability and severity of punishment). The criminal does not commit the crime because he or she owns a gun. It is not at all surprising, in light of this argument, to note Magaddino and Medoff's findings that current gun control laws in the United States do not reduce crime. Neither the Federal Gun Control Act of 1968 nor existing state gun laws appear to have any significant impact on violent crime.[1]

But the analogy between jogging and firearms goes even further. Many people jog in order to prevent heart attacks. Evidence indicates that far more heart attacks will be prevented because people jog and improve their circulatory system than will occur while people are jogging. Of course, it is not possible to know how many heart attacks do not occur because people jog, since we cannot count things that do not happen. But certainly the existence of a positive correlation between the level of jogging (or jogging shoe ownership) and the number of heart attacks would not demonstrate a causation running from jogging to heart attacks. At most, it would suggest that, as the threat of other diseases is gradually eliminated, so people live longer and heart attacks become more likely, and as the life style of the American people becomes more tense and more sedentary (and therefore physical condition declines), the *threat* of heart attacks rises. The growing *fear* of heart attacks *causes* more people to take up jogging in order *to protect themselves.*

Analogously, individuals buy firearms in an effort to protect themselves and their property from criminals. This, in turn, may deter criminals, at least from confrontation-type crimes. Of course, it is not possible to know how effective such self-protection efforts are, since it is impossible to count how many crimes do not occur (or, perhaps, are shifted to other areas where people have not taken such precautions). Many individuals *believe* that their ownership of guns can help to protect them from crime, however. For example, Lizotte, Bordua, and White found that several variables, including fear of crime and previous violent experiences, were statistically significant predictors of gun ownership for protection.[2] Feagin argues that fear of crime may be the primary motive for home defense, and conse-

1. Joseph Magaddino and Marshall Medoff, "An Empirical Analysis of Federal and State Firearm Control Laws," in this volume.

2. Alan Lizotte, David Bordua, and Carolyn White, "Firearm Ownership for Sport and Protection: Two Not so Divergent Models," *American Sociological Review* 46 (August 1981): 499–502.

quently for firearm ownership.[3] Even when fear of crime is put aside, Reiss and Bordua point out that those people who believe the criminal justice system is ineffective might take measures to defend themselves.[4] Since the *threat* of crime is perceived to be on the rise, the growing *fear* of crime causes more individuals to buy firearms in order to protect themselves.

One obvious impetus to the rising fear of crime is crime statistics. These showed crime rising very rapidly through the 1960s and early 1970s, and remaining at a very high level since. There has been a definite correlation between increasing gun ownership and increasing crime during the 1960s and early 1970s. But the question few people have addressed is which way does the causation run. It certainly seems just as reasonable to argue, at this point, that causation runs from rising crime to increasing gun ownership for protection, as to argue that causation runs from increasing gun ownership to rising crime. Actually, there could be causation running in both directions.

Many scholars apparently started with the assumption that guns lead to crime and, upon discovering a correlation between firearm ownership and crime rates, jumped to the conclusion that their assumption was borne out.[5] Tonso argues that social scientists who have addressed the area generally are predisposed to support gun control and then search for evidence for their biases, rather than neutrally appraising the issue.[6] Underlining Tonso's contention is an

---

3. Joe Feagin, "Public Reaction to Crime in the Streets," *American Behavioral Scientist* 13 (1970): 797–814.

4. Albert Reiss and David Bordua, "Environment and Organization: A Perspective on the Police" in David Bordua, ed., *The Police: Six Sociological Essays* (New York: Wiley, 1967).

5. In fact, correlation does not necessarily imply any causation. For example, handgun ownership rose by about 250 percent between 1937 and 1963. During that period homicide rates fell by 35.7 percent (Don B. Kates, Jr., *Why Handgun Bans Can't Work*, Bellevue, Wash.: Second Amendment Foundation, 1982, p. 23). Clearly, rising gun ownership did not lead to more homicides during that period, so this data tends to deny the direction of causation claimed by gun control advocates. Of course, falling homicide rates did not result in falling gun ownership either, so one might also question the argument of causation flowing from crime rates to guns. However, there are other reasons for buying firearms besides protection, so gun ownership very well could rise even when ownership for protection declines. For instance, a large portion of the increased ownership during the 1937–1963 period involved the collection of war souvenirs from World War II and Korea. So, while these numbers cast doubt on the argument for causation running from guns to crime, they cast less doubt on the crime to guns for protection causal theory.

6. William R. Tonso, "Social Problems and Sagecraft: Gun Control as a Case in Point," in this volume.

assumption that the causation running from firearms to crime has rarely been questioned. A recently completed massive survey of the existing gun control literature finds the evidence totally inadequate to justify the guns-to-crime causality assumption.[7] Kleck, on the other hand, found evidence of causation running both ways using time series analysis.[8] He first concluded as a result of this study, that rising crime leads to large increases in gun ownership, and that rising gun ownership in turn leads to relatively small increases in crime. Kleck extended the same time series analysis with new data for this volume and found with the additional data that the only significant causation is from rising crime to increased gun ownership.[9]

There is, in fact, no strong a priori reason to expect a causal connection between rising gun ownership and rising crime. After all, such causation requires us to assume that "increased gun ownership somehow caused increasing numbers of ordinary law-abiding people to commit rapes, robberies, and murders which they otherwise would not have done."[10] But there is a strong a priori reason to expect a causal relation in the direction that Kleck deduces. One purpose of this presentation is to explain and support that expectation.

In this connection it is relevant to look at other private sector protection efforts to supplement public protection services, which are also on the rise. In fact, it appears that gun ownership for protection is just one small part of a large and growing process of privatization of crime prevention and protection. Government's inability to bring crime rates down has led citizens to turn increasingly to the private sector. They are hiring private police, buying burglar alarms and other anti-intrusion devices, learning self-defense, joining neighborhood watches and patrols, *and* buying firearms and other protection equipment in growing numbers. Such private sector efforts may be desirable. They could, over time, lead to a reduction in crime rates. Thus, attempts to suppress any of these private sector protection

7. James Wright, Peter Rossi, Eleanor Weber-Burdin, and Kathy Daly. *Weapons, Crime and Violence in America: A Literature Review and Research Agenda* (Washington, D.C.: National Institute of Justice, 1981).

8. Gary Kleck, "Capital Punishment, Gun Ownership, and Homicide," *American Journal of Sociology* 84 (January 1979): 882–910.

9. Gary Kleck, "The Relationship Between Gun Ownership Levels and Rates of Violence in the United States," in this volume.

10. Kates, *Why Handgun Bans Can't Work*, p. 19.

efforts, including reduction of gun ownership, could be very undesirable.

PRIVATE SECTOR RESPONSES
TO RISING CRIME

The most obvious and visible example of private sector production of protection is the private security industry. Sherman pointed out that "few developments are more indicative of public concern about crime—and declining faith in the ability of public institutions to cope with it—than the burgeoning growth in private policing."[11] An estimated one million people were employed for private security in the United States during 1982 as compared to 650,000 public law enforcement officers.[12] In 1976 approximately 6.6 billion dollars was spent on private guards, an increase of 46 percent in five years, and "in essence, most of the growth can be attributed to increases in crime in the United States."[13] A 1982 estimate put expenditures on private police at 10 billion dollars annually.[14] These private police are employed primarily by individuals and firms. However, recently an entire neighborhood in St. Louis bought the streets and hired private police to protect the area.[15]

In addition to the purchase of protection services from private firms, individuals are increasingly supplementing government protection with efforts of their own. This often involves purchases by individuals of capital or training to enhance their ability to protect themselves. As already noted, fear of crime is inducing more and more citizens to buy firearms for protection. Burglar alarms are being installed and guard dogs purchased. Approximately $5.3 billion in intruder-detection sales alone are anticipated by the industry for the

11. Lawrence Sherman, "Watching and Crime Prevention: New Directions for Police," *Journal of Contemporary Studies* 80 (Fall 1982): 87.

12. Christopher Dobson and Ronald Payne, "Private Enterprise Takes on Terrorism," *Reason* (January 1983): 36.

13. Robert Hair, "Private Security and Police Relations," in John O'Brien and Marvin Marous, eds., *Crime and Justice in America: Critical Issues for the Future* (New York: Pergamon Press, 1979), pp. 113–114.

14. Dobson and Payne, "Private Enterprise Takes on Terrorism," p. 36.

15. In addition, some local governments have opted to purchase police services from private firms rather than produce such services themselves. This phenomenon is discussed later.

1980–85 period, with half those purchases being made in North America.[16] Individuals are learning self-defense, carrying whistles and other noisemakers, and buying self-protection devices such as mace dispensers. There is a growing business in the provision of bulletproof cars and security systems for those in positions of power and wealth who face high risks of assassination and/or kidnapping. There are about a dozen U.S. firms now specializing in armoring cars, for example, at prices ranging between $32,000 and $250,000 depending upon the degree of safety required, and many other privately provided forms of protection equipment and services are available to those willing to pay.[17]

Private individuals' protection efforts need not require monetary outlays for services and equipment, of course. Activities like neighborhood or tenant watches and patrols (for example, the Guardian Angels) and escort groups are becoming increasingly prevalent. A recent Gallup poll found that 17 percent of those surveyed reported participation in one or more of these voluntary neighborhood crime prevention efforts, leading Lawrence Sherman to conclude that "the recent emphasis on voluntary watching efforts suggests a diminishing confidence in the ability of the publicly empowered police to perform. . . ."[18]

In light of these phenomena, gun ownership for protection is an obvious component of the overall privatization trend. Let us return to the jogging analogy. People who fear heart attacks do many things in an attempt to protect themselves from the danger. They get physical examinations, diet, take medication for high blood pressure, have bypass surgery, donate their time and money to support heart research, and exercise. Some of these protection efforts may involve risk. Jogging can bring on a heart attack under the right circumstances, even though in the majority of cases it helps prevent one. Individuals' efforts to protect themselves from crime can be similarly characterized. They have many options available, as noted above. Some are relatively risky options. Gun ownership for protection clearly involves some risk insofar as it may lead an individual, who would otherwise have submitted to a rape or robbery, to resist.

The question is therefore whether the expected benefits of gun ownership and other private sector protection efforts are sufficient

16. Dobson and Payne, "Private Enterprise Takes on Terrorism," p. 36.
17. Ibid., pp. 34–41.
18. Sherman, "Watching and Crime Prevention: New Directions for Police," p. 87.

to offset the risk. The fact that the causation runs from crime to guns rather than vice versa does not necessarily imply that gun controls are not desirable. If privatization of protection, including gun ownership, is an ineffective or inefficient means of protecting people, perhaps because of the high cost of risk, then this question of causality may be irrelevant. It clearly damages the main argument made by gun control advocates (that guns cause crime so gun control will reduce crime), but if private protection efforts are ineffective and excessively costly, then perhaps we should protect people from wasting their money in these areas. Rushforth et al., for example, claim (without any support) that "this goal of security through gun possession is illusory."[19] Is this true?

THE BENEFITS OF PRIVATE SECTOR CRIME PREVENTION AND PROTECTION EFFORTS

There are many reasons to expect that private sector crime prevention and protection efforts will be both relatively effective and relatively efficient as compared to public sector efforts. The private sector tends to be relatively effective because of specialization, which improves productivity. Private sector efficiencies arise from this specialization, but efficiency is also enhanced because private sector individuals tend to be much more cost conscious than public sector decisionmakers. Additional benefits may arise from privatization as well, since private sector efforts may tend to make public protection more effective and efficient. In part, private sector crime prevention activities may complement public police and therefore improve their ability to prevent or solve crimes. In addition, competition from the private sector may force bureaucrats to make a greater effort to produce at low costs. Let us explore each of these potential benefits in turn.

Privatization and Specialization

Public police perform many many functions that have nothing to do with prevention of, and protection against, violent crimes and crimes

19. Norman Rushford, Amasa Ford, Charles Hirsch, Nancy Rushford, and Lester Adelson, "Violent Death in a Metropolitan County," *New England Journal of Medicine* 297 (September 1977), p. 537.

against property. In Blumberg's words, "Much police work is of the social worker, caretaker, babysitter, errand boy variety; almost 80 percent of police time is expended in this fashion."[20] The police are responsible for such matters as traffic control, aiding injured, lost, and helpless individuals, and for enforcing nonviolent "victimless" crime laws such as those against prostitution, gambling, marijuana use, and so on. With so many duties to perform, police may not be able to gather the expertise in any one area (e.g., violent crime categories) that a private specialist can. Of course, large police departments do undertake a great deal of specialization with their homicide, burglary, robbery, vice, narcotics, and traffic divisions. But even these police departments must concentrate at least some resources in nonviolent and nonproperty crime areas (e.g., vice, narcotics, and traffic), and police are always expected to provide information and assistance to virtually anyone who demands it.

One advantage of private sector crime prevention and protection efforts is that they can be very specialized. Private individuals can concentrate their resources and those that they hire or purchase in areas that they perceive to be the greatest threat to themselves and/ or their property. Naturally, then, all private sector efforts will be concentrated on (that is, specialized in) prevention of and protection against violent crimes and property crimes. This concentration of effort can be very effective. Consider, for example, the success of the railroad police.

Railroad police were complete and autonomous police forces dating from the end of World War I. Wooldridge observed that

> Railway police compiled a remarkable record of effectiveness: between (the end of WWI) and 1929 they succeeded so well that freight claim payments for robberies decreased 92.7 percent, from $12,726,947 to $704,262. . . . Statistically, arrests by railroad police have resulted in a higher percentage of convictions than those of their municipal counterparts. A five-year sample from the Pennsylvania Railroad showed an 83.4 percent conviction rate, while a thirteen-year sample from another line revealed a conviction rate of 97.47 percent. . . .[21]

The railroad police have a "widespread reputation for good character and high ability," which "poignantly contrasts with the present

20. Abraham Blumberg, *Criminal Justice*, (Chicago: Quadrangle, 1967), p. 185.
21. William Wooldridge, *Uncle Sam, The Monopoly Man* (New Rochelle, N.Y.: Arlington House, 1970), p. 116.

status of many big-city public forces."[22] Wooldridge noted that primary reason for the success of the railroad police is that they specialized in one area of enforcement and, in the process, developed "an expertise not realistically within the grasp of public forces."[23] Such specialization and consequent gain in proficiency (and efficiency) often characterizes existing private sector police firms.

Similar gains from specialization should also arise when individuals concentrate their own efforts and resources in areas from which they face the greatest threat. If persons perceive a significant threat of burglary, then they may purchase burglar alarms and substantially reduce that threat. If they fear violent crime, they may wish to make purchases that enable them to better protect themselves, like training in self-defense, or mace dispensers, or guns. These purchases of specialized equipment are little different from a banker hiring an armed guard and installing cameras and alarms.

Such specialization has two impacts. First it makes it less likely that a criminal will be successful in an attempt at theft or violence. In other words, increasing levels of private protection efforts increase the potential cost of crime by increasing the probability of capture (and in the case of guns for protection, the probability of personal injury or death for the potential criminal). This leads to a second impact of such private efforts. As the potential cost of committing crime rises, potential criminals may be less likely to become actual criminals. In other words, there is a deterrent impact of such private sector protection.

Unfortunately, most studies of crime deterrence have been concerned with the effects of public sector efforts. However, there is some evidence that private sector production of protection does deter crime. One interesting study along these lines was done by Hannan.[24] Using a Tobit maximum likelihood statistical procedure, he found that the presence of guards in banks "significantly reduce[s] the risk of robbery. Accepting point estimates, the magnitude of this reduction is approximately one robbery attempt a year for those offices which would have otherwise suffered a positive number of robbery attempts."[25] This empirical result supports findings ob-

---

22. Ibid., p. 117.
23. Ibid., p. 121.
24. Timothy Hannan, "Bank Robberies and Bank Security Precautions," *Journal of Legal Studies* 11 (January 1982): 83–92.
25. Ibid., p. 91.

tained by Camp, who interviewed imprisoned bank robbers.[26] Camp found that most of the robbers (77 percent) checked to find out whether the bank had a guard before committing the robbery. In contrast, only 6 percent of those interviewed bothered to learn the police routine in the area before the robbery. Apparently these criminals were more concerned with this private protection measure than with public enforcement. (Of course, this may be because information about police routine is both more costly to obtain and less valuable because police may change their routines).

Firearm ownership is a very specialized form of protection that clearly generates benefits detailed below in the form of preventing successful completion of crimes, as well as deterring crime. In John Sneed's words,

> As in any other industry (other than crime prevention and protection), there will be specialization on the basis of the economies to be derived from the division of labor. Each consumer will balance his purchases of protection services (and those provided by public police) relative to self-supplied defense so as to maximize his utility. For example, many purchasers of personal property defense will keep a gun in their homes in order to deal with situations where delayed action by a specialist (private or public police) is useless or less preferred than immediate, though more risky, action by a nonspecialist.[27]

The Sneed statement raises a number of important points about the role that gun ownership for protection may play in the overall privatization picture. For one thing gun ownership allows the individual to respond very quickly to a crime situation. The response is generally much more immediate than public police are able to provide.

There is some evidence to indicate that the immediate response of gun owners can be quite effective. Private citizens *legally* shoot almost as many criminals as police do, and in some places citizens justifiably kill up to two or three times as many violent criminals as do police. There were 126 justifiable homicides by private citizens in California during 1981, for example, as compared to 68 justifiable homicides by police.[28] In addition, there are many more nonfatal than fatal justifiable assaults. The numbers here are very difficult

26. G.M. Camp, "Nothing to Lose: A Study of Bank Robbery in America" (Ph.D. dissertation, Yale University, 1968).

27. John Sneed, "Order Without Law: Where Will the Anarchists Keep the Madman?" *Journal of Libertarian Studies* 1 (1977): 17.

28. California Department of Justice, *Homicide in California, 1981* (Sacramento: Bureau of Criminal Statistics and Special Services, 1981).

to establish, of course, but an approximation might be gained by considering that there are an estimated 38 nonfatal handgun assaults for every fatal one.[29] If approximately the same ratio holds for justifiable assaults as for all assaults, then about 4,788 (38 × 126) justifiable handgun assaults would have occurred in California alone in 1981.

Although information on the relative success of private use of firearms to interrupt crime and apprehend criminals is very scarce, it appears that such private efforts are at least as successful as police efforts. Kates compared the success rates of police and private citizens by examining every story printed in forty-two of the nation's largest newspapers between January and June 1975 and May and July 1976, which were concerned with uses of firearms for protection or prevention of crime. He estimated that 68 percent of the times that police used their firearms, they successfully prevented a crime or apprehended a criminal, while private citizen firearm use resulted in an 83 percent success rate.[30] So it seems apparent that the private use of firearms for crime protection does generate benefits in contrast to the claims made by some (e.g., Rushford et al.). Of course, as Sneed noted, firearms can be a risky means of protection. If the risk to the individual exceeds the benefits, then gun controls may be desirable. However, Silver and Kates have presented some evidence indicating that the use of handguns for protection may be very beneficial relative to the risk to society arising from criminal handgun use. They concluded that it " . . . appears that the number of instances in which handguns were used for defense exceeds the number in which they were misused to kill (between 1960 and 1975) by a factor of 15–1."[31]

Furthermore, the above discussion does not consider one of the most important benefits arising from gun ownership for protection— the deterrent effect. Naturally the deterrent effect cannot be accurately measured, since we cannot count the number of crimes not committed for fear of confronting an armed victim. However, there

29. Gary Kleck, "Handgun-Only Gun Control: A Policy Disaster in the Making," in this volume.

30. Don B. Kates, Jr., Unpublished tables, no date.

31. Carol Silver and Don B. Kates, Jr., "Self-Defense, Handgun Ownership and the Independence of Women in a Violent, Sexist Society," in Don B. Kates, Jr., ed., *Restricting Handguns: The Liberal Skeptics Speak Out* (New York: North River Press, 1977), p. 158. [Editor's note: Wright, ch. 11, concludes that crimes/accidents each year are equalled by total self-defense handgun uses.]

is some powerful evidence that gun ownership deters crime. Let us begin with what may be the weakest evidence and advance through the most convincing. Cook used cross section data and looked at the relationship between armed robbery rates and the strength of gun controls.[32] He found that areas with strong gun controls have higher levels of armed robbery than areas with weaker controls. One might interpret this to mean that when individuals' ability to defend themselves with guns is limited, they become more vulnerable to crime and therefore are more likely to become crime victims. That is, gun ownership is a deterrent. Of course, there is a danger in such an interpretation. After all, as stressed throughout this chapter, correlation does not necessarily mean causation. In this case the correlation may arise because the strictest gun controls have been established in high crime areas in an unsuccessful effort to reduce crime.

There is more persuasive evidence of a deterrent effect arising from gun ownership, however. For example, surveys of prisoners "uniformly find felons stating that, whenever possible, they avoid victims who are thought to be armed, and that they know of planned crimes that were abandoned when it was discovered that the prospective victim was armed."[33] This is not surprising in light of the risk criminals face when confronting an armed victim. Cook provided us with an idea of the magnitude of this risk with his calculations based on Atlanta data. He concluded that a robber doubles his chances of dying by committing only seven robberies, because of the risk of being attacked by a victim.[34]

Some of the best evidence of the deterrent effect of gun ownership for protection comes from the impact of publicized programs to provide training in firearms use for potential victims. One such effort was sponsored by the Orlando police department between October 1966 and March 1967. The program was designed to train women in the safe use of firearms because of the sharp increase in rapes in the city during 1966. This program was widely publicized in Orlando newspapers. Kleck and Bordua recently examined the deterrent im-

32. Philip Cook, "The Effect of Gun Availability on Robbery and Robbery Murder: A Cross-section Study of 50 Cities," *Policy Studies Review Annual* (1979): 743–781.

33. Silver and Kates, "Self-Defense, Handgun Ownership and the Independence of Women in a Violent, Sexist Society," p. 151. Such surveys include Van den Haag, "Banning Handguns: Helping the Criminal Hurt You," *New Woman* (November–December 1975): 80.

34. Cook, "The Effect of Gun Availability on Robbery and Robbery Murder," p. 755.

pact of this publicized training program.[35] They found that the rape rate in Orlando fell from a 1966 level of 35.91 per 100,000 inhabitants to only 4.18 in 1967. This was clearly not a part of any general downward trend, since the national rate was increasing and rates in surrounding metropolitan areas and in Florida as a whole (excluding Orlando) were either constant or increasing over the same period. Furthermore, this decrease did not reflect a continual downward trend for Orlando, since the trend had been erratic but upward for the previous several years. It seems obvious that the knowledge that a potential rape victim might have a gun and might know how to use it was a significant deterrent.

Further evidence of the deterrent effect of the Orlando program can be obtained by comparing the change in the rape rate, which was the crime category targeted by the program, to other Orlando crime rates.[36] Rates for virtually all crimes were rising or constant in Orlando, the surrounding metropolitan area, and Florida over the 1966–67 period. There was one exception. The Orlando burglary rate also declined. But this is not particularly surprising. In fact, it tends to strengthen the argument that gun ownership for protection has a deterrent effect, since burglary would seem to be the most likely crime category other than rape in which a criminal might confront an armed female victim.

The Orlando example is not unique. Publicized training programs in the use of firearms have led to a reduction in armed robberies in Highland Park, Michigan, drugstore robberies in New Orleans, and grocery store robberies in Detroit.[37] When potential criminals become aware that potential victims might be willing and able to protect themselves with a gun, the increased perceived risk of committing a crime can lead to the abandonment of the crime effort. Of course, it may also lead to the choice of another victim, perhaps in another area where guns for protection are less likely. As a consequence, location-specific gun control could easily lead to higher crime rates in that area, as the Cook results cited earlier may imply.

This brings up an important point. Wealthy individuals typically have many options at their disposal for protecting themselves. They

---

35. Gary Kleck and David Bordua, "The Factual Foundation for Certain Key Assumptions of Gun Control," *Law and Policy Quarterly* 5 (August 1983): 271–98.

36. Ibid.

37. Ibid.

often live in high income communities where the tax base allows for a well-financed public police department. The number of police per crime committed is probably very high in most high income suburbs, relative to most inner-city low income neighborhoods. In addition, wealthy individuals can buy alarms, guard dogs, bulletproof cars, and so forth, and they can hire private police for protection. Gun control advocates do not appear to seek to disarm private police, so gun control laws will not deprive the wealthy of gun-armed defense and crime deterrence.

The impact could be significant for middle and lower income individuals, however. Typically they live in areas not as well protected by the public police, and they have far fewer self-protection options available due to their relatively limited buying power. Evidencing the relative importance of guns for protection for lower income individuals are the facts that, of the 126 justifiable homicides by private citizens in California during 1981, 28.6 percent were committed by Hispanics, 47.6 percent by blacks, but only 21.4 percent by whites.[38] There is no genetic reason to expect that certain races are more likely to be crime victims or to kill criminals than other races. However, a much larger percentage of blacks and Hispanics are in the lower income classes in California than are whites, so we might conclude that lower income individuals, approximated here by blacks and Hispanics, tend to turn to firearms for protection more often than higher income individuals simply because their choices are much more limited. In addition, of course, the poor are more likely to be the victims of crimes, so they are more likely to seek some means of self-protection.

If strict handgun prohibition is enacted, lower income individuals will be forced to choose between giving up their primary tool for protection of their persons and property, or becoming criminals themselves by disobeying the gun ban. Faced with such a choice, and realizing that gun control laws will be virtually unenforceable anyway (as Kates has pointed out[39]), most will probably choose to disobey the ban.

One other piece of evidence of the deterrent impact of gun ownership for protection must be noted. Kennesaw, Georgia's, city council passed a highly publicized ordinance on March 15, 1982, which re-

---

38. California Department of Justice, *Homicide in California, 1981*, p. 74.

39. Don B. Kates, Jr., "Handgun Banning in Light of the Prohibition Experience," in this volume.

quired each household to keep a firearm. The ordinance, just like a gun ban, is probably unenforceable, but the publicity surrounding its passage apparently dramatized to potential criminals in the area the fact that many Kennesaw residents owned firearms and were willing to use them for protection. Consequently, crime in Kennesaw has dropped at what has to be called a dramatic rate. Serious crime in Kennesaw dropped by 74.4 percent from 1981 to 1982.[40] Residential burglaries fell from fifty-five in 1981 to nineteen in 1982, while aggravated assault was down from nine to two, rapes fell from three to zero, armed robberies declined from four to zero, and homicide from one to zero. In the seven months immediately following the passage of the ordinance there were only five burglaries as compared to forty-five during the same seven month period during the previous year.[41] Reviewing the evidence from Orlando, Kennesaw, and other sources led Kleck and Bordua to conclude,

> Given the data on private citizens' use of firearms against criminals and evidence on the slight risks of legal punishment associated with most crimes, it is a perfectly plausible hypothesis that private gun ownership currently exerts as much or more deterrent effect on criminals as do the activities of the criminal justice system. The gun-owning citizenry is certainly more omnipresent than the police, and the potential severity of private justice is at least as severe or more severe than more formal legal justice, given the frequency of citizen shootings of criminals and the de facto near-abolition of capital punishment by the federal judiciary. In short, there is the distinct possibility that although gun ownership among the crime-prone may tend to increase crime, gun ownership among the noncriminal majority may tend to depress crime rates below the levels they otherwise would achieve.[42]

Gun ownership specifically, and private sector crime protection and prevention efforts in general, do appear to have considerable benefits then—benefits arising from specialization, which tend both to increase the likelihood that attempted crimes will be unsuccessful and to deter potential crimes. There are other benefits as well, as indicated by Sneed. Competition for consumer protection dollars among alternative sources of protection is one factor among many which indicates that private sector protection efforts will be produced relatively efficiently.

40. "Kennesaw's Crime Down 74 Percent," *Gun Week* (January 28, 1983): 3.
41. Kleck and Bordua, "The Factual Foundation for Certain Key Assumptions of Gun Control."
42. Ibid.

Privatization and Cost Minimization

For obvious reasons, private sector production of protection is likely to be relatively efficient in a cost-effectiveness sense, when compared to public sector production. First, private firms producing protection services and devices can only survive if they make a profit. To maximize profits, the private entrepreneur will attempt to produce protection at the lowest possible cost. If successful, the seller reaps benefits of the excess profit. Citizens do not expect a public police department to make a profit, however. Taxes are collected to cover costs. The police department survives no matter what those costs might be (at least up to some level, as noted below). The police chief does not have to make a profit to survive. Furthermore, he reaps no special reward by successfully producing at the lowest possible cost, so his cost-minimizing incentives are extremely weak relative to those of a private producer. This does not imply that the police chief will be completely unconcerned with the level of costs his department generates. It simply means that he is likely to put less emphasis on reducing wasted time and resources (and at monitoring employees), so waste will be greater and costs higher than for a comparable profit-maximizing private firm.

The expectation of more cost-effective production by private sector firms is borne out. In fact, budget pressures are forcing many community officials to consider at least partial private sector provision of services typically provided by public police.[43] Recently, virtually complete privatization of police services has taken place in two communities. Reminderville, Ohio (and the surrounding Twinsburg Township), contracted with a private security firm in 1980. This arrangement was established following an attempt by the Summit County Sheriff's Department to charge the community $180,000 per year for the emergency response service and an occasional patrol by one car that it had been providing. The community turned to a private firm, Corporate Security, for help. For $90,000 a year the firm provided twice as many patrol cars and a six minute emergency response rather than the sheriff department's forty-five minute response time. The firm selects trained, state-certified candidates for

---

43. Theodore Gage, "Cops, Inc." *Reason* (November 1982): 23–28.

the police positions, and the village chooses among the candidates. Corporate Security then pays the seven chosen officers' salaries, provides and maintains two patrol cars, maintains the department's electrical, communications, and radar equipment, and carries the auto and liability insurance for the police force. The 1980 contract has been renewed once at only a slightly higher yearly fee, and a third contract will be negotiated soon.[44] The arrangement has been challenged by the Ohio Police Chiefs Association, but they have not been able to find anything in Ohio law to prevent it. The community is well satisfied with their private police force. In fact, despite many arrests, traffic tickets, and other actions typical of police, no complaints or charges have been registered.

A similar but even more completely private sector police force was established in Oro Valley, Arizona, in 1975. In Reminderville, the village officials maintained their autonomy in hiring, firing, disciplining, and organizing the police force, but Rural/Metro Fire Department, Inc. (a private firm that provides fire protection for approximately 20 percent of Arizona's population) took responsibility for full operations management of Oro Valley's police force, replacing services previously provided by the County Sheriff. Rural/Metro kept all the records required by the state and decided what equipment and how many officers were needed, what salaries to pay, and when to use non-police personnel (e.g. routine work like writing parking tickets and directing traffic was not performed by police officers). All these services were provided for $35,000 per year. Under policies established by Rural/Metro's police chief (e.g. twice a day check of homes whose residents were away) burglary rates in the 3.5 square mile town dropped from 14 to 0.7 per month and stayed at that level.[45] The Oro Valley-Rural/Metro arrangement was challenged by the Arizona Law Enforcement Officers Advisory Council, which argued that under Arizona law an employee of a private firm could not be a police officer. Rural/Metro decided that they could not bear the high court fees required to fight the challenge, so in 1977 the arrangement was ended. The 1982 Oro Valley police budget was $241,000 as compared to the $35,000 price tag for Rural/Metro's provision of police services in 1975. Inflation might account for a doubling of the cost of these services over seven years, but it

44. Ibid., p. 25.
45. Ibid., p. 26.

cannot account for the 500 percent increase in costs. Theodore Gage's conclusion that "in short, Oro Valley has become a typical police operation with typical costs"[46] seems warranted.

The profit motive provides strong incentives to produce at low costs. There is another reason to expect efficiency in regard to private sector production of protection as well. This reason does not apply to the above examples of government purchase of police services (which are only intended to serve as illustrations of the lack of incentives on the part of public police to minimize production costs), but it clearly could apply if the communities had held competitive bids before awarding the contracts.

The reason is that private sector producers of protection are often subject to competition. Since consumers are free to choose among private protection options, the only way that a private firm can legally obtain customers is by persuading people that they offer a quality service at a reasonable price. Government producers of protection have another option—they can use the government's power of coercion to collect taxes and produce protection whether it is valued at the price paid or not.

Resources are most efficiently used when they are guided to the use that generates the greatest benefit to members of society. Competitive markets tend to guide resources to their highest and best uses because the price consumers are willing to pay for goods or services reflects the benefits they expect to obtain from their consumption. Public police departments are *not able* to take advantage of price signals in deciding how to allocate resources, and they really do not have any other signals that are as effective as prices are at telling producers what consumers want. Private providers of protection services and equipment, on the other hand, are *forced* to pay attention to price signals. Gustave de Molinari, a nineteenth century French economist and perhaps the earliest advocate of protection provided by the private sector, wrote that the " . . . option the consumer retains of being able to buy security wherever he pleases brings about a constant emulation among all producers, each producer striving to maintain or augment his clientele with the attraction of cheapness or of faster more complete and better . . . " services.[47]

---

46. Ibid., p. 26.
47. Gustave de Molinari, "De la Production de la Securite," *Journal des Economistes* (February 1849): 277–290. This article has been translated into English and published as

The importance of price signals and competition for clientele should not be overlooked in a discussion of efficiency. Most police departments have not perceived the pressures of competition (except in terms of competition for a share of the budget that other bureaucracies are also seeking), since their clientele (taxpayers) is guaranteed. However, all private sector firms selling protection services or devices must compete for consumer dollars. Consumers then choose among all the options available. If, under these circumstances, a consumer decides to buy a gun for protection, then that decision implies a rational, efficient allocation of protection resources. Such a decision reflects the previously noted fact that a firearm is a specialized tool of protection that provides benefits the public police (and many other private protection options) cannot provide.

So competition has beneficial efficiency impacts, since it forces private sector providers of protection services and equipment to keep costs and prices down and the quality of their products up. If competition among private firms can also be directed at public police, there may be some positive efficiency gains there as well.

Privatization and Public Sector Efficiency

Suppose that local governments all over the country had the legal right to contract with private firms for the provision of police services (as they do in Ohio but perhaps do not in Arizona). As the threat of private contracting becomes apparent to public police departments, we should see considerably more attention being paid to efforts at reducing costs for the level of service quality being supplied. This is an extreme example meant to illustrate the potential impact of expanding private sector production of protection services. But even without going this far, competitive pressures should arise and cost-reducing incentives result. As citizens turn to the private sector in increasing numbers in order to supplement the protection they receive from the public sector, they should come to realize that privatization has advantages. In particular, private sector protection will be specialized and, consequently, relatively more effective than public police at protecting individuals from the crimes they fear the

---

Gustave de Molinari, *The Production of Security,* tr. J. Huston McCullock (New York: The Center for Libertarian Studies, 1977), and this citation comes from that translation, p. 13.

most. Furthermore, private sector efforts will generally be available at relatively low cost. Therefore, citizens will become increasingly reluctant to pay taxes for public protection. The threat of loss of budgets and jobs may become sufficient to induce public police to monitor costs more closely. So, some of the benefits of private sector competition may spill over into public sector production.

There is another reason to expect that many private protection efforts will improve the effectiveness of the public police. Many of the private sector activities that are developing are actually complementary to public sector production. Neighborhood watches and patrols, for example, generally involve private cooperative actions by individuals in a particular area in an effort to deter crime by visibly patrolling. However, when a crime is observed, the individual on patrol calls the public police. Since crimes are more likely to be observed in progress than discovered after completion, the police are more likely to apprehend and successfully prosecute the criminal. So neighborhood watches are likely to reduce crime in the area because of the deterrent effect of the visible patrol. They are also likely to increase the effectiveness of the police in responding to crimes actually committed. It is not surprising to find police departments actively supporting neighborhood watch organizations and aiding in their formation.

Many private sector efforts can complement and improve the effectiveness of public police. "Operation ID" involves individuals marking their property so it can be easily identified when stolen. Such projects have been actively promoted by police departments in many communities, because they increase the likelihood of catching a criminal after a robbery when he or she tries to sell the stolen property. However, for our purposes, perhaps the most interesting private sector crime protection activity that serves as a complement to the public police is gun ownership.

As noted earlier, gun ownership is a specialized form of self-protection. It allows the individual to respond much more quickly to a crime in progress than the response time characterizing most public police efforts. In fact, "the odds are better than 1000-to-1 that the officer won't be there when it happens; indeed, most violent criminals will do some scouting and make sure there are no policemen around."[48] The potential for a relatively quick response by a gun

---

48. Massad F. Ayoob, *The Experts Speak Out: The Police View of Gun Control* (Bellevue, Wash.: Second Amendment Foundation, 1981), p. 4.

owner increases the likelihood of apprehending the criminal. In light of this, it is not surprising to find an overwhelming majority of police officers opposing gun bans.

A number of polls by police and independent organizations indicate that this is the case. One such poll, performed by the Second Amendment Foundation in 1977 and verified by the GMA Research Corporation, found that approximately 64 percent of the 34,000 police officers surveyed believed that an armed citizenry serves as a deterrent to crime; 86 percent indicated that even if they were not police officers, they would keep a gun for protection; and more than 83 percent indicated that banning handguns would benefit criminals rather than citizens.[49] A 1976 survey commissioned by Boston Police Chief Robert di Grazia (an active gun ban advocate) and conducted by the Planning and Research Division of the Boston Police Department found that over 66 percent of the nation's leading police administrators favored possession of handguns by the citizenry, and 80 percent approved of possession of handguns in homes and business places.[50] So, the majority of public police believe that gun control will help criminals and hurt noncriminals, since gun controls will reduce the private citizen's self-protection ability and make it more likely that a criminal will be successful in crime efforts. Therefore crime becomes more likely, since gun ownership is a deterrent.

Thus it appears that privatization of protection, including gun ownership, can have positive spillover impacts on the success of public sector law enforcement efforts in addition to the benefits it provides directly to citizens. It seems clear that privatization should be encouraged and supported rather than limited. Gun control laws are likely to have precisely the opposite impact on crime rates to that which control advocates claim.

CONCLUSIONS—HOW MUCH PRIVATIZATION?

The preceding discussion had two purposes. First it was contended that there are strong reasons to expect that the direction of causality in the relationship between gun ownership and crime rates runs from crime to guns for protection. This is demonstrated by the fact that individuals are increasingly turning to the private sector for protec-

49. Ibid., p. 7.
50. Ibid., pp. 7–8.

tion supplementing the protection they get from public police. This growing privatization of protection is taking many forms. The private police and security industry is expanding quite rapidly. Sales of crime detection and protection devices (e.g. burglar alarms, firearms) are on the rise. Voluntary neighborhood watches are involving increasing numbers of private citizens. With all the growth in privatization, the argument that guns are being bought for protection seems to be very reasonable. One problem with the arguments for (and some of them against) gun control is that they focus only on the gun-crime relationship and ignore many related phenomena that are also occurring.[51] Rising gun ownership is just one part of a large trend toward greater private sector involvement in crime prevention, detection, and protection which is taking place due to the growing fear of crime (and, of course, increasing crime rates generate greater fears).

The second point stressed was that the overall privatization trend, including rising gun ownership, generates some very important benefits. Private sector protection efforts tend to be concentrated on

51. For example, if rising gun ownership does lead to more crime, it is likely to be a very insignificant factor at best, in light of all the other changes that have taken place over the last few decades. The economic theory of crime proposed by Gary Becker ("Crime and Punishment: An Economic Analysis," *Journal of Political Economy* 78 [March/April 1968]: 526–536) and subsequently expanded upon and tested by several others, indicates that crime rates rise if (1) the expected payoff to crime rises; (2) opportunities for legitimate income-generating possibilities decline, as for example, in an economic downturn characterized by high unemployment; or (3) the deterrents to crime such as the chances of capture and conviction, and/or the severity of punishment are diminished. Empirical findings demonstrate that all these factors are clearly important. For example, let us emphasize the third point. There has, over the last few decades at least, been a reduction in the chances of capture and conviction when violent crimes are committed. Criminals are increasingly likely to get away with their crime. Over the past twenty years the percentages of reported total crimes cleared by arrest have diminished considerably from 26.1 percent in 1960 to 19.2 in 1980. The violent crime categories show even sharper declines, with murder and nonnegligible manslaughter arrests falling from 92.3 to 72.3 percent of those reported, rape declining from 72.5 to 48.8, robbery from 38.5 to 23.8, and aggravated assault from 76.8 to 58.7. Similarly, total conviction rates in the federal courts peaked in 1952 and have declined since, while dismissal rates have been increasing over the period. Similar trends characterize many state courts. The severity of punishment has also been on the decline. The use of capital punishment has fallen dramatically over the last fifty years, for example. The length of prison terms *actually served* has also diminished despite the fact that the average length of sentence has been rising. These changes have, in turn, been associated with an increase in crime. It is interesting to note, in this context, that the two countries most often cited by gun control advocates as having effectively held violent crime rates down through gun controls are Japan and Great Britain. However, these two countries solve 81 and 90 percent of their violent crimes, respectively, as compared to our 45 percent (David Hardy, "Gun Control: Arm Yourself With Evidence," *Reason* [November, 1982]). The economic theory of crime would predict relatively low crime rates with such high probabilities of being caught, regardless of what the gun laws might be.

what individuals perceive as the greatest threat to their persons and property. This concentration (or specialization) improves the overall effectiveness of the crime protection system. Furthermore, private sector providers of protection (including individuals protecting themselves) have relatively strong incentives to be much more cost conscious than public sector producers. Between the cost-minimizing efforts of private sector producers and the specialization of private protection resources, it is likely that a dollar spent on protection in the private sector will have a greater impact on preventing or protecting against violent crime than a dollar spent on the public police.

But the benefits go even further. Privatization also tends to improve the efficiency and effectiveness of the public sector's production of protection. Many private sector protection activities (including gun ownership) are complements to police actions and enhance the likelihood of both deterring potential criminals and catching actual criminals. Other private sector activities compete with public police for the attention of the consumer-taxpayer protection dollar, and as a consequence, public police are forced to become more concerned about trying to keep the costs of their services down.

With all these benefits from privatization, one might ask how much privatization should be allowed. There certainly are conflicting views as to the answer to this question. Consider, for example the study by Marshall Clinnard which contrasted crime rates in Switzerland and Sweden and attempted to explain observed differences in crime rates by noting differences in the social and political makeup of the two countries.[52] Crime rates, and especially violent crime rates, are much higher in Sweden. It is also interesting to note that most Swiss households have a gun, because about two thirds of all males are part of the militia from age 20 to 50 or 55, and they keep their weapons at home. Thus, a lack of firearms availability cannot be the explanation for low crime (and especially violent crime) rates in Switzerland. Clinnard's explanation for the low crime rate in Switzerland relative to Sweden stressed the different degrees of government control. He observed that Sweden has a strong central government that has tended to inhibit individual initiative and responsibility in all areas, including crime. The Swiss have relied much more on individual efforts with a much weaker central government. In fact, private sector provision of police services is rather common in

52. Marshall Clinnard, *Cities With Little Crime: The Case of Switzerland* (Cambridge: Cambridge University Press, 1978).

Switzerland, with more than thirty Swiss villages and townships currently purchasing protection at what the Swiss Association of Towns and Townships describes as "substantial savings."[53] This led Clinnard to conclude that "Communities or cities that wish to prevent crime should encourage greater political decentralization by developing small government units and encouraging citizen responsibility for obedience to the law and crime control. The increased delegation and responsibility for crime control to the police and to governmental agencies . . . should be reversed."[54] So Clinnard's findings clearly support even greater privatization.

These conclusions are in sharp contrast to the claims made by others, including Raymond Kessler. He contended that the "basic sources of crime" are "rooted in the political economy of capitalism."[55] However, crime in socialized countries is a significant problem, so it is difficult to justify Kessler's claim that crime is "rooted in the political economy of capitalism." One Soviet writer on crime, for example, reported an "almost continuous growth of alcoholism and crime" and that far from "being eliminated, bribery and corruption increased, particularly in the work of many economic and trade organizations, in institutions of higher learning, in various state organizations and enterprises, and even within the party."[56] Another author wrote of "the spreading epidemic of senseless, brutal hooliganism and crime."[57]

Crime statistics from Russia are typically unreported or unreliable, but Peter Juviler compared conviction rates in the United States and

53. Gage, "Cops, Inc.," p. 26.

54. Clinnard, *Cities With Little Crime: The Case of Switzerland*, p. 156. Clinnard's findings concerning the benefits of decentralization and use of small police forces is supported by several studies of the United States as well. For example, Elinor Ostrom, William Baugh, Richard Guarasci, Roger Parks, and Gordon Whitaker report that "smaller, community-controlled police departments are able to provide consistently higher levels of service to smaller neighborhoods" ("Community Organization and the Provision of Police Services," *Administrative and Policy Studies Series* 1 [1973]: 66). Also see Ostrom and Parks, "Suburban Police Departments: Too Many and Too Small?" *Urban Affairs Annual Reviews* 7 (1973), and Ostrom and Whitaker, "Does Local Community Control of Police Make a Difference? Some Preliminary Findings," *Midwest Journal of Political Science* 17 (1973).

55. Raymond Kessler, "The Ideology of Gun Control" (Paper presented at the 1981 Annual Meeting of the American Society of Criminology, Washington, D.C., November 1981).

56. Roy A. Medvedev, *On Socialist Democracy*, tr. and ed. Ellen de Kalt (New York: Alfred A. Knopf, 1975), pp. 25, 339.

57. Andrei D. Sakharov, *My Country and the World*, tr. Guy V. Daniels (New York: Vintage Books, 1975), p. 25.

the Soviet Union for 1971 and concluded that "if actual crime rates followed anywhere near these conviction rates then . . . one would be safer from violent crimes in the United States."[58] In fact, it is interesting to note that Soviet citizens are adopting private sector protection techniques because of fear of crime. Juviler cites several Soviet writers in reporting that—

> It is not uncommon for people living in an apartment house to have keys to the elevator, equip apartment doors with peepholes and double locks, chip in for someone to run the elevator and lock and guard the door by 1:00 A.M. Soviet car owners remove windshields from their machines except when driving in the rain. They keep kids off the streets as much as possible . . . gates on many a high garden fence carry a sign, ZLAYA SOBAKA (Beware of the Dog). Some homeowners go to the extent of sleeping outdoors with shotguns or stringing up electrical fences when fruit and vegetables are temptingly ripe. . . . Residents in factory barracks and distant collective villages become accustomed to thieving, violence, and drunkenness among the young and not so young, and try to protect themselves accordingly.[59]

Since Russia has suppressed private market (capitalist) activity significantly, replacing it with government, and crime remains a significant and growing problem, it seems unlikely that capitalism can be blamed for crime. Thus, the argument for greater privatization seems to be the strongest. However, we still do not have an answer to the question of how much more privatization should be allowed (or even encouraged).

A growing number of scholars advocate complete privatization.[60] That is, they contend that government should have no role whatever in the crime protection area. Their argument is an appealing one. It stresses the advantages of freedom of choice and competition, the cost-minimizing incentives of profit seekers, and the benefits of spe-

58. Peter H. Juviler, *Revolutionary Law and Order: Politics and Social Change in the USSR* (New York: The Free Press, 1976), p. 140.

59. Ibid., pp. 136–137.

60. A few examples of exponents of total privatization are Murray Rothbard, *For a New Liberty* (New York: Macmillan, 1973); David Friedman, *The Machinery of Freedom: Guide to a Radical Capitalism* (New Rochelle, N.Y.: Arlington House, 1970); John Sneed, "Order Without Law: Where Will Anarchists Keep the Madman?" *Journal of Libertarian Studies* 1 (1977): 117–124; George Smith, "Justice Entrepreneurship in a Free Market," *Journal of Libertarian Studies* 3 (Winter 1979): 405–426; Randy Barnett, "Justice Entrepreneurship in a Free Market: Comment," *Journal of Libertarian Studies* 3 (Winter 1979): 439–451; and William Wooldridge, *Uncle Sam, The Monopoly Man* (New Rochelle, N.Y.: Arlington House, 1970).

cialization. (Much of the argument is briefly summarized in the preceding section.) This point of view stresses the efficiency and effectiveness of supply by private producers relative to supply by public producers. However, some would contend that it tends to overlook certain problems that may emanate from the demand side of the market.

Private sector production of protection generates external benefits for which private suppliers may be unable to charge. For example, suppose a few individuals hire a private security firm to patrol their neighborhood. This patrol deters criminals, both for the individuals paying the firm and for the individuals in the neighborhood who do not pay. Thus, there are strong free rider incentives associated with many private sector protection efforts. If everyone paid for the benefits received, the firm would patrol more often and prevent more crime, but since individuals can reap benefits without paying, they have strong incentives not to enter into the neighborhood group that hired the security firm.

The free rider problem arises to one degree or another with the production of many private sector protection attempts. Neighborhood watches face considerable free rider problems, for example, as individuals refuse to participate or drop out but still receive benefits. There are even spillover benefits associated with individual purchases of firearms for protection. Suppose that an area of small retail shops is plagued by robberies, for example, and some of the store owners decide to purchase firearms for protection. Further, assume that in the course of a few weeks robberies are attempted at two or three of the stores whose owners have guns, and that the guns are used in an effort (whether successful or not) to prevent the robbery. Potential criminals realize that a number of shop owners in this retailing area have guns and are willing to use them. Rather than take a chance of running into one of these store owners, criminals may choose to concentrate their efforts in another area. Thus, all the store owners in the area are better off, including those who chose not to buy a gun. Still, if more store owners owned guns for protection, rather than free riding off those who do, more crime would be deterred. The free rider problem actually means that *too little* private sector protection is purchased and produced. Therefore, it *does not* justify suppressing private sector protection efforts further, as gun control would do. Instead, efforts to encourage more privatization are appropriate. More guns for protection are needed, rather than less.

Furthermore, in contrast to what many people claim, the free rider problem *does not justify government production.* The problem arises because individuals cannot be persuaded to cooperate in buying the good or service in question, not because the private sector would not produce it if producers were fully compensated for the benefits they provide. For example, it was argued earlier that the private sector will concentrate resources in the areas of greatest perceived threat, so such resources will be deployed against potential violent and property crimes. One function of police is to enforce traffic laws. Under the existing system of rights and liabilities it is doubtful that anyone would voluntarily contribute to the purchase of the services of a private firm to enforce traffic laws. Yet there are obviously tremendous benefits generated by a traffic system in which people must obey at least a minimum level of rules or be punished. This would generate classic free rider problems if traffic control were left completely to the private sector. However, it does not mean that government must enforce the traffic laws. It simply means that given current rights and liabilities, people will have to be *coerced into paying* for this service since they cannot be persuaded to cooperate. Government is the only entity that is widely recognized to have the power to coerce. Thus, government involvement may be required to collect taxes and pay for enforcement of traffic laws. Once a private firm is appropriately paid, it will provide the service, and in all probability it will do it at a lower cost than the public police. For example, during the mid-1960s Kalamazoo, Michigan, contracted with a private company to patrol its streets and enforce traffic laws.[61] The process worked well until it was declared illegal. Wooldridge reported that "the judge who administered the *coup de grace* was offended that anyone should make a profit out of law enforcement, and apparently did not consider it relevant that a profit making company might do the job more cheaply than a non-profit-making sheriff."[62]

This is an important point. Even *if* total privatization would lead to too little protection because of the free rider problem, there are considerable benefits to be gained from higher levels of private production. Communities should have the right to contract with private police firms if the firms can offer services that are adequate in the mind of the taxpayers and are produced more efficiently than by the

61. Wooldridge, *Uncle Sam, The Monopoly Man*, p. 122.
62. Ibid., p. 123.

public police. This would not necessarily eliminate all public police, of course, but it should force them to compete for the right to supply the service and therefore to become considerably more cost effective. Furthermore, individuals should have the right to own firearms for protection.

It should be stressed that the free rider problem arises because of the existing systems of rights and liabilities. Externalities exist when property rights are unclearly or incompletely defined (or when they are communally assigned). Thus, with an appropriate and clearly delineated structure of rights and liabilities, the free rider problem could conceivably be overcome so private sector protection systems could provide the optimal amount of protection. For example, Anderson and Hill examined several private cooperative organizations that established private protection and enforcement systems in the western part of the United States during the period between 1830 and 1880, including land clubs, cattlemen's associations, and both wagon train and mining camp justice systems.[63] In order to internalize the benefits of each system, and thereby minimize costs and generate a sufficient level of protection, these organizations' justice applied to anyone within the community. In effect, entry into the community (e.g. wagon train, mining camp, etc.) required cooperation in the establishment of law enforcement and protection against crime.

Anderson and Hill found the perception many of us have of the West as a wild society to be incorrect. Instead, private agencies saw to it that persons and property were protected and order prevailed. In the West, "competition rather than coercion insured justice," and many "voluntary, extra-legal associations provided protection and justice without apparent violence and developed rules consistent with the preferences, goals, and endowments of the participants."[64] So, the advocates of complete privatization may be right in their contentions, *if* appropriate property rights structures can be instituted. Whether they are or not is irrelevant for the question at hand, however. The benefits from increasing privatization, including greater gun ownership for protection, can be substantial. Privatization of protection should be encouraged rather than discouraged through restrictions like gun controls.

63. Terry Anderson and P.J. Hill, "An American Experiment in Anarcho-Capitalism: The *Not* So Wild, Wild West," *Journal of Libertarian Studies* 3 (1979): 9–29.

64. Ibid., pp. 17, 25.

SELECTED BIBLIOGRAPHY
(PART VI)

Alviani, Joseph D., and William R. Drake. *Handgun Control: Issues and Alternatives.* Washington, D.C.: United States Conference of Mayors, 1975.

Anderson, T., and P.J. Hill. "An American Experiment in Anarcho-Capitalism: The *Not* So Wild, Wild West." *Journal of Libertarian Studies* 3 (1979): 9-29.

Ayoob, M.F. *The Experts Speak Out: The Police View of Gun Control.* Bellevue, Wash.: Second Amendment Foundation, 1981.

Barnett, R. "Justice Entrepreneurship in a Free Market: Comment." *Journal of Libertarian Studies* 3 (Winter 1979): 427-31.

Becker, G.S. "Crime and Punishment: An Economic Approach." *Journal of Political Economy* 76 (March/April 1968): 169-217.

Blumberg, A. *Criminal Justice.* Chicago: Quadrangle, 1967.

Cambridge Reports, Inc. *An Analysis of Public Attitudes Toward Handgun Control.* Cambridge, Mass.: Cambridge Reports, Inc., 1978. (Prepared for the Center for the Study and Prevention of Handgun Violence.)

Camp, G.M. "Nothing to Lose: A Study of Bank Robbery in America." Ph.D. dissertation, Yale University, 1968.

Clinnard, M. *Cities with Little Crime: The Case of Switzerland.* Cambridge: Cambridge University Press, 1978.

Cook, Philip J. "The Effect of Gun Availability on Robbery and Robbery Murder: A Cross-section Study of Fifty Cities." In Robert Haveman and B. Bruce Zellner, eds., *Policy Studies Review Annual*, vol. 3, pp. 743-81. Beverly Hills, Calif.: Sage Publications, 1979.

————. "Reducing Injury and Death Rates in Robbery." *Policy Analysis* 6 (Winter 1980): 21-45.

_____ . "The Effect of Gun Availability on Violent Crime Patterns." *Annals of the Academy of Political and Social Sciences* 455 (May 1981): 63-79.

Decision/Making/Information (DMI). *Attitudes of the American Electorate Toward Gun Control, 1978.* Santa Ana, Calif.: DMI, 1979.

Deiner, Edward, and Kenneth W. Kerber. "Personality Characteristics of American Gun Owners." *Journal of Social Psychology* 107 (1979): 227-38.

Dobson, C., and R. Payne. "Private Enterprise Takes on Terrorism." *Reason* (January 1983): 34-41.

Ehrlich, Isaac. "Participation in Illegitimate Activities: A Theoretical and Empirical Investigation." *Journal of Political Economy* 81 (May-June 1973): 521-65.

Feagin, J.R. "Public Reaction to Crime in the Streets." *American Behavioral Scientist* 13 (1970): 797-814.

Formani, R. "George Smith's Justice." *Journal of Libertarian Studies* 3 (Winter 1979): 439-51.

Friedman, D. *The Machinery of Freedom: Guide to Radical Capitalism.* New Rochelle, N.Y.: Arlington House, 1970.

Gage, T. "Cops, Inc." *Reason* (November 1982): 23-28.

Hannan, T. "Bank Robberies and Bank Security Precautions." *Journal of Legal Studies* 11 (January 1982): 83-92.

Hardy, David T. "Gun Control: Arm Yourself With Evidence." *Reason* (November 1982): 37-41.

Juviler, P.H. *Revolutionary Law and Order: Politics and Social Change in the U.S.S.R.* New York: Free Press, 1976.

Kates, Don B., Jr. *Why Handgun Bans Can't Work.* Bellevue, Wash.: Second Amendment Foundation, 1982.

Kleck, Gary. "Capital Punishment, Gun Ownership, and Homicide." *American Journal of Sociology* 84 (January 1979): 882-910.

_____ . "Guns, Homicide, and Gun Control: Some Assumptions and Some Evidence." Paper read at the annual meeting of the Midwest Sociological Society, Minneapolis, Minn., 1979.

Kleck, Gary, and David Bordua. "The Factual Foundation for Certain Key Assumptions of Gun Control." *Law and Policy Quarterly* 5 (August 1983): 271-98.

Lizotte, Alan J., and David J. Bordua. "Firearms Ownership for Sport and Protection: Two Divergent Models." *American Sociological Review* 45 (April 1980): 229-44.

Lizotte, Alan J.; David J. Bordua; and Carolyn S. White. "Firearms Ownership for Sport and Protection: Two Not So Divergent Models." *American Sociological Review* 46 (August 1981): 499-503.

Marks, Alan, and C. Shannon Stokes. "Socialization, Firearms, and Suicide." *Social Problems* 23 (June 1976): 622-29.

Massachusetts Council on Crime and Correction, Inc. *A Shooting Gallery Called America.* Boston: Massachusetts Council on Crime and Correction, Inc., 1974.

Medvedev, R.A. *On Socialist Democracy.* Translated and edited by E. deKalt. New York: Alfred A. Knopf, 1975.

Molinari, G. *The Production of Security.* Translated by J.H. McCullock. New York: Center for Libertarian Studies, 1977.

Newton, George D., and Franklin Zimring. *Firearms and Violence in American Life.* A Staff Report of the Task Force on Firearms, National Commission on the Causes and Prevention of Violence. Washington, D.C.: Government Printing Office, 1969.

Northwood, Lawrence K.; Richard Westgard; and Charles E. Barb, Jr. "Law-abiding One-man Armies." *Society* 16 (November–December 1978): 69–74.

Ostrom, E.; W. Baugh; R. Guarasci; R. Parks; and G. Whitaker. "Community Organization and the Provision of Police Services." *Administrative and Policy Series* 1 (1973).

Ostrom, E., and R. Parks. "Suburban Police Departments: Too Many and Too Small?" *Urban Affairs Annual Review* 7 (1973).

Ostrom, E., and G. Whitaker. "Does Local Community Control of Police Make a Difference? Some Preliminary Findings." *Midwest Journal of Political Science* 17 (1973).

Reiss, A., and David J. Bordua. "Environment and Organization: A Perspective on the Police." In D. Bordua, ed., *The Police: Six Sociological Essays.* New York: Wiley, 1967.

Rothbard, Murray N. *For a New Liberty.* New York: Macmillan, 1973.

Rushford, Norman; Charles Hirsch; Amasa Ford; and Lester Adelson. "Accidental Firearms Fatalities in a Metropolitan County (1958–1973)." *American Journal of Epidemiology* 100 (1975): 499–505.

Sakharov, A.D. *My Country and the World.* Translated by G.V. Daniels. New York: Vintage Books, 1975.

Sherman, L. "Watching and Crime Prevention: New Directions for Police." *Journal of Contemporary Studies* 88 (Fall 1982): 87–101.

Silver, Carol Ruth, and Don B. Kates, Jr. "Self-defense, Handgun Ownership, and the Independence of Women in a Violent, Sexist Society." In Don B. Kates, Jr., ed., *Restricting Handguns: The Liberal Skeptics Speak Out,* pp. 139–69. Croton-on-Hudson, N.Y.: North River Press, 1979.

Smith, G. "Justice Entrepreneurship in a Free Market." *Journal of Libertarian Studies* 3 (Winter 1979): 405–26.

Sneed, J. "Order Without Law: Where Will Anarchists Keep the Madman?" *Journal of Libertarian Studies* 1 (1977): 117–24.

Spiegler, Jeffrey H., and John J. Sweeney. *Gun Abuse in Ohio.* Cleveland, Ohio: Governmental Research Institute, 1975.

Tittle, Charles R. "Crime Rates and Legal Sanctions." *Social Problems* 16 (1969): 409–23.

Williams, J. Sherwood, and John H. McGrath III. "Why People Own Guns." *Journal of Communication* 26 (Autumn 1976): 22–30.

Wooldridge, W. *Uncle Sam, The Monopoly Man.* New Rochelle, N.Y.: Arlington House, 1970.

Wright, James D. "Public Opinion and Gun Control: A Comparison of Results from Two Recent National Surveys." *Annals of the American Academy of Political and Social Science* 455 (May 1981): 24–39.

Wright, James D., and Linda L. Marston. "The Ownership of the Means of Destruction: Weapons in the United States." *Social Problems* 23 (October 1975): 93–107.

Wright, James D.; Peter H. Rossi; Eleanor Weber-Burdin; and Kathleen Daly. *Weapons, Crime, and Violence in America: A Literature Review and Research Agenda.* Washington, D.C.: National Institute of Justice, 1981.

Wright, James D.; Peter H. Rossi; Sonia R. Wright; and Eleanor Weber-Burdin. *After the Clean-Up: Long-Term Effects of Natural Disasters.* Beverly Hills, Calif.: Sage Publications, 1979.

Yeager, Matthew G.; Joseph D. Alviani; and Nancy Loving. *How Well Does the Handgun Protect You and Your Family?* Washington, D.C.: United States Conference of Mayors, 1976.

PART VII

GUN OWNERSHIP AS A DETERRENT TO DESPOTISM

Chapter 13

THE SECOND AMENDMENT AS A PHENOMENON OF CLASSICAL POLITICAL PHILOSOPHY

Stephen P. Halbrook

Scholarly interpretation of the Second Amendment has tended to concentrate on its language, the very limited debates on the amendment, some reference to the general thought of the Founding Fathers on militias and standing armies, and brief generalizations about the political and philosophical background in seventeenth and eighteenth century England.[1] Pertinent as such evidence is, it is necessary to consider it in the broader context of the concept of "the armed people" as that concept appears in classical political philosophy.

The Bill of Rights, like the Declaration of Independence, derived its basic philosophy from what Thomas Jefferson described as "the elementary books of public right, as Aristotle, Cicero, Locke, Sidney etc."[2] In fact, the importance of the "right to keep and bear arms"

---

1. See, for example, David T. Hardy and John Stompoly, "Of Arms and the Law," *Chicago-Kent Law Review* 51 (1972): 62–114; David I. Caplan, "Restoring the Balance: The Second Amendment Revisited," *Fordham Urban Law Journal* 5 (1976): 31–53; John Levin, "The Right to Bear Arms: The Development of the American Experience," *Chicago-Kent Law Review* 48 (1971): 148–198; John C. Santee, "Right to Keep and Bear Arms," *Drake Law Review* 423 (1977): 26; and Lawrence H. Tribe, *American Constitutional Law* (Mineola, N.Y.: Foundation Press, 1978), pp. 226, 567–68.

2. Thomas Jefferson, *Living Thoughts*, ed. J. Dewey (Greenwich, Conn.: Fawcett, 1940), p. 42. For general references on the influence of Aristotle, Cicero, Machiavelli, Locke, Sidney, Trenchard, and Gordon on the founding fathers, see B. Bailyn, *Ideological Origins of the American Revolution* (Cambridge, Mass.: Harvard University Press, 1967); E. Corwin, *The "Higher Law" Background of the American Revolution* (Ithaca, N.Y.: Cornell University Press, 1955); and C. Mullett, "Classical Influences on the American Revolution," *Classical Journal* 35 (1939): 93–112.

to republican institutions was attested not just by these luminaries of republicanism but by the authoritarian philosophers, for example Plato, Jean Bodin, and Thomas Hobbes. Of course, those who drafted and supported the Bill of Rights rejected the thinking of Plato, Hobbes, and others, in favor of the libertarian tradition represented by the line of philosophers from Aristotle through Machiavelli to Rousseau. The essential point, however, is that *all* the political philosophers whom the Founding Fathers knew, whether proponents or opponents of the republican form of government, affirmed the indispensability of an armed people to it.

PLATO AND ARISTOTLE

Plato saw political institutions naturally (but undesirably) moving from oligarchy to democracy to despotism. Essential to each of these stages was the tendency of the unjust state to win privilege and power through "armed force" and the opposition thereto of "the armed multitude." According to Plato, oligarchy arises when privilege based on wealth is fixed by statute. "This measure is carried through by armed force, unless they have already set up their constitution by terrorism." The abuse consequent on the state monopoly of violence leads to a disunited state wherein the rich and poor continuously plot against each other. If a war with outside forces arises, the oligarchs are faced with a dilemma: "Either they must call out the common people or not. If they do, they will have more to fear from the armed multitude than from the enemy; and if they do not, in the day of battle these oligarchs will find themselves only too literally a government of the few."[3]

The arming of the common people is a prerequisite for the development of oligarchy into democracy. There are former members of the ruling class who lose their wealth and power and "long for a revolution; these drones are armed and can sting." Finally, "whether by force of arms or because the other party is terrorized into giving way," the poor majority overcomes and establishes a democracy, which grants the people "an equal share in civil rights and government." "Liberty and free speech are rife everywhere; anyone is allowed to do what he likes."[4]

3. Plato, *Republic*, F. Cornford translation (London: Oxford University Press, 1945), p. 275.
4. Ibid., pp. 280–81, 282.

Plato's negative attitude toward democracy is based not only on rejection of characteristics that today would be considered laudable, but on the belief that democracy inevitably leads to tyranny. After the old oligarchy is replaced by a society progressing toward democracy, a strong leader arises who "begins stirring up one war after another, in order that the people may feel their need of a leader, and also be so impoverished by taxation that they will be forced to think of nothing but winning their daily bread, instead of plotting against him."[5] Finally the despot wins complete victory by reestablishing the state monopoly of arms:

> Then, to be sure, the people will learn what sort of a creature it has bred and nursed to greatness in its bosom, until now the child is too strong for the parent to drive out.
>
> Do you mean that the despot will dare to lay hands on this father of his and beat him if he resists?
>
> Yes, when once he has disarmed him.[6]

Though Plato pictures this tyranny as the ultimate degeneration of the state, it is actually similar in form to his ideal, the reign of the philosopher king. Both despotism and Plato's ideal monarchy involve rule by one person, the only difference being the alleged good intention of the latter. Indeed, Plato himself suggested that a young, educated despot be transformed into the philosopher king[7] — an experiment that Plato tried with little success and at great personal cost with both Dionysius I and Dionysius II of Syracuse. Attacking the democratic ideal where "one man is trader, legislator and warrior all in one,"[8] Plato proposes instead a normative social structure with the ruling philosophers at the top, the soldier auxiliaries in the middle, and the working masses at the bottom. This pyramid sets the royal elite over the professional warriors and requires the "inferior multitude" to "mind their own business." The stage is thereby set for the elite to control and tyrannize the majority.[9]

---

5. Ibid., p. 293.
6. Ibid., p. 295.
7. Ibid., p. 210.
8. Plato, *Republic*. B. Jowett translation (Cleveland: Fine Editions Press, 1946), p. 149.
9. Plato, *Republic*, Conford translation, pp. 125–29. Thus Plato praises the ancient way of only two classes — the Guardians are the military class as well, and all others are workers. Plato, "Critias," *Plato* (Cambridge: Harvard University Press, 1929), vol. 9, p. 271.

Plato would have admitted women into the royal or warrior classes, advocating their training in bodily exercise and in "bearing arms and riding on horseback." Plato also advances the abolition of legal actions for assault or outrage among the Guardians, "for we

Plato's practical proposals are set forth in the *Laws*, which anticipates a state of just over 5,000 citizens in addition to slaves.[10] While at one point singling out warriors as a specialized class,[11] elsewhere Plato anticipates that the Director of Children and other instructors will discipline all girls, boys, women, and men with compulsory military exercises.[12] Discussing the Pyrrhic (war-dance), pankration (fighting with hands and feet), and armed contests, Plato mandates that "the techniques of fighting" are "skills which all citizens, male and female, must take care to acquire."[13] While the possession by the citizens of martial skills would suggest a mode for some form of popular control, the overwhelming power of the Guardians of the Laws would provide for state domination over every aspect of life. To assure this domination, the individual would have no right to keep arms and would be allowed to bear them only for the temporary purpose of exercise once per month at the instance of the State which would issue them, apparently from some secure armory or armories.[14]

By thus carefully circumscribing the right to keep and bear arms, Plato hoped to avoid the conundrum he saw as inevitable in oligarchy – providing the individual with arms necessary to support the state from external attack inevitably would lead to popular liberty. The *Laws* insists that "freedom from control must be uncompromisingly eliminated from the life of all men." Following the militaristic examples of Sparta and Crete, rather than the example of Athens, Plato dictated that "no one, man or woman, must ever be left without someone in charge of him; nobody must get into the habit of acting independently in either sham fighting or the real thing, and in peace and war alike we must give our constant attention and obedi-

---

shall pronounce it right and honorable for a man to defend himself against an assailant of his own age, and in that way they will be compelled to keep themselves fit." Plato, *Republic*, Conford translation, pp. 149, 160.

10. Plato, *Laws*, P. Saunders translation (New York: Penguin, 1970), p. 218. While Plato does not literally state this, Aristotle interpreted him to mean that "those bearing arms," i.e., having citizenship, would be limited to 5,000 (in Plato's *Laws*) and 1,000 (in Plato's *Republic*) (Aristotle, *Politics*, T. Sinclair translation [New York: Penguin, 1962], p. 69). While Plato may not have held, as did Aristotle, that the bearing of arms was necessary for full citizenship, clearly Plato anticipates that the great body of slaves and other workers would have neither arms nor citizenship.

11. Plato, *Laws*, p. 218.

12. Ibid., pp. 282, 305.

13. Ibid., p. 306; also 280-82, 307, 322-29.

14. Ibid., p. 324.

ence to our leader. . . . "[15] Thus Plato's ideal state would foster attitudes that would direct the populace away from its desire to possess
arms individually or to use them to obtain liberty and equality.
"Everyone is to have the same friends and enemies as the state."[16]
In sum, in the *Republic* and the *Laws* Plato proposes an authoritarian
state whose existence depends upon the absence of an individual
right to keep and bear arms.

Plato's ideal state was critically analyzed by Aristotle in the *Politics*, which posed popular participation as a political ideal. As opposed to the strict division between rulers, warriors, and workers in
the Socratic dialogue, Aristotle's concept of polity was based on a
large middle class wherein each citizen fulfilled all three functions of
self-legislation, arms bearing, and working. According to Aristotle,
"there are many things which Socrates left undetermined; are farmers and craftsmen to have no share in government . . . ? Are they or
are they not to possess arms . . . ?" In accord with his broad philosophical ideal of the mean, Aristotle saw in the right to keep and
bear arms the true basis of political equality. "The whole constitutional set-up is intended to be neither democracy or oligarchy, but
midway between the two—what is sometimes called 'polity,' the
members of which are those who bear arms."[17]

On the same basis Aristotle rejected the "Best State" advocated
by Hippodamus: "Hippodamus planned a city with a population of
10,000 divided into three parts, one of skilled workers, one of agri-
culturalists, and a third to bear arms and secure defense." This restriction of the right to keep and bear arms to one class entrusted
with the defense of all would inevitably lead to that class tyrannizing
the others: "the farmers have no arms, the workers have neither
lands nor arms, this makes them virtually the servants of those who
do possess arms. In these circumstances the equal sharing of offices
and honors becomes an impossibility."[18]

In analyzing the elusive concept of the constitutional kingship,
Aristotle commented on its opposite, tyranny, one characteristic of
which was a professional standing army. Thus, "a king's bodyguard
is composed of citizens carrying arms, a tyrant's of foreign mercenaries." The citizens protect the king, but they need protection from

15. Ibid., p. 489.
16. Ibid., p. 507.
17. Aristotle, *Politics*, pp. 68, 71.
18. Ibid., pp. 78, 79.

the tyrant. Even the armed force of the monarch must not be "strong enough to overpower . . . the whole population."[19]

Since all true citizens possess arms, the class of arms bearers is not limited to those who defend the state in war. Just after referring to "the class which will defend in time of war," Aristotle states that "it is quite normal for the same persons to be found bearing arms and tilling the soil."[20] By contrast, "oligarchial devices" exist in "regulations . . . made about carrying arms," to the effect that "it is lawful for the poor not to possess arms; the rich are fined if they do not have them." Since arms were essential to polity for full participation, "in principle citizenship ought to be reserved for those who can afford to carry arms."[21] Yet Aristotle immediately went on to recognize the ill treatment of the poor that would result from such a property qualification. Thus, in Aristotle's ideal polity, each citizen is to personally keep his own arms which would not be owned by the State.

Every city requires food, tools, and arms. "Arms are included because members of the constitution must carry them even among themselves, both for internal government in the event of civil disobedience and to repel external aggression."[22] In polity and democracy, those who are members of the constitution and thereby have arms are many, while in oligarchy and tyranny only a few possess these attributes. Whether the few or the many, those with arms are sovereign: "For those who possess and can wield arms are in a position to decide whether the constitution is to continue or not."[23] And since he argued that no free person submits to a tyrant and that rule without consent is neither rightful nor legal, Aristotle deemed arms possession a requisite to obtain or maintain the status of being a freeman and citizen.[24]

Recognizing the political implications of material factors, including territory and military technology, Aristotle contended that conditions that promote use of cavalry and hoplites result in oligarchy due to the respective expenses of horses and heavy armor. "But the light-armed infantry and service in ships are democratic. And so in

19. Ibid., pp. 136, 146.
20. Ibid., pp. 156–58.
21. Ibid., p. 177.
22. Ibid., p. 272.
23. Ibid., p. 274.
24. Ibid., pp. 120, 260.

practice, wherever these form a large proportion of the population, the oligarchs, if there is a struggle, fight at a disadvantage." The possession of light arms by the people allows them to overcome oligarchy: "It is by the use of light infantry in civil wars that the masses get the better of the rich; their mobility and light equipment give them an advantage over cavalry and the heavy-armed."[25]

Thus, tyranny derives from oligarchy "mistrust of the people; hence they deprive them of arms, ill-treat the lower class, and keep them from residing in the capital. These are common to oligarchy and tyranny." Through war, taxation, and public works, the people are kept poor and preoccupied by the tyrant, whose power is thereby perpetuated. "It is also in the interests of a tyrant to keep his subjects poor, so that they may not be able to afford the cost of protecting themselves by arms and be so occupied with their daily tasks that they have no time for rebellion."[26]

In the *Athenian Constitution*, Aristotle described the manner in which Peisistratus seized power by force and set up a tyranny by disarming the Athenians. Having been exiled for establishing a tyranny, Peisistratus hired soldiers and returned.

> Winning the battle of Pallenis, he seized the government and disarmed the people; and now he held the tyranny firmly, and he took Naxos and appointed Lygdamis ruler. The way in which he disarmed the people was this: He held an armed muster at the Temple of Theseus, and began to hold an Assembly, but he lowered his voice a little, and when they said they could not hear him, he told them to come up to the forecourt of the Acropolis, in order that his voice might carry better; and while he used up time making a speech, the men told off for this purpose gathered up the arms, locked them up in the neighbouring buildings of the Temple of Theseus, and came and informed Peisistratus.[27]

Peisistratus then told the people that henceforth only he would manage public affairs.

Peisistratus was tyrant for almost two decades and was succeeded by his sons, Hippias and Hipparchus. After Hipparchus was assassinated during a procession, Hippias resorted to torture and execution, "but the current story that Hippias made the people in the proces-

---

25. Ibid., p. 248.
26. Ibid., pp. 218, 226.
27. Aristotle, *Athenian Constitution*, H. Rackham translation (Cambridge: Harvard University Press, 1935), p. 47.

sion fall out away from their arms and searched for those that retained their daggers is not true, for in those days they did not walk in the procession armed, but this custom was instituted later by the democracy."[28] In short, the Athenians were disarmed under tyranny and armed under democracy.

Aristotle also described the similar methods resorted to by the Thirty Tyrants to perpetuate their power. Under their rule, citizenship was limited to 3,000 persons who favored the tyranny. Opposition naturally arose from the majority of the people who were deprived of citizenship, and the multitude found an able spokesman in Theramenes, whom the Thirty feared would lead the people to destroy the oligarchy. After being defeated in an expedition against armed exiles, the Thirty "decided to disarm the others and to destroy Theramenes," in part by giving themselves "absolute powers to execute any citizens not members of the roll of Three Thousand. . . ."[29] "Theramenes having been put out of the way, they disarmed everybody except the Three Thousand, and in the rest of their proceedings went much further in the direction of cruelty and rascality."[30]

THE ROMANS

To eighteenth century thinkers of European origin, classical antiquity (particularly Rome) represented the highest point yet achieved by human civilization. Cicero, Livy, and other Roman philosophers and historians were particularly studied by the Founding Fathers, for the Roman Republic provided at once an ideal and a condign warning of the frailty of republican institutions.[31] Cicero's general vindi-

---

28. Ibid., p. 57.
29. Ibid., p. 105.
30. Ibid., p. 107.
31. This ideal was exemplified in the image (so frequently evoked in early American oratory) of Cincinnatus called from his plow to save the Republic and then returning to pick up the plow again after the deed was done. To the generation that succeeded the Founding Fathers the heritage of the Roman militia was exemplified by the Battle of New Orleans. There about 3,500 militiamen, hastily gathered, bearing their own personal weapons, soundly defeated about 8,500 of Wellington's best Peninsular veterans, led by a distinguished British general of the Peninsular War. Although the casualty lists are unreliable, the militiamen lost somewhere between 25 and 70 of their number and the British somewhere between 2,000 and 3,000 of theirs. Compare the account given by a British military historian (J.F.C. Fuller, *Decisive Battles of the U.S.A.* [New York: Yoseloff, 1942], pp. 123–24)

cation of resistance to tyranny implicitly presupposed the imperative of an armed citizenry. In *De Officiis*, written after Caesar's death, Cicero referred to him as "that king who with the Roman People's army brought the Roman People themselves into subjection,"[32] justified tyrannicide,[33] and asserted that tyrants who rule by armed force are bound to be overthrown by those who want to be free.[34]

As a lawyer, Cicero upheld the right of individuals to bear and use arms against tyranny and in self-defense in at least two murder trials. His client Gaius Rabirius had (or had at least claimed that he had) ended the coup d'etat of L. Saturnius by taking his head. Arguing that "the taking up of arms was lawful," Cicero pointed out that besides the knights "every single other Roman citizen who existed proceeded to take up arms in the same cause"; they "took up arms to defend freedom of every one of us."[35]

In defense of Titus Annius Milo, Cicero argued that the right of self-defense is inborn, derived from nature, and known by intuition, and that arms bearing was justified absent any criminal motive. Referring to "the swords we carry" to meet violence with violence, Cicero stated:

> I refer to the law which lays it down that, if our lives are endangered by plots or violence or armed robbers or enemies, any and every method of protecting ourselves is morally right. . . . Indeed, even the wisdom of the law itself, by

---

with that given by an American (John W. Ward, *Andrew Jackson: Symbol for an Age* [London: Oxford University Press, 1953], pp. 16–17).

Before the battle Jackson had enthused his troops with an address aptly entitled "To the Embodied Militia." After it the Roman virtues of the citizen militia were evoked in countless turgid orations, like the following from Congressman Troup:

> It was the yeomanry of the country marching to the defense of the City of Orleans leaving their wives and children and firesides at a moment's warning . . . the farmers of the country triumphantly victorious over the conquerors of the conquerors of Europe. I came, I saw, I conquered, says the *American Husbandman*, fresh from his plow. The proud veteran who triumphed in Spain and carried terror into the warlike population of France was humbled beneath the power of my arm. The God of Battles and of Righteousness took part with the defenders of their country and the foe was scattered as chaff beneath the wind. It is, indeed, a fit subject for the genius of Homer or Ossian or Milton . . . that regular troops, the best disciplined and most veteran of Europe, should be beaten by undisciplined militia with the disproportionate loss of a 100 to 1 . . . (Ward, *Decisive Battles*, pp. 7–8).

32. Cicero, *De Officiis*, trans. Walter Miller (New York, 1921), p. 359.

33. Ibid., pp. 287, 299.

34. Ibid., pp. 191–99.

35. Cicero, *Murder Trials*, trans. M. Grant (New York: Penguin, 1975), pp. 279–80, 285.

a sort of tacit implication, permits self-defense, because it does not actually forbid men to kill; what it does, instead, is to forbid the bearing of a weapon with the intention to kill. When, therefore, an inquiry passes beyond the mere question of the weapon and starts to consider the motive, a man who has used arms in self-defense is not regarded as having carried them with a homicidal aim.[36]

Civilized people, barbarians, and wild beasts "learn that they have to defend their own bodies and persons and lives from violence of any and every kind by all the means within their power."[37] In short, Cicero held it a natural right to bear arms and to use them for individual self-defense.

From a plethora of ancient sources, the founding fathers learned that the greatness of the Roman Republic was based upon its citizen army, and its decline coincided with the replacement of the citizen army by a standing army of professionals. As Livy remarks, the institution of an armed populace whose members would provide and keep their own arms was initiated by Servius Tullius. "Formerly the right to bear arms had belonged solely to the patricians. Now plebeians were given a place in the army, which was to be reclassified according to every man's property, i.e., his ability to *provide himself* a more or less complete equipment for the field."[38] According to Livy, all the citizens "capable of bearing arms" registered in a census, and "these men were required to provide" their own swords, spears, and other armour.[39] In *De Re Publica*, Cicero relates that Servius organized a "large group of knights from the main body of the people" and that "the rest of the population" was divided into centuries.[40]

MACHIAVELLI

Subsequently the republican political philosopher Machiavelli, who heavily influenced Algernon Sidney, John Adams, and other British and American Whigs, took from the Roman example the lesson that

36. Cicero, *Selected Political Speeches*, trans. M. Grant (New York: Penguin, 1962), p. 222.
37. Ibid., p. 234.
38. Livy, *Books*, trans. B. Foster (Cambridge: Harvard University Press, 1919), vol. 1, p. 148 n. 2.
39. Ibid., pp. 151, 155.
40. Cicero, *On the Commonwealth*, trans. Sabine and Smith (Columbus: Ohio State University Press, 1929), pp. 174–75.

the armed people was an essential safeguard for republican institutions. On this theme, Machiavelli develops several interconnected points.[41]

The first of these, which appears in his earliest work, *The Art of War*, is that an armed people will not forfeit their liberties to a domestic tyrant:

> Rome remained free for four hundred years and Sparta eight hundred, although their citizens were armed all that time; but many other states that have been disarmed have lost their liberties in less than forty years.[42] [This was also the fate of the Romans when they allowed themselves to be disarmed.] For Augustus, and after him Tiberius, more interested in establishing and increasing their own power than in promoting the public good, began to disarm the Roman people (in order to make them more passive under their tyranny) and to keep the same armies continually on foot within the confines of the empire.[43]

Referring to contemporary examples in the *Discourses,* Machiavelli cites the Florentines, Venetians, and French as people forced to pay tribute and despoiled by tyrants: "This all comes from depriving the people of arms. . . . Such are the inconveniences that arise from depriving your people of arms. . . . [F]or he who lives in the aforesaid way treats ill the subjects who reside within his domain. . . . "[44]

A second and related point that Machiavelli took from the Roman experience is that a government that trusts all its people with arms promotes unity, civic virtue, and patriotism; but where only a few groups are armed (including, inevitably, factions secretly armed) they will vie to conquer each other and oppress the unarmed multitudes. Thus, in *The Art of War*, Machiavelli comments:

> So that by establishing a good and well-ordered militia, divisions are extinguished, peace restored, and some people who were unarmed and dispirited,

---

41. As to Machiavelli's importance to the founding fathers, see note 2 and note 85. The founders were familiar with Machiavelli both directly (see J. Adams, *A Defense of the Constitution of the United States of America* [London: C. Dilly, 1787-1788], vol. 4, pp. 57, 410, 416–20; and H. Granter, "The Machiavellianism of George Mason," *William and Mary Quarterly* 17 [1937] : 239) and as his thought was transfused to them through Harrington, Neville, Rousseau, et al. (Cf. J. Pocock, *The Machiavellian Moment* [Princeton, New Jersey: Princeton University Press, 1975], p. 528).

42. Niccolo Machiavelli, *The Art of War*, E. Farnsworth translation (Indianapolis: Bobbs-Merrill, 1965), p. 30.

43. Ibid., p. 20.

44. Niccolo Machiavelli, *Discourses*, trans. L. Walker (New York: Penguin, 1970), pp. 373, 374.

but united, continue in union and become warlike and courageous; others who were brave and had arms in their hands, but were previously given to faction and discord, become united and turn against the enemies of their country those arms and that courage which they used to exert against each other.[45]

Returning to the same theme in the *Discourses*, Machiavelli again refers to the Roman example:

> If a city be armed and disciplined as Rome was, and all its citizens, alike in their private and official capacity, have a chance to put alike their virtue and the power of fortune to the test of experience, it will be found that always and in all circumstances they will be of the same mind and will maintain their dignity in the same way. But, when they are not familiar with arms and merely trust to the whim of fortune, not to their own virtue, they will change with the changes of fortune. . . . [46]

By the same token, Machiavelli saw the armed people as a republic's most effective defense against foreign enemies. Machiavelli's third point was that an enemy, or combination of enemies, who relied solely on professional armies, could not remotely equal the numbers of soldiers that could quickly be raised in a state where all citizens had arms and were accustomed to their use. A republic that relied on its armed citizenry would have sufficient numbers to defend its own borders, no matter how numerous its opponents. And if the army were bested in the field, it could fall back on its ever-available supply of armed citizens. On this point, Machiavelli referred to the Second Punic War, in which Rome managed to sustain itself for sixteen years during Hannibal's invasion, sending against him army after army so that his forces were eventually hemmed in and neutralized (though never defeated), whereas Carthage was forced to sue for peace after one disastrous battle when the Romans invaded North Africa:

> For either I have my country well equipped with arms, as the Romans had and the Swiss have; or I have a country ill-equipped with arms, as the Carthagians had, and as have the King of France and the Italians today.
>
> But, when states are strongly armed, as Rome was and the Swiss are, the more difficult it is to overcome them the nearer they are to their homes: For such bodies can bring more forces together to resist attack than they

45. Machiavelli, *The Art of War*, p. 41.
46. Machiavelli, *Discourses*, p. 492.

can to attack others. . . . [I]n attacking a foreign country [the Romans] never sent out armies of more than fifty thousand men; but for home defense they put under arms against the Gauls after the first Punic war, eighteen hundred thousand [i.e., 1.8 million].[47]

Revolutionaries such as Jefferson took Machiavelli's advice that "all armed prophets have conquered and unarmed ones failed." In the final analysis, states are founded on "good laws and good arms. . . . [T]here cannot be good laws where there are not good arms. . . ."[48]

THE AUTHORITARIANS

The work of the great French sixteenth century absolutist, Jean Bodin, represents, in some respects, the mirror image (i.e., reversal) of Machiavelli. His *Six Books of a Commonweale* (1576) lists his recommendations for preservation of monarchical power, among which are disarming the people and suppression of speech:

> Another and the most usual way to prevent sedition, is to take away the subject's arms: howbeit, that the Princes of Italy, and of the East cannot endure that they shall at all have arms; as do the people of the North and the West. . . . [Wise is the Turkish practice] not in only punishing with all severity the seditious and mutinous people, but also by forbidding them to bear arms. . . . [Y]et another [cause of rebellions and seditions is] the immoderate liberty of speech given to orators, who direct and guide the people's hearts and minds according to their own pleasure.[49]

Using several historical examples to show how arms and speech had "translated the sovereignty from the nobility into the people, and changed the Aristocracy into a Democratic or Popular state," Bodin complained that "we have seen all Germany in arms . . . after that the mutinous creatures had stirred up the people against the nobility."[50]

In addition to the adverse effect an armed people would have on despotism, Bodin saw in the wearing of arms "the cause of an infi-

47. Ibid., pp. 308, 309.

48. Niccolo Machiavelli, *The Prince*, trans. L. Ricci (New York: New American Library, 1952), pp. 50, 72.

49. Jean Bodin, *The Six Books of Commonweale*, trans. R. Knolles (London: G. Bishop, 1606), pp. 542, 543.

50. Ibid., p. 544.

nite number of murders." Joining this criminological assertion to his political concerns, he described legislation punishing weapons possession by all but soldiers and guards with death as "so to take away the fears of murders and seditions. . . ." As to any supposed advantages that an armed people would have against foreign enemies, Bodin dismissed these with pacifistic horror at the bloodshed wreaked by soldiers: "I see no reason why we should instruct citizens in this cruel and execrable kind of life, or to arm them. . . ." Citing the example of the Egyptians and the teaching of Plato he concluded that it should be illegal for most subjects "to use and bear arms"[51] and that society should be divided into distinct classes with only the few trained to arms.[52]

Although Bodin's considerable influence on Thomas Hobbes' *Leviathan* is clear, distinct elements of English policy and tradition concerning the right to keep and bear arms made it impossible for Hobbes to follow the Frenchman on this point. From at least 1500, the French monarchy had consistently sought to disarm the common citizen on the rationale that "since an imposing array of royal officers was charged with the protection of his life and property, he did not need to undertake this protection himself."[53] But the more frugal English kings, from Alfred the Great (871–899) through the earlier years of George IV (1820–1830), required the ordinary citizen to maintain arms and perform all these functions with the constant aid of "watch and ward" organizations and the general supervision of the constables and shire reeves (sheriffs).[54] Bodin's policy of disarmament was obviously impractical in a country that had only the sketchiest rudiments of a standing army or police force and whose laws required the ordinary citizen to maintain arms in order to perform the police function himself.

Thus Hobbes could join Bodin only in condemning sedition and repudiating Aristotle's and Cicero's belief in the right to overthrow tyranny by armed force. Hobbes could not deny the duty of the English citizen to enforce both the King's law and the natural law by arms. Thus, Hobbes acknowledged as the "summe of the Right of

51. Ibid., pp. 106, 389, 542, 599.
52. Ibid., pp. 610–11, 614.
53. Lee Kennett and James La Verne Anderson, *The Gun in America* (Greenwich, Conn.: Fawcett, 1975), pp. 8–16.
54. Colin Greenwood, *Firearms Control: A Study of Firearms Controls and Armed Crime in England and Wales* (London: Routledge and Kegan Paul, 1972), pp. 7–14.

Nature" that "By all means we can, to defend ourselves." Indeed, he regarded this right as so fundamental as to be inalienable, that is, not subject to waiver under any circumstances: "a covenant not to defend my selfe from force, by force, is always voyd."[55]

THE LIBERTARIANS

John Locke's 1689 refutation of absolutism in the *Second Treatise on Civil Government* demonstrated the difficulty in Hobbes' attempt to reconcile the popular possession of arms and this right of self-defense with authoritarian theory. Locke's primary contribution in the minds of the English revolutionaries of 1688, and the Americans of 1776, was his argument that tyranny may of right be resisted in the same manner as private aggression. If private persons "have a right to defend themselves and recover by force what by unlawful force is taken from them,"[56] then they have the right to reclaim by force the liberties of which the state has unlawfully deprived them. Tyranny, being illegal, may be resisted by force just as people may resist robbers or pirates.[57] As even the pro-monarchist Barclay conceded: "self-defense is a part of the law of nature; nor can it be denied the community, even against the king himself."[58]

The only work that might conceivably have rivaled Locke in influence upon the founders of the American republic is Algernon Sidney's *Discourses Concerning Government*, published in 1698, fifteen years after his execution by Charles II. That Sidney was viewed as a martyr, and that the manuscript of the *Discourses* had been used by the prosecution in his trial, added a patina of romance to the work's unquestionable philosophic import. Sidney resembles Machiavelli in seeing the armed populace as at once the ultimate guarantee against domestic tyranny and the best possible defense against foreign enemies. Like Machiavelli, Sidney lauded the popular sovereignty of republican Rome based on an armed citizenry and deplored the seizure of power by Caesar by means of a corrupt standing army. Rome could have never reached its height "if the People had not

55. Thomas Hobbes, *Leviathan* (New York: Washington Square Press, 1964), pp. 88, 95.

56. John Locke, *Of Civil Government* (Chicago: Henry Regnery Company, 1955), p. 174.

57. Ibid., pp. 177–93.

58. Ibid., p. 195.

been exercised in arms. . . . Such men as these were not to be used like Slaves, or oppressed by the unmerciful hand of Usurers."[59]

While the absolute monarch seeks to render his subjects powerless,[60] "in a popular or mixed Government every man is concerned," which means that everyone participates in politics and that "the body of the People is the public defense, and every man is armed and disciplined. . . ." Continuing his references to the republics of classical antiquity, Sidney notes that the Romans "had as many soldiers to fight for their Country as there were freemen in it."[61] Among the Greeks, "there was not a Citizen of *Athens* able to bear arms" who did not join in the defense against invasion.[62]

Sidney cites numerous examples to demonstrate that the people "by the use of Arms" maintain their defense and that "no numbers of men, though naturally valiant, are able to defend themselves, unless they be well arm'd, disciplin'd and conducted." An armed populace may maintain its independence longest, while defeat of a mercenary army is decisive; among an armed people "when one head is cut off, many rise up in the place of it."[63]

Only an armed people can maintain freedom, not only from foreign invasion but also from domestic tyranny. "Peace is seldom made, and never kept, unless the Subject retain such a Power in his hands, as may oblige the Prince to stand to what is agreed. . . ."[64] Sedition is appropriate where supreme power is seized by a tyrant: "The Laws which they overthrow can give them no protection; and every man is a soldier against him who is a public Enemy."[65] Should no right to resist tyranny exist, "twere better for every man to stand in his own defense, than to enter into societies." Sedition is an extraordinary but righteous mode "of delivering an oppressed People from the violence of a wicked Magistrate, who having armed a Crew of lewd Villains," kills and confiscates the property of his opponents.[66] In sum: "Nay, all Laws must fall, human Societies that subsist by them be dissolved, and all innocent persons be exposed to the violence of the most wicked, if men might not justly defend them-

59. Algernon Sidney, *Discourses Concerning Government* (London, 1698), p. 134.
60. Ibid., p. 146.
61. Ibid., p. 157.
62. Ibid., p. 159.
63. Ibid., pp. 163, 165, 167.
64. Ibid., p. 173.
65. Ibid., p. 175.
66. Ibid., pp. 180–81.

selves against injustice by their own natural right, when the ways prescribed by public authority cannot be taken."[67]

Sidney based his realist theory of arms and freedom on the premise that "Swords were given to men, that none might be Slaves, but such as know not how to use them."[68] The arms question is central to Sidney's critique of royal absolutism in England. Monarchy originally did not exist there. The Britons who fiercely defended their liberty from Roman conquest "could not otherwise be subdued, than by the slaughter of all the inhabitants that were able to bear arms." The people themselves, rather than leaders, made the laws, and "that no force might be put upon them they met arm'd in their general Assemblies. . . ."[69] Even after monarchy was established following the Norman conquest, the people were expected to have arms. Referring to the ancient nobility as "composed of such men as have been ennobled by bearing Arms in the defense or enlargement of the Commonwealth," Sidney mentions the obligation "according to their several degrees and proportions, to provide and maintain Horses, Arms and Men for the same uses. . . ." He described this nobility as "such Gentlemen and Lords of Mannors, as we now call Commoners, together with the Freeholders."[70] Referring to the subversion of the English constitution in his own times, Sidney wrote: "The Law was plain, but it has been industriously rendered perplex: They who were to have upheld it are overthrown, that which might have been easily performed when the people were armed, and had a great, strong, virtuous and powerful Nobility to lead them, is made difficult, now they are disarmed, and that Nobility abolished."[71]

Like Locke, Sidney held that each individual is naturally free, that by the law of nature each person has a right to his own life, liberty, goods, and lands, and that tyrannical governments may rightfully be abolished. Ultimately, each person must guarantee his own freedom, which is why the ancients "carried their Liberty in their own breasts, and had Hands and Swords to defend it." "Let the danger be never so great, there is a possibility of safety while men have life, hands, arms, and courage to use them; but that people must certainly perish, who tamely suffer themselves to be oppressed. . . ."[72]

67. Ibid., pp. 266–67.
68. Ibid., p. 270.
69. Ibid., p. 380.
70. Ibid., p. 395.
71. Ibid., p. 420.
72. Ibid., pp. 407, 434.

Among the English Whigs influenced by Algernon Sidney were John Trenchard and Thomas Gordon, whose joint essays known as *Cato's Letters* (1721–22) in turn influenced American critics of standing armies and were highly regarded by John Adams and Thomas Jefferson.[73] Trenchard and Gordon concisely stated their views on the role of the armed people in the preservation of liberty: "Our Armies formerly were only a Number of the People armed occasionally; and Armies of the People are the only Armies which are not formidable to the People."[74] Contending that only civil liberty produces military virtue, the two Whigs observed that "when a tyrant's army is beaten, his Country is conquered: He has no Resource; his Subjects having neither Arms nor Courage, nor Reason to fight for him. . . ." By contrast, "In Attacks upon a free State, every Man will fight to defend it, because every Man has something to defend in it."[75] Standing armies they saw as existing solely to oppress the people domestically and to meddle in the affairs of foreign peoples, and their absence is requisite for a people to retain their liberties.[76]

Finally to be mentioned is Rousseau, who in some respects upheld the Machiavellian republican tradition in *The Social Contract* arguing that "In a State truly free, the citizens do all with their own arms and nothing with their money. . . ."[77] And in *Discourse on Political Economy*, "Having become enemies of the peoples for whose happiness they were responsible, tyrants established standing armies, in appearance to repress foreigners and in fact to oppress the inhabitants." Seeing the citizen's army or militia as protective of freedom at home and nonaggressive abroad, Rousseau attributed the demise of ancient Roman liberty to the growth of a murderous standing army and foresaw the pernicious effects of standing armies for the next two centuries: "To maintain them [standing armies], it is no less necessary to oppress the peoples. And in recent times, these dangerous establishments have been growing so rapidly in all our coun-

---

73. John Trenchard and T. Gordon, *The English Libertarian Heritage*, ed. D. Jacobson (Indianapolis: Bobbs-Merrill, 1965), pp. liv–lv.

74. Ibid., pp. 71–72.

75. Ibid., p. 152.

76. Ibid., pp. 215–30.

77. Jean Jacques Rousseau, *The Social Contract*, anonymous 1791 translation (New York: Hafner, 1947), p. 84.

tries that one can foresee only the future depopulation of Europe and, sooner or later, the ruin of the peoples who inhabit it."[78]

CONCLUSION

Jefferson's comment on the Declaration of Independence that "all its authority rests then on the harmonizing sentiments of the day," including "the elementary books of public right, as Aristotle, Cicero, Locke, Sidney, etc.," would apply equally to the Bill of Rights. The classical republican political philosophers strongly influenced the founding fathers generally in the direction of a libertarian vision of individual rights coupled with a fundamental distrust of government, and particularly in regard to the necessity of an armed populace to effect popular sovereignty.[79]

Concurring with the seventeenth century English Whig Marchamont Nedham "that the people be continually trained up in the exercise of arms, and the militia lodged only in the people's hands," John Adams cited Nedham favorably on the Greek and Roman sources of this principle:

> "As Aristotle tells us, in his fourth book of Politics, the Grecian states ever had special care to place the use and exercise of arms in the people, because the commonwealth is theirs who hold the arms: the sword and sovereignty ever walk hand in hand together." This is perfectly just. "Rome, and the territories about it, were trained up perpetually in arms, and the whole commonwealth, by this means, became one formal militia. There was no difference in order between the citizen, the husbandman, and the soldier."[80]

Adams went on to note approvingly that "arms in the hands of citizens may be used at individual discretion" for various purposes, including "private self-defense."[81]

While relying to a great extent on Cicero, "the greatest orator, statesman, and philosopher of Rome,"[82] the founders probably

---

78. Jean Jacques Rousseau, *Discourse on Political Economy*, trans. J. Masters (New York: St. Martin's Press, 1978), p. 229.

79. See note 2.

80. Adams, *Defense of the Constitutions*, vol. 3, p. 471.

81. Ibid., p. 475.

82. J. Adams, *Works*, ed. C. Adams (Boston: Little, Brown and Company, 1856), vol. 1, p. 26.

based their thinking on the role of the militia in the Roman experience more on the lengthy accounts of Machiavelli. The influence of Machiavelli was clear in George Mason's speech to the Fairfax Independent Militia Company,[83] which was composed of volunteers who supplied their own arms and elected their officers. When the "essential maxims" of the Roman Commonwealth were undermined, according to Mason, "their army no longer considered themselves the soldiers of the Republic, but as the troops of Marius or Sylla, of Pompey or of Caesar, of Marc Antony or of Octavius."[84] John Adams praised Machiavelli for his constitutional model for Florence (which included a popular militia), wherein "the sovereign power is lodged, both of right and in fact, in the citizens themselves."[85] Considering these influences, it is no wonder that our leading authority on Machiavelli has stated that the Second Amendment "affirms the relation between a popular militia and popular freedom in language directly descended from that of Machiavelli. . . . "[86]

Great reliance was also placed on the seventeenth century English republicans, who themselves had been influenced by Aristotle, Cicero, and Machiavelli. Jefferson saw to it that Locke and Sidney would be required reading at the University of Virginia, for "as to the general principles of liberty and the rights of man, in nature and in society, the doctrines of Locke, in his 'Essay concerning the true original extent and end of civil government,' and of Sidney in his 'Discourses on Government,' may be considered as those generally approved by your fellow citizens of this, and the United States. . . . "[87] Relying on Locke to deny any governmental right to be absolutely arbitrary, Samuel Adams related: "Mr. Locke has often been quoted in the present dispute between Britain and her colonies, and very much to our purpose."[88] Like the Declaration of Independence, the Virginia Declaration of Rights of 1776 by George Mason contains specific phrases from Locke and from *Cato's Letters* by Trenchard and Gordon.[89] In his last will and testament, Josiah Quincy, Jr., left "to my son when he shall arrive to the age of fif-

83. See note 41.

84. G. Mason, *Papers*, ed. R. Rutland (Chapel Hill, N.C.: University of North Carolina Press, 1970), vol. 1, p. 231.

85. Adams, *Works*, vol. 5, p. 183.

86. Pocock, *Machiavellian Moment*, p. 528.

87. C. Robbins, "Algernon Sidney's Discourses," *William and Mary Quarterly* 4 (3d series, 1947), pp. 267, 269.

88. S. Adams, *Writings* (New York: G.P. Putnam's Sons, 1904), pp. 210, 298–99.

89. Mason, *Papers*, vol. 1, pp. 279–80.

teen years, Algernon Sidney's works, John Locke's works, . . . and *Cato's Letters*. May the spirit of liberty rest upon him!"[90]

In summary, the two categorical imperatives of the Second Amendment—that a militia of the body of the people is necessary to guarantee a free state, and that all of the people have a right to keep and bear arms—were derived from the classical philosophical texts concerning the experiences of ancient Greece and Rome and seventeenth century England. Aristotle, Cicero, Machiavelli, Locke, Sidney, Trenchard, and Gordon provided the philosophical vindication of an armed populace to counter oppression which found expression in the Declaration of Independence and Bill of Rights. In this sense the people's right to have their own swords was based on the sharpest intellectual swords known to the founding fathers.

90. Robbins, "Algernon Sidney's Discourses," p. 270.

Chapter 14

THE RIGHT OF THE PEOPLE TO KEEP AND BEAR ARMS
The Common Law Tradition

Joyce Lee Malcolm

INTRODUCTION*

Every generation suffers to some degree from historic amnesia. However, when the history of a major political tradition, along with the assumptions and passions that forged it, are forgotten, it becomes extraordinarily difficult to understand or evaluate its legacy. This is particularly unfortunate when that legacy has been written into the enduring fabric of government. The Second Amendment to the United States Constitution is such a relic, a fossil of a lost tradition. Even a century ago its purpose would have been clearly appreciated. To nineteenth century exponents of limited government the checks and balances that preserved individual liberty were ultimately guaranteed by the right of the people to be armed. The preeminent Whig historian, Thomas Macaulay, labelled this "the security without which every other is insufficient," [1] and a century earlier the great jurist, William Blackstone, regarded private arms as the means by which a people might vindicate their other rights if these were sup-

This chapter has appeared in *Hastings Constitutional Law Quarterly* (vol. 10, no. 2, 1983), and is part of a larger project on the history of the right to bear arms. It is herewith reprinted by permission of the editors.

1. T. Macaulay, *Critical and Historical Essays, Contributed to The Edinburgh Review* 154, 162 (Leipzig 1850).

pressed.[2] Earlier generations of political philosophers clearly had less confidence in written constitutions, no matter how wisely drafted. J. L. De Lolme, an eighteenth century author much read at the time of the American Revolution[3] pointed out:

> But all those privileges of the People, considered in themselves, are but feeble defences against the real strength of those who govern. All those provisions, all those reciprocal Rights, necessarily suppose that things remain in their legal and settled course: what would then be the recourse of the People, if ever the Prince, suddenly freeing himself from all restraint, and throwing himself as it were out of the Constitution, should no longer respect either the person, or the property of the subject, and either should make no account of his conversation with the Parliament, or attempt to force it implicitly to submit to his will?—It would be resistance ... the question has been decided in favour of this doctrine by the Laws of England, and that resistance is looked upon by them as the ultimate and lawful resource against the violences of Power.[4]

This belief in the virtues of an armed citizenry had a profound influence upon the development of the English, and in consequence the American, system of government. However, the many years in which both the British and American governments have remained "in their legal and settled course," have helped bring us to the point where the history of the individual's right to keep and bear arms is now obscure. British historians, no longer interested in the issue, have tended to ignore it, while American legal and constitutional scholars, ill-equipped to investigate the English origins of this troublesome liberty, have made a few cursory and imperfect attempts to research the subject.[5] As a result Englishmen are uncertain of the circumstances surrounding the establishment of a right to bear arms and the Second Amendment to the Constitution remains this country's most hotly debated but least understood liberty.

2. *See* W. Blackstone, *Commentaries* 139–40 (1st ed. Oxford 1765).

3. De Lolme's book, *The Constitution of England*, was first published in 1771 and quickly went through an impressive number of editions. D'Israeli later referred to De Lolme as "the English Montesquieu." *See* Oxford University Press, *The Concise Dictionary of National Biography* 332 (2d ed. 1903); 7 *Encyclopaedia Britannica* 970 (11th ed. 1910).

4. J. De Lolme, *The Constitution of England* 227 (New York 1792).

5. See, e.g., L. Kennett and J. Anderson, *The Gun in America* 25–27 (1975); G. Newton and F. Zimring, *Firearms and Violence in American Life; A Staff Report Submitted to the National Commission on the Causes and Prevention of Violence* 255 (1968); Levin, *The Right to Bear Arms: The Development of the American Experience* 48 *Chi-Kent L. Rev.* 148 (1971); Weatherup, *Standing Armies and Armed Citizens: An Historical Analysis of the Second Amendment*, 2 *Hastings Const. L.Q.* 961 (1975).

In a report on the legal basis for firearms controls, a committee of the American Bar Association observed:

> There is probably less agreement, more misinformation, and less understand-
> ing of the right of citizens to keep and bear arms than on any other current
> controversial constitutional issue. The crux of the controversy is the con-
> struction of the Second Amendment to the Constitution, which reads: "A
> well-regulated militia, being necessary to the security of a free State, the right
> of the people to keep and bear arms, shall not be infringed."[6]

Few would disagree that the crux of this controversy is the construction of the Second Amendment, but, as those writing on the subject
have demonstrated, that single sentence is capable of an extraordinary number of interpretations.[7] The main source of confusion has
been the meaning and purpose of the initial clause. Was it a qualifying or an amplifying clause? That is, was the right to arms guaranteed
only to members of "a well-regulated militia" or was the militia
merely the most pressing reason for maintenance of an armed community? The meaning of "militia" itself is by no means clear. It has
been argued that only a small, highly trained citizen army was
intended,[8] and, alternatively, that all able-bodied men constituted
the militia.[9] Finally, emphasis on the militia has been proffered as
evidence that the right to arms was only a "collective right" to
defend the state, not an individual right to defend oneself.[10] Our
pressing need to understand the Second Amendment has served to
define areas of disagreement but has brought us no closer to a consensus on its original meaning.

The fault lies not with the legal, but with the scholarly community. For if the crux of the controversy is the construction of the
Second Amendment, the key to that construction is the English tradition the colonists inherited, and the English Bill of Rights from
which much of the American Bill of Rights was drawn. Experts in
English constitutional and legal history have neglected this subject,
however, with the result that no full-scale study of the evolution

6. Miller, Sec. III *The Legal Basis for Firearms Controls*, in *Report to the American Bar Association* 22 (1975).

7. *See, e.g.*, Caplan, *Handgun Control: Constitutional or Unconstitutional. A Reply to Mayor Jackson*, 10 *N.C. Cent. L.J.* 53, 54 (1978); Weatherup, *supra* note 5, at 973–74; Whisker, *Historical Development and Subsequent Erosion of the Right to Keep and Bear Arms*, 78 *W. Va. L. Rev.* 171, 176–78 (1975).

8. *See* Miller, *supra* note 6, at 25–28.

9. *See* Caplan, *supra* note 7, at 54–55.

10. *See, e.g.*, Levin, *supra* note 5, at 154, 159; Weatherup, *supra* note 5, at 973–74.

of the right to keep and bear arms has yet been published. Conse-quently, there is doubt about such elementary facts as the legality and availability of arms in seventeenth and eighteenth century England and uncertainty about whether the English right to have arms ex-tended to the entire Protestant population or only to the aristocracy. Experts in American constitutional theory have nevertheless endeav-ored to define the common law tradition behind the Second Amend-ment without the benefit of research into these basic questions. These experts' findings are contradictory, often involve serious mistakes of fact, and muddle, rather than clarify, matters. For example, in their report to the National Commission on the Causes and Prevention of Violence, George Newton and Franklin Zimring insist that any tradi-tional right of Englishmen to own weapons was "more nominal than real,"[11] while the authors of *The Gun in America* conclude that few Englishmen ever owned firearms because prior to the adoption of the English Bill of Rights in 1689 firearms were expensive and inefficient, and thereafter guns were not considered "suitable to the condition" of the average citizen.[12] Neither set of authors provides more than cursory evidence.[13] On the other hand, one British author found that until modern times his countrymen's right to keep arms was "unim-paired as it was then [in 1689] deliberately settled"[14] and a second noted that with only "minor exceptions" the Englishman's "right to keep arms seems not to have been questioned."[15]

The continuing confusion is apparent in the articles that have appeared on this subject in American law journals. David Caplan, writing in the *North Carolina Central Law Journal*, finds that "the private keeping of arms was completely guaranteed by the common law as an 'absolute right of individuals,'"[16] while James Whisker

11. G. Newton and F. Zimring, *supra* note 5, at 255.

12. L. Kennett and J. Anderson, *supra* note 5, at 25-27.

13. For example, Newton and Zimring fail to cite a single seventeenth or eighteenth century source for the critical assertion that the English Convention Parliament of 1688 intended to guarantee only a general, not an individual, right to have arms. *See* G. Newton and F. Zimring, *supra* note 5, at 254-55, n. 12. Kennett and Anderson conclude that in the seventeenth century firearms "were not generally held . . . because of their inefficiency, costliness, and general scarcity," but provide no evidence of their efficiency, cost, or avail-ability in that period. *See* L. Kennett and J. Anderson, *supra* note 5, at 27.

14. J. Paterson, *Commentaries on the Liberty of the Subject and the Laws of England Relating to the Security of the Person* 442 (London 1877).

15. C. Greenwood, *Firearms Control: A Study of Armed Crime and Firearms Control in England and Wales* 10 (1972).

16. Caplan, *supra* note 7, at 54.

argues in the *West Virginia Law Review* that long before the American Revolution "Englishmen came to view the retention of arms by individuals or by private groups as productive only of rebellion or insurrection."[17] There is a temptation to superimpose the debate over the Second Amendment's militia clause back onto the English guarantee of the right to have arms although the English guarantee contained no such clause. Roy Weatherup, for example, interprets the clear English guarantee that "Protestant subjects may have arms for their defence" to mean "Protestant members of the militia might keep and bear arms in accordance with their militia duties for the defense of the realm."[18] Despite the fact that the Convention Parliament which drafted the English Bill of Rights purposely adopted the phrase "their defence" in preference to "their common defence"[19] he could find "no recognition of any personal right to bear arms."[20] In short, there is disagreement over who could, or did, own firearms both before and after passage of the English Bill of Rights.

Nearly all writers agree, however, that an accurate reading of the Second Amendment is indispensable to resolving current debates over gun ownership, and that a clarification of the common law tradition is necessary to that reading.[21] There are compelling reasons for this consensus. To begin with, the royal charters that created the new colonies assured potential emigrants that they and their children would "have and enjoye all Liberties and Immunities of free and naturall Subjects . . . as if they and every of them were borne within the Realme of England."[22] Furthermore, the entire body of common law, with the exception of those portions inappropriate to their new situation, crossed the Atlantic with the colonists.[23] The perilous circumstances of the infant colonies made the common law tradition of

---

17. Whisker, *supra* note 7, at 176.

18. Weatherup, *supra* note 5, at 973–74. For the precise English guarantee of the rights of the subject to have arms, *see* The Bill of Rights, I W. & M., sess. 2, ch. 2 (1689).

19. 10 *H. C. Jour., 1688–93*, 21–22; 1 W. & M., sess. 2, ch. 2 (1689).

20. Weatherup, *supra* note 5, at 974.

21. *See, e.g.*, Caplan, *supra* note 7, at 53–54; Emery, *The Constitutional Right to Keep and Bear Arms*, 28 *Harv. L. Rev.* 473–75 (1915); Hays, *The Right to Bear Arms, A Study in Judicial Misinterpretation*, 2 *Wm. & Mary L. Rev.* 383 (1960); Levin, *supra* note 5, at 148; Weatherup, *supra* note 5, at 964; Whisker, *supra* note 7, at 175–76.

22. Charter of Connecticut, Charles II, 1 *The Public Records of the Colony of Connecticut* 7 (Hartford 1850) [hereinafter cited as *Records of Connecticut*]. *See also* Charter of the Province of Massachusetts-Bay, William and Mary, 1 *Acts and Resolves of the Province of Massachusetts Bay* 14 (Boston 1869).

23. *See* T. Barnes, *The English Legal System: Carryover to the Colonies* 16 (1975).

an armed citizenry both appropriate and crucial to the survival of the plantations.[24] Indeed, the colonies began very early requiring residents to keep firearms and establishing militias.[25]

There is a further reason for examining the Second Amendment in the light of English legal traditions. Not only did colonists arrive in the new land equipped with an elaborate legal framework, they were for the most part imbued with that attitude of anti-authoritarianism that had fueled the traumatic upheavals of the seventeenth century, the English Civil War of 1642, and the Glorious Revolution of 1688. This general distrust of central power resulted in the English Bill of Rights in 1689 and was to produce the American Bill of Rights a century later. Bernard Bailyn, in *The Ideological Origins of the American Revolution*, is emphatic about there being a connection between English opposition philosophy and American political thought:

> To say simply that this tradition of opposition thought was quickly transmitted to America and widely appreciated there is to understate the fact. Opposition thought, in the form it acquired at the turn of the seventeenth century and in the early eighteenth century, was devoured by the colonists. . . . There seems never to have been a time after the Hanoverian succession when these writings were not central to American political expression or absent from polemical politics.[26]

When they had won their battle to retain the rights of Englishmen, and came to write the federal and state constitutions and draw up the federal Bill of Rights, American statesmen borrowed heavily from English models.[27] Since the federal Bill of Rights, including the

---

24. *See, e.g., Records of Connecticut, supra* note 22, at 285–86; 19 *The Colonial Records of the State of Georgia* 137 *passim* (Atlanta 1911); *The Book of the General Lawes and Libertyes Concerning the Inhabitants of the Massachusetts* 39–41 (Hunt. Lib. reprint 1975) (1st ed. Boston 1648); 1 *Records of the Colony of Rhode Island and Providence Plantations in New England* 77, 94 (Providence 1856); W. Billings, *The Old Dominion in the Seventeenth Century* 172 (1975).

25. *See, e.g., Acts of the Grand Assembly of Virginia 1623-24*, Nos. 24 & 25; *Acts of the Grand Assembly of Virginia 1673*, Act 2; *The Compact with the Charter and General Laws of the Colony of New Plymouth* 44–45 (1836); 8 *Records of Connecticut* 380; 1 *Colonial Laws of New York* 161 (1894); South Carolina Stat. No. 206 (1703).

26. B. Bailyn, *The Ideological Origins of the American Revolution* 43 (1967).

27. *See, e.g.*, 2 *The Records of the Federal Convention of 1787*, 509, 617 (M. Ferrand ed. 1911); *Debates and Proceedings in the Convention of the Commonwealth of Massachusetts, Held in the year 1788*, 198–99 (Boston 1856); *Debates and Other Proceedings of the Convention of Virginia, 1788*, 271 (2d ed. Richmond 1805); *The Federalist* Nos. 26, 84 (Hamilton).

Second Amendment, is to a very great extent an example of such borrowing, it behooves us to take a closer look at their English models.

THE TRADITIONAL OBLIGATION
TO BE ARMED[28]

During most of England's history, maintenance of an armed citizenry was neither merely permissive nor cosmetic but essential. Until late in the seventeenth century England had no standing army, and until the nineteenth century no regular police force. The maintenance of order was everyone's business and an armed and active citizenry was written into the system. All able-bodied men between the ages of sixteen and sixty were liable to be summoned to serve on the sheriff's posse to pursue malefactors or to suppress local disorders.[29] For larger scale emergencies, such as invasion or insurrection, a civilian militia was intermittently mustered for military duty.[30] While all able-bodied males were liable for this service, the practice during the late sixteenth and seventeenth centuries had been to select a group of men within each county to be intensively trained.[31] Whenever possible, members of these trained bands were supposed to be prosperous farmers and townsmen, but in practice, the rank-and-file were usually men of modest means — small freeholders, craftsmen or tenant-farmers.[32] They were, however, invariably led by prestigious members of their community, and commanded by lords lieutenants, who were peers appointed by, and directly responsible to, the Crown.[33] The effectiveness of the militia varied with the need for their services, the interest of particular monarchs, and even with the

28. Earlier versions of sections I, II, & III of this article appear in Malcolm, *Disarmed: The Loss of the Right to Bear Arms in Restoration England* (Bunting Inst., Radcliffe College 1980).

29. *See* R. Burn, 2 *The Justice of the Peace and Parish Officer* 16–20 (London 1755); F. Maitland, *The Constitutional History of England* 276–77 (1968) (1st ed. Cambridge 1908).

30. *See Assizes of Arms*, Hen. 2 (1181); *Statute of Winchester*, Edw. (1285); 4 & 5 Phil. and M., ch. 3 (1557).

31. *See* C. Cruickshank, *Elizabeth's Army* 24–25 (2d ed. 1966).

32. Manuscripts of the sixteenth and seventeenth centuries contain repeated complaints to this effect. For printed comment, see, e.g., J. Morrill, *Cheshire, 1630-1660*, 26 (1974); G. Trevelyan, *England Under the Stuarts* 187–88 (1928).

33. *See* C. Cruickshank, *supra* note 31, at 19–20; H. Hallam, *The Constitutional History of England* 386 (London 1870).

enthusiasm of individual muster masters and captains.[34] During some reigns, the trained bands were scarcely mustered from one year to the next; while at other times, as in the 1630s for example, a major effort was made to re-equip these citizen-soldiers and have them instructed in the latest European military tactics.[35]

The militia and the posse were summoned only occasionally, but English subjects were involved in more everyday police work. The old common law custom persisted that when a crime occurred citizens were to raise a "hue and cry" to alert their neighbors, and were expected to pursue the criminals "from town to town, and from county to county."[36] Villagers who preferred not to get involved were subject to fine and imprisonment.[37] As an additional incentive to aid in crime prevention, local residents were expected to make good half the loss caused by robbers or rioters.[38]

The most frequent police duty was the keeping of watch and ward. Town gates were closed from sundown until sunrise and all householders, "sufficiently weaponed" according to the requirement, took turns standing watch at night or ward during the day.[39] Widows, disabled men, and other townsmen unable to carry out the task had to hire substitutes to serve in their stead.[40]

Citizens were not only expected to have suitable weapons at the ready for these duties, but, since passage of the Statute of Winchester in 1285, were assessed according to their wealth for a contribution of arms for the militia.[41] When not in use for musters or emergencies, nearly all of this equipment remained in private hands. A series of later statutes spelled out in detail the arms each household was required to own and the frequency of practice sessions.[42] During the reign of Queen Elizabeth, for example, every family was commanded to provide a bow and two shafts for each son between the ages of seven and seventeen and to train them in their use or be subject to a

---

34. *See, e.g.*, R. Ashton, *The English Civil War* 55–59, 66 (1978); L. Boynton, *The Elizabethan Militia* 212 *passim*, 264–65 (1967); C. Cruickshank, *supra* note 31, at 5–11.

35. *See* L. Boynton, *supra* note 34, at 245–54.

36. *See* R. Burn, *supra* note 29, at 17–20.

37. *See* id.

38. *See* id.

39. *See* id. at 512.

40. *See* id.

41. *See Statute of Winchester*, Edw. (1285).

42. *See, e.g.*, 2 *Acts & Ords. Interregnum* 397–402 (London 1911); *An Act for Setling the Militia of the Commonwealth of England* (London 1650); 4 & 5 Phil. & M., ch. 3 (1557); *An Act Declaring the Sole Right of the Militia to Be in the King*, 14 Car. 2, ch. 3 (1662).

fine.[43] To promote proficiency in arms, Henry VIII and his successors ordered every village to maintain targets on its green at which local men were to practice shooting "in holy days and other times convenient."[44]

The obligation to own and be skilled in the use of weapons does not, of course, imply that there were no restrictions upon the type of weapon owned or the manner of its use. A statute passed in 1541, for instance, cited the problem of "evil-disposed" persons who daily rode the King's highway armed with crossbows and handguns—weapons easily concealed beneath a cloak—and preyed upon Henry VIII's good subjects. The new law limited ownership of such questionable weapons to persons with incomes over one hundred pounds a year—citizens presumably more trustworthy—whereas those with less income were not to carry a crossbow bent, or a gun charged "except it be in time and service of war."[45] This law, often misinterpreted as restricting all ownership of firearms to the upper classes, merely limited the use of those weapons most common in crime. Indeed, the statute specifically states that it is permissible not only for gentlemen, but for yeomen, servingmen, the inhabitants of cities, boroughs, market towns, and those living outside of towns "to have and keep in every of their houses any such hand-gun or hand-guns, of the length of one whole yard."[46] The use of shot was forbidden, as was the brandishing of a firearm so as to terrify others, and the use of guns in hunting by unqualified persons.[47] It is notable that in cases in which crossbows, handguns, or other weapons were confiscated because of improper use, the courts were at pains to specify that the weapon in question was "noe muskett or such as is used for defence of the realm."[48]

The kingdom's Catholics formed an important exception to the tolerant attitude toward individual ownership of weapons. After the English Reformation they were regarded as potential subversives, and as such were liable to have their arms impounded. They were still assessed for a contribution of weapons for the militia, but were not permitted to keep these in their homes or to serve in the trained

43. *See* G. Sharp, *Tracts, Concerning the Antient and Only True Legal Means of National Defence, by a Free Militia* 12 (London 1782).

44. Id. at 13.

45. 33 Hen. 8, ch. 6 (1541).

46. Id.

47. 2 & 3 Edw. 6, ch. 14 (1549); 1 *Statute of Northampton*, 2 Edw. 3, ch. 3 (1328).

48. W. Fisher, *The Forest of Essex* 214–15 (1887).

bands.[49] They were allowed to keep personal weapons for their defense, although in times of extreme religious tension their homes might be searched and all weapons removed.[50] The various restrictions on Catholic subjects are significant for demonstrating that a particular group could be singled out for special arms controls, but they did not disadvantage a substantial proportion of the community, for, by the second half of the seventeenth century, Catholics seem to have comprised not more than one in fifty of the English population.[51]

For the great majority of Englishmen there was a natural tendency during tranquil years or in periods of government indifference to become blasé about military duties; complaints of widespread negligence echo through the years. In 1569, a jury presented a grievance "that there is to much bowling and to little shoting,"[52] and fifty years later, in the 1620's, Charles I had to resort to the closure of alehouses on Sundays to keep men at their shooting practice.[53] In 1621 Sir James Parrett complained of the lamentable decline in the numbers of armed retainers maintained by the wealthy. "Those gentlemen whose grandfathers kept 15 or 17 lusty serveing men and but one or 2 good silver boules to drinke in," he notes, had been succeeded by "grand-children fallen from Charity to impiety [who] keepe scarce 6 men and greate Cubards of plate to noe purpose." Worse still, Parrett reported that public complacency had reached the stage where "in two shyres [there was] not a barrell of Gunn-powder to bee seene."[54]

During the 1620's and 1630's there was a serious effort to modernize the militia, but the increased expenses and requirement of additional participation aroused popular resistance. Robert Ward, author of a military manual published just prior to the Civil War, was distressed at the failure of many bandsmen to appreciate

49. *See* C. Cruickshank, *supra* note 31, at 24.

50. This occurred, for example, just prior to the outbreak of the English Civil War in 1642. *See* Manning, *The Outbreak of the English Civil War*, in *The English Civil War and After* 1642-1688, 16 (R. Parry ed. 1970). Charles I empowered Catholics who had been disarmed to rearm in 1642. *See A Discourse of the Warr in Lancashire*, 62 *Chetham Soc.* 12-14 (1864); *Tracts Relating to Military Proceedings in Lancashire during the Civil War* 2 *Chetham Soc.* 38-40 (1844).

51. *See* J. Jones, *The Revolution of 1688 in England* 77 n. 2 (1972).

52. *See* G. Roberts, *The Social History of the People of the Southern Countries of England in Past Centuries* viii-ix (London 1856).

53. Id.

54. 6 *Commons Debates 1621*, 318 (1935).

how deeply every man is interested in it, for if they did, our yeomandrie would not be so proud and base to refuse to be taught, and to thinke it a shame to serve in their own armes, and to understand the use of them; were they but sensible, that there is not the worth of the peny in a Kingdome well secured without the due use of Armes.[55]

Two years later, with the commencement of frantic preparations for civil war and party struggles over public arsenals, the public's attitude had completely altered. Wails of despair were heard from city after city as the royal army confiscated public magazines and disarmed local residents. "The best of it is," a disarmed and distraught townsman of Nantwich wrote, "if we stay at home, we are now their slaves. Being naked they will have of us what they list, and do with us what they list."[56] Forewarned was forearmed, and from 1642 Englishmen learned to hide their firearms and to stockpile weapons.

Nearly twenty years later, this proliferation of privately owned weapons would be regarded by the restored monarch and his supporters as a menace. It was their efforts to control weapons that convinced Englishmen that the duty to keep arms must be recognized as a right. The events of the Restoration period, therefore, are of crucial importance.

ROYAL EFFORTS AT ARMS CONTROL

To grasp the magnitude of the problem that awaited Charles II upon his return in 1660 it is useful to get some idea of the numbers of firearms kept in private homes. In ordinary times each household was expected to possess arms suitable to its defense, but what was considered suitable? It is possible to obtain an indication of what was regarded as a minimal arsenal by examining the responses of those charged by Charles II's government with stockpiling weapons. For example, in 1660, in reply to allegations that he had concealed weapons, one Robert Hope pleaded that in the past he had, indeed, kept guns for neighbors, but at present he had only "one light rapire and a

55. R. Ward, *Animadversions of Warre, or a Militarie Magazine of the Truest Rules and Ablest Instruction for the Managing of Warre* 150 (London 1639).
56. *The Latest Remarkable Truths from Worcester, Chester, Salop* in *Tracts Relating to the Civil War in Cheshire, 1641-1659*, reprinted in 65 *Chetham Soc.* new series, appendix B, 238 (1909).

small birdinge gunne."[57] Hope obviously considered this small stock
beyond exception. In 1667, a Catholic subject informed an official
that he was "not so well furnished with arms" as formerly, having
only two fowling pieces and two swords.[58] Those not suspected of
disaffection had, or at least admitted to having, comparatively more
weapons. A Buckinghamshire squire kept for private use a pair of
pocket-pistols, another pair of "screwed" pistols, a suit of light
armour, a sword, and a carbine.[59] A country curate in the early eighteenth century, unqualified to hunt and certainly no soldier, nonetheless owned two guns and a blunderbuss.[60] While wealthier citizens
usually owned more weapons, firearms seem to have been well-dis-
tributed throughout the community.[61] Quarter Session records reveal
that men charged with illegal use of a gun for hunting were most
often poor laborers, small farmers, or craftsmen.[62] This is not surprising, since guns abounded during and after the Civil War[63] and seem
not to have been beyond the means of the poorer members of the
community. In 1664 a musket could be purchased for ten shillings,
a sum that would take only a little over a week for a foot soldier in
a militia band to accumulate from his wages, and a little more than
two weeks for a citizen to afford with the modest wages paid for
standing night watch.[64] Used weapons could probably be bought
even more cheaply.

The anxious period between Cromwell's death and the arrival of
Charles II was no ordinary time, and many citizens began to assemble

57. William Cavendish, Earl of Devonshire, *Correspondence as Lord Lieutenant of
Derbyshire from 1660 to 1666*, fol. 12, Additional MS. 34, 306, British Library, London.

58. LeFleming MS, *Historical Manuscripts Commission, 12th Report*, pt. 7, 44 (1890).

59. *See* 4 *Memoirs of the Verney Family* 167 (1899).

60. *See* E. Thompson, *Whigs and Hunters* 71 (1975).

61. Much evidence of the widespread ownership of firearms is scattered throughout the
personal and public documents of this period. The most accessible proof is found in the
county quarter session records, some of which are in print, which cite English men and
women from all walks of life for misuse of firearms. *See, e.g., Minutes of the Proceedings in
Quarter Sessions Held for the Parts of Kesteven in the County of Lincoln, 1674-1695*,
reprinted in *Lincoln Record Soc.* 25, 26 (1931); *Quarter Session Records for the County of
Somerset, 1607-77*, reprinted in *Somerset Rec. Soc.* 23-24, 28, 34 (1907-19); *Warwick
County Records: Quarter Session Order Books, 1625-90*, reprinted in *Warwick County
Council* 6, 7 (1935-53); *Worcestershire County Records Division 1: Documents Relating
to Quarter Sessions*, in *Worcestershire Hist. Soc. passim* (1899-1900).

62. *See* sources cited *supra* note 61.

63. *See, e.g.,* E. Thompson, *supra* note 60, at 71; J. Western, *The English Militia in the
Eighteenth Century* 4, 5, (1965); 4 *Memoirs of the Verney Family* 167 (1899); Letter from
West to Fleming, Jan. 27, 1667, LeFleming MS, *supra* note 58, part 7 at 44.

64. *See* 92 Clarendon MS 143, Bodleian Library, Oxford.

caches of weapons, some of which turned up years later in homes, churches, and guildhalls throughout the realm.[65] In 1660 a Bristol prebendary notified authorities that the stables of his predecessor's house were full of cannon balls and, even twenty years later, a Shropshire man and his son were found with a cache of some thirty muskets and other guns and admitted to having owned and burned fifty pikes.[66] City officials stockpiled weapons as well, and Northampton and Exeter were among those communities later embarrassed by the disclosure of stocks of arms hidden in public buildings. In 1661 the city of Exeter surrendered 937 musket barrels only to have another hoard of weapons discovered shortly afterwards in the guildhall.[67]

If his subjects and the republican army of some 60,000 men who waited to greet their new monarch were "armed to the teeth," Charles II found himself virtually unarmed. In the months before his arrival public arsenals had suffered such extensive embezzlements that the King's men were unable to find in them "firearms enough... to arm three thousand men."[68] The King was careful to conceal the fact "that it might not be known abroad or at home, in how ill a posture he was to defend himself against an enemy."[69]

It is scarcely surprising, therefore, that the wild rejoicing that greeted Charles II upon his return to London in May, 1660[70] failed to disguise from the King the precariousness of his position. He was painfully aware that many of these same citizens had gathered for his father's execution eleven years earlier and that despite its obedient professions Parliament had never been at "so high a pitch," for "the power which brought in may cast out, if the power and interest be not removed."[71] A proposal sent to his Court recommended the removal of that power. The anonymous author argued that no prince could be safe "where Lords and Commons are capable of revolt," hence it was essential to disarm the populace and establish a professional army. "It is not the splendor of precious stones and gold, that makes Ennemies submit," he observed, "but the force of armes. The

65. *See* J. Western, *supra* note 63, at 4–5.

66. *See* id.

67. *See* 2 Privy Council Registers 55, fol. 520 Public Record Office, London; J. Western, *supra* note 63, at 4.

68. E. Hyde, 2 *The Life of Edward Earl of Clarendon* 117 (Oxford 1827).

69. Id.

70. *See* 3 *Memoirs Illustrative of the Life and Writings of John Evelyn* 246 (deBeer ed. 1955).

71. *Two Treatises Addressed to the Duke of Buckingham*, fol. 79, 805 Lansdowne MS, British Library, London.

strength of title, and the bare interest of possession will not now defend, the stres will not lye there, the sword is the thing."[72]

Charles agreed completeiy. But to achieve a shift in the balance of armed might from the general populace to reliable supporters, he needed an obedient police establishment and a series of legal or quasi-legal enactments that would permit the disarmament of his opponents, among whom he counted members of the republican army.[73] In this latter task he had help from Parliament, whose members had learned a lasting distrust of all armies at the hands of Cromwell's soldiers. Parliament speedily devised a scheme to pay off regiments by lot, taking care to secure their weapons "for his Majesty's service."[74] While Charles was relieved to have this particular army disbanded, he was anxious to launch a permanent establishment of his own, and shortly after his return to England secretly began to plan for a force of eight thousand men. A loophole in the disbandment bill permitted the King to maintain as many soldiers as he liked, provided he paid for their upkeep.[75]

The militia was a knottier problem. Both King and Parliament were eager to re-establish the old trained-band system, but Parliament was reluctant to confront the numerous difficulties any militia act would have to resolve. A bill submitted at the time of the Restoration had been rejected because many representatives believed its provision for martial law might make Englishmen "wards of an army."[76] The struggle over control of the militia had driven the realm to war in 1642;[77] this would have to be clarified and a militia assessment set, which would involve an evaluation of every subject's property. Despite vigorous pressure from the Court, members of Parliament refused to approve even a temporary militia bill for more than a year.[78] The King, however, was unwilling to wait even a few days before establishing a militia, and was reported within ten days of his return to London to be "settling the militia in all counties by Lords Lieutenants."[79] His right to do so, even in the absence of a

---

72. Id.

73. *See* 8 *H. C. Jour.* 5–6; E. Hyde, *supra* note 68, vol. 1 at 335.

74. *See* 8 *H. C. Jour.* 142–43, 161, 163, 167.

75. *See* id. at 167.

76. 4 *Parl. Hist. Eng.*, 145 (London 1808–20).

77. *See* J. Kenyon, *The Stuart Constitution* 196 (1966); J. Malcolm, *Caesar's Due: Loyalty and King Charles 1642-1646*, 17–21 (1983).

78. A militia act was not passed until the spring of 1662, although a temporary measure was passed a year earlier. *See* 13 Car. 2, ch. 6 (1661); 13 & 14 Car 2, ch. 3 (1662).

79. *Historical Manuscripts Commission, 5th Report* 153 (1876).

valid militia act, does not seem to have been questioned. All candidates for the post of lord lieutenant were carefully screened and officers were instructed to select bandsmen of unblemished royalist complexion.[80] The resulting force should in no way be seen as representative of the people.

In conjunction with this purged and loyal militia, Charles created a new military body as large again as the militia for which there was far less precedent. It was composed of regiments of volunteers who met at their own, rather than the county's, expense and drilled alongside the regular militia.[81] Both the size of this private army and its longevity are impressive. It continued as an organized force well after the Militia Act of 1662 took effect, and at least through 1667, when the entire militia fell into decline.[82] Although the official task of the volunteers was "to assist on occasion," occasion occurred with great frequency, particularly when such controversial and unpopular duties as the disarmament of fellow subjects were involved.[83]

Charles II employed his militia and volunteer regiments differently from the manner in which militia had been used before the Civil War. In place of the occasional muster in time of peace and mobilization during an invasion or rebellion, his men were to be ready for action at an hour's warning.[84] Their main task was to police possible opponents of the regime. Their first order was to monitor the "motions" of persons of "suspected or knowne disaffection" and prevent their meeting or stockpiling weapons.[85] All arms and munitions in the pos-

---

80. *See* id.; *State Papers Domestic, Charles II*, S.P. 29, vol. 11, fols. 146-74 (August 1660), Public Record Office, London; *Instructions to Lords Lieutenants, Whitehall, 1660*, fol. 512, *Nicholas Papers*, Egerton MS 2542, British Library, London.

81. *See* sources quoted in Malcolm, *supra* note 28, at 8-9.

82. *See, e.g., Letter Book of Thomas Belasyse, Viscount Fauconberg Lord Lieutenant of the North Riding of Yorkshire, 1665-84*, fols. 20-22, Additional MS 41, 254, British Library, London, which reported that the militia had not been ordered to muster for several years. *See also* J. Western, *supra* note 63, at 48.

83. *See, e.g., Norfolk Lieutenancy Journal, 1661-1674*, fol. 29, Additional MS 11, 601, British Library, London; *Earl of Westmorland Letter Book, 1660-1665, Northamptonshire Militia*, fols. 25-26, 32, Additional MS 34, 222, British Library, London; Westmorland to Vane, July 21, 1662, *Clarendon State Papers*, vol. 77, fol. 66a, Bodleian Library, Oxford.

84. Additional MS 34, 306, *supra* note 57 at fol. 14. The King went still further and, for a time, required militia commanders to keep a portion of their men on duty at all times. This scheme proved unworkable. *See* Additional MS 34, 222, *supra* note 83, at fol. 43; Additional MS 34, 306, *supra* note 57 at fol. 44; D. Ogg, *England in the Reign of Charles II* 253 (1967).

85. *Instructions to Lords Lieutenants, Whitehall, 1660*, Egerton MS 2542, *supra* note 80, at fol. 512.

session of such suspects beyond what they might require for personal defense were to be confiscated.[86]

With this police apparatus in place the King turned to the royal proclamation, a device of uncertain legal status, to tighten arms control. In September, 1660, he issued a proclamation forbidding footmen to wear swords or to carry other weapons in London.[87] In December another proclamation expressed alarm that many "formerly cashiered Officers and Soldiers, and other dissolute and disaffected persons do daily resort to this City."[88] All such soldiers and others "that cannot give a good Account for their being here" were to leave London within two days and remain at least twenty miles away indefinitely.[89] At the same time the royal government launched a campaign to control firearms at the source. Gunsmiths were ordered to produce a record of all weapons they had manufactured over the past six months together with a list of their purchasers.[90] In future they were commanded to report every Saturday night to the ordnance office the number of guns made and sold that week.[91] Carriers throughout the kingdom were required to obtain a license if they wished to transport guns, and all importation of firearms was banned.[92]

Events then played into Charles' hands, for on January 6, 1661, an uprising by a handful of religious zealots provided the perfect excuse to crack down on all suspicious persons and to recruit his own standing army. Thomas Venner, a cooper, had led his small band of Fifth Monarchists into the streets of London to launch the prophesied fifth universal monarchy of the world. Although the group was soon

---

86. *See* Id.

87. "A Proclamation For Suppressing of disorderly and unseasonable Meetings, in Taverns and Tipling Houses, And also forbidding Footmen to wear Swords, or other Weapons, within London, Westminster, and their Liberties," Sept. 29, 1660, B.M. 669, fol. 26 (13), British Library, London. This and subsequent proclamations cited in this article are calendared in R. Steele, *Tudor and Stuart Proclamations* (1910). Originals can be found at the British Library and the citations will be to these.

88. "A Proclamation commanding all cashiered Soldiers and other Persons that cannot give a good account of their being here to depart out of the Cities of London and Westminster," Dec. 17, 1660, B.M. 669, fol. 26 (37), British Library, London.

89. *See* Id.

90. *See* Privy Council Registers, P.C. 2, vol. 55 (1660–1662), fol. 71, Public Record Office, London.

91. *See* Id.

92. *See* Privy Council Register, P.C. 2, vol. 55, fol. 187 (Sept. 4, 1661), fol. 189 (Mar. 29, 1661), Public Record Office, London.

subdued,[93] the Court administration blatantly exaggerated the threat they had posed. Speaking to Parliament six months later, the Lord Chancellor characterized the pitiful uprising as the "most desperate and prodigious Rebellion . . . that hath been heard of in any Age" and insisted the plot had "reached very far," and that "there hath not been a Week since that Time in which there hath not been Combinations and Conspiracies formed."[94]

The timing of the Fifth Monarchist uprising was especially opportune, for it occurred the very day the last regiments of the Commonwealth army were due to be disbanded. In response to this visible danger, these regiments were retained and twelve more companies were recruited to form the nucleus of a royalist army.[95] The militia and volunteers throughout the realm were ordered to carry out a general disarmament of everyone of doubtful loyalty.[96] By January 8, 1661, two days after the Venner uprising, Northamptonshire lieutenants reported that all men of known "evill Principles" had been disarmed and secured "so as we have not left them in any ways of power to attempt a breach of the peace."[97]

By the autumn of 1661, with his enemies in prison or at least disarmed and under surveillance, with strict monitoring of both production and distribution of weapons, and with a small standing army and a large police establishment, Charles was ready to disarm the most dangerous element of the population – the thousands of disbanded soldiers of the republican army. Acting by proclamation on November 28, he ordered all veterans of that army and all those who had ever fought against the Stuarts to depart from the capital within the week and to remain at least twenty miles away until June 24, 1662.[98] During their six months of banishment the veterans were warned not to "weare, use, or carry or ryde with any sword, pistoll or other

93. *See* Burrage, *The Fifth Monarchy Insurrections*, 25 *The English Hist. Rev.* 722–47 (1910).

94. 11 *H. L. Jour.* 243.

95. *See* 1 J. Clarke, *The Life of James the Second, King of England, etc. Collected out of Memoirs Writ of His Own Hand* 390–91 (London 1816).

96. *See* Additional MS 34, 222, *supra* note 83, at fol. 15.

97. Id. at fol. 17. The seizure of arms and persons was so zealously carried out – a Derbyshire man claimed his house had been searched nine times in one week – that in mid-January the King had to issue a proclamation to reassure outraged Londoners that the customary restrictions against unwarranted search and seizure were still in effect. *See* B.M. 669. Fol. 26 (49), British Library, London.

98. *See* B.M. 1851 ch. 8 (133), (134), (135), British Library, London.

armes or weapons."[99] Two days before this proclamation was due to expire, another appeared which extended the ban and the prohibition against carrying arms for an additional six months.[100] The scope of these bans was so broad it is doubtful whether the militia and volunteers were capable of enforcing them. Nevertheless, the proclamations had the practical effect of depriving a large portion of the male population of its legal right to carry firearms.

Charles II's program to police his realm and control its arms demonstrated skill, timing and resourcefulness. Arriving unarmed in 1660 to confront an armed nation and a veteran republican army, he succeeded within two years in molding the militia and volunteers into a police force of unprecedented size and effectiveness. All possible adversaries were watched, harassed, disarmed, and in many instances imprisoned. And the men of Oliver Cromwell's army, once the pride of England and terror of Europe, were flattered, disbanded, psychologically disarmed and then actually deprived of their right to carry weapons.

Endless alarms of plots provided an excuse to keep the militia on full alert, to impose restrictions on the production, importation, and movement of arms, and to create a standing royal army. Parliament cooperated in this policy by passing militia acts in 1661 and 1662 which reaffirmed the King's control of that force and specifically authorized bandsmen to continue the seizure of arms that Charles' militia had been undertaking on the King's orders alone.[101] Any two deputy lieutenants could initiate a search for, and seizure of, arms in the possession of any person whom they judged "dangerous to the Peace of the Kingdom.[102] This definition of those who could be disarmed was less precise than that of any former militia act, and permitted lower ranking officers great latitude in disarming their neighbours. Many members of Parliament were skeptical about the need for such broad powers or the actual danger of rebellion[103]

---

99. Id.

100. This proclamation was issued on June 22, 1662. There is no record of a proclamation for 1663, but on November 18, 1664, June 28, 1665, and June 10, 1670, the proclamation was reissued. *See* R. Steele, *supra* note 87.

101. 13 Car. 2, ch. 6 (1661); 14 Car. 2, ch. 3 (1662).

102. Id.

103. Sir John Dalrymple observed that in government rhetoric, "mobs were swelled into insurrections, and insurrections into concerted rebellion." 1 J. Dalrymple, *Memoirs of Great Britain and Ireland* 26 (2d ed. London 1771-73).

but were content to give the King what he wished as long as their own interests were protected.

PARLIAMENT'S CAMPAIGN TO REGULATE ARMS

The royalist aristocrats who flocked to welcome Charles II on his return had every reason to rejoice, for his restoration was theirs as well. After twenty years during which their prestige, pocketbooks, and property had been ravaged by war, revolution, and a republican government, they had an opportunity to restore, and even enhance, their former position. The royalists were to be so successful in this aim that their position by 1688 was described as like that of the barons of Henry III.[104] In Order to restore order they were prepared to concede much to the Crown, but jealously guarded the power of the sword and mastery of the localities. They administered local justice, staffed the militia, served in the royal volunteers, and sat in Parliament.[105] The King was dependent upon them to carry out his policies and shore up his regime.[106] For the sake of maintaining their political dominance they acquiesced in the King's program of arms control and, in the Militia Act of 1662, extended the power of militia officers to disarm suspects.[107] But the aristocracy went beyond approving the royal controls. On its own initiative, Parliament passed a game act in 1671, that, for the first time, deprived the vast majority of Englishmen of their legal right to keep weapons.[108]

Game acts had been passed from time to time and were ostensibly designed to protect wild game and to reserve the privilege of hunting for the wealthy. But disarming the rural population was sometimes an underlying motive for their passage.[109] Game acts of the sixteenth

104. *See* J. Plumb, *The Origins of Political Stability, England, 1675-1725*, 21–22 (1967).

105. *See* id. at 20–21. *See also* C. Hill, *Reformation to Industrial Revolution* 110–11 (1967).

106. The English monarch had only a small bureaucracy and was dependent upon the nobility and, in particular, the gentry throughout the realm to carry out numerous functions of government as unpaid volunteers. In reference to the militia itself, *see* J. Western, *supra* note 63, at 16–17, 63.

107. *See* 13 & 14 Car. 2, ch. 3 (1662–63).

108. *See* 22 & 23 Car. 2, ch. 25 (1671).

109. The very first game act to set a property qualification on the right to hunt appeared in 1389, eight years after that century's devastating peasant rebellion. The preamble to 13

and early seventeenth centuries had made possession of certain breeds of dog and of equipment specifically designed for hunting illegal for all those not qualified by income to hunt.[110] However, since guns were acknowledged to have legitimate purposes, they were confiscated only if used illegally.[111]

The Game Act passed in 1671 differed from its predecessors in several important respects. To begin with, it raised the property qualification necessary to hunt from forty pounds to one hundred pounds annual income from land, a figure so high that only the nobility, gentry, and a very few yeomen could qualify, whereas all those whose wealth came from a source other than land—such as lawyers and merchants—were forbidden to hunt.[112] This extraordinarily high qualification divided the rural population into two very unequal groups and placed the aristocracy at odds with everyone else. Many critics would later express astonishment that "the legislature of a mighty empire should require one hundred [pounds] a year to shoot a poor partridge, and only forty shillings to vote for a senator!"[113] The qualification to hunt was fifty times that required to vote.

Of more importance, this game law stated that all persons unqualified to hunt, at least ninety-five percent of the population, were not qualified to keep or bear arms. In the language of the statute: "[A]ll and every person and persons, not having Lands and Tenements of the clear yearly value of One hundred pounds . . . are . . . not allowed to have or keep for themselves, or any other person or persons, any Guns, Bowes, . . . or other Engines."[114] It was no longer necessary to

---

Ric. 2, ch. 13, "None shall hunt but they which have a sufficient living" read: "Item for as much as divers artificers, labourers, and servants, and grooms, keep greyhounds and other dogs, and on the holy days, when good christian people be at church, hearing divine service, they go hunting in parks, warrens, and connigries of lords and others, to the very great destruction of the same, and sometimes under such colour they make their assemblies, conferences, and conspiracies for to rise and disobey their allegiance." *See* J. Chitty, *A Treatise on the Game Laws, and on Fisheries* 368 (2d ed. London 1826); 4 W. Holdsworth, *A History of English Law* 505 (1924).

110. *See* 19 Hen. 7, ch. 11 (1495); 5 Eliz., ch. 21 (1562); 3 Jac. ch. 13 (1605); 7 Jac. ch. 13 (1609); 13 Car. 2, ch. 10 (1663).

111. *See* sources cited *supra* note 110.

112. The game act of 1609, in effect until the act of 1671, provided that those who had personal property of £400 were entitled to hunt. This permitted merchants and professionals whose wealth was not based on land to hunt. The act of 1671, however, abolished this category. Compare 7 Jac., ch. 13 (1609) with 22 & 23 Car. 2, ch. 25 (1671).

113. J. Chitty, *Observations on the Game Laws, with Proposed Alterations for the Protection and Increase of Game, and the Decrease of Crime* 180 (London 1816).

114. 22 & 23 Car. 2, ch. 25 (1671).

prove illegal use or intent; the mere possession of a firearm was illegal. The new act also empowered owners of forests and parks to appoint gamekeepers who, by warrant, could search the homes of persons suspected of harboring weapons, and confiscate any arms they found.[115]

There can be little doubt that it was the intention of the promoters of the Game Act to give themselves the power to disarm their tenants and neighbors and to bolster the position of their class with respect to that of the King and of the wealthy members of the middle class. They had begun to be suspicious of Charles II by 1671 and frightened by a spate of rural violence.[116] Hence, the provision of the Game Act that enabled country squires to set up their own gamekeeper-police and to confiscate the weapons of unqualified persons at their discretion must have seemed most desirable. As James II was to demonstrate, however, it was a statute with great potential for the Crown.

There appears to have been no overt protest or widespread alarm over the royalist program of arms control. While this may have been due to the conviction that such controls were necessary, it seems more likely that the real reason was that the program was not rigidly enforced during the reign of Charles II. It would have been difficult to carry out the proclamations against the carriage of arms by parliamentary veterans, and the militia's disarmament of suspicious persons was always selective.[117] The prosecution of the Game Act of 1671 was left to the gentry and from the scant evidence available appears to have been sporadic.

115. Id.
116. From at least 1665 there was growing distrust of the regime of Charles II. At the beginning of 1667, Samuel Pepys, a civil servant, found the royal court "[a] sad, vicious, negligent Court, and all sober men there fearful of the ruin of the whole kingdom this next year; from which good God, deliver us!" Cited by D. Witcombe, *Charles II and the Cavalier House of Commons, 1663-1674*, 55 (1966); *see* D. Ogg, *supra* note 84, at 313; 22 & 23 Car. 2, ch. 7 (1671).
117. Persons judged to be suspicious by the royal administration were those active in the parliamentary party during the Civil War and its aftermath, and those who belonged to the Protestant sects that refused to remain within the Church of England. The Quakers were prominent sufferers. *See, e.g.*, fol. 18, Additional MS 34, 306, British Library, London, *and* 13 Car. 2, ch. 6 (1661), a militia act which noted that since June 24, 1660, less than a month after Charles II's return, "divers persons suspected to be fanaticks, sectaries or disturbers of the peace have been assaulted, arrested detained or imprisoned, [by the militia] and divers arms have been seized and houses searched for arms." The militia had specifically been ordered to disarm all persons "notoriously knowne to be of ill principles or [who] have lately . . . by words or actions shewn any disaffection to his Majestie or his Government, or in any kind disturbed the publique peace." Additional MS 34, 222, *supra* note 83, at 15.

After 1680, however, Charles II began to use the Militia Act to disarm his Whig opponents, and in 1686, James II made use of both the Militia Act and the Game Act to disarm his Protestant subjects.[118] Englishmen were outraged and alarmed, and finally convinced of the need to guarantee their right to own weapons. After James II had fled from the kingdom, members of the Convention Parliament convened by William of Orange[119] felt it incumbent upon them to shore up the rights of English subjects before a new monarch ascended the throne. During their discussions the need for Protestant subjects to have arms came up repeatedly.[120] When the many rights considered most in need of reaffirmation had been pared to thirteen, and a Declaration of Rights presented to William and Mary, the seventh among the "true, ancient, and indubitable" rights proclamed was the right of all Protestants "to have Arms for their Defence suitable to their Conditions and as allowed by Law."[121]

118. *See* J. Western, *supra* note 63, at 48–51; *Calendar of State Papers Domestic, 1686–87,* 314 (1964), Public Records Office, London.

119. James II decided to abandon his kingdom in the face of a growing army of his subjects led by William of Orange and the desertion of his own army. The realm was thrown into a constitutional crisis, as no parliament was in session and only the king could legally summon a parliament. William consulted with the nobility and former members of the Commons and on their advice summoned a "Convention" Parliament to meet to resolve the kingdom's succession. He promised to abide by its decision. A "convention" parliament had been called in 1659 by George Monck, again in the absence of a reigning monarch, and it was this body that invited Charles II to return as king. Unlike its predecessor, however, the Convention Parliament of 1688 was determined to ensure the rights of subjects and to prevent any infringement by future monarchs. *See infra* sources cited in n.120.

120. We have only sketchy records remaining of the debates of the Convention Parliament. The best of these in print are the notes made by John Somers, chairman of the committee that drafted the English Bill of Rights reprinted in 2 *Miscellaneous State Papers from 1501 to 1726 passim* & esp. 407–18 (London 1778). Somers's notes are punctuated with the angry comments of members at the use of the Militia Act in particular to disarm law-abiding citizens. Sir John Maynard was furious that "an Act of Parliament was made to disarm all Englishmen, whom the Lieutenant should suspect, by day or night, by force or otherwise" and branded it "an abominable thing to disarm a nation, to set up a standing army." Id. at 407. Another member argued that there was "no safety but the consent of the nation – the constitution being limited, there is a good foundation for defensive arms – It has given us right to demand full and ample security." Id. at 410. *See also* L. Schwoerer, *The Declaration of Rights, 1689* (1981), a recent study of the Convention Parliament.

121. 1 W. & M., Sess. 2, ch. 2, (1689). The English Declaration of Rights drawn up by the Convention Parliament was approved by the first parliament summoned by William and Mary and incorporated with the legislation recognizing them as king and queen. It was thereafter known as the English Bill of Rights.

THE ENGLISH BILL OF RIGHTS AND
THE PRESENT CONTROVERSY

As an article of the English Bill of Rights, the right to have arms was part and parcel of that bundle of rights and privileges that Englishmen carried with them to America and which they later fought to preserve. Much of the present confusion over the Second Amendment to the United States Constitution stems from the failure to understand the meaning or to determine the effect of the English right — problems that can both be finally solved by a careful reading of the historic record.

Roy Weatherup is one of several authors who fail in the attempt to fix the meaning of the English right by slipping into the common trap of imposing a modern controversy upon past events.[122] Weatherup is so caught up in the debate over the reference to the militia in the Second Amendment and the attendant quarrel over whether that amendment conveys a collective or an individual right[123] that he totally ignores the fact that the English right to arms makes no mention whatsoever of the militia. Undeterred, Weatherup insists that the English right conveyed "no recognition of any personal right to bear arms on the part of subjects generally" but merely granted members of the militia the right to "keep and bear arms in accordance with their militia duties.[124] Such an interpretation ignores the clear language of the English right and disregards the accompanying historic record. The militia was certainly of grave concern to members of the Convention Parliament, but this was not because members of the militia had been disarmed. Quite the contrary. The militia was a problem because the Militia Act of 1662 had permitted its officers wide latitude to disarm *law-abiding citizens.* The correction of this abuse and many others that preoccupied the members required new legislation which, they reluctantly admitted, in the present emergency they did not have the leisure to draft.[125] Instead, they decided to

122. *See* Weatherup, *supra* note 5.
123. *See* id., at 962–64.
124. *See* Id., at 973–74.
125. *Anonymous Account of the Convention Proceedings, 1688,* fol. 10, Rawlinson MS D1079, Bodleian Library, Oxford. The committee was instructed "to distinguish such of the . . . heads (of grievances) as are introductory of new laws, from those that are declaratory of ancient rights." The revised version of their report can be found in 10 *H. C. Jour. 1688-93,* 21-22.

concentrate their energies upon reaffirming those ancient rights most recently imperiled through a declaration of rights they hoped would be "like a new magna carta."[126] Legislative reform was meant to follow when time allowed.

Weatherup is somewhat nearer the mark in his assertion that a collective right was intended.[127] A collective right to arms was discussed by the Convention, but it was rejected in favor of an individual right alone. The Whig members of the Convention had pressed hard for a collective as well as an individual right[128] and the first version of the arms article adhered to their view that the public should be armed to protect their rights:

> It is necessary for the publick Safety, that the Subjects which are Protestants, should provide and keep Arms for their common Defence. And that the Arms which have been seized, and taken from them, be restored.[129]

The second version of this article retreated somewhat from this stance. It stated:

> That the Subjects, which are Protestants, may provide and keep Arms, for their common Defence.[130]

All mention of arms being "necessary for the publick Safety" was omitted although this version still asserts that arms could be kept for "common" defense; instead of the exhortation that citizens "should" provide and keep arms, the permissive "may" is used.

It was the third, and final version, however, that constituted a complete retreat from any collective right to have arms. It read:

> That the Subjects which are Protestants may have Arms for their Defence suitable to their Conditions, and as allowed by Law.[131]

The reference to a need for arms for "their common Defence" was replaced by the right to keep arms for "their Defence," and two

---

126. *See* 2 G. Burnet, *Bishop Burnet's History of His Own Time* 522 (London 1840).

127. *See* Weatherup, *supra* note 5, at 974.

128. The Whigs had sizable majorities on the committees which drafted the Declaration of Rights, and those most outspoken in favor of a general possession of arms for the purpose of resisting tyranny were Whigs. *See* L. Schwoerer, *supra* note 120, at 152; and members quoted in J. Somers, *supra* note 120, at 107–18, with their affiliation as described by Schwoerer. *See also* D. Lacey, *Dissent and Parliamentary Politics in England, 1661–1689*, 382–83, 422–23 (1969).

129. Rawlinson MS D1079, *supra* note 125, at fol. 8.

130. 10 *H. C. Jour.*, 1688–93, 21–22.

131. 1 W. & M., Sess, 2, ch. 2 (1689).

modifying clauses were added at the last moment at the instigation of the cautious House of Lords.

In the opinion of a modern British scholar, the retreat from a collective to an exclusively individual right to have arms "emasculated" the article: "The original wording implied that everyone had a duty to be ready to appear in arms whenever the state was threatened. The revised wording suggested only that it was lawful to keep a blunderbuss to repel burglars."[132] The Whigs continued to press for the notion that it was necessary for the safety of the constitution that subjects be armed and, in the course of the eighteenth century, Blackstone among others reinterpreted the English right to arms to include that position.[133] At the time it was drafted, however, the English right to have arms was solely an individual right. By the outbreak of the American Revolution it had been transformed into both an individual and a collective right.

The actual impact of the English right as stated in the new Bill of Rights is far more difficult to determine than its meaning. Modern critics have argued that the limitation to Protestants of the right to have arms and the qualifying clauses further restricting lawful possession by Protestants to those weapons "suitable to their conditions" and "as allowed by Law" made this right so exclusive and uncertain as to be "more nominal than real."[134] But if, at first glance, the article's exclusiveness appears striking, much hinges on how these clauses, added at the last moment, were in fact interpreted. There is no doubt that "as allowed by law" included those sixteenth century laws which placed certain restrictions on the type of arms subjects could own, but did not deprive Protestant subjects of their right to have firearms.[135] However, the Game Act of 1671 was in direct conflict with that right. Since the Convention Parliament had agreed to restate rights but leave legislative reform for the future,[136]

---

132. J. Western, *Monarchy and Revolution: The English State in the 1680's*, 339 (1972).

133. For examples of Whig efforts to incorporate into legislation their view that the citizenry must be armed to prevent tyranny, see 10 *H.C. Jour.* 621; 5 *Parl. Hist., Eng. supra* note 76, at 344. N. Luttrell, *The Parliamentary Diary of Narcissus Luttrell, 1691-1693*, 444 (H. Horwitz ed. 1972); *see also* 2 W. Blackstone, *Commentaries* 441 (E. Christian ed. London 1793-95) (editor's comment); and 1 W. Blackstone, *supra* note 2, at 143-44.

134. G. Newton & F. Zimring, *supra* note 5, at 255 (quoting from 2 J. Story, *Commentaries on the Constitution* 678 (3d ed. 1858)).

135. These acts were: 33 Henry 8, ch. 6 (1541) and 2 & 3 Edw. 6, ch. 14 (1549). For evidence of their continued enforcement, see sources cited *supra* note 61 (relating to quarter session records); G. Sharp, *supra* note 43, at 17-18; Rex v. Alsop, 4 Mod. Rep. 51 (K.B. 1691).

136. *See supra* notes 125-26 & accompanying text.

it is not surprising that the right to have arms contradicted laws still on the statute books. The best means of determining the extent to which the qualifying clauses limited ownership of firearms is to examine subsequent legislation and those legal cases that decided permissible use.

Early in the reign of William and Mary, Parliament approved two acts affecting arms ownership: "An Act for the better securing the Government by disarming Papists and reputed Papists" in 1689,[137] and, in 1692, "An Act for the more easie Discovery and Conviction of such as shall Destroy the Game of this Kingdom."[138] A militia act was also approved by the House of Commons in July 1689, but failed to pass the House of Lords.[139] The first of these acts, the act for disarming Catholics, was meant to secure the realm against a rising on behalf of the deposed Catholic king, James II. It prohibited Catholics from keeping all "Arms, Weapons, Gunpowder, or Ammunition," but did permit a Catholic to retain those weapons that local justices at Quarter Sessions thought necessary "for the Defence of his House or Person."[140] This exception is especially significant, as it demonstrates that even when there were fears of religious war, Catholic Englishmen were permitted the means to defend themselves and their households; they were merely forbidden to stockpile arms. The need for individual self-defense was conceded to have precedence over other considerations. Furthermore, while the Bill of Rights excluded Catholics from any absolute right to have arms, members of that faith were, in practice, accorded the privilege of retaining some weapons.

In 1692 Parliament passed a game statute designed to supersede all previous game acts.[141] This act incorporated many articles of the Game Act of 1671, but altered that act's ban on ownership of firearms by persons unqualified to hunt by omitting all mention of guns

---

137. 1 W. & M., ch. 15 (1689).

138. 4 & 5 W. & M., ch. 23 (1692).

139. In July 1689, members of the House of Commons passed a measure "for ordering the Forces in the several Counties of this Kingdom," which was designed to make the militia more efficient, to strengthen local control over it, and to eliminate its powers to search for and seize weapons of so-called suspects. The measure ran into opposition in the House of Lords and was lost when the King dissolved Parliament. *See* J. Western, *supra* note 132, at 340 n. 1, 343; J. Western, *supra* note 63, at 85–89; 5 *Parl. Hist. Eng., supra* note 76, at 344.

140. 1 W. & M. ch. 15 (1689).

141. 4 & 5 W. & M., ch. 23 (1692).

from the list of forbidden devices. Whereas the Game Act of 1671 stated that persons not qualified to hunt were "not allowed to have or keep for themselves, or any other person or persons, any Guns, Bowes, Greyhounds . . . or other Engines," [142] the new act prohibited such persons from keeping and using "any bows, greyhounds . . . or any other instruments for destruction of . . . game." [143] According to the rule of law of that era, a later statute expressed in terms contrary to those of a former statute takes away the force of the first statute even without express negative words. [144] Of course, it was possible that guns could be included among "other instruments for destruction of . . . game." All evidence, however, points to the intentional exclusion of firearms from the terms of the statute.

The House of Commons journals reveal the sensitivity of members to the new act's potential for disarming Englishmen. At the time of the bill's third reading, an engrossed clause, offered as a rider, stated that "any Protestant may keep a Musquet in his House, notwithstanding this or any other Act." [145] This was a very sweeping proposal, as it made no allowance for factors such as the sanity or previous criminality of the gun owner, and would, moreover, have purportedly bound future parliaments—something no session was really at liberty to do. [146] On the question of whether this rider should have a second reading, there was sufficient controversy to compel a division. The proposal lost by sixty-five votes to one hundred sixty-nine. [147] Despite its failure to become part of the new game act, it is of interest for two reasons: first, because it indicated the awareness of members that a game act could jeopardize the right of Protestants to have arms; second, because although it was an extreme proposal, it was not dismissed out of hand but occasioned a rare division in the House of Commons.

There is a frustrating lack of commentary or cases bearing on the issue of whether the omission of guns from the list of proscribed devices in the Game Act of 1692 should be regarded as legalizing

---

142. 22 Car. 2, ch. 25 (1671).
143. 4 & 5 W. & M., *supra* note 141.
144. H. Rolle, *Reports* 91 (London 1675).
145. 10 *H. C. Jour.* 824.
146. A future parliament was always at liberty to amend a statute or to repeal it. During the debate on this rider an opponent of the measure argued that it "savours of the politics to arm the mob, which I think is not very safe for any government." *See* N. Luttrell, *supra* note 133, at 444. The Whig view expressed later by Blackstone did not yet prevail.
147. 10 *H. C. Jour.* 824.

their ownership, or whether firearms ought to be included under "any other engine." But the fact that there is no recorded instance of anyone charged under the new act for mere possession of a firearm, coupled with decisions from cases under a later law with similar language,[148] lends weight to the conclusion that guns were meant to be excluded from the terms of the statute.

In reference to the successor to the Game Act of 1692, "An act for the better preservation of the game" passed in 1706,[149] Joseph Chitty, an expert on game law, notes: "We find that guns which were expressly mentioned in the former acts were purposely omitted in this because it might be attended with great inconvenience to render the mere possession of a gun *prima facie* evidence of its being kept for an unlawful purpose."[150] Two cases brought under that game act dealt specifically with the question of the inclusion of firearms under prohibited devices. Perhaps the most important of these was *Rex* v. *Gardner*,[151] in which the defendant had been convicted by a justice of the peace for keeping a gun in alleged violation of the game act. There was no evidence that the gun in question had been wrongfully used. But it was argued that a gun was mentioned in the 1671 Game Act[152] and considered there as an engine, and that the use of the general words "other engines" in the 1706 act should be taken to include a gun.[153] It was objected "that a gun is not mentioned in the statute [of 1706], and though there may be many things for the bare keeping of which a man may be convicted, yet they are only such as can only be used for destruction of the game, whereas a gun is necessary for defence of a house, or for a farmer to shoot crows."[154]

---

148. *See* 5 Ann, ch. 14 (1706). This statute levied a fine against any person or persons "not qualified by the laws of this realm so to do" who "shall keep or use any greyhounds, setting dogs . . . or any other engines to kill and destroy the game." Id.

The Devonshire Quarter Sessions clearly regarded the possession of firearms as legal after passage of the 1692 Game Act, for in 1704 it explained that while the houses of unqualified persons could be searched for dogs, nets and other "engines," no Protestant was to be deprived of his gun. *See* A.H.A. Hamilton, *Quarter Sessions from Queen Elizabeth to Queen Ann*, 289 (1878).

149. 5 Ann, ch. 14 (1706).

150. J. Chitty, *supra* note 109, at 83.

151. Rex v. Gardner, Strange, 2 *Reports* 1098, 93 Eng. Rep. 1056 (K.B. 1739); 1 R. Burn, *supra* note 29, at 442–43.

152. *See supra* text accompanying note 114.

153. Rex v. Gardner, 93 Eng. Rep. at 1056.

154. Id.

The court concluded that "a gun differs from nets and dogs, which can only be kept for an ill purpose, and therefore this conviction must be quashed."[155] The justices reasoned:

[I]f the statute is to be construed so largely, as to extend to the bare having of any instrument, that may possibly be used in destroying game, it will be attended with very great inconvenience; there being scarce any, tho' ever so useful, but what may be applied to that purpose. And tho' a gun may be used in destroying game, and when it is so, doth then fall within the words of the act; yet as it is an instrument proper, and frequently necessary to be kept and used for other purposes, as the killing of noxious vermin, and the like, it is not the having a gun, without applying it in the destruction of game, that is prohibited by the act.[156]

Indeed, Lord Macclesfield commented in this regard that he himself was in the House of Commons when that game act was drafted and personally objected to the insertion of the word gun therein "because it might be attended with great inconvenience."[157]

In *Wingfield* v. *Stratford & Osman*,[158] appellant challenged his conviction under the game act and the confiscation of his gun and dog, the dog being a setting dog, the gun allegedly "an engine" for killing of game. The prosecution's plea was held faulty because it amounted to a general issue,[159] but the court pointed out that it would have held for appellant in any case as the prosecution had not alleged that the gun had been used for killing game:

It is not to be imagined, that it was the Intention of the Legislature, in making the 5 Ann.c.14 to disarm all the People of England. As Greyhounds, setting Dogs . . . are expressly mentioned in that Statute, it is never necessary to alledge, that any of these have been used for killing or destroying the Game; and the rather, as they can scarcely be kept for any other Purpose than to kill or destroy the Game. But as Guns are not expressly mentioned in that Statute, and as a Gun may be kept for the Defence of a Man's House, and for divers other lawful Purposes, it was necessary to alledge, in order to its being

155. Id.
156. Id.
157. 1 R. Burn, *supra* note 29, at 443. Lord Macclesfield sat on an earlier case, King. v. King, 3 Geo. 2, in which the question of whether guns were intentionally omitted from the statute was raised but never determined. This is noted in the *Gardner* decision, along with his comments. *See* 93 Eng. Rep. at 1056.
158. Wingfield v. Stratford & Osman, Sayer, *Reports* 15–17, 96 Eng. Rep. 787 (K.B. 1752).
159. Id. at 16, 96 Eng. Rep. at 787.

comprehended within the Meaning of the Words "any other Engines to kill the Game", that the Gun had been used for killing the Game.[160]

By the middle of the eighteenth century, therefore, English courts could not "imagine" that Parliament intended to disarm the people of England.

In 1775, the American colonists fought for what they regarded as the rights of Englishmen.[161] Fortunately, there is ample contemporary evidence defining exactly what the rights of Englishmen were at that time in respect to the keeping and bearing of arms. In 1782, Granville Sharp, an English supporter of the American cause, wrote that no Englishman "can be truly Loyal" who opposed the principles of English law whereby the people are required to have "arms of defence and peace, for mutual as well as private defence."[162] He argued that the laws of England "always required the people to be armed, and not only to be *armed*, but to be *expert in arms*."[163] Edward Christian noted in his edition of Blackstone's *Commentaries* published in 1793 that "ever since the modern practice of killing game with a gun had prevailed, everyone is at liberty to keep or carry a gun, if he does not use it for the destruction of game.[164] But the most definitive opinion on the rights of Englishmen "to bear arms, and to instruct themselves in the use of them" came from the Recorder of London, the chief legal adviser to the mayor and council, in 1780. He stated:

> The right of his majesty's Protestant subjects, to have arms for their own defence, and to use them for lawful purposes, is most clear and undeniable. It seems, indeed, to be considered, by the ancient laws of this kingdom, not only as a *right*, but as a *duty*; for all the subjects of the realm, who are able to bear arms, are bound to be ready, at all times, to assist the sheriff, and other civil magistrates, in the execution of the laws and the preservation of the public peace. And that right, which every Protestant most unquestionably possesses, *individually, may*, and in many cases *must*, be exercised collectively,

160. Id. (Lee, C.J., concurring).

161. For extensive treatment of this subject *see* B. Bailyn, *supra* note 26. Bailyn writes, for example: "For the primary goal of the American Revolution, which transformed American life and introduced a new era in human history, was not the overthrow or even the alteration of the existing social order but the preservation of political liberty threatened by the apparent corruption of the [English] constitution, and the establishment in principle of the existing conditions of liberty." Id. at 19.

162. G. Sharp, *supra* note 43, at 27.

163. Id. at 18.

164. 2 W. Blackstone, *Commentaries* 411 (E. Christian ed. 1793–95).

is likewise a point which I conceive to be most clearly established by the authority of judicial decisions and ancient acts of parliament, as well as by reason and common sense.[165]

CONCLUSION

Prior to the Restoration, Englishmen had the obligation to be armed for the public defense and the privilege of keeping arms for their personal defense. During the reigns of Charles II and James II, from 1660 to 1688, the Court and Parliament passed laws and issued proclamations that severely restricted the rights of the people to possess firearms, and followed a policy designed to control production and distribution of weapons. The English Bill of Rights of 1689, however, not only reasserted, but guaranteed, the right of Protestant subjects to be armed. The qualifying clauses of the Bill that appear to limit arms ownership were, in fact, interpreted in a way that permitted Catholics to have personal weapons and allowed Protestants, regardless of their social and economic station, to own firearms. The ancillary clause "as allowed by Law" merely limited the type of weapon that could be legally owned to a full-length firearm, enforced the ban on shot, and permitted legal definition of appropriate use. The right of Englishmen to have arms was a very real and an individual right. For all able-bodied men there was also the civic duty to bear arms in the militia. The twin concepts of a people armed and an armed militia were linked, but not inseparably.

If one applies English rights and practice to the construction of the Second Amendment to the United States Constitution, it is clear that the amendment's first clause is an amplifying rather than a qualifying clause and that a general rather than a select militia was intended. In fact, every American colony formed a militia that, like its English model, comprised all able-bodied male citizens.[166] This continued to be the practice when the young republic passed its first uniform militia act under its new constitution in 1792.[167] That act stipulated that "each and every free able-bodied white male citizen" between the ages of 18 and 45 "shall severally and respectively be enrolled in the

165. W. Blizard, *Desultory Reflections on Police* 59–60 (London 1785) (emphasis in original).

166. *See supra* notes 24–25 & accompanying text.

167. Act of May 8, 1792, 2d Cong., 1st Sess., ch. 33.

militia." Such a militia implied a people armed and trained to arms. The American government could rely upon its population being armed, for along with the belief in a citizen militia Americans had inherited the English conviction that every citizen was entitled to have arms for personal defense. Indeed, Americans had been unfettered by the English restrictions on the arms Catholics could own, on who might own a handgun, or on who could hunt game. Their right to have arms lacked those few restraints that clung to the English right. Of chief importance, however, were not these restraints, but that the English right was, at base, an individual right, albeit in the course of the eighteenth century it had grafted onto it the Whig notion that the citizenry must be armed against the time when, in Blackstone's words, "the sanctions of society and laws are found insufficient to restrain the violence of oppression."[168] It was these two beliefs that the Second Amendment of the American Bill of Rights, reflecting the tradition of the English Bill of Rights, was attempting to preserve, a right intended to protect government by and for the people.

168. 1 W. Blackstone, *Commentaries, supra* note 2, 143–44.

Chapter 15
WEAPONS, TECHNOLOGY, AND LEGITIMACY
The Second Amendment in Global Perspective

William Marina

The hope of the future does not rest, as commonly believed, in winning the peoples of the "buffer fringe" to one superpower or the other, but rather in the invention of new weapons and new tactics that will be so cheap to obtain and so easy to use that they will increase the effectiveness of guerrilla warfare so greatly that the employment of our present weapons of mass destruction will become futile and, on this basis, there can be a revival of democracy and of political decentralization in all three parts of the world.[1]

Carroll Quigley, 1961

INTRODUCTION

Today many Americans perceive the increase in violence in our society and attribute it to the general availability of firearms, especially handguns. They further believe that handgun prohibition would effectively deal with the problem. These beliefs are called into question by much of the data in this volume. Moreover, even conceding that firearms prohibitions could result in violence reduction, there would remain the question of constitutionality within the Second Amendment. Regardless of whether the courts today would honor

1. Carroll Quigley, *The Evolution of Civilization: An Introduction to Historical Analysis* (New York: Macmillan, 1961), p. 258.

the Founders' belief in a personal right to arms, the philosophical and public policy issues underlying that belief remain. Might it not still be the case that the costs of widespread firearms availability must be endured if we are to maintain the conditions necessary to preserve a free society?

To understand the reasoning of those who framed the Second Amendment, we need to comprehend their view of social behavior, based upon their distinctive interpretation of history and their own political experience. In essence they believed the lesson taught by both history and experience was that an armed citizenry is both necessary against the perennial threat of tyrannical government, and the ultimate protection against foreign invasion.

Were the authors of the Second Amendment wrong in their deep suspicion of political power or in their view of history and human behavior? In the wake of Vietnam and Watergate should we reject out of hand the notion that those who hold political power in the United States are susceptible to its abuse like the rulers of the nations or civilizations studied by the Founding Fathers? If so, how are today's politicians different? But of course many who are little less suspicious of government (or governors) than were the Founding Fathers nevertheless reject the notion that private possession of arms represents any meaningful check, at least today. A populace armed with only handguns and rifles cannot, they argue, be expected to stand up to a modern army with tanks, planes, and the other formidable equipment of war today.[2]

The purpose of this essay is to demonstrate that technology, correctly understood, has not outmoded the basic insights of those who framed the Second Amendment's guarantee of the people's right to hold and bear arms. In fact, recent history has corroborated the validity of these insights. Much of violence today, in America and elsewhere, actually stems not from firearms but rather from a legitimacy crisis in the state itself. At the same time, certain objective conditions make government control of goods—from weapons to marijuana—virtually impossible nationally, let alone internationally. These considerations, which entail far-reaching historical and global perspectives, severely undercut the case for prohibition of firearms.

---

2. Leroy D. Clark, "Reducing Firearms Availability: Constitutional Impediments to Effective Legislation and an Agenda for Research," Chapter 1 in this volume.

THE REVOLUTIONARY POTENTIAL
OF WEAPONS TECHNOLOGY

Technology is a *technique* rather than any specific *object* such as a tank or airplane. In terms of general systems theory, technology is a process rather than a structure. In military medicine, for example, the application of the technique of "triage" (making quick, difficult decisions about allocating medical treatment to those who can most benefit from it) in Korea, and later in Vietnam, probably saved more lives than did any particular new medicine or medical device.[3] Revolutionary warfare, much emphasized in the last few years but dating back to ancient times, is better regarded as a technique than as the use of any particular weapon. When technology is viewed in this perspective, we see that it clearly is not a new factor in history nor one that arose only with the Industrial Revolution.[4] Those with political power seek to control any technology perceived as a threat to their dominance.

For example, recently there has been considerable discussion about why China, which was far more technologically advanced than the West in the early years of the modern era, fell behind and did not experience an industrial revolution. The destabilizing potential of technology may provide the answer. The mandarin leadership perceived that any wide application of such technology—and that certainly included weapon technology—would threaten the established system.[5] Chinese science, at least at the theoretical level, was seldom, if at all, very far behind the West. But scientific knowledge was never allowed to develop into a technology whose wide application might benefit the entire population.[6]

In short, if man as a tool maker very early emphasized weaponry, as has been suggested by some ethologists, then those at the top of a

3. Triage is simply a specific instance of a decisionmaking technique for allocating time or other scarce resources.

4. Technology as technique is evident in the original French title of Jacques Ellul's *The Technological Society* (New York: Knopf, 1964), which is *L Technique.*

5. Carlo M. Cipolla, *Guns and Sails in the Early Phase of European Expansion, 1400–1700* (London: Collins, 1965), p. 117.

6. Immanuel Wallerstein, *The Modern World-System: Capitalist Agriculture and the Origins of the European World-Economy in the Sixteenth Century* (New York: Academic Press, 1974), p. 61.

social order would understand that various technologies of weaponry pose a threat to the status quo.[7]

THE FLEXIBILITY OF SHOCK VERSUS MISSILE WEAPONS

The discussion of numerous kinds of weapons has tended to obscure the fundamental dichotomy into which all weapons can be divided. As Carroll Quigley emphasized, the two categories are "shock" weapons and "missile" weapons. While it might seem curious, for example, to suggest that a slingshot is more like a handgun or an ICBM than it is to a stick or billy club, there is a sense in which this is, indeed, the case.[8] Shock weapons can be used only at close range. As such, they tend to offer flexibility in inflicting injury and therefore offer flexibility in social control. Missile weapons, on the other hand, employ a velocity that enables them to be used over distance. Aim cannot be perfectly controlled over distance, however. Once launched, a missile may kill, thereby giving less flexibility as a means of social control. The above has long been understood by police in Great Britain, who, if armed at all, have preferred shock weapons and only reluctantly have employed missile weaponry.[9]

THE VARYING TYPES AND PARAMETERS OF THE ARMED FORCES

This preliminary analysis brings us to the role of the military in history and its relationship to the question of weapons technology and control. In the United States, recent discussion about the role of the military has narrowly focused around the question of a voluntary versus a conscripted army. Many people with libertarian or anti-military leanings have tended to oppose restoring the draft because of its obvious impingement upon freedom of choice. Despite the

---

7. Carroll Quigley, "Weapons Systems and Political Stability: A History." (Unpublished manuscript, Quigley Papers, Georgetown University, Washington, D.C.).

8. Quigley, "Weapons Systems."

9. John Alderson, *Policing Freedom: A Commentary on the Dilemmas of Policing in Western Democracies* (Plymouth: MacDonald and Evans, 1979), p. 25.

importance of individual choice, more is at issue than this simple dichotomy.

THE HISTORICAL CONTEXT: COUNTRY AND REPUBLICAN IDEOLOGY

Citizen-Militias versus Standing Armies

Those who pressed for the Second Amendment transcended the previously mentioned dichotomy. It was not that they valued freedom of choice less, but rather that history suggested to them a different set of issues. In the eighteenth century context of the framing of the Second Amendment, those who advocated what some have called the "Country" as opposed to "Court" ideology opposed conscripted standing armies. Yet they were aware that, historically, in the republics of the ancient world, the shift from conscripted armies to volunteers as a source of manpower was accompanied by a corresponding shift toward empire. In the process, citizens had eventually lost their sense of liberty.[10] There was, however, a third alternative – the citizen-militia. Analogous to Thomas Paine's differentiation in *Common Sense* between society, or the people, and government, or the state, was the concept of the citizen-militia. Here the authority emanated from the people upward, versus the standing army, where authority rested above with the state. Participation in the people's militia was thus an integral aspect of citizenship in what was perceived as a republican culture.[11]

The realization that historically volunteer armies become instruments of imperialism precludes reducing the issue to a narrow debate over volunteerism versus conscription. As a society becomes more affluent, the wealthy seek to avoid conscription by buying themselves out of military service. Volunteerism accommodates this. A citizen-militia is amateur-oriented service (the conscript is also an amateur in the sense that he is there for a limited time). Volunteer

10. The importance of the Anglo-American "Country" ideology is discussed below. See especially Lois Schwoerer, *"No Standing Armies!" The Antiarmy Ideology in Seventeenth Century England* (Baltimore: Johns Hopkins University Press, 1974).

11. The changing republican world view from the Renaissance in Italy through England and America is discussed in J. G. A. Pocock, *The Machiavellian Moment: Florentine Political Thought and the Atlantic Republican Tradition* (Princeton: Princeton University Press, 1975).

armies, when they assume imperial responsibilities, quickly become professionals with a career orientation.

To the differences arising from *source* and *composition* of armed forces may be added the importance of *structure*. The grass-roots orientation of the citizen-militia derives from society rather than the state. Forces deriving from the state can be either decentralized or centralized, but the tendency of imperial structure is toward centralization.

Finally, there is the question of *function*: how is the armed force to be utilized? Citizen-militia forces are by their source, composition, and structure local defense forces. George Washington, who complained about the inefficiency of the citizen-militia, insisted on using these forces for imperial ventures, such as capturing the Ohio Valley in the war with France or taking Canada during the American War for Independence. He experienced first-hand the complaints by conscripts who, having lost their liberty, had little stomach for long-range imperial adventure.[12] As every republic in history has discovered, there is a drawback in using volunteers for imperial purposes: those who have to do the bleeding and dying to extend or defend the empire demand that those who have the courage to defend the empire ought also to run it.

The four factors of armed forces mentioned above—source, composition, structure, and function—have to be related to changes in the technology of weaponry and the way in which, especially in the short run, a new technology may facilitate power by a minority in control of the state. Analysis of these factors exhibits the historical relationships among weapons, technology, and legitimacy.[13]

China

Technology in general, and military technology in particular, played an important role in the ebb and flow of Chinese civilization. China

---

12. Murray N. Rothbard, *"Salutary Neglect": The American Colonies in the First Half of the 18th Century*, Vol. 2 of *Conceived in Liberty* (New Rochelle: Arlington House, 1975), p. 236.

13. After this essay was drafted, the author received a review copy of William H. McNeill, *The Pursuit of Power: Technology, Armed Force, and Society Since A.D. 1000* (Chicago: University of Chicago Press, 1982). McNeill offers considerable data to support the view here, but his emphasis is on professional armies rather than insurgency or people's war concepts.

offers one of the best examples of cyclical patterns in history, with dynastic cycles occurring roughly every 300 years. Revolts culminating in the emergence of a new dynasty invariably meant mobilizing and arming a significant portion of the populace. The immediate problem of the new dynasty was the disarming of this militialike force and its displacement by a more traditional professional army. Some of the techniques of achieving this disarmament showed considerable imagination. One ruler proclaimed that to celebrate the victory, a great metal statue of himself would be erected derived from melting down the weapons of those who had helped him to achieve power. This interesting variant of the notion of swords into plowshares was repeated by the Japanese ruler Hideyoshi in the sixteenth century to cement his newly won power.

Another recurrent theme first emerged during the second century B.C. One mandarin advised the ruler that rapidly increasing criminality could be stemmed by depriving the populace of arms. The proposal was dropped when another adviser replied that outlaws would always find weapons so only the honest citizenry would be disarmed, thereby actually facilitating criminal attack upon them—shades of "when guns are outlawed, only outlaws will have guns."[14]

Chinese authorities very early recognized the differential importance of missile over shock weaponry. While the cost of a bow put it beyond the means of the vast majority of peasants, Confucianism stressed archery as one of the skills to be acquired by the gentleman-scholar. With the majority of the people disarmed most of the time, the principal threat to the hegemony of the mandarin bureaucracy came from the military. The Confucian system of legitimacy, unlike that of the West, sought to place the soldier virtually outside of the social system, thus the Confucian aphorism, "One does not use good iron for nails, nor good men for soldiers."

Of course, the military could never be totally controlled by that system. This meant a threat of warlordism from within, arming a portion of the dissatisfied population in order to establish a new Chinese dynasty. Later, with the effort to control technology, it meant the dominance of foreign regimes that had developed the technology, starting with the Mongols, then the Manchus, and finally the Westerners.

---

14. The ways in which the mandarin bureaucracy maintained control is discussed in Etienne Balazs, *Chinese Civilization and Bureaucracy* (New Haven: Yale University Press, 1964).

Chinese circumstances would have made possible an industrial revolution several centuries before the West, which borrowed heavily from China. Iron technology and gunpowder developed within an expanding market culture, involving improved manufacture, transportation, and trade.[15] These developments, which included the wide-ranging naval expeditions that had taken Chinese ships as far as the Indian Ocean, threatened bureaucratic control to the point that they ultimately had to be stifled.[16] Having denied herself the market environment necessary for an industrial revolution, China began to fall behind the evolving West. One of the first areas in which this became evident was iron technology, especially in cannon manufacturing.

The means of achieving power and establishing legitimacy have changed with the triumph of the Communists under Mao Tse-tung. More so than in previous dynasties, the "mandate of heaven" of Mao's regime is closely tied to the state's ability to control the potential violence of the river systems. As in earlier rebellions, arming the peasantry was the key to Chinese Communist victory. Mao brilliantly united the lower, middle, and upper class peasantry in a people's war. But despite the pervasive ideology of an ever-continued revolution, Mao early realized that the peasant guerrillas' desire for land must be undercut by disarming them under the centralized control of the regular army. This, in turn, would be controlled by the Party. Thus in 1936, he made the following observation on guerrilla warfare: "One (of its aspects) is irregularity, that is decentralization, lack of uniformity, absence of strict discipline. . . . As the Red Army reaches a higher stage we must gradually and consciously eliminate them so as to make the Red Army . . . more popular in character. . . . Refusal to make progress in this respect and obstinate adherence to the old stage are impermissible and harmful."[17]

Mao moved to eliminate some of the grass-roots structure of his movement more than a decade before its final triumph. The militia since has been used as a frontier-colonizing force along those borders where tensions with the Soviet Union remain high. Authority is from the Party downward.

15. Perhaps the best description is in Mark Elvin, *The Pattern of the Chinese Past* (Stanford: Stanford University Press, 1973).

16. See especially McNeill, *Pursuit of Power*, Chapter Two. Not all Chinese entrepreneurs accepted this control. McNeill (p. 41) describes an ironmaster, employing over 500 workers, who mobilized them to defend themselves against state control late in the twelfth century.

17. Cited in John Ellis, *Armies in Revolution* (London: Croom Helm, 1973), p. 223.

Greece

The Greco-Roman world provided much of the historical data for those who wrote the Second Amendment. From this classical history, it would appear that democracy derived not so much from philosophy as from the sociotechnology of weaponry. The Greeks developed the phalanx as a method of fighting. That tight formation of spears demanded disciplined participation, out of which grew the idea of citizenship: one spear equaled one vote. Characteristically, Socrates, for instance, defined himself as a hoplite, or heavily armed infantry soldier, and that social change leading to shared decision-making is known as the hoplite revolution.[18]

The use of infantry tends toward greater citizen participation than does the use of cavalry and mounted archers. In contrast to incipient Greek democracy, Asia quickly moved from shock to missile weaponry, with an emphasis on cavalry and bowmen.[19] Technology, however, does not guarantee greater citizen participation. With increased affluence and the passage of time, volunteer, paid professional armies began to appear, whose ranks could spend long hours mastering the skills of keeping the phalanx together. The Greeks were caught in what has sometimes been called "the law of the retarding lead," that is, the ability of one organization or nation to surpass a more advanced organization or nation by the former profiting from the institutionalization of the advantages of the latter. So it was the Macedonian monarchy that brought the professional phalanx to its utlimate fulfillment.[20]

Not all Greeks accepted changes in military tactics and techniques as inevitable. In the face of Macedonian growth at the end of the fourth century, the Athenian orator Demosthenes "pleaded in vain for a citizens' army instead of the mercenaries so unsuited for the polis, much as Machiavelli eighteen hundred years later demonstrated

18. Carol G. Thomas, "War in Ancient Greece," in L. L. Farrar, Jr., ed., *War: A Historical, Political, and Social Study* (Santa Barbara: ABC-Clio, 1978), p. 83.

19. Quigley, "Weapons Systems."

20. The law of the retarding lead refers to the fact that those who adopt a new technique tend to institutionalize it so that as others later improve upon the idea, the originators find it difficult to change and keep pace. This is especially true if the changes have been institutionalized by state sanction. American concern over Japanese growth is but a recent example of this historical phenomenon.

against Florentine reliance on hired soldiers."[21] Unless they abandoned the technique of the phalanx, the smaller city-states with citizen-militia could not hope to compete with larger nation-states, which were able to afford professional standing armies. What was once a new technology that aided the rise of self-government had become institutionalized into a tactic favoring despotism and a hired, professional standing army.[22]

Rome

Elsewhere the spirit of the citizen-soldier flourished. The example of republican Rome demonstrates that such an army was not inherently unable to cope with a professional phalanx. The Romans developed a much more flexible use of the infantry—the legion.[23] With this innovation they defeated the Carthaginians and later the Macedonians and Greeks. It is interesting to note that the Aetolians, and later the Corinthians, held out longest against Roman imperialism. They did so not as mercenaries employing either the phalanx or legion, but as a citizen-militia largely using irregular, partisan, guerrilla, and people's war tactics.[24]

As Rome moved from a policy of defense to one of imperialism, she found herself caught in the same structural changes as had the Greeks. The formal shift from republic to empire, which occurred in the first century A.D., was already foreshadowed at the beginning of the first century B.C.[25]

Away for long years of service, often abroad, the citizen-soldier found it increasingly difficult to function as a farmer, if indeed he had not already lost his farm to one of those who had stayed behind to accumulate war profits. Plunder and a promise of new land upon

21. Robert G. Wesson, *State Systems: International Pluralism, Politics, and Culture* (New York: Free Press, 1978), p. 38.

22. It was not the first time such a cycle would occur. Rigidity of institutionalization was not limited to military affairs but affected other areas of Greek life. In music, and especially sports, professionalism also replaced the amateur spirit. See Wesson, *State Systems*, p. 39.

23. Richard A. Preston, Sydney F. Wise, and Herman O. Werner, *Men in Arms: A History of Warfare and Its Interrelationships with Western Society* (New York: Praeger, 1956), p. 35.

24. Wesson, *State Systems*, pp. 39–40.

25. Emilio Gabba, *Republican Rome, the Army and the Allies* (Berkeley: University of California Press, 1976), p. 39.

retirement became the stimuli of the volunteer, professional standing imperial strike force. The system flourished as long as it could expand its empire, based on a growing welfare state at home and taxation of the provinces. At home the Pax Romana was characterized by a "cultural sterility" and a loss of liberty.[26]

Rome was so weakened by the defeat of her soldiers at the hands of the Germans in the Teutoburg Forest in A.D. 9 that she was never able to replace the three legions lost there. Further territorial gains at weaker areas of the periphery masked the fact that her "grand strategy" had shifted to trying to hold what she already had.[27] That the Roman Empire remained in existence so long is attributable to three factors: the rise of Christianity within the Empire, the vitality of cities on the periphery, and the barbarians' lack of any alternative system of legitimacy.[28] The peasant-barbarian volunteers of the late Empire army were themselves such a violent group that cities hesitated to request them to help restore order.

The Dark Ages and the First Industrial Revolution

The "Dark Ages" was actually a period of considerable technological development.[29] The slave system of the Roman Empire, which had inhibited technological advancement, was swept away in the development of the decentralized social system generally referred to as feudalism. By the tenth century, technological growth had reached such a point that this era has been termed "the first industrial revolution."[30]

The millenium of infantry dominance in Europe, roughly 600 B.C. to A.D. 500 which accompanied the rise of republicanism and democratic participation in the classical world, was followed by a return of cavalry (the mounted knight) to military predominance for close to another millenium, 500–1450.[31] Technological development in the military area mainly served to refine this aristocratic paradigm rather

26. Chester G. Starr, *Civilization and the Caesars* (New York: Norton, 1965).
27. Ibid.
28. Ibid.
29. L.S. Stavrianos, *The Promise of the Coming Dark Age* (San Francisco: W.H. Freeman, 1976).
30. Jean Gimpel, *The Medieval Machine: The Industrial Revolution of the Middle Ages* (New York: Holt, Rinehart and Winston, 1976).
31. Quigley, "Weapons Systems."

than to aid in the growth of the wider citizen-soldier participation such as had characterized the ancient world.

Economic development during the latter years of this medieval period (the late thirteenth to the late fifteenth century) unlike that of the previous three centuries, was characterized by an overall economic stagnation of the system, which lasted until the expansion and colonization of the New World. This stagnation was directly related to governmental economic regulation pushed by the guilds in the cities and to increased efforts at taxation resulting from the wars launched by the aristocracy.[32] Though the majority of the people revolted against these conditions in a series of "peasant revolts" during this 200-year downturn, they simply did not have the weapons to challenge the dominance of the state and its aristocratic cavalry. The Peasants' Revolt in England in 1381 provides a typical example.

A Bourgeois Tax Revolt?

During 1348–50, the Black Death swept through England, killing one third of the population. This resulted in a shortage of labor, coupled with a rise in wages and considerable discontent among those who were tied to the "villein" system. To resolve the socioeconomic woes King Edward III tried wage controls, with penalties for those employers who paid more than the old wage. As the *Chronicon* of the age observed, "But the labourers were so arrogant and so hostile that they took no notice of the King's mandate; and if anyone wanted to employ them, he was obliged to give them whatever they asked, and either to lose his fruit and crops or satisfy at will the labourers' greed and arrogance."[33]

Thus the common people had access to jobs, and the revolt broke out not in the feudal North but in the more economically advanced areas of the Southeast in Suffolk and Norfolk. History tends to confirm the often-made observation that rebellion tends to break out among those whose recent improvement is suddenly threatened. Young Richard II, on the advice of Parliament, instituted a poll tax on every adult to help pay for the war with France. "There was much evasion and loud complaint of the arrogance of the tax asses-

---

32. Gimpel, *The Medieval Machine.*
33. Richard West, "Why the Peasants Revolted," *Spectator* (May 30, 1981), p. 15.

sors, and still more of the special commissioners who were given a cut of the money collected."[34]

The revolt started in the market town of Essex near London. Led by a baker, over one hundred merchants and artisans from three towns gathered to protest to one of the tax collectors that they would neither "deal with him nor give him any money." When the collector ordered arrests, the people took up arms and killed two tax men. Other towns soon joined, and an army was quickly formed. Its major problem was that the men lacked weapons, for as one observer recounted, "some carried only sticks, some swords covered with rust, some merely axes and others bows more reddened with age and smoke than old ivory, many of their arrows had only one plume."[35]

The *Anonimaille Chronicle* notes that the rebels "proposed to kill all the lawyers, jurors and royal servants they could find." From the beginning the revolt was aimed not at the landowners but at the government and against the arbitrary taxes levied by Parliament and the King. Despite later efforts by radical priests such as John Ball, who talked of attacking "gentlemen," the revolt was not a class struggle; it was the merging of middle segments of the society against the government. As one historian says, "Personal attacks on secular landlords were indeed extremely infrequent throughout the course of the rebellion."[36] The tax revolt was neither started nor led by peasants. In the Southeast it was led by craftsmen and artisans, "while elsewhere in England the leadership of the revolt came from clerics, landowners, above all the 'burghers' of the towns, or what we would now call the bourgeoisie."[37]

Within a few weeks the revolt was put down through bloody repression by the government. What is significant is the evidence of how few weapons, and those of poor quality, were possessed by the people. Almost 400 years later a similar group of American colonial leaders would stage a revolt against economic regulation and arbitrary taxation. One difference would determine their success: they were armed!

34. West, "Why the Peasants Revolted," p. 15.
35. Ibid., pp. 15–16.
36. Ibid., pp. 15–16.
37. Ibid., pp. 15–16.

THE REVOLUTION IN WEAPONRY

In the period from Machiavelli's early sixteenth-century Florence to England in the eighteenth century, technological developments, especially in weaponry, caused considerable social changes and significant problems of social control.

Cavalry—with or without an armored knight—is very expensive. In all but the most nomadic groups, a horse's cost limits its use to an elite, usually an aristocracy. Castle defense and a mounted knight reinforced the decentralizing tendency of feudalism and the power of the aristocracy.[38]

The rise of centralized, absolutist, monarchical states saw several concomitant tendencies in the area of weapon technology and control. One was the continued introduction of new technologies with respect to missile weaponry, essentially the cannon and firearms. The cannon's ability to penetrate castle walls and the ease with which a ball could pierce armor undercut the supremacy of the knight.

In the long run it was such technologies that weakened the power of the feudal aristocracy relative to that of the monarch and the national state. Just as in the classical world the city-states had been less able than larger states to pay for standing professional armies, so in the early modern period the emerging national states were better able to afford the new firearms technology and the professionals to use it.[39]

DISARMAMENT AND SOCIAL CONTROL

At the same time that costs limited a widespread ownership of the new firearms, governments on a global scale sought to disarm their populace as a means of social control. In Japan, for example, as a prelude to the Tokugawa Shogunate, Hideyoshi in the "famous

---

38. Quigley, *The Evolution of Civilizations*, pp. 224-26.

39. The historical cycle of republican citizen militia devolving into a volunteer professional army for empire was evident in Renaissance Italy in the fourteenth and fifteenth centuries and explains the relevance of Machiavelli's analysis to later generations. In a brilliant description of this process McNeill describes how as each city-state pushed out farther to control as much as fifty miles away, it became necessary to hire full-time professionals to replace the militia (*The Pursuit of Power*, pp. 66-67). This was repeated in the rise of centralized monarchy all over Europe.

'sword hunt'" disarmed the farmers and gave the professional samurai class the sole right to wear swords. In France and England, authoritarian monarchs attempted systematically to disarm the people as a basic safeguard against unpopular regimes.[40] Shortly before the American Revolution, a British officer named Charles Lee, who later fought with the Americans and became an advocate of people's war, was an observer of the Poles' valiant sturggle against the Russian invaders. He commented upon how effectively the Poles might have fought had they not been essentially disarmed beforehand. The lesson was not lost on Lee.

It was not just the cost or availability of firearms that strengthened the rise of central government and professional armies. Early weapons were inaccurate over any great range and took a long time to reload, even by a skilled soldier. Rain might render the firing mechanisms useless. As late as the American Revolution, professionals hoped for rain so that a musket exchange could be dispensed with and bayonets fixed for a charge. Pikes and pikemen remained an important part of professional armies well into the seventeenth century.

Prior to the American Revolution, the one military struggle that did engage a significant segment of the population was the English Civil War. Shock weapons still predominated over missiles. The basic weapons of the 1640s included the sword, the pike, and, to a lesser extent, the arquebus. As John Ellis has observed, "Because the level of technology was not high the manufacture of such equipment was in the hands of ordinary craftsmen rather than specialized, government supervised production units. Such crafts were spread about the country and . . . each side had access to adequate amounts of military materials."[41]

"COUNTRY" VERSUS "COURT" IDEOLOGY AND ARMAMENTS

Ellis's study *Armies in Revolution* examines both the revolutionary struggle *between* each side in major events such as the English, American, and Chinese revolutions and the tension and struggle *with-*

---

40. Alfred Crofts and Percy Buchanan, *A History of the Far East* (New York: David McKay, 1958), Chapter Six, and the author's conversations with Professor Crofts spanning a number of years.
41. Ellis, *Armies in Revolution*, p. 5.

in the factions of the revolutionary coalitions themselves. "Country" ideology—from the English Revolution through the framing of the Second Amendment—was cognizant that opposition from within the revolutionary coalition was a major reason for the defeat of some of the more equalitarian goals of the revolution.

During the English Revolution, Oliver Cromwell and other conservative parliamentarian leaders pressed for more aristocratic powers for the officers as opposed to the sense of equality of the rank and file of the army represented by the Levellers.[42] The turning point of the Revolution was the triumph of the more conservative elements. The restoration of the monarchy affirmed that change of emphasis. If the events of 1688–89 established the ultimate hegemony of Parliament, they also set the oligarchical nature of British politics.

"Court" and "Country" ideologies fought out these eighteenth century political battles at three levels—the monarchial/bureaucratic, the parliamentarian, and the public. The Court ideology dominated the first level and the Country ideology the last, with an ongoing struggle in the Parliament. In the face of continuing disarmament of the people carried on by the police and local officials, the Country party rediscovered a technique of fighting that developed, in both Europe and America, into a very sophisticated political weapon—the "organized mob" or crowd.[43] Although the struggle continued in England and other parts of the British Empire, the real home for this equalitarian-Leveller-Commonwealthman-Country-True Whig world view became the American colonies—the scene of its greatest triumph.

THE AMERICAN REVOLUTION AS A PEOPLE'S WAR: COUNTRY IDEOLOGY CONTEXT OF THE SECOND AMENDMENT

Although some writers continue to misinterpret John Adams's views about the Revolution as a majoritarian movement, the 1976 Bicen-

42. Ellis, *Armies in Revolution*, p. 39. The Leveller emphasis on equality or equity is striking. Ellis quotes a passage from one of their leaders, Richard Overton, in which "equity" and "equitable" is used four times in several sentences.

43. Richard Maxwell Brown, "Violence in the American Revolution," in S. Kurtz and J. Hutson, eds., *Essays in the American Revolution* (Chapel Hill: University of North Carolina Press, 1973).

tennial year witnessed a renewed interest in the subject.[44] In breaking free from England, the Country-Court debate was re-created *within* the American revolutionary coalition, was incorporated into the structure of American politics in the new republic, and is still very much with us today.[45] The difference between Country and Court world views lies at the very heart of the debate over firearms prohibition, and this fundamental difference should not be overlooked by a narrow, ad hoc perspective on the Second Amendment debates of today. In the case of the American Revolution, the philosophical, political, economic, and social differences between these world views had a distinctive military dimension as well: a long, simmering, often acrimonious struggle over strategy and tactics (technique) involving goals and how the war ought to be conducted. Again, these debates are germane to the framing of the Second Amendment and its historical, ideological context.

At one extreme were those like Washington and Franklin who thought in terms of fighting a traditional, European-style, eighteenth-century war with a standing army. The key to understanding their bias for traditional standing army tactics lay in their perception of what the war was all about. A key division or "fault line" in the revolutionary coalition was between those who wished only independence and those who wanted independence *and* empire.[46] Thus a peace negotiation in 1778 failed partly because men like Franklin wanted not only independence but also Canada and Florida. By the end of the war, the farmers who formed the bulk of the militia had learned how to deal with this issue. In 1778, when Washington sent Lafayette north to launch another crusade against Canada, members of the Vermont militia, which had played a major role in defeating Burgoyne the year before at Saratoga, told Washington they would go along only for "double pay, double rations and . . . plunder!"[47] That demand stopped the entire campaign.

Washington's "standing" army's numbers went up and down. It swelled with farmers in the spring, but these men went home in the

44. William Marina, "The American Revolution and the Minority Myth," *Modern Age* 20 (Summer 1976).

45. William Marina, "Revolution and Social Change: The American Revolution as a People's War," *Literature of Liberty* 1 (April/June 1978): 5–39.

46. Weldon A. Brown, *Empire or Independence: A Study in the Failure of Reconciliation, 1774–1783* (Berkeley and Los Angeles: University of California Press, 1942).

47. Cited in Page Smith, *A New Age Now Begins* (New York: McGraw-Hill, 1976), p. 1,079.

fall. It was never able to function as an instrument of empire. Those who stayed through the bitter winters, such as at Valley Forge, were predominantly displaced or marginal men with nowhere else to go.[48]

The skirmishing and irregular partisan warfare that characterized much of the success of the Revolution was more a contribution of the militia than of the standing army.[49] This has recently been brought out in an important essay by John Shy.[50] Concern with harassment by militia was a major reason the British seldom ventured inland following the clashes at Lexington and Concord. When they did so, they lost an army at Saratoga and later at Yorktown—the culmination of a number of battles and skirmishes across the South during which considerable men and equipment were lost. Militia attacks on supply convoys into Philadelphia were significant in the British decision to withdraw from that city.

In terms of counterinsurgency warfare, the British never were able to achieve the first step in subduing America. After dark, they dared not to venture out in less than battalion strength.[51] At times, when troops were being shifted by ship, there were virtually *no* British soldiers in North America. The British never came close to challenging the legitimacy of the American revolutionary coalition. The Americans thus were free to pursue regular, irregular, and partisan warfare because the British controlled so little territory and even that for a relatively short time. There was therefore no need for Americans to pursue real guerrilla warfare—living among the occupier and fighting him, often at night—the classic use of an armed citizens' militia.

The one exception can be found described in Adrian Leiby's brilliant study of Bergen County, New Jersey, where the British foraged during the years they held New York City. Leiby shows how in five years the militia turned itself into a more formidable fighting force than either the British or American regular army units.[52]

48. Allan Bowman, *The Morale of the American Revolutionary Army* (Washington, D.C.: American Council on Economic Affairs, 1943).

49. Marina, "Revolution and Social Change," pp. 23–27.

50. John Shy, *A People Numerous and Armed: Reflections on the Military Struggle for American Independence* (New York: Oxford University Press, 1976).

51. Eric Robson, *The American Revolution in Its Political and Military Aspects* (London: Cambridge University Press, 1953), p. 83.

52. Adrian Leiby, *The American Revolutionary War in the Hackensack Valley: The Jersey Dutch and the Neutral Ground, 1775–1783* (New Brunswick: Rutgers University Press, 1963). A recent study using Leiby's work as a data base for exploring guerrilla-people's war

There were no "free riders"; all had to commit themselves one way or another. The farmer militia was paid in gold, not inflated paper money. The commander of the militia had a better understanding of the essentials of people's war than did George Washington.[53]

It is interesting to speculate, given the importance of weapons technology, what might have been the results had the revolt occurred a half century earlier or later. From roughly the latter part of the seventeenth century until well into the nineteenth century, the standard weapon piece of the British and other armies was a basic musket — the famous "Brown Bess." Ownership of the musket, which underwent little technological development during that long period, was widely dispersed in America. But early in that period the government held predominant control of the weapon, as it did later when percussion caps, cartridges, and repeating weapons were invented.[54]

THE SECOND AMENDMENT — WHAT DOES IT MEAN?

In light of the struggle between the Court and Country ideology, which extended into the Federalist-Antifederalist debate at the time of the Constitution and into the Federalist-Republican party battles of the early Republic, the discussion about the meaning of the Second Amendment takes on a new significance.

A number of articles have been written arguing whether the Second Amendment right to bear arms is restricted to a state-derived militia or extends to the whole populace.[55] Based on the Country ideology background and the context of the debate, the latter interpretation is correct.[56] One recent analysis appeared in the *Journal of*

---

in the American Revolution is William Marina and Diane Cuervo, "The Dutch-American Guerrillas of the American Revoltuion," in Gary North, ed., *The Theology of Christian Resistance: A Symposium*, Vol. 2 of *Christianity and Civilization* (Tyler, Texas: Geneva Divinity School Press, 1983), pp. 242–65.

53. Leiby, *American Revolutionary War.*

54. McNeill, *Pursuit of Power*, pp. 142–43.

55. See, for example, Roy G. Weatherup, "Standing Armies and Armed Citizens: An Historical Analysis of the Second Amendment," *Hastings Constitutional Law Quarterly* 2 (Fall 1975): 961–1061; and James B. Whisker, "Historical Development and Subsequent Erosion of the Right to Keep and Bear Arms," *West Virginia Law Review* 78: 171–90.

56. Stephen P. Halbrook, "To Keep and Bear Their Private Arms: The Adoption of the Second Amendment," *North Kentucky Law Review* 10 (1982): 13–39. Two recent studies of the Country ideology are worth noting. Rodger Durrell Parker, "The Gospel of Opposition: A Study in Eighteenth Century Anglo-American Ideology" (doctoral dissertation,

American History.[57] Historian Robert Shalhope's summary of the case is so well stated, and its relationship to the overall thrust of this essay so evident, that it is worth examining in some detail.

Shalhope notes that while some have found the Second Amendment "obsolete," "defunct," and "with no meaning for the twentieth century," others have found it "vital" to the debate over gun control. Ultimately, he observes, "disagreements over gun legislation reveal disparate perceptions of American society that rest upon, or inspire, dissimilar interpretations of the Second Amendment." Gun control advocates stress "collective rights" or, as one Presidential Commission put it, the Amendment acts "only as a prohibition against Federal interference with State militia and not as a guarantee of an individual's right to keep or carry firearms." Shalhope suggests that an examination of both sides in their historical context—the eighteenth century context and the several centuries prior to that—might offer some insights into the debate.

In the last several decades numerous scholars have contributed toward a reconstruction of the American Revolution as seen by its participants:

> As a result we now recognize the importance of "republicanism," a distinctive universe of ideas and beliefs, in shaping contemporary perceptions of late-eighteenth-century society. Within such a political culture thoughts regarding government were integrated into a much larger configuration of beliefs about human behavior and the social process. Drawing heavily upon the libertarian thought of the English commonwealthmen, colonial Americans believed that a republic's very existence depended upon the character and spirit of its citizens. A people noted for their frugality, industry, independence, and courage were good republican stock. Those intent upon luxury lost first their desire and then their ability to protect and maintain a republican society. Republics survived only through a constant protection of the realm of Liberty from the ceaselessly aggressive forces of Power. America would remain a bastion of Liberty, in stark contrast to the decadent and corrupt societies of Europe, only so long as its people retained their virility and their virtue.

Wayne State University, 1975), discusses the broadest aspects of this world view, while John Todd White, "Standing Armies in Time of War: Republican Theory and Military Practice During the American Revolution" (doctoral dissertation, George Washington University, 1978), examines the military facet of that paradigm.

57. Robert E. Shalhope, "The Ideological Origins of the Second Amendment," *Journal of American History* 69, 3 (December 1982): 599–614. All of the quotations that follow are taken from Shalhope's piece.

In the vast literature on republicanism Shalhope finds two ideas significant to understanding the Second Amendment: "the fear of standing armies and the exaltation of militias composed of ordinary citizens." An "equally vital theme" is also found in this Revolutionary "libertarian literature which, except in the work of J.G.A. Pocock, has been largely ignored in the recent literature dealing with republicanism. *This is the dynamic relationship that libertarian writers believed existed between arms, the individual, and society"* (emphasis added). Machiavelli's "sociology of liberty," which emphasized the "role of arms in society" and the "arming of all citizens," and precedes the libertarian tradition expressed by James Harrington, John Trenchard and Thomas Gordon, Walter Moyle, James Burgh, and Richard Price, among others, down to the period of the Revolution itself. Even literary figures like the American poet Joel Barlow dwelt upon this relationship between an armed citizenry as a republic, "not only *permitting* every man to arm, but *obliging* him to arm." Barlow believed that "only tyrannical government disarmed their people."

Thus when James Madison wrote the amendments that became the Bill of Rights, "he did not do so within a vacuum" but rather in "an environment permeated by the emergent republican ideology," and with numerous suggestions from citizens, local groups, and state conventions. As Shalhope states, "These sources continually reiterated four beliefs relative to the issues eventually incorporated into the Second Amendment: the right of the individual to possess arms, the fear of a professional army, the reliance on militia controlled by the individual states, and the subordination of the military to civilian control." The resolutions at state conventions cited by Shalhope demonstrate that the Americans of that generation linked the individual's right to keep arms with a grass-roots militia as the means to maintain civilian control over the military and the internal threat of a standing army.

Madison and those on the select committee writing a bill of rights "were anxious to capture the essence of the rights demanded by so many Americans in so many different forms." What disturbed many since then, from Timothy Dwight to Joseph Story, was the indifference of Americans at exercising the right to keep and bear arms, which they believed was the only way to check internal tyranny or to repel a foreign invader.

The debate continues today, and as Shalhope observes: "Whether the armed citizen is relevant to late-twentieth century American life is something that only the American people–through the Supreme Court, their state legislatures, and Congress–can decide." He warns, however, "But advocates of control of firearms should not argue that the Second Amendment did not intend for Americans of the late eighteenth century to possess arms for their own personal defense, for the defense of their states and their nation, and for the purpose of keeping their rulers sensitive to the rights of the people."

Which view of history, the Country view or the collectivist view, has proved the more relevant in explaining what has happened in America over the last 200 years? The answer is obvious. In gaining many of the goals of the collectivist view–a large, centralized, active government with a growing global military presence–American history has experienced many of the developments that those of the Country persuasion warned would occur.

Richard Kohn has shown how the militia system was "murdered" as early as the 1790s.[58] While the notion of the militia as a grass-roots derivation from the people has smothered, even at the state level, it lost further ground to the growing power of the national government. The New England militia refused to participate in that renewal of the imperial adventure to take Canada known as the War of 1812. The removal and policing of the Indians, the War with Mexico for more expansion, were minor enough or short enough to avoid using the militia. The regular volunteer standing army, small though it was, was sufficient.

The Civil War was a watershed of centralization. The Spanish-American War and the "benevolent pacification" of the Philippines were small enough to be handled by the volunteer standing army. This last conflict engendered a considerable protest about the perils of empire.[59] It is intriguing to speculate how well the Filipinos might have done–having turned in most of their weapons in an earlier truce with the Spanish–had they had even the 5,000 rifles promised to them by the Japanese. American soldiers in the field often seemed embarrassed, as did the British in Africa, at shooting down men armed so poorly.

58. Richard H. Kohn, "The Murder of the Militia System in the Aftermath of the American Revolution in Stanley J. Unterdal, ed., *Military History of the American Revolution* (Colorado Springs: United States Air Force Academy, 1974).

59. William Marina, "U.S. Interventions: Aberrations or Empire?" *Reason* 8 (February 1976): 40–45. See also Harold A. Larrabee, "The Enemies of Empire," *American Heritage* 11 (June 1960): 28–33, 76–80.

Americans were bewildered that participation in two world wars had not brought global security nor made the world safe for democracy, and were equally frustrated that, given their hegemony after 1945, conflicts in China, Korea, Cuba, Vietnam, and elsewhere could not be "won" in any meaningful sense. The reason for this had very much to do with another revolution in weaponry. Far from technology "antiquating" the Second Amendment, the Country ideology was being validated on a global scale. Put succinctly, as the superpowers emphasized ever more massive missile weapons of enormous sophistication and terrible destructiveness, these weapons, when they functioned at all, had virtually no flexibility in bringing power to bear. At the same time, a global arms race, often pushed by the superpowers and prodded by competition from lesser states, was making weapons of an intermediate or appropriate technology available at lower costs to virtually anyone. To talk about national control in the face of this international competition is pointless.

THE SECOND REVOLUTION IN WEAPONRY

The first revolution in weaponry aided the rise of the monarchical national state and volunteer standing army at the expense of the aristocracy and mounted knight. In the American and French Revolutions, muskets were still unwieldy enough to give advantages to those with professional training. As Page Smith noted with respect to the American Revolution, the role of artillery in battles of position has been underemphasized. Even experienced infantry would break and run under bombardment.[60]

The real technological breakthrough occurred in the nineteenth century and included mass-produced guns, interchangeable parts, repeating and automatic rifles and machine guns with easy-to-load, dependable, mass-produced bullets. As Carroll Quigley observed, the battle of Petersburg in the American Civil War was the harbinger of the defensive stalemate when Western armies fought each other to a bloody standstill in World War I.[61] This stalemate was disguised by the ease with which western gunboats and advanced weapons opened up previously closed areas such as Japan and that great riverine giant, China, which appeared pitifully helpless.

60. Smith, *A New Age Now Begins*, p. 688.
61. Quigley, *The Evolution of Civilization*, p. 256.

The process is also evident in Africa. For centuries, labor (slaves) had been exported from Africa. Disease made it difficult to explore the interior, but quinine and the steamboat changed that. Antislavery sentiments caught hold with English leaders just as technologies provided the opportunity to open up this area, necessitating the labor of blacks at home. The new weapons allowed small groups of Europeans to govern large groups of natives.

Three kinds of confrontations took place between whites and blacks. Tribes like the Zulu chose to use their traditional spears against the British. The resulting kind of butchery embarrassed even the imperialist. In northern Africa, tribes with firearms inferior in kind and number tried to confront the British. This resulted in some European defeats, such as that of "Chinese" Gordon at Khartoum, but eventually the Europeans triumphed. In contrast to the use of traditional military technique that characterized the American Revolution, some tribes chose to fight a guerrilla, people's war with weapons supplied by some of the lesser powers such as the Belgians, and the effectiveness of this practice is only now beginning to gain recognition. The British and French were not able to defeat these guerrillas until they put sufficient pressure on the guerrillas' sources of arms and cut off the relatively meager supplies.[62]

That preeminent volunteer imperial rapid deployment force—the U.S. Marines—found much the same problem in confronting the guerrilla leader Sandino in Nicaragua. Sandino's arms came from Mexico, and a stalemate ensued even though the Marines used the best counterinsurgency tactics of the 1920s and employed technology such as the autogyro, an early prototype of the helicopter. This stalemate, which was, in effect a victory, morally won Sandino recognition throughout Latin America.

The emphasis on traditional military history has tended to obscure the revolutionary, people's warfare aspects of World War II, yet the Japanese were suffering enormous losses against the Chinese guerrillas.[63] In the European war this was also true as the numerous partisan resistance groups took an increasing toll on the Germans. When

---

62. Daniel R. Headrick, "The Tools of Imperialism: Technology and the Expansion of European Colonial Empires in the Nineteenth Century," *Journal of Modern History* 51 (June 1979): 231-63.

63. Crofts and Buchanan, *A History of the Far East*, p. 434. Large numbers of Japanese troops simply went "over the hill" and married Chinese women. This was similar to the American Revolution, where an estimated 5,000 Hessian troops deserted, many going into western Pennsylvania in search of wives.

the resistance in many countries began, some sought to cooperate with the Allies. Tensions growing out of Allied army efforts to control these movements aided German efforts to monitor, penetrate, and destroy the resistance leadership infrastructure. After losing several precious years to German success, the resistance had to build its own infrastructure relatively free of outside control and interference. This is a painful lesson that has had to be learned in every people's war throughout history. It takes time to establish legitimacy, build a political organization, and develop an effective fighting force. Without that initial costly setback, resistance forces would have played an even greater role in World War II. Taken in its entirety, though, the role of popular resistance was larger than acknowledged in most histories, and the details of that contribution are still emerging.

Vietnam demonstrated what organization and outside help can achieve in a war. Vietnam guerrillas proved too large an insurgency to be put down by volunteer troops, forcing the United States to resort to conscription. By the late phases of the war, "fragging" of officers was on the increase and middle-echelon officers sometimes joined the infantry "grunts" going off to smoke marijuana and evade, rather than search out and destroy, the enemy.

Recent events in Nicaragua and El Salvador show how little revolutionary warfare and its relationship to an armed citizenry are understood. Ellis was cited earlier regarding how oligarchical leadership in revolutions has attempted to control weapons within its own coalition. Communists have always done this—for example, in Spain in the 1930s as pointed out by George Orwell in *Homage to Catalonia*. Trotsky said it most clearly in arguing that centralization was possible only by smashing the peasant units whose individualism and love of freedom had made them among the most effective fighting units in the Red Army during the civil war.[64]

The United States tends to arm the political right, while the Soviets arm the left. In some cases, as in Nicaragua, many arms come from outside the control of either superpower. Those in the middle, often the peasantry, are without arms. They are prey to the army from the right and the guerrillas from the left, who have, like Trotsky, a much different agenda in mind once they seize power. As the international arms trade increases—the United States will earn at least $30 billion this year from the trafficking—more people will

64. Ellis, *Armies in Revolution*, pp. 165–99.

obtain access to guns as governments lose control over the great number of arms being traded.[65]

The Soviet state has its share of problems: rampant alcoholism, terrible morale throughout the army, the party, and society, millionaires flourishing on the black market, protests in client states, a succession crisis because of a lack of legitimizing institutions, a decrepit economy, an inability to feed itself, and a rebellion in Afghanistan. Recent events in Communist societies—certainly in Poland—suggest the difficulty civilian officials face in keeping control from the military with its monopoly on weaponry.[66] In Afghanistan, as was the case during the American Revolution, there is a widespread ownership of firearms. The latest reports indicate a growing insurgency, with the rebels now controlling whole villages.

It is difficult to assess the psychological effects on Russian society as veterans of the more than 100,000-man Soviet force filter back into their own country. That problem may prove more difficult than the economic cost of the continuing struggle. When the French Revolution broke out, it was particularly strong in those areas of France with concentrations of veterans who had fought in America a decade before.

The difference between an essentially nonprofessional citizen's army and a professional standing army is perhaps best seen in the Israeli army's reaction to the decision to occupy parts of Lebanon. Elements in the army discussed whether a foreign invasion and occupation was a good idea, and a vigorous investigation was conducted into any Israeli responsibility for a massacre of Palestinians. Contrast that with the performance of professional armies, for example, the United States armed forces in Vietnam, where efforts were made to cover up atrocities.

A CRISIS IN LEGITIMACY

The increasing level of violence that people perceive is not caused by the availability of firearms; rather, it is fundamentally a crisis in the

---

65. See, for example, Andrew J. Pierre, *The Global Politics of Arms Sales* (Princeton, N. J.: Princeton University Press, 1982).

66. The concern of the military, however, is not only the threat of Solidarity, whose mass following presents an alternative legitimacy, but specifically the indigenous Catholic militia, which sprang up from the grass roots to maintain order during the Pope's visit. It is no wonder the military tries to keep the people disarmed. Such an already in existence, organized militia—if armed—would pose a grave threat to Communist hegemony.

legitimacy of the state, a crisis that is economic, political, military, and moral. Without a sense of legitimacy, it is impossible to have any real degree of stability, for force alone cannot restore order but will only create stagnation and repression.[67]

Western civilization has never experienced the kind of all-encompassing universal empire that characterized other civilizations in their declining phases. That kind of pervasive centralization has been the most stifling of all.[68] Yet each of the Western states in the nation-state system has attempted a degree of centralization and governmental control that has created stagnation and near collapse of the whole system.

The current breakdown in virtually every facet of life resulting from the loss of legitimacy is very similar to what occurred in the Roman Empire, a comparison that has been made from the pulpit, by writers, and even by politicians. Around A.D. 150, the government in Rome had difficulty in organizing the collection of garbage, a sight that would be familiar to many urban dwellers today. One of the few functioning organizations at that time was the Christian Church, which went on about its business and ignored directives from the state. It fed over 1,500 widows and orphans in the city of Rome alone, another task that was beyond the ability of the government. But just as Roman civic humanists discussed the decline of the Empire and what to do about it without arriving at a workable solution, so does no program curing modern social ills seem to have emerged today.

With government regulation failing to produce desirable results in so many areas, it seems curious to imagine that government control of weapons would effectively reduce social instability or that possession of weapons is in any sense the cause of this instability. Huge economic entities, once boasting of their managerial techniques, now stagnate and ask for subsidies and/or protection. Monetary and fiscal policies—inflation and deficits—lurch out of control while a growing underground economy flourishes both in the Communist and "free" worlds, at a rate in the United States that some suggest may make it more than one fourth of the economy. Illegal immigration reaches one million a year, and it is evident this flow across the border cannot be stopped short of an identity card system of Orwellian police-

67. William Marina, "Surviving in the Interstices," *Reason* 7 (June 1975): 34–40.

68. Robert G. Wesson, *The Imperial Order* (Berkeley and Los Angeles: University of California Press, 1967).

state proportions. Furthermore, a number of nations that only a few years ago were hailed as undergoing economic "miracles" such as Mexico and Brazil, have in effect declared themselves bankrupt and unable to pay their international debts.

The symptoms of breakdown and the efforts at control are virtually endless, but take one item alone – the United States' determination to eradicate marijuana – as a parallel to the problem that would be faced in attempting to ban firearms. Estimated at $8.5 billion, marijuana is now America's fourth largest cash crop, just behind corn, soybeans, and wheat. Less than 10 percent, it is estimated, is confiscated from among the tons being traded. This nation now exports marijuana seeds even to Colombia, and many local government officials are urging the police to refrain from enforcement of the law, since the economic value of this crop to farmers in some areas is increasingly recognized as important in an economy experiencing hard times.[69]

While the effort to ban firearms bears a similarity to the attempt to control sex, alcohol, or drugs – all items to which a significant portion of the society wishes to have access – at an international level it differs in one respect. Late in the nineteenth century, businessmen and government officials began to develop what we now refer to as the military-industrial complex, commencing with naval armaments in Great Britain.[70] The technology and the capital needed were so great that government and business became jointly involved. At the same time, profits from so large an undertaking could only be made by competing for sales internationally. It was this need that drove Belgians to sell weapons to Africans, even though they thereby aided the latter against other Europeans encroaching the African continent.

The need for international sales is even greater today than it was then. Thus when the Carter administration attempted to cut sales of arms abroad, France and other countries stepped in to exploit the markets, which are essentially in the Third World. International trade makes the prohibition of firearms a dubious if not impossible proposition in any given country, and certainly in one with the personal freedoms long enjoyed by Americans.

69. "The Grass Was Never Greener," *Time* (August 9, 1982): 15.
70. McNeill, *The Pursuit of Power*, Chapter Eight.

AN EMERGING PARADIGM

Those who talk about the "fall" of a civilization are often the same ones who bemoan the state's inability to control some facet of an individual's life. Even noted historian William H. McNeill complains of the relationship between the market and the technological development of weapons throughout history. But it was precisely those periods of relative market development, as opposed to state control, that made possible technological growth of which weapons advances were only one part.[71] With the present system of international trade in arms, governments cannot control the flow of arms downward. Eventually the peasantry in every society—that most oppressed group at the bottom—will find weapons available to them. The Afghanis have long had a cottage industry in relatively crude weapons. There is a certain irony in the fact that Russian Kalishnakov submachine guns procured from Egypt are now being smuggled into Afghanistan for use against the Soviet invaders.

No one has ever seen a civilization fall. That image is completely an illusion in the human mind. According to different historians, the decline of Rome, for example, can be placed at anywhere from 202 B.C. to A.D. 1453. Crises, as the Chinese ideograph suggests, are a time of danger and a time of opportunity. In the midst of global crisis we are witnessing the emergence of a new paradigm. In many ways this paradigm is an updating of the "Country" ideology, yet bridges a spectrum from left to right and includes many who would view themselves as nonpolitical. Some of the advocates of this paradigm are late in fully understanding—as were those who formed the Country ideology—that possession of weapons for self-defense is integral to any plan of individual independence.

Many of the key ideas of this new paradigm—people participation, decentralization, smallness of scale, and appropriate/intermediate technology as a means of "doing one's thing" in a less than free world—are similar to the earlier Country would view. These emerging cooperative networks tend simply to bypass or ignore government in ways reminiscent of the early Christians or the ancient Chinese Taoists. The new paradigm is closely linked to science and to an eco-

71. McNeill, *The Pursuit of Power*, p. 263.

logical, general systems world view. Its literature, spanning a wide spectrum of seemingly unrelated areas, is growing.[72]

Decentralization and human scale thus return, despite the efforts of imperial centralizers to stop the process. The term "dark age" was invented by those who dislike such periods of fundamental growth and change, but students of history can appreciate that the low point of human dispiritedness has usually been in the stagnation-accompanying epochs of empire.

In all this change, the larger philosophical outlook underlying the Country interpretation of the Second Amendment takes on a new meaning and relevance. In today's international context, any such effort at arms prohibition by the state against the individual, in violation of the spirit of the Second Amendment, is bound to fail. As with a number of other such crusades and evasion of larger questions of causation, that failure is apt to have far more serious repercussions on the legitimacy of those seeking prohibition than upon the actions or existence of those whose lives they seek to regulate.

It is ironic that the broader application of the Second Amendment to the global confrontation between superpowers with large standing armies, huge stockpiles of nuclear weapons, and growing international trade in arms should be the result of what began as a debate over handguns. But that is indeed the case.

In general, the Amendments to the Constitution were pushed by those who shared the Country ideology and who thought broadly of creating an atmosphere that would promote the growth of a republican *culture*.[73] In one sense the Amendments were negatives, as they sought to prevent the central government from doing certain things that, in the authors' reading of history, had meant the death of republican culture. In the context of the Second Amendment in particular, what the great jurist Joseph Story said in 1833 is still relevent: "The right of a citizen to keep and bear arms has justly been considered the palladium of the liberties of a republic, since it offers a strong moral check against the usurpation and arbitrary power of

---

72. For example, E.F. Schumacher, *Small Is Beautiful: Economics As If People Mattered* (New York: Harper, 1973); Marilyn Ferguson, *The Aquarian Conspiracy: Personal and Social Transformation in the 1980s* (Los Angeles: Tarcher, 1980); Fritjof Capra, *The Turning Point: Science, Society, and the Rising Culture* (New York: Simon and Schuster, 1982); and Leopold Kohr, *The Breakdown of Nations* (New York: Dutton, 1978).

73. The best summary of the ideas making up that cluster of values and culture is in Parker, "Gospel of Opposition," Chapter Fourteen.

rulers, and will generally, even if these are successful in the first instance, enable the people to resist and triumph over them."[74]

But clearly the specific *negative* against which the Second Amendment was directed was the notion of a standing army. As great as were Country-Whig fears of the Bank of England and the financial jobbery that accompanied monopoly mercantilism and empire, these arbitrary actions were made possible by the existence of a standing army.

The whole Second Amendment debate is taking place within, and stimulating, a growing literature about the historical interrelationship of such issues. A recent study has focused on the way in which English colonization was part of an overall military policy,[75] while research into the coming of the American Revolution has emphasized the American concern about standing armies as *the* catalyst that led to war.[76]

Any reader of that controversy cannot but marvel at the similarities with our own times. At the end of the Great War for Empire (1763), the British government had a bloated officer corps and army that it hoped to keep intact and had to pay for, but could not station at home. It decided to dump much of the cost on the Americans and the Irish, and the army itself was thus drawn into politics and defending its bureaucratic prerogatives.

The growth of the American state in the twentieth century has created the same dilemma. The sheer size of the military and its budget has led to a deep involvement in politics, often to defend officer pensions and "double-dipping," much as was true in the late eighteenth century. Even in a severe budget crisis, it is argued that the military cannot be cut back, while the government refuses to examine alternative paradigms that might make a rational defense possible.

---

74. Joseph Story, *Commentaries on the Constitution of the United States*, 5th ed. (Boston: Little, Brown, 1897), Vol. 3.

75. Stephen Saunders Webb, *The Governors-General: The English Army and the Definition of the Empire, 1569-1681* (Chapel Hill: University of North Carolina Press, 1979). This is the first volume, with a second promised, which brings the story up to the American Revolution. The essentials of Webb's interpretation are outlined, however, quite clearly in the first volume. As one noted American historian concluded, if Webb's fascinating thesis about the role of the army is even partially correct, then a great deal of our early history will need rethinking.

76. John Phillip Reid, *In Defiance of the Law: The Standing Army Controversy, The Two Constitutions, and the Coming of the American Revolution* (Chapel Hill: University of North Carolina Press, 1981).

Just as British policymakers understood it was important to keep a standing army and military presence outside the home Islands, so the vast American military buildup has benefited from the low profile at home (even military hospitals for the maimed are placed far out in the countryside), with the great bulk of the bases and troops in Europe and Asia. These constitute by far the largest part of the military budget, over $80 billion for Europe alone.

But the military consensus is breaking down in the face of crisis. Sam Cohen, "father" of the neutron bomb has recently "jumped ship" with respect to American "defense" strategies.[77] He maintains that American troops become hostages and a liability if Europe chooses not to seriously involve itself in its own defense, and should be brought home. Cohen's demand for a rethinking of our defense, involving technology, appropriate tactics, and a citizen participation—in the past one might have called it a militia—is in many ways reminiscent of the Country ideology embodied in the Second Amendment.

This chapter began by suggesting that even if one conceded a relationship between handgun availability and violence, a case far from proved, there is a larger historical argument about liberty in a republic that influenced those who framed the Second Amendment. Justice Story's observation about the Second Amendment as a bulwark of liberty in a republic is as relevant today as it was when it was written. That the present fiscal and armaments crises of the state system have led to a renewed debate over this question is, indeed, grounds for hope.

In the current debate over volunteer versus professional standing armies, little attention has been given to a citizen force derived from a grass-roots militia. There is evidence that such a force could certainly master much of the appropriate technology of modern weaponry. The military as it now stands hires skilled civilians for certain technological jobs. If nuclear weapons are reduced, a new emphasis must be given to conventional forces. A citizen militia on the Swiss model, for example, is not coercion; rather, it is an effort to define the rights and responsibilities of citizenship. History, especially the era of the American Revolution, suggests that such a force is unlikely to consent to taking part in global interventionism. Rather, it will maintain its foundation in the right of the citizen to keep and bear arms.

77. Sam Cohen, *The Truth About the Neutron Bomb*, especially Chapter Eight.

SELECTED BIBLIOGRAPHY
(PART VII)

Adams, J. *A Defense of the Constitutions of the United States of America.* London: C. Dilley, 1787-1788.

Alderson, John. *Policing Freedom: A Commentary on the Dilemmas of Policing in Western Democracies.* Plymouth, England: Macdonald and Evans, 1979.

Aristotle. *Politics.* Translated by T. Sinclair. New York: Penguin, 1962.

Bailyn, Bernard. *Ideological Origins of the American Revolution.* Cambridge, Mass.: Harvard University Press, 1967.

Balazs, Etienne. *Chinese Civilization and Bureaucracy.* New Haven, Conn.: Yale University Press, 1964.

Beccaria. *On Crimes and Punishments.* Translated by H. Paolucci. New York: Bobbs-Merrill, 1963.

Bodin, Jean. *The Six Books of Commonweale.* Translated by R. Knooles. London: G. Bishop, 1606.

Bowman, Allan. *The Morale of the American Revolutionary Army.* Washington, D.C.: American Council on Economic Affairs, 1943.

Brown, Richard Maxwell. "Violence in the American Revolution." In S. Kurtz and J. Hutson, eds., *Essays on the American Revolution.* Chapel Hill: University of North Carolina Press, 1973.

Brown, Weldon A. *Empire or Independence: A Study in the Failure of Reconciliation, 1774-1783.* Berkeley and Los Angeles: University of California Press, 1942.

Burgh, James. *Political Disquisitions.* London: Edward and Charles Dilly, 1774.

Capra, Fritjof. *The Turning Point: Science, Society and the Rising Culture.* New York: Simon and Schuster, 1982.

Caso, Adolph. *America's Italian Founding Fathers.* Boston: Brandon Press, 1975.

Cicero. *Selected Political Speeches.* Translated by M. Grant. New York: Penguin, 1962.

_____. *Murder Trials.* Translated by M. Grant. New York: Penguin, 1975, p. 75.

Cipolla, Carlo M. *Guns and Sails in the Early Phase of European Expansion, 1400-1700.* London: Collins, 1965.

Cohen, Sam. *The Truth About the Neutron Bomb.* New York: Morrow, 1983.

Corwin, Edwin. *The "Higher Law" Background of the American Revolution.* Cambridge, Mass.: Harvard University Press, 1967.

Crofts, Alfred, and Percy Buchanan. *A History of the Far East.* New York: David McKay, 1958.

Ellis, John. *Armies in Revolution.* London: Croom Helm, 1973.

Ellul, Jacques. *The Technological Society.* New York: Knopf, 1964.

Elvin, Mark. *The Pattern of the Chinese Past.* Stanford: Stanford University Press, 1973.

Ferguson, Marilyn. *The Aquarian Conspiracy: Personal and Social Transformation in the 1980s.* Los Angeles: Tarcher, 1980.

Fletcher, Andrew. "A Discourse of Government with Relation to Militias." In *Political Works.* London: Robert Urie, 1749.

Gabba, Emilio. *Republican Rome, the Army and the Allies.* Berkeley and Los Angeles: University of California Press, 1976.

Gimpel, Jean. *The Medieval Machine: The Industrial Revolution of the Middle Ages.* New York: Holt, Rinehart and Winston, 1976.

Granter, H. "The Machiavellianism of George Mason." *William and Mary Quarterly* 17 (1937): 239.

Halbrook, Stephen P. "The Jurisprudence of the Second and Fourteenth Amendments." *George Mason University Law Review* 4 (1981): 1-69.

_____. "To Keep and Bear Their Private Arms: The Adoption of the Second Amendment." *Northern Kentucky Law Review* 10 (1982): 13-39.

Headrick, Daniel R. "Tools of Imperialism: Technology and the Expansion of European Colonial Empires in the Nineteenth Century." *Journal of Modern History* 51 (June 1979): 231-63.

Kohn, Richard H. "The Murder of the Militia System in the Aftermath of the American Revolution. In Stanley J. Unterdal, ed., *Military History of the American Revolution*, pp. 110-34. Colorado Springs: United States Air Force Academy, 1974.

Kohr, Leopold. *The Breakdown of Nations.* New York: Dutton, 1978.

Leiby, Adrian. *The American Revolutionary War in the Hackensack Valley: The Jersey Dutch and the Neutral Ground, 1775-1783.* New Brunswick, N.J.: Rutgers University Press, 1963.

Locke, John. *Of Civil Government.* Chicago: Henry Regnery, 1955.

Machiavelli, Niccolo. *The Prince.* Translated by L. Ricci. New York: New American Library, 1952.

_____ . *The Art of War.* Translated by F. Farnsworth. Indianapolis, Ind.: Bobbs-Merrill, 1965.

_____ . *Discourses.* Translated by L. Walker. New York: Penguin, 1970.

Marina, William. "Surviving in the Interstices." *Reason* 7 (June 1975): 64-69.

_____ . "U.S. Interventions: Aberrations or Empire?" *Reason* 8 (February 1976): 40-45.

_____ . "The American Revolution and the Minority Myth." *Modern Age* 20 (Summer 1976): 298-309.

_____ . "Revolution and Social Change: The American Revolution as a People's War." *Literature of Liberty* 1 (April/June 1978): 5-39.

_____ . "Egalitarianism and Empire." In K.S. Templeton, Jr., ed., *The Politicization of Society,* pp. 125-65. Indianapolis, Ind.: Liberty Press, 1979.

_____ . "William Appleman Williams." In Clyde N. Wilson, ed., *Twentieth-Century American Historians,* vol. 17 of *Dictionary of Literary Biography,* pp. 450-58. Detroit: Gale Research/Bruccoli Clark, 1983.

Marina, William, and Diane Cuervo. "The Dutch-American Guerrillas of the American Revolution." In Gary North, ed., *The Theology of Christian Resistance: A Symposium,* vol. 2 of *Christianity and Civilization,* pp. 242-65. Tyler, Tex.: Geneva Divinity School Press, 1983.

McNeill, William H. *The Pursuit of Power: Technology, Armed Force, and Society Since A.D. 1000.* Chicago: University of Chicago Press, 1982.

Mitchell, Terence R. *People in Organizations: Understanding Their Behavior.* New York: McGraw-Hill, 1978.

Montesquieu. *The Spirit of the Laws.* Translated by T. Nugent. New York: Colonial Press, 1899.

Mullett, Charles. "Classical Influences on the American Revolution." *Classical Journal* 35 (1939): 93-112.

Orwell, George. *Homage to Catalonia.* New York: Harcourt Brace, 1952.

Palmer, Dave Richard. *The Way of the Fox: American Strategy in the War for America, 1775-1783.* Westport, Conn.: Greenwood, 1974.

Parker, Rodger Durrell. "The Gospel of Opposition: A Study in Eighteenth Century Anglo-American Ideology." Ph.D. dissertation, Wayne State University, 1975.

Pierre, Andrew J. *The Global Politics of Arms Sales.* Princeton: Princeton University Press, 1982.

Plato. *Republic.* Translated by F. Cornford. London: Oxford University Press, 1945.

Pocock, J.G.A. *The Machiavellian Movement: Florentine Political Thought and the Atlantic Republican Tradition.* Princeton, N.J.: Princeton University Press, 1975.

_____. "Between Machiavelli and Hume." In G.W. Bowersock, ed., *Edward Gibbon and the Decline and Fall of the Roman Empire.* Cambridge: Harvard University Press, 1977.

_____. *The Political Works of James Harrington.* London: Cambridge University Press, 1977.

Preston, Richard A.; Sydney F. Wise; and Herman O. Werner. *Men in Arms: A History of Warfare and Its Interrelationships with Western Society.* New York: Praeger, 1962.

Quigley, Carroll. *The Evolution of Civilizations: An Introduction to Historical Analysis.* New York: Macmillan, 1961.

_____. "Weapons Systems and Political Stability: A History." Quigley Papers, Georgetown University, Washington, D.C. (Unpublished.)

Reid, John Phillip. *In Defiance of the Law: The Standing Army Controversy, the Two Constitutions, and the Coming of the American Revolution.* Chapel Ilill: University of North Carolina Press, 1981.

Robbins, C. "Algernon Sidney's Discourses." *William and Mary Quarterly* 4 (3rd series, 1947): 267.

Robson, Eric. *The American Revolution in Its Political and Military Aspects.* London: Cambridge University Press, 1953.

Rothbard, Murray N. *"Salutary Neglect": The American Colonies in the First Half of the 18th Century,* vol. 2 of *Conceived in Liberty.* New Rochelle, N.Y.: Arlington House, 1975.

Schumacher, E.F. *Small is Beautiful: Economics as If People Mattered.* New York: Harper, 1973.

Schwoerer, Lois G. *"No Standing Armies!" The Antiarmy Ideology in Seventeenth Century England.* Baltimore: Johns Hopkins University Press, 1974.

Shalhope, Robert E. "The Ideological Origins of the Second Amendment." *Journal of American History* 69 (December 1982): 599–614.

Shy, John. *A People Numerous and Armed: Reflections on the Military Struggle for American Independence.* New York: Oxford University Press, 1976.

Sidney, Algernon. *Discourses Concerning Government.* London: n.p., 1968.

Smith, Page. *A New Age Now Begins.* New York: McGraw-Hill, 1976.

Starr, Chester G. *Civilization and the Caesars.* New York: Norton, 1965.

Stavrianos, L.S. *The Promise of the Coming Dark Age.* San Francisco: W.H. Freeman, 1976.

Story, Joseph. *Commentaries on the Constitution of the United States,* 5th ed., 3 vols. Boston: Little, Brown, 1897.

Thomas, Carol G. "War in Ancient Greece." In L.L. Farrar, Jr., ed., *War: A Historical, Political, and Social Study.* Santa Barbara, Calif.: ABC-Clio, 1978.

Trenchard, John, and T. Gordon. *The English Libertarian Heritage.* Edited by D. Jacobson. Indianapolis: Bobbs-Merrill, 1965.

Wallerstein, Immanuel. *The Modern World System: Capitalist Agriculture and the Origins of the European World-Economy in the Sixteenth Century.* New York: Academic Press, 1974.

Weatherup, Roy G. "Standing Armies and Armed Citizens: An Historical Analysis of the Second Amendment." *Hastings Constitutional Law Quarterly* 2 (Fall 1975): 961-1061.

Webb, Stephen Saunders. *The Governors-General: The English Army and the Definition of Empire, 1569-1681*. Chapel Hill: University of North Carolina Press, 1979.

Wesson, Robert G. *The Imperial Order*. Berkeley and Los Angeles: University of California Press, 1967.

_____. *State Systems: International Pluralism, Politics, and Culture*. New York: Free Press, 1978.

West, Richard. "Why the Peasants Revolted." *Spectator* (May 30, 1981).

Whisker, James B. "Historical Development and Subsequent Erosion of the Right to Keep and Bear Arms." *West Virginia Law Review* 78: 171-90.

White, John Todd. "Standing Armies in Time of War: Republican Theory and Military Practice During the American Revolution." Ph.D. dissertation, George Washington University, 1978.

PART VIII
POLITICAL AND SOCIAL ASPECTS OF GUN OWNERSHIP

Chapter 16

THE POLITICAL FUNCTIONS OF GUN CONTROL

Raymond G. Kessler

INTRODUCTION

The use of law for social control is most obvious in the case of criminal law, and most of the controversy about firearms laws centers around whether or not they will reduce crime. The main focus has thus been on the crime control functions of gun laws. However, an additional dimension of social control through law is the attempt by government to control dissident political activity. The purpose of this discussion is to focus attention on this much-ignored aspect of firearms laws and conduct a preliminary examination of some of the "political"[1] functions of gun control.

"Gun control"[2] refers to laws, usually criminal statutes, that regulate some or all of the following: manufacturing, assembling, selling,

1. As used herein, the term "political" refers to the violent and nonviolent processes by which individuals and groups seek to share in, capture, change, or destroy the apparatus of the state (see Max Weber, *From Max Weber*, ed. and trans. H.H. Gerth and C. Wright Mills [New York: Galaxy, 1958], p. 78; Randall Collins, *Conflict Sociology* [New York: Academic Press, 1975], p. 333). The term includes such processes at all levels of government (e.g., federal, state, local). Much of the material follows Don Kates, Jr., ed., *Restricting Handguns: The Liberal Skeptics Speak Out* (Croton-on-Hudson, N.Y.: North River Press, 1979); Lee Kennett and James L. Anderson, *The Gun in America: The Origin of a National Dilemma* (Westport, Conn.: Greenwood Press, 1975); and Stephen P. Halbrook, "The Armed People and the State Monopoly of Violence," 1977. (Unpublished) and was presented at the 1980 Annual Meeting of the Mid-South Sociological Association.

2. The terms "firearms laws," "firearms controls," "gun laws," and so forth are used interchangeably with the term "gun control." The term "weapons" includes not only firearms but also larger more sophisticated weapons of war as well as daggers and swords.

transferring, receiving, possessing, or carrying of firearms by all or certain categories of persons. Most, if not all, nations have such laws, and in the United States all three levels of government have various gun control statutes and ordinances.[3]

Since gun control refers to laws, and since laws are creations of the state, the main focus herein will be on the manner in which firearms control is functional for the government, that is, the groups and individuals who share in the exercise of the power of the state and act in its name.

As discussed herein, gun control has at least five political functions. It (1) increases citizen reliance on government and citizen tolerance of increased police powers and abuses. Such laws (2) help prevent opposition to government and (3) facilitate repressive action by government and its sympathizers. Gun control laws (4) lessen the pressure for major or radical reform and (5) can be selectively enforced against those perceived to be a threat to government.

No claim is made that this list exhausts all the possible political functions of gun control, that the functions are mutually exclusive, that gun control has only political functions, or that some or all of these functions are operative in jurisdictions with firearms controls. At any time, gun control may serve none, some, or all of these political functions (as well as other functions), and these may change over time, including a change from manifest to latent or vice-versa.

The Context of Gun Laws

In times of political or social crisis, governments may enact or strengthen laws on political activity and political crime (e.g., insurrection, treason, sedition). Martial law or a state of emergency may be declared. Such crises often precede and/or follow radical or violent changes in government. If gun controls are enacted or more stringently enforced contemporaneously with these laws and/or events, it is likely that the controls have political functions.[4] For in-

3. See George Newton and Franklin Zimring, *Firearms and Violence in American Life: A Task Force Report to the National Commission on the Causes and Prevention of Violence* (Washington, D.C.: GPO, 1970), ch. 16; see Bureau of Alcohol, Tobacco and Firearms, *Your Guide to Firearms Regulation – 1978* (Washington, D.C.: GPO, 1978).

4. This is not to say that even under these circumstances gun control might not serve crime control functions. Ordinary (i.e., nonpolitical) crime might also increase during times

stance, confiscation of civilian weapons or other strict control followed the 1944 Communist takeover in Bulgaria, Castro's successful revolution in Cuba, the 1967 military coup in Greece, and the shooting of Ugandan President Milton Obote in 1969.[5]

Four Forms of Gun Laws

From the perspective of the political functions of gun laws, it can be said that such laws take four basic forms. No claim is made that this list is comprehensive, or that the forms are mutually exclusive. Some nations use or have used various combinations at the same time.

First, some gun control laws specifically refer to certain groups, thus suggesting that the laws have political functions. In the first part of this century, the massive influx of immigrants from eastern and southern Europe caused much fear of crime, anarchy, and revolution among established groups in the United States and Canada. Symptomatic of this reaction was firearms legislation explicitly discriminating against aliens.[6]

In the second form, the laws speak in political terms and often give officials discretion as to the granting of permits. For instance in Poland, permits to possess firearms are not issued to those who may use firearms "for purposes inconsistent with the security of the state or of public order."[7] In New Jersey an applicant for a permit to purchase a handgun and for a firearms purchaser identification card must, under N.J.S.A. 2C: 58–3 (e), state, inter alia, "whether he presently or ever has been a member of any organization which advocates or approves the commission of acts of force or violence to overthrow the government of the United States or of this State. . . ."

A third form includes laws that are apolitically worded and include or exclude no groups by name. Some of these explicitly provide discretion to officials in granting permits, licenses, and so forth.

---

of political crisis when authorities are paralyzed, demoralized, or too concerned with political activity and political crime to do much about ordinary crime.

5. Library of Congress, *Gun Control Laws in Foreign Countries* (Washington, D.C.: Library of Congress, 1976), p. 33; Robert B. Kukla, *Gun Control* (Harrisburg, Penn.: Stackpole Books, 1973), p. 442; "Uganda Curbs Firearms," *New York Times*, 22 December 1969, p. 36.

6. See Kennett and Anderson, *The Gun in America*, pp. 167–89; Don B. Kates, "Handgun Prohibition in the United States," in Kates, ed., *Restrcting Handguns*, pp. 16–19.

7. Library of Congress, *Gun Control Laws in Foreign Countries*, p. 157.

As suggested by the fifth function, the intentionally or unintentionally biased manner in which such laws are administered or enforced could have political consequences. For instance, there is suspicion that gun laws in the United States are enforced in a discriminatory manner against blacks.[8] Even if the laws give little or no discretion and are administered and enforced neutrally, the results nonetheless may be those suggested by the first four functions.

Finally, there are laws that ban firearms possession and so forth, by civilians in certain specific areas or types of facilities. As discussed below, Malaysia has such a law. In the United States, many state legislatures responded to the carrying of weapons by militant students and the massive and frequently violent student unrest of the 1960s with legislation prohibiting guns on campus except when carried by police, security guards, and the like.[9]

GUN CONTROL INCREASES CITIZEN DEPENDENCE ON GOVERNMENT

One of the functions of the state is to control "disruptive" behavior, some of which is defined as criminal. However, since government does not provide a bodyguard for every citizen and cannot deter, incapacitate, or rehabilitate every criminal, the protection offered by government is supplemented by the activities of groups (e.g., neighborhood patrols) and private individuals.[10] In all American jurisdictions, private citizens are authorized to use force to defend themselves, their families, and their property under certain circumstances. This authorization is usually reflected in the criminal defenses of self-defense, defense of others, defense of habitation or property, and so forth.[11] Crime control is thus a mixture of governmental and private activity.

---

8. See David T. Hardy and Kenneth L. Chotiner, "The Potentiality for Civil Liberties Violations in the Enforcement of Handgun Prohibition," in Kates, ed., *Restricting Handguns*, pp. 210–11.

9. See "Campus Violence Spurs New Laws Across the Nation," *New York Times*, 1 September 1969, p. 1.

10. Don B. Kates, Jr., "Can We Arrest Police Budgets," *Taxing and Spending* (April 1979): 2–7.

11. Charles E. Torcia, ed., *Wharton's Criminal Law*, 14th ed., vol. 2 (Rochester, N.Y.: Lawyers Cooperative, 1979), pp. 138–52, 316–24.

In view of the above, consider a jurisdiction that severely limits possession of firearms. Those who are law-abiding will, by definition, not possess proscribed weapons. If alternative defensive weapons, devices, or techniques are not available (or are not perceived to be effective), the more law-abiding citizens will have to look to government, rather than themselves, for protection. In general, the more citizens are dependent on government, the more likely they are to accept expanded police powers and abuses to deal with crime and the less likely they are to challenge the status quo.[12]

If government should succeed in keeping crime at a tolerable level, citizens will support the government because of its success. On the other hand, if unarmed citizens are severely dissatisfied with government protection, they may press for change in government. If dissatisfied, unarmed citizens place the blame for crime on those outside government (e.g., unpopular minority groups, "communists"), they will call on government to suppress these "causes," thus again increasing their dependence on government.

It is also conceivable that the effect of a weapons ban in a violent political situation would be to increase citizen dependence on government and ultimately to polarize the political situation. The rebels will not obey firearms laws and may obtain additional weapons from foreign interests or powers, as appears to be the case in Northern Ireland, Israel, Afghanistan, and El Salvador. The government will further arm itself and arm and protect its supporters.

Groups and political figures caught in the middle may better represent the majority and be able to effectuate a peaceful solution. However, the ability of the moderates to defend themselves and to act and speak out may be severely impaired by gun laws. Government may not consent to their arming for self-defense. Or, it may allow them to arm after obtaining concessions. Taking government arms or accepting permission to arm, however, may ruin the ability of the moderates to act as neutral go-betweens. They cannot obtain weapons from other sources without risking prosecution or their neutrality. Disarmed and in a volatile situation, they may be denied the protection of either side and be attacked by either side as long as they attempt to play the role of neutral peacemaker. As the violence

---

12. This is not to imply that all persons who are dependent in some way on government are politically passive. For instance, welfare recipients have challenged the government in lawsuits and have formed activist organizations such as the Welfare Rights Organization.

escalates, the defenseless moderate elements may either be silenced or driven into the ranks of government or its opponents.

Although this brief discussion cannot do justice to the complexity of the issue, there may be some situations in which gun control leads to increased dependence on government for protection. This dependence may, in turn, deter or moderate challenges to the governmental status quo and abuses of police powers.

GUN CONTROL HELPS PREVENT OPPOSITION TO, AND FACILITATES REPRESSIVE ACTION BY, GOVERNMENT

The second and third functions of gun control are closely related, and when it has one of these functions it is likely to have the other. For the sake of brevity, they are discussed together.

These political functions have been at least implicitly recognized by individuals and commissions seeking solutions to the problems of riots and terrorism.[13] The Task Force on Disorders and Terrorism of the National Advisory Commission on Criminal Justice Standards and Goals recommends legislation designed to reduce the possibility of illegal acquisition and utilization of firearms by "subversive groups" and effective search policies to implement laws making the carrying of concealed weapons a serious offense.[14]

In democratic societies, those on the political extremes often perceive that they have little chance of victory through the electoral or other peaceful processes. They may thus seek violent means of attaining their goals.[15] Firearms facilitate terrorist or revolutionary activity, and thus violent groups on the far left and far right could be expected to strongly resist efforts to disarm them. Those extremist groups who want easy access to weapons are thus going to oppose restrictions on firearms—at least to the extent it affects them. It is thus not surprising that a number of such groups, at both extremes

13. For example, David Schoendiger, "Riot Control Legislation: A Necessary Evil," in M. Cherif Bassiovni, ed., *The Law of Dissent and Riots* (Springfield, Ill.: Charles C. Thomas, 1971), p. 344; Arnold Kotz, "Firearms, Violence and Civil Disorders," Stanford Research Institute Report, 1968, pp. 11–15. (Unpublished.)

14. Task Force on Disorders and Terrorism, *Disorders and Terrorism* (Washington, D.C.: GPO, 1975), pp. 85–86.

15. Arnold Forster, "Violence on the Fanatical Left and Right," *Annals of the American Academy of Political and Social Sciences* 364 (1966): 141–48.

of the political spectrum, have opposed gun control.[16] (This is not to imply that all who oppose gun controls are extremists. Opposition to gun control can be found among both conservatives and liberals in the mainstream of American politics. By the same token, all who support firearms control do not do so because they are conscious of its political functions.) In nondemocratic societies, it may be the majority, not just the extremists, who seek to arm for violent revolt if peaceful processes cannot bring change.

From the government's perspective, the best way to deal with a violent attempt at political change is to prevent it from occurring. Propaganda and the granting of limited autonomy to potentially rebellious regions are two well-known techniques for preventing disorder. Another is to attempt to disarm the potentially rebellious through firearms controls.

If government wants to make a strong, unpopular political move against the population or segments thereof, it would be wise policy to disarm the populace first. An armed population may deter government action; a disarmed population is less of a deterrent.[17] The greater the extent to which potentially violent dissidents are denied access to weapons, the less likely they are to perceive that violence will be successful against well-armed military and police forces. The reduced likelihood of success may deter these groups from issuing a violent challenge to government. Tilly points out, for instance, that a government can raise a contending group's mobilization costs (and thereby raise its costs of collective action) by "freezing necessary resources such as guns and manpower."[18]

If government cannot prevent the start of rebellion through firearms control or other nonviolent means, it may be compelled to act with force against the rebels, their sympathizers, and potential converts. The potential of government success (and the inability of dissidents and others to resist) would seem to be inversely proportional to, among other factors, the amount of weaponry available to the rebels. In other words, when government or its sympathizers react with violence or threats of violence, they have a higher probability of success if opponents have little or no firepower. Common sense

16. Newton and Zimring, *Firearms and Violence in American Life*, App. F.
17. David T. Hardy, "The Second Amendment as a Restraint on Federal Firearms Restrictions," in Kates ed., *Restricting Handguns*, p. 184.
18. Charles Tilly, *From Mobilization to Revolution* (Reading, Mass.: Addison-Wesley, 1978), p. 100.

would lead the heads of any government to realize that "the greater the coercive resources—including private armies, weapons and segments of the national armed forces—controlled by the revolutionary coalition, the more likely a transfer of power."[19] Gun control is obviously one way to limit the coercive resources of opponents or, to use Gurr's terms, to influence the "coercive balance."[20] While it is unlikely that confirmed revolutionaries would voluntarily comply with or be deterred by it, gun control may have some effect on those in sympathy with the rebels and those who are currently neutral but later go over to the revolutionary side.

There are other more individualized ways in which gun control laws may assist government in dealing with either violent efforts at political change or, as described in the following section, peaceful reform efforts. Firearms violations can be trumped up to harass and discredit opponents and justify their arrest, detention, trial, and punishment. Searches for weapons, whether bona fide or not, can provide a "cover" for invading political headquarters and the homes of dissidents in order to harass or assault them and to collect membership lists, correspondence, and "subversive" publications. Undercover agents can offer illegal weapons to militants and then have them arrested for possessing the weapons. Agents for the government can urge dissidents to obtain illegal weapons and assist them in doing so. They can also "plant" illegal weapons in selected places so as to justify searches for weapons and arrests for weapons offenses. Infiltrators can provide information on the presence of weapons that can justify searches and arrests and can assist authorities in planning raids to search for and seize weapons.[21]

GUN CONTROL LESSENS THE PRESSURE FOR REFORM

Another strategy the government can use to defuse potentially explosive situations is to grant reforms beneficial to dissatisfied groups. Gurr points out that if dissidents have arms and sympathy from some

---

19. Ibid., p. 216.
20. Ted Robert Gurr, *Why Men Rebel* (Princeton, N.J.: Princeton University Press, 1970), ch. 8.
21. Such potential abuses are not limited to gun laws. Any possessory offense (e.g., narcotics, pornography) lends itself to this type of activity.

of the military and police, the coercive capacity of the dissidents may increase to the point where they can "obtain major concessions without having full-fledged revolutionary organizations or even revolutionary motives."[22] If these groups are poorly armed, because of gun control or for other reasons, they pose less of a threat. Thus, in general, if the government imposes gun control early, it may find it necessary to grant fewer concessions later when previously passive or nonviolent groups begin seeking arms.[23]

There is another manner in which gun control might lessen the pressures for reform. As a panacea for violent crime, gun control can be touted as the only solution or at least as an alternative to the solution of eliminating poverty, unemployment, racism, and other possible causes of the violence. The primary victims of these causes are, almost by definition, the politically powerless, and elimination of these causes might require drastic reform. Such reform might involve a decrease in the wealth and power of those segments of the population which disproportionately influence government policy. If gun control could minimize violent crime, it would eliminate a justification for radical reform. Even if unsuccessful, the existence of gun control laws could be perceived as an attempt by government to do something about the problem and might help divert attention and support from proposals for radical reform as a solution to the crime problem.

GUN CONTROL CAN BE SELECTIVELY ENFORCED

Because gun control offenses involve possessing, carrying, selling, and so forth, they are crimes in which the persons involved are participating voluntarily and do not feel victimized. The individuals possessing weapons or those involved in illegal firearms transactions are generally not going to inform on themselves. These are thus "complainantless" crimes, which are not easily detected. The police must seek out these offenses by aggressive techniques such as entrapment and the utilization of undercover agents and informers. Law enforcement

---

22. Gurr, *Why Men Rebel*, p. 261.
23. Some of the earlier discussion of violent and nonviolent routes to change in the section on the second and third functions is also relevant to this function.

personnel can thus choose the individuals or groups they want to investigate.[24]

Just as the laws against marijuana were selectively enforced against unpopular groups, gun control laws that are seemingly nondiscriminatory and apolitical can be selectively enforced against persons who are perceived to constitute a threat to government.[25] Even though there might be some enforcement against neutral or pro-government groups and individuals to maintain an appearance of fairness, the bulk of the enforcement efforts could be directed against actual and potential opponents.[26]

Salter and Kates point out that

> [a]dvocacy of controversial political or social views frequently provokes violent antagonisms. Although they are usually unwilling or politically unable to suppress these views, officials can covertly withdraw police protection, leaving the job [of suppression] to such groups as the Ku Klux Klan, the White Citizens Council, the Cherry Society and the Black Hand.[27]

At the same time, pro-government extremists could be given de facto immunity from gun control and other laws to promote their intimidation of and attacks on opposition or nonconformist groups. Simultaneously, gun control and other laws could be selectively enforced against opposition groups. If opposition groups could be stripped of their means of self-defense, government could then unleash well-armed pro-government terrorists on the opposition. For instance, in 1969, hundreds of demonstrators were machine-gunned by right-wing extremists in Mexico City. Both possession of automatic weapons and murder are strictly forbidden by law in Mexico. "Nevertheless, the police made no arrests—either on the scene or when the attackers later invaded hospitals to finish off the wounded."[28]

24. Raymond G. Kessler, "Enforcement Problems of Gun Control: A Victimless Crime Analysis," *Criminal Law Bulletin* 16 (March-April 1980): 135–40.

25. John Kaplan, *Marijuana: The New Prohibition* (New York: World, 1970), pp. 41–42.

26. Hardy and Chotiner, "The Potentiality for Civil Liberties Violations in the Enforcement of Handgun Prohibition," pp. 202, 209–11.

27. John Salter and Don B. Kates, Jr., "The Necessity of Access to Firearms by Dissenters and Minorities Whom Government is Unwilling or Unable to Protect," in Kates, ed., *Restricting Handguns*, p. 127.

28. Ibid.

Unfortunately, selective enforcement is difficult to detect. Officials can usually be expected to attempt to conceal such practices. Intensive case studies may reveal individual instances, but detailed, large-scale studies are needed to prove systematic discrimination with regard to gun laws. Thus far, no adequate large-scale studies have been conducted.

EXAMPLES OF THE POLITICAL FUNCTIONS

The political functions of gun control are worldwide phenomena and can be traced at least as far back as the mid-sixteenth century, when firearms were crude, bulky devices. While a few examples were presented earlier, the following material makes clear the historic and geographic pervasiveness of the political functions of gun control and briefly attempts to place the examples in their social and political context. Examples from both left- and right-wing governments are presented.

England and France

In England, from the 1500s through the early 1800s, various governments took numerous steps to disarm religious and political opponents.[29] Further, some of the controversy over the composition, size, utilization, and arming of the militia was related to the political functions of gun control.[30] Even as early as the mid-sixteenth century, when firearms were still mechanically imperfect, there existed a deep-seated fear among the ruling classes about putting such dangerous weapons into the hands of the people at large.[31] Western points

---

29. Disarming individuals then meant seizure not only of firearms but of broadswords, axes, and so forth. This analysis of France and England follows Kennett and Anderson, *The Gun in America*, pp. 20–25.

30. See Lindsay Boynton, *The Elizabethan Militia* (London: Routledge and Kegan Paul, 1967), p. 57. This controversy highlights a firearms policy not usually thought of as gun control but which has political implications. Rather than taking away weapons, the government refuses to allow certain disfavored segments of the population to become part of the militia. In addition to shutting off a supply of or excuse for having firearms, the policy denies disfavored segments the training in arms use that favored groups will obtain.

31. Boynton, *The Elizabethan Militia*, p. 57.

out that a civil population in arms represented a constant threat of disorder or worse.[32]

For financial, administrative, and political reasons, "it was impossible to maintain a standing force strong enough to disarm or entirely overawe the nation." The only alternative was to arm and organize the allies of government as a sort of amateur gendarmerie to counterbalance the malcontents. If there was an uprising, the loyalists were to come together and beat it down. At other times the militia was "to try to anticipate trouble by searching for and confiscating the arms of likely troublemakers" and more generally to deter the disaffected by "showing the flag" and making it seem that force was on the side of the government. For example, some of the tasks of the militia of the Restoration during the period 1660–1670 in opposing the republicans were "in part preventive—the seizure of their arms" and the disruption of their organization.[33]

Even the game laws in England had political functions. These laws had an inhibiting effect on the ownership of firearms, since mere possession of hunting weapons was sometimes the basis for prosecution. The purpose of the game laws was at least in part to keep the masses disarmed.[34] The eminent eighteenth-century jurist Sir William Blackstone noted that one of the reasons for the existence of these laws was that they aided in the "prevention of popular insurrections and resistance to government by disarming the bulk of the people. . . ."[35]

Later, in response to radical demonstrations in 1819, Parliament passed the notorious Six Acts, which, among other things, empowered magistrates to search homes for weapons, confiscate them, and arrest their owners.[36] During the long debates on the Acts, reference to the French Revolution was made repeatedly; Was the government, asked the ministers, to imitate the weakness of Louis XVI and go along idly while the throne and altar perished as they had in France?[37] Referring to the Acts, Wellington wrote, "Our example

32. J. R. Western, *The English Militia in the Eighteenth Century* (London: Routledge and Kegal Paul, 1965), p. 5.

33. Ibid.

34. Kennett and Anderson, *The Gun in America*, p. 25.

35. Sir William Blackstone, *Commentaries on the Laws of England*, 1783, 9th ed., reprint (New York: Garland, 1978), p. 412.

36. T. A. Critchley, *The Conquest of Violence: Order and Liberty in Britain* (New York: Schocken Books, 1970), p. 117.

37. Frederick B. Artz, *Reaction and Revolution, 1814–1832* (New York: Harper, 1934), p. 126.

will render some good in France as well as in Germany, and we must hope that the world will escape the universal revolution which seems to menace us all."[38]

Although space limitations prohibit detailed analysis, the French experience during the sixteenth through eighteenth centuries paralleled that of England in many respects. As in England there was great reluctance to utilize the masses in the militia, numerous laws and edicts restricting firearms, especially among the lower classes, and attempts to disarm political opponents.[39] While the French monarchy was sincere in the belief that banning firearms would reduce crime, it would be misleading to conclude that this was the sole reason for the reiterated prohibitions; "What the law did not say, but what the King knew very well, was that his subjects were all too capable of insurrection and rebellion."[40]

Kennett and Anderson conclude that these anti-weapons policies in England and France are understandable in the context of "paternal governments, social hierarchies and restless masses"; a monarch could "scarcely risk confiding the ultimate coercive power in the state" to those masses to whom he denied representation and political power.[41]

The Nazi Example

In twentieth-century Europe, one of the most controversial yet most poorly researched topics is the use of firearms controls by the Nazis. Fairly strict firearms controls predated the 1933 Nazi takeover in Germany, and the Library of Congress could find nothing in its collection that would indicate statutory confiscation of privately owned firearms when Hitler came to power.[42] However, according to a commentary of Nazi firearms laws, after the Fuhrer's takeover the government acted decisively and took away "weapons still remaining in the hands of people inimical to the State . . . "[43]

---

38. Ibid., p. 126.
39. Kennett and Anderson, *The Gun in America*, pp. 8–16.
40. Ibid., p. 14.
41. Ibid., p. 26. Although Kennett and Anderson are referring to "pre-1789 Europe," the conclusion applies to later events such as the Six Acts of 1819.
42. Library of Congress, *Gun Control Laws in Foreign Countries*, pp. 77–80.
43. Ibid., p. 80.

By 1938 the government felt secure enough to pass new gun laws, which would permit some segments of the population to obtain firearms.[44] For instance, under the 1938 "Law of Weapons" and subsequent decrees, licenses to obtain or carry firearms could be issued to persons whose reliability was not in doubt and who could prove a need for them. Among the classes who were to be denied licenses were "gypsies," persons

> for whom police surveillance has been declared admissible, or upon whom the loss of civil rights has been imposed, for the duration of the police surveillance or the loss of civic rights; [and] persons who have been convicted of treason or high treason, or against whom facts are under consideration which justify the assumption that they are acting in a manner inimical to the state.[45]

Jews were also excluded from eligibility for firearms licenses, and since they could not depend on the government for protection, unarmed Jews were left virtually defenseless against official and unofficial violence.[46] Another Nazi firearms law denied licenses to trade in, assemble, or repair firearms or ammunition "if the applicant, or the persons intended to become the commercial or technical managers of the operation or trade, or any one of them, is a Jew."[47] Later, when German Jews and those from occupied countries were forced into ghettos in Poland, both individual and collective punishment were meted out when any resident was found in possession of weapons.[48] Although there was violent resistance by many Jews, they were often plagued by a lack of arms.[49]

With regard to countries occupied by the Nazis, neither Bakal nor the Library of Congress could find evidence that the Nazis used gun

44. Ibid.

45. Library of Congress. Exhibits. In *Federal Firearms Legislation Hearings Before the Subcommittee to Investigate Juvenile Delinquency of the U.S. Senate Committee on the Judiciary*. Washington, D.C.: GPO, 1968, pp. 491–92.

46. Salter and Kates, "The Necessity of Access to Firearms by Dissenters and Minorities," pp. 185, 188.

47. Library of Congress, *Federal Firearms Legislation Hearings*, p. 490. While it can be argued that this law was merely symptomatic of a general attempt to drive Jews out of the trades, businesses, and professions, it is still significant that a special provision for firearms was felt necessary.

48. Isaiah Truck, "The Attitude of the Judenrats to Problems of Armed Resistance against the Nazis," in *Jewish Resistance During the Holocaust* (Jerusalem: Yad Vashem, 1971), p. 203.

49. Yuri Suhl, ed., *They Fought Back* (New York: Schocken Books, 1967), pp. 5–6; Ber Mark, *Uprising in the Warsaw Ghetto* (New York: Schocken Books, 1975), pp. 7, 15, 112, 118.

registration lists to seize firearms.[50] On the other hand, Kukla concludes that the Nazi occupiers forced the Danish government to
enact gun registration and then used these lists to facilitate confiscation.[51] It is clear, however, that the Nazis issued proclamations
ordering the submission of firearms and implements of war to the
authorities and carried out searches to enforce them.[52] These bans
on firearms were often accompanied by bans on political activities,
thus highlighting the political functions of the firearms prohibitions.
For instance, in German-occupied Serbia, a 1941 decree provided
military punishment for

1. Violations of the order for the surrender of radio transmitters, guns, and
   other implements of war. . . .
7. Street meetings, distribution of leaflets, arrangement of public assemblies
   and demonstrations without previous approval by a German commander
   . . .
8. Inducing work stoppages, malicious stoppage of work, strikes and lock-
   outs.[53]

Similar decrees were planned for England, where immediate execution was to be the fate of anyone who failed to turn in firearms
within twenty-four hours.[54] Exceptions to the firearms prohibitions
were, however, made for those whom the occupying forces could
trust. For example in Norway, exceptions were granted "to such
persons as have been given permission by German military commanders (for the protection of works) or from the German Security
Police."[55]

The Library of Congress concluded:

This sampling of German statutes, decrees and other documents concerning
firearms indicated two points: first, the profound importance the German
invaders attached to the possession of firearms. Second, the importance of

50. Bakal (1969), p. 277; Library of Congress, *Federal Firearms Legislation Hearings*,
p. 483.
51. Kukla, *Gun Control*, p. 440.
52. Library of Congress, *Federal Firearms Legislation Hearings*, p. 488; Raphael Lemkin, *Axis Rule in Occupied Europe* (Washington, D.C.: Carnegie Endowment for International Peace, Division of International Law, 1944), pp. 163, 318, 422, 566. When U.S.
forces occupied Germany at the end of World War II, they issued similar decrees (Bakal
Federal Firearms Legislation, p. 278).
53. Lemkin, *Axis Rule in Occupied Europe*, p. 591.
54. William H. Shirer, *The Rise and Fall of the Third Reich* (New York: Simon and
Shuster, 1959), p. 782.
55. Library of Congress, *Federal Firearms Legislation Hearings*, p. 487.

these proclamations and decrees as a technique used by the Germans to obtain and limit weapons in the possession of the nationals of the invaded country. . . . A totalitarian society, and particularly a totalitarian society occupying a country against its will, simply cannot permit the private possession of weapons to any great extent, except by those who have proven their loyalty.[56]

The Soviet Union

In the Soviet Union peaceful dissident political activity is subject to severe sanctions, and the acquisition and possession of firearms are "subject to severe restrictions and limitations by the state."[57] The laws essentially ban all private ownership of handguns.[58] In 1978 Soviet dissident Alexander Podrabnick was the subject of an alleged blackmail attempt by the Soviet government when the KGB (Soviet Secret Police) arrested his brother Kirill on a trumped-up charge of illegal possession of firearms. Because Alexander was known and respected around the world in the human rights movement and psychiatric profession, the KGB was reluctant to move directly against him. Their tactics were to pressure him into emigrating. When he refused, the KGB planted a pistol and ammunition in his brother Kirill's apartment. After Kirill was arrested, the KGB promised to drop the charges if Alexander would leave the country.[59]

Soviet dissidents are often subjected to harassment and assault by vigilantes.[60] Although there is no hard evidence, the dissidents suspect government acquiescence in if not encouragement of the vigilante activity and doubt the police will do anything about it.[61] The vigilante action and gun control laws place dissidents in a "can't win" situation. If they arm for portection, they will be arrested for

56. Ibid., p. 488.
57. See Amnesty International, *Report 1980* (London: Amnesty International, 1980), pp. 302–09; Library of Congress, *Gun Control Laws in Foreign Countries*, p. 181.
58. Charles J. Hanley, "Gun Controls More Stringent Abroad," *Kansas City Star*, 2 December 1980, p. 28A.
59. *St. Louis Post Dispatch*, 29 January 1978, p. 28. Podrabnick was later tried, convicted, and sentenced to five years internal exile for his expose of psychiatric abuses in the Soviet Union. This type of blackmail is not limited, of course, to firearms. The same result could be obtained by planting any illegal item (e.g., narcotics) in the residences or on the persons of dissidents or their families.
60. *Los Angeles Times*, 29 September 1980, p. 1.
61. Ibid.

violating the gun laws. If they do not arm, they may not be able to defend themselves and deter the vigilantes. The easiest solution to the dilemma is, of course, the one that would please the government most—stop dissenting.

Examples from Asia

Since late December 1979, Soviet military forces have occupied Afghanistan under two different puppet regimes. When the loyalty of some Afghan military battalions was questioned, Soviet commanders ordered that they be disarmed.[62] Although the Soviets have utilized tanks, helicopter gunships, etc., the rebels have put up stiff resistance in all parts of the country, even though their basic weapon is the locally made version of the Lee-Enfield rifle—a bolt action .30 caliber weapon not much different from many American hunting rifles.[63] After general strikes, nightly firefights, and ambushes the government declared martial law in the capital city. All residents of Kabul were ordered to surrender their firearms to police within twenty-four hours.[64]

In the Philippines, one of the countermeasures used by the government in dealing with the "Huk" rebellion of the 1950s was gun control. To preclude the possible flow of additional arms and ammunition to subversive hands, the government increased the penalty for illegal possession of firearms and ammunition.[65] In 1972, in response to alleged conspiracies to overthrow the government by violence and subversion, President Marcos instituted martial law and announced that "the carrying of firearms outside residences without the permission of the Armed Forces of the Philippines is punishable with death."[66] While this edict was later modified, subsequent measures completely outlawed private possession of most large caliber hand-

---

62. *Time*, 28 January 1980, p. 34.

63. *Kansas City Times*, 26 December 1980, p. B3.

64. *Time*, 3 March 1980, pp. 34–35.

65. Jesus Vargas and Rizal Tarciano, *Communism in Decline: The Huk Campaign* (Bangkok: SEATO, 1957), p. 18.

66. In January 1981 President Marcos announced the end of martial law in the Philippines; quoted in F.D. Pinpin, *The First 107 Presidential Decrees Consequent to Proclamation Nos. 1081/1104.* Consolidated edition, Book One Series, no. 7 (Mandaluyong, Rizal, Philippines: published per approval of the Department of Public Information, dated November 27, 1972), pp. XXXIV-XXXV.

guns and other firearms.[67] At the present time, more than 2,000 people are being detained for political reasons, and many individuals engaging in nonviolent expression of their political beliefs have been detained without trial for alleged criminal offenses, including firearms possession.[68] Allegations of violations of firearms law and rebellion were used against at least one prominent political opposition leader, former Senator Benigno S. Aquino.[69]

The government of Malaysia has been engaged in an armed struggle with communist insurgents since 1948 and since 1969 has been operating under a "state of emergency," which permits severe restrictions on individual rights. Insurgents kill or maim large numbers of military personnel and police each year. After widespread violence in 1975, amendments to the 1960 Internal Security Act included one of the world's most severe gun control laws.[70] A death sentence is mandatory for individuals convicted of possessing firearms in designated "security areas" or in circumstances which give rise to a "reasonable presumption that the [person] intends or is about to act, or has recently acted in a manner prejudicial to public security."[71] Since enactment, at least seven communist insurgents have been executed and others are awaiting execution.[72]

South Africa

In the Republic of South Africa, 4.4 million whites exercise almost complete economic and political control over 19.4 million Africans, 2.4 million Coloreds (mixed race), and 0.7 million Asians.[73] Although whites comprise only 16 percent of the population, they alone elect the government (which is entirely white), consume 60

67. Pinpin, *The First 107 Presidential Decrees*, p. 448.

68. Amnesty International, *Report 1980*, p. 225.

69. *New York Times*, 9 May 1980, p. A26. Following his three-year self-exile in the United States, Aquino returned to the Philippines and was assassinated there August 20, 1983.

70. See U.S. Department of State, *Country Reports on Human Rights Practices* (Washington, D.C.: GPO, 1981), pp. 657–58; Amnesty International, *Report 1980*, pp. 216–19.

71. Amnesty International, *Report 1980*, p. 219.

72. U.S. Department of State, *Country Reports*, p. 658; *Kansas City Star*, 2 May 1981, p. A5.

73. United Nations, "Women and Apartheid," *Objective Justice* 12 (August 1980): 25–27; Jim Hoagland, *South Africa* (Boston: Houghton Mifflin, 1972).

percent of the nation's income, and occupy 86.5 percent of the land.[74]

The white population, particularly the dominant Afrikaners (Dutch descent), have fashioned "white power into an enduring force based on the Bible and the gun"; officially enforced segregation (apartheid) and the Afrikaners' traditional way of life are aimed at keeping blacks politically powerless.[75] Because of fear of the Africans and Coloreds, whites have developed an internal security apparatus that rivals that of the Soviet Union in its single-minded and ruthless repression of dissidents.[76] Although the government uses a wide variety of means of stifling dissent, such as banning, detention without trial, and torture, it is not above the unnecessary shooting and killing of unarmed demonstrators (including children) for political purposes.[77] A white South African observed that the police "think they can shoot, arrest and beat the black back into submission, and on the past record, you have to conclude that they are right."[78]

For many segments of the white population, the severe measures taken by the government against nonwhites are not enough to provide security. "Fear of revolution pervades much of South African life."[79] The white community is one of the world's most heavily armed.[80] After every black disturbance, fearful whites besiege gun shops.[81] White vigilantes patrol white neighborhoods and engage in a variety of other activities ranging from surveillance to assault with firearms on dissidents.[82] While the government and white citizens spend millions to arm themselves, the government has mounted against nonwhites "one of the world's most effective gun control

74. Ibid., p. 26.

75. *Washington Post*, 11 January 1977, p. A12.

76. *Washington Post*, 14 January 1977, p. A12. Nothing herein is meant to imply that there is not white opposition to apartheid. White dissidents, however, are generally treated less severely. See Hoagland, *South Africa*, ch. 5.

77. Amnesty International, *Report 1980*, p. 74; Hoagland, *South Africa*, ch. 5; *Washington Post*, 14 January 1977, p. A12; Ambrose Reeves, "A Massacre Recalled" *Objective Status* 2 (January 1970): 32–35; Dennis Herbstein, *White Man, We Want to Talk to You!* (London: Andre Deutsch, 1979); chs. 1 and 6.

78. *Washington Post*, 14 January 1977.

79. William Frye, *In Whitest Africa* (Englewood Cliffs, N.J.: Prentice-Hall, 1968), p. 44.

80. Herbstein, *White Man*, p. 159; Frye, *In Whitest Africa*, p. 44.

81. *Washington Post*, 11 January 1977.

82. Jim Hoagland, "Mood of Fear Begins to Grip South African Whites," *Washington Post*, 13 January 1977, p. A20; Herbstein, *White Man*, pp. 159, 216; United Nations, "The Soweto Massacre and its Aftermath," *Objective Justice* 8 (Spring 1976): 6.

campaigns."[83] Even the black superhero of a black-oriented comic book series published by whites speaks out against firearms ownership; some liberals in South Africa suspect that the comics are aimed at promoting black subservience to white authorities.[84]

As the discussion above makes clear, the South African government has utilized unfettered police power as a substitute for responding to the basic political demands of urbanized Africans.[85] If nonwhites were not hindered from obtaining firearms, they could arm themselves and, because of their superiority in numbers, perhaps obtain concessions. Even though the whites have military hardware, they are still outnumbered by more than five to one, and armed rebellion might encourage military intervention by surrounding nations to assist the black insurrectionists.

Although there is a "Black Power" movement in South Africa, it has "proven no match for the guns and economic pressure" the white power structure uses to destroy it.[86] Even though blacks outnumber whites, Hoagland concludes that the "odds against a black population that is barred from obtaining arms seem enormous." When asked why the blacks and Coloreds do not revolt, a Colored leader responded, "The white man has all the tanks, the jets and the guns. We don't have anything. In a revolt, the blood that would be shed would be the blood of nonwhites."[87] A white opponent of apartheid responded: "Power does not grow out of the barrel of a gun if you do not have a gun."[88]

GUN CONTROL AND AMERICAN BLACKS

In the United States, the experience of blacks from slavery through the 1960s was one of the clearest and best-documented examples of the political functions of gun control.

83. *Washington Post*, 13 January 1977, p. A20.
84. "Africa: The Caped Crusader," *Newsweek*, 14 June 1976, p. 48.
85. *Washington Post*, 12 January 1977, p. A6.
86. Ibid.
87. Hoagland, *South Africa*, p. 145.
88. Ibid. This is not to imply that weapons are not smuggled or carried in from neighboring countries. The government, however, conducts raids to find the arms caches and uses military force against infiltrators (see Herbstein, *White Man*, pp. 233–35, 242). Note also the similarities to the nineteenth-century American South described in a later section.

Seventeenth Through Early Twentieth Centuries

In his study of slave revolts, Aptheker concludes that a ruling class, often subjected to periods of crisis arising from doubt of its ability to maintain its power, may be expected to develop complex and thorough systems of control.[89] America's slaveocracy developed a number of methods of suppression and oppression: one of these methods was gun control.[90] In fact, the first recorded legislation concerning blacks in Virginia (1640) excluded them from owning guns.[91] Throughout the South, the intense fear of slave revolts resulted in additional legislation, which included provisions further restricting the access of slaves to firearms.[92] The political functions of these laws were often indicated in their titles, for example, "An Act for the better preventing of Insurrections by Negroes."[93] In 1850 an Alabama legislator recognized the political functions of gun control when he attempted to minimize fears of the slave population by pointing out that slaves were disarmed, unaccustomed to the use of arms, and thus could be easily suppressed.[94]

Slave rebellions frightened the ruling class into granting concessions, such as the establishment of minimal legal protections for slaves.[95] Had the slaves not been restricted in their access to firearms, their actual and potential revolts might have been even more devastating, and even greater concessions might have been obtained.

At the close of the Civil War, Frederick Douglass was concerned that legislatures in the South still had power to pass laws discriminating against blacks and predicted that, in addition to other disabili-

---

89. Herbert Aptheker, *American Negro Slave Revolts* (New York: International Publishers, 1963), p. 53. It should be noted that slavery was not simply "an economic institution; it was a social, and by exclusion, a political one as well" (Don B. Kates, Jr., "Abolition, Deportation, Integration: Attitudes Toward Slavery in the Early Republic," *Journal of Negro History* 53 [January 1968] : 37). This analysis of gun control and blacks follows Kennett and Anderson, *The Gun in America*, chs. 2 and 6; Kates, "Handgun Prohibition in the United States"; and Robert Sherrill, *The Saturday Night Special* (New York: Charterhouse, 1973).
90. Apetheker, *American Negro Slave Revolts*, pp. 53, 70–74.
91. Kennett and Anderson, *The Gun in America*, p. 50.
92. Ibid.
93. Aptheker, *American Negro Slave Revolts*, p. 71.
94. Ibid., p. 36.
95. Herbert Aptheker, *Essays in the History of the American Negro* (New York: International Publishers, 1964), p. 64.

ties, the freedmen would be restricted in their access to firearms.[96] Immediately after the war, provisional governments set up militia organizations that excluded former slaves and were used to disarm the freedmen.[97] Later, however, radical state governments in some Southern states were able to abolish the provisional militia and set up Negro militias.[98] Eventually, however, abandoned by the national government and subjected to violent attack and intimidation, as well as some legitimate politicking, the black militias and radical governments succumbed.[99] One contemporary observer stated, "It is no longer with them [anti-Reconstruction forces] the number of votes but the number of guns."[100] When white supremacists captured the legislatures, they confirmed Douglass' fears.

The use of firearms by blacks had "social and political implications," and among the laws designed to maintain what Southern legislators "considered due subordination of the freedmen" were prohibitions against Negroes handling firearms.[101] For blacks, firearms had been both a symbol and means of keeping their freedom and political power; they were also instruments of suppression by whites seeking to reestablish the old order. In the end, whites triumphed and blacks were effectively disarmed.[102] Since they were forbidden to possess firearms, blacks "were rendered defenseless against assault," and in "parts of the country remote from observation, the violence and cruelty engendered by Slavery found free scope for exercise upon the defenseless Negro."[103] Public officials "stood by while murders, beatings and lynchings were openly perpetrated."[104] From the 1870s until well into this century, the handgun laws of "Alabama, Arkansas, Mississippi, Missouri and Texas deprived the victims of the means of self-defense, cloaking the specially deputized Klansmen in the safety of their monopoly of arms."[105]

96. Frederick Douglass, speech, May 9, 1865, in Harold M. Hyman, ed., *The Radical Republicans and Reconstruction, 1861-1870* (New York: Bobbs-Merrill), pp. 242-46.

97. Otis A Singletary, *Negro Militia and Reconstruction* (New York: McGraw-Hill, 1957), pp. 4-5.

98. Ibid., pp. 6-16.

99. Ibid., pp. 129-52.

100. Ibid., pp. 143-44.

101. Kennett and Anderson, *The Gun in America*, p. 154; John H. Franklin, *Reconstruction* (Chicago: University of Chicago Press, 1961), p. 49.

102. Kennett and Anderson, *The Gun in America*, p. 155.

103. Lyman Abbott, "Survey of the Freedman's Bureau Work," in Hyman, ed., *The Radical Republicans and Reconstruction*, pp. 220-21.

104. Kates, "*Hand Gun Prohibition in the United States*," p. 19.

105. Ibid.

The Black Panthers

As we move to more recent times, when the nation makes some attempt to solve the "American Dilemma" and open racism becomes less socially acceptable, the political functions of gun control with regard to blacks become less clear. Some hypotheses are examined briefly below.

The 1960s saw the beginnings of a militant black power movement, and one of the most controversial segments of that movement was the Black Panther Party (BPP). In response to perceived oppression by white society and alleged brutality by its agents, the police, the BPP organized for radical reform and black consciousness-raising and armed themselves for self-defense.[106] The Panthers were anti-racist, anti-capitalist, anti-imperialist, and openly hostile to the police. They opposed the Viet Nam war, offered aid to the Viet Cong, and talked openly about obtaining weapons to use in violent revolution.[107]

Vice President Agnew called the Panthers "a completely irresponsible, anarchistic group of criminals"; Assistant Attorney General Leonard concluded that the Panthers were "nothing but hoodlums and we've got to get them"; FBI Director Hoover stated that the Panthers "without question represent the greatest threat to internal security of the country [among] violence-prone black extremist groups"; and Attorney General Mitchell ruled that the Panthers were a threat to national security and thus subject to FBI wiretapping.[108]

A number of observers concluded that at least some of the government activity against the Panthers was not justified by legitimate law enforcement concerns and was aimed at destroying the Panthers as a political force.[109] The BPP was one of the main targets of the FBI's nationwide counterintelligence operation known as COINTELPRO. Although some of COINTELPRO's activities were politically neutral, one of its objectives was to neutralize, disrupt, and destroy various targeted groups such as the BPP. The program's unexpressed major

106. Gene Marine, *The Black Panthers* (New York: New American Library, 1969), pp. 34–37, 74.

107. See Louis G. Heath, *Off the Pigs!* (Metuchen, N.J.: Scarecrow Press, 1976).

108. Commission of Inquiry into the Black Panthers and the Police, *Search and Destroy* (New York: Metropolitan Applied Research Center, Inc., 1973), p. 11.

109. L.F. Palmer, Jr., "Out to Get the Panthers," *The Nation* 29 (July 28, 1969): 78–82; Robert Justin Goldstein, *Political Repression in Modern America* (Cambridge, Mass.: Schenkman, 1978), pp. 523–24.

premise was that "a law enforcement agency has the duty to do whatever is necessary to combat perceived threats to the existing social and political order."[110] COINTELPRO information was frequently shared with local police to facilitate their actions against the BPP.[111]

As the BPP and police engaged in a steadily escalating cycle of confrontation and violence, the Panthers sought and obtained additional arms—partly at least for self-defense.[112] Obtaining weapons, however, rendered the Panthers vulnerable to both bona fide and politically motivated enforcement of firearms laws. Although the Panthers were raided, arrested, prosecuted, and punished for a wide variety of alleged offenses, enforcement of firearms laws played a large part in the campaign against the BPP.[113] Between 1967 and 1969, BPP members were charged with at least 130 firearms and weapons offenses.[114] In addition, anti-Panther sentiment was a factor in the enactment of some new firearms laws.

The BPP was formed in Oakland in 1966, and by 1967 a bill was introduced in the California legislature to prohibit the carrying of loaded weapons within incorporated areas of the state. The bill—later enacted—was, in fact, an anti-Panther bill instigated by the Oakland police and given impetus by the appearance of numerous armed Panthers in Contra Costa County.[115] The Panther response to the bill recognized the political functions of gun control. The Party

---

110. U.S. Senate, *Final Report of the Select Committee to Study Governmental Operations with Respect to Intelligence Activities*, Senate Report No. 94–755, book III (Washington, D.C.: GPO, 1976), p. 3.

111. Ibid., pp. 220–23.

112. Ed Cray, *The Enemy in the Streets* (Garden City, N.Y.: Doubleday, 1972), p. 198.

113. COINTELPRO and firearms raids and arrests were not limited to black groups. The Ku Klux Klan and other right-wing groups were also targets. Further, activity against left-wing groups was not limited to black groups (see U.S. Senate, *Final Report*, pp. 246–51; Martin Waldron, "Militants Stockpile Illegal Guns Across the U.S.," *New York Times*, 28 December 1969, p. 42). For instance, in 1969, Yippie leader and "Chicago Eight" defendant Abbie Hoffman was arrested on charges of possessing guns and blackjacks after an early morning raid on an apartment five doors away from the local police precinct. Hoffman was not present during the raid, and a detective justified Hoffman's arrest by maintaining that since the apartment was in Hoffman's name, Hoffman was legally responsible for the guns. Hoffman termed the charges a police frame-up. They were later dismissed because of insufficient evidence. (See *New York Times*, 24 March 1969, p. 37; *New York Times*, 16 December 1969, p. 4.)

114. Martin R. Haskell and Lewis Yablonsky, *Criminology* (Chicago: Rand McNally, 1978), p. 229.

115. Marine, *The Black Panthers*, p. 63.

condemned the bill as "fascist" and contended that its aim was to keep "black people disarmed and powerless at the same time that racist police agencies are intensifying the . . . repression of black people."[116]

When carrying weapons legally, the Panthers were sometimes harassed and falsely charged with weapons offenses.[117] In a number of cases, undercover agents offered and/or provided illegal guns to BPP members.[118] For example, in April 1969, undercover agents sold machine guns to party members and then arrested them.[119]

The mayor of Seattle turned down a request by the Alcohol, Tobacco and Firearms Unit of the Internal Revenue Service that the city cooperate in an "information gathering" raid on Panther headquarters where illegal firearms were allegedly being stored.[120] While this raid never occurred, a number of actual raids were based on searches for weapons and resulted in seizures of weapons and arrests for weapons offenses.[121] Some of these raids were justified or facilitated by COINTELPRO information.[122] The most controversial raid, however, occurred on December 4, 1969, in Chicago.

Since at least 1960 the relationship between Chicago police and the black community had been one of increasing tension and distrust. In 1969, police-community relations had reached crisis proportions, and violence between Panthers and police had escalated steadily.[123] A pàid COINTELPRO informer who had infiltrated the BPP urged the party to obtain more weapons and, when they did so, reported to authorities that illegal weapons could be found at a particular Panther apartment. The informant also provided a diagram of the apartment and other intelligence. A search warrant for sawed-

---

116. Reginald Major, *A Panther is a Black Cat* (New York: William Morrow, 1971), p. 289.

117. Marine, *The Black Panthers*, pp. 40–43, 64–65.

118. See Waldron, "Militants Stockpile Illegal Guns"; Goldstein, *Political Repression*, p. 529.

119. Waldron, "Militants Stockpile Illegal Guns."

120. See *New York Times*, 9 February 1970, p. 30; *New York Times*, 10 February 1970, p. 27.

121. See Waldron, "Militants Stockpile Illegal Guns"; Edward J. Epstein, "The Panthers and the Police: A Pattern of Genocide?" *The New Yorker* (February 13, 1971), p. 45; Heath, *Off the Pigs!*, pp. 89, 181–82.

122. U.S. Senate, *Final Report*, pp. 220–23, 246.

123. See Commission of Inquiry, *Search and Destroy*, pp. 14, 26–30; Heath, *Off the Pigs!*, pp. 178–79.

off shotguns and illegal weapons was then obtained.[124] The Commission of Inquiry concluded that it was probable that the real purpose of the raid was to conduct a surprise attack on the Panthers and that the execution of the search warrant for weapons was merely a guise.[125]

The Commission determined that, contrary to police testimony, the first shot was fired accidentally by a police officer and that only one shot was fired by the Panthers.[126] After the police had fired between 80 and 100 shots, the shooting stopped. Some of the raiders began seizing not only Panther weapons but also Party books and files.[127] Two policemen had suffered minor injuries. Dead were Chicago BPP leader Fred Hampton and member Mark Clark. Four other Panthers were wounded. The body of Fred Hampton was found on his bed. He had been shot four times—twice in the head. There was evidence that at the time of the raid Hampton was in an unconscious, drugged state.[128] The Commission of Inquiry concluded there was probable cause to believe Hampton was murdered—shot by an officer or officers who could see his prostrate form lying on his bed.[129]

Federal Gun Laws

Robert Sherrill's analysis of the federal Gun Control Act of 1968 suggests that Congress passed the Act because of its anticipated political functions.[130] Sherrill points out that in the 1960s, white America became concerned about the "black problem." The black population had a high rate of illegitimacy, was blamed for the welfare problem, and was growing faster than the white population. The high index crime rates for blacks caused concern, and the intelligence of blacks was openly questioned.[131]

124. See *Hampton v. Hanrahan.* 600 F.2d 600, U.S. Court of Appeals, Seventh Circuit, 1979.
125. Commission of Inquiry, *Search and Destroy*, p. 242.
126. Ibid., pp. 243–45.
127. Hampton v. Hanrahan, p. 616.
128. See Commission of Inquiry, *Search and Destroy*, chs. 4, 5, 6, 9.
129. Ibid., pp. 3–4, 122, 129, 246; see *Hampton v. Hanrahan* for a review of the legal action following this incident. By the end of 1971, the Panthers were, for a variety of reasons, no longer an influential force (see Goldstein, *Political Repression*, p. 530).
130. Sherrill, *The Saturday Night Special.*
131. Ibid., p. 285.

Because of the massive riots by blacks, reports of snipers, and threats of revolution by black militants (including the Black Panthers), many Americans, both liberal and conservative, were apprehensive of black insurrection and guerilla warfare.[132] One aspect of these apprehensions was a fear of guns in the hands of insurrectionist blacks. For example, *U.S. News and World Report*, in an article entitled "Black Militants Talk of Guns and Guerillas," noted that "open rebellion has been declared by black power advocates."[133] After the 1967 riot in Plainfield, New Jersey, Governor Hughes ordered a warrantless house-to-house search of black areas by the National Guard to find forty-six carbines allegedly stolen from a nearby arms factory. No carbines were found, but many residences were left in shambles.[134] In an editorial entitled "Disarm the Sniper," *The New York Times* called for federal regulation of the domestic gun traffic.[135] The National Advisory Commission on Civil Disorders recommended further restrictions on the sale of firearms and the emergency closing of stores selling firearms during civil disorders.[136]

In reaction to this domestic crisis, Congress panicked and passed the Gun Control Act of 1968—a law they hoped would close the routes by which blacks were getting guns.[137] Congress assumed that ghetto blacks were getting cheap imported military surplus and mail-order guns and thus decided to cut off these sources while leaving over-the-counter acquisition open to the affluent. Although the Gun Control Act came shortly after the murders of Robert Kennedy and Martin Luther King, Jr., the Act did nothing about the types of guns used in those assassinations. Sherrill thus concludes that the law was directed against "that other threat of the 1960s more omnipresent than the political assassin—namely the black rioter."[138] In sum, Sherrill's thesis is, quite simply, that the Act was passed not to control guns but to control blacks.[139]

132. Ibid., pp. 283, 286–90.
133. *U.S. News and World Report*, 7 August 1967, p. 32.
134. National Advisory Commission on Civil Disorders, *Report* (New York: Bantam Books, 1968), pp. 523, 525.
135. *New York Times*, 2 August 1967, p. 36.
136. National Advisory Commission, *Report*, pp. 523, 525.
137. *The Saturday Night Special*, p. 283.
138. Ibid., p. 282.
139. Ibid., p. 280.

The Civil Obedience Act of 1968

Although the preceding analysis may exaggerate the role of white fear of black violence and revolution in the passage of the Gun Control Act of 1968, there is another piece of firearms legislation whose roots in white reaction to the riots and threats of black militants were quite explicit. Section (a) (2) of the Civil Obedience Act of 1968 provides criminal penalties for "Whoever transports or manufactures for transportation in commerce any firearm, or explosive or incendiary device knowing or having reason to know that the same will be used unlawfully in furtherance of a civil disorder. . . . "[140]

The Act was offered on the Senate floor by conservative Democrat Russell Long of Louisiana as an amendment to the Civil Rights Act of 1968.[141] In the Senator's remarks and articles he placed in the record there is frequent mention of riots and black militant leaders H. Rap Brown and Stokely Carmichael, and references to "open revolt," "violent and bloody revolution," "aggressive guerilla warfare," and the stockpiling of arms for use in next summer's riots.[142] Long stated that his proposal of the Civil Obedience Act stemmed from "the riotous conditions that have plagued the United States for the past four years, and which were predicted for the summer of 1967."[143]

Although there was at the time some exaggeration of the use of firearms by and the political consciousness of rioters, as well as of the potential for black revolt, those perceptions helped secure reform beneficial to blacks (e.g., the Fair Housing Provisions of the Civil Rights Act of 1968) as well as new criminal laws such as the Civil Obedience Act.

If Sherrill's thesis and the above analysis are correct, the parallel with the slaveowners' response to slave revolts is striking. In both

140. 18 U.S.C.A. Sec. 231.
141. U.S. Congress, Senate, *Congressional Record*, 90th Congress, second sess., vol. 114 (Washington, D.C.: GPO, 1968), pp. 5531-32.
142. Ibid., pp, 1294-97, 3360, 5530-36.
143. Ibid., p. 3360. The Civil Obedience Act was enacted April 11, 1968, more than five months *before* the Gun Control Act. Thus, both were born of the same national mood. Long's amendment was offered on the Senate floor and was overshadowed by other parts of the Civil Rights Act of 1968. The Act was then passed quickly by the House. There are, therefore, no reports or hearings on the Civil Obedience Act and little debate. Both liberals and conservatives in the Senate voted for Long's amendment (see U.S. Senate, *Congressional Record*, pp. 5539, 6484).

cases, more firearms control follows outbreaks of violence by blacks. The difference is, of course, that by the 1960s, gun laws directed only at blacks would have been held unconstitutional and would have damaged the nation's image abroad. There can be little doubt, however, that all concerned knew quite well that the rioters and snipers were overwhelmingly black.

Black crime, rioting, and revolutionary movements indicate problems in the black community and white-dominated society that certain vested interests would prefer to ignore. If this crime, rioting, and threats of revolt can be minimized by gun control without the necessity of major reform beneficial to blacks, it is a victory for those who have an interest in the political and economic status quo. If the black population is armed and potentially volatile, it cannot be ignored as it was for so many years. Such a population places tremendous pressure on government to grant beneficial reforms and can defend itself against white vigilantes as it did in the South in the 1960s.[144]

CONCLUSION

Five functions or effects of gun control have been discussed herein: (1) increasing citizen reliance on government and citizen tolerance of increased police powers and official abuse; (2) helping prevent opposition to government; (3) facilitating repressive action by government and its sympathizers; (4) lessening the pressure for major reform; and (5) selective enforcement against those perceived as a threat by government.

While there are numerous other examples of the second and third functions of gun control—for example, Native Americans and Palestine/Israel—clear, well-documented examples of the first, fourth,

---

144. See Salter and Kates, "The Necessity of Access to Firearms by Dissenters and Minorities," pp. 188, 190, 192. Although space limitations preclude analysis herein, an aspect that deserves further study is discriminatory enforcement of gun laws against blacks (see Hardy and Chotiner, "The Potentiality for Civil Liberties Violations in the Enforcement of Handgun Prohibition," pp. 210–11). Two studies that found no evidence of *increased* discrimination against blacks under Massachusetts' new tougher gun law (Bartley-Fox) are D. Rossman, P. Froyd, G. L. Pierce, J. McDevitt, and W. Bowers, "Massachusetts Mandatory Minimum Sentence Gun Law: Enforcement, Prosecution and Defense Impact," *Criminal Law Bulletin* 16 (March-April 1980); 150–63; and Beha (1977). For some insight into the pitfalls of such studies, see Joan DeFleur, "Biasing Influences in Drug Arrest Records," *American Sociological Review* 40 (1975): 88–103.

and fifth functions are hard to find.[145] Further research may reveal additional examples.

One aspect given inadequate attention herein is the possible discrepancy between what the government intends to achieve by enacting firearms controls and what it is able to achieve by enforcing them. Whether the political effects be intentional or not, the difficulties and costs of enforcing gun laws may result in a large discrepancy between the effects hypothesized by observers (including this author) and the actual results.[146] Detailed qualitative and quantitative studies are needed to determine the existence, exact nature, and extent of the effects hypothesized in this discussion. Such studies may confirm or disprove the interpretations presented herein and reveal additional political functions.

Additional weaknesses of this study are its primary reliance on secondary sources and lack of a broad theoretical base. A comprehensive theory of political repression incorporating the second, third, fourth, and fifth functions of gun control is sorely needed, as is a theoretical niche for the first function.

Further, at times the analysis makes assumptions about the motives of police, legislators, and so forth. This is always risky and necessitated the inclusion of general background material to support inferences as to motive. Motives are difficult to prove, and "bad" or illegal motives are rarely admitted by public officials. Others have interpreted some of the events and motives described herein in a different fashion. Such differences, however, should not obscure the fact that gun control can have political functions, even in the absence of political motivation on the part of legislators or police.

With regard to the literature on revolution, repression, and political violence, it is disturbing how little many well-respected authors deal with firearms and firearms controls. Readers of these works could easily arrive at the impression that revolts, violent political repression, and the like are weaponless affairs carried on without any concern by either side as to their own or their opponent's firepower. Little is said about where opponents of governments obtain firearms and what governments do to try to stop such acquisitions. Far too

145. See Kennett and Anderson, *The Gun in America*, pp. 51–52, 167; Yonah Alexander, "From Terrorism to War: The Anatomy of the Birth of Israel," in Yonah Alexander, ed., *International Terrorism* (New York: Praeger, 1976), pp. 230–34; Library of Congress, *Gun Control Laws in Foreign Countreis*, p. 122.

146. Kessler, "Enforcement Problems of Gun Control."

little has been done to research and analyze how the availability or unavailability of firearms influences the course of political change. Individuals and organizations concerned about civil and human rights ignore the fact that in addition to political power and oppression, political freedom, defense against injustice, and a more just society may also grow out of the barrel of a gun.

The relative lack of scholarly attention to these issues may reflect not only the anti-gun bias flowing from a cosmopolitan life style but also from the fact that academicians are largely dependent on (and perhaps members of) the more fortunate segments of society who feel some uneasiness not only about street crime but also about the "armed masses." Given the fact that government forces (i.e., police, military) are going to have guns for the near future at least, the essentially conservative bias of advocacy of gun control becomes clear.[147] Many comfortable individuals (including scholars and academicians) are willing to barter away the potential for resistance to oppressive government and its partisans in return for an uncertain promise of less crime. The exchange may also mean the loss of the means of self-defense for unpopular minorities and dissenters and the potential for riot and revolt by those being exploited or oppressed. The comfortable almost always have more to fear from those below them than they do from those above them. It is thus easy for the "haves" to give away freedoms for which they see no need. It is also easy for the "haves" to bargain away freedoms the "have nots" may need— especially when those freedoms pose a threat to the class structure.

Finally, in view of the need for further research, it is hoped that the controversial nature of gun control and the ideological implications of its political functions will not inhibit attempts at dispassionate examination of this subject.

147. Stephen P. Halbrook, "The Armed People and the State Monopoly of Violence," 1977. (Unpublished.)

Chapter 17

FIREARMS USE AND THE POLICE
A Historic Evolution of American Values

Frank T. Morn

INTRODUCTION

Guns and gun usage have become a significant issue in American society. More than most cultures, Americans seem enamored with the gun. The gun control controversy, whether in 1780, 1880, or 1980, is a highly sensitive historic issue that still goes unresolved. This is an historical exploration of the rise of gun carrying and displaying by the police, as part of the American gun phenomenon.

As one observer has indicated, there is a tantalizing dichotomy in America: Americans are law-abiding people prone to violence. A certain degree of violence and even criminality in America has become permissible as a moral necessity. Many heroes, especially those found in literature and media, are placed in situations in which some form of violence or criminality is condoned. Several subordinate themes support this legitimization of violence.[1]

American society, its institutions and people, periodically has been perceived as being cleansed through violence. The American Revolution stands as a violent declaration and act of independence. Only the violence of the Civil War could alter the social arrangements of the South. Violence to "make the world safe for democracy," or to

---

1. John Cawelti, "Myths of Violence in Popular Culture," *Critical Inquiry* 3 (1975): 525.

stop the evils of Nazism or Communism are part of this redeemer attitude justifying violence. In an almost religious way, Americans see purgation and regeneration through violence.[2]

In addition, regarding individual deviants from societal norms, there is the conviction that criminals must meet appropriate and exemplary ends. Such feelings gave rise to the formal institutions of criminal justice: the law and courts, jails and penitentiaries, and finally the police. In fact, these institutions were created to substitute for the violent resolution of grievances and disputes. American institutions, however, were not always sufficiently effective in such tasks, and vigilante justice emerged. Private citizens performed criminal justice chores in response to the weaknesses and corruption of public institutions. Of course, from the English common law was inherited a long tradition of private involvement in criminal justice. Responding to the hue-and-cry, and participating in the *posse comitatus* are only two forms that survive today in common expressions.

Vigilante organizations are privately constituted criminal justice systems. Most often these have been collective efforts, but the possibility of individuals becoming self-appointed avengers always has been present. The main act of such extralegal criminal justice systems was violence. In short, to combat violence, counterviolence was necessary. Violence, therefore, is implicit in the American experience, and as John Cawelti claims, "the gun is our prime symbol of moral violence." This adoration of the gun as a tool of protection and patriotism he calls the "six gun mystique."[3]

Other values existed, however. Police in America began unarmed. Only in response to the growing dangers of their work environment did they begin to arm. That work environment was made dangerous, in part, because of America's adoration of the gun. Americans, in the formative years of police development, had firmly established attitudes. As mentioned previously, an ongoing gun mystique had developed and even had been sanctified in the Constitution. A gun-owning citizenry was considered a safeguard against foreign invasion of the country and governmental invasion of the citizenry. An "anti-standing army" mentality prevailed, under which the average citizen, armed with his gun, was considered the primary defense for the nation.[4] This also militated against a strongly armed, militarized

    2. Ibid., pp. 537–40.
    3. Ibid., p. 525.
    4. Lois G. Schwoerer, *"No Standing Armies!": The Antiarmy Ideology in Seventeenth Century England* (Baltimore: Johns Hopkins University Press, 1974), pp. 195, 197, 198.

police. The police, like those newly formed in England, were to be unarmed. The United States, as one prominent historian noted, long exhibited "the interesting spectacle of an armed population juxtaposed to feeble police and military establishments, a remarkable testimony to public confidence in the loyalty of the citizens and in their disposition, if they were to use their arms at all, to use them only against each other and not against civil authority."[5]

Respectable citizens, therefore, wanted their guns, but at the same time they did not want guns for their police. Disreputable citizens, however, soon took advantage of such a cultural environment, using guns as tools of the criminal craft. In response, the police began to arm. At first it was not an overt policy but a covert adjustment to dangerous conditions. Only slowly did the general public accept the necessity of a gun-carrying police. Even here that acceptance took on the dimensions of a masquerade. At a time when civilian concealed weapons were increasingly becoming a social issue, the police were to keep their weapons concealed. The fears of militarism were still very strong in the nineteenth century. Furthermore, in spite of the growing menace of guns in the wrong hands, government did little more than threaten meaningful legislation to end private firearm ownership. Most states opted only to regulate and not to ban. As regulation proved ineffective, the police steadily increased their armament, though they would not bring their guns out into open view until the twentieth century.

AMERICA'S GUN CULTURE

Colonial America was in many respects a transplanted England. The new land, however, was a hostile place, and guns were not a luxury of the few but a necessity for many. The musket (whether a wheellock, matchlock, or flintlock) was an indispensible if not perfect tool in the civilizing process. Colonial governments did not provide such tools, so each individual was required to furnish his own arms and ammunition as security from hostile attack. Hunting very early became a crucial activity, and colonists were encouraged in such activities to perfect their gun skills as well as to provide food. Since the

5. Richard Hofstadter, "Reflections on Violence in the United States," in Richard Hofstadter and Michael Wallace, eds., *American Violence: A Documentary History* (New York: Random House, 1970), p. 25.

British army played little part in colonial America, local governments passed militia laws. The citizens were to be soldiers at a minute's notice, and they needed skills in firearms. As the primary historians of the gun in American history have said, "The frontier had led the American to believe his personal safety lay with his gun; by 1776 he would take it up as a symbol of civic obligation."[6] Ideologically speaking, he would never put the gun down again.

In colonial times, citizen soldiers became increasingly important. Militias fought most of the colonial wars and became popular symbols. The famed minutemen were militia, and the skirmishes at Lexington and Concord were fought between American citizen soldiers and British professional troops. The American Revolution, especially as it retreated into the past, enshrined the citizen soldier "intimate with his gun from his infancy."[7] In the new states, militias, being both inexpensive and democratic, were perpetuated as an American ideal. In such a spirit, the Second Amendment to the Constitution declared, "A well-regulated militia being necessary to the security of a free state, the right of the people to keep and bear arms shall not be infringed." Gun ownership was acclaimed not just as a practical necessity for a frontier people, but as the basis of a free society and the attribute of free men.[8]

In terms of honor the gun emerged in another peculiar way at the onset of the nineteenth century. Very little dueling occurred in colonial America. It arose in the 1770s and grew rapidly after the Revolution, particularly in the South. Charleston, South Carolina, and Savannah, Georgia, became dueling capitals, especially among military and naval officers of the middling ranks. Vanity and vengeance were important ingredients of the duel, which in America was conducted with guns.[9]

Some duels became spectacular events. Dueling grounds, like Blandensburg, Maryland, near Washington, D.C., became tourist attractions. The Hamilton-Burr duel, between high government officials in 1804, ended most dueling in the North. Thereafter, the duel, like slavery, became unique to the South. Andrew Jackson, a future

6. Lee Kennett and James LaVerne Anderson, *The Gun in America: The Origins of a National Dilemma* (Westport, Conn.: Greenwood Press, 1975), p. 56.

7. Ibid., p. 66.

8. Ibid., pp. 76–82.

9. William Oliver Stevens, *Pistols at Ten Paces: The Story of the Code of Honor in America* (Boston: Houghton Mifflin Co., 1970), pp. 9, 12, 14, 33.

President of the United States, shot and killed Charles Dickinson in 1806. Thomas Hart Benton, a United States Senator, killed Charles Lucas in 1817. Second only to the Hamilton-Burr incident for notoriety was the 1820 duel in which naval hero Stephen Decatur was killed by Commodore James Barron. Senator John Randolph and Secretary of State Henry Clay dueled in 1826; both survived. Congressman Jonathan Cilley and William Graves fought in 1838. Graves was censured by Congress after he killed Cilley, and the Northeast demanded passage of an anti-duel law. The South filibustered such attempts, and the duel almost as much as slavery represented the growing demarcation between the two regions.[10]

In addition, a number of semi-duels — conflicts not adhering to the formalities of the gentlemanly code — occurred in antebellum America. Such assaults among notable figures captured public attention and set a national tone for public behavior. Andrew Jackson and Tennessee governor Jack Servier exchanged shots on the steps of the state capitol in 1810. Five years later Jackson and Thomas Hart Benton exchanged blows and bullets without resort to *code duello.* Later, the first presidential assassination attempt would be made against Jackson with guns. In short, the man whom historians have used to personify the pre–Civil War epoch was very much involved with guns and violence.

With few exceptions, the duel and assaults among famous politicians declined after the Civil War. It was as if the Civil War, something of a grand duel in itself, exhausted energies for such activity among notables. The less notable, however, continued to resolve disputes through assault and mayhem. The cheap sale of enormous numbers of surplus arms after the Civil War, and the subsequent development and sale of very cheap revolvers, resulted in increasing use of these weapons in assaults.

As they had been in the colonial frontier period, guns were significant items on the outward boundaries of trans-Mississippian settlement. Into this new frontier came the revolving pistol, invented by Samuel Colt of Connecticut in the mid-1830s. But the price was too high and eastern market demand too low for such a device, and Colt went out of business. Even the military, ever conservative when it came to adopting new weapons, ignored Colt. In the 1839–41 period, the Texas Rangers, needing a light and reliable rapid-firing

10. Ibid., pp. 165–66, 173, 210, 212, 219.

weapon, ordered enough to enable Colt to reopen his business.[11] By the late 1840s and early 1850s, Colt, Remington, Sharpe, Lawrence, and Robbins, and the forerunners of the Winchester Arms Company, began to replace the older private contractors and armories in production of arms.[12] These men introduced modern industrial management, production, and distribution to their enterprises. But in these formative years, prices still remained too high for a mass gun market to develop. As late as 1860, for example, the Colt revolver was priced at $15.00 – down from the $35.00 of 1835, but still a very substantial investment in terms of contemporary wages. Older "hand-me-down" guns remained common, and the more modern handguns became prized possessions.

War and the tools of war have profound impacts on society. The Mexican-American war, and especially the Civil War, introduced thousands of young men to firepower. Ralph Waldo Emerson's metaphor was appropriate when he said in 1864 that "the cannon will not suffer any other sound to be heard for miles and for years around it. Our chronology has lost all old distinctions in one date – Before the war, and since."[13]

The skirmishes in "Bloody Kansas," in the years immediately preceding the Civil War, won fame for Sharps rifles, called "Beecher's Bibles" after Henry Ward Beecher who professed to see "more moral power in one of those instruments so far as the slave-holders were concerned than in a hundred Bibles." During the war America's gun production soared from 30,000 small arms in 1861 to 700,000 annually at war's end. Throughout the war soldiers and citizens became accustomed to guns.

Additional new cultural ingredients increased the importance of guns. As before, hunting was important, but now there were celebrated hunters. Buffalo Bill Cody, for example, was estimated as killing 4,200 buffalo in one eighteen-month period.[14] Western towns, as will be described in a following section, were not as volatile as they have been portrayed to be. Nonetheless, there were numerous

11. Roger Burlingame, *Machines That Built America* (New York: Signet Books, 1953), pp. 82–94.

12. Alfred D. Chandler, Jr. *The Visible Hand: The Managerial Revolution in American Business* (Cambridge, Mass.: Harvard University Press, 1977), p. 77.

13. Ralph Waldo Emerson, *Journals of Ralph Waldo Emerson with Annotations, 1864–1876*, vol. 10, ed. Edward Waldo Emerson and Waldo Emerson Forbes (Boston: n.p., 1914), p. 33.

14. Lee Kennett and James LaVerne Anderson, *The Gun in America*, p. 119.

boom-and-bust mining camps known for violence. Various wartime guerrillas turned their guns to more or less apolitical crime, the most famous being the gangs led by the infamous brothers, Youngers and Daltons.[15]

Perhaps more important is that the gun industry continued to develop. Samuel Colt's revolver was light, accurate, and easy to repair. He not only invented the revolver but exploited the principal of interchangeable parts. Others followed, and the manufacture of guns moved from a craft with custom-made products to a mass-production industry. By 1890 there were 239 firms producing small arms.[16] In 1892, 750,000 pistols, 400,000 shotguns, and 500,000 rifles were purchased. One correspondent for the *New York Daily Tribune* observed that "for a quiet, peace-loving nation, it is surprising how many firearms are sold in this country every year."[17] Winchester, Colt, and Remington, in the late 1890s, set up regional sales offices, which improved scheduling of deliveries.[18] Advertising programs became aggressive, and traveling shows of marksmen became an advertising feature. Frank Butler and Annie Oakley became living testimonies for Remington. Adolph and Elizabeth Tapperwein did the same for Winchester. Products and personalities were being associated together, and profits soared.[19]

By the 1880s and 1890s the gun culture of America was proceeding in two directions. First, the adoration of the rifle flourished. Hunting continued to be a significant pastime in the East as well as the West. One estimate is that hunters were taking 15,000 ducks a day from the Chesapeake area as late as the 1870s. The National Rifle Association was formed in 1871 to stimulate citizen/marksmanship. Rifle ranges became an important place in urban settings, and shooting events sprung up, making shooting an organized sport. By the 1880s, the .22 caliber and the air rifle were developed to promote a greater youth market.[20]

Second was the rise of concern over the "pocket pistol." Guns made by Colt, Smith & Wesson, Savage, and Marlin were still beyond

15. Eugene W. Hollen, *Frontier Violence: Another Look* (New York: Oxford Universiry Press, 1974), pp. 106-123.
16. Chandler, *The Visible Hand*, pp. 77, 314, 434, 438.
17. *New York Daily Tribune*, 12 September 1892.
18. Alfred D. Chandler, Jr. *The Visible Hand*, p. 134.
19. Lee Kennett and James LaVerne Anderson, *The Gun in America*, p. 136.
20. Ibid., pp. 137-38.

the means of most people, and very few of them were pocket sized. Soon, however, less prestigious firms began making cheaper and smaller models stamped with names like "Tramps Terror" and "Little Giant." These so-called "suicide specials" were sold at prices that brought the handgun within the reach of everyone. As the chief historians of the gun in America have stated, "by 1900 the 'Two dollar pistol' was a fixture in American life."[21] That pistol came to have a major impact on urban society and urban police.

FOREIGN EXPERIENCE WITH FIREARMS AND POLICING

From ancient times, conventional wisdom taught that democratic states had been protected by armed citizens while despotic governments relied on hired soldiers. For eighteenth and nineteenth century Americans, this observation seemed strengthened by French and English history. France, much like other continental powers in the seventeenth and eighteenth centuries, had a strong centralized government. At first, many of its social arrangements continued out of the medieval past. Nobles and members of the upper classes, due to their ancient roots in militarism and their hunting privileges, were allowed, with certain restrictions, to carry arms. Particularly under Louis XIV in the mid-seventeenth century, however, an arms policy developed that continues to this day.

This policy was determined by two institutional devices. First, Louis and his successors created a professional standing army. The noble's military powers and privileges became outdated. Like the lower classes, he now had no particular responsibility for protecting the realm. Second, by 1667 Louis had created out of a contingent of his army France's modern police. Now all citizens were freed from the obligation to preserve law and order by the presence of a professional police. Henceforth the citizens of France were required to look to the strength and power of the monarch for protection from both foreign and domestic enemies. With the exception of time-honored hunting rights of the aristocracy, no one had a right to maintain arms except this militarized police. France, and those countries throughout the world that followed its model, therefore exer-

21. Ibid., p. 98.

cized a comprehensive power to prohibit arms ownership by the common citizen. Arms wearing by the police, on the other hand, was prevalent and visible.[22]

England also developed a monarchy early, but stronger elements of localism and decentralization remained. Such fundamental documents as the Magna Carta (1215), the Petition of Rights (1628), and the Bill of Rights (1689) counteracted excessively authoritarian tendencies of the English monarchy. In addition, because of England's insular geography, a strong navy with its skills and technology was more important than an army. When, under Cromwell and the Stuarts, a standing army did develop, its excesses made it unpopular. It was never expanded into a police force, except for occasional enforcement of smuggling and other legislation that could not be left to the citizenry, which from Anglo-Saxon days, had performed the police function. In local areas, through the "watch-and-ward" (a local citizen police) and *posse comitatus*, citizens were actively involved in policing. Common people, therefore, early acquired the right to arms.

English society was a class-structured society. Local elites had greater rights to arms ownership. In fact, throughout English history one's social rank determined the types and quantities of arms one could own. Crossbows, for example, were regarded as ungentlemanly and thus subject to regulation or restriction, to be reserved for military use. Even those not in the gentleman classes, it would appear, had a sense of appropriateness. Only the "dangerous classes" (or so respectable people reasoned) would resort to such devices. Even had England's seventeenth and eighteenth century rulers had the same proclivities of their French counterparts, historic and cultural restraints determined the future of guns and police.[23]

Throughout the eighteenth century, England experimented with a variety of policing mechanisms. The most persistent form was the ancient constable-night watch. Daytime constables detected, and nighttime watchmen protected urban society. These police were unarmed. King Charles's "Charlies," the Stuart king's experimentation

22. Howard C. Payne, *The Police State of Louis Napoleon Bonaparte, 1851-1860* (Seattle: University of Washington Press, 1966), pp. 3-33; George Lefebvre, *The Coming of the French Revolution*, trans. R. R. Palmer (Princeton University Press, 1971), pp. 18, 113-14.

23. Colin Greenwood, *Firearms Control: A Study of Armed Crime and Firearms Control in England and Wales* (London: Routledge & Kegan Paul, 1972), pp. 7-10.

with a soldier police, were too militaristic and Jonathan Wild's thief takers too corrupt to remain long-lasting models. Henry Fielding's Bow Street Runners were effective, but the rampant crime and disorder of eighteenth century England soon outdistanced a magistrate-directed force. Parliamentary investigations in 1750, 1772, and 1777 pointed out the inadequacies of the existing police systems, but little was done in the eighteenth century.

Urban disorder always had been a problem, but tolerance diminished, especially in a generation experiencing the American and French Revolutions. Events in France, with the Reign of Terror and the rise of Napoleon, indicated the ominous power of the masses to disrupt and drastically change established order. In the first two decades of the nineteenth century, London became the scene of riots almost every year. During the Peterloo Massacre of 1819, for example, eleven people had been killed. More parliamentary investigations focused on both the law and order crises and the supposed dangers from revolutionary groups. Such public and political concern led to two developments. First, the Seizure of Arms Act of 1820 was enacted. Magistrates were now allowed to seize arms that might be used by revolutionaries. This would be the only "gun control" law in England before the twentieth century.[24] The second development was the creation of the London Metropolitan Police by Robert Peel.

ENGLAND IN THE NINETEENTH CENTURY

In 1829, responding to the crime problem, Home Secretary Peel finessed a police bill through Parliament. It was restricted to London but would become a model for urban police throughout England. Charles Rowan and Richard Mayne, the first two police commissioners, actually created the new police. They had to parry considerable public fear of "Peel's bloody gang" and create acceptable models of the bobby. To assuage popular concerns over police spies, the police were quickly uniformed. These early policemen were dressed in civilian cut suits of tails-and-trousers. A top hat, in keeping with contemporary middle class styles, would be worn, and in no way did the policeman resemble the red-coated soldier. In addition, weapon carrying was forbidden. Order was to be maintained with a minimum of

24. Ibid., p. 14.

violence. The truncheon was to be carried in the tail pocket of the uniform and would not emerge into public view until 1863. Persuasion rather than intimidation was to be the rule.[25]

The police could be unarmed because English criminals did not use firearms against them. Criminal weapons were largely hands, knives, bludgeons, brickbats, and paving stones. It has been suggested that because the police did not feel threatened by a gun-carrying criminal, the pattern of a heavily armed police did not develop in England as it did in America.[26] Handguns, of course, were present in Great Britain, but the extremes of violence that once characterized England had largely abated by the time the revolver and other modern firearms began to be produced sufficiently cheaply to be available to criminals. Firearms crime, therefore, was never so grave a problem as to overcome the strong English resistance either to arming the police or to disarming the citizenry.

Only under extraordinary circumstances did the bobby carry weapons other than batons. During the Chartist tensions of 1842 and 1848, for example, bobbies patrolled the streets at night armed with cutlasses. Police officers on dangerous assignment might carry a pistol. Rural crime involving the enforcement of unpopular "game laws" against armed poachers was sometimes dangerous; by the 1850s some rural policemen had guns. Finally, during the Fenian scares of 1867 and 1868 police were issued firearms, but they gave them up as the crisis subsided. In short, during ordinary times the English police relied heavily on the truncheon and not the revolver.[27]

It cannot be suggested that England was free from armed crime. "Foreign refuse" and "reckless characters from America" were blamed for introducing firearms as criminal weapons, and some attempts were made to restrict guns.[28] But the number of legitimate firearms owners was sufficient to make resistance to any such governmental regulation strong. The Regulation of Carrying Arms bill (1881), the Firearms bill (1883), the Felonious Use of Firearms bill (1887), and the Pistols bill (1893) all failed passage in Parliament.

---

25. Wilber R. Miller, *Cops and Bobbies: Police Authority in New York and London, 1830-1870* (Chicago: University of Chicago Press, 1973), pp. 2, 3, 13, 14.
26. Ibid., pp. 51, 114-15, 170-71.
27. Ibid., p. 50.
28. Ibid., pp. 114-15.

England entered the twentieth century with no gun control legislation and no massively armed police system.

THE NINETEENTH CENTURY UNITED STATES

The American police, shortly after they were created, took a very different path from that of England. Early policing in America consisted of the unarmed citizen system of constable-night watch. It would not be until the 1840s and 1850s, patterning somewhat after the London police, that America would modernize its police. The New York City police were reorganized in 1844, in response to the growing crime and disorder in the streets. The old constable-night watch could do nothing.

The contrast with the ordinary citizenry was striking. Shortly before the police were reformed, local newspapers were commenting that "the gunshops and hardware stores, where firearms are to be found, have had a most extraordinary increase of business."[29] At one party in 1845, it was reported that four fifths of the gentlemen present were armed with pistols for protection against thieves, yet for nearly a decade of its formative years the New York police were neither uniformed nor armed. In 1853 the officers were officially uniformed, but gun carrying was still forbidden. The truncheon was the official weapon.[30]

Near the end of the 1850s New York officers experienced considerable problems. An epidemic of crime hit the city in the winter of 1857. Garroting and highway robbery on the streets caused a panic. George Templeton Strong, one of the more observant respectable people of the city, felt that "most of my friends are investing in revolvers and carrying them about at night, and if I expect to have to do a great deal of late street-walking off Broadway, I think I should make the like provision; though it's a very bad practice carrying concealed weapons." The number of criminal attacks on police increased, and it was felt that "nearly every ruffian carries a concealed weapon of destruction about his person."[31]

---

29. *New York Herald*, October 1844.

30. Wilbur R. Miller, *Cops and Bobbies*, pp. 3, 10-11, 16-24.

31. George Templeton Strong, *The Diary of George Templeton Strong: The Turbulent Years, 1850-1859*, ed. Allan Nevins and Milton Halsey Thomas (New York: Macmillan, 1952), p. 320.

The police were at once distracted by political turmoils. Mayor Fernando Wood and Governor John King fought for control of the police. George Templeton Strong was aghast, seeing Mayor Wood's police as "drilled desperadoes with their stout locust clubs or truncheons in their belts and protuberances about the breasts of their coats that indicated revolvers and sling shot within." For a short time New York City had two police systems: a city-controlled one vying with King's state-controlled system. Chaos resulted until King's system emerged as the dominent police for over a decade.[32]

While Wood's old police and King's new police were still in turbulent transition, riots occurred. Various gangs, such as the Dead Rabbit Club and the Five Pointers, were involved. As the police attempted to put these riots down, the urban warriors turned on them, and many guns and pistols were evident. The police withdrew, and the militia was called upon to restore order. Many police officers resented the timidity of their commanders.[33] George Matsell, who commanded the police from 1845 to 1847, had a policy that gun usage by his police was a sign of cowardice, grounds for dismissal.[34]

Because of the turbulence a new superintendent in 1857, Frederick Tallmadge, attempted to arm the police with revolvers. But to the Board of Police a gun-carrying police resembled too closely the dreaded standing army, and Tallmadge's policy was stymied.[35] Officially the policy was that of an unarmed police. After the 1857 violence, however, the unofficial policy was discretionary with police captains, and night patrolmen began carrying concealed weapons. By 1860, then, many New York police officers were carrying privately obtained concealed guns. It became an operational necessity in a work environment characterized by hostile criminals and suspicious citizens.

The 1860s escalated these trends. The Civil War acquainted and accustomed thousands to gun usage. Stolen or surplus military firearms became available in greater profusion and more cheaply than ever before. As more criminals used guns, more respectable citizens began to tolerate police use of guns.

The New York Draft Riots in 1863 proved the necessity of an armed police. For five days in July of 1863 New York City experi-

32. Ibid., p. 344.
33. Ibid., p. 349.
34. Wilbur R. Miller, *Cops and Bobbies*, p. 51.
35. James Richardson, *The New York Police: Colonial Times to 1901* (New York: Oxford University Press, 1970), p. 113.

enced one of its bloodiest riots. In what has been called "the second rebellion," approximately 1000 people died and millions of dollars worth of property was destroyed. Police Chief George W. Walling later recalled that his officers responded to the armed mobs with revolvers. The militia eventually was called in, but the police had held their own. Guns figured importantly in the police success.[36]

Increasingly, guns became important among the civilian population. In 1866 the *New York Times* complained that "one of the most fruitful causes of crime in this City is the practice, tolerated by law, of carrying concealed firearms." Apparently a concealed weapon law was on the books, but guns had been omitted from the list of forbidden items. The dangerous classes were fully armed, and it was among them that most shooting affrays occurred. "Being armed," the *Times* observed, "they rush eagerly into quarrels and fights, and at the first opportunity draw their weapons and fire promiscuously about them." The *Times* offered an early version of a now-familiar argument. "Hundreds of shooting cases have been reported in our columns within the last few months, and it is safe to say that scarcely a dozen of them would have occurred had not the parties implicated been armed at the moment of excitement. Deliberate, premeditated murder does not occur in the City more than once or twice a year. Yet sudden passion and ready pistols lead to homicides almost innumerable."[37]

In such an environment police officers had a difficult task. They patrolled alone some distance from headquarters. Patrol wagons and communications systems were primitive or nonexistent. Arrest was difficult in neighborhoods where citizens might side with the offender rather than the officer. On numerous occasions criminals were released by the local citizenry and the arresting officer was put in jeopardy. Apparently there were more "rum-crazed ruffians" reeling through the city heavily armed than there were armed police.[38]

On January 13, 1874, the Tompkins Square riot pointed up the fact that the police were not as yet fully committed to firearms. Hundreds of workers gathered in Tompkins Square to protest the city government's lack of sensitivity to those unemployed due to the

36. James McCague, *The Second Rebellion: The Story of the New York Draft Riots of 1863* (New York: Dial Press, 1968), pp. 36–43, 108–10.

37. *New York Times*, 16 August 1866.

38. Edward Crapsey, *The Nether Side of New York: or the Vice, Crime and Poverty of the Great Metropolis* (New York: Sheldon and Company, 1872), pp. 29–30.

existing economic depression. The police used their clubs and were even accused of "excessive brutality," but any firearm activity was left to the militia. After the riot, demands for stronger militias were heard, and one outside newspaper reminded New Yorkers that "when clubs are in vain, bullets are potent."[39]

Even by the mid-1870s the police gun was still a hidden artifact, and not only in New York. In 1876 the Philadelphia Centennial Exposition contained a police exhibit, a general portrayal of American police equipment at that time. A police rattle and whistle, a police shield and lattern, and a pair of handcuffs, were displayed. In the category of weapons, however, only clubs were evident. A police belt and club, plus seven additional varieties of police clubs were exhibited. There were no revolvers to be seen. It is noteworthy, however, that one of the more popular displays in the Exposition was the Navy's new Gatling gun. Guns were important in America, but their suitability for police work remained a questionable issue.[40]

For New York City dubiety ceased in 1879. A number of labor-related disturbances occurred during this and the next decade, making policing even more dangerous and difficult. A sense of seige prevailed, and the police acted accordingly. Numerous complaints had been made about officers promiscuously swinging their clubs. Since the Tompkins Square affair, police brutality had become a recurrent problem. In response, a member of the Police Board, the administrative agent of the department, proposed that the baton be carried in a belt or a pocket on the right side of the trousers. This proposal, however, stimulated a general debate over police and weapons. Disorder in the streets, especially since the strikes of 1877, had strained public tolerances, and a remarkable change of official policy occurred. An amended rule to the Rules and Regulations of the Police was issued: "In addition to the ordinary baton of a patrolman, each member of the Police force shall be armed while on duty, with a revolving pistol. Neither baton nor pistol shall be taken in the hand except in case of need."[41] Therefore, throughout the 1880s New York City police could officially carry guns. They remained con-

39. Herbert F. Gutman, "The Tompkins Square 'Riot' in New York City on January 13, 1874: A Re-examination of its Causes and its Aftermath," *Labor History* 6 (1965): 54-55, 68.

40. J. S. Ingram, *The Centennial Exposition, Described and Illustrated, Being a Concise and Graphic Description of this Grand Enterprise, Commemorative of the First Centennary of American Independence* (Philadelphia: Hubhard Brothers, 1876), pp. 195-96.

41. *New York Times*, 29 October and 1 November 1879.

cealed, however, and no standard revolver was prescribed. The police carried all kinds of guns, and their skills in firearms usage were as varied.

Much police history is the story of corruption. Riotous conditions throughout the 1880s, however, forestalled exposé. When a semblance of stability returned in the early 1890s, revelations of scandal forced a reform of police administration. From 1895 to 1897, Theodore Roosevelt, a firearms aficionado and strong supporter of law and order, dominated the Police Board. In little over a decade, as President of the United States, Roosevelt would create what would later become the F.B.I. During his tenure as police commissioner, Roosevelt introduced many reforms, including the Bertillion system of criminal identification and the formation of a bicycle squad. More germane to this discussion, he standardized the police pistol as the .32 caliber Colt. Furthermore, Roosevelt wrote, "we introduced a system of pistol practice by which, for the first time, the policemen were brought to a reasonable standard of efficiency in handling their revolvers." This pistol practice school would eventually become the police academy where all forms of police instruction would occur. Therefore, by the end of the century the New York police were fully armed and trained to use pistols as part of police work. Still the guns remained concealed under the coats.[42]

Other cities had similar histories. Detroit police, for example, were not issued guns, but violence on officers led to their unofficial arming in the 1870s and 1880s.[43] One collector of antique guns has found 1880 vintage pistols from Atlanta, Washington, D.C., Kansas City, Missouri, and Providence, Rhode Island, with inscriptions indicating they were police property.[44]

The Boston police when created were authorized to carry only a club. In 1857 one officer was killed, and Bostonians were shocked to learn that the police had to confront armed criminals armed only with clubs. During the Boston Draft Riots in 1863 the police were generally unarmed. The next session of legislature authorized the police to carry arms as the alderman of their district might direct. Thereafter about one third of the force carried revolvers. Not until

42. Theodore Roosevelt, "Administrating the New York Police Force," in *American Ideals and Other Essays* (New York: Putnam, 1897): p. 185.

43. John C. Schneider, *Detroit and the Problem of Order, 1830-1880: A Geography of Crime, Riot, and Policing* (Lincoln: University of Nebraska Press, 1980), pp. 117-18.

44. Dr. Richard Marohn, Chicago, Illinois.

1884 did the City Council vote to provide the police with sidearms at public expense. Eight hundred Smith and Wesson .38 caliber pistols were issued, and for the first time every member of the patrol was armed. As in New York, however, the guns remained discreetly under the officers' coats.[45]

In Philadelphia, the Nativist riots of 1844 were a crisis of violence for most residents. Between 1839 and 1845 there had been nine homicides by guns in the city; six of those deaths occurred during the 1844 riots. One Philadelphia blueblood felt, "now that firearms have been once used and become familiar to the minds of the mob we may expect to see them employed on all occasions." Between 1846 and 1852 there was a slight decrease in gun deaths, but from 1853 to 1859 gun felonies rapidly increased. In that period there were ninety-three homicides involving guns, and one historian, Roger Lane, using statistical data, calculated that twenty of these would not have occurred if not for the pistol. In response to these trends, the Philadelphia modern police were created and the men told by the chief to buy guns for self-protection. The City Council balked, however, and any gun carrying had to be unofficial. The police did use guns, and while nineteen officers were investigated for line-of-duty killings between 1839 and 1901, only one was indicted. It would not be until the 1880s and 1890s that the Philadelphia police could carry their concealed weapons officially.[46]

Some comment should be made about the West because it has the historical reputation as the gun-crazed section of the country. Actually two areas must be differentiated: the western town and the western city. The cattle towns of Kansas offer some interesting perspectives. Between 1867 and 1885, for example, Abilene, Caldwell, Dodge City, Ellsworth, and Wichita, Kansas, had only forty-five homicides. These towns depended upon transient traffic, especially the cattle drivers from Texas, and had to prevent violence but not suppress it to such an extent as to drive the cattle barons elsewhere. At first, vigilante action prevailed, but by the early 1870s these towns incorporated. Law against gun carrying came quickly. In 1871,

---

45. Roger Lane, *Policing the City: Boston, 1822-1885* (Cambridge, Mass.: Harvard University Press, 1967), pp. 18, 103, 134, 164, 203.

46. Roger Lane, *Violent Death in the City: Suicide, Accident and Murder in Nineteenth Century Philadelphia* (Cambridge, Mass.: Harvard University Press, 1979), pp. 60-62, 79, 88, 106-07; David R. Johnson, *Policing the Urban Underworld: The Impact of Crime on the Development of the American Police, 1880-1887* (Philadelphia: Temple University Press, 1979), p. 139.

Wichita forbade weapons within town limits and began a program of exchanging guns for a metal token to be redeemed as the visitor left town.

Law enforcement officers were established early. Abilene, in 1870, set up the first cattle town police force. Though smaller, it was patterned after Eastern models. The deadly reputation of these legendary law officers considerably exceeded their actual activities. Wild Bill Hickock as marshall of Abilene killed just two men. Wyatt Earp, while at Wichita and Dodge City, killed only one. William "Bat" Masterson killed no one in his several years at Dodge City. In eighteen years only six law officers were slain in these cities combined, and half of these killings were accidental. Classic gunfights in the cattle towns were not as common as the western myth would have it. Nonetheless, the western citizen and police officer more readily accepted the gun as a tool of law enforcement, and less subterfuge on the issue was needed.[47]

At the same time, the West and the "militant South" had numerous gun control laws. As early as 1801 Tennessee forbade the terrorizing of people with weapons. A little over a decade later Louisiana declared it illegal to carry concealed weapons, and Alabama did so in 1841. The territory of Arizona prohibited concealed gun carrying within towns, villages, and cities. New Mexico made it unlawful to carry weapons, concealed or otherwise, in 1880. Oklahoma forbade handguns in 1890; ownership of rifles and shotguns was limited to hunting and militia service. By 1890 all western and southern states had some concealed gun law.

Some southern states went considerably farther toward prohibition. By 1880, Mississippi had forbidden sale or gift of firearms or ammunition to minors, and in 1906 it enacted the country's first handgun registration law. In 1870 Tennessee, and in 1881 Arkansas banned cheap, short-barrelled guns. Alabama in 1893 and Texas in 1907 imposed prohibitive taxes on the sale of such guns. Tennessee in 1870, Texas in 1871, and Arkansas in 1875 prohibited the carrying of handguns whether concealed or openly. The only area not having some consistent form of gun regulation on a state basis was the East. Four states (Rhode Island, New Jersey, Connecticut, and New

---

47. Robert R. Dykstra, *The Cattle Town* (New York: Atheneum, 1970), pp. 114–48.

York) had no law by 1890.[48] New Jersey did not enact one until 1924.

In addition to the cattle towns there were real cities in the West by 1880. San Francisco, the largest, had over 200,000 population. Oakland, California, Denver, Colorado, St. Joseph, Missouri, and Omaha, Nebraska, had over 30,000 persons each. Sacramento, California, Galveston and San Antonio, Texas, and Salt Lake City, Utah, had over 20,000 inhabitants. Portland, Oregon, Houston, Texas, and Atchison, Leavenworth, and Topeka, Kansas, had over 15,000 people each.[49]

These western cities were no more violent than the larger cities of the East. In 1880, New York City led the nation with thirty-seven homicides; New Orleans was second with twenty. At the same time, Atchison, Kansas had five, while both San Jose, California, and Galveston, Texas, had two each. In Omaha, Nebraska, the mayor could rejoice that no commission of capital crime occurred in his city during 1880.[50]

The western urban areas patterned police development after the East, and this occurred rapidly in the 1870s and 1880s. But the western police were uniformed and carried a club and revolver. Only Stockton, California (population 10,282), police went unarmed. In Portland, Oregon, the chief of police ran the clothing concession and sold his men their uniforms. Each man, however, had to supply his own club and gun. A historian of these western cities points out that police casualties were few. It was safer to be a policeman in the West than in New York and Chicago.[51]

Chicago offers additional information on the history of guns in American policing. Between 1837 and 1855 Chicago was policed by a constable-night watchman system. As the city grew rapidly in size and diversity, such a village police system became inappropriate. In March, 1855, Levi Boone, standard bearer for the Know-Nothing and Law and Order tickets, became mayor. Part of his campaign was to "Americanize" the police by removing the Irish and German elements from the constable-night watch. Boone's promise to reform

48. Philip Dillon Jordan, *Frontier Law and Order* (Lincoln: University of Nebraska Press, 1970), pp. 2-7, 17-22.

49. Lawrence H. Larsen, *The Urban West at the End of the Frontier* (Lawrence: Regents Press of Kansas, 1978), p. 8.

50. Ibid., pp. 88-89.

51. Ibid., pp. 81, 82, 84.

the police was quickly implemented, but further tampering was unsuccessful. For example, attempts at uniforming police personnel were rejected by the City Council. One month later, riot and disorder caused a reversal in the attitude toward professionalization.[52]

On April 22, 1855, large numbers of Germans demonstrated in front of the city courthouse, protesting the closing of several taverns. The "Lager Riots" resulted, and guns were evident in the melee. Within days Chicago's modern police was created. Constables and night watchmen were abolished, and an integrated system like that of New York and London was established. The booklet of rules and regulations declared that "no police officer shall carry any weapon other than the policeman's club, unless by permission of the mayor, marshal or captain of police, nor to [sic] carry any cane or umbrella, or to wear any cloak while on duty." At this point the police were neither armed nor uniformed, both of which were characteristics of a standing army.[53]

For the next twenty years the Chicago police were at the mercy of local politicians. Departmental rules changed often (the police were finally uniformed in 1861), but the prohibition on gun carrying remained. The official weapon of the police remained the club or baton, which was never to be used except in self-defense. Guns in civilian hands, however, increased, and a city ordinance was enacted in August, 1871, to control handguns in the city. The ordinance was ineffective. Apparently the police had guns for emergency situations, however. During the great fire of October, 1871, for example, the department reported losing 620 muskets. Nevertheless, in the first phase of Chicago police development, the gun was prohibited or was allowed only in an extraordinary situation.[54]

The years 1877 to 1887 were crucial times for the Chicago police. Railroad strikes spread throughout the country in the summer of 1877. Roaming bands raided gunshops in Chicago. At first, police were sent out with orders not to use weapons. They were so ineffective that the mayor called upon all law-abiding citizens to form armed patrols. The police then were successively told to fire blanks,

---

52. John J. Flinn, *History of the Chicago Police* (Chicago: Police Book Fund, 1887), pp. 70-71.

53. *Police Ordinance and Rules and Regulations for the Government of the Police Department, and Instruction as to the Powers and Duties of Police Officers of the City of Chicago* (Chicago: Daily Democratic Printer, 1855), p. 59.

54. John J. Flinn, *History of the Chicago Police*, p. 130.

then to fire high, and finally to fire upon the crowds. The *Chicago Tribune* felt that such use of guns "had a most admirable effect on the mobs and convinced them that the police were at last in earnest and meant business." Guns should have been used sooner against these "radicals," concluded the *Tribune*. Five police officers had been shot and killed and four others wounded during the strikes. Similar violence occurred in other cities.[55]

One response to the strikes of 1877 was a new city ordinance regulating the carrying of concealed weapons. It was estimated that 50,000 people (or one out of ten) in the city carried weapons. Cognizant of the constitutional right to have arms, the policymakers wanted to draw distinctions between the honest possessor of a pistol and the thug. The ordinance required the purchase of a license. This would bring added revenue to the city and make it more difficult and dangerous for criminals to carry guns. It would also allow the police to arm themselves unofficially by confiscating guns of people they arrested.[56]

The chief of police, in the meantime, asked the City Council for money to purchase 500 rifles for future riots. He received permission to buy 300. The Citizens Association of Chicago, an organization of business leaders, gave the department money for an additional 100 Springfield rifles. The police, according to a nineteenth century historian, was reorganized along more military lines, including its dress and codes of discipline. Public respect, expectations, and tolerance of police power increased due to the strikes.[57]

An urban arms race began between radicals, criminals, businessmen, and police in Chicago. In 1878, Officer Albert Race was shot by a thief, and Superintendent V.A. Seavey complained to the City Council "that the practice of carrying concealed weapons, especially firearms, not only by adults, but by minors and boys, has become so prevalent of late that something must be done to suppress it." Seavey felt there were some occasions for carrying guns, but it had become too prevalent; "the average young man of the present time will not

55. Ibid., p. 203; Robert V. Bruce, *1877, Year of Violence* (Chicago: Quadrangle Books, 1970), pp. 239–40.

56. *Chicago Tribune,* 4 August 1877.

57. John J. Flinn, *History of the Chicago Police*, pp. 198–99, 202–03; *Report of the General Superintendent of Police* (Chicago: Clark and Edwards, 1877), pp. 21–22, 33–34, 53.

regard his outfit complete until his 'pistol-pocket' is adorned with an 'improved seven-shooter'."[58]

The 1880s were turbulent in heavily armed Chicago. For the first five years of the decade at least one officer was shot with a handgun each year. During a strike in 1885 a large crowd threatened an officer during an arrest. Several private citizens, drawing their guns, had to come to his rescue, verifying the importance of an armed respectable citizenry as an aid to police.

When called upon to justify his officers' extensive use of the baton, Captain John Bonfield told the mayor, "a club today to make them scatter may save the use of a pistol tomorrow."[59] Police guns increased in importance, and Lieutenant George W. Hubbard testified during the Haymarket hearings in 1886 that police officers now kept "regular revolvers" in their pockets, discreetly hidden. For extraordinary times, like the situation at Haymarket, a larger revolver was kept visible in their belts. The official weapon, the club, remained on the right side, while this extraordinary weapon was kept on the left side — the "unofficial" side of the officer.

By the 1890s, then, the carrying of guns by criminals and by police was well established. In 1891 a state bill was introduced making the carrying of deadly weapons a felony, because "every crook now carries weapons and do [sic] not hesitate to use them on police officers."[60] By 1892 a new pistol permit law was in effect requiring the approval of the mayor to carry a firearm. These laws and ordinances, however, were either not enforced or not enforceable, and the "revolver habit" continued into the new century.[61] Youth gangs had periodic wars in the ghetto areas.

In the summer of 1903 the Car Barn robbery and murder incident shook Chicago. It was the first time in the city that a crime had been committed with one of the "new automatic" pistols. Substantial changes in the police department resulted from the crime. A murder bureau, one of the first in the country, was established. Fingerprinting for criminal identification was introduced. Finally, the police pistol was standardized at a .38 caliber. Two years later, as though to

58. *Report of the General Superintendent of Police* (Chicago: Clark and Edwards, 1878), pp. 18–19.

59. John J. Flinn, *History of the Chicago Police*, p. 246.

60. *Chicago Tribune*, 25 January 1891.

61. *Chicago Record Herald*, 9 December 1904.

acknowledge the danger of police work, Casimer Zeglen's new bullet-proof vest was widely advertised in local police journals.[62]

As of 1908, Chicago was considered the most dangerous city in the country for police work. Someone had even tried to shoot the police chief. Six police officers had been shot and killed by holdup men by the middle of the year. Chief of Police Shippy frequently called upon his colleagues at the International Association of Chiefs of Police to "devise some way to put a stop to this most dangerous habit" of carrying concealed guns. In response to the increasing number of police fatalities, the City Council passed another gun control ordinance. An owner had to have a license, issued by the mayor, to carry a gun. A Firearms Bureau in the police department was put in charge of all licensing records. The chiefs in the International Association of Chiefs of Police considered Chicago a model for gun control law and petitioned for similar controls nationwide. The federal government balked, but many chiefs used the Chicago code to pattern similar legislation in their own jurisdictions.[63]

Gun use by and against the police continued in the next ten years, forcing substantial changes in Chicago policing. Amid growing complaints of "overfree gun play on the part of policemen," a police school was created in 1910. The new school, it was hoped, would make it plain that "the weapons dedicated to public use [were] not a legitimate instrument for settling the bearer's domestic and monetary difficulties."[64] Furthermore, changes in the uniform were occurring. New overcoats were designed in 1910 so that officers would not have to lift aside their coats in order to draw revolvers. There was to be an outside pocket for carrying the gun.[65] But this was still a cumbersome arrangement, and in 1916 holsters were introduced in Chicago police paraphernalia. Two holsters appeared: the "cowboy holster" placed below the left armpit and the "belt slung holster" hanging on the hip. It was felt that this new innovation would give the police an "even break" when confronting the criminal and would decrease the number of police deaths.[66] The coat, however, still

62. *Chicago Tribune*, 12 March 1906; *Chicago American*, 22 April 1904; *The Detective*, December 1906.

63. *International Association of Chiefs of Police: Proceedings (1908)*, pp. 60, 61, 67–68, 84, 85.

64. *Chicago Record-Herald*, 5 November 1910.

65. *Chicago Tribune*, 26 September 1910.

66. Ibid., 3 February 1916.

covered the gun. A study of drawings and photographs indicates that not until the late 1920s did the pistol become a more visible attribute of police dress. By the outbreak of World War I, however, the Chicago police were fully armed and militarized, a process that would become more obvious and dramatic in the turbulent 1920s.

CONCLUSION

The gun is an important artifact of American culture. Future archeologists may interpret it as a symbol of America and American civilization. In a society dedicated to egalitarianism, the gun represents democracy. Its power and presence brings all (citizens versus citizens and citizens versus government) to a common level. The inscription on early Winchester rifles captured this feeling:

> Be not afraid of any man,
> No matter what his size.
> When danger threatens, call on me
> And I will equalize.[67]

The gun not only represented democracy, however; it pointed up a dilemma. Perceived as essential for security and order, the gun frequently became a tool bringing about insecurity and disorder. To many police officials, national disarmament was the obvious solution. Attempts at lesser control or regulation were futile. Police executives discussed the gun issue for years, but only one dared to suggest a return to police disarmament as a corollary to citizen disarmament. In 1912, while speaking about the "unnecessary use of clubs and firearms by the police" before a convention of police chiefs, George H. Bodeker, Police Chief of Birmingham, Alabama, caused a ripple of amusement and disbelief throughout the auditorium. Guns spur people to violence, he observed, and "a lack of arms has a tranquilizing effect on many people." The ideal would be a disarmed police like that of England. The public, however, would have to be "de-educated" and learn to accept an unarmed police. But such a task was almost impossible, Bodeker conceded. Regardless of real or perceived dangers from criminals, Americans had been conditioned by 1912 to accept an armed police. The evolution, therefore,

---

67. Quoted in Lee Kennett and James LaVerne Anderson, *The Gun in America*, p. 108.

was complete as Americans accepted a policing system that would have been unacceptable fifty years earlier.[68]

The historic solution, thus far, has been to arm police but to keep that armament invisible. The American people and police have taken different paths from their cultural cousins in Great Britain. Both British and American police began unarmed because of strong public feeling. British police continued to be unarmed because societal violence in general, and violence against the police in particular, steadily diminished after the institution of policing. The strong reluctance to arm American police was overcome only by the patent necessity of doing so as the violence that they were expected to control, and the violence directed at them, continued unabated year after year.

England, in spite of the fact it had been compelled by historical forces to pass its first Pistol Law in 1903, remained the ideal. Well into the twentieth century there were attempts by American police to at least look like the London police, and the guns remained hidden. But it would be easier, as subsequent history would show, to educate the English into arming than to educate Americans into disarming. Commitments to an unarmed police in America had ended, and soon the police pistol would be brought out into the open. By the mid-1920s, in Chicago at least, the revolver would be a conspicuous part of the police uniform. Heavily armed persons walked ominously throughout the cities. An evolution—some might say revolution—of American values had occurred.

68. *International Association of Chiefs of Police: Proceedings (1912)*, pp. 135–37.

SELECTED BIBLIOGRAPHY
(PART VIII)

"Abbie Hoffman Cleared." *New York Times*, 16 December 1969, p. 4.

Abbott, Lyman. "Survey of the Freedman's Bureau Work." In Harold M. Hyman, ed., *The Radical Republicans and Reconstruction, 1861–1870*, pp. 212–29. New York: Bobbs-Merrill, 1967.

"Africa: The Caped Crusader." *Newsweek*, 14 June 1976, p. 48.

Alexander, Yonah. "From Terrorism to War: The Anatomy of the Birth of Israel." In Yonah Alexander, ed., *International Terrorism*, pp. 211–57. New York: Praeger, 1976.

Amnesty International. *Report 1980*. Amnesty International, 1980.

Aptheker, Herbert. *American Negro Slave Revolts*. New York: International Publishers, 1963.

_____. *Essays in the History of the American Negro*. New York: International Publishers, 1964.

Artz, Frederick B. *Reaction and Revolution, 1814–1832*. New York: Harper, 1934.

"Black Militants Talk of Guns and Guerrillas." *U.S. News and World Report*, 7 August 1967, p. 32.

Blackstone, Sir William. *Commentaries on the Laws of England*. 1783. 9th ed. Reprint. New York: Garland, 1978.

Boynton, Lindsay. *The Elizabethan Militia*. London: Routledge and Kegan Paul, 1967.

Bruce, Robert V. *1877, Year of Violence*. Chicago: Quandrangle, 1970.

Burlingame, Roger. *Machines That Built America*. New York: Signet Books, 1953.

Bureau of Alcohol, Tobacco and Firearms. *Your Guide to Firearms Regulation, 1978*. Washington, D.C.: Government Printing Office, 1978.

"Campus Violence Spurs New Laws Across the Nation." *New York Times*, 1 September 1969, p. 1.

Cawelti, John G. "Myths of Violence in Popular Culture." *Critical Inquiry* 1 (March 1975): 521-41.

Chandler, Alfred D., Jr. *The Visible Hand: The Managerial Revolution in American Business*. Cambridge, Mass.: Harvard University Press, 1977.

Chevigny, Paul. *Cops and Rebels*. New York: Pantheon, 1972.

Collins, Randall. *Conflict Sociology*. New York: Academic Press, 1975.

Commission of Inquriy into the Black Panthers and the Police. *Search and Destroy*. New York: Metropolitan Applied Research Center, Inc., 1973.

Crapsey, Edward. *The Nether Side of New York: Or the Vice, Crime and Poverty of the Great Metropolis*. New York: Sheldon, 1872.

Cray, Ed. *The Enemy in the Streets*. Garden City, N.Y.: Doubleday, 1972.

Critchley, T.A. *The Conquest of Violence: Order and Liberty in Britain*. New York: Schocken Books, 1970.

"Deeper into the Quagmire." *Time*, 3 March 1980, pp. 34-35.

DeFleur, Joan. "Biasing Influences in Drug Arrest Records." *American Sociological Review* 40 (1975): 88-103.

"Detained Philippine Politician Allowed to Fly to U.S." *New York Times*, 9 May 1980, p. A26.

"Disarm the Sniper." *New York Times*, 2 August 1967, p. 36.

Douglass, Frederick. Speech, May 9, 1865. In Harold M. Hyman, ed., *The Radical Republicans and Reconstruction, 1861-1870*, pp. 242-46. New York: Bobbs-Merrill, 1967.

Dykstra, Robert R. *The Cattle Towns*. New York: Atheneum, 1970.

Emerson, Ralph Waldo. *Journals of Ralph Waldo Emerson with Annotations, 1864-1876*, vol. 10. Edited by Edward Waldo Emerson and Waldo Emerson Forbes. Boston: n.p., 1914.

Epstein, Edward J. "The Panthers and the Police: A Pattern of Genocide?" *The New Yorker* (February 13, 1971): 45ff.

Flinn, John J. *History of the Chicago Police*. Chicago: Police Book Fund, 1887.

Foster, Arnold. "Violence on the Fanatical Left and Right." *Annals of the American Academy of Political and Social Sciences* 364 (1966): 141-48.

Franklin, John H. *Reconstruction*. Chicago: University of Chicago Press, 1961.

Frye, William. *In Whitest Africa*. Englewood Cliffs, N.J.: Prentice-Hall, 1968.

Gillette, Robert. "Soviet Protesters Risk Vigilante Action, Prison." *Los Angeles Times*, 29 September 1980, p. 1.

Goldstein, Robert Justin. *Political Repression in Modern America*. Cambridge, Mass.: Schenkman, 1978.

Greenwood, Colin. *Firearms Control: A Study of Armed Crime and Firearms Control in England and Wales*. London: Routledge and Kegan Paul, 1972.

Gurr, Ted Robert. *Why Men Rebel.* Princeton, N.J.: Princeton University Press, 1970.

Gutman, Herbert F. "The Tompkins Square 'Riot' in New York City on January 13, 1874: A Re-examination of its Causes and its Aftermath." *Labor History* 6 (Winter 1965): 44–47.

Halbrook, Stephen P. "The Armed People and the State Monopoly of Violence." 1977. (Unpublished.)

Hampton v. Hanrahan. 600 F.2d 600, U.S. Court of Appeals, Seventh Circuit, 1979.

Hanley, Charles J. "Gun Controls More Stringent Abroad." *Kansas City Star,* 2 December 1980, p. 28A.

Hardy, David T. "The Second Amendment as a Restraint on Federal Firearms Restrictions." In Don B. Kates, Jr., ed., *Restricting Handguns: The Liberal Skeptics Speak Out,* pp. 171–84. Croton-on-Hudson, N.Y.: North River Press, 1979.

Hardy, David T., and Kenneth L. Chotiner. "The Potentiality for Civil Liberties Violations in the Enforcement of Handgun Prohibition." In Don B. Kates, Jr., *Restricting Handguns: The Liberal Skeptics Speak Out,* pp. 194–216. Croton-on-Hudson, N.Y.: North River Press, 1979.

Haskell, Martin R., and Lewis Yablonsky. *Criminology.* Chicago: Rand McNally, 1978.

Heath, G. Louis. *Off the Pigs!* Metuchen, N.J.: Scarecrow Press, 1976.

Herbstein, Dennis. *White Man, We Want to Talk to You!* London: Andre Deutsch, 1979.

Hoagland, Jim. *South Africa.* Boston: Houghton Mifflin, 1972.

_____. "Rising Dissent on Apartheid Splits South Africa's Ruling Tribe." *Washington Post,* 11 January 1977, p. A12.

_____. "Black Power in South Africa." *Washington Post,* 12 January 1977, p. A6.

_____. "Mood of Fear Begins to Grip South African Whites." *Washington Post,* 13 January 1977, p. A20.

_____. "Police are Feared Guardians of White Power, Privilege." *Washington Post,* 14 January 1977, p. A12.

Hofstadter, Richard. "Reflections on Violence in the United States." In Richard Hofstadter and Michael Wallace, eds., *American Violence: A Documentary History.* New York: Random House, 1970.

Hollon, W. Eugene. *Frontier Violence: Another Look.* New York: Oxford University Press, 1974.

Ingram, J.S. *The Centennial Exposition, Described and Illustrated, Being a Concise and Graphic Description of this Grand Enterprise, Commemorative of the First Centenary of American Independence.* Philadelphia: Hubbard Brothers, 1876.

Johnson, David R. *Policing the Urban Underworld: The Impact of Crime on the Development of the American Police, 1800–1887.* Philadelphia: Temple University Press, 1979.

Jordan, Philip Dillon. *Frontier Law and Order.* Lincoln: University of Nebraska Press, 1970.

Kaplan, John. *Marijuana: The New Prohibition.* New York: World, 1970.

Kates, Don B., Jr. "Abolition, Deportation, Integration: Attitudes Toward Slavery in the Early Republic." *Journal of Negro History* 53 (January 1968): 33–47.

_____. "Can We Arrest Police Budgets." *Taxing and Spending* (April 1979): 2–7.

_____. "Handgun Prohibition in the United States." In Don B. Kates, Jr., ed., *Restricting Handguns: The Liberal Skeptics Speak Out*, pp. 7–30. Croton-on-Hudson, N.Y.: North River Press, 1979.

_____, ed. *Restricting Handguns: The Liberal Skeptics Speak Out.* Croton-on-Hudson, N.Y.: North River Press, 1979.

Kennett, Lee, and James L. Anderson. *The Gun in America: The Origins of a National Dilemma.* Westport, Conn.: Greenwood Press, 1975.

Kessler, Raymond G. "Enforcement Problems of Gun Control: A Victimless Crime Analysis." *Criminal Law Bulletin* 16 (March–April 1980): 131–49.

Kotz, Arnold. "Firearms, Violence and Civil Disorders." Stanford Research Institute Report, 1968. (Unpublished.)

Kukla, Robert B. *Gun Control.* Harrisburg, Penn.: Spackpole Books, 1973.

Lane, Roger. *Policing the City: Boston, 1822–1885.* Cambridge: Harvard University Press, 1967.

_____. *Violent Death in the City: Suicide, Accident and Murder in Nineteenth Century Philadelphia.* Cambridge: Harvard University Press, 1979.

Larsen, Lawrence H. *The Urban West at the End of the Frontier.* Lawrence: The Regents of Kansas Press, 1978.

Lefebvre, George. *The Coming of the French Revolution.* Translated by R.R. Palmer. Princeton: Princeton University Press, 1971.

Lemkin, Raphael. *Axis Rule in Occupied Europe.* Washington, D.C.: Carnegie Endowment for International Peace, Division of International Law, 1944.

Library of Congress. Exhibits. In *Federal Firearms Legislation Hearings Before the Subcommittee to Investigate Juvenile Deliquency of the U.S. Committee on the Judiciary.* Washington, D.C.: Government Printing Office, 1968, pp. 480–505.

_____. *Gun Control Laws in Foreign Countries.* Washington, D.C.: Library of Congress, 1976.

Major, Reginald. *A Panther is a Black Cat.* New York: William Morrow, 1971.

Marine, Gene. *The Black Panthers.* New York: New American Library, 1969.

Mark, Ber. *Uprising in the Warsaw Ghetto.* New York: Schocken Books, 1975.

McCague, James. *The Second Rebellion: The Story of the New York Draft Riots of 1863*. New York: Dial Press, 1968.

Miller, Wilbur R. *Cops and Bobbies: Police Authority in New York and London, 1830–1870*. Chicago: University of Chicago Press, 1973.

National Advisory Commission on Civil Disorders. *Report*. New York: Bantam Books, 1968.

Newton, George D., and Franklin Zimring. *Firearms and Violence in American Life*. A Staff Report of the Task Force on Firearms, National Commission on the Causes and Prevention of Violence. Washington, D.C.: Government Printing Office, 1969.

"One Year Later, Analysts Groping for Answers to Afghanistan." *Kansas City Times*, 26 December 1980, p. B3.

Palmer, L.F., Jr. "Out to Get the Panthers." *The Nation* 29 (July 28, 1969): 78–82.

"Panther Raid Confirmed by U.S." *New York Times*, 10 February 1970, p. 27.

Payne, Howard C. *The Police State of Louis Napoleon Bonaparte, 1851–1860*. Seattle: University of Washington Press, 1966.

Pinpin, F.D., ed., comp. *The First 107 Presidential Decrees Consequent to Proclamation Nos. 1081/1104*. Consolidated edition, Book One Series, number 7. Mandaluyong, Rizal, Philippines: published per approval of the Department of Public Information, dated November 27, 1972.

Police Ordinance and Rules and Regulations for the Government of the Police Department, and Instruction as to the Powers and Duties of Police Officers of the City of Chicago. Chicago: Daily Democratic Printer, 1855.

"Props for Moscow's Puppet." *Time*, 28 January 1980, p. 34.

Reeves, Ambrose. "A Massacre Recalled." *Objective Status* 2 (January 1970): 32–35.

Report of the General Superintendent of Police, (Yearly). Chicago: Clark and Edwards.

Richardson, James. *The New York Police: Colonial Times to 1901*. New York: Oxford University Press, 1970.

Roosevelt, Theodore. "Administering the New York Police Force." In *American Ideals and Other Essays*. New York: Putnam, 1897.

Rossman, David; Paul Froyd; Glen L. Pierce; John McDevitt; and William Bowers. "Massachusetts Mandatory Minimum Sentence Gun Law: Enforcement, Prosecution and Defense Impact." *Criminal Law Bulletin* 16 (March–April 1980): 150–63.

Salter, John, and Don B. Kates, Jr. "The Necessity of Access to Firearms by Dissenters and Minorities Whom Government is Unwilling or Unable to Protect." In Don B. Kates, Jr., ed., *Restricting Handguns: The Liberal Skeptics Speak Out*. Croton-on-Hudson, N.Y.: North River Press, 1979, pp. 186–91.

Schneider, John C. *Detroit and the Problem of Order, 1830–1880: A Geography of Crime, Riot, and Policing*. Lincoln: University of Nebraska Press, 1980.

Schoendiger, David. "Riot Control Legislation: A Necessary Evil." In M. Cherif Bassiouni, ed., *The Law of Dissent and Riots.* Springfield, Ill.: Charles C. Thomas, 1971, pp. 337-56.

Schwoerer, Lois G. *"No Standing Armies!" The Antiarmy Ideology in Seventeenth Century England.* Baltimore: Johns Hopkins University Press, 1974.

"Seattle Mayor Says He Refused to Raid Panthers." *New York Times,* 9 February 1970, p. 30.

Sherrill, Robert. *The Saturday Night Special.* New York: Charterhouse, 1973.

Shirer, William H. *The Rise and Fall of the Third Reich.* New York: Simon and Schuster, 1959.

Singletary, Otis A. *Negro Militia and Reconstruction.* New York: McGraw-Hill, 1957.

"Soviet Dissident Asks for Help Against KGB Blackmail." *St. Louis Post Dispatch,* 29 January 1978, p. 28.

"Soviet Dissident Finds His Home in a Shambles." *New York Times,* 19 September 1976, p. 15.

Stevens, William Oliver. *Pistols at Ten Paces: The Story of the Code of Honor in America.* Boston: Houghton Mifflin, 1970.

Strong, George Templeton. *The Diary of George Templeton Strong: The Turbulent Years, 1850-1859.* Edited by Allan Nevins and Milton Halsey Thomas. New York: Macmillan, 1952.

Suhl, Yuri, ed. *They Fought Back.* New York: Schocken Books, 1967.

Task Force on Disorders and Terrorism. *Disorders and Terrorism.* Washington, D.C.: Government Printing Office, 1975.

"Three Hanged in Malaysia for Firearms Convictions." *Kansas City Star,* 2 May 1981, p. A5.

Tilly, Charles. *From Mobilization to Revolution.* Reading, Mass.: Addison-Wesley, 1978.

Torcia, Charles E., ed. *Wharton's Criminal Law.* 14th ed., vol. 2. Rochester, N.Y.: Lawyers Cooperative, 1979.

Truck, Isaiah. "The Attitude of the Judenrats to Problems of Armed Resistance Against the Nazis." In *Jewish Resistance During the Holocaust.* Jerusalem: Yad Vashem, 1971, pp. 202-20.

"Uganda Curbs Firearms." *New York Times,* 22 December 1969, p. 36.

United Nations. "The Soweto Massacre and Its Aftermath." *Objective Justice* 8 (Spring 1976): 6-11.

_____ . "Women and Apartheid." *Objective Justice* 12 (August 1980): 25-27.

U.S. Congress. Senate. *Congressional Record—Senate.* 90th Congress, second session, vol. 114. Washington, D.C.: Government Printing Office, 1968.

_____ . Senate. *Final Report of the Select Committee to Study Governmental Operations with Respect to Intelligence Activities.* Senate Report No. 94-755, Book III. Washington, D.C.: Government Printing Office, 1976.

U.S. Department of State. *Country Reports on Human Rights Practices.* Washington, D.C.: Government Printing Office, 1981.

Vargas, Jesus, and Rizal Tarciano. *Communism in Decline: The Huk Campaign.* Bangkok: SEATO, 1957.

Waldron, Martin. "Militants Stockpile Illegal Guns Across the U.S." *New York Times*, 28 December 1969, p. 42.

Weber, Max. *From Max Weber.* Edited and translated by H.H. Gerth and C. Wright Mills. New York: Galaxy, 1958.

Wertenbaker, Thomas Jefferson. *The First Americans.* New York: Macmillan, 1927.

Western, J.R. *The English Militia in the Eighteenth Century.* London: Routledge and Kegan Paul, 1965.

"Yippie Leader Held in Raid on Lower East Side." *New York Times*, 24 March 1969, p. 37.

CONCLUSION

It is not the purpose of this book to offer definitive solutions to the knotty problems of gun control.[1] Had such a perspective been desired, a single author would have sufficed. Moreover, attention would necessarily have been substantially focused on the specifics of present gun laws (defined by Magaddino and Medoff in Chapter 9) and details of alternative or supplementary proposals.

1. It may be useful to begin by defining "gun control." Not a few analytical problems stem directly from the semantic confusions and unexamined assumptions connected with the use of this phrase. Being an inanimate object, a gun is always "controlled" by the individual who owns or possesses it. But in general usage, "gun control" is taken to mean a broad range of legislative policies whereby that individual is controlled by the state, as opposed to having full freedom of choice. Even this definition is somewhat too narrow, since the individual's freedom of choice may alternatively or cumulatively be governed by that of other individuals. For instance, one rationale for laws requiring the individual to carry weapons openly, rather than concealed, is that it allows others the freedom to choose to exclude that individual from their businesses, homes, and so forth, so long as he or she is armed.

A further unexamined assumption of common usage is that somehow gun control can only refer to legislative policies designed to limit or restrict. In fact, the five or six small towns that now require every household to possess a firearm are engaged in gun control no less than those that require registration of every firearm or every handgun.

But the single most important semantic confusion is the equation of gun control with policies designed not simply to regulate firearms but to eliminate or drastically reduce their ownership by the general citizenry. This confusion has created what is sometimes considered the most baffling paradox in the area: why confiscation proposals are invariably defeated both electorally and in legislatures when the public repeatedly answers affirmatively to opinion polls ambiguously asking whether it supports gun control. The paradox disappears when,

Frankly, I have not asked, and therefore do not know, the positions of the other contributors on particular firearms policy options.[2] It is fair to say that each of them supports the concept of "gun control" in the abstract. But they tend to be skeptical of the extravagant claims that have sometimes been made for the efficacy of certain control mechanisms, and particularly of whether the benefits of moving from control to general prohibition (confiscation) would outweigh the costs. By and large, then, the papers in this volume do not speak from either of the conflicting viewpoints that have (to my mind unfortunately) so dominated the American gun control debate.

The following comments are by way of exercising an editor's prerogative of summing up. It is understood, of course, that the views expressed are my own. Other contributors, as well as readers, may feel that entirely different conclusions are justified by the material presented herein.

LEGAL CONSIDERATIONS

Absent specific constitutional restraints, the states unquestionably have plenary authority to regulate, and even prohibit and confiscate, civilian firearms under the police power (legislation on public health, safety, and welfare). The power of Congress to so legislate is somewhat more doubtful, since the federal government has only limited criminal jurisdiction. But it appears that power would exist under the Commerce Clause, at least as to all firearms that have ever traveled

---

as has been done by Bordua in Chapter 3 and Tonso in Chapter 4, such polls are compared to ones probing more deeply for public attitudes toward specific firearms policies. It turns out that the public does not support confiscation but only controls designed to regulate general firearms ownership for preventing misuse and denying firearms to high-risk groups such as juveniles and criminals.

Accordingly, in both the title and text of this conclusion, I use the phrase "gun control" to denominate governmentally imposed restrictions that are merely regulatory in nature as opposed to confiscatory or prohibitory (see my discussion in Chapter 6, n. 3). Terms like "gun laws" or "firearms policies" are used to describe the entire gamut of policy options, from totally prohibiting gun ownership, to mandating it, to leaving it open to individual choice.

2. To this there are two exceptions: Leroy Clark's avowed support for handgun prohibition (see Chapter 1, n. 1) and the Kleck-Bordua explicit endorsement of strategies designed to deprive convicted felons of all firearms, not just handguns, without affecting gun ownership by responsible adults generally (see Chapter 2).

in interstate commerce or been fabricated from materials that have so traveled.[3]

A greater obstacle to federal and state legislation is presented by the Second Amendment. Halbrook in Chapter 13, Malcolm in Chapter 14, and Marina in Chapter 15 demonstrate that, despite much partisanly obscurantist literature to the contrary, this amendment clearly was intended to protect individuals and particularly the "militia" (a term that in eighteenth century usage included the entire able-bodied adult male population) in the possession of ordinary firearms. *United States* v. *Miller*, 307 U.S. 182 (1939), suggests the further qualification that right of possession is guaranteed of only those civilian weapons that are closely analogous to standard military weapons. In other words, even home possession of gangster weapons such as sawed-off shotguns and Saturday Night Specials, might not be protected by the Second Amendment.[4]

In Chapter 1, Clark suggests that the amendment's original purposes have been rendered obsolete by technological change, which makes it impossible for an armed citizenry to war against a tyrannical government or foreign conqueror. But this can only be based upon the gratuitous assumption that a handgun-armed citizenry will eschew guerrilla warfare in favor of throwing themselves headlong under the tracks of advancing tanks. As Marina and Kessler (Chapters 15 and 16) note, in the vast majority of instances, twentieth century military establishments have failed to suppress popular revolutionaries who started out with only small arms. Consider the success of Irish (1920) and Jewish (1948) rebels against British authority, the Algerians and the Viet Minh against the French, the Viet Cong against the United States, Mozambique and Angola against the Portuguese, the Afghans against the Soviets, and the Iranian and Nicaraguan revolutions.

In any case, though courts sometimes give constitutional rights *additional* scope in order to effectuate their intent; courts have no authority to reduce or eliminate the plain terms of a constitutional guarantee because it is no longer deemed important. For instance,

---

3. *Scarborough* v. *United States*, 431 U.S. 563 (1973); see also *Katzenbach* v. *McClung*, 379 U.S. 294 (1964).

4. As to these and the much more substantial qualifications on the right to carry firearms (as opposed to keeping a gun in the home) see Kates, "Handgun Prohibition and the Original Meaning of the Second Amendment," in the November 1983 issue of *The Michigan Law Review*.

although the Seventh Amendment's requirement of jury trial in any controversy involving more than $20 is clearly obsolete, the courts continue faithfully to apply it in all cases fairly covered by its literal wording and original spirit. The judicial function is to enforce the Constitution as written, not to effectuate the deletion of provisions they may deem obsolete. The prerogative of deleting the Second Amendment as obsolete belongs to the people through the amendatory process.

In addition to the direct barrier presented by the Second Amendment, the Fourth, Fifth, and Sixth Amendments limit police-prosecutorial-judicial behavior in ways that impede controls and would likely frustrate general gun prohibition and confiscation. Thus a distinguished federal appellate judge has suggested that confiscation would be enforceable only by creating a special constitutional "gun exception" to make illegal searches permissible (see my discussion, Chapter 6). Likewise, the former executive director of the American Civil Liberties Union (ACLU) has noted that "since such reprehensible police practices are probably needed to make antigun laws effective, my proposal to ban all guns should probably be marked a failure before it is even tried."[5]

But those who have argued that the cost of compensating handgun owners for confiscating their property would be prohibitive are proceeding from an erroneous premise. There is no requirement of compensation. Whether it is a gun collection or a stamp collection—and regardless of value—the state may declare private property contraband and destroy it. Compensation is required only if the property is taken for actual use by the government.[6]

CRIMINOLOGICAL CONCLUSIONS

One of the viewpoints referred to earlier holds that the mere possession of firearms somehow causes homicide (whether because it distorts the psyche or for other reasons) and that increased homicide can be attributed to increased firearm or handgun sales. What is commonly offered in demonstration of this position is so circular as to be little more than an *ipse dixit*. The correlation between increased

---

5. A. Neier, *Crime and Punishment: A Radical Solution* (New York: Stein and Day, 1976), p. 76.
6. See, for example, *Miller v. Schoene*, 276 U.S. 272 (1928) (grove of valuable trees).

crime and increased handgun sales and ownership is baldly adduced as evidence that the latter causes the former (i.e., that buying handguns turns formerly law-abiding people into robbers, rapists, and murderers) without consideration of the inherently more plausible alternative (see Benson, Chapter 12) that increased crime is causing increased gun ownership.

As indicated in the Introduction, Kleck's *American Journal of Sociology* article was the first systematic attempt to sort out these cause-and-effect relationships through the application of sophisticated computer-assisted modern statistical technique. Although Kleck's article concluded that increased gun ownership modestly increases homicide, Kleck reaches a different conclusion in Chapter 5, based on post–1973 data that was unavailable at the time of his initial study. It now appears that gun ownership by the general populace does not cause or increase homicide.[7]

I hasten to add that this refutation of one group's claim does not justify the other group's claim that gun laws are necessarily useless and irrelevant. Even taking Kleck's present finding as conclusive, it negates causation only as to gun possession *by the general citizenry.* Obviously gun possession *by violent criminals* (a subsection of our population too small to be easily analyzed as part of the general citizenry) does play an important part in life-threatening crime. Beyond stringent legislation targeting such individuals for disarmament (which Kleck himself suggests in Chapters 5 and 7), it is arguable that popular ownership of firearms or of certain categories thereof, should be prohibited, lest the guns be transferred to the criminal milieu through burglary. A less extreme proposal might be the imposition of a mandatory prison sentence for knowing possession of a stolen firearm. This would dissuade burglars from stealing them.[8]

7. See also J. Wright, et al., *Weapons, Crime, and Violence: Literature Review and Research Agenda* (Washington, D.C.: GPO, 1981) and D. Kates, *Why Handgun Bans Can't Work* (Seattle: Second Amendment Foundation, 1982), pp. 18–24 (supplying figures indicating both a 37% decrease in overall homicide in the period 1937-1962, in which handgun ownership increased by 250%, and a decrease in domestic homicide [the type most frequently attributed to handgun availability] during the period 1964-1974).

8. In general I am quite skeptical of the increasingly popular concept of mandatory penalties. The National Rifle Association sees this as a panacea, arguing that criminals would eschew firearms if misuse thereof (e.g., gun robberies) were punished by a mandatory five-year sentence. But mandatory penalties quickly reach a point of diminishing return. When attached to crime that is very common, the costs to the criminal justice system, in terms of increased jury trials, monopolization of prison cells, and so forth, are so egregious that avoidance mechanisms (e.g., plea bargaining down to nonmandatory penalty offenses) be-

(Even more important would be a complementary provision making it easier to convict for this offense by erecting a rebuttable presumption of knowledge that the guns were stolen if a person were found in possession of two or more. The effect of such a presumption-cum-mandatory penalty would be to deter "fences" from accepting stolen firearms, which in turn would induce thieves to concentrate on other items.)

One of the few areas of agreement between the opposing viewpoints (though, predictably, they draw opposite conclusions from it) is that present gun laws have not had the desired effect of eliminating or reducing American violence. This is confirmed regarding both federal and state laws by Magaddino and Medoff in Chapter 9. The conclusion that gun laws cannot dramatically reduce crime necessarily follows from the other findings in this volume, for example Wright's findings discussed in Chapter 11 that the vast majority of gun owners are responsible adults who neither misuse nor want to misuse their guns. To reiterate Kleck's conclusion in Chapter 5, gun possession does not "cause such people to commit violent crime." Homicide is overwhelmingly committed by those with long criminal violence histories, as Kleck and Bordua show in Chapter 2. Such violent criminals represent a tiny portion of our population, perhaps one fifth of one percent.

These facts impose insuperable limitations upon firearms law, particularly prohibitionist-confiscatory strategies. Even in a very violent society the number of potential misusers is so small that the number of firearms legally or illegally available to its members will always be ample for their needs, regardless of how restrictive gun laws are or how strenuously they are enforced.[9] (This generalization applies equally to my scheme of mandatory penalties for gun theft or fenc-

---

come necessary. When criminals find that the sentence is only mandatory in theory, its deterrent effect disappears.

Also, where mandatory imprisonment is provided for an ever-widening number of offenses, the comparative disincentive against the commission of the more serious of these tends to disappear. Thus the mandatory penalty suggested here, like other proposed mandatory penalty devices, will be efficacious only so long as few other crimes are mandatorily punished.

9. Bringing up to date the figures used by Bruce-Briggs in "The Great American Gun War," *The Public Interest* (Fall 1976), the ratio of handgun criminals to handguns is perhaps 1 to 600 (and of handgun murderers to handguns 1 to 5,400) (see Kates, Chapter 6, *supra*, n. 22). Thus, making the over-optimistic assumption that a complete handgun ban would result in a 90 percent diminution through surrender and confiscation, there would still be 60 handguns left for every handgun criminal and 540 for every murderer.

ing. I propose the scheme in the hope of drastically reducing firearms theft, not because I believe that such theft can be eliminated altogether, which is what would be required in order to prevent the tiny minority of violent criminals from obtaining firearms.) The determinants of violence are the fundamental economic, sociocultural, and institutional differences that cause as many as 0.2 percent of one nation's population to be willing to use such extreme violence while only 0.02 percent or even 0.002 percent of another nation's population is so inclined. Since gun laws, by definition, do not focus on these kinds of fundamental determinants, their potential benefits can be no more than marginal.

By no means, however, does this bring us to the "no controls" position of the pro-gun militants. Marginal benefits are not to be despised, particularly when they reduce instances of behavior that may threaten human life. The question of whether we should have more or less gun control cannot be answered in the abstract. It requires a painstaking assessment of whether the inherently marginal benefits of any particular control mechanism are likely to exceed the costs (including costs to civil liberties and to other life-protective criminal justice programs, as well as fiscal costs). Yet another variable that should be included in the formulation of control policies is the deterrent effect that civilian handgun ownership has for the gun owner and society at large. San Francisco Supervisor Carol Ruth Silver estimates that between 1960 and 1975, the number of instances where handguns were used for defense exceeded the cases where they were misused to kill by a ratio of fifteen to one. Because of that premise, the cost of reducing the legitimate defensive uses of guns must also be factored into cost-benefit analysis of gun control strategies.

Even in the case of burglars, who generally take care to strike only at unoccupied premises, handgun ownership appears to provide a deterrent effect against crime that is at least as great as the risk of imprisonment. Kleck and Bordua calculate that a burglar's small

---

Greenwood who, as a Chief Inspector of British Police, was invited to research the effectiveness of handgun prohibition in that country for the Cambridge University Institute of Criminology, concludes (rather more pessimistically than do I): "The number of firearms required to satisfy the 'crime' market is minute, and these are supplied no matter what controls are instituted. . . . There is no case, either in the history of this country or in the experience of other countries, in which controls can be shown to have restricted the flow of weapons to criminals or in any way reduced armed crime." (In D. Kates, ed., *Restricting Handguns* [Croton-on-Hudson: North River Press, 1979], p. 39.)

chance of being confronted by a gun-armed defender probably exceeds that of being apprehended, tried, convicted, and actually serving any time. Which, they ask, provides more of a deterrent: a slim chance of being shot or an even slimmer chance of being punished?

Specific localities have experienced dramatic reductions in crime following publicized handgun-training programs. The best known is probably the Orlando program undertaken because of an abnormally high rate of rape in that area. Between October 1966 and March 1967, police trained women in the use of handguns and rape fell from a level of 35.91 per 100,000 inhabitants in 1966 to 4.18 in 1967. The surrounding areas and Florida in general experienced either constant or increasing rape rates during the same period, as did the United States in general. Burglaries dropped in the Orlando area as well, though publicity surrounding the training program centered around rape-defense. Similar programs have resulted in decreasing store robberies by as much as 90 percent in Highland Park and Detroit, Michigan, and in New Orleans.

Perhaps the most publicized case comes from Kennesaw, Georgia, where every noncriminal head of household is required to keep a gun. In the ten months following this widely publicized enactment, there was an 89 percent decrease in crime. Kleck's and Bordua's calculations imply that police services do not provide the level of crime protection that widespread gun ownership does. This proposition is given increased weight when police and civilian accomplishment are compared. According to a study of incidents reported in the nation's largest newspapers between June 1975 and July 1976, 68 percent of the times when police used firearms they successfully prevented a crime or caught a criminal. But the success rate for private citizens in comparable situations was 83 percent. This is not particularly surprising since the police must usually be summoned to the scene of criminal activity while the private gun owner is more likely to be there when it occurs. Nationwide, 1981 FBI statistics show that citizens justifiably kill 30 percent more criminals than do police. Even this statistic substantially underrepresents the phenomenon: it counts only robbers and burglars killed, excluding personal self-defense—for example a woman who kills a boyfriend to keep him from beating her to death. The whole range of justifiable homicide appears in 1981 California statistics that show citizens justifiably kill twice as many felons as do police; in Chicago and Cleveland it is three times as many. At the same time, Kleck and Bordua conclude that citizens who resist crimes with weapons are much less likely to suffer victimization without being more likely to be injured than those who do not resist at all (as well as less likely to be injured than those who resist without weapons). While these incidents are not meant to give the impression that I am in favor of coercive arming of the populace as in Switzerland, they provide an insight into the societal benefits of civilian gun ownership that must be included in calculus of the value of projected gun control measures.

Grandiose prohibitionary schemes based on the illusion that enormous resources poured into the enforcement of a ban can produce commensurately enormous violence reductions are counterproductive. But controls carefully tailored to produce marginal benefits at only marginal costs are not. The remainder of this discussion will be given over to concrete examples illustrating this balancing process and to the unfortunate political dynamic that has resulted in the substitution of raw political power for rational evaluation of gun control proposals.

THE CALCULUS OF AN IDEAL GUN POLICY

The Kleck-Bordua proposal discussed in Chapter 2 to ban the possession of any kind of firearm for persons who have been convicted of violent crime provides a paradigm of a cost-effective gun control.[10] A wide degree of voluntary compliance cannot realistically be anticipated. But insofar as there is any compliance at all, the law has achieved the direct and palpable benefit of disarming persons who have a high potential for gun misuse. At the same time, the cost to the criminal justice system of enforcement against the noncompliant is minimal, or may even be looked upon as a benefit. This law directs attention to a discrete and comparatively small group upon which it is desirable to focus police attention in any case, particularly when it begins acquiring deadly weapons.

As to gun policies affecting the populace in general, the law against taking firearms onto a commercial airliner also exemplifies for cost-effectiveness. The projected benefit is the elimination of a practice involving a peculiarly grave threat to the public. This

10. This is, theoretically, accomplished by the Federal Gun Control Act of 1968, but in fact, prosecutions for violations of the particular sections are given very low priority by the enforcing agency (see n. 17 *infra*).

projection is not chimerical but highly realizable, for it is possible to closely monitor, and mechanically inspect, those entering commercial airliners.[11]

Although the existing airport monitoring process is both extremely expensive and moderately inconvenient to passengers, most people seem willing to endure these costs for the margin of extra security achieved. (Anyone who is not willing may simply eschew the option of flying commercially.) As to other costs, the prohibition does not prevent legitimate owners from transporting their firearms because it allows the arms to be placed (unloaded) in checked baggage. Despite Wright's demonstration in Chapter 11 that firearms ownership may be widely useful for self-defense and crime deterrence, there is less justification for such weapons on commercial airliners where muggings and other violence are virtually nonexistent. Therefore, those most likely to be apprehended and punished under this law are potentially dangerous criminals rather than decent citizens engaged in the "victimless crime" of carrying a handgun for self-defense. A palpable instance of the marginal utilities such a carefully designed control can confer is the case of John Hinckley. Had he been prosecuted in 1980 when caught sneaking a handgun on board an airliner, he would have been in federal prison in 1981 instead of shooting President Reagan.[12]

Regarding gun restrictions applicable to the populace in general, the key factor is the likelihood of voluntary compliance-enforceability. Only one out of 600 handguns is misused, while the proportion of long gun misuse is much smaller yet (see n. 9). Assuming that 50 to 75 percent of handgun owners would defy a ban (compare Kates, *supra* n. 65 to Bordua, Chapter 3), achieving the public benefit of confiscating the one handgun that would otherwise have been mis-

---

11. In recognizing this response, however, we should be mindful of the fact that prior to the federal statutes, such monitoring by private airlines acting on their own was prohibited due to the public municipal status of metropolitan airports. Private handgun restrictions were simply illegal on public airport property. Hence, if no such restrictions had previously existed, and/or if airports were operated solely in the private sector, private airline monitoring would no doubt have become commonplace as prudent management and competition would have had to respond to hijacking or any other threat to air travel and airline profits.

12. The unresolved caveat to this successful story may be a substitution effect similar to Kleck's findings in Chapter 7. Where the level of hijacking has resumed, potential hijackers have switched from guns to far more dangerous but less detectable gasoline and other bombs. Hence, in some ways monitoring may actually increase the danger to air travel from hijackers. Such a possibility is clearly in need of further study.

used will require the disproportionate expenditure of the enforcement resources necessary to forcibly confiscate at least 299 others. Even if this were not an uneconomic expenditure of resources per se, the resources simply do not exist to be expended. Clearly it is not feasible for a criminal justice system that is currently staggering under the burden of dealing with a comparatively tiny number of violent criminals (perhaps 0.2% of our population) to deal with the 25 million handgun owners who would probably defy it.

In a free society, at least, the criminal justice system is designed to cope with only the tiny minority of antisocial deviants. It works on the assumption that the rest of the citizenry will more or less voluntarily comply with the laws. This necessarily limits laws to those that do not outrage any substantial proportion of the populace so as to cause massive noncompliance.[13] Grave problems are presented for such a criminal justice system even by antiprostitution and similar laws that the general citizenry supports in the abstract, though many shamefacedly violate. The system will be overwhelmed (as the failure of the crusades against alcohol and marijuana demonstrates) by trying to enforce prohibitions against things any substantial minority of the population believes to be right and values deeply. As with marijuana and alcohol Prohibition, to ignore these principles in the gun area will result only in (1) criminalization and alienation of people who would otherwise be responsible citizens; (2) diversion against such people of criminal justice resources needed to contain real crime; and (3) eventually, either outright repeal or detumescence into "selective," that is, discriminatory, enforcement.

EXTREMISM POISONS THE WELL

Unfortunately, the terms and possibilities by which we conceive of gun regulation have been limited by the two opposing sets of viewpoints espoused by those who have been able to virtually drown out all perspectives and alternatives except their own. One group consists of militant gun owners who know nothing about crime except that guns are the solution, not the problem. They oppose any new control

---

13. Exceptions to this generalization are such regulatory measures as tax and traffic laws. Violations of these are readily discoverable and can effectively be punished by easily imposed financial penalties.

proposal, however rational it may be, out of the paranoid delusion that it forms part of an insidious step-by-step program for eventual confiscation.

The other group consists of those (denominated by Tonso in Chapter 4 as the "sages") who have been largely dominant in intellectual circles and the media. They know nothing about guns (and, therefore, about the feasibility of their own and others' legislative proposals) except that the fewer there are, the better off society will be. In fact, many "sages" are unconcerned with the feasibility, or even the crime-reductive potential, of particular proposals. Ironically, they support such proposals indiscriminately for reasons that validate their opponents' paranoia; however ill-designed or costly a gun policy may be (gun registration is a case in point), they welcome it as a step leading toward eventual confiscation.[14] At the very least, it will throw up red tape, obstruct or delay gun possession or acquisition, and discomfit the gun owners, whom the "sages" despise so openly as to virtually assure his or her defiance of any law that receives their support.[15]

14. Predictably, the sages' statements to this effect are assiduously publicized and commented upon by their opponents. See, for example, "Forum Told Total Ban is Goal," *Gun Week* (December 25, 1981), quoting an Illinois legislator endorsing various seemingly moderate new controls on the ground "that all the small steps taken in handgun control aim at the same goal: a complete ban on all handguns"; "Just How Moderate are Kennedy, Rodino, Post?" *Gun Week* (July 17, 1981), contending that legislators' and newspapers' current endorsement of moderate restrictive legislation can be understood only in light of their past advocacy of total prohibition and confiscation.

15. Characteristic are the innumerable political cartoons and columns caricaturing and ridiculing people who keep guns for family protection or excoriating them as "anti-citizens, traitors." However well-meaning Mike Royko, Russell Baker, Herblock, Oliphant Garry Wills, and others may be, they are playing directly into the hands of the gun lobby, which avidly reprints their diatribes for any gunowner who has not already seen them. The gun lobby knows there is no better way of poisoning the well for any new gun regulation – not to mention filling its own coffers and assuring its supporters' fervor – than by convincing the 54 million American handgun owners that they are a beleaguered, despised minority with their backs to the wall. Politicians (except for the few prohibitionist zealots) understandably shy away from embracing a cause that will lead one-fourth of the American people to view them as enemies. Nor, if new regulations were enacted, would politicians be willingly obeyed by people who have been convinced that such laws are motivated by hatred and contempt for them.

This is not to deny that vituperation against gun owners is often provoked, or matched, by gun owner vituperation against control advocates. The issue with which I am concerned is not good manners or courtesy, but enforceability. Although gun owners often damage their own arguments through vituperative presentation, this is not *monumentally* counterproductive. The vital distinction is that they are not seeking anything from the people they are irretrievably alienating. In contrast, the gun prohibitionists are caluminating the very people whom they must convince to comply if the laws they advocate are ever to be effective.

Polarization of the debate into these contending extremes gives us not a set of coherent and workable policies, but a crazy quilt of irrational "compromises" representing only how much one side could power through over the virulent resistance of the opposing militants.[16] The malignant effect of a debate degraded into a mere tug-of-war between opposing proponents (with more moderate or rational perspectives virtually excluded) is illuminated by two examples — one state and one federal.

Some years ago a mentally disturbed man attempted to buy a handgun in a San Francisco gun store. Upon being informed that state law requires a several-day predelivery "cooling-off" period, he bought a rifle for which no such requirement existed. Loading it as he walked onto the street, he killed four strangers. A "cooling off" period is a reasonable control when applicable to *all* guns. Had it existed in that situation, such a law might conceivably have saved four lives.

But consider the policy implications of Kleck's findings in Chapter 7. Because long guns are so much more deadly, a law hypothetically eliminating all handgun assaults would actually increase homicide if it caused attackers to susbtitute long guns in only one third of the assaults that would otherwise have been perpetrated with handguns. Because California's law applied only to handguns, four people died of wounds from which at least three of them would probably have recovered had they been inflicted with the less deadly handgun the killer originally wanted. Thus a basic dictate of any rational gun policy must be that, in general, restrictions should not be applied to handguns unless at least equally stringent ones are applied to long guns. This is, of course, particularly true of restrictions like the cooling-off period, which are specifically formulated with regard to enraged or irrational people who are the least likely to care about the concealability difference between handguns and long guns. Thus, had they focused on the avowed object of saving lives, the gun lobby should have accepted a cooling-off period on all firearms, while the anti-gun lobby should have abandoned its cooling-off period proposal when it became apparent that it could only be enacted as to handguns. Another danger associated with upgrading of weaponry due to

16. Generally speaking, it is the "sages" who seek new legislation and the militant gun owners who oppose it. Occasionally, however, the roles switch, as in the case of reform of the Gun Control Act of 1968, which is backed by the gun owner organizations (see discussion at text accompanying n. 12 *infra*).

a handgun ban is the increased risk of accidental wounds and fatalities do to the increased power of shotguns and rifles. While a shot from a handgun that misses its target will usually come to rest in a wall, a shotgun or rifle blast will continue on to impact whatever is on the other side of the wall. Even now, long guns are involved in 90 percent of all accidental firearms deaths, though they probably represent less than 10 percent of the weapons kept loaded at any one time. Unfortunately, the object of rationally formulating policy gets lost in a legislative process dominated by opposing groups who agree only in evaluating proposals not on their own merits but as steps forward or backward on the path toward firearms prohibition and confiscation.

In the case of the federal example, the Gun Control Act of 1968 includes a number of ill-designed, vaguely written, and/or overbroad provisions that have given rise to serious enforcement abuses.[17] Corrective legislation should have encountered little difficulty, since gun prohibition advocates have regarded the 1968 Act as virtually useless—an appraisal that Magaddino and Medoff corroborate in Chapter 9. But, simply because the gun organizations sought reform, the prohibitionists *volte faced*, declaring their uncompromising allegiance to an Act they have continually derided for fifteen years and poohpoohing abuses that would have excited their outrage in the enforcement of drug laws, for instance. In the topsy-turvy world of gun control, it is the National Rifle Association that supports civil liberties legislation and the National Coalition to Ban Handguns (of which the ACLU is a member organization) that opposes it. While many academicians tend to support handgun confiscation, a national study conducted by the Boston Police Department showed that a majority of high-ranking police administrators and police chiefs not only

---

17. See Report No. 97-476 of the Committee on the Judiciary, United States Senate, to accompany S.1030 (June 18, 1982), pp. 14-15 ("the mandate for the addition of civil liberty guarantees to the Gun Control Act of 1968 was documented" in several hearings from which "it is apparent that the enforcement tactics made possible by current firearms laws are constitutionally, legally, and practically reprehensible." It is far easier to catch unwary shopkeepers in the Act's many vague, hypertechnical requirements—minor record-keeping, violations of which are felonies—than felons obtaining guns in violation of the Act. As a result, "a former Treasury official estimated that 75 percent of" prosecutions brought under the Act involve victimless crime, "individuals whose violations, if any, were unintentional.") An exhaustive, if highly partisan, discussion concentrating on the more serious abuses is David T. Hardy's *The BATF's War on Civil Liberties* (Seattle, Wash.: Second Amendment Foundation, 1979). See also Robert Sherrill, *The Saturday Night Special* (New York: Charterhouse, 1973), p. 274.

oppose handgun control but a bare majority actually favor allowing law-abiding citizens to carry guns for self-protection.

Needless to say, these political dynamics (which Bruce-Briggs has aptly termed "the great American Gun War") significantly reduce the likelihood that the fundamentally important research done over the last decade will bear legislative fruit. Although vast lacunae remain, that research has enormously enriched our understanding of the characteristics of violent offenders, of the nature of firearms crime in particular, and of how and why gun laws do or do not achieve their desired results. The time is ripe for experimentation with, and perhaps thoroughgoing reform of, our gun laws. (I hasten to add that "reform" means not multiplication of burdensome, useless red tape as an obstacle to gun ownership, but abandoning it even as promising policies are extended and intensified.) Unfortunately, to date the political dynamic has left little room for optimism that such will occur.

INDEX

Detroit, 38, 111, 341, 504, 530
Deutsch, Stuart J., 227–28
De Zee, M., 213
Dickinson, Charles, 493
Di Grazia, Robert, 64, 149 n. 33, 349
Dionysius I, 365
Dionysius II, 365
Discourse on Political Economy, 380
Discourses, 373, 374
Discourses Concerning Government, 377
Dissidents
application of firearms legislation to, 467–85
discrimination against, by firearms legislation, 459, 460, 466
government repression of, 462–64
importance of firearms to, 486–87
reformist concessions to, 464–65
District of Columbia. *See* Washington, D.C.
District of Columbia Crime Commission, 189
Dodd, Thomas, 169, 170
Dodge City, Kansas, 505, 506
"Doonesbury," 73
Douglass, Frederick, 142, 477–78
Drinan, Robert, 165
Drugs. *See* Prohibition, substance.
Dueling, 492–93
Dwight, Timothy, 437

Earp, Wyatt, 506
Edward III, 428
Egypt, 376, 445
Ehrlich, Isaac, 232, 234
Ehrlich, L., 269
Eighth Amendment, U.S. Constitution, 163
Eisenhower, Milton, 81, 87
Eisenhower Commission. *See* National Commission on the Causes and Prevention of Violence.
Elitism, 154–55
Elizabeth, 392
Ellis, D.P., 28
Ellis, John, 431–32, 441
Ellsworth, Kansas, 505
Ellul, Jacques, 419 n. 4
El Salvador, 441, 461
Emerson, Ralph Waldo, 494

England, 5, 6, 86–87, 350n., 430, 431, 444, 471, 491, 525
African wars of, 438, 440
and American Revolution, 433, 434–35
colonial armies of, 447, 448
militias of, 389–95 *passim*, 398–402 *passim*, 407–8, 415–16
monarchy of, 376, 379
peasants' revolt in, 428–29
police of, 420, 497–500, 512, 513
political/philosophical traditions of, 363, 382–83
posses of, 391, 392
restoration of monarchy in, 397–403
right to arms in, 387–90, 406–16
stockpiling of arms in, 395–97
volunteer regiments of, 399–400, 401, 402
weapons restrictions in, 393–406 *passim*, 410–14, 415, 467–69
English Bill of Rights, 387–90 *passim*, 407–16, 497
English Civil War (1642), 390, 395, 396, 431, 432
English Reformation, 393
Enloe, E., 145 n. 24
Ennis, Philip, 104, 105 (Table)
Entrapment, 464, 465
Erskine, Hazel, 52, 53 (Table)
Essex, England, 429
Europe, defense of, 448
Evanston, Illinois, 210
Exeter, England, 397
Externalities of protection market, 354–56

"Factoring-Criteria-for-Weapons" test, 203 n. 7
Fairfax Independent Militia Company, 382
Family violence, 21, 22, 41, 131, 145, 206, 207–9 (Table), 213, 216, 317–19
FBI Uniform Crime Reports, 9, 42, 113, 172, 204, 530
Feagin, Joe, 330–31
Federal Bureau of Investigation, 233 n. 15, 479, 504. See also *FBI Uniform Crime Reports.*

ABOUT THE EDITOR

Don B. Kates, Jr. attended Reed College, received his J.D. from Yale University Law School (1966), and has been Associate Professor of law, St. Louis University (1976-1979). He previously has worked for civil rights lawyer William Kunstler of Kunstler, Kunstler & Kinoy (1964-1965) and California Rural Legal Assistance (1966-1973), where he served as Director of Legal Research and Senior Litigation Attorney. Currently, he is with O'Brien & Hallisey (1979-present) and is a partner in Benenson, Kates and Hardy (1981-present).

He has served as civil rights consultant to the Judiciary Committee of the U.S. House of Representatives (1965-1966); member, Project Director's Advisory Group, Legal Services Division, U.S. Office of Economic Opportunity (1969-1972); Trustee, Poverty Lawyers for Effective Advocacy (1969-1972); member, California State Advisory Committee to the U.S. Civil Rights Commission (1971-1972); Director of Litigation and Deputy Director, San Mateo Legal Aid Society (1973-1975); police legal advisor, San Francisco Sheriff's Department (1973-1976); and Consultant to the legal services program for Seattle, Washington, Berkeley, California, and the state of Alaska.

He is the author of the book, *Restricting Handguns: The Liberal Skeptics Speak Out* and a contributor to the volumes, *The Relevant*

Lawyer (ed. A. F. Ginger), *Mexican-Americans and the Administration of Justice in the Southwest* (U.S. Civil Rights Commission), and the *Encyclopedia of the American Constitution* (eds. L. Levy and K. Karst, forthcoming). His recent article entitled "Handgun Prohibition and the Original Understanding of the Second Amendment" appears in *Michigan Law Review* 82 (1983): 1701-70.

ABOUT THE AUTHORS

Steven Balkin is Assistant Professor of economics at Roosevelt University of Chicago. He received his B.S. in finance and his M.A. and Ph.D. in economics from Wayne State University. In addition, he has been Assistant Professor of criminal justice and economics at the University of Illinois-Chicago (1974–1983), has served as a Criminal Justice Specialist for the Illinois Law Enforcement Commission, Division of Planning and Evaluation (1974), and has conducted research for the Chicago Cook County Criminal Justice Commission (1977) and the Illinois Institute for Development Disabilities (1978). Specializing in economics of crime, urban-regional economics, and human resources economics, Dr. Balkin has written numerous articles appearing in *Journal of Behavioral Economics, Journal of Police Science and Administration, Journal of Urban Economics, Judicature, Policy Analysis,* and *Social Problems.*

Bruce L. Benson received his B.A. and M.A. in economics from the University of Montana and his Ph.D. in economics from Texas A&M University. Currently Associate Professor of economics at Montana State University, he has also taught at Texas A&M University and Pennsylvania State University. Dr. Benson's research interests focus primarily on the analysis of regulatory policy, decision-making behavior in the public sector, law and economics, and spatial price theory. His publications in these areas have appeared or are to

565

appear in such journals as *American Economic Review, Antitrust Bulletin, Appalachian Business Review, Industrial Organization Review, Journal of International Economics, Journal of Libertarian Studies, Journal of Urban Economics, Public Choice, Public Finance Quarterly, Review of Regional Studies,* and *Southern Economic Journal.*

David J. Bordua is Professor of sociology at the University of Illinois, Urbana-Champaign. He received his B.A. and M.A. from the University of Connecticut, and his Ph.D. from Harvard University. Professor Bordua has previously taught at the University of Connecticut, University of Michigan, and as a Visiting Professor at the Stanford University Law School. A consultant to numerous commissions, foundations, and committees on law enforcement and criminal justice, he is the author of three research reports to government agencies: *Prediction and Selection of Delinquents* (1961), *Comparative Police Supervision Systems* (1970), and *Patterns of Firearms Ownership* (1979). In addition, he is the editor of *The Police: Six Sociological Essays* (1967). A contributor to numerous scholarly volumes, Professor Bordua's many articles have appeared in *American Behavioral Scientist, American Journal of Sociology, American Sociological Review, The Annals, Connecticut Law Review, Journal of Political and Military Sociology, Journal of Research on Crime and Delinquency, Law and Policy Quarterly, Law and Society Review, Social Forces, Social Problems, Sociological Inquiry,* and *Sociometry.*

Leroy D. Clark is Visiting Professor of law at the University of Maryland. He received his B.A. from City College of New York and his LL.B. from Columbia University. He has been Staff Counsel for the Civil Rights Division of the Attorney General's Office, State of New York (1961-1962); Assistant Counsel, N.A.A.C.P. Legal Defense and Educational Fund, Inc. (1962-1968); Professor of Law, New York University (1968-1979); Arbitrator, American Arbitration Association (1974-present); General Counsel, Equal Employment Opportunity Commission (1979-1981); and Professor of Law at Catholic University (1981-1983).

Author of *The Grand Jury: The Use and Abuse of Political Power* and co-author of *Employment Discrimination Law—Cases and Materials*, 2nd edition (with A. Smith, Jr. and C. Craver), Professor Clark has also prepared numerous articles for scholarly publications such as

A.B.A. Journal, Adherent, Civil Liberties, Denver Law Journal, Howard Law Journal, Journal of Urban Law, Kansas Law Review, and *Rutgers Law Review.*

Stephen P. Halbrook received his B.S. in business and his Ph.D. in philosophy from Florida State University, and his J.D. from Georgetown University. Currently specializing in firearms litigation with offices in Fairfax, Virginia, Dr. Halbrook is a member of the Virginia State Bar and the bars of the U.S. Courts of Appeals for the Fourth, Fifth, and Seventh Circuits and the U.S. Supreme Court. He has been an Assistant Professor of philosophy at Tuskegee Institute (1972–74), Howard University (1974–79), and George Mason University (1980–81).

Dr. Halbrook's writings on gun control have appeared in the volumes *The Right to Keep and Bear Arms: Report of the Subcommittee on the Constitution of the Senate Judiciary Committee* and *The Victims of Crime* (forthcoming), as well as in numerous journals including *George Mason University Law Review, Gun Week, Hamline University Law Review, Libertarian Forum*, and *Northern Kentucky Law Review.*

Raymond G. Kessler is a consultant from El Paso, Texas, specializing in gun control and related issues. He holds a J.D. degree from Temple University School of Law and a M.A. in sociology from the University of Texas-El Paso. Dr. Kessler has served as chairperson of the Administration of Justice Department at Rockhurst College, was an Assistant District Attorney in Lehigh County, Pennsylvania, and taught at Arkansas State University. Coauthor of *Law-Abiding Criminals* and *The Etiology of Alcoholism*, he has also written numerous papers and articles on gun control, including selections in *Criminal Law Bulletin* and *Law and Policy Quarterly.*

Gary Kleck is Associate Professor of criminology at Florida State University. He received his B.A., M.A., and Ph.D. in sociology from the University of Illinois, Urbana-Champaign. He has served as an editorial consultant for the *American Sociological Review* and as a grants consultant for the National Science Foundation. His research interests on violent behavior have involved the areas of capital punishment, deterrence and crime control, and gun ownership and violence.

His studies have appeared in such journals as *American Journal of Sociology, American Sociological Review,* and *Contemporary Sociology.*

Joseph P. Magaddino received his Ph.D. from Virginia Polytechnic Institute and State University, and is Chairman and Professor of economics at California State University, Long Beach. He has taught at the University of Connecticut, Virginia Polytechnic Institute, and the University of California, Irvine, and his studies on violent crime have been presented at meetings of the Southern Economic Association and Western Economic Association. In addition to his teaching activities, Professor Magaddino was a University Fellow at the University of Connecticut. A contributing author to *Restricting Handguns: The Liberal Skeptics Speak Out* (ed. D.B. Kates, Jr.), he has also written articles for such journals as *Public Choice, Public Policy,* and *Public Finance Quarterly.*

Joyce Lee Malcolm received her B.A. in history from Barnard College and her M.A. and Ph.D. in history from Brandeis University. The recipient of Fellowships from Radcliffe Institute at Harvard University (1979–1980), the National Endowment for the Humanities (1979–1980), and Harvard Law School (1980–1982), she has also taught at Boston University, Northeastern University, and Cambridge University.

Currently preparing a book on the history of the right to keep and bear arms, Dr. Malcolm is the author of *Caesar's Due: Loyalty and King Charles, 1642–1646,* and has contributed articles to the *Bulletin of the Institute of Historical Research, The Historical Journal, Irish Historical Studies,* and *Hastings Constitutional Law Quarterly.*

William Marina is Professor of public administration at Florida Atlantic University. He served as Senior Economist with the Joint Economic Committee of the U.S. Congress (1981), taught at the University of Texas at Arlington (1962–1964), and was Liberty Fund Senior Research Scholar at the Institute for Humane Studies (1975–1977). He received an A.B. in American studies from the University of Miami, and an M.A. and Ph.D. in that field from the University of Denver where he was an N.D.E.A. fellow (1959–1962).

An educational consultant to the Office of Economic Opportunity Adult Migrant Programs in Tennessee, Georgia, and Texas, Dr. Marina is a contributor to numerous scholarly volumes, the author of *Egalitarianism and Empire* and *American Statesmen on Slavery and the Negro* (with N. Weyl), and Associate Editor of *News of the Nation: A Newspaper History of the United States.* His articles have appeared in *Law and Liberty, Libertarian Review, Literature of Liberty, Modern Age, Reason,* and *Reason Papers.*

Paula D. McClain is currently Associate Professor of public affairs and Director, Division of Policy Analysis and Evaluation, Center for Urban Studies at Arizona State University, and received her B.A., M.A., and Ph.D. in political science from Howard University. Previously, she has been Assistant Professor of political science at the University of Wisconsin-Milwaukee (1980–1982) and Assistant Professor of political science and Afro-American studies at the University of Wisconsin-Milwaukee (1977–1980).

Dr. McClain's publications include *Alienation and Resistance: The Political Behavior of Afro-Canadians,* and numerous articles in a wide variety of journals such as *Death Education, Ethnicity, Journal of Criminal Justice, Journal of Environmental Studies, Law and Policy Quarterly, Omega, Victimology,* and *The Western Journal of Black Studies.*

John F. McDonald received his B.A. in economics from Grinnell College and both his M.Phil. and Ph.D. in economics from Yale University. In addition to his current position as Professor of economics at the University of Illinois, he has served as Chairman of the Committee on Economic Analysis and Forecasting of the Mayor's Council of Manpower and Economic Advisors, City of Chicago; Consultant to Mathematica Policy Research, Inc.; and a member of the Research Advisory Board, Chicago Urban League.

Author of *Economic Analysis of an Urban Housing Market,* Dr. McDonald's articles and reviews concerning urban and labor economics have been published in *American Economic Review, Annals of Economic and Social Measurement, Annals of Regional Science, Economics Letters, Educational and Psychological Measurement, Growth and Change, Journal of Human Resources, Journal of Urban Economics, Review of Economics and Statistics,* and *Urban Studies.*

Marshall H. Medoff is currently Associate Chairman and Professor of economics at California State University, Long Beach, and has previously taught economics at Northwestern University and the University of California, Berkeley and Irvine. He received his B.S. from the Illinois Institute of Technology (Chicago), his M.S. from the University of Illinois (Urbana-Champaign), and his Ph.D. from the University of California (Berkeley). In addition to having served as reviewer for both the *Southern Economic Journal* and the *Review of Economics and Statistics*, Dr. Medoff has authored scholarly articles for *Applied Economics, Atlantic Economic Journal, Economic Inquiry, Journal of Black Studies, Journal of Human Resources, Journal of Urban Economics, Quarterly Review of Economics and Business, Review of Black Political Economy, Review of Economics and Statistics,* and other journals.

Frank T. Morn is Assistant Professor of criminal justice at the University of Illinois-Chicago. He received his B.A. and M.A. in history from Brigham Young University and his Ph.D. in history from the University of Chicago, and has served as Consultant to the National Advisory Committee on Criminal Justice Standards and Goals. Specializing in American history, Dr. Morn is the author of *The Eye That Never Sleeps: A History of the Pinkerton National Detective Agency* and *Debates and Disciplines: An Essay on Criminal Justice and Criminology as Academic Professions in Higher Education*. Currently he is writing a history of criminal justice education.

William R. Tonso, Associate Professor of sociology at the University of Evansville, received his B.S. in industrial education, his M.S. in business administration, and his Ph.D. in sociology from Southern Illinois University, Carbondale. His research interests are primarily focused on the study of deviance, ethnicity, ethnic interaction, and popular culture. Dr. Tonso is the author of *Gun and Society: The Social and Existential Roots of the American Attachment to Firearms*, a cross-cultural, social-historical, phenomenologically oriented exploration of the social and existential origins of the practical, recreational, and symbolic functions of firearms.

James D. Wright is Professor of sociology and Director of the Social and Demographic Research Institute at the University of Massachusetts. He received his B.A. in philosophy from Purdue University, and his M.A. and Ph.D. in sociology at the University of Wisconsin. Recipient of a Ford Foundation Graduate Fellowship (1970–1973), Dr. Wright has also served as Investigator to various projects sponsored by the Social Science Research Council (1975), Comprehensive Employment and Training Administration (1978), U.S. Department of Justice (1978–1980), and National Science Foundation (1976–1978). He is the author of *The Dissent of the Governed, New Directions in Political Sociology* (with R. Hamilton), *After the Cleanup: Long-Range Effects of Natural Disasters* (with P. Rossi, S. Wright, and E. Weber-Burdin), and *Social Science and Natural Hazards* (with P. Rossi). His many articles and reviews have been published in *American Journal of Sociology, American Sociological Review, Annals of the American Academy of Social and Political Science, Contemporary Sociology, Dissent, Human Behavior, Journal of Political and Military Sociology, The Nation, Polity, Public Opinion Quarterly, Qualitative Sociology, Revue francaise de sociologie, Social Policy, Social Problems, Social Science Quarterly, Sociology and Social Research, Youth and Society, Zeitschrift für Soziologie*, and other journals.